LOVE AND HISSES

Other books by the National Society of Film Critics

**Foreign Affairs:
The National Society of Film Critics'
Video Guide to Foreign Films**

**Produced and Abandoned:
The National Society of Film Critics Write on
the Best Films You've Never Seen**

The Movie Star

Movie Comedy

Film 73/74

Film 72/73

Film 71/72

Film 70/71

Film 69/70

Film 68/69

Film 67/68

LOVE AND HISSES

THE NATIONAL SOCIETY OF FILM CRITICS SOUND OFF ON THE HOTTEST MOVIE CONTROVERSIES

Edited and with Introductions by
PETER RAINER

MERCURY HOUSE
San Francisco

Published in the United States by
Mercury House
San Francisco, California

United States Constitution, First Amendment: Congress shall make no law
respecting an establishment of religion, or prohibiting the free exercise
thereof; or abridging the freedom of speech, or of the press; or the right of
the people peaceably to assemble, and to petition the Government for a redress of grievances.

Mercury House and colophon are registered trademarks
of Mercury House, Incorporated

Design by Sharon Smith
Typesetting by Stanton Publication Services
Printed on recycled, acid-free paper
Manufactured in the United States of America

Library of Congress Cataloging-in-Publication Data
Love and hisses : the National Society of Film Critics sound off on the hottest movie controversies / edited by Peter Rainer.
   p.   cm.
Includes index.
  ISBN 1-56279-031-5
  1. Motion pictures. 2. Motion pictures—Reviews. I. Rainer, Peter,
1951–   . II. National Society of Film Critics.
PN1995.L66   1992
791.43'75—dc20   92-11175
                                   CIP

5 4 3 2 1

PN
1995
.L66
1992
c.1
9200551

CONTENTS

ACKNOWLEDGMENTS

For the care and enthusiasm they have shown for this project, I would like to express my gratitude to the Mercury House team: executive editor Thomas Christensen, editor David Peattie, and art director/ designer Sharon Smith. Production coordinator extraordinaire Zipporah Collins was indispensable in keeping the book on track. Much appreciated, too, is Barbara Fuller's contribution in helping copyedit the manuscript.

Maureen Sullivan and Chris Koseluk contributed their considerable research skills and lickety-split efficiency to the task of tracking down photos, and photo and article permissions. Kirsten Janene-Nelson was also quite helpful in obtaining permissions. For their assistance in obtaining stills, my thanks also extend to Susan King and to Andy Klein, film critic of the *Los Angeles Reader*. (Andy, with Peter Keough of the *Boston Phoenix,* was elected to the National Society of Film Critics too late for inclusion in this book.) Susan Salter Reynolds gets the credit for the title *Love and Hisses*. She worries that her facility for coming up with snappy titles is a sign of shallowness. I have assured her it is not.

Mindy Pomper, manager of International Distribution Services for Dino De Laurentiis Communications, was instrumental early on in securing just the right *Blue Velvet* art for the book's cover. Photographer Kirk McKoy provided his considerable talents for the "About the Editor" mug shot. Helping out, too, were Linda Sweeten, Gaile Robinson, Joanna Dendel, and Mary Rourke. For the fine example they set as editors of the first two Mercury House–National Society collections, I owe a debt to the late Kathy Schulz Huffhines (*Foreign Affairs*) and to Michael Sragow (*Produced and Abandoned*), who also volunteered many invaluable production tips and shortcuts. The cooperation of the entire National Society, and its executive director, Elisabeth Weis, was unstinting.

For their unwavering support and encouragement throughout this project, I would like to express my deepest appreciation to Donna Perlmutter, Dick Ravin, Ed Tobinick, and, most of all, to my parents, John and Barbara Rainer.

INTRODUCTION

"Did we see the same movie?"

It's the question that crackles between friends, family, lovers, dating couples, as we edge out of the theatre into the nippy night air and wonder if perhaps we are not made for each other after all. It's the wail of someone who has seen in a movie everything you wish you had seen; or of someone blinded to your bliss.

It's also what audiences continually ask critics on the opposing side of their own opinion. And it's what critics often ask huffily of each other. For, make no mistake, few critics are so ecumenical that they do not believe in their blood that their judgments alone will be embraced by posterity. William Faulkner once asked about book critics, "Do they enjoy reading each other?" His conclusion: "One can as easily imagine barbers shaving each other for fun."

The premise of *Love and Hisses* is that collisions of critical opinion *are* fun. Even more, they are *fundamental* to criticism, to the play of ideas that gives criticism its vitality.

The National Society of Film Critics, founded in 1966, consists of critics representing many of the major general-interest magazines and daily and weekly newspapers across the country. The thirty-six men and women who contributed to this book, all members of the NSFC as the project went into production, range in age from early thirties to early seventies, and their publications range from Brooklyn's *City Sun* and the *Village Voice* to the *Wall Street Journal* and *Time*.

Working within the constraints of their forums, these critics bring to their reviews and essays not only their craft and intelligence but also all of the peculiarities and particularities that go into making up a writer. They create out of their own history and the history that surrounds them.

Is it any wonder, then, that movies about sex and race and madness, movies about Vietnam and JFK and Christ, should boost these critics into their bumper cars? How could it be otherwise? The films and filmmakers covered in these pages were selected because they provoked the controversies and raised the issues that delivered the most juice to those bumper cars.

We live at a time when film criticism, or what passes for it, has never been more ubiquitous. Our newspapers and magazines, our airwaves, are heady with the gabble of screening-room scribes and soothsayers. And yet there may be a neutralizing effect in all this ubiquity; for many in the mass audience, criticism has become a kind of hum in the background of the moviegoing event. It is perceived as a part of the overall media blitz. (Some reviewers, feeling insufficiently stroked, are not above conspiring in the blitz. Their socko blurbs are all-of-a-piece with the movies' ad copy.) The Hollywood studios, despite their increasing reliance on market research test screenings and demographic flowcharts, still fancy they need critics to help sell their movies. (The independent film companies certainly need them.) But they're not too worried: With so many critics writing reviews now, it's a cinch that any movie, no matter how putrid, will draw a few blurbable raves.

For the incurious legions who automatically equate a movie's popularity with its worth and feel no need to move beyond that equation, criticism—real criticism, that is, practiced with taste and intelligence—may be close to irrelevant anyway. Virtually all the major media outlets now feature weekly rankings of the five or ten top-grossing films; these lists, which both reflect and determine a movie's media push, have become the nation's true critics-of-choice. They carry a the-People-have-spoken certitude that regular critics can't hope to match.

Even if they could, it would be a bad match. A critic, to be of any real value, must speak only for the critic. Maybe this is why criticism in this country is often perceived as persnickety, undemocratic—yea, un-American. Yet honest criticism may be the only line of defense against the studio *parfumeurs* whose job it is to sweeten a stinker and turn it into a movie that everybody wants to sniff.

Which is not to say that honest criticism is "objective" criticism. You hear a lot of noise these days about how critics should be objective. In a technological age, the personal and expressive nature of criticism—its subjectivity—can seem wimpy and inexact to people who want it to be a science. After all, if you can't *prove* that *Citizen Kane* is a greater achievement than, say, an episode of "Gilligan's Island," what's the point?

The point is that good criticism is less about the judgment one finally arrives at than about the journey one takes to get there. The journeys in *Love and Hisses* are double-tracked. The kick of the book is that its pieces, most of them contrasting pairs on a single film or subject, work off each other even though they generally were not written with that view in mind. Their heated, reasoned contrariness makes the films more vivid no matter which side of the fence you fall on. This byplay, far from being a sign of critical disarray, is a sign of health. (Indeed, as this book demonstrates, the current state of film criticism, despite the ascendancy of the blurbmeisters and pushover populists, is probably healthier right now than the state of the movies.) For the most part, the isms and schisms in *Love and Hisses* are hitched to a working journalist's rhythms; almost all the reviews and essays were written in the quick of the moment, and they probably gain from that immediacy. The to-and-fro between these pieces is sometimes mimicked by the to-and-fro within a particular review, as the critic reaches for a way to synthesize his — or her — own dueling intuitions.

This synthesis may not be possible: Movies are a combination of all the arts; they connect with so many different things in our lives that, finally, they may take in more than we can handle. (This is what makes them so unreasonably exciting.) A movie critic, perhaps more than a critic for any of the other arts, is bound to fail.

Still, the failures can be bracing. Some of the best pieces in *Love and Hisses* have a narrowed focus that allows us to see only one thing sharply. And that pinpoint sharpness can almost be enough to satisfy us. Then, too, some of the best pieces have a wide-open, almost expeditionary quality. There's a crazy, indispensable valor in the way a critic will risk looking foolish for a lost cause, as in the chapter "On the Contrary," which consists primarily of love pats for such hiss-a-thons as *Heaven's Gate* and *Hudson Hawk.*

In television now, the preferred mode of critical debate over just about anything is sound-bite-sized talking-heads rancorousness. *Love and Hisses* seeks to reclaim the value of rancor in criticism by deepening the terms of the debate. Starting with *The Wild Bunch* and *Last Tango in Paris* and going right up to *JFK* and *Basic Instinct,* films were chosen not simply because they divided critics but also because the divisions brought out the critics' leopard spots. The films define the ways these writers approach both movies and criticism.

Although the pro-and-con format predominates, with the pros consistently preceding the cons, the critical differences sometimes hinge on approach rather than evaluation. A number of pieces, such as the essays on Brian De Palma (in "Psycho Dramas") and Bertrand Blier (in "Auteur/Hauteur"), stand unopposed because they take into account so many of the reservations of those directors' detractors. A few of the controversial films represented singly, such as *Pink Flamingos,* are included as historical markers.

The art of film is served by the art of criticism. Both advance as much by their wars as by their truces. It may be in the nature of "difficult" works to create a critical front that other critics move against. What may at first seem to be a mistake or misperception in a review can turn out to be an essential response to something new on the screen. The critical climate surrounding directors such as De Palma and Robert Altman and Jean-Luc Godard and Oliver Stone and Spike Lee incorporates the confusions and passions and wrong turns and sneak attacks of both their admirers and their loathers. We probably can't come close to doing justice to filmmakers like these unless we are prepared to inhale the gunsmoke on both sides of the skirmish.

A critic's needs may be served by writing from a position of judicious authority; this may even be a necessary stance for doing any writing at all. But in the back of everything should be the humbling afterthought that, though we rage to be definitive, there is always more to be said.

In that spirit, then, accept this book as an offering — and a provocation.

Peter Rainer
Los Angeles
1992

PSYCHO DRAMAS

The movies have always been ferociously adept at frightening us. Scare pictures, even inept ones, can get inside us, like some David Cronenbergian homunculus, and root out our dungeons.

Because of their suggestiveness and power, horror films have always been both championed and targeted. Is the violence that we see exploration or exploitation? Does the on-screen depiction of a horrific act encourage its off-screen counterpart? Can you separate aesthetic responsibility from moral responsibility?

Since horror in the movies is often also eroticized, there's a double whammy built into a reviewer's attempt to do justice to these films: He knows he's going to be getting it from all sides. A critic who hails a director like Brian De Palma—such as Stephen Schiff in his pieces here on *Dressed to Kill*—may quickly discover he has become an Enemy of the People.

Most of the horror films discussed in this chapter revolve around Hollywood's current maniac of choice: the deranged obsessive who commits unspeakably squishy atrocities. Is the depravity that we witness in Jonathan Demme's Oscar-laden *The Silence of the Lambs* and Martin Scorsese's *Cape Fear* and David Lynch's *Blue Velvet* and *Wild at Heart* and John McNaughton's *Henry: Portrait of a Serial Killer* worth the ride?

For some time now, flapdoodle maniacs like Freddy Krueger (of the *Nightmare on Elm Street* films) and Jason (of the *Friday the 13th* cycle) have been faves on the teen-movie circuit. Detractors of a film like *The Silence of the Lambs* would argue that it simply co-opts the teen-horror attitudes: For all its pseudosophistication and mind-meld mumbo jumbo, it's essentially a ghoul movie for adults. The difference between Freddy Krueger and Hannibal Lecter is more a matter of diction than of conception. Demme's film is just higher-grade pulp, with a higher-browed bogeyman. Like *Cape Fear*, it's a movie made by an artist who has trashed his gifts in pursuit of a hit.

Those who champion these films *as a class,* while disagreeing on the merits of specific movies, argue that they provide a coherent critique of America's underside. They reflect a dread in the atmosphere that can't be expressed in our movies in any other way right now. Modern life terrorizes you; all roads to sanity have been blockaded. You can't even retreat to the small-town backwaters and bayous because, as in Lynch's films, the loonies have overrun them, too. The vagrant serial killers who figure in many of these movies are a relatively new phenomenon in the annals of crime; they fit into a world where randomness and rootlessness have taken hold. Technology has failed to order our lives; there's no way to keep track of the chaos. In *The Silence of the Lambs,* the newfangled police gadgetry pales beside Lecter's brainwaves.

Do these social critiques hold up? Is it fair to locate, as *Henry: Portrait of a Serial Killer* does, the murderous heart of America in the anomic working class? (Its centerpiece rape-murder scene is lifted from Stanley Kubrick's notorious *A Clockwork Orange,* an earlier example of porno-violent class bashing.) What does it say about the sixties that the children of the counterculture in *River's Edge* are more like the Children of the Damned?

The problem many people have with these films often has as much to do with their technique as with their content. How can Lynch be so facetious about such awfulness? How can De Palma be so comic? Isn't McNaughton's deliberately artless, flattened realism a form of sadism?

Lurking behind these movies' various approaches is the same uncertainty: What is an appropriate *style* to encompass modern horror?

BLUE VELVET

Peter Rainer

David Lynch's *Blue Velvet* is a great movie, and one of the rare American films of the past decade to make a difference in the medium. It gets into areas of dread and shock and torment that are so profoundly dislocating and dreamlike that, watching it, you feel as if you're coiled right up inside the vision of an artist with a live feed to the unconscious. The moviemaking has a hushed, incantatory quality, even when the action is rabid; Lynch's imagery is continuous with the unwakened states that most filmmakers (and audiences) censor. The movie has a stark, hallucinatory clarity. You think back on it as you would think back on a particularly fervid dream.

Blue Velvet, like most great movies, alters our way of seeing. Lynch's vision seems pulled by the very nature of the movie medium itself, which has always been coexistent with dream states. By making those states shockingly evident on film, Lynch risks disturbing audiences and, sure enough, the people who don't like *Blue Velvet* don't just dislike it — they detest it. Still, that detestation may be one of the truest responses to the film.

Recent Hollywood movies, even the few good ones, look like they were made to be shaken off, but *Blue Velvet* isn't a movie you can shake off; it's actually more disturbing on a second viewing. A film that fuses sexual terror with murderous, bottomless-pit anxiety is so far from the easy-viewing fare we've been getting at the movies that *Blue Velvet* has the effect of a sick, black joke on an industry that has given up on the magic of movies. Lynch is saying that movies don't only have the capacity to coddle us; they also have the power to leave us aghast, not in the pop-gruesome way of the horror cheapies, but in the deeper way of artists, by drawing on our dark dreams and bringing them to a simmer.

The slowed-down opening images in *Blue Velvet* — the shots of yellow tulips, fire trucks, grade schoolers crossing the street — glow with a heightened nostalgia. Not for long. Lynch quickly gives us the theme of the movie in miniature: A middle-aged man watering his lawn is suddenly stricken, clutching his throat in a paroxysm of pain before collapsing. The ratchety whir of warring insects takes over the sound track, as the camera scurries deep into the lawn's underbrush, with its battalions of festering horrors. We've been given a glimpse under nature's rock, and soon the glimpse will magnify—only the creatures will be bigger, life-size. The human hellions in *Blue Velvet* will crawl out from under the rock of consciousness and take over the screen.

Jeffrey Beaumont (Kyle MacLachlan), the college-age son of the man who collapsed, returns to his Middle American hometown, Lumberton. He spends a sad, wordless session with his father in the hospital and then, cutting through a field on his way home, finds a detached ear in the grass. This ear, with its poetic association from the Buñuel/Dali movies and the surrealist painters, is Jeffrey's latchkey into a mystery. He shows it to the town's police chief (George Dickerson) and, aided by the chief's teenage daughter Sandy (Laura Dern), tries to solve the enigma. In the course of his voyaging, he encounters a beautiful local nightclub chanteuse, Dorothy Vallens (Isabella Rossellini), whose specialty is singing "Blue Velvet." He discovers that, in exchange for sexual favors, her husband and child are being held hostage by a maniac, Frank Booth (Dennis Hopper), and his scuzzy minions. Jeffrey's detective work becomes more and more obsessive. The netherworld he slips into has a sensual, trancelike pull on him; he's transfixed by the horrors of which men are capable—of which *he* is capable.

Blue Velvet is conceived as a poetic allegory. "Why are there people like Frank?" Jeffrey asks. Frank is everything that perverts goodness—he's malevolence incarnate. He's also Jeffrey's unadmitted animus. To save himself, and right the world, Jeffrey must destroy him. Lynch's poetics have a Freudian cast, but they're not doctrinaire: If they connect with any of the hallowed psychosexual totems, it's at their most basic level—at the same source of fear and anxiety that fairy tales draw on. Frank is Jeffrey's dark double, and his false father; when the boy is in the maniac's clutches, Frank is keyed up, seething. His favorite song is Roy Orbison's "In Dreams," which he carries on cassette; he smears lipstick on his face and mashes his face against Jeffrey's, spitting out, tonelessly, "In dreams I walk with you . . . in dreams you're mine." Frank's omnisexual ferocity is directed at Jeffrey, at Dorothy, at the whole world. The sour, sick fury of his impacted sexuality makes the screen tremble.

In the movie's centerpiece scene, Jeffrey hides in Dorothy's closet and, through the slats, watches Frank, enraged, inhale a gaseous stimulant through a face mask as he batters Dorothy while he copulates. Just before this scene, Dorothy had discovered the boy in her apartment (he was searching for clues) and, holding out a carving knife, orders him to strip. Swooning, she fondles him, knife poised. Lynch goes so far into depravity in this scene that you can't believe what you're watching; your jaw drops.

Lynch gets deeper inside the scourge of sexual terror than any director ever has—the only comparison is with Bernardo Bertolucci's *Last Tango in Paris,* where the sexuality had an emotional violence that also stunned audiences into absolute silence. For Lynch, sex is the force that draws you into life's dark mystery, and at the pit of that mystery is horror. Frank and Dorothy call each other "Mommy" and "Daddy" in that apartment scene; what Jeffrey the voyeur witnesses is like a child's first frantic, uncomprehending glimpse of sex.

What makes such scenes so dreadful for audiences—the reason some people will recoil from them and call the movie exploitative trash—is that Lynch has eroticized them. For Lynch, all fascinations contain a sexual secret. That certainly doesn't mean that he endorses what goes on in this movie. If one feels compelled to look at an auto accident on the freeway, and receives a thrill up the spine, that doesn't mean one endorses auto accidents. Lynch doesn't attempt to deny the horrid fascination of what he shows us. Before he administers the antidote, he wants us to taste the poison.

Lynch has worked with the awful allure of rot in his previous films—*Eraserhead, The Elephant Man,* and *Dune*—but *Blue Velvet* carries his themes so far that it's almost a career apotheosis. It enlarges his obsessions. Dorothy's apartment has the same steady-state creepiness as the apartment in *Eraserhead.* (It even has the same radiator.) It's a chamber of horrors, with Jeffrey appearing in the corridors like a dream walker out of a Cocteau film. The apartment's colors, the mauves and deep greens, are lurid and mesmerizing—these colors still have some blood in them. Inside her apartment, Dorothy seems as trapped and transfixed by her fears as Jeffrey does, and they go at each other like co-conspirators in a mutual nightmare.

Compared to this world, Laura Dern's Sandy, and the whole straight-arrow Lumberton community, pale. Lynch doesn't have the same feeling for paradise as he does for hell, and the lack makes *Blue Velvet* a slightly lopsided allegory. Laura Dern, lovely as she is, should be more transcendent. So should Kyle MacLachlan: He's too blank to register Jeffrey's morbid stirrings. (MacLachlan, who resembles Lynch, functions as the director's alter ego; it's a stand-in role.) But Isabella Rossellini, with her big black wig and crimson lips, is a ripe, ravaged image. She seems to understand exactly what Lynch wants;

her acting is a series of poetic moods. Dennis Hopper certainly knows what Lynch wants. From *Easy Rider* to *Apocalypse Now* to *Blue Velvet,* Hopper has epitomized the aberrant archetypes of each era. He gives one of the most infernal performances ever seen on film.

Blue Velvet comes out at a time when sex and violence in pop culture have come under increasing attack. The force of *Blue Velvet* is, in a way, a testament to what the bluenoses are attacking: It demonstrates the awful power in what the whole Reagan eighties culture is trying to deny. Lynch's movie is presumably contemporary, but he gives it a slightly wacky fifties time-warp ambiance, as if to seal the correspondence between then and now. And yet Lynch hankers for fifties tranquillity. That's the irony of *Blue Velvet.* He's a small-town regular guy except for one crucial thing: He's got an incubus inside him that won't allow him to accept that tranquillity. Like Jeffrey moving to Dorothy's noxious flame, he's compelled to root out all the dirty little secrets.

Los Angeles Herald Examiner, September 19, 1986

BLUE VELVET

Roger Ebert

Blue Velvet contains scenes of such raw emotional energy that it's easy to understand why some critics have hailed it as a masterpiece. A film this painful and wounding has to be given special consideration. And yet those very scenes of stark sexual despair are the tip-off to what's wrong with the movie. They're so strong that they deserve to be in a movie that is sincere, honest, and true. But *Blue Velvet* surrounds them with a story that's marred by sophomoric satire and cheap shots. The director is either denying the strength of his material or trying to defuse it by pretending it's all part of a campy in-joke.

The movie has two levels of reality. On one level, we're in Lumberton, a simpleminded small town where people talk in television clichés and seem to be clones of 1950s sitcom characters. On another level, we're told a story of sexual bondage, of how Isabella Rossellini's husband and son have been kidnapped by Dennis Hopper, who makes her his sexual slave. The twist is that the kidnapping taps into the woman's deepest feelings. She finds that she is a masochist who responds with great sexual passion to this situation.

Everyday town life is depicted with a deadpan irony; characters use lines with corny double meanings and solemnly recite platitudes. Meanwhile, the darker story of sexual bondage is told absolutely on the level in cold-blooded realism.

The movie begins with a much-praised sequence in which picket fences and flower beds establish a small-town idyll. Then a man collapses while watering the lawn, and a dog comes to drink from the hose that is still held in his unconscious grip. The great imagery continues as the camera burrows into the green lawn and finds hungry insects beneath—a metaphor for the surface and buried lives of the town.

The man's son, a college student (Kyle MacLachlan), comes home to visit his dad's bedside and resumes a romance with the daughter (Laura Dern) of the local police detective. MacLachlan finds a severed human ear in a field, and he and Dern get involved in trying to solve the mystery of the ear. The trail leads to a nightclub singer (Rossellini) who lives alone in a starkly furnished flat.

In a sequence that Hitchcock would have been proud of, MacLachlan hides himself in Rossellini's closet and watches, shocked, as she has a sadomasochistic sexual encounter with Hopper, a drug-sniffing pervert. Hopper leaves. Rossellini discovers MacLachlan in the closet and, to his astonishment, pulls a knife on him and forces him to submit to her seduction. He is appalled but fascinated; she wants him to be a "bad boy" and hit her.

These sequences have great power. They make *9½ Weeks* look rather timid by comparison, because they do seem genuinely born from the darkest and most despairing side of human nature. If *Blue Velvet* had continued to develop its story in a straight line, if it had followed more deeply into the implications of the first shocking encounter between Rossellini and MacLachlan, it might have made some real emotional discoveries.

Instead, director David Lynch chose to interrupt the almost hypnotic pull of that relationship in order to pull back to his jokey, small-town satire. Is he afraid that movie audiences might not be ready for stark S&M unless they're assured it's all really a joke?

I was absorbed and convinced by the relationship between Rossellini and MacLachlan, and annoyed because the director kept placing himself between me and the material. After five or ten minutes in which the screen reality was overwhelming, I didn't need the director prancing on with a top hat and cane, whispering that it was all in fun.

Indeed, the movie is pulled so violently in opposite directions that it pulls itself apart. If the sexual scenes are real, then why do we need the send-up of the "Donna Reed Show"? What are we being told? That beneath the surface of Small Town, USA, passions run dark and dangerous? Don't stop the presses.

The sexual material in *Blue Velvet* is so disturbing, and the performance by Rossellini is so convincing and courageous, that it demands a movie that deserves it. American movies have been using satire for years to take the edge off sex and violence. Occasionally, perhaps sex and violence should be treated with the seriousness they deserve. Given the power of the darker scenes in this movie, we're all the more frustrated that the director is unwilling to follow through to the consequences of his insights. *Blue Velvet* is like the guy who drives you nuts by hinting at horrifying news and then saying, "Never mind."

There's another thing. Rossellini is asked to do things in this film that require real nerve. In one scene, she's publicly embarrassed by being dumped naked on the lawn of the police detective. In others, she is asked to portray emotions that I imagine most actresses would rather not touch. She is degraded, slapped around, humiliated, and undressed in front of the camera. And when you ask an actress to endure those experiences, you should keep your side of the bargain by putting her in an important film.

That's what Bernardo Bertolucci delivered when he put Marlon Brando and Maria Schneider through the ordeal of *Last Tango in Paris.* In *Blue Velvet*, Rossellini goes the whole distance, but Lynch distances himself from her ordeal with his clever asides and witty little in-jokes. In a way, his behavior is more sadistic than the Hopper character's.

What's worse? Slapping somebody around, or standing back and finding the whole thing funny?

Chicago Sun-Times, September 19, 1986

WILD AT HEART

Peter Travers

Imagine *The Wizard of Oz* with an oversexed witch, gun-toting Munchkins, and love ballads from Elvis Presley, and you'll get some idea of this erotic hellzapoppin from writer-director David Lynch. Lynch's kinky fairy tale is a triumph of startling images and comic invention. In adapting Barry Gifford's book *Wild at Heart* for the screen, Lynch does more than tinker. Starting with the outrageous and building from there, he ignites a slight love-on-the-run novel, creating a bonfire of a movie.

All that's left of the book is a chunk of pungent dialogue. Lynch dramatically alters the characters; adds liberally from his own wickedly demented imagination; pumps up the violence and erotica; throws in a Toto look-alike, a good and a bad witch, and the ruby slippers from *The Wizard of Oz;* and then watches the sparks fly. Though lacking the organic clarity of *Blue Velvet, Wild at Heart* is a breathtaking display of movie magic that steadily tightens its hypnotic hold. Lynch, the man who shook TV by exposing the pits of cherry-pie America in "Twin Peaks," revels in finding the logic in the random, the beauty in the broken. He's a cockeyed pessimist, both appalled and thrilled by the dark secrets he uncovers.

The story, which begins in North Carolina, revolves around the love of Sailor Ripley (Nicolas Cage) and Lula Pace Fortune (Laura Dern). "Jeez Louise, Sailor," says Lula after one of their marathon sex bouts, "you are something else." Sailor is equally besotted. Between the sex and the chain-smoking, these two seem in danger of burning themselves down. "You really are dangerously cute, Peanut," he tells Lula as she paints her toenails red before doing the same to the town. They're just two sweet, horny kids, except for their Lynch-load of psychological baggage. Raped at thirteen by her father's business partner, Lula has a monster mother, Marietta (Diane Ladd), who arranged to have Lula's father killed in a fire. And Sailor, despite his tender way with a Presley ballad ("Treat me like a fool / Treat me mean and cruel / But love me"), has a hidden past and a rebel streak. He wears a snakeskin jacket as "a symbol of individuality and my belief in personal freedom." But his hot temper has a way of crimping his options.

At a dance hall, Marietta makes a lewd proposition to Sailor in a toilet. When he rejects her, she dispatches a hood to gut him. Sailor bashes the man's head in, not once but repeatedly — Lynch is not one to skimp on the gore. Convicted of manslaughter, Sailor spends the next twenty-two months and eighteen days in prison. When his parole finally comes, the faithful Lula is waiting. They hop in her car and hit the road for California, encountering a mysterious collection of grotesques along the way. Recalling their favorite movie, they lament that "it's too bad we couldn't visit the Wizard of Oz to get good advice."

They certainly need guidance. Marietta has sweet-talked her private-detective boyfriend Johnnie Farragut (the ever-eccentric Harry Dean Stanton) into trailing the runaways. Ladd, who is Dern's real-life mother, squeezes her juicy role with scene-stealing zest. "No tongue — my lipstick," says Marietta as Johnnie tries to steal a kiss. When Johnnie proves slow at finding Lula, Marietta takes more drastic action. "I'm gonna hire me a hit man," she cackles like the Wicked Witch. That's when she calls on her onetime lover Marcello Santos (J. E. Freeman), a mobster of surpassing repugnance.

Sailor and Lula are traveling a metaphorical yellow brick road that Dorothy and Toto would hardly recognize. By the time the lovers reach New Orleans, they're being pursued by several outsize creeps, including Mr. Reindeer (W. Morgan Sheppard), a hit man who lives in a whorehouse with bosomy topless valets, and a trio of ritual killers, played by Calvin Lockhart, David Patrick Kelly, and Grace Zabriskie, who don't spell good news for Johnnie or viewers with weak stomachs.

Wild at Heart abounds in Lynchian peculiarities. In a flashback, we meet Lula's cousin Dell, played by that gifted oddball Crispin Glover. Dell is a nervous type who wishes that every day could be Christmas and relieves his anxiety by making countless sandwiches and putting cockroaches in his underwear. Lynch regards Dell's perversities with the same detached, nonjudgmental wonder with which he views a decapitated head, a severed hand, or flies on vomit.

Lynch's special angle on the world is sometimes repellent but often smashingly effective. One roadside sequence, in which Sailor and Lula encounter the staggering victim of a car accident — played by Sherilyn Fenn, Audrey on "Twin Peaks" — resonates with a ghostly, poetic terror. Lynch's gorgeously lurid style is superbly complemented by the photography of Frederick Elmes, who worked with Lynch on *Eraserhead, Dune,* and *Blue Velvet,* and by the eerily evocative score of the "Twin Peaks" maestro Angelo Badalamenti.

Lynch wisely avoids letting technique overshadow emotion. Cage and Dern deliver phenomenal performances—they're the hottest, oddest movie couple in years. Even those who can't abide Cage—I found him an adenoidal horror in *Peggy Sue Got Married*—may have to capitulate to his daring in playing Sailor. He's tried before to make his yearning eyes, choked voice, and basset-hound deadpan add up to a unique personal style, most notably in *Raising Arizona* and *Vampire's Kiss.* But this time it works awesomely. Cage gives Sailor an animal vibrancy that jumps off the screen. And Dern is his match. Meltingly lovely in *Smooth Talk* and *Blue Velvet,* Dern doesn't overplay fragility the way she did in *Haunted Summer* and *Fat Man and Little Boy.* In fact, nothing she has done before prepares us for the lusty vividness she brings to Lula. Dern is a raunchy, radiant wonder. She makes us see that Lula is just as turned on by trading stories and experiences with Sailor as she is by jumping him in bed. "You move me, Sail, you really do," she says. "You mark me the deepest."

Lynch is clearly moved by the plight of these beleaguered innocents, but that doesn't stop him from heaping on misfortunes. The worst comes in the boomed-out town of Big Tuna, Texas, where Sailor and the now pregnant Lula meet Bobby Peru, a psycho former marine ferociously acted by Willem Dafoe, and Bobby's jealous girlfriend Perdita, played by the delicious Isabella Rossellini with blond hair and a bad attitude. "Big Tuna isn't exactly Emerald City," says Lula. No argument. After nearly raping Lula, Bobby involves Sailor in a robbery that results in shocking bloodshed, death, and another five years in the pen for Sailor.

Some may be bothered by Lynch's fantastical ending. It wouldn't be fair to say more than that the final moments include another meeting of the lovers, a visit from the Good Witch, played by Sheryl Lee (Laura Palmer on "Twin Peaks"), and a heartfelt version of "Love Me Tender" from Sailor. In any universe but one created by Lynch, the audience might feel stranded. But Lynch has a knack for heightened reality that keeps us attuned to the pleasures of the unexpected. "This whole world is weird on top and wild at heart," says Lula. And who better to chart such a world than David Lynch? Even over the rainbow, he finds his own kind of truth.

Rolling Stone, September 6, 1990

WILD AT HEART

Armond White

From the opening scene of *Wild at Heart,* David Lynch crosses the line between art and obscenity. A white man beats a Black man to a literal pulp—blood oozes, bones crack, body crumples. Taken on Lynch's neosurreal level, these aren't anonymous men fighting. Their physical aspects are drastically symbolic, highly connotative, and their actions carry definitive meanings. This knock-down-and-drag-out is an epic battle of the races. Not only does the white man win; in Lynch's view, he *should* win. The Black victim has no personality, little identity (besides wielding a knife and uttering the film's first few cuss words), and his death is never mourned.

Some people want to call this art in the postmodern age, but no matter how inflated with esteem Lynch becomes, his art isn't so great that it transcends political reading or vicious, regressive, conservative meaning. *Wild at Heart* is a road movie about Lula and Sailor (Laura Dern and Nicolas Cage; she of the gaping mouth, he of the annoying voice) on the run from Lula's hysterical, controlling mother (Diane Ladd). The situation isn't real—it's taken from one of the more recurrent themes of movies for the past thirty years: dark-haired man and blonde speed toward their destiny.

Lynch adds contemporary quotients of violence and sex, making Lula a childlike nympho and Sailor an insular Elvis imitator. But instead of these traits signaling an all-too-human compulsion or neurosis, they lapse into cliché: Lynch can't redeem them. Without the surprise of insistent banality where the mundane takes on such a distinctive bathos that the commonplace (and the laws of the universe) seem to be redefined, Lynch's storytelling becomes literal. (Lynch returns too often to a conflagration visual motif—matches, arson, car crashes, heat—that reduces sensation to meaningless mannerism.)

In *Wild at Heart,* America's white trash culture sets the terms through which Lynch sees the world. This can only be praised as insightful or inspired if one shares Lynch's blinkered, regressive unconscious. Not only is it simplistic to depict the most virulent aspects of contemporary society at loose in the lower classes (that's ready-made condescension), but the approach ignores the recent political reality

(*Where the Heart Is, Metropolitan*) that recognizes even antisocial impulses in middle- and upper-class behavior.

Lynch's white working-class identification masquerades as chic nostalgia for the conservative fifties-era inhibitions and repression. (Soon after *Blue Velvet,* a neophyte director such as Bob Balaban was able to copy this approach in *Parents,* his own fifties paranoia film about red meat.) The presumed timeliness of this view is disingenuous. If Lynch were an instinctive artist of this era (rather than a solipsistic expressionist), he would make movies about people trying to put the lid on their libidos instead of seeking to relieve themselves of inhibitions. Lula and Sailor are constantly on the offensive, lashing out at others, striking out for the road. They're Lynch's id monsters, representing aspects of social and political degeneracy that the current era connects with historical hypocrisy. In Lynch, the repressed is returning without irony just as Reagan returned repression as fact rather than neoconservative wish.

The conservative's tendency to coddle and contain his subjectivity shows in Lynch's fondness for outrageous — rather than eccentric — actions. As Lula and Sailor wheel across the Southwest encountering gimpy prostitutes, odious mobsters, and porn stars, they're haunted by images out of *The Wizard of Oz.* These threats from the subconscious (ruby slippers, good and wicked witches, crystal balls, etc.) infantilize their social guilt, make it toylike. Lula and Sailor are trying to get back to the way things used to be; they envision a sentimental, family-centered, Boy Scout, pop-music America.

In *Wild at Heart,* Lynch adheres to the idea of camp (implying its seriousness) as a neocon answer to Jonathan Demme's *Something Wild,* which, even back in 1986, some of us thought was superior to Lynch's *Blue Velvet.* Instead of Demme's intelligent reconciliation with the diversity and instability of the world at large, Lynch retreats into the isolation of fantasy and erotic immaturity where adults are unclean, lecherous monsters. This sexual envy is localized in the way Lynch uses Sailor's adoption of the Elvis Presley persona as a representation of youth's superiority. He's going back to an old idea of rebellion. But the Elvis Presley figure is no longer iconoclastic; it symbolizes, instead, a period of "safe" social progress — specifically just before the revolution of racial and sexual politics. The Presley figure, already domesticated into official Americana, allows yuppie conservatives to cling to a vestige of radicalism as an idea that yet is rooted to a status quo mind-set.

Lynch has fallen markedly from being an avant-garde artist. His "daring" vision was consumed by the mass audience too easily for it to have posed much challenge. *Blue Velvet* can now be seen as an evocation of the era's self-consciousness, which is why postmodernists love it so. It made obvious the psychological dysfunctions that people learned to live with during an era of personal political isolation. It wasn't a movie about solving crimes or ridding the world of evil but about accommodating evil by learning to ignore it. At the end of that picture, Laura Dern's vision of robins and happiness — a consciously manufactured placebo — coincided with the confirmation of Republican-era fantasy.

Because of Lynch's stunningly contrived obviousness in *Blue Velvet* (it was a good picture, no more than that), the mainstream (including Woody Allen, no less) could recognize and eventually appropriate his vision with no trouble. His spring 1990 television series "Twin Peaks" continued the postmodern putsch by further domesticating social problems. It was the perfect TV show for a society well aware of chaos and decay yet seeking some emotional distance from such perceptions — which is exactly what Lynch's facetious art allowed them to do.

Wild at Heart congratulates that sophisticated insensitivity by overdoing delirium and using excesses of violence and sex to entertain decadent tastes. It's tempting to suggest that the perceived anomaly of an arty TV show like "Twin Peaks" actually, in fact, wound up subverting Lynch himself, but that's true only in part. Actually, his most comprehensible work scrupulously avoids being transgressive or truly radical. And just as *Something Wild* explored society's infrastructure better than *Blue Velvet,* one can see a superior example of *Wild at Heart*'s generational conflict in Brian De Palma's 1978 masterpiece, *The Fury.*

De Palma's control of genre stereotypes and thriller-teen-flick kinetics enabled him to make comment on the effect of pop mythology while spinning a tale about the adult world (government authority) attempting to co-opt the sexual energy (innocence, righteousness) of youth. The measure of Lynch's failing can be taken by the triviality and meaninglessness of the pop references throughout *Wild at Heart.* It's a postmodern world Lula and Sailor inhabit, all right — decentered and disgustingly fake.

Meaningful art gives a sense of the artist's ideas and facts of life being at stake. David Lynch isn't an artist who makes that happen, but Public Enemy certainly does — almost regularly, most of all in their "Fight the Power" theme song for *Do the Right Thing,* where the denunciation of Elvis Presley drew a line through American popular culture. "Fight the Power" was the single work of art in the past ten years to demand that the public (and other artists) declare themselves for a progressive view of culture or a traditionalist, politically conservative view. Lynch's paean to fifties values in *Wild at Heart* shows exactly where his heart is: deep in the darkness of a lily-white paranoid America.

Undeniably there is a psychological connection between the scarcity of Black people in Lynch's "Twin Peaks" worldview and the matter-of-fact racial killing that opens *Wild at Heart.* His vision coheres around the self-centeredness (and racism) that signifies bad art. To excuse Lynch on the basis of his "profundity" is to be as blind to the intricacies of popular art, and its social function, as the blissfully ignorant Lula and Sailor. When Godard took his trio of young lovers and crooks on the road in *Band of Outsiders* (1964), he didn't divorce them from the political world: Godard made a great movie by facing contemporary politics head-on. For Lynch to use art as a sinecure — displacing and suppressing politics — indicates shallowness or dishonesty. It certainly limits the value of his work and makes his complex strategies offensive in the most ordinary way.

Some people like Lynch's moralistic method of exposing the dirty, sexual secrets of his characters, but that's not much of an approach these days; corruption and insensitivity no longer misrepresent themselves in the Oliver North/Donald Trump era. But I think the sex in Lynch's movies is as much a dead giveaway as the racism. His exposés aren't enlightening, merely uptight. Anyone who gets as out of joint over sex as Lynch isn't a seer but a prude.

City Sun, August 22–28, 1990

THE SILENCE OF THE LAMBS

J. Hoberman

Jonathan Demme's *The Silence of the Lambs* is a thriller as somber as it is frightening. The film has a dark, brooding momentum. Superbly terse and moody, it's troubling for reasons that are not always apparent. Given the shock material and Demme's visceral direction, the movie is unexpectedly affecting, with its burden of grief unusual for its genre; beneath the narrative, there's a river of tears.

A revisionist version of the psycho-slasher woman-in-danger flick, adapted by Ted Tally from Thomas Harris's 1988 best-seller (the sort of book you avidly consume in two sittings, then stop to wonder why), *The Silence of the Lambs* reverses the form's customary mode. Here, a young woman tracks the monster as well as vice versa: Jodie Foster stars as Clarice Starling, a resourceful FBI trainee drafted into the search for a crazed serial killer nicknamed Buffalo Bill for his trademark kink of skinning the women he abducts and murders.

Although, as imagined by Harris, Clarice is strikingly beautiful, Foster's isn't a glamorous portrayal. Her hair is lank, she speaks with a flat, Appalachian twang, and she's under strain in every sequence — ostentatiously unsmiling, sharp features focused to a point. (As the actress herself was a victim of American pathology, her character's mixture of beleaguered cool and intense isolation takes on additional resonance. In any case, the movie is inconceivable without her.) The credit sequence, with solitary, sweat-suited Clarice pushing herself through the obstacle course on the wooded grounds of the FBI academy, signals that the movie will be her ordeal. If *Blue Velvet* was something like "The Hardy Boys on Mars," then *The Silence of the Lambs* is "Nancy Drew Meets the Minotaur" — a chthonic quest through back wards and backwoods, rural funeral parlors and make-shift morgues, abandoned rooms in decrepit Rust Belt towns and storage facilities so moldy the cobwebs look like jungle creepers, into the ultimate basement of death.

The film exudes irresolvable crisis. No one is safe. It only takes five minutes for a cop to be surprised, overpowered, butchered, and trussed like an angel to the top of a holding cage. Seldom have so many SWAT teams been deployed to so little avail. More than a haunted terrain where the bleak winter landscape is unsoftened by snow, Demme's America is a charnel house of flayed, fragmented, mutilated bodies — their baroque torment typically preserved in su-permarket tabloids or 8×10 glossies. With its manicured grounds and clean, functional buildings, the FBI academy where Clarice receives her Spartan training is the lone citadel of rationality. Everyplace else reeks of menace: The interiors are characterized by longtime Demme-collaborator Tak Fujimoto's black-on-black, Ad Reinhardt lighting; most of the exteriors were shot at night, and even the sunshine seems as pallid as a lifer's complexion.

The Silence of the Lambs has a heavy infusion of gothic elements, although Clarice—the daughter of a small-town West Virginia cop, killed when she was a child—is the opposite of the archetypically helpless gothic heroine. For starters, she's sent by her mentor, special agent Jack Crawford (Scott Glenn), to consult the most sinister of oracles, Dr. Hannibal Lecter (Anthony Hopkins), a psychotic psychiatrist who is himself a mass murderer, with a penchant for eating his victims. (*The Silence of the Lambs* is a movie in which all men have their hidden agendas.) Lecter is locked in the dungeon of a suitably dank and turreted Baltimore mental hospital and, in a scene worthy of *Shock Corridor,* Clarice must run a gauntlet of gibbering crazies—one hissing "I can smell your cunt"—to find him standing at ironic attention, a chilly twinkle in his dead blue eyes.

Largely faithful to the novel (in this scene particularly), Tally's adaptation is necessarily compressed. Although the script renders character psychology even more schematic than originally written, it also has the effect of heightening Harris's nightmarish imagery—the movie's strongest sequences have intimations of *Un Chien Andalou* and *Vampyr*—as well as reinforcing the book's Grimm's-tale subtext. In essence, *The Silence of the Lambs* is a bloody *Kindermärchen* in which, to resolve the question of her own identity, the fatherless heroine is compelled to rely upon the dangerous advice of two duplicitous surrogates. (That the memory of Clarice's mother is so repressed as to preclude a flashback underscores the movie's lone example of maternity—the distant and powerful U.S. senator whose daughter is Buffalo Bill's ultimate victim.)

As Crawford, Clarice's daytime dad, Scott Glenn is paper dry and dourly uptight. His intentions masked by a vinegary smile and expression hooded behind clear plastic glasses, he might be Grant Wood's farmer in a three-piece suit. (The film script relieves him of his tragic burden: in the novel his wife is terminally ill.) More attractive is the nocturnal Anthony Hopkins. The urbane mutant to whom the script hands its best lines, he more than fulfills the gothic archetype of the charismatic suitor who may also be a crazed murderer. With his shiny, outsize head, Hopkins's Lecter seems at once advanced and devolved—he listens to the Goldberg Variations as he contemplates devouring his jailer.

While Crawford sets Clarice specific tasks, playful Lecter amuses himself by messing with her mind, doling out encoded information while conducting a bizarre form of psychoanalysis. Avuncular where Crawford is evasive, Lecter demands that Clarice relive her childhood traumas as the price for his insights into Buffalo Bill. As compared to the novel, however, Lecter has been considerably softened – if not sentimentalized. Demme cuts from a scene of Buffalo Bill taunting his captive to one of Lecter, his face imprisoned in a grotesque hockey mask, mocked by *his* keeper, the smarmy Dr. Chilton (played with open-mouthed gusto by Anthony Heald).

The Silence of the Lambs has been described as a departure for Demme, although his early drive-in movies, not to mention *Something Wild,* exhibited a marked flair for violence. The film is not exactly freewheeling – but neither is it devoid of Demme humor (most creepily when we're introduced to one victim driving her heap through the rainy night, singing along as her car radio blasts the Tom Petty headbanger "American Girl"). There's a subtle, sci-fi flavor reminiscent of *Melvin and Howard.* Characters hurtle through the air like missiles – Clarice and Crawford uncomfortably squeezed together in the back seat of a small plane, examining photographs of the killer's latest victim; Lecter, bound to a hospital stretcher, being flown through the night to a top-secret rendezvous; Crawford at the console of an airborne FBI fortress zooming over the Midwest. The film locates itself close to the source of planetary power – but, if the Capitol is shrouded in darkness and the Smithsonian full of reconstructed dinosaur skeletons, the woods and towns of the Beltway are even darker boneyards.

Demme is good on clutter – the ghastly photos and lurid clippings on Crawford's office wall, the shelf of cheap china kittens in a murdered girl's chilly room, the various breeding tanks, dress mannequins, and wall hangings of Buffalo Bill's lair. As vivid as that bilious green hellhole is, the film's weakest, most problematic element is precisely its denizen. Meant to be the personification of evil, Buffalo Bill (Ted Levine) is a jarring billboard of discordant signs – a figure stitched together, like the Frankenstein monster, taking elements from Robert Mitchum in *The Night of the Hunter, Psycho*-prototype Ed Gein (who also used to dress in the skins of the women he murdered), the post-Manson hippie killers of the early seventies, and, most offensively, a Hollywood homosexual from the same era, complete with pet poodle and nipple ring.

The characterization is crude, but then Buffalo Bill's pathology, even less developed here than in the novel, only makes metaphoric sense. In his bloody quest for self-actualization, the serial killer is Clarice's nightmare opposite. Film theorist Linda Williams has written persuasively on the horror movie's implicit equation of monster and woman – the monster, "one of many mirrors held up [to women] by patriarchy" being "a biological freak with impossible and threatening appetites that suggest a frightening potency precisely where the normal male would perceive a lack." Thus, the desire that defines Buffalo Bill's illness is what Clarice's desire must overcome. She too is a freak, a woman alone in a man's world. (Demme includes several shots in which she is surrounded by male officers.)

Ultimately, what makes *The Silence of the Lambs* so potent is the heroine's inconsolable unhappiness, her solitude and sense of abandonment, the rescue fantasies she nurtures, the defensive posture she's forced to maintain. Not the least of *The Silence of the Lambs*'s reversals is that, although Clarice is the heroine, the movie's final image of freedom does not belong to her.

Village Voice, February 19, 1991

THE SILENCE OF THE LAMBS

Dave Kehr

It's on the second viewing that films usually reveal their undertones — the background emotions that may heighten, offset, or even contradict the feelings the director has self-consciously placed up front.

In the case of Jonathan Demme's *The Silence of the Lambs* — which seems, on the first pass, a particularly brutal, inhuman thriller — a second look reveals a layer of sadness and exhaustion, a pervasive, dispiriting sense of resignation.

This sadness of *The Lambs* is, perhaps, a sadness of surrender, the despair of an immensely gifted filmmaker who has (only for the moment, one hopes) decided to abandon the struggle. It's a film that contradicts almost everything Demme has stood for as an artist, in such superbly realized films as *Something Wild, Melvin and Howard,* and *Handle with Care,* and yet, in the three weeks it has been in release, it is well on its way to becoming the most commercially successful of Demme's films — his only real hit.

It's sad, too, that the film's success doesn't seem surprising in the least. Give the people what they want — which, in this case, apparently, is a cannibalistic serial killer as the hero of a major motion picture — and they'll turn out every time.

For those who haven't yet seen *The Silence of the Lambs* (and it is, for all of its disturbing implications, a film that deserves to be looked at and taken seriously), the plot might be quickly summarized as follows:

Baffled by a series of murders, in which the killer removes the skin of his victims, FBI agent Jack Crawford (Scott Glenn) assigns eager young FBI trainee Clarice Starling (Jodie Foster) to establish a relationship with captured serial killer Dr. Hannibal "The Cannibal" Lecter (Anthony Hopkins), a brilliant psychiatrist who enjoyed devouring the internal organs of his victims. Crawford hopes that Lecter may have some special insights into the killer's personality, which he might share with a beautiful, vulnerable young woman.

As it turns out, somewhat too conveniently, Dr. Lecter not only possesses those insights, but also knows the killer's identity, having treated one of his early victims. Clarice must convince him to give her the name before Buffalo Bill, as the new killer has been nicknamed, can execute his latest kidnap victim.

Demme, following Ted Tally's screenplay adapted from Thomas Harris's novel, cuts among the on-the-scene investigations of Crawford and Clarice; Buffalo Bill (Ted Levine) in his infernal cellar, preparing for his latest kill; and Dr. Lecter's grisly attempts to escape. But the core of this film is the relationship between Clarice and Lecter, as it is played out on opposite sides of glass walls and prison bars.

The Silence of the Lambs was described by *Village Voice* critic Amy Taubin as "deliberately, unabashedly, and uncompromisingly a feminist movie," an interpretation that Demme himself has clung to in his interviews. The film establishes a clear, if somewhat exaggerated, parallel between Clarice's exploitation at the hands of her employer Crawford (who is also portrayed as a father figure and potential lover) and Buffalo Bill's treatment of his victims as objects or animals (he is "harvesting" their skin to make a dress for himself).

Only Clarice's inner strength and feisty independence save her from the predatory impulses of the males who surround her; she is allowed — and this is the greatest anomaly for a Hollywood film of 1991 — to survive the film without entering into a romance, without being claimed and redeemed by a man.

But is that really true? Clarice earns Lecter's complicity by striking a strange bargain: For every bit of information Lecter grants her, he will be allowed another question about the most intimate aspects of her emotional history. It's hard to see the feminist thrust of a heroine who allows herself to be raped, mentally if not physically, in exchange for access to the male's superior intelligence and insight.

The perverse dynamics of the Clarice–Lecter relationship become the central focus of the film. On one side of the glass partition that fronts Lecter's infernal prison cell there is power and desire, on the other vulnerability and submission.

The exploitative relationship is reflected in the literary names Harris has chosen for his characters: *Hannibal Lecter* links the irresistible power of a legendary military leader (with the free side effect of some phantom elephant imagery) to a sinister intellectualism — Hannibal is a reader (a *lecteur* in French) of both books and souls. *Clarice Starling* trembles with a quaint, bygone femininity — a bird about to vanish under the elephant's foot.

Clarice makes herself valuable to her FBI superiors to the degree that she enjoys a "special" closeness to Lecter (although she clearly has other investigative talents). As a couple, she empowers him and he validates her; they become a unit, and we are made to feel troubled when Clarice seems to betray him with a phony deal involving a furlough on a disease-ridden island. It's like a lovers' quarrel, a senseless spat in an Astaire-Rogers film, and we want to see it resolved as quickly as possible.

Luckily, the pair is able to kiss and make up. The consummation of their relationship comes when Clarice yields her ultimate emotional secret (the traumatic childhood event that gives the film its protectively poetic title) and Lecter responds with the suggestion that finally allows her to track the new killer to his lair. There is even a happy ending, one that reaffirms the bond between the characters by means of a quick, sick joke. Lecter promises to kill (and devour) the one character they both dislike — the one character who has tried to come between them.

One of the principal themes of Demme's work is precisely this sense of exchange between the partners in a romantic relationship, an exchange that produces a couple that is greater — stronger, more stable, and more alive — than the sum of its parts. The incurable dreamer (Paul Le Mat) marries the hopeless pragmatist (Mary Steenburgen) in *Melvin and Howard;* the tense businessman (Jeff Daniels) is seduced by the dangerous free spirit (Melanie Griffith) in *Something Wild;* another uptight FBI agent (Matthew Modine) succumbs to the funky ethnicity of a gangster's wife (Michelle Pfeiffer) in *Married to the Mob.*

The Silence of the Lambs parodies and perverts that process. The exchange is not free, but horribly forced, sadistically inflicted; the couple produced is sterile and monstrous.

We know that Clarice has finally absorbed all that Lecter has to teach when Demme confers Lecter's signature shot upon her: a huge, looming close-up, taken through a space-compacting telephoto lens. This is an image of total domination — the subject's forehead seems to hang over the audience, the burning eyes fix us directly — and it sums up Demme's style in *The Silence of the Lambs,* a style of intimidation, control, manipulation. He will tell us exactly where to look, down to the precise millimeter, and exactly what to feel, down to the smallest tremor.

That's hardly an unusual technique in American movies, but in the context of a Jonathan Demme film it seems almost shocking, so thoroughly and deliberately does it contradict the approach Demme has developed over the course of his career.

Like Renoir and Rossellini in Europe, and McCarey and Sturges in Hollywood, Demme belongs to a profoundly democratic tradition of filmmaking, in which the basic unit is a long shot, filled with a number of characters and a multiplicity of points of view, that allows the viewer to make his own choices, forge his own identifications, and arrive at his own judgments. It is an open, free style, as opposed to the closed-off, authoritarian technique of a Hitchcock or Lang. And most audiences don't like it, because it requires too much work.

In *The Silence of the Lambs,* Demme has finally given up: He's succumbed to the temptations of movie authoritarianism, making a film about domination that seeks itself to dominate its audience. Clarice's compassion is only the alibi; the film's deepest appeal lies in the dream of complete callousness, of irresistible power and perfect freedom from moral constraint, that Lecter represents. Ultimately, the film is a power fantasy barely distinguishable from the crudest Arnold Schwarzenegger or Eddie Murphy vehicle, though aimed at a more knowing, more sophisticated public.

There is one shot in *The Silence of the Lambs* that bears Demme's signature, and it comes at the very end of the film: Looking down from above, the camera watches the people passing through the narrow main street of a Caribbean village, quietly observing as Lecter disappears into the crowd. The camera continues to record the spectacle for several minutes, as the end credits pass, even though there is now nothing to see (that is, nothing to do with the narrative).

As the character disappears, so does the director: His authority melts away, leaving only an open, uninflected view of a real world living in its own time and its own rhythm. This is a shot that could have been taken by Louis Lumière on the first day of the invention of the movies (and Lumière did take many like it). Returning a sudden, startling sense of innocence to this deeply contrived, brutally calculated film, the shot is almost heartbreaking. Here, in one image, is what Jonathan Demme has lost.

Chicago Tribune, March 10, 1991

CAPE FEAR

J. Hoberman

The young Jean-Luc Godard wrote of Nicholas Ray that if the cinema no longer existed, Ray alone would be capable of inventing it — and, what's more, of wanting to. Looking at the roster of current American directors, the same might be said (and often is) of Martin Scorsese. Steven Spielberg has made more money, Woody Allen has received more accolades, Oliver Stone (a former student) has reaped bigger headlines — but nobody has made better movies. Scorsese is Hollywood's designated maestro: the most celluloid-obsessed and single-minded filmmaker in Hollywood, the one American director that Spike Lee would deign to admire.

Although *Taxi Driver* and the title song from *New York, New York* are the only Scorsese artifacts to embed themselves in American mainstream consciousness (a television series based on *Alice Doesn't Live Here Anymore* barely lasted one season), Scorsese has never lacked for critical support. *Mean Streets* was the most highly praised debut of the seventies; *Raging Bull* topped several polls as the best American movie of the eighties; *GoodFellas* received virtually every critics' award in 1990. Even his so-called flops — the brilliant *King of Comedy,* engaging *After Hours,* and heartfelt *Last Temptation of Christ* — have had their defenders.

Perhaps hoping to repay Universal for bankrolling his magnificent obsession, *The Last Temptation of Christ,* Scorsese has entered into an exclusive six-year directing and producing deal with the studio and succumbed, at last, to remakitis. With his edgily overwrought *Cape*

Max Cady (Robert De Niro) awaits a secret rendezvous with the unsuspecting daughter of the family he is terrorizing in *Cape Fear*. (Photo by Phil Caruso, courtesy of Universal Pictures.)

Fear remake, he has concocted an admittedly commercial thriller more skillful than inspired and at least as cerebral as it is gut twisting.

The first *Cape Fear* (1961, released by Universal-International) was knocked off by British director J. Lee Thompson between the martial epics *The Guns of Navarone* and *Taras Bulba*. The hero, Sam Bowden (Gregory Peck), was an upstanding Georgia prosecutor who, some years before, had testified against one Max Cady (Robert Mitchum) in a particularly vicious rape case. The plot thickens when Cady, having served his time, comes looking for revenge, presumably to be inflicted on Bowden's wife and daughter.

Undeniably disturbing (the original trailers promised moviegoers that they were going to "Feel Fear!"), Thompson's movie derived much of its frisson from Cady's antisocial assault on the good-good culture of the fifties. With the judicious Peck seemingly preparing for his Oscar-laureate role as the saintly Southern lawyer in Universal's *To Kill a Mockingbird,* which opened six months later, and his wife and daughter (TV personalities Polly Bergen and Lori Martin) so sitcom wholesome, one might well sympathize with the villain—at least at first.

The heavy, deceptively somnolent Mitchum—an action star with a hipster edge, having been busted for pot in the late forties—brought a brute physicality and unprecedented sexual sadism to his characterization. Barry Gifford, who would later pay homage to *Cape Fear* by incorporating its eponymous location in his meta-noir novel *Wild at Heart,* calls Mitchum "the angel of death-with-pain, put on earth to give men pause." But although *Cape Fear* is as much horror film as thriller—with Mitchum's virtually unkillable monster anticipating the slashers of the late seventies—there is another, equally disturbing subtext lurking in the film.

Cady wants to spook Bowden before he destroys him, and for much of the movie he is protected by the very law he places himself beyond. Set in the South and released at the height of the struggle for desegregation, *Cape Fear* conjures up the bogie of a terrifying rapist—albeit white—who proved inconveniently conversant with his "civil rights." In its nightmarish way, *Cape Fear* managed to suggest both what terrified the white South and the terror the white South itself inspired. "You won't forget this movie," Gifford ends his critique, "especially if you're a Yankee Jew."

In general, *Cape Fear* was received with trepidation. The film's British opening was delayed until early 1963, while Thompson and Lord Morrison, president of the British Board of Censors, argued over cuts. (The movie was eventually released with six minutes trimmed.) Calling it "a nasty film," Lord Morrison objected to the sexual threat Mitchum posed to Lori Martin. Nor was the British censor alone. Pit in *Variety,* Dwight MacDonald in *Esquire,* and Bosley Crowther in the *New York Times* all warned readers against bringing their children, Crowther adding that *Cape Fear* was "one of those shockers that provoke disgust and regret."

Of course, disgust and regret are scarcely emotions to make Martin Scorsese flinch, and he would doubtless endorse the sense the 1962 movie left that civilization's veneer is somewhat less sturdy than the shell of an egg.

Scorsese's *Cape Fear* opens with the camera rising from the depths of the primordial swamp where all the protagonists will ultimately swim. Although the ensuing sense of beleaguered middle-class territoriality is as strong as ever, the new *Cape Fear* complicates the moral equation by shifting focus from Max Cady, flamboyantly played by Robert De Niro, to the Bowden family. In this *Cape Fear,* the Bowdens' lives are built on quicksand. Scorsese undermines their solidarity, wipes his hands on their reputations, sullies their laundry with a miasma of guilt.

Not simply a concerned citizen, the new Sam Bowden turns out to have been Cady's public defender against a particularly brutal charge of rape, who buried evidence of the victim's promiscuity so as not to jeopardize his client's conviction. The self-righteousness inherent in sensitive Peck has here coalesced into uptight Nick Nolte—a man built to absorb punishment, even as his menacing bulk suggests Mitchum's. As his wife Leigh (renamed for Janet?), Jessica Lange looks just as classy as precursor Polly Bergen, but she's considerably more bitter and a lot less supportive. Their teenage daughter Danielle, played by Juliette Lewis, is ripe and disheveled, braces gleaming out of her unformed face. (Does Marty know how to pick them? Not long after *Cape Fear*'s release, Lewis replaced Emily Lloyd as the nymphet in Woody Allen's current project.)

Whereas in 1962 evil stalked the Bowden family from without, the threat is now to be found within. They are, as current parlance would have it, "dysfunctional." Leigh not irrationally suspects Sam of having an affair; to block out their screaming, Danielle—who is recovering, it is suggested, from a precocious drug problem—locks herself in her bedroom, flicks on both MTV and the radio, and begins compulsively dialing her Swatch phone, as instinctive an ostrich as the rest of her clan. Meanwhile, his release from prison heralded by a drumroll of thunder, Cady is the return of Bowden's repressed self—telling him later that while the judge and DA "were just doing their jobs," Bowden betrayed his trust.

Even more than in the original, it's difficult not to feel a sneaky sympathy for Cady, particularly when the more physically imposing

Bowden is trying to buy him off, or, later, hiring goons to run him out of town. This Cady is less the snake in the Bowden family Eden and more the projection of their unconscious fears. Indeed, he first appears to them in precisely that fashion. Shuffling into a movie house (showing the horror comedy *Problem Child*), Cady positions himself directly in front of the family, blocks the screen, and, brandishing his cigar while laughing like a hyena, subjects them to what must be the film buff's ultimate violation. "Dad, you should have just punched him out," Lewis admonishes Nolte, unaware that they've just encountered implacable evil.

Cross splayed across his back, religious mantras inscribed on his arms, De Niro's Cady is a self-taught psychopath and a refugee from Kafka's penal colony, as much a mythological beast as any unicorn or yeti. Although it's tempting to read his character as Scorsese's revenge on the Christian fundamentalists who attacked *The Last Temptation of Christ,* it's difficult to conceptualize the sort of born-again Baptist who would pray to Jesus beneath a Stalin pin-up and augment the scriptures with a combination of *Thus Spake Zarathustra* and Henry Miller. A two-bit de Sade with delusions of grandeur, Cady sees himself as avenging angel. By opening the family up to his blandishments, *Cape Fear* has perverse intimations of *Teorema* as well as *Straw Dogs.*

Johnny Boy and Travis Bickle, Jake La Motta and Rupert Pupkin have nothing on this nut. With his long black hair slicked back under a white yachting cap, mouth wrapped around the world's biggest cigar butt, and torso draped in a flaming aloha shirt, De Niro is a cracker from hell. The conception is wildly baroque, and most of the time De Niro's Cady is more crazy than menacing. Although his tattooed slogans and religious rants evoke Mitchum's career performance as the psychotic preacher in *The Night of the Hunter,* De Niro lacks Mitchum's insolent ease as a performer. His Max Cady is a riff and, half camping on his southern drawl, he never lets you forget it.

The movie, too, is knowing without seeming felt. The rough sex here looks a lot rougher than it did in the original, but is actually less visceral. Where Mitchum cracks an egg on one of his victims, De Niro (like Dracula) takes a bite out of a woman's face. More overt too is his suggestion, repeated in various contexts throughout the film, that when a rape is reported, it is actually the victim who goes on trial. (Note: Even though *Cape Fear* opened the very day the American public was transfixed by allegations of sexual harassment and achieved box-office saturation during the William Kennedy Smith rape trial, the operative movie metaphor for such cases remained *Fatal Attraction. Cape Fear*'s critique is softened by the use of the daughter's voice-over to frame the movie—the entire nightmare can thus be read as the hysterical fantasy of a teenage girl.)

In the movie's most daring set piece, De Niro makes a call to Lewis in the guise of her new drama coach (one more instance of subtext overwhelming narrative). The stunt nature of this self-reflexive turn is literalized by having the actor chat on the phone and even cue records while dangling upside down on his chinning bar (eventually the camera flips over as well). It's followed by another hot-dog scene in which, having lured Lewis down into her high school's basement and onto the stage where a play is to be rehearsed, De Niro seems determined to out-creep Willem Dafoe's "seduction" of Laura Dern in *Wild at Heart.* This fairy-tale sequence in the make-believe gingerbread house ("I'm the Big Bad Wolf," De Niro begins) has received near-universal acclaim. What's far more effective, however, is Nolte's subsequent rage at the nubile daughter with whom he can never quite make eye contact. "Did he touch you? Wipe that smile off your face!" he screams when he discovers what happened. It's an indignity Gregory Peck never had to suffer—the autumn of the patriarch.

Does it sound as if *Cape Fear* is overdirected? The movie is undeniably gripping and it certainly looks great. Shot by Freddie Francis, director of the Hammer horror flicks beloved by Scorsese in his youth, it's a heady succession of extreme close-ups and artful reflections, luridly shimmering sunsets lit by flickers of heat lightning. If an unknown had signed *Cape Fear,* it would have been heralded as an impressive debut. (Consider the delirious overpraise that greeted *Dead Again.*) But Scorsese is no twenty-five-year-old retooling antique genres, and more than one observer has attributed *Cape Fear*'s manic formalism to the director's alienation from the material (a similar hyperkinetic frenzy is evident in his last commercial assignment, the 1986 *The Color of Money*).

Scorsese's relationship to *Cape Fear* is, however, more self-conscious and complex. No less than Godard, Scorsese is prodigiously movie-literate. His VCRs work overtime, he employs a full-time film archivist, spends thousands on prints, and has supervised the restoration and re-release of movies as varied as *Peeping Tom, Once Upon a Time in the West,* and *Le Carrosse d'Or.* His grasp of film history far exceeds that of most American critics and is far too sophisticated for him to attempt anything so crude as an un-self-conscious remake—let alone a heedless obliteration of the original version. If anything, the new *Cape Fear* assumes that the viewer has seen the earlier one, perhaps even as recently as Scorsese himself.

In effect, Scorsese has taken a piece of hack work and, like the archetypal *auteur,* filled it with his own directorial touches and perhaps subversive notions of guilt and redemption. Douglas Sirk is quoted in the film. As *The Nation*'s Stuart Klawans observed in his suitably ambivalent review, "History robbed Scorsese of the chance to be an *auteur* in the full, oppositional sense of the term. So now, as compensation, he's gone back thirty years and inserted himself into a studio product, *Cape Fear,* giving it the one thing it lacked in 1962 — a star performance by the director."

The new *Cape Fear* oscillates between a critique of the original and a variation on a common text: It's a choreographed hall of mirrors, an orchestrated echo chamber. The first version resonates throughout the second — often literally. Elmer Bernstein stridently reworks the original Bernard Herrmann score. An aged Robert Mitchum appears as the local chief of police, and his deep drawl, first heard over the telephone, haunts the movie. Martin Balsam, who played the police chief in the 1962 version, has here been promoted to judge.

Scorsese's witty casting includes using the archetypal southern vigilante, star of *Walking Tall,* Joe Don Baker, as a sleazy private eye whose idea of a mixed drink is Pepto-Bismol laced with Jim Beam. But the film's vertiginous sense of inversion is completed by the appearance of Gregory Peck as the enthusiastically slippery criminal lawyer who represents De Niro's smirking Cady. (It's as if Peck has become what he beheld.) Scorsese's remake thus contains its own negative image — a trope that's more than once utilized in the cinematography. *Cape Fear*'s tumultuous climax — a *tour de force* for De Niro, Scorsese, and mainly editor Thelma Schoonmaker — completes the role reversals by putting the lawyer Nolte on trial, even while the boat of civilization spins out of control and cracks up on the rocks.

Although De Niro's final scene is as powerfully crafted an exit as that actor has ever made, the movie — like his performance — is a good deal more spectacular than terrifying, and somewhat less than the sum of its parts. Blood is not an abstraction; De Niro is. (I never thought I'd say this, but what *Cape Fear* needs is a shot of Paul Schrader — Cady's particular nexus of evangelical fervor, sexual guilt, and class resentment is more alluded to than fleshed out.) Like the villain, the location lacks specificity: It's a curiously all-white South.

Budgeted at $34 million, *Cape Fear* is Scorsese's most expensive movie, and his first commissioned project since *The Color of Money.* The project originated with Steven Spielberg, who interested De Niro in playing Cady, who then persuaded Scorsese to undertake a commercial thriller. And indeed, *Cape Fear* is structurally quite similar to Spielberg's *Hook.* A careerist father's failure to spend quality time with his children brings down a baroque threat to the family that can only be defeated by the father's capacity for regression. The difference is that *Hook* is filmically more impoverished, but psychologically far richer.

That absence of pathology seems to have left Scorsese with a guilty conscience. "I think a lot of the pictures I've made are good," he recently told *Premiere.* "But they're not *The Searchers.* They're not *8½. The Red Shoes. The Leopard.*"

Although it's a disservice to consider *Cape Fear* more than middling Scorsese, the film has received near-universal raves. The major exception is *New Yorker* critic Terrence Rafferty, who, no less hysterical than those who hailed *Cape Fear* a masterpiece, termed the film "a disgrace . . . ugly, incoherent, dishonest." Rafferty echoes the original's reviews — including the brief mention that appeared in the *New Yorker* back in 1962: "Everyone concerned with this repellent attempt to make a great deal of money out of a clumsy plunge into sexual pathology should be thoroughly ashamed of himself." And money has been made. *Cape Fear,* which seems headed for a $70 million domestic gross, needed barely six weeks to surpass *The Color of Money* as Scorsese's most financially successful film. (His reassuringly outré follow-up project is an adaptation of Edith Wharton's novel, *The Age of Innocence.*)

Directors are manipulative by definition, but I've never met a filmmaker more adept at enlisting critical sympathy than Scorsese. "For Scorsese, there's no such thing as a throwaway," Peter Biskind wrote in *Premiere.* "He couldn't sell out if he wanted to," enthused Richard Corliss in *Time.* Their characterizations are not exaggerated; neither is their support unwarranted. Other directors wax self-servingly sentimental about the art of the movies; Scorsese repeatedly pledges allegiance, spending time and money on the job of preservation.

In extolling Nicholas Ray, Godard was reviewing his less than epochal *Hot Blood*—"a semi-successful film to the extent that Ray was semi-uninterested in it." *Cape Fear* is a similar sort of semiotext. More than a critic's darling, Scorsese is a national treasure — the only director in Hollywood whose devotion to cinema justifies everyone's notions of popular art. We need him. He needs a hit. *Cape Fear* is a semi-sacrifice to that faith.

Sight and Sound, February 1992

CAPE FEAR

Terrence Rafferty

Martin Scorsese's *Cape Fear* is a remake of a bluntly effective 1962 thriller about a middle-class family — husband, wife, teenage daughter — who are terrorized by a devious, implacable psychopath. This looks like Scorsese's attempt to make a crowd-pleasing commercial film, to apply his intense, kinetic style to the relatively undemanding job of scaring audiences out of their wits. The movie is a disgrace: an ugly, incoherent, dishonest piece of work. The original picture, directed by a skillful journeyman, J. Lee Thompson, is memorable without being especially artful. Thompson's movie (adapted, by James R. Webb, from a John D. MacDonald pulp novel called *The Executioners*) is no-frills suspense. The story couldn't be simpler. An ex-con named Max Cady arrives in a Southern town in search of the man he holds responsible for his imprisonment, the lawyer Sam Bowden. There's no doubt that Cady is out for revenge. We understand that his dedication to his task is utterly single-minded, but he's too smart to do anything that would allow the authorities to lock him up or run him out of town; he conveys his intentions to Bowden through suggestions and insinuations rather than explicit threats. Calmly and cruelly, he does everything he can to undermine Bowden's sense of security. From the moment Cady appears in town, Bowden is constantly aware of him. Cady is furtive and unscrupulous, and he has the unnerving quick-strike elusiveness of a guerrilla fighter — the now-you-see-it-now-you-don't quality that can give human malevolence the aura of the demonic. He's a monster, a bogeyman, and the original *Cape Fear* has the straight-ahead construction of a horror movie. It aims low, meaning only to produce the most fundamental, uncomplicated sort of tension: There's something out there; we don't know how to stop it; here it comes again. Bowden (played by Gregory Peck in his best pillar-of-rectitude manner) is so civilized and rational that initially he is almost helpless against Cady's animal cunning; as the movie goes along, though, his rock-solid principles erode, and what replaces them is a fierce, basic instinct to defend himself and his family by whatever means may be necessary.

Like all truly scary movies, the original *Cape Fear* is essentially conservative, even reactionary. It works by evoking the childish, primal fears that are strong enough to override reason, moral discrimination, faith in the social contract—to make every consideration other than that of survival seem irrelevant, effete. A good part of the horror that movies of this sort induce is horror at the baseness and violence of our own reactions; we feel as if we had regressed to some primitive state of consciousness. For an educated middle-class audience—those of us, that is, who are meant to identify with the besieged Bowden family—the original *Cape Fear* is the guiltiest pleasure imaginable, more shameful than pornography; it brings out the vigilante, the redneck, the caveman lurking inside our liberal-humanist selves. There's a strange purity to the dishonorable intentions of Thompson's picture: It frames the conflict in the starkest terms and proceeds inexorably from there, without bothering to provide the distractions of wit, imagination, or psychological nuance. Its terrifying momentum is fueled by our fascination with Robert Mitchum's Cady. Mitchum is amazing; he uses all his customary mannerisms for profoundly disturbing effects. The danger that Cady poses to the Bowden family is largely sexual: The crime he was sent up for was the rape of a teenage girl, and his plan for revenge clearly includes the violation of Bowden's daughter. Mitchum's characteristic air of relaxed masculine confidence takes on really foul overtones in *Cape Fear.* His star power has always depended on the hint of sexual threat expressed by his drawling, ambling, heavy-lidded presence. Here his lazy machismo is appalling, and yet, unsettlingly, he's still attractive. He is the sole source of excitement in *Cape Fear,* and a constant reminder that the pleasure we're deriving from this brutal thriller is corrupt, helplessly perverse. There's a remarkable scene near the end of the picture in which Cady, who has traced the Bowdens to a houseboat on the Cape Fear River, peels off his shirt and slips quietly into the water, hoping to sneak up on his prey. In the moonlight, he looks simultaneously like a gleaming, bare-chested stud, a grimly determined commando, and some sort of prehistoric reptile—a cold-blooded predator that we thought had disappeared from the earth a few geological ages ago.

The 1962 *Cape Fear* isn't complex—morally, psychologically, or cinematically. The picture makes a mockery of the very notion of complexity; it's constructed to dissolve all emotional and intellectual distinctions, to throw everything back into the undifferentiated primal ooze of terror and survival. This is not an admirable aim, but the movie certainly has the courage of its low convictions: It never pretends that what it's doing is good for us. Scorsese's remake muddies the waters with self-consciousness. He has loaded *Cape Fear* with apparent moral ambiguities, facile ideas about guilt and redemption (themes that link the movie, forcibly, to his previous work), and explicit attempts to portray his scuzzy villain as a mythic nemesis. In the new script (which is credited to Wesley Strick), the Bowdens aren't innocent victims of an irrational evil. The seeds of evil are within them, and Cady no longer seems to have come out of nowhere like a hurricane, an unforeseeable natural disaster; in this picture, he appears to have sprung forth from the Bowdens' dirty little souls. Sam Bowden (Nick Nolte) isn't quite the straight arrow he was in the first movie. He once almost wrecked his marriage with his philandering, we learn, and it's not clear that he has entirely reformed: He's enjoying a heavy flirtation with a law clerk named Lori (Illeana Douglas) —a relationship teetering between friendship and romance. And he isn't a paragon of legal integrity, either. The basis of Cady's grudge against him has been changed from that of the original story. In the novel and the 1962 film, Bowden witnessed Cady's assault on the teenager and gave testimony in court. In the new version, Bowden has not witnessed the crime; he was Cady's defense attorney in the rape trial, and he suppressed evidence that could have led to his client's acquittal. Bowden's wife, Leigh (Jessica Lange), is now an edgy, unhappy-looking woman; she hasn't forgiven her husband for his past infidelities, and she's quick to accuse him of new ones. Fifteen-year-old Danielle Bowden (Juliette Lewis), Cady's ultimate prey, has been given a sullen, pouty teenage sexuality, and she's alienated from her parents. She's more repelled by the hostile vibes between Sam and Leigh than she is by Cady's advances to her. In one long, loathsome scene, Cady, posing as Danielle's new drama teacher, comes perilously close to seducing her. Halfway into the sequence, she sees through the impersonation and realizes that this man is her family's tormentor, but she isn't turned off; she kisses him anyway. And this Cady (Robert De Niro) is more than a sadistic, amoral cracker; he is also an avenging angel (his body is covered with tattooed biblical quotations like "Vengeance Is Mine" and with Christian symbols like the cross) and the trickster figure common to many of the world's mythologies.

Of course, educated middle-class moviegoers like a little subtext in a genre picture: It adds spice. Picking up intimations of dark psychological "truths," identifying mythic patterns and narrative archetypes — these are ways of making ourselves feel smart while we enjoy dumb movies, of asserting our superiority to gut-level, cheap-thrills storytelling. They're also ways of neutralizing the visceral, wholly irrational kick of powerhouse trash like the original *Cape Fear:* they enable us to dismiss the damning evidence of our emotional reactions — to deny that we've been lured, momentarily, into wholehearted acceptance of some pretty crude notions. Thompson's *Cape Fear* turns the audience as well as the hero into yahoos, and it doesn't supply us with any convenient excuses for our feelings. It ends, after a climactic battle in which Sam vanquishes the monster, with a brief, bleak shot of the Bowdens, their faces expressing exhaustion and degradation rather than triumph. The new *Cape Fear* is all excuses. You couldn't say that Scorsese's treatment is a desecration of a great, pure work of the human spirit; it's more like a consecration of something debased and profane. This *Cape Fear* is much flashier and more assaultive than the original (and it's also, at two hours and eight minutes, a hell of a lot longer), but the Christian/mythological subtext that Scorsese dredges up and places in the foreground has the effect of increasing our emotional distance from the story. And it isn't true subtext; it's stuff that has been imposed on, rather than discovered in, the material. The idea that Cady is a monster who has bubbled up out of the unconscious of a dysfunctional family seems at first to be just glib, fashionable pop psychology. As the movie goes along, though, Scorsese keeps hammering away at the Bowdens' frailties, and it becomes harder and harder to ignore the implication that they somehow *deserve* the vengeance that's being visited on them. There's a gruesome sequence in which Cady picks up Lori, the law clerk, in a bar and then handcuffs her in bed and beats her senseless, and the movie gives us to understand that Sam is indirectly responsible for this atrocity: Lori allowed herself to be seduced by Cady because she was frustrated by the unsatisfying ambiguity of her relationship with Sam. In this movie, flirting with a coworker can leave a guy with blood on his hands. And what makes the long scene between Cady and Danielle so surpassingly ugly is that it turns the normal confused sexuality of a teenage girl into something unclean: As Danielle begins to respond to the advances of her would-be rapist, the movie unavoidably suggests that she, like the unfortunate Lori, is *asking for it.*

There's no way to recast this story in Christian terms without reducing it to moral (and aesthetic) nonsense. The stain of original sin on the Bowdens' souls seems to justify Cady's viciousness. Sam's breach of legal ethics in his conduct of Cady's defense makes the lawyer's later descent, first into shady extralegal tactics and then into plain violence, seem far less dramatic. The whole story is now constructed to illustrate the Christian idea that suffering is good for the soul: Battling Cady provides a kind of spiritual catharsis for the Bowdens. In the end, they've been reborn: They've wrestled with the demons of their corrupt natures and exorcised them, spewed the poison out of their mouths. If that devil, that tattooed man, had not come along, Lord knows what might have become of these lost children; they would still be wandering in the wilderness of sin. The Christian implications that Scorsese lays on this elemental story actually serve to make the message more reactionary: Violence is no longer just a matter of survival—it's now the instrument of salvation. (If Scorsese were making *Taxi Driver* today, would he present Travis Bickle's spooky calm in the aftermath of the massacre without irony, as if this serenity were a sign of grace?) These ideas may be among Scorsese's most deeply held convictions, but they aren't integral to this kind of movie or this particular story. The new *Cape Fear* is still, at heart, a picture whose sole aim is to give its audience huge, bowel-loosening shocks; the veneer of moral seriousness and psychological complexity that Scorsese brings to the enterprise feels like an attempt to convince himself that he's not doing what he's doing.

It's hard to find the pleasure, or value, in a horror picture that keeps providing us with high-toned justifications for our basest reactions —insisting that the grueling experience it's putting us through is really meant to edify us. De Niro's frenetic but thoroughly uninteresting performance is emblematic of the movie's inadequacy. He's covered with tattooed messages and symbols, but he doesn't seem to have a body. We could feel Mitchum's evil in all its slimy physicality; De Niro's is an evil that we merely read. Despite the movie's relentless pace and the ingenious staging and editing of its violent sequences, *Cape Fear* has a peculiarly antiseptic quality. It drags us into the mud and then tells us that we haven't got dirty. Our messy primitive responses have been cleaned up, rationalized away; we're guilt free—washed in the blood of the bogeyman. The pretense of moral purity in Scorsese's *Cape Fear* is far more sordid than the honest, un-self-conscious shockmongering of the original. Scorsese seems to want to make a gut-wrenching thriller and yet duck the responsibility for the sleazy thoughts it might churn up in us. He's asking absolution for the wrong sin. He shouldn't be ashamed of having made a mass-audience horror movie; he should be ashamed of having made one that sends its viewers home feeling morally complacent and intellectually superior.

The New Yorker, December 2, 1991

DRESSED TO KILL

Stephen Schiff

In François Truffaut's celebrated book-length interview with Alfred Hitchcock, he and the Master of Suspense discuss the opening of *Psycho*—you remember, the scene in which Janet Leigh, in her iron-plated bra, has an illicit lunch-hour fling with John Gavin. Hitchcock notes that the scene "allows the viewer to become a Peeping Tom," and there follows this revealing exchange:

> **Truffaut:** Jean Douchet, a French film critic, . . . wrote that since John Gavin is stripped to the waist, but Janet Leigh wears a brassiere, the scene is only satisfying to one half of the audience.
>
> **Hitchcock:** In truth, Janet Leigh should not have been wearing a brassiere. I can see nothing immoral about that scene and I get no special kick out of it. But the scene would have been more interesting if the girl's bare breasts had been rubbing against the man's chest.

To which readers the world over have probably murmured, "And how!" Somewhere in that chorus, no doubt, one might have discerned the voice of Brian De Palma, the director of such Hitchcockian films as *Carrie, The Fury,* and *Sisters.* In fact, De Palma's rich, seductive new thriller, *Dressed to Kill,* turns out to be a sort of fantasy remake of *Psycho*—*Psycho* as De Palma would have liked to have experienced it, as it lives on in his dreams.

The film even begins the way *Psycho* does, with our slow entry into the intimate lives of a pair of lovers. But as De Palma's creeping camera rounds the corner of a bourgeois bedroom, it keeps going, straight into the bathroom beyond, and there, in the shower, is the perfect Hitchcock blonde — not Janet Leigh, this time, but elegant Angie Dickinson — washing herself, caressing herself: voluptuously naked. Her husband, a dark, muscular sort with a male model's bland handsomeness, is at the sink shaving with an alarmingly silvery straight razor, and Dickinson is staring at him through the steam and the water, hungrily, sensually. Here, De Palma finally satisfies the dirty longings of twenty years. He gives us languorous shots of breasts being soaped, rinsed, and massaged, shots of tummy and thighs and — well — everything. Pino Donaggio's hilariously schmaltzy music rises to a crescendo. And suddenly a man is standing behind Dickinson in the shower, grabbing her by the throat, handling her brutally, holding her in a grip that's half erotic, half terrifying — half desire, half murder.

No, she doesn't die. This is *a* shower scene, not *the* shower scene. (That will come later, and it won't involve Dickinson at all.) In fact, it's merely a sex fantasy, one of many that Dickinson's Kate Miller has every day. Kate, you see, is terribly frustrated. Every morning her hunky husband gives her the old "wham-bam special" and leaves her angry and panting. Her expensive psychoanalyst, Dr. Elliott (Michael Caine), tells her that she should *express* her anger, release those repressed emotions. But he only frustrates her further. Dr. Elliott, it seems, is another of her fantasies. She wants to sleep with him and he responds to her tentative attempts at seduction with a lot of prim bluster about how he's a married man and a doctor, and, you know, it would be wrong. Repression. *Dressed to Kill* takes place in a world of repressions, a world of prurience and heat and pent-up desire. To De Palma, repression breeds monsters — monsters who kill. The more sexually alive you are, the more you attract them. And in sexy, steamy New York City, there are monsters around every corner.

De Palma has walked this line between sex and violence — the locus of so much of what's exciting in movies — before, most notably in 1976's *Carrie.* There, the wallflower's mother, played by Piper Laurie, was herself a murderous demon of repression, a sexy, once-beautiful woman who could almost have been a sweltering belle out of a Tennessee Williams play — if only she didn't view sexuality as a sort of malignancy. To her, lust was something that had to be cut out of a person—with a knife, if necessary. Here, in *Dressed to Kill,* the weapon is a straight razor and the killer a transsexual—in sunglasses and a ratty blond wig, yet—whose female half wants to do in the women its male half finds desirable. (In *Psycho,* you'll recall, Norman Bates's "mother" wanted to kill the women Norman pined for.) It sounds awful, I know, or spoofy, or puerile. And so perhaps I should say right here that this movie is not only better than *Carrie* and, in fact, better than any other Brian De Palma film: It's the best new American movie I've seen this year. *Dressed to Kill* is as scary and funny and self-conscious as *Carrie* was, but it's not for kids, and you don't feel embarrassed at the implausibilities and trivialities and trashiness, because none of it is childish. De Palma has grown up. His virtuosity is more controlled, his gliding, sensuous style more judiciously used, his eagerness to manipulate an audience tempered by a willingness to please. He has always been a show-off, a kid who knows all the tricks and wants us to *know* he knows. But here the tricks are so pretty, so kinky, so lurid, and finally so absurd that they tickle us and make us laugh.

Photographed by Ralf Bode (who captured a certain slummy glamour in *Saturday Night Fever* and *Rocky*), the murder scenes are slow and bloody and beautiful. They're shot in the same circling-camera style as the sex scenes, and they have the same dreamy, lingering pace. De Palma isn't afraid to make a thriller move slowly, and the laziness of it all adds to the horror; even though the murder is lasting forever, there's still no time to get away. Watching the violence in *Dressed to Kill,* it's as though we were seeing the world through the eyes of some monstrous aesthete, a voyeur for whom the glistening textures of blood and blade and torn flesh are as enchanting—even as arousing—as those of skin caressing skin. Here, sex, violence, and even, perhaps, a casual conversation all have the same pornographic allure. They all create a poetry of surfaces, a beauty beyond meanings and morals. De Palma toys with us: joshes, nudges, winks. He cannibalizes not only *Psycho* but also the museum scene from *Vertigo* and the spying camera of *Rear Window.* He even cannibalizes *Carrie,* giving us one reprise of that film's final shocker right where we expect it—and then another, right where we do not. And it's fun watching De Palma make us jump, even when we're in midair. Though some of his underlying themes are dead serious, he knows that if we take them seriously, as real life instead of as an off-color dream, we'll hate the way he manipulates us. So he wants us to think of his film as unimportant, trashy, a throwaway movie that's like a tabloid magazine you pick up in the supermarket because the headline is so tantalizing. Grown-ups, he knows, don't have *clean* sex fantasies.

Tantalizing this movie certainly is — and almost meretriciously offensive. De Palma's notion of transsexuality, for instance, seems almost calculated to anger people: It reduces a very real sexual confusion to a psycho-movie scare device. De Palma doesn't care. He's willing to offend; he even goes about it with a kind of subversive glee, the way Buñuel does. This is a *movie,* he cackles — just a movie. A tough young call girl named Liz (Nancy Allen, who is Mrs. De Palma) witnesses the first murder and is chased by the killer. In one scene, she runs into the subway, dressed in her fancy-tawdry "working clothes," and tries to hide near some young black men. Irritated by her provocative flippancy, the men decide to rape her, and they chase her into a subway car. It's a gorgeous scene. De Palma turns the dark, elusive stretches of the subway platform into hiding places from which anything might emerge — a bag lady or a madman — and there's a claustrophobic chase through the subway cars that's made all the more creepy by our knowledge that the black dudes aren't the only ones stalking poor Liz: Somewhere, between the cars perhaps, that killer in the fright wig is waiting. But the implications here are bound to drive some people up the wall. I mean, the only blacks we see in this movie find the very sight of an attractive white woman an inducement to rape.

Moreover, even though this is a movie about women, it views them with a very sardonic eye. Feminists who begin by applauding De Palma's acknowledgment of sexual fantasies and frustrations may end up wanting to throw eggs. Dickinson is cool, womanly, and restrained; Allen pouty, forward, itching for excitement. But they both have the same sex dreams: of cigarette-ad men and warm showers and razors. No doubt about it: In this movie, what women dream of is rape. Some will find that notion repugnant. But if it's viewed simply as a movie device (which is exactly what it is), it seems as outlandish and funny as one of those hot-and-bothered Frank Tashlin comedies of the fifties, the ones in which several different sorts of men — a milkman, an intellectual, a nightclub owner — all flip for the same insanely busty blonde. *Dressed to Kill* takes its luxurious imagery from the erotic fantasies of women and then extends that imagery to its spooky-funny extremes. It takes sex seriously, but it also understands it as a kind of humiliating joke. Desire is what reduces us all to pathetic clowns. It's the greatest indignity, the thing that catches us with our pants down. And because it makes us vulnerable, it attracts danger.

De Palma mocks his female characters in order to distance us from them. If we can love them and at the same time laugh at them, he thinks, we won't find their perils painful. Dickinson and Allen are both extraordinarily likable characters, but they're also a little silly. De Palma pokes fun, for instance, at Allen's bubble-headed financial schemes: Even with a killer on her trail, she's desperate to get her hands on some Autotron stock, and she has purchased a dreadful painting that she thinks will be worth a million dollars some day — more, if the painter dies. Dickinson's silliness lies in the contrast between her apparent intelligence and her actual banality. In one scene, we find her deep in thought. Magic flashes in those breathtaking eyes, and, inspired, she removes a little black book from her purse and jots something down in it. The music rises and De Palma gives us a tight close-up of that mysterious little book: "Pick up turkey," reads the reminder she's scribbled. Pursuing romance, Dickinson is living out soap operas. But she's also the sort of woman who might spend the day watching them.

Still, De Palma sympathizes with his women. They, at least, have desires, feelings, ambitions. His men, on the other hand, are all sexual dead ends. Dr. Elliott may be attractive and intelligent, but he's also a hopeless prig, sexually unavailable to the women who need him most. And Michael Caine plays him beautifully: arms held stiffly by his sides, mouth crinkling in feigned jollity; eyes lit by a twinkle that's much too carefully controlled. Dickinson's husband, that handsome nothing, is awful in bed, and the detective on the case, perfectly overplayed by Dennis Franz, is a plug-ugly caricature of a cynical cop. Dressed in a shiny leather coat, with a polyester disco shirt and enough gold chains to strangle Steve Rubell, he's so sarcastic that every word he utters seems to mean its opposite. He even pronounces people's names with a sort of leaden irony, as if he knew they were aliases but was willing to go along with the charade. There is, however, a handsome, lusty hunk who actually turns out to be good in bed — whereupon De Palma smirks and lets us know that Mr. Dream Date has syphilis *and* gonorrhea. Men! You can't live with 'em and you can't live without 'em.

Well, there is *one* decent fellow. Peter is intelligent, strong-willed, and kind — trouble is, he's a high school kid. Played with remarkable assurance by a young actor named Keith Gordon, Peter is Kate's son, and his characterization is another of De Palma's little jokes. Gangly, lonely, a brilliant tinkerer whose relationship with his mother seems more than a little Oedipal — this is Norman Bates all over again: *Psycho*'s twisted killer returning a hero. Moreover, this voyeuristic whiz kid is also De Palma's on-screen representative (like Peter, De Palma spent his high school years designing computers). He watches the action quietly, devising new cameras to track the killer with, and finally, as in every adolescent's fantasy, he saves the damsel in distress. But of course, Peter's voyeurism does not reflect just De Palma's. It's ours, too. We are peering through fancy lenses with him, feeling frightened and relieved as he does — participating in our own porny-scary fantasy of *Psycho*. In *Psycho,* our voyeurism joined us to the monster: Norman Bates, too, was a voyeur, and his murder, in part, a substitute for rape. But *Dressed to Kill* presents a lighter, more exhilarating view of kinky sexuality, and here our voyeurism puts us in complicity with a hero. Relax, enjoy, this movie seems to be saying. Nothing wrong with a little fantasizing.

But what if watching makes you want to participate? De Palma answers in his most spectacular sequence, a bit of storytelling magic that covers fifteen minutes and relates a whole love affair — with no dialogue to speak of. Angie Dickinson is in the Metropolitan Museum. Paintings stare down at her; she stares back. Watching. As she glances around the museum, she sees a boy give his girlfriend a squeeze, a mother lose her tiny daughter, a man pick up a woman. Just then, a striking gentleman sits down beside her, and Donaggio's music begins: Our lovely watcher is about to become a doer. The man gets up and, flirtatiously, Kate pursues him; what follows is a beautifully handled cat-and-mouse game through the silent museum. Everything is told in gestures, expressions, the way Dickinson walks or bites her lip or shifts her gaze. It's a luscious, almost lyrical passage (though that soap-opera banality gives it a humorous edge), but it ends in a shock: in Dickinson's first confrontation with something unimaginably evil. Fantasy is safe, De Palma seems to be saying. Acting out your fantasies isn't.

That's a very moral, sensible message for a movie that revels in such seaminess. Could it be that De Palma is making a subtler point here, one about the relationship between movies and audiences? People are going to be outraged that he has depicted female fantasies as being about rape; they are going to be outraged that he makes violence unutterably beautiful. But if this movie has a theme, it's that there's a vast difference between fantasy and reality, and hence a vast difference between the screen and real life. Dickinson and Allen both dream of violence, but that doesn't mean they welcome violence in their lives. And we may go to the movies to indulge our own naughty fantasies, but that doesn't mean we want to go home and enact them. In fact, the people who refuse to soften up and let themselves enjoy a dirty dream like this one—they, De Palma says, are the dangerous ones. Refuse fantasy, and you get twisted inside.

De Palma himself wrote the screenplay for *Dressed to Kill,* and though there are some stupefying puns and some stilted lines, the camera seems to wink at us whenever they occur. Then too, some of the verbal twists are downright spectacular. Early on, Kate walks into Peter's room, where she finds him hard at work inventing a new kind of circuit, a thingamajig with a dizzying array of lights and switches. What are you going to call it? Kate asks. It needs a name. Napoleon called his pastry a Napoleon. Peter considers and decides to name his whatzit a Peter. Whereupon Kate leaves, saying that if his grandmother asks after him, "I'll just say you're working on your Peter." It's a joke that ripples, because, in retrospect, we appreciate the way Peter's marvelous blinking contraption is a substitute for his sex life. Everybody in this movie does *something* with all that pent-up sexual energy, and Peter works on his Peter. But if Peter, the character, is De Palma's screen surrogate, the joke takes on an extra resonance. De Palma, too, has churned his sexual fantasies—and a few old parts—into a wonderful whirring gizmo. In *Dressed to Kill,* he's invented a perfect Brian.

Boston Phoenix, July 29, 1980

POSTSCRIPT: I first found out I was an enemy of the people on Tuesday, August 12. That morning, when my clock-radio went off, a newscaster announced that the night before, about thirty picketers, all women, had marched around in Park Square, denouncing me because of a movie review I had written. This sort of thing really wakes you up. My surprisingly tranquil informant sketched the details: The protesters had been picketing the Sack Cinema 57, and they had advocated that people boycott Brian De Palma's murder thriller *Dressed to Kill,* as well as all Sack theaters. They even demanded a boycott of the *Phoenix,* because I had praised *Dressed to Kill* (in a July 29 review) and had allegedly called a rape scene in it "gorgeous." On this particular morning, I should add, my mouth felt as though someone had mistaken it for a Maytag and had stuffed three weeks' worth of soiled socks in it. Nevertheless, I managed to mutter, "Rape scene? What rape scene?" You see, there is no rape scene in *Dressed to Kill.*

I was just trying to get my nose to work when the phone rang. "Have you heard?" a friend at the office inquired.

"About the picketers?" I gurgled.

"Well, yeah. But not just that. Someone spray-painted the windows of the *Phoenix* classified-ads office."

"Someone what?"

"Yeah. They sprayed, 'Stiff Schiff Porno.' "

I wasn't sure what that meant, but I thanked this bearer of glad tidings and hung up the phone. The morning paper brought a picture of a woman carrying a sign that read, "No Excuse for Woman Abuse." Apparently, the picket line at Cinema 57 had included members of Women Against Violence Against Women, the Transition House for the Shelter of Battered Women, and the Massachusetts Coalition for Battered Women Service Groups. They had distributed a release stating, "We are picketing the movie *Dressed to Kill* because of its portrayal of violence against women as erotic and entertaining."

The object of their anger, besides yours truly, is a work that I have called "the best new American movie I've seen this year." *Dressed to Kill* is about two women who are stalked by a killer—a crazed transsexual with a straight razor. It's De Palma's fantasy remake of Hitchcock's *Psycho,* and it's full of sex, suspense, naughty wit, and, yes, violence. Part of what's touched off so many tempers is one of its central jokes: that although its two heroines (played by Angie Dickinson and Nancy Allen) are very different, they both have the same baroque sex fantasy, one involving glistening razors and steamy showers and men who look as though they just stepped out of cigarette ads. For De Palma, the very improbability of this extravagant coincidence is funny. How could he foresee that some literal-minded sorts would take it as a sociological statement—that they'd think he was seriously asserting that *all* women have such fantasies?

De Palma has shot the violence in the same languorous, surreal style he's used for the sex scenes. It's a sensual style: an erotic, even pornographic one. And it gives the violence a certain prettiness. But that doesn't mean the movie depicts violence itself as being erotic or entertaining. Violence in this movie is terrifying and repugnant, and so is its perpetrator. In fact, in photographing it so splendidly, De Palma heightens its hypnotic horror. His gliding camera reminds me of the lovely, swaying undulations of a cobra when it's about to strike. The cobra's dance fascinates, it even beguiles, but it doesn't for a moment lessen one's dread.

On August 17, when I appeared on WBCN's "Boston Sunday Review" program, Ellen Herman of Women Against Violence Against Women called in to deliver an "official" statement. It said, in part, "That Stephen Schiff finds no fault whatsoever in this raw depiction of violence against women is unacceptable to us. . . . We somehow doubt that Schiff would be as enthusiastic about a film glorifying KKK violence against blacks or Hitler's mass slaughter of Jews." That's perfectly true. Nor would I be as enthusiastic about a film glorifying violence against women. *Dressed to Kill* does not. It *depicts* violence against women, and it does so with extraordinary skill. And I applaud its extraordinary skill. I would applaud this skillful a depiction of "KKK violence against blacks or Hitler's mass slaughter of Jews," because extraordinary skill would almost certainly make these atrocities feel more atrocious. And if people can't understand the distinction between portraying something and glorifying it, then we're in real trouble.

In print, this distinction may sound subtle. On the screen, it's not subtle at all. Anyone can grasp it: instantly, instinctively. But to realize this, you have to have seen the movie. And many of the people objecting to De Palma's work don't seem to have bothered. How do I know? Well, a lot of the nasty letters and phone calls I've received since I became an enemy of the people have come right out and said as much.

Then too, no one who had seen the movie could have criticized me for saying that a rape scene in it is gorgeous. Because I didn't. Here's the passage in my review that the picketers are referring to: "A tough young call girl named Liz (Nancy Allen, who is Mrs. De Palma) witnesses the first murder and is chased by the killer. In one scene, she runs into the subway, dressed in her fancy-tawdry 'working clothes,' and tries to hide near some young black men. Irritated by her provocative flippancy, the men decide to rape her, and they chase her into a subway car. It's a gorgeous scene. De Palma turns the dark, elusive stretches of the subway platform into hiding places from which anything might emerge—a bag lady or a madman—and there's a claustrophobic chase through the subway cars . . . " It's a gorgeous chase scene; it's not a rape scene at all.

The protesters marched again on Friday, August 15. The day before, I had tiptoed out of my bunker in order to tape a telephone interview for a radio program called "WGBH Journal." Reporter Becky

Rohr also talked with Natalie Paven, a representative of Transition House, who said she had noticed that when men are killed on TV (and presumably in the movies), it's usually in long shot — we see them fall off a building or get run over by a car — and when women are killed, there are lots of close-ups, lots of panting and running and fear. Of course, there are so many exceptions to this "rule" — from Dustin Hoffman's heavy-breathing victim in *Marathon Man* to all the poor lads who are so gruesomely dispatched in *Friday the 13th* — that one hardly knows where to begin disputing it. But even if Paven's observation were accurate, wouldn't it suggest just the opposite of what she thinks it proves? Men have always been more "acceptable" as objects of violence than women. Men are the ones who are buttoned into uniforms and sent out to die; men are the faceless cops who are killed in long shot and then forgotten. And doesn't showing imperiled women close up, panting and running, personalize and humanize their terror? Shouldn't the violence against them seem more terrible than that perpetrated against the distant SWAT officer or the private eye's hapless sidekick? For every movie that, in the words of Ellen Herman's statement, "reinforces the cultural assumption that women are acceptable, appropriate, and ever-willing victims," there are a dozen that do the same thing for men.

Well, even a hardened enemy of the people would tire of blowing holes in such ragged arguments. A more interesting question is what's behind them. The strain of violence in American life is appalling, and our best efforts to control it — or protect ourselves against it — seem bootless. People are afraid, as well they should be, and they're frustrated. They want to stamp out violence at its source, but they don't know where that source is. And since our culture reflects the violence in our lives, cultural artifacts become scapegoats: People mistake the mirror image of violence for its cause. But can anyone really believe that a peaceful, law-abiding type would be turned into a criminal by seeing a movie? Or that not seeing one would stay a rapist or murderer from his crime? Of course, we must also consider those whom the vociferous letter-writers keep calling "unstable personalities." Would a movie drive them over the edge? Possibly. But I wonder what in our culture would be safe for them. Certainly television is full of pernicious influences, and newspapers too. And novels and plays and music: anything that reflects the society that has created unstable personalities in the first place — anything, in fact, that sets off a strong emotional response. Should we then do away with all effective art, since so much of it excites the emotions? After all, we have to keep those unstables calm. Surely Dostoyevsky's description of the impulse to murder in *Crime and Punishment* is as dangerous as the elevator scene in *Dressed to Kill.*

We've all absorbed such a load of received wisdom about violence and its sources that we're turning into a nation of knee-jerk behaviorists: We automatically trace criminality to this or that movie or TV show when the real causes are far more complex. The current controversy brings to mind the much larger one in February and March of 1979 over Walter Hill's gang movie, *The Warriors,* which was said to have resulted in the murder of sixteen-year-old Marty Yakubowicz. Yakubowicz was stabbed on February 15, 1979, outside the Fields Corner MBTA subway station in Dorchester by a man who was part of a gang that had gone to see *The Warriors* earlier that evening. Hearings were held and marches marched and speeches delivered. And months later, when the sound and fury died down, the murder case came to trial. There it was discovered that the alleged murderer had been dead drunk and had slept through the movie.

On that WBCN program, Ellen Herman made a statement that I thought astonishing. "*Dressed to Kill,*" she said, " . . . is killing us on the streets, in our homes, and at our workplaces." This isn't just a benign figure of speech. It's a dangerous oversimplification. Movies don't kill people or cause rape — but something does. And we desperately need to know what that something is. Violence has real sources, sources that have to a large degree eluded our discovery. And to me, it seems outrageous to waste time and energy picketing movies — and movie critics.

In fact, I must say that the recent celebrity — and notoriety — of film critics has given me the willies. Our readers take us to be high priests when we usher them into the sanctified world of a beloved film, and Judases when we pan something they've cherished. Because everyone has opinions about movies — because everyone is a film critic — those of us who actually practice the trade for a living find that we've become cultural politicians, voting pro or con, representing our factions well or poorly. And in an age when so many people misunderstand movies, liking only the ones that agree with them and hating those that don't, the film critic finds himself in a strange position. I recall the anger of people who hated *The Deer Hunter* because it didn't reflect the Vietnam War they knew, or the people who cried out against *Kramer vs. Kramer* because their divorces weren't like that at all. When I like or dislike a film, I find I'm suddenly aligning myself with a whole range of deeply felt responses in my readers, with prejudices and assumptions to which I may not subscribe.

When a movie critic is recognized as an enemy of the people, he gets letters like the unsigned one I received the other day. Addressed to "Despised Person," it read, "*Re Dressed To Kill,* another 'let's kill, mutilate, and rape women' promotional film, which you gave a four-star rating again this week. I was threatened with a razor and raped a few years ago, and the only rape fantasy I have *ever* had is of breaking every bone in a would-be rapist's body—and making hamburger out of people like you, who *cause* rape as much as rapists by giving it endless public approval and support. Let's hope more women don't start acting out their *actual* rape fantasies, eh? Worry. We aren't putting up with this stuff anymore."

Apparently, if my reviews give rise to any sort of crime, it's likely to be directed against me.

Boston Phoenix, August 26, 1980

RIVER'S EDGE

David Ansen

The teenagers in Tim Hunter's unnerving *River's Edge* think their small-town school's a joke, hold their parents in contempt, and are so alienated it doesn't occur to them: Alienation implies there's a world you could imagine being attached *to.* They live in a kind of blurry present, scoring beer and weed, their heads full of pop-culture trash. If there's any code they adhere to, it's *Don't narc on your friends.* Then one of them—a big, lumbering guy named John (Daniel Roebuck)—strangles his girlfriend for no good reason, leaves her naked body by the riverbank, and starts boasting about it to his friends. But instead of outrage, their reaction is numbness. And instead of reporting the body, they decide—prodded on by their leader, Layne (Crispin Glover)—that their duty is to protect the killer. "Jamie's dead. John's still alive. Can't you see that?" argues Layne. Nobody cries; nobody mourns their dead friend; only one boy, Matt (Keanu Reeves), finally decides to call the cops, and when his demonic little twelve-year-old brother finds out, he vows to kill Matt for his disloyalty.

It would be comforting to think of *River's Edge* as a kind of science fiction, but in fact it's based in part on an actual 1981 incident in Milpitas, California. This is the scariest vision of youth since the alarming Brazilian movie *Pixote,* but there one could point a finger at the appalling poverty that drove kids into crime. Hunter, working from a tough, authentic script by Neal Jimenez, isn't a finger pointer, and he doesn't approach the subject in the "problem-solving" style of TV sociology. *River's Edge* pitches the audience inside this nightmare world of affectless, middle-class kids and lets us watch them wallow their way through moral dilemmas they can only half articulate. The sixties-generation adults don't have answers: They helped create the mess. What's doubly disturbing is the movie's streak of jet-black humor: The values on display are so upside down the movie reaches moments of near-surreal comedy. When the twelve-year-olds break out the guns and the karate moves, it's like watching a suburban *Bugsy Malone* played for keeps — nothing cute about it. As a kind of warped moral spokesman, the movie provides Dennis Hopper as the dope-peddling one-legged hermit Feck, who once killed his girlfriend and now lives with an inflatable doll. The difference between him and John, he desperately points out, is that he *loved* the woman he killed.

Feck is the movie's most literary conceit (that life-size doll is too symbolically insistent for its own good), but Hopper plays the part with such spooked conviction you excuse the excess, as you excuse other moments when the script seems in danger of piling on the grotesquerie. As the unhinged Layne, Glover gives a dangerously over-the-top performance that's both riveting and almost Kabuki-like in its stylization. But none of the film's flaws dilute its power. Hunter never exploits the material for cheap thrills — his camera keeps a sober, clear-eyed detachment. Detail by appalling detail, he creates a vivid, stunted world where banality and horror intermingle. "I cried when that guy died in *Brian's Song,*" one of the girls says. "You'd figure I'd at least be able to cry for someone I hung around with." Some may gag on this daring, disturbing movie; few will be able to shake it off.

Newsweek, May 22, 1987

RIVER'S EDGE

Owen Gleiberman

At the opening of *River's Edge,* an odd-looking, preadolescent kid (he's a boy but looks more like a girl) stands on a concrete bridge and drops a tattered doll into the brown river below. It's an overcast day, frighteningly gray and bleak, and as the kid looks over at one of the banks, he sees a huge older boy sitting there like a mean, teenage Buddha. The film cuts over to this ambiguous figure and reveals an image of tabloid ugliness: There, lying next to him on the grass, is the nude corpse of a teenage girl — the girl he's recently strangled (and probably raped). Her eyes are wide open (looking into them, you know why they close the eyes of corpses), and her face is already developing blue-and-purple splotches. The scene is grisly yet detached; watching it, you're chilled, yet you can't help wondering at the portentous atmosphere. Why is the older kid just sitting there? Does he want to get caught, or has he gone catatonic? Why does the younger boy offer him a comradely shout, as if the dead body were nothing more than stolen merchandise — isn't he the least bit shocked or upset or even intrigued? And what about the doll? We've just been confronted with an image of clinical death, yet the way the camera keeps lingering over the waxy white corpse, it's hard not to observe that the girl looks — well, *like a doll.* The film has barely started, and already it's rife with "meaning."

River's Edge, which is about the girl's murder and (more than that) its aftermath, is a true-life nightmare, one of the few films that's attempted, in a serious, nonexploitative way, to poke into some of the darker aspects of teenage life during the last fifteen years — that is, in the era of post-sixties permissiveness and nihilistic burnout, when adolescents have indulged in sex and substance abuse with unprecedented freedom, and the very notion of values (even rock-and-rollish, rebellious values) has crumbled, leaving a pervasive numbness and a dispirited, punked-out anger. The film is sincere and very ambitious. It is also, I think, a dismal failure — a slovenly, lurching mess, and so nakedly pretentious about what it's "saying" that hardly a scene in it plays naturally, fluidly, with the indelible rhythm of life unfolding. Taking off from an incident that occurred in California in 1981, screenwriter Neal Jimenez and director Tim Hunter have fashioned a group portrait of moral deadness, a story of characters so fried they can barely muster a reaction when their friend is murdered—or when they learn that a boy in their group did the deed. For several days, the kids don't go to the police (as they didn't in the California incident). More important, they act as if the girl had, say, been killed in a car crash—they treat her murder not as an outrageous crime but as a bum accident, a "drag." (Whether this precisely mirrors the emotional reality of what happened is more questionable.) And what's oppressive about the film is the explicit, moralistic way it clobbers you with their indifference; the kids keep insisting on their own jadedness, announcing it to the world and to one another. The filmmakers aren't TV-movie prigs. They're sympathetic to the characters—they want to get inside the kids' hardened, damaged souls. Yet they're in such a rush to deliver the shocking truth of how far gone some kids are today that they haven't made the story *dramatically* true. In place of the old, hokey myth of the misunderstood kid they've concocted a new myth of the teenager as stoned, alienated slug—they lay on the kids' affectlessness with a trowel, never locating the glints of life behind it. They put you in a stupor too.

The murderer, Samson "John" Tollette (Daniel Roebuck), is chunky and scary, a psychopath who has strangled Jamie, his fourteen-year-old girlfriend, because it made him feel powerful—like a man. The film isn't really about him, though. It's about the gang of friends, the half dozen or so delinquents (some boys and some girls) he proudly leads to the riverbank so he can show them the corpse. At first, they think it's a hoax; the body must be a prop in some crude practical joke—it looks so *unreal*. But no, it's real all right. The movie is set up to suggest that if you dismiss the way the characters react to Jamie's death, if their response seems too empty, too malformed, then you're just not willing to accept what things have come to. Well, perhaps I'm not, but the whole movie struck me as showy and hyped up. The characters are thinly "believable" without being empathetic, universal—they never become projections of our own indifference (as in the great 1981 Brazilian film *Pixote*). The leader of the gang (and the main character) is a long-haired druggie named Layne (Crispin Glover) who wears driving gloves and a ski cap and speaks in the slurry-emphatic, David Lee Roth–Jeff Spiccoli stoner style. Like the killer, he's a kid with clear psychotic tendencies, so when he starts babbling on about how they all owe "loyalty" to John, his raving at least has a demented integrity. (Certainly it has little to do with any genuine, compassionate sense of loyalty—this kid is simply a head case.) On the other hand, the two girls in the group are hardly pill-popping weirdos like Layne. The sly flirtatious Clarissa may enjoy hanging out with reckless boys, but as played by the exquisitely pretty Ione Skye Leitch she comes across as a creature of feeling, and she's supposed to have been fairly close to Jamie. It's inconceivable that a girl like this wouldn't be distraught — indeed, probably in tears — over her friend's violent death. The film makes Layne a mythic figure, an apotheosis of modern-youth zombiehood, but then arbitrarily smears his malaise all over the other characters.

If I've drifted immediately to the thematic aspects of *River's Edge,* that's because the story itself is sketchy — a ramshackle frame to prop up a message. It's a teen-gang art film, like Coppola's *The Outsiders,* a series of self-conscious nihilist flourishes. The way the movie takes off from that opening corpse scene is a mistake. If the filmmakers hadn't begun with the murder, if they'd spent, say, the first third of the story showing how the characters interacted *before* Jamie was killed, and also how the slobby, menacing John (who barely seems interested in conversation) fitted into the group, we'd have a better feeling for what the murder meant — a sense of how their shock could mingle with indifference, and how they might use one another to insulate themselves from something this lacerating. As it is, their blankness has no underpinnings, no resonance; the movie just plays the same glum tune in every scene.

The screenwriter, Neal Jimenez, wrote the original draft of the script for a class at UCLA, and a number of the incidents (a little girl erecting a maudlin grave for her doll, an ex-hippie high school teacher offering a lecture on the lost glories of the peace-and-love generation) are ponderously metaphoric in a style common to young writers. But most of *River's Edge* is just laborious and inert, with patches of bizarre black comedy that call too much attention to themselves. (The film's humor seems to spring from its overstatement.) There's really no plot. Instead, Jimenez builds an episodic structure meant to mirror the searching, existential emptiness of the kids' lives, as they group off in twos and threes, cruise around the nameless town at night, drink and play video games and battle their divorced parents, return to the scene of the crime, or try to score some pot from the only adult they can stand — a one-legged ex-sixties biker named Feck (Dennis Hopper) who shares his bombed-out house with a party doll. Hopper plays the same sort of glassy-eyed burnout he did before *Blue Velvet* offered him a chance to give a performance, and the scenes in which he clutches his beloved doll or speaks about the woman he shot in the head for love are so campy-ghastly they seem to knock his status as an actor right back down.

There's much hand-wringing over the question of whether any of the kids will "narc" on John. And when one of them does, Layne and a couple of the others are incensed: According to them, this betrayal is unforgivable. But how can they work up so much steam over narcing if even murder didn't make a dent in them? The answer is supposed to be that their youthful bond means more to them than ties to any adult authority (i.e., the police, the whole official system they'd have to turn John over to). Yet it's here you can feel the filmmakers brush up against — and bypass — their true subject: not just the moral indifference of today's teens but the intense, almost erotic closeness kids in the drugs-and-heavy-metal subculture can share; with no pretense toward pleasing their parents, or of joining the majority of (straight) kids at school, they live for one another in a way that more middle-of-the-road youths don't. The director, Tim Hunter, co-scripted 1979's *Over the Edge,* a far livelier and more organic film, and one with a better feeling for what the new breed of amoral teens share. *River's Edge* is too sloppy and theme-heavy to establish a convincing pattern of camaraderie, even in an era as fractured and decadent as this one. The film falls over itself trying to reveal what's important to the characters, but it never finds the pulse of their friendship. It's like spending two hours staring at a bomb blast: After a while, you want to see the site before the thing went off—to know what's been destroyed.

Daniel Roebuck cuts an authentic figure as the vacant killer (the scenes in which he tries to bully a liquor-store clerk into selling him beer are among the strongest in the movie), and Keanu Reeves has some moments as the shuffling, long-haired Matt, who shows a groggy nobility. He comes closest to suggesting what the real-life urchins did in the extraordinary documentary *Streetwise*—that even the most shell-shocked contemporary kids live by a layered set of habits and codes, their indifference a natural (even innocent) response to the world they've grown up in. But the star of the movie is Crispin Glover, and I don't think most audiences will know what to make of him. Glover, who gave a masterful performance as the wimpy, earnest father in *Back to the Future,* is the damnedest actor. He's out in the ionosphere somewhere, but even when he gives a flamboyantly terrible performance (as he does here), it's hard to take your eyes off him. A majestic flake, he's willing to go off the edge into flaming, rhapsodic camp, like a junior (and freakier) Eric Roberts. With his androgynous bone structure, his seesawing voice, his popping-yet-sensitive eyes, he's mesmerizing, and he convinces you that Layne is a group leader just by giving him a pet gesture: When the character wants to make a point and take control, he'll extend his index finger and pinky outward in a goalpost shape and then whip his arm around — it's as if the two bent-down fingers symbolized the missing section of his consciousness. As exciting as he can be to watch, though, Glover is such a stylized performer that it's simply impossible to believe in most of what he does here. (Indeed, it's hard to see him succeeding outside a mythic-cartoon environment like that of *Back to the Future*.) His wild, operatic performance seals you out of the movie — it isn't ultimately about anything but the private, eccentric joy he takes in acting.

Boston Phoenix, May 22, 1987

HENRY: PORTRAIT OF A SERIAL KILLER

Henry Sheehan

Henry: Portrait of a Serial Killer is certainly the most disturbing and possibly the best film to play Los Angeles so far this year. It is unquestionably the most thought-provoking. A microbudgeted 16mm feature shot in Chicago in 1985 and 1986, it is the story of a morose psychotic killer who murders without regret, first alone, but soon in tandem with a garrulous roommate. Between the murders, he conducts a desultory and chaste courtship with his partner's unknowing sister, and together the three live a life of soulless poverty in Chicago's Uptown neighborhood, the haunt of moneyless Appalachians and other rejected social groups.

The principal action of the film is murder, brutal and graphic murder at that. But though the plot is a familiar one — it is essentially the bare-bones parable of punished sociability that informs every slasher film — and the visual style at first appears utilitarian or even crude, this movie is one of the most sophisticated accusations of audience — and by implication, societal — blood lust since Alfred Hitchcock's *Frenzy*.

The typical thriller or horror film today delivers its scenes of killing and butchery the same way: through a blistering flurry of sharp, jangly edits that construct a total picture of devastation out of minutely assembled peaks of action. Beyond that, the consequences of violence are never displayed for very long. Shots of violated bodies appear for only a few seconds, and at that they are more displays of wounds than of the wounded.

Henry departs from this routine with its very first shot, a long, slow, almost sensuous zoom away from the corpse of a bludgeoned woman. There is nothing flashy about the shot, though despite its apparent simplicity it does have an insinuating cleverness to it. Long before the shot is completed, it is obvious what we are going to look at. But director (and cowriter) John McNaughton clearly does not just want the audience to *know* what it is looking at, for it is that very knowing he is trying to disrupt. This opening shot, like one horrifying, similarly unblinking one to come later, is meant to cause us to really look at violence in a way that most other films try to prevent. Throughout the film, quick cutting to action and away from effects is eschewed in favor of an almost flat, unswerving stare that measures a killing not just in the flash of a moment, but in the exposure of prologue and consequence. Henry is not only the killer on the screen; he is the killer inside us.

In a performance so full of understated psychosis that even his muscled torso and blandly handsome features look somehow sickly, Michael Rooker plays Henry as an inarticulate drifter, living out his days in a bleak Chicago apartment. His roommate is the unceasingly gabby Ottis (Tom Towles), whom Henry met in prison and whose gas jockey job is just a cover for his only slightly more lucrative small-time drug deals.

In contrast to Henry's movie-hero stoicism, Ottis is a typical sidekick, a caricature of the colorful character type, always coming up with harebrained schemes that are already pitiful in the scuzziness of their petty ambitions before they inevitably backfire. Contrasted to this is the manly, silent, and purposeful pursuit of Henry.

Of course, that pursuit is death, cold-blooded, efficient, and random. Henry prowls through the Chicago area, picking up female hitchhikers or talking to women on the street, and then proceeds to rape and agonizingly murder them, either with a knife or with his own hands. Yet, in a style both audacious and austere, McNaughton maintains a cool and analytical detachment from Henry, filming his activities with a documentarian's distance, yet at the same time positioning Henry as the hero of the drama.

Henry is forced into a heroic dilemma when Ottis's sister Becky

Michael Rooker plays the title character in John McNaughton's *Henry: Portrait of a Serial Killer.* (Photo courtesy of Greycat Films.)

(Tracy Arnold, in a portrait of a victim of rural southern poverty that is both harsher and more honest than anything in a Hollywood movie) arrives in town. More or less on the run from an abusive husband, Becky has left her daughter back home with her mother while she tries to make a few bucks in the big city. She is immediately attracted to Henry, such a self-contained and deliberately polite man — with all women, Henry is unfailingly courteous, thus making the most devious and most ancient use of manners — particularly when contrasted with her undoubtedly vicious husband and crude and sexually suggestive brother.

After setting up this curious trio, and establishing an unsettling sympathy for Henry, the film proceeds to take its audience identification figure and essentially indict the audience for murder. However, this is not accomplished merely by camera placement or by gussying up the action with complex camera movements, a lush orchestral musical score, fantasy sequences, or other stylistic sleights of hand that confuse the seduction of form with the appetite for violence.

The first murder that plays off the audience sympathy occurs when Henry and Ottis visit a fence and the fat oafish fellow abuses them verbally after he tries to trick them financially. Being brutes, Henry and Ottis attack the man and kill him. But not only has sympathy for attackers been firmly established — they are, after all, potential victims in the scene themselves — but the killing itself, which involves shoving a television set over the head of the mountainous victim, is actually funny, a fairly typical cinematic conjunction of humor and horror.

However, having set us up to expect more of the same, McNaughton suddenly switches tacks. Ottis has been drawn into Henry's insane world of death when, angrily frustrated over a rebuffed homosexual pass he has made at a high school student, he accompanies Henry to the dank underpass of Chicago's Lower Wacker Drive. There, Henry lures a motorist to the side of the road by feigning car trouble and, once he has cornered him, has Ottis kill him.

One taste of blood proves insufficient for Ottis's newly whetted appetite, and he accompanies Henry on a suburban home invasion. This scene is simply the most indescribably horrifying sequence I, for one, have ever seen in a movie. Shot in unbroken take, from Henry's point of view, the scene shows Ottis raping a woman as Henry kicks the head of her husband, who lies bound and hooded on the floor. As if that were not bad enough, a twelve-year-old boy, obviously the couple's son, rushes upon the carnage, only to live just long enough to see what is happening to his parents before he gets his neck broken.

What keeps this scene from being merely sadistic is the revelation that what we are watching is not the brutal multiple murder "live," but a videotape made by Henry. The wild swings of the camera are caused by Henry's own swings of attention — which, of course, match the audience's — and the climactic child murder is accompanied by a clump as the camera slips from Henry's clutching fingers.

McNaughton tracks his camera to show Ottis and Henry, in the film's "present," watching the videotape on their television and laughing at the ghastly predicament of their victims, just as their last murder had itself provoked laughter.

The film is more than a moralistic put-down of audience taste. For one thing, its exposure of audience sadism is not a condemnation so much as a restless examination. Although repulsive, both Henry and Ottis, and the far more sympathetic Becky, are given a kind of peculiar psychological openness. Although there is an early scene, during which Becky tries to swap childhood stories with Henry, in which it is established that both were victims of childhood abuse, McNaughton holds that only the neurotic, nonpsychotic Becky can be fully comprehended by a conventional character analysis.

So the director compensates by showing us Henry in the fullness of his daily routine. What he talks about, what kind of food he wants, what kind of courtesy he expects from others around him, and particularly his peculiar notions about the proper treatment of women all receive careful attention in the way that daily minutiae get as much screen time, and as much patient contemplation, as the murder scenes.

The unbearable tension brought about by the unblinking witnessing of the camera, coupled with the strange mixture of the trivial and terrifying, finally leads to a climax of closet Götterdämmerung. Henry and Becky are beginning to fall in love; to Henry, sexual intercourse is the trigger that rouses his implacable murderous impulses, but to blowsy Becky, it is virtually the only sign of affection she knows how to make. But as Henry fights off his darker urges in order to achieve some sort of fractured romantic state with Becky, her brother Ottis intervenes with depraved and violent sexual advances of his own.

This inevitable collapse of the triangle sets off another murder, this time combining both the elements of the first two, the urge to root for one of the killers and horrified repulsion at the drawn-out and gruesome nature of what the putative hero is accomplishing. Reaching its gory crescendo, the film then stretches out to an almost peaceful, if deadly, denouement, in which all the issues are finally buried on the edge of an endless highway. The confusion we feel over our own reactions to violence can never be fully resolved and so, in its way, neither can this movie.

While *Henry: Portrait of a Serial Killer* is a rough film to take—and I would never think of allowing anyone young or squeamish to see it—it is also pertinent. The lust for violence overtakes us all, either singly or in mass, either as a seizure of reaction or as a paroxysm of revolution. Every day, the happy murderer commits his bloodless execution over and over again on television. In this dark and horrifying film, John McNaughton brilliantly depicts how that actor can never be happy, and his act can never be bloodless.

Los Angeles Reader, April 13, 1990

HENRY: PORTRAIT OF A SERIAL KILLER

Terrence Rafferty

John McNaughton's *Henry: Portrait of a Serial Killer* has a stark, relentless quality that is sometimes mistaken for art; the movie, a low-budget independent feature originally made for the home-video market, has been "discovered" by critics at various film festivals and has had enthusiastic reviews from its recent theatrical release. But it isn't a terribly interesting movie. The film it most resembles is Leonard Kastle's *The Honeymoon Killers,* which enjoyed a comparable cult success in 1970. Like that picture, *Henry* is a deliberately flat, affectless treatment of gruesome true-crime material. *The Honeymoon Killers,* which was shot in low-contrast black-and-white, was an oddly memorable freak show — shocking, but with a distinctively wobbly half-lurid, half-comic tone. McNaughton's movie, loosely based on the criminal career of a mass murderer named Henry Lee Lucas, is more conventionally realistic: It's grisly, unrelieved horror. After an introductory sequence of graphic tableaux of murder victims, McNaughton gets down to the everyday life of his protagonist (Michael Rooker), a beefy, moronic-looking lug who lives in a miserable apartment with a creep named Ottis (played, by Tom Towles, in a style that suggests a syphilitic Warren Oates) and Ottis's sister, Becky (Tracy Arnold). The members of this depressing household drink enough beer and watch enough TV for us to figure out that this isn't just a splatter movie but, you know, a vision of America. Every now and then, Henry gets a sort of funny look in his eyes and goes out to kill somebody. Eventually, he starts taking Ottis along, and Ottis has a whale of a time; for a while, they videotape their exploits and watch them at home afterward. Becky thinks Henry is sweet, because he defends her from Ottis's incestuous advances. Henry doesn't respond to her attempts to seduce him, though; he must have some kind of sexual problem. That's about all there is to the movie.

Henry plays like a hybrid of *Blood Feast* and *Stranger than Paradise;* it mixes gore-movie carnage with Jarmusch-style aimless minimalism. (Its cleverest dialogue exchange goes like this: "Where you going?" "Nowhere. You wanna come?") It might appeal to fans of both styles. When it's over, though, and you've staggered out of the theatre, you may wonder what this queasy exercise was supposed to be all about. Sure, it's compelling; the nature of the material guarantees that. But it doesn't seem to be telling us much more than that the world is a scary place and murder is ugly. We knew those things. The most sickening murder takes place in an upper–middle-class house; we see the grim-faced Henry and the obscenely whooping Ottis eliminate an entire family in their cozy living room. Is the movie also telling us that happy bourgeois homeowners should be more suspicious of lower-class beer-drinking men? *Henry,* both hip and deeply conservative, is consistent only in its bad faith. It's tabloid chic.

The New Yorker, April 23, 1990

SEX WARS

The movie medium is perhaps the most sensual and hot-diggity of all art forms, and yet there have been few truly memorable erotic works. Sex as a fuse, as an instigator, as a kick, an obsession, sex as an explicit and implicit part of our lives—where are the movies that speak to us of these things?

There were many in the audience in 1973 who hoped *Last Tango in Paris* would inaugurate a time when film artists would finally be able to confront the rawness and shock of sexual emotion with the same power employed by writers like Henry Miller and D. H. Lawrence. It didn't happen. In a buddy-buddy movie era such as the current one, when men and women rarely get to do much of *anything* together on-screen, the dream has practically faded from view. This despite the fact that, in October of 1990, the Motion Picture Association of America, under increasing fire to revise its ratings code, replaced the dread porno-tinctured X with the NC-17 (which sounds like a hemorrhoid ointment).

But it's one thing to sanction more adult-oriented movies; it's another thing to make them. Since Philip Kaufman's *Henry & June* became the first film to be rated NC-17, there has not been, as this book goes to press, a single major studio-financed, studio-distributed NC-17–rated movie.

The films discussed in this section, ranging from *Last Tango in Paris* and *Swept Away* to the (gasp) partially National Endowment for the Arts–funded *Poison* and *Basic Instinct,* demonstrate some of the ways in which sex in the movies has been trumpeted, camouflaged, coopted, politicized, brutalized, lyricized. In perhaps no other film realm has there been such critical double vision.

Is the rape scene in *The Accused* exploitation or condemnation? Is *Pretty Woman* essentially harmless or essentially degrading? Is *Tie Me Up! Tie Me Down!* (one of the last major movies to receive an X rating) a metaphor for the ties that bind, or something uglier? Is the portrayal of the gay S&M subculture in *Cruising* hateful or just politically inexpedient? (The controversy surrounding this film was a forerunner of the gay activist picket-protests that accompanied *Basic Instinct,* with its phalanx of lesbian killers, more than a decade later.)

In *Swept Away,* was Lina Wertmuller equating sex warfare with class warfare, or was she just indulging in some satirical, slaphappy misogyny? Did *Henry & June* deserve all that NC-17 ruckus, or was it more chi-chi than carnal? Does *sex, lies, and videotape* have anything to say about sex, lies, *or* videotape?

The movies in this chapter made some of their critics hot—and some of them just plain hot under the collar.

LAST TANGO IN PARIS

Charles Champlin

The trouble is that by now it is very nearly impossible to *see Last Tango in Paris.* So much has already been written in extravagant praise and even more extravagant damnation of the movie, and so much has been reported on the making of the movie (covers on both *Time* and *Newsweek*), about what Marlon did and didn't do, would and wouldn't do, about the heroine and her incessant private life and the director and his politics and his intentions real or postdated, that *Last Tango* is not a movie any longer, it is a tourist attraction like Pigalle or North Beach.

I am one of the culprits, self-confessed, and I am not really trying to lay off the blame on to those who have written so inflammatorily about a movie they have not seen or who unfairly represented a movie they had seen. But the sad fact is that it is now monstrously difficult to watch *Last Tango* calmly, on its own terms, without taking sides from the start on the grave question of whether it is the greatest debut since Stravinsky's *Rite of Spring,* as Pauline Kael has said, or whether it is only a *Deep Throat* for intellectuals, as the most waspish of the Eastern critics has charged. (It would be hard to think of another movie that needs to be defended quite so urgently from both its enemies and its friends.)

What would be useful would be to clear the dance floor just for a minute and then start all over again, refreshed and cleansed, trying to see the film as it is.

The tone is established during the titles themselves, which are illuminated, as it were, by some of the famous and tortured paintings of the English artist, Francis Bacon, with their distended faces that resemble spoiled meat or melted plastic and that suggest decadence, disintegration, and despair.

Last Tango is a film of decay and despair, in which the activities of the adults are time-serving rituals on the edges of an empty and pointless center, and in which the young seem already to be infatuated with their own pasts for lack of a future or of a present that contains anything more than casual sexual contacts.

As he did previously in *The Conformist,* Bernardo Bertolucci finds sexual behavior symptomatic of the situation of society. In *The Conformist,* sexual anxieties and frustrations seemed to be the makings of a fascist. In *Last Tango,* a kind of sexual abandonment seems to characterize lives (or at least a life) that have ceased to have real meaning.

How far the readout from the particular lives in *Last Tango* is to be taken is left finally to the viewer; what must be kept clear, I think, is that sexual behavior is being examined and commented upon in *Last Tango* and not — in the film itself — exploited. Bertolucci's film is remarkably beautiful to watch. The aura, most often, is somehow autumnal, golden but thin and unwarming, with the city seen most often at night or at the ends of the day in the partial light of dawn or dusk and with the interiors murky beneath dim lamps or shuttered against the sun.

We see Brando first walking zombielike beneath an elevated tramline. He is unshaven, red eyed, weeping; except for the expensive camel's-hair coat he could be a wino, a drifter. (The plot has now been summarized so often that it is easy to forget how catching and how mystifying Bertolucci's exposition is. The sense of discovery, the gradual revelation of character, is one of the strong points of the film.)

A young girl in a floppy hat and long coat and boots strides by, aware, as we are, of Brando. She enters a block of flats, has a demented exchange with a dippy old concierge (Darling Legitimus, say the credits), goes up to investigate a vacant apartment. There, by design or more likely by accident, is Brando again, still in a trancelike state, or hiding like a hurt animal.

The apartment, ratty, dusty, peeling, empty except for some draped and junky furniture, is to be the center of the movie, the place Brando establishes as an oasis for himself and the girl (round-faced Maria Schneider), in which they have no names, no identities, no links with anything beyond the apartment walls.

There is a good deal of surrounding action. The girl seems to be starring in a television documentary about her own life (she is the daughter of a French army officer), which is being made by her young lover (Jean-Pierre Léaud, from the Antoine Doinel films of François Truffaut). Brando, as we are to discover, is in flight from the messy suicide of the French wife he loved. Paul, the Brando character, had led a life of vagabondage, which took him from a Midwest farm to Cuba to Tahiti and then — happily — into the small, shabby residential hotel owned by his wife's mother (Maria Michi).

The relationship he establishes with the girl in the deserted apartment is brutally, coarsely, impersonally sexual. The language is probably unprecedented in its abrasive candor, and we are left in no doubt that some intricate and unconventional things are going on. But even to identify them is to give them an explicitness which they do not really have. Ultimately, what is happening is left mostly to our imagination. The graphics are less specific than those in *I Am Curious (Yellow),* although that is probably not the most helpful comparison in the world.

But what is crucial is the emotional coloring of these goings-on. And the coloring is pale, chilly, off-putting rather than erotic. The images are designed to convey not the physical specifics but the complicated, contradictory, and highly charged emotional states of the protagonists.

If I may repeat myself, *Last Tango* more than any film I have yet seen deals with sexuality coolly and objectively as it dominates the relationship (as initially it *is* the relationship) of two complex, fully realized, and entirely credible contemporary characters. They may be extraordinarily unusual figures, and yet they are believable; and whether or not we accept them as making a comment on their society, it is hard not to accept that they have some things to say about the relationship between men and women.

Brando and the girl have tried to create an entirely physical relationship, and it does not work. It begins for Brando in a kind of terrible anguish, which he hopes to mask with a brutally impersonal sexual association, and the scenes in which he tries to assert the nature of this association are cruel and discomforting.

But if there is a brief release, there is no relief and no escape, no alternative to the need for a deeper sharing. Both of them recognize this; but it is the girl who cannot cope with the truth of it. Bertolucci, as I suggested earlier, has set up a reversal of roles, in which for once it is the woman rather than the man who flees from deeper needs that impose a dependency on her. Brando as a free and equal love object might have been acceptable; Brando as a creature of pathos is not.

The ending, which I do not intend to give away, is the least satisfactory part of *Last Tango,* I think, because it simply avoids the long-term implications of everything the movie has seemed to be about. It is unpersuasive as story and evasive as a conclusion.

If *Last Tango* is chilly in its detached examination of the characters, it is also finally very affecting indeed, thanks overwhelmingly to the strength of Brando's portrayal. His performance as the Godfather was a particular triumph for the actor as craftsman and technician, creating a character with guile and the tools of voice and visage. But it is impossible not to believe that much of Paul grew out of Brando's own innards. There are two or three extended scenes—Brando suggesting that he ought never to have had a name, another recalling his boyhood and his mother — that feel like improvisations that have gotten out of hand, gone beyond the needs of the exercise and beyond make-believe.

No one, you think, could possibly have written or even outlined them. Whether they are truly autobiographical becomes a matter of gossip; what is important is that they have a clenching sincerity and intensity that seems to leave mere craft far behind. Brando is always impressive on the screen; it is hard for me to remember when he has been so moving.

Schneider is a triumph of casting—petulant, self-indulgent, and convincingly terrified as someone who has gotten in beyond her depth. Massimo Girotti has some very effective moments as Brando's wife's sad lover. Luce Marquand is colorful as an old-crone friend of the girl's. Gitt Magrini is the girl's mother, and Michi is convincingly emotional as the wife's mother.

Vittorio Storaro did the exquisite cinematography, and Gato Barbieri, who did the music and its urging, noodling sax solo, has made a crucial contribution to the mood of the film.

Last Tango does not betoken a revolution but it is a long evolutionary step forward in the screen's ability to deal not exploitively but coolly with human sexuality in the context of complicated human relationships. Indeed, what Bertolucci's story says is that sexuality can be neither a refuge from nor an alternative to more thoroughgoing relationships and responsibilities.

The sadness and the danger is that even though *Last Tango,* seen as coolly as it regards its events, looks to be shocking but not exploitational, it certainly has been treated exploitationally. Movies are a marketplace commodity and profit is their iron law of survival. And United Artists, which is distributing *Last Tango,* is also stuck with $11 million or more worth of *Man of La Mancha* and cannot be blamed for wanting to extract every dime the dance will yield. Yet allowing the impression to stand that *Last Tango* is somehow more prurient than it really is invites a double backlash — from the disgruntled young studs who are already tossing beer cans at the screen in New York (according to a published report from Rex Reed) and from those forces in the society who are already unhappy with the freedom of the screen and who imagine, sight unseen, that *Tango* is glorifying a kind of behavior that it, in fact, is not.

Last Tango is a strong, disconcerting, sobering motion picture, an examination of some of the most guarded but universal fears, desires, and pains in human nature. It acknowledges the pleasures of the flesh, but acknowledges also that they are never without consequences, and that, as I said when I wrote about *Last Tango* before, nothing we do is without consequence.

For the mature audience for which the film was made, it ought to be possible to see it that way.

Los Angeles Times, March 11, 1973

LAST TANGO IN PARIS

Judith Crist

For starters, let's cut through all the official and semiofficial pre-sell stuff about *Last Tango in Paris,* ranging from orgasmic cineastic euphoria after its New York Film Festival showing (noneuphoric reactions don't get reprinted in the ads) to cover stories (it's post-Inauguration dulltime on the national and international scenes) to smarmy witties on the Johnny Carson show (where sodomy is still one of the taboo topics—at the moment).

We are not facing an ultimate cultural milestone: *Le Sacre du Printemps* or even *Nude Descending a Staircase,* this is not. Nor is it a moral milestone. The year, need we note, is 1973, ten years since we thought *La Dolce Vita* a bit racy and *The Silence* "dirty"; *I Am Curious (Yellow),* with its simulations (and dreary moviemaking and mediocre actors), has come and long gone, and *Deep Throat,* with its actualities (and idiot moviemaking and awful actors) is upon us. To each his own erotica and shock threshold. It would be a pity — more specifically, an insult to this new Bernardo Bertolucci film and a disappointment to the thrill seeker—if those who haven't worked up the courage to go to one of the hard-core movies plan to get their kicks the respectable way (the price, by the by, is the same five dollars) by going to see *Last Tango.* For this newest Marlon Brando film is a highly personal work by him and by the thirty-one-year-old filmmaker whose talents have become more and more apparent, his artistry more and more mature with *Before the Revolution, Spider's Stratagem,* and *The Conformist.*

Because this is so personal a work, reactions must be more subjective than ever: Rest assured, even you who still believe that nonsense about critical objectivity, that you may well learn more about the reviewers than about the film in the case of *Last Tango.* To call the film "adult" is a disservice, for who but adults are riddled with the sexual hang-ups, inhibitions, prejudices, and blocks that turn them off or infuriate or sicken them when they are confronted by even *Carnal Knowledge* or *Sunday Bloody Sunday.* It is, however, a strong film in its sexual depictions. Not, mind you, that you're going to see the "real" thing, as in *Schoolgirl* or *Mona* or *Throat,* although indeed Brando and Maria Schneider create the illusion. And although the Brando backside is bared, the privacy of his pubic parts is sustained even at the sacrifice of truth, in that great male chauvinist tradition that of course presents us with all of Schneider that there is to see. Where new sexual ground is broken in this "respectable" film, however, is in the simulation of sodomy and anal stimulation, both in sadomasochistic terms and in the spewing of language and verbal imagery more usually associated with the sewer and with more esoteric sexual practices.

The foregoing is part warning, part preparation, for it is not what *Last Tango* is all about. If you cannot accept this sort of content, however, you can thereafter reduce this film to simply a depiction of everyman's (and undoubtedly somewoman's) erotic fantasy. A brooding expatriate American and a feckless Parisienne of twenty meet in a vacant apartment; their attraction is instant, their sexual encounter overwhelming. The man moves in minimal furniture, including a large mattress, establishes the rule of no names and no self-identity, and they meet regularly, the girl in complete subjection to the man's every wish and desire. Her degradation continues until—here the filmmaker particularizes the fantasy—she decides to break away. The man—let us be simplistic—realizes that sexuality cannot exist in a vacuum and that he "loves" the girl. He pursues her with drunken ardor but, after a cursory "homage" to their past passion during an interlude in a tango palace where a contest is being held (the title moment), they race on to a melodramatic—indeed, near-operatic—tragic ending.

This is what an antagonist can reduce the film to—and in lesser, or indeed any other, hands, it would bear this reduction. For the film is Brando, and he provides not only the most satisfying and complete characterization since his *Streetcar, On the Waterfront,* and *One-Eyed Jacks* performances, but also two sequences of such power, of such piercing emotional intensity and perception, that he brings an aura of greatness to the entire film. It is, alas, only an aura, for the film is all machismo filled with such detestation of and contempt for women that its universality is limited; its plot detailing and mechanics tend to the pop and the slick and the self-indulgent, marred by the contrivances of theatricals that replace the insights of drama, and so the artistry is flawed.

Brando's Paul is, in effect, Stanley Kowalski grown world-weary quite literally, much in the Brando biography manner, with writing, boxing, bongo playing, and women of exotic places in his past; he has settled down as the kept husband of the proprietress of a fleabag hotel, with her lover ensconced in a room of his own. And his wife has, at the film's outset, committed the ultimate inhumanity: She has committed suicide without apparent motive or explanation. And it is in a monologue at the side of the bed where her body has been laid out in necrophiliac loveliness that Brando, spewing forth the love-hatred of guilt, the agony of complete rejection, the desperation of one faced with final silences, gives the film its raison d'être and proves his greatness.

Small wonder that the guilt-ridden man is ready to wreak his vengeance and prove his manhood upon the willing flesh and vacuous mind of the compliant girl, determined to give nothing of himself beyond the masterful maleness. And yet he cannot prevent the slipping of the mask — again in a monologue, soft and moody, of a Midwest boyhood recalled, a moment of injustice and humiliation remembered. And the actor as magician is apparent.

The girl, a lovely frizzy-haired creature, is a far less interesting character, incredible to me and, I suspect, a contrivance and tool for the moviemen. She is all of the flesh, dashing about Paris with her fiancé, ultraboyish of course in Jean-Pierre Léaud's embodiment, who, for the convenience of the film, is busily making a movie about her for television. This device, obviously, permits Schneider to reveal her past and present, offers us all sorts of pleasing interludes away from the love nest, and allows the plot to thicken with the location of a gun that belonged to her father. But the girl as person is never quite credible; so "open" a girl (and I refer not merely to her lack of underpants) would hardly be in such instant sexual thrall even to Brando, let alone the brooding Paul. Even her decision to marry seems more plot device than self-determination and certainly her final act is totally out of the character that has drifted in and out of experience without introspection, that would, in fact, revel in the final reversal of needs. But perhaps even the drift to tragedy is to the point.

Nor are the surrounding women any more than "service" characters. The dead wife remains an enigma and thereby a villain; her mother, a kindly woman, is a religious fool to be tormented; the girl's mother is a babbling bourgeoise; and even a prostitute who comes to the hotel must be so revolting a specimen that even her prospective client rejects her.

This antiwomanism permeates the film but admittedly it is in keeping with its personal viewpoint and, if anything, enforces the essential theme of the rejected man seeking to reassert himself and discovering that it is the human rather than sexual response that man must live by. One can, if belief in the girl is sustained, see the lesson through her eyes and realize an almost instinctual rejection of the commonality of sensual experience alone, even though her final act of rejection comes after the man has offered her his person instead of his body. For his person, made foolish by drink and as outdated as the rituals of the tango, is not to the taste of a chic video-oriented daughter of the discreet bourgeoisie.

There are any number of avenues to explore in retrospect, the question of middle-aged machismo, of public performance and private image — and the reverse thereof. For the duration of the film Brando and Bertolucci, past masters at holding the viewer's eye, hold one's attention to their chosen path. It is not a pleasant one but it is a fascinating and absorbing one — and it stays to nag at the mind. This is the excellence of their achievement, their bold approach to an intimate experience in terms that cause us to explore ourselves. And that, of course, is the point.

New York, February 5, 1973

SWEPT AWAY

Judith Crist

Fortunately there's flesh and blood in contemporary terms in *Swept Away . . . by an Unusual Destiny in the Blue Sea of August.* Lina Wertmuller's newest foray into the class struggle becomes a fierce battle of the sexes that is as witty as it is wise, as ferocious as it is funny, and as touching as it is truthful. No holds are barred in this entertaining tale of the lady and the sailor, and the blows strike close to home, whatever your sex or politics.

Wertmuller — Fellini's gifted protégée who came into her own here last year with *Love and Anarchy* and the delightful *The Seduction of Mimi* — is that rare creative filmmaker who dares to keep her partisanship private and her view of the human comedy impartial. Still working with the stars of her earlier films, Mariangela Melato and Giancarlo Giannini, she offers us a delightful seventies version of the kind of interclass love story that Hollywood doted on in the thirties. The lady is not a lady; she's a loudmouthed self-sufficient capitalist from Milan out yachting with the beautiful people. The sailor is no prince in disguise; he's a macho communist from the south who despises women and capitalists with equal fervor. She is, of course, in the catbird seat on the yacht, doing her "Marie Antoinette" number on a captive audience; but when, through a whim of hers, the two are stranded on a deserted Mediterranean island, the tables turn.

It isn't quite *Admirable Crichton* time as the sailor triumphs with survival skills. Wertmuller has no romantic view of women, and feminists may well rebel against the lady's seeming acceptance first of slavery, then of sex, and then of love, preceded though it is by one of the funniest knock-down drag-out name-calling fist-flying battles on screen record. I say "seeming," because ultimately Wertmuller makes it quite clear that the women call the final tune, making their choices and thereby sealing man's fate.

If the love affair lacks total credibility, it's the getting there that provides the basic fun of the film. Wertmuller is ruthless and Melato immaculate in their portrait of the ultimate shrike, with Giannini the complete primitive in social response and male ego. And that sun-soaked blue sea of August has enough sparkle to warm you through a chilly fall.

Saturday Review, November 1, 1975

SWEPT AWAY

Gary Arnold

Giancarlo Giannini spends so much time slugging Mariangela Melato during their would-be romantic island idyll in Lina Wertmuller's *Swept Away* that you begin to wonder why the film wasn't called something appropriate, like *Out Cold* or *The 500 Blows.* Resounding, unrelenting, and unpleasant as they are, these blows are also weirdly gratuitous and unreal. After sustaining a battery of punches that sounds like thunder in the Rockies, Melato's face ought to be hideously bruised and pulpy. Since it remains unmarked, one can't take all the walloping literally, but how is it supposed to be taken?

Typically, Wertmuller herself doesn't seem to have a coherent, comprehensible point of view. Ironically, her ability to equivocate in the process of exploiting modern sexual and political dogmas and resentments may be the secret of her success with New York film critics and art-house audiences, a success that may or may not spread.

It would certainly be easier to criticize Wertmuller if one could get a clear impression of what she felt and stood for. *Swept Away,* for example, could inspire knee-jerk gratification among mutually exclusive groups. Although one assumes that feminists would be repelled by the physical abuse dished out to Melato, certain kinds of sophistic or masochistic feminists might be inclined to go along with the picture as a parable of sexual victimization, demonstrating what brutes men are. Unregenerate male chauvinists might interpret the scenario, with rather more justification, as a parable of "what women really want," i.e., a traditional masculine Lord and Master.

Those who aren't choosing sides might see a slapstick put-down of both extremes. Incurable romantics may be able to groove on the late-blooming hints of a great love thwarted by cruel, fickle fate. Erotic fantasists may be the luckiest group of all: After a raucous beginning, *Swept Away* drifts into a semipornographic reverie that resembles nothing so much as the fantasies of dominance collected by Nancy Friday in her best-selling anthologies of women's sexual fantasies, *My Secret Garden* and *Forbidden Flowers.* Perhaps *Swept Away* is simply Lina Wertmuller's contribution to the garden.

Wertmuller has borrowed the plot mechanism of a durable Victorian social satire, James M. Barrie's play *The Admirable Crichton,* in which an English household is shipwrecked on a desert island, compelling a shift in authority from the least able member of the household, the foolishly liberal Lord Loam, to the most able, the resolutely aristocratic butler Crichton. In *Swept Away,* a pair of vehemently ignorant antagonists — Melato as a lazy, opinionated, insulting Milanese plutocrat and Giannini as a seething, resentful, vindictive Sicilian proletarian — are marooned together on an island in the Mediterranean.

As usual, Wertmuller comes on like gangbusters, but she has formulated this supposedly up-to-date battle of the sexes in a way that makes it unlikely that the story can go anywhere except downhill, which it does with a vengeance. While the opening reels have a brassy, perky, crudely effective kind of comic energy, they also establish a severely limited comic and human framework. Wertmuller's characters are not particularly sensitive or sympathetic, and the only notes in her repertoire seem to be acrimonious ones.

Melato, the hostess on a yachting party, makes herself generally disagreeable, but Giannini, one of the crewmen, becomes the special target of her outrageous spite and condescension. By the time these two characters are finally isolated in a state of nature, the man, who proves amazingly resourceful, has taken so much verbal abuse from the woman, who proves utterly helpless, that the movie would fall apart if he didn't try to get even.

As it happens, getting even isn't enough for either Wertmuller or her hero. The male demands total submission. The female not only submits, after undergoing that more or less incessant pounding, but also learns to love her new role. Taken at face value, this seems to be such a hackneyed porno twist, with the rich bitch and poor slob fulfilling every obscene delusion about one another, that you assume Wertmuller must have intended it satirically.

On the contrary, she appears to endorse it as the ultimate emotional imperative of woman. When the castaways are rescued and Melato regretfully rejects Giannini's proposal to return to their island of love, the atmosphere is dreadfully sentimental. Far from believing the obvious — that a dopey erotic bubble has burst — we're encouraged to believe the absurd — that a great romantic betrayal has taken place.

The fact that Wertmuller could even entertain a notion this mawkish with a set of characters this dislikable may be the surest available clue to her conventional turn of mind. She has a sentimental side as well as a funny side, but her sensibility and techniques are perfectly consistent: She remains a crude, heavy-handed operator whether she's jerking tears or forcing laughs.

Wertmuller affects a topical tone that may help to camouflage her commonplace sentiments, particularly with foreign audiences. It takes a while before you realize that these argumentative, prejudiced Italian types have a vaguely familiar ring: the ring of Archie Bunker and Norman Lear comedy. The language may be exotic, but the drift is just as single-minded. What may obscure the issue even more is a sympathetic element of prejudice in American audiences. The heroine's humiliation may seem excusable to some people because she's portrayed as an upper-class bitch.

Wertmuller's concept of sexual antagonism gets inextricably mixed up with class hatred. The woman goes out of her way to insult the man when he's at a social disadvantage, and he goes out of his way to make her grovel when the tables are turned. When you return to Barrie's play, you're struck by both its clarity of vision and its lack of class hatred. The humor derives from the fact that it's Crichton the servant who believes absolutely in the class system and is pained by his master's infatuation with ideas of social equality. When the family is marooned, Crichton doesn't abandon his principles; he simply takes over the position of leadership that Lord Loam is incapable of filling in primitive surroundings.

Barrie succeeded in developing the premise more amusingly and resolving it more poignantly. When the party is rescued, it pains Crichton to return to the old arrangement, but he doesn't hesitate to see it through. Unlike Barrie's characters, Wertmuller's characters don't have convictions; they simply have prejudices, and their idyll turns into a kind of erotic celebration of those class and sexual prejudices.

The lack of women film directors no doubt accounts for the way Lina Wertmuller is being overrated at the moment. Some critics, particularly male critics, may find it both a relief and a convenience to jump on the Wertmuller bandwagon, and there's certainly nothing subtle or mysterious about her style, which suggests Norman Lear or Mel Brooks with a profane Italian accent.

Nevertheless, it is disturbing to think that Wertmuller may be creating a less professional following, that a large number of men and women may derive emotional satisfaction from an essentially hateful image of modern sexual conflicts. Amusing as they are to watch, Melato and Giannini are embodying a relationship that is not in the least amusing, because it suggests that erotic fantasy is becoming the only focus of interest one sex has in the other. In an atmosphere where young men and women may be encouraged to distrust and avoid one another, this tendency is more than a little ominous.

The Washington Post, February 4, 1976

CRUISING

David Ansen

There is *Cruising* the movie and there is *Cruising* the controversy; before discussing the flick, one must acknowledge the flap. Angry debate has surrounded William Friedkin's movie since it first went into production last summer along the waterfront back-room gay bars in New York's Greenwich Village. It was Friedkin's intention to explore a series of grisly murders of homosexuals who frequent those bars in pursuit of some of the more outré forms of sadomasochistic pleasure.

Gay activists cried foul, fearing that Hollywood was once again out to exploit them by presenting a lurid, distorted slice of the gay sub-subculture; homosexuals took to the streets to protest the filming. Liberal journalists saw the protest as a threat to the First Amendment and defended Friedkin's right to make his movie. The producers, hearing the sweet crackle of controversy, fanned the flames for all the publicity they could get. To add to the confusion, the largest theater chain in the United States, General Cinema Corporation, recently took a look at the film and pronounced it "unsuitable for our clientele." General Cinema Corporation felt that the film should be X-rated and has canceled its thirty-three bookings.

The movie itself will not quiet the storm. It is going to anger, disturb, and confuse a lot of people—but few, it's safe to say, will be entertained or enlightened. Friedkin tells the story of a young cop (Al Pacino) on an undercover assignment to infiltrate the bars as a decoy; because he bears an astonishing resemblance to the killer's victims, the police hope the murderer will be drawn into Pacino's trap. It was the thesis of Gerald Walker's 1970 novel, upon which the film is only loosely based, that the bigoted, aggressively heterosexual cop and the father-haunted, aggressively heterosexual killer were two sides of the same coin—counterparts whose identities increasingly merged as they each confronted their similarly pathological homophobia. The novel was perhaps too tidy and symmetrical for its own good, but it was a thriller with a very clear point.

What Friedkin's film is about is anybody's guess. If he just wanted to make a thriller, he has made a clumsy and unconvincing one. If he wanted to explore the psychology of his characters, he has left out most of the relevant information. If he intended to illuminate the tricky subject of S&M, he hasn't even scratched the surface. *Cruising* is quite effective in working up an atmosphere of dread: the ominous bar scenes are butch Grand Guignol, full of sweaty flesh, menacing shadows, and barely glimpsed acts of degradation performed by glowering, bearded men in black leather and chains. But who are these people and why are they doing all these kinky things? Friedkin isn't interested in explaining his milieu; he merely offers it up as a superficially shocking tableau for the titillation and horror of his audience.

Friedkin obviously thinks he has made a daring and honest film, but he has made a deeply evasive one. *Cruising* does look unflinchingly at the violence and kinkiness, but it avoids answering all the key dramatic questions about its hero. How far does Pacino have to go in his role as decoy? Why doesn't his unknowing girlfriend (Karen Allen), a sophisticated Manhattanite, wonder why her boyfriend comes home dressed in heavy leather? What is Pacino feeling as he enters into the gay scene? We know he's upset, and we assume he's experiencing some sexual confusion, but that's it. Friedkin's screenplay is so taciturn that not even Pacino's formidable skills can fill in the blanks: It's his most opaque, unadventurous performance.

The most puzzling evasion occurs at the end. After the killer has been caught, another homosexual is found murdered, and Friedkin plants the suggestion that the killer may have been either Pacino or the jealous lover of the dead man. If it's Pacino, nothing whatsoever has prepared us for this. If it's the lover, then *Cruising* seems to be pushing the absurd message that any homosexual is a potential killer. Asked last week at a press conference who committed the murder, Friedkin said he didn't know. Asked why he wanted a deliberately ambiguous ending, he said he didn't know if it *was* deliberate. Asked why the novel's heterosexual killer had been pointedly changed into an active homosexual, he said the killer was heterosexual.

No wonder *Cruising* is murky. Friedkin shows no signs of having digested or thought through his material. If *he* doesn't know what his movie is about, how are we to know? Though the film is now preceded by a statement that the story is not meant to be an "indictment" or "representative" portrait of the homosexual world, it does succeed in creating a new homosexual stereotype: not the limp-wristed, effeminate pansy of old, but a menacing, macho muscleman who pursues sex with surly ferocity and barely suppressed violence. Like *The Exorcist,* this is—for all its harshly lit authenticity of location—another of Friedkin's urban Gothic fantasies, and, like *The Exorcist,* its principal aim is to scare us. At that it succeeds—although it's not an accomplishment to boast about.

Newsweek, February 18, 1980

THE ACCUSED

Roger Ebert

The Accused demonstrates that rape victims are often suspects in their own cases. Surely they must have been somehow to blame. How were they behaving at the time of the crime? How were they dressed? Had they been drinking? Is their personal life clean and tidy? Or are they sluts who were just asking for it?

I am aware of the brutal impact of the previous sentence. But the words were carefully chosen because sometimes they reflect the unspoken suspicions of officials in the largely male criminal justice system. *The Accused* is a movie about Sarah Tobias, a young woman who is not a model citizen. One night she has a fight with her live-in boyfriend, who is a drug dealer. She goes to a sleazy bar and has too much to drink, and does a provocative dance to the jukebox, and begins to flirt with a man in the bar's back room.

And then things get out of hand. The man, also drunk, picks her up and lays her down on top of a pinball machine, and begins to assault her. Two other men hold her down, helpless. The music pounds. The other guys in the back room begin to cheer and chant and egg him on, and when he is finished they push another guy forward, and then another. Finally she escapes and runs weeping out onto the highway, crying for help.

The film shows most of this sequence only later, in a flashback. Its opening scenes deal with the immediate aftermath of the rape, as the woman (Jodie Foster) is moved through the emergency care and legal systems, where she meets professionals who are courteous and efficient, but not overly sympathetic. Then she meets Kathryn Murphy (Kelly McGillis), the assistant district attorney who will handle her case. McGillis is not impressed with some of the things she discovers, such as Tobias's previous conviction on drug possession charges, or her drinking on the night of the crime. And one of the rape suspects is a young fraternity man whose parents hire a good lawyer. In conference, the assistant DA agrees to reduce charges to "aggravated assault."

Sarah Tobias feels betrayed. She was raped, brutally, repeatedly, in front of many witnesses. It was not "aggravated assault." And the argument of the movie is that although a young woman may act improperly, even recklessly, she should still have the right to say "no" and be heard. This is something the McGillis character has difficulty in understanding at first; she is so comfortable with the informal compromises of the criminal justice system that she has lost some of her capacity for outrage.

In a sense, the movie is about the relationship between these two women, one an articulate lawyer, the other an inarticulate, angry alcoholic who sometimes lacks the words for the things she feels. One of the interesting choices in the screenplay by Tom Topor was to make it so hard for the Foster character to express herself, so that when she speaks we can almost feel each word being wrung out of her emotions. During the course of the film, the woman attorney comes to identify some of her client's feelings as actual experiences, not simply legal evidence. And the rape victim begins to see herself as others see her; we feel it is possible that the relationship between the two women will eventually lead the Foster character to clean up her act, stop drinking, and start taking responsibility for herself.

The other current in the film is equally interesting. This is the first film I can remember that considers the responsibility of bystanders in a rape case. The drunken fraternity boys and townies who climb on the furniture and chant and cheer are accessories to rape, although our society sometimes has difficulty in understanding that. When the McGillis character finally decides to bring some of them to trial, she gets no support at all from the chief district attorney, and many of her colleagues feel she's lost her mind. Assistant DAs are supposed to try cases they can win, not go looking for lost causes. But the lesson learned in the movie's second trial may be the most important message this movie has to offer.

I wonder who will find the film more uncomfortable—men or women? Both will recoil from the brutality of the actual scenes of the assault. But for some men, the movie will reveal a truth that most women already know. It is that verbal sexual harassment, whether crudely in a saloon back room or subtly in an everyday situation, is a form of violence—one that leaves no visible marks but can make its victims feel unable to move freely and casually in society. It is a form of imprisonment.

Chicago Sun-Times, October 14, 1988

THE ACCUSED

Julie Salamon

During the big scene in *The Accused,* a young woman is jammed up against a pinball machine by a man she's been flirting with. He rapes her, then relinquishes his place — on top of her — to two other drunks. They rape her, too, while their drinking buddies egg them on.

It's already been noted earlier in the movie that the name of the game the pinball machine was really designed for is Slamdunk; when players score many points, bells ring and lights flash, illuminating a cartoon drawing of a half-naked woman whose backside swishes into a basketball net.

Like almost everything in this loaded — and powerful — melodrama, the point is slam-dunked. Everyone is guilty: the rapists, certainly; their cheering pals; the waitress who pretends it isn't happening; and even the pinball machine manufacturers who subtly encourage rape by subliminally connecting their thrusting, sweating pinball play with a full-court press against a woman. The picture seems to be making a strong case for preventive castration.

It was produced by Sherry Lansing and Stanley R. Jaffe, the same team that previously capitalized on the public's general nervousness about sex by turning a casual adultery into a homicidal nightmare, in *Fatal Attraction.* Now, the same filmmakers say they want to use this graphic rape in *The Accused* to examine the social problem of people who just stand by and do nothing while crimes take place in front of them — or worse, become cheerleaders. But this is no dispassionate investigation of moral complexity. In this movie the bystanders are portrayed as loathsome louts, more vile than the actual rapists. The filmmakers have taken all the intellectual and moral depth out of the issue they say they wanted to explore. Nor does the movie get at the real problem in rape trials — of convincing juries that the nice-looking men sitting there at the defense table with their female attorneys could hurt anyone. These movie defendants look like the creeps that they are; the scuzziest among them has a red scorpion tattooed on his arm.

By saving the visualization of the rape until the end of the movie, director Jonathan Kaplan (*Heart Like a Wheel, Project X*) and screenwriter Tom Topor (*Nuts*) pretend to the seriousness of a documentary while slyly milking the squalid incident as hard as any tabloid headline writer ever could. In addition to The Scene itself, the movie starkly presents the messy aftermath of rape — the hospital exams, the legal maneuverings. The picture also gets at the class snobbery that lowers a rape victim's revenge percentages if she is working class, uneducated, and "ill-bred." Yet, because the victim finally gets to retaliate, women are supposed to take this movie as a Clint Eastwood flick (not *Bird*) where the girl gets to be Dirty Harry — but without guns.

Since she was stalked in real life by would-be presidential assassin John Hinckley, actress Jodie Foster has apparently decided that victims are going to be her specialty as an actress (*Five Corners, Stealing Home*). She is almost eerily perfect as the working-class girl who hasn't got much in life; she drinks and does drugs and goes to cheap dives and flirts provocatively with men. (It is depressing to think about what will happen to this woman when the trial is over and she's back alone with herself and her sad sex fantasies.) As the earnest prosecutor who takes her case, Kelly McGillis doesn't get a chance to do much besides look big and authoritative and repressed, all of which she accomplishes handily.

What's most unsettling about the picture has been the way some men are responding to it. A friend of mine reports that on a Saturday night in the well-heeled suburb of Upper Montclair, New Jersey, the young men around him started cheering during the rape. He also noticed an usher letting in a couple of men who showed up just for that part of the movie.

This makes me think the moviemakers would have done better by their subject — though probably not better at the box office — if they'd more closely followed the facts of the much-publicized 1983 rape case in New Bedford, Massachusetts, which partly inspired the picture. That was the case in which bystanders purportedly cheered while a woman was gang-raped on a pool table. It turned out there weren't really any heckler accomplices.

The even more relevant part of the case was something that didn't get written about much. While the national press was quick to jump on the phenomenon of onlooker culpability, the prosecutors were hard pressed to make the rape charge stick in court (though they eventually did).

Unlike the virile rapists these filmmakers have put on screen to teach us a lesson, the New Bedford attackers were too overcome by drink and, perhaps, the anxiety of public performance to technically complete the rape. Reality was far less titillating, and much more

difficult to exploit, than the spectacle made so horrifyingly "real" in
The Accused.

Wall Street Journal, October 20, 1988

sex, lies, and videotape

Jay Carr

Take a look at the exclusively lowercase lettering in the title of Steven
Soderbergh's *sex, lies, and videotape* and you'll start to understand the
secret of its success. It's full of purpose, but never comes on strong,
never raises its voice. Astonishingly, with one feature film, Soderbergh redefines romantic comedy for the late eighties, and probably
for a good part of the nineties, too, with a distinct, original, and
thoroughly contemporary sensibility. In new ways, he does what the
great old sophisticated comedies did. He provides a subtle context for
the sex. It's intriguing, slyly amusing, unexpectedly erotic, and ultimately quite moral. *sex, lies, and videotape* makes *Dangerous Liaisons*
look like a Jerry Lewis movie, but what makes it modern, apart from
its essential earnestness, is Soderbergh's virtuosic use of indirection,
his extraordinary ear for hesitations and charged silences, his awareness of how sexy, under the right circumstances, talk can be.

As *sex, lies, and videotape* begins, nobody is experiencing the right
circumstances. Skewed, repressed Ann (Andie MacDowell) sits in
her shrink's office, obsessing about garbage. When he asks her how
things are going with her husband, John, she says, "They're fine, except I'm goin' through this period where I don't want him to touch
me." She's on to something she doesn't realize consciously. While she
sits in her flowered belle-of-the-South frock in the new yuppie Baton
Rouge, smug, pouty, two-timing lawyer John (Peter Gallagher) sits
in his office, twirls his wedding ring on his expensive desk, and heads
off for sex in the afternoon with his wife's sister, Cynthia.

Cynthia, a painter who works as a bartender, is as brazenly voluptuous as Ann is prudish. Although tiny, Laura San Giacomo's Cynthia is a mini-lioness. Her moves grow more luxuriantly feline and
her husky voice expands, thickens, and drops one register when sex
enters the picture. She's confident, but not really relaxed. To her, sex

is a weapon in a never-ending sibling war with her sister. Although he never makes a big thing of it — or anything — Soderbergh is amusing about the way each sister defines herself as the sexual opposite of the other. Both sisters are confused, but Ann distances herself not only from sex, but from her own blinkered life.

When Graham (James Spader), an old college buddy of John's, shows up as a houseguest, Ann is first annoyed, then intrigued when it becomes apparent that her husband regards Graham as a dropout loser he's sorry he invited. After Graham denounces lying and encourages intimate exchange by telling Ann over coffee that he's impotent, Ann is hooked. Finding him sympathetic and irresistibly safe, she can't resist tiptoeing downstairs in the middle of the night to scope him out. Soderbergh, who says his film is based on incidents from his own recent past, isn't cynical. Graham isn't faking impotence as a seductive ruse, although Spader's soft, spidery, confidential tone leaves no doubt that he's a seducer, and knows it.

He travels with a stock of videotapes, he explains, because he's too blocked by his own rage and disgust to have sex. Instead, he encourages women to talk about their sex lives, and tapes the interviews. Only in private, when he plays the tapes back, can he find sexual release. The tapes — they're not porn — work as interviews, it becomes obvious, because the women don't have to worry that he's coming on to them. When she learns about the tapes, Ann retreats. But when Cynthia hears about Graham, she loses interest in John. Having enjoyed Ann's husband in Ann's bed, she now wants the new man to whom Ann is attracted.

From this modern sexual quadrille, Soderbergh's design becomes clear. He means to use the videotapes to get the lies out of the sex. While Graham may not immediately seem the hero type, he's clearly the salutary catalyst here, the stranger in black who rides into town and challenges the essentially rotten status quo. He gets women to confess because confessing comes so naturally to him, and his gentle hesitancy keeps him unthreatening even though he's pretty persistent beneath his diffident politeness and formality. Yet he's not just soft. There's something faintly sinister in his muted style. Spader's beautifully gauged and layered performance keeps us off balance.

One could debate the notion of impotence as a new form of romantic purity, challenging to a certain kind of woman. But Soderbergh succeeds by never overstating, and he doesn't on this point. Successful at leaving things unsaid, he's just as successful at leaving them unseen. We only see small parts of the videos until it becomes important to see the video Ann makes. When we do see her, we're struck — but not surprised — at how sexy she finally looks, at how she and Cynthia finally look like sisters. (Even though their exchanges are catty, Soderbergh has a good enough ear to make them sound like sisters, too.) The economy of Soderbergh's fluent camera heightens his film's feeling of offhand intimacy. He sees things with the cool but far from unfelt reflexes of a product of the TV generation. The acting — which, by the way, achieves with insolent ease that much-cited but seldom realized ensemble ideal — is flawless. I'd give them all Oscars in a minute. *sex, lies, and videotape* is a cool, fresh, funny, almost unnervingly assured treat.

Boston Globe, August 11, 1989

sex, lies, and videotape

Gary Arnold

Despite its catchy lowercase title, *sex, lies, and videotape* proves to be about as schematic, shallow, and insufferably dinky as a movie can get. Not to mention a movie that also gets away with faking an exploitable pretense of titillating solemnity.

Obviously, sarcastic congratulations are in order for everyone who's been instrumental in helping this pseudoshocking and pseudo-profound trifle overcome its conspicuous inertia and emerge as a bandwagon sleeper, presumably rolling in the general direction of fashionable success. Get out those unfinished screenplay notes and drafts. If a picture as starved for substance and originality (and, incidentally, erotic gratification) as *sex, lies, and videotape* can luck into the grand prize at the Cannes Film Festival and earn its self-evidently groping and tentative creator, twenty-six-year-old Steven Soderbergh, an instantly inflated reputation as prodigy of the moment, then outrageous good fortune could smile on all of us.

Inspired myself, I took a few moments before starting this appreciation to dash off soul-searching treatments called *sex, truth, and screenings* and *sex, bills, and other financial obligations,* which try to come to terms with the traumatic pathos implicit in reconciling oneself to life as a movie critic and family man, respectively. I expect several lucrative nibbles before the month is out, especially from producers shrewd enough to perceive the commercial potential in those sexy, sexy titles.

Soderbergh's stunted little celebration of contemporary sexual hang-ups from frigidity to infidelity to passivity to avidity to blithering idiocy begins with the word "Garbage," followed by the say-what rejoinder "Garbage?" and the explanation, "We've got so much of it." How true, and so much of the so much seems to take a cinematic form and be swallowed whole by excessively credulous and cooperative members of both the critical fraternity and the movie-going public. Would that it were otherwise, but the prevailing tilt toward positive promotional reinforcement does make it interesting when you feel moved to accent the negative.

The "garbage" exchange takes place between one of the principal characters, a prosperous but sexually blocked young housewife named Ann (Andie MacDowell), and her psychotherapist. While she dithers on, exposing herself as at best a sweet-natured airhead, the filmmaker slips in teasing introductions to his other principals, played by James Spader, Peter Gallagher, and Laura San Giacomo, a genuinely promising newcomer who gives the film its only credible source of diversion and distinction.

Spader is a deceptively subdued catalyst named Graham, the mysterious interloper destined to awaken Ann from her Sleeping Beauty trance of marital discontent and sexual immaturity by making such a mock-nonchalant fetish of his own sexual dysfunction—alleged impotence aggravated by collecting the sexual confessions of women acquaintances on videotape—that Ann will take pity on his wretchedness and emerge as an impromptu therapist, bringing the hope of interpersonal salvation to both of them. Gallagher is Ann's cheating husband John, once a college chum of Graham's but now such a transparent Yuppie whipping boy that we don't need to waste pity on him, thank heaven. San Giacomo is Ann's shamelessly slutty sister Cynthia, busy carrying on a torrid affair with brother-in-law John and entrusted with such provocative, though ultimately overstated, remarks as "The idea of doing it in my sister's bed gives me a perverse thrill" and "I wish I could come right out and say, 'My sister's a lousy lay.' "

Delightful couplet, that, and as far as one can tell, no one's stopping her from abusing her sister up one side and down the other. However, Soderbergh absentmindedly discards this initial note of rather pathological sibling hostility when it becomes necessary to hook up

Graham with both women and he can't think of any subterfuge except making the girls sexual confidantes, at least as far as plot convenience demands. Dropping by Graham's apartment, Ann can't help but observe his cache of tapes and Graham can't help confessing their shameful significance.

Ann tells Cynthia, whose filthy mind is irresistibly aroused. She drops by and submits to an interview, beginning with this opening volley of fascinating questions: "When did you finally see a penis? What did you think? Was it what you expected?" What a technique! Adapted from Barbara Walters, perhaps? Incredibly, it seems to work even more effectively than Billy Crystal's blatantly obnoxious form of sexual presumption in *When Harry Met Sally*. At least it took twelve years of desperation before poor Sally evidently decided to weaken. Brazen Cynthia finds Graham's dolorous line of prurient inquiry so stimulating that she allegedly stimulates herself for his camera and then goes off to fornicate the afternoon away with potent, albeit despicable, John.

Then Cynthia tells Ann about doing the video dirty with Graham, and despite herself Ann feels sufficient consumer, sibling, or merely libidinous incentive to become an interview subject herself. It helps when she also catches on to her husband's affair, very conveniently finding the telltale pearl earring that Cynthia very conveniently lost in Ann's very own bedroom. The upshot of all this incestuous humbug is that Graham evidently gets even with John for bygone rivalries by alienating first his mistress and then his wife. Although it appears that the slyboots will only get to keep Ann as his reward, forming a relationship of exemplary intimacy and fidelity pointing toward the model sexual alliance of the twenty-first century, you can't help suspecting that a return of potency might not preclude a spot of hanky-panky with an incorrigible as available as Cynthia. Meanwhile, John's law practice seems to be falling apart, and good riddance.

If Soderbergh were capable of sustaining a satiric conception, this setup might have paid perversely funny dividends. But the prevailing tone of *sex, lies, and videotape* is therapeutic banality. We're supposed to take solicitous pity on Graham in concert with Ann, believing not only his woe-is-me impotence hustle but also his claims of character reformation. Where once he was a male chauvinist liar and opportunist like John, now he has humbled himself into a salvation-hunting voyeur, compulsively asking women what it is they find sexy until freed from this slavish curiosity by the compassionate love of a compatibly dim-witted woman. Hallelujah!

The whole skimpy, ridiculous contraption suggests *Play It Again, Sam* rewritten by the world's most humorless (or dishonest) sex counselor. Moreover, I wouldn't trade any single gag in a long list of playful sex farces from *Sam* through *Women on the Verge of a Nervous Breakdown* for Soderbergh's film in its portentous, overrated entirety. It doesn't just compare poorly with frivolous entertainments of style and integrity — *The Secret of My Success,* for example. Elevate the comparison by recalling film comedies that managed to combine insight and affection while observing the obsessive, kinky side of things — *Bob & Carol & Ted & Alice, Citizens Band,* and *Tin Men,* to name an admirable trio. The slightness of *sex, lies, and videotape* is thrown into such stark relief that it's difficult to imagine anyone recommending it without a fistful of apologetic reservations.

On the contrary, one can encounter the most extravagant gush. Witness this outpouring in the current issue of *Film Comment:* "[Soderbergh] has showed us our skin, how it wants to be touched with truth and beauty and eternity, and the consequences of that time called our twenties. That is to say, it is about the end of the first time, and the beginning of wisdom." There's no telling what kind of immortal nonsense will get written if you can fashion a cinematic cocktail that spikes a big gulp of psychoanalytic cliché with a little carbonated prurience.

Spader's best-actor prize at Cannes will surely endure as one of the enigmas of the age. Was the jury belatedly honoring his nonsluggish, nonmawkish work in movies like *Pretty in Pink, Mannequin,* and *Less Than Zero?* Not that any members of the cast finesse their straitjacket roles more than momentarily, but Graham is certainly the dud role of the quartet. I did enjoy one take in which Andie MacDowell seemed to take an eternity to register the significance of finding that pearl earring, but the only positive feature of the show is Laura San Giacomo's debut, which gives us an expressively striking and amusing new face, plus a personality that could provide healthy competition for Holly Hunter.

Soderbergh's precociousness seems to express itself in synthetic forms of confrontation and stilted patterns of close-up, slowly panning composition that strike me as deadly on arrival. Maybe he's got a bright future ahead, but this mannered, trifling first work doesn't inspire much confidence. "I guess it's all downhill from here," Soderbergh cracked amiably after winning at Cannes. For some of us the disillusion has already begun.

The Washington Times, August 11, 1989

PRETTY WOMAN

Carrie Rickey

The reason to see *Pretty Woman* is the gal who plays her, Julia Roberts, the first American actress with both Audrey Hepburn's gamine air and Ava Gardner's earthy sexuality—a killer combination.

About the movie itself: Well, it used to be that Hollywood made Cinderella movies about a chambermaid or a waitress who captured a millionaire's imagination. Today, Hollywood stoops lower and lower to elevate Cinderella higher and higher.

In *Pretty Woman,* Roberts portrays Vivian, a hooker who snares playboy Edward Lewis (Richard Gere), a corporate raider. That's right: Hollywood stoops lower and lower to elevate Prince Charming higher and higher, too.

Vivian works without a pimp, wears a midriff-baring minidress tighter than a sausage casing, and sports a blond wig that makes her resemble a drag-queen Carol Channing. Her thigh-high patent-leather footwear sings "These boots are made for streetwalking."

The potentially subversive quality of this conventional romantic fantasy is that its heroine is literally a Hollywood Boulevard whore and its hero is figuratively a Wall Street pimp. When Edward picks up Vivian on the boulevard (supposedly he's lost and can't find Beverly Hills), she jumps into his car and offers to take him to Rodeo Drive—for twenty dollars.

Edward tells Vivian what he does for a living and she nods in understanding, "Buying companies and selling off the parts is like stealing cars and selling off the parts." Noting the parallels between their professions, he says, "You and I are such similar creatures—we both screw people for money."

Although *Pretty Woman* has a residue of caustic comic dialogue, this Disney Touchstone comedy is sanitized for your protection. Vivian is the most wholesome hooker in the history of the profession, and flosses her teeth regularly. Good gums are essential in her line of work.

Naturally, Edward, a failure at intimacy, figures that buying Vivian's companionship is more cost-effective and emotionally economical than courting a love object, which takes time and commitment.

He makes Vivian a deal to be his "beck-and-call girl" for his week in Los Angeles, during which he plans to raid a company owned by James Morse (Ralph Bellamy). Call her the American gigola.

A gal can't wear a sausage casing to tony restaurants and polo matches; thus Vivian needs a new wardrobe. Fortunately, under her Carol Channing fright wig, she has a dazzling auburn mane. More fortunately, she finds a fairy godfather in the manager (Hector Elizondo) of the fancy hotel where Edward is registered. He coaches Vivian in what ladies wear, how ladies speak, and which forks ladies use.

Yes, the film has the requisite shopping spree, which replaces the romantic montage in this romantic comedy.

In this Garry Marshall movie, his most crisply directed film since *The Flamingo Kid,* the scenes between eye-catching Roberts and watchful Elizondo are more affecting than those between her and Gere. Likewise for those sequences between the brash Gere and the solid Ralph Bellamy. Vivian and Edward must learn to love their father figures before they can love each other.

Although *Pretty Woman* is as contrived and cynical a film as Disney has had the chutzpah to make, there is nothing bogus about Roberts's performance, which redeems the movie in a way that its plot cannot redeem Vivian and Edward. Gere is relaxed, perhaps relieved that he doesn't have to carry the movie by himself.

The movie's other pleasures are Elizondo and the delightful Laura San Giacomo (the sultry sister in *sex, lies, and videotape*) as Kit, Vivian's sister streetwalker, whose face has a paint job straight from Earl Scheib. When she sees the transformed, natural-beauty Vivian in her designer duds, Kit squeals, "You can clean up real nice."

Would that this could be said about *Pretty Woman*, which cloaks its dirty deals under an immaculate mantle. Even on Hollywood Boulevard, Julia Roberts's Vivian is so well scrubbed that she might be playing Snow White at Disneyland.

Philadelphia Inquirer, March 23, 1990

PRETTY WOMAN

Jay Carr

The disturbing thing about *Pretty Woman* is that apparently nobody at the Disney studio saw it as anything but a light romantic comedy. Actually, it's a film whose real message is startlingly at odds with its nominal story, in which smooth, icy takeover tycoon Richard Gere comes to Los Angeles, takes over sweet, fresh-faced prostitute Julia Roberts, and does a Pygmalion number on her. Picking her up on Hollywood Boulevard, then realizing he needs an escort for business dinners, he throws some money at her for stylish clothes. She's also smart enough to seek tutelage on table manners from the kindly manager of the Beverly Wilshire Hotel, in whose penthouse they're ensconced. In this landscape of remade appearances signifying self-transformation, she literally becomes a six-day wonder, transformed from gum-chewing klutz to country-club goddess in less than a week.

What's wrong with this picture is that it's an astonishingly self-oblivious piece of woman-bashing. Its real message is that money rules, that it can buy anything. It goes through the motions of endowing Roberts's character with dignity—in the end, she refuses to be a kept woman, holding out for marriage. But its real view is that without this rich guy, she's nothing. And she needs not only a rich guy, but one who'll tell her what to wear and how to behave. She can't even fight her own battles on Rodeo Drive. After a couple of snooty saleswomen show her the door, Gere makes it possible for her to go back and humble them (more woman-bashing!), reinforcing the film's credo that money and appearances are what counts, that if the prostitute trades in her tie-dyed miniskirt for the right cocktail dress, her problems will be solved.

Not that she has many problems. Possibly with an afterthought to its image, this Disney studio prostitute is the most squeaky-clean ever put on film. Only once toward the end, when Gere's sleazy lawyer, played by Jason Alexander, jumps her, is there even a hint that the world of the prostitute is filled with anything unpleasant, much less ugly. Prostitution isn't so much glamourized as sanitized—no drugs, no disease, no nasty pimps. It's almost as if Disney is packaging a new theme park attraction—Hooker World. Sure enough, there's a flash of cheap insight as Gere's character mutters, "You and I are such similar creatures — we both screw people for money." After this, and a couple of passages allowing him to be sensitive to music and explain why he hated his father, we're supposed to believe that her warmth gets him to change the habits of a lifetime and become a better human being. At bottom, though, this remains a film in which she shops — and he approves or rejects. His money means she'll take his orders — and his contempt.

In short, he remakes and reshapes her while she slightly tempers his rapaciousness. Continuing his improvement program, he immerses her in opera and chess, presumably to decrease the chances that she'll prove a social embarrassment to him. In a way, it all seems even more meretricious because the actors are charming — Gere in his muted, ironic way; Roberts in her heartfelt vitality; Hector Elizondo as the avuncular hotel manager; Laura San Giacomo recycling her *sex, lies, and videotape* appeal at a much lower level here as the prostitute's roommate. Somehow, you feel *Pretty Woman* is being honest only when the prostitute slips into submissiveness, that only here do its real intentions emerge. Alfred Hitchcock was called kinky for the way he molded Kim Novak into the cool blonde of his dreams in *Vertigo*. What are we to make of the spectacle of a studio molding another beauty even more imperiously into a figure of gorgeous powerlessness? At best, *Pretty Woman* is condescending. It's a misogynist's delight.

Boston Globe, March 23, 1990

TIE ME UP! TIE ME DOWN!

Henry Sheehan

Pedro Almodóvar's *Tie Me Up! Tie Me Down!* despite the presence of the filmmaker's typically free-wheeling, eccentric, and sexually frank characters, is an oddly deterministic film, suggesting we are all prisoners of dark lusts so hidden within us and within misleadingly cheerful or sociable notions of love that it takes a crisis for us to discover their very existence. I have never been much of a fan of Almodóvar, and the director's vaunted shifts in tone and wacky

Antonio Banderas and Victoria Abril are locked in carnal captivity in Pedro Almodóvar's *Tie Me Up! Tie Me Down!* (Photo by Paco Navarro, courtesy of Miramax Films.)

characters have always appeared to me to be more a symptom of shaky technique than the controlled expression of a comic satirist. However, there has been a progressive narrowing of focus and accompanying intensity to his work, and in *Tie Me Up! Tie Me Down!*

the filmmaker has achieved a clarity that has been missing from earlier films. In fact, Almodóvar's intentions are so clear here that he may finally actually succeed in upsetting the complacent audiences who have previously been chuckling along at his ruthless send-ups of their most cherished romantic notions.

Victoria Abril, unconventionally sexy, stars as Marina, a former porno star who is paddling over into the mainstream under the tutelage of director Maximo Espejo (Francisco Rabal), a wheelchair-bound tyrant whose past reputation for greatness contrasts with his current diminished capacity to raise funds. He has ensconced Marina as the leading lady in an action-adventure potboiler, complete with a masked marauder, hairbreadth escapes, and tortured confessions of unrequited love.

Into the middle of this crisis-strewn movie set wanders Ricky (Antonio Banderas), recently paroled from a sort of orphan's mental institution. Long obsessed with Marina, dating back to her lustier days, Ricky kidnaps her, ties her up to her bed, and patiently waits for her to acknowledge her love for him while the world scurries about looking for her.

Although it is Ricky who has been gazing upon Marina from afar for years, Almodóvar begins treating him as a love object from his first appearance on screen when the female staff of his former institution bid tearful farewells to their in-house stud. In fact, Banderas, a rough-looking but boyish young man, has appeared in three previous Almodóvar films, and though he has not always been the central object of affection, Almodóvar's treatment of him has always made it clear that, for the director at least, Banderas, and hence Ricky, embodies clear-cut notions of sexuality and desirability.

Thus Almodóvar, after establishing Marina's credentials as a working love object, pulls a shift, creating a reluctant voyeur out of a willing sex object. Marina's status as an unattainable goal is emphasized by her own do-it-yourself love life, which reaches a zenith in a bathtub scene in which she graphically (too graphically for the ratings board, which branded the film with an absurdly out-of-line X) reaches climax with a persistent battery-operated scuba diver. Likewise, later Almodóvar shows her watching one of her old porno tapes in which she looks back over her naked haunches as she acts out a love scene with an unseen fellow partner.

The placid solitude of her masturbatory sequences is in stark contrast to the full-fledged soap opera that accompanies her imprisonment. Although she is left alone for hours to contemplate her bound plight, the worst parts of Marina's condition, at least as she sees it, are the wild protestations of affection and insane assurance that they will be returned that Ricky insists on making. Pulled kicking and screaming, literally and figuratively, from her lonely pleasures, Marina does eventually begin to respond, if not to Ricky, then to the depths of the passion that he swears she has aroused.

A pair of contradictions lurks at the bottom of all this. The richer one, deliberately unresolved, concerns the very nature of the relationship between Marina and Ricky. Obviously a metaphor for the coercive and debilitating nature of marriage, the bond between kidnapper and victim very clearly answers a need not just for Ricky, but for Marina as well. Fighting the passivity that Ricky demands — despite the unusual courtship, he seeks a traditional role-playing marriage at its end — Marina eventually succumbs to it with pleasure, partly because of the paradoxical control submission allows her to extend over Ricky, but also because she enjoys it for herself. While hip filmgoers may have no problems with the description of marriage as a repressive institution, they might have a hard time swallowing Almodóvar's explicit contention that the repression is self-generating, the result of the voluntary suasion of neurosis.

More troubling, as always with Almodóvar, is the way the director puts his characters through their paces with such detached vigor. The entire first portion of the movie, featuring the exasperated director Espejo's frustrated attempts to bend Marina to the needs of his film, is obviously Almodóvar's declaration that his characters are beyond his control, with the fictional director's wheelchair suggesting, furthermore, that such control is always beyond the power of the filmmaker. Well, in a perfect cinema, maybe, but though the *Tie Me Up! Tie Me Down!* loosey-goosey comic melodrama appears an accommodating baggy fit for its characters, there are times when it is as restricting as any fashionably tailored suit.

Los Angeles Reader, May 11, 1990

TIE ME UP! TIE ME DOWN!

Stuart Klawans

Condemned by her beauty to be a figure of fantasy, a young woman must choose between the roles assigned her by two different men, one an impotent septuagenarian with a head full of porn, the other a psychotic who dreams of turning her into a housewife. She eventually accepts the latter role, not only because the psychotic is young and handsome and has a knife but also because he's willing to supply heroin for a toothache that's killing her.

Once more, we have entered the land of Pedro Almodóvar, this time on an excursion titled *Tie Me Up! Tie Me Down!* In previous works such as *What Have I Done to Deserve This!* and *Women on the Verge of a Nervous Breakdown,* the events I've just summarized might have zipped past as only one of a dozen gaudy diversions. Here, they have become the whole film. Having parked the careening vehicle of his moviemaking in front of one particular fun house, Almodóvar this time conducts his tour on foot, slowly, almost respectfully, asking the sightseers to observe every detail of the architecture and look into the eyes of the inhabitants. I very much fear he's becoming serious.

Yes, he still insults Spanish religiosity. The very first image is of rows of identical pictures of the Sacred Hearts of Mary and Jesus; later on, these turn into icons of sadomasochism, as they hang over the bed where the crucial action takes place. You also get to laugh at one of Almodóvar's fake TV commercials—but only one. For the most part, *Tie Me Up! Tie Me Down!* tries to be a well-made character study. It's intelligent and sensitive but also—heroin or no heroin—just a little stodgy.

Marina, played by the sleek and pouty-mouthed Victoria Abril, is a porn star and reformed junkie who has just broken through to respectability, acting in the latest film by the legendary director Maximo Espejo (Francisco Rabal). But nobody on the set, Marina included, seems to want to be all *that* respectable. Maximo has an undisguised admiration for her former productions; he also wants his new film, a psycho-killer story, to pay tribute to B movies. Obviously, he feels Marina should stay true to her past. And so does she—though the past she cherishes has less to do with being a trash queen than with her rural background. She's a woman of the people, who still remembers how to treat an abscess on a mule's hoof.

The only person around who seems to long for middle-class repose is Ricky (Antonio Banderas), who has just won release from a mental hospital. He seems to owe his freedom to an improved attitude and also a willingness to grant sexual favors to the asylum's keeper. No sooner has he hit the street than he swipes a heart-shaped box of candy and a knife, the better to woo Marina. He just knows she will learn to love him.

Now, some viewers have professed outrage at Ricky's method of courtship. Others, though willing to see such violence portrayed, are upset that Marina eventually yields to it, especially given her now-notorious gesture of submission. Instead of "I love you," she murmurs "Tie me up." Though you might claim this is meant to render literal the condition of marriage, I doubt it's possible this time to mount a defense on the grounds of travesty—the overall tone of the picture is too earnest for that, the plot's resolution too sentimental. These characters really are supposed to live happily ever after, or as happily as such people can. That, I suppose, is the point. Marina, like Ricky, turns out to hunger for a traditional role—for respectability, in the bourgeois sense—since she, too, has suffered too much from being an outsider. So *Tie Me Up!* might be seen as a taboo-breaking director's provisional endorsement of taboos—his reminder that some people have been hurt so badly that social conventions seem to them a refuge.

If this reading is correct, it also would explain Almodóvar's uncharacteristically plodding direction. For the moment, he's turned against the artifice that old Maximo represents, the artifice that his own films have celebrated. (Unless my eyes deceive me, Maximo is shooting his B movie on the living-room set from *Women on the Verge*.) The Madrid in which Marina lives is a society of fakery, in which people change their identities at will. "You're a journalist now?" a performer asks the reporter who is interviewing him—to which the reporter replies, "And you're an actor?" Ricky, too, takes part in this playacting, donning a succession of dumb-looking disguises. But he clearly would prefer *real* life. So, ultimately, would Marina, leading the film to conclude not on Maximo's soundstage but in a rural village.

When jaded sophisticates start longing for the authenticity of rustic life, I get nervous. Of course, the real problem with *Tie Me Up!* is not political. Who but Zippy the Pinhead would go to an Almodóvar film for its ideology? But there seems to be a disturbing change of attitude, all the same, that has led Almodóvar to tone down his beloved mockery and outrage and titillation. I hope the change is temporary and that he'll soon be back in form. If not, I wonder if the Falangism that he's so grandly ignored might start to make a delayed entrance into his films, and not in the way you would have expected. What's next for Almodóvar — *Ricky and Marina Return to the Soil?*

The Nation, May 28, 1990

HENRY & JUNE

Michael Sragow

Philip Kaufman's *Henry & June* is a gorgeous piece of work — a tough-minded, ironical, tremendously enjoyable vision of sex, love, and creation and the roving, improvisatory life of the expatriate artist in Paris circa 1931.

This is the film that propelled the Motion Picture Association of America rating system into the twenty-first century. The prospect of having this ebullient, uncorrupted rhapsody by America's most talented (and honorable) director stigmatized with an X, and thus barred from mainstream theaters and advertising outlets, hastened the acceptance of NC-17, a new adult rating that replaces the X. *Henry & June,* the first to sport that rating, is the perfect test case.

Kaufman focuses on the three-way love story of Henry Miller, Anaïs Nin, and Miller's second wife, June: two writers and a muse. He refuses to turn his fabulously talented actors — Fred Ward (Henry), Maria de Medeiros (Anaïs), and Uma Thurman (June) — into conventional erotic objects. What's sexiest about the movie is its charged, captivating atmosphere.

This film is a mind-opener and a sense-opener. It's about characters who pull themselves inside out, in life as well as in literature. Once Henry and Anaïs hit their groove, everything they do is sexy, from making love against a wall at sunrise to unraveling a measuring string for the great chronicler of Paris in the thirties, the photographer Brassaï. *Henry & June* heightens the act of observation into a sensual experience.

Anaïs talks about her need to feel innocent. But this movie isn't about the conflict between innocence and experience — a subject often perverted in pornography. It's about characters who find innocence through experience, sexual and otherwise. *Henry & June* combines life-embracing American rhythms — the roiling, wisecracking rumble of Miller's prose and of Kaufman's moviemaking — with a grizzled ambiance of mortal frailty. That's what Miller himself loved most about French films.

Like all of Kaufman's features — recently, *The Right Stuff* (1983) and *The Unbearable Lightness of Being* (1988) — this funny, large-spirited beauty is seductively compelling. It draws and holds you in without an obvious plot. *Henry & June* is brimful with details that lodge in the mind because they're redolent of character. It brings to life a Bohemian existence surging with human appetites and fueled by art, magic, and rebellion, just as the Prague Spring scenes did in *The Unbearable Lightness of Being*.

Ticklish, lyrical side moments, like the petty crimes and tomfoolery of unemployed magicians and street comics, snowball in importance as the film goes on. The sidewalk wizards contrast with more earthbound artists like Henry and Anaïs, who must discover their own ways of astonishing an audience. *Henry & June* is 1990's most satisfying film. It allows you to absorb an artist's existence through the pores.

The 1986 publication of Anaïs's first unexpurgated journals under the title *Henry & June* — which revealed her passionate affair with Henry and the depths of her sexual fascination with June — provided Kaufman with a springboard for comedy and drama, high and low. Kaufman and his cowriter and wife, Rose Kaufman, haven't shaped the material merely as an "untold story" of famous writers or a love poem to Paris.

In a meticulously wrought, exuberant style, it's a thought-out, felt-out celebration of adult experience — of grown-ups using their brains and bodies, their notions and sensations, to find out who they are and who they can be.

Employing Anaïs's multivolumed diary and Henry's Rabelaisian novels and essays as a base, yet bringing his own wry, adventurous sensibility to it, Kaufman is able to salute self-liberation without getting pompous or gassy. *Henry & June* is rooted in the texture of real events. It boasts the firm, rich grain that most explorations of selfhood lack.

Kaufman views Anaïs, Henry, and June with affection and without

Henry Miller (Fred Ward) is the recipient of the strategically placed hand-shake of Anaïs Nin (Maria de Medeiros) and June (Uma Thurman) in Philip Kaufman's *Henry & June*. (Photo by Etienne George, courtesy of Universal Pictures.)

moralism. Yet he doesn't treat them to an easy ride — he opens up their behavior to question. The characters do horrible things and lie about them: Anaïs betrays her husband — and June — by having affairs not just with Henry but also with her cousin Eduardo; June gives Henry his inspiration while castrating him psychically as she goads him to portray her as a noble heroine; Henry is an incorrigible scrounger of emotions as well as sex and money.

All three are self-dramatists — they forge their own racks and stretch on them. They're ideal subjects for a movie that lives through gestures and shadings. Even when they rest, they express themselves.

Henry & June is an unusual triangle story — every corner is equal in unpredictable ways. June is at first the strongest: a streetwise Brooklyn taxi-dancer who would do anything to put Henry in clover, even prostitution. She's an artist without an art; she's adept at making scenes only in real life. She's also an enigma within an enigma. Even though she takes Anaïs to a lesbian bar and rouses the writer's same-sex curiosity, you can't be sure if she's a lesbian, or bisexual, or just fooling around. June's inability to channel her imagination leaves her more vulnerable than Henry or Anaïs.

Anaïs is physically tiny compared with June, and sheltered, but with her secrecy and cunning she's more than a match for Henry's wife. Henry, the blustery male, turns out to be tender and needy. The movie salutes their joint creativity. Anaïs and Henry strengthen each other, not just as lovers or as connoisseurs of the erotic but also as writers who, more literally than the pilots in *The Right Stuff*, "push the outside of the envelope."

The film is never precious. *Henry & June* is the exceptional work about artists that honors them not for God-given gifts but for their urgent articulations of humanity. It also acknowledges how artists exploit the ones they love.

Partly because of Maria de Medeiros's performance, and partly because of the brilliantly oblique way the Kaufmans have built their script, the movie has an intensity that goes beyond the art of the turn-on. Anaïs asserts her independence from her banker-husband Hugo (played by Richard E. Grant), enters Henry's circle, is entranced by June and Henry, and finds her sexuality tugging every which way. First subtly and then vividly, the Kaufmans put you through Anaïs's twists and turns—you're with her as she bends the contours of her own life.

Medeiros has an amazing face for the camera—you never tire of looking at her, you always discover something new—and she's such a consummate actress that she magnifies Anaïs's impulses without distortion, and embodies her dilemmas without special pleading. Medeiros is a rara avis who's not rarefied. Although she's exquisite, with hummingbird bones and sculpted features, she shows formidable power.

From the opening shot of Anaïs looking toward her pipe-smoking publisher against the eerie opening chords of Stravinsky's *The Rite of Spring,* the movie strikes a multileveled tone. The juxtaposition of that music with these characters is both fresh and funny. Kaufman is cuing us in to the libidinal content of his film, bringing us back to a time when Stravinsky's music was considered scandalous, and indicating that those notes were still reverberating in the heads of the cultured—that the woman who's just written a book about D. H. Lawrence and the man who wants to publish it are always thinking about sex.

It's humorous when the publisher assumes from the way she writes about Lawrence that Anaïs must be a woman of vast experience. And there's a liberating burst of giddiness after she explains that what little experience she has comes from books. He abruptly kisses her. Still, the publisher reads Anaïs correctly — she's yearning for excitement. When she takes a Spanish dance class, she can't keep body and soul together, and the ritualized energy of the dance can help her only as a stimulus. She needs someone like Henry — someone intoxicated by life.

As Henry Miller, Fred Ward gets you smiling from the moment he lights a match on the sole of his shoe. He's not just the Miller of *Tropic of Cancer* — a self-portrait of an artist as a hungry, horny mutt. He's the Miller of his generation's dreams: an energizing force for Everyman.

Like the grasshopper in the fable, Ward's Miller feels that the world owes him a living, albeit a basic one — he hugs the pavement as snugly as an ant. He savors life's simple and complex pleasures with a growl. More than anyone since Wallace Beery or Gary Cooper, Ward has mastered the music of the "Hm-m-m-m" — he makes it register everything from quizzicality to satisfaction. He's got a beguilingly sturdy, open manner. There's a proud tilt to Ward's chin and mouth when Henry stands next to June.

The glorious Uma Thurman makes you see why. She manages to embody each of June's woman-of-mystery poses with conviction, while imparting the threat of the sly street fighter underneath — and the cry of the frightened woman below that. In her first full-scale dramatic role, Thurman uses her towering presence to allure as well as to dominate. She makes June's knowing mannerisms and affectations haunting and amusing at the same time. It's maddening and touching to hear her say that she sacrificed and slaved so that Miller could be her Dostoyevsky.

☆

The film could use more of Kevin Spacey's riotous lunacy as Miller's buddy and meal ticket, Osborn, and perhaps less of Richard E. Grant as Anaïs's husband. Grant doesn't put any oomph behind Hugo's straight-arrow goodness; even after Hugo gets into Anaïs's let's-try-anything spirit (he ultimately became a noted experimental filmmaker), he fails to convey the glints of wit or temperament that would explain why Anaïs married him.

In every other way, *Henry & June* is an engulfingly romantic movie. The script puts Anaïs through the gamut of desire without ignoring the danger and violence that lurk around the edges of ecstasy. Kaufman syncs everything to her emotional panorama: the pulsating hues of Philippe Rousselot's cinematography, the superbly apposite pop, jazz, and classical passages selected by the Kaufmans and Alan Splet (who also did the refreshingly pellucid sound design), and the sometimes staccato, sometimes gliding rhythms of the empathic editing (by Vivien Hillgrove, William S. Scharf, and Dede Allen).

The film is replete with mirror images that clarify two or more points of view, and with skewed variations that enrich and deepen the action. At times, the scenes emerge from the dark like the characters' ids leaping from the primal murk. Kaufman uses the camera expressively, coming up with reflected compositions that shimmer with passion, or bluesy flashbacks and confrontations rendered in otherworldly blue lighting. The beating drums and gyrating Spanish dancers that sometimes accompany the lovemaking have a fiery atavism—they're true to a period when culturemongers were discovering the sexual drive of African and Hispanic rhythms.

☆

With its re-creation of a bit from *Ecstasy* and its clips from *Mädchen in Uniform, The Passion of Joan of Arc,* and *Un Chien Andalou,* this movie beckons you into an era when the avant-garde was unembarrassed about ardor. Kaufman is the rare artist who uses modernist techniques, like pastiche and irony, to illuminate what William Faulkner called the subject of all good writing—the human heart in conflict with itself.

In these dehumanized times, this period film functions, in the best sense, as a contemporary fantasy. After watching *Henry & June,* you may want to see it again, right away. You may even want to live in it.

San Francisco Examiner, September 30, 1990

HENRY & JUNE

John Powers

Director Philip Kaufman discovered Henry Miller as an undergraduate at the University of Chicago and, enthralled by that writer's "life force," so he says, carried *Tropic of Cancer* in his knapsack through France in the late 1950s. He adored Miller's vitality, his desire to open modern society to the animal spirits it tries to deny. Kaufman's early crush on Miller obviously never went away. A shame, then, that *Henry & June,* Kaufman's love letter to his early hero, should be exactly what Henry Miller was not: cold, torpid, and utterly unsexy, despite the naked-femme huffing and puffing that earned it the first-ever NC-17 rating. Devoutly humorless, it's even less fun than Joseph Strick's 1970 version of *Tropic of Cancer,* a breezy piece of brutality, which at least had some good laughs.

Henry & June actually approaches Miller on the rebound — through the diary of his sometime lover Anaïs Nin. The movie centers on Nin's self-liberation, a process that leads her away from her likable stick of a husband, Hugo ("Estate planning can be very creative!"), and into a self-mythologizing erotic triangle with Miller and his second wife, June, a secretive beauty who plays glowering Thanatos to Henry's spontaneous Eros.

"I am tempted by unknown pleasures," Nin tells us, eyes popping like Concord grapes, and the Millers help her get to know them. June takes her to a plush lesbian bar (swoony dreams follow) and teaches her that one can do "the foulest things" and still feel "innocent," a theme the script never develops. For his part, Henry insists that "sex is natural, like boith and death" (he's from Brooklyn); he teaches Anaïs to literally let down her hair, to say "fuck you, Jack," and to achieve orgasm from a stand-up quickie under a moonlit bridge. Seared by all this liberation, Anaïs "becomes a woman" (her words, not mine).

Even today, this is an explosive idea — fucking as the royal road to self-discovery — and I'd love to see a movie spunky and alive enough to do it justice. Had Kaufman been able to shoot *Henry & June* as a young director still scornful of Money, Beauty, and Art, he might have come close to making such a movie, a bold, passionate *something* — a precocious masterpiece, or anyway a memorable mess. But by now, I'm afraid, he's had too long to think about it, and like many of us he's spent years buying into the values that Miller once encouraged him to mock. Whatever the reason, he's taken exactly the wrong approach to Nin and Miller: He's gone reverent, *tasteful. Henry & June* comes doused with artistic rosewater — neat period costumes and nifty decor, tactful music and handsome photography by Philippe Rousselot, shots modeled on Brassaï's famous photos of brothels and bars. Even the sex is decorous: Henry never once uses words like "twat" or "muff"; exquisitely lit women make graceful love, their nudity reflected in a fishbowl. (You might have thought that *The Unbearable Lightness of Being* would have satisfied Kaufman's yen for extensive scenes of naked women frolicking together. As Voltaire said: "Once, a philosopher; twice, a pervert.")

Kaufman leaves no room in this movie for the rudeness of spontaneous life. In 135 minutes of adultery, braggadocio, and passion writ large, the only vulgar moments are inadvertent: Henry and Anaïs humping on a chair in slow motion, a kettle steaming beside them; Henry pounding away at the typewriter, then finally writing the words "Tropic of Cancer" across the front page — in close-up. Sad to say, these gaucheries are much funnier than the rare deliberate jokes such as Hugo obliviously eating a phallic bread roll while Henry and his wife go at it upstairs.

Kaufman is a polished filmmaker, and has done remarkably well at evoking 1931 Paris on a budget of only $10 million. But just because he's re-created Paris doesn't mean anybody lives there. Granted, Maria de Medeiros is a dead ringer for Nin and is splendid at capturing that writer's absurd yet compelling Betty-Boop-in-heat feverishness. But Fred Ward's Miller never transcends the most obvious animalistic clichés — a walking life force with the booming laugh of Zorba the Brooklynite. As June, Uma Thurman falls hopelessly short of the fatal glamour on which the film depends. In fact, with her "Honeymooners" dialect and weltschmerzy vamping, she comes off less as Henry and Anaïs's dark muse than as a slightly overblown fishwife.

The first few times we see June with Henry, their earthy physicality is laughably overdone — leave them alone for a second and they're already in midrut, while Anaïs's big eyes get bigger. Kaufman keeps pumping up his characters so they'll reach the size of his fantasies: bigger-than-life figures in a wondrous Paree where passing magicians pull doves from newspapers and art students scamper through the streets wearing nothing but coats of blue paint. In this attempt at mythmaking, *Henry & June* cheats us out of the Henry Miller and Anaïs Nin that their readers care about: The movie's tiptoeing solemnity couldn't be further in spirit from the purple-prose orgasmics of Nin's *Diaries* or the big-cocked rhetorical rush of *Tropic of Cancer,* which Miller called "a prolonged insult, a gob of spit in the face of Art, a kick in the pants to God, Man, Destiny, Time, Love, Beauty . . . what you will." By design, those books challenged and shocked the people who read them; they changed, however slightly, the consciousness of a whole culture. Nobody will be changed in the least by *Henry & June,* which may be a blessing.

LA Weekly, October 13, 1990

POISON

David Ansen

The besieged National Endowment for the Arts is once again under assault. Its sin, in the eyes of the Reverend Donald Wildmon, who has made a career of attacking things he hasn't seen, was providing a $25,000 grant to a $250,000 experimental film called *Poison.* A jury at the Sundance Film Festival in Park City, Utah, awarded *Poison* its grand prize. This held no weight with Wildmon, who has said he was first turned off by the movie when he read a description of it as "the most important and acclaimed gay American movie in years." That alone was enough to put the head of the American Family Association in a rage. Upping the ante with characteristic imagination, he denounced the movie for its "explicit porno scenes of homosexuals involved in anal sex." While one of the film's three interrelated stories, inspired by the writing of Jean Genet, involves homoerotic passions in a 1940s prison, anyone rushing out to see an explicit porno film is going to wonder what Wildmon's been eating for breakfast.

This time around, even NEA Chairman John Frohnmayer, who has managed to irritate both the art world and the religious right with his hapless vacillations, discovered his spine. He unambiguously defended the artist, calling the movie "the work of a serious artist." *Poison* is not for all tastes — even in Park City it had its detractors — but it's precisely the kind of imaginative, form-stretching, and increasingly endangered species of filmmaking the NEA ought to be supporting.

The flap, as these things do, will guarantee Todd Haynes's 16mm movie a healthy audience. What you will see is a disturbing, highly stylized art film that deals with transgression and punishment — while simultaneously asking us to consider how movies themselves deal with these themes. Boldly self-conscious, *Poison* switches channels among its three stylistically varied but thematically linked tales with cumulative, claustrophobic power.

The tale called "Hero" is filmed in mock documentary style. It's an inquiry into the fate of Richie Beacon (who's never seen), a much-picked-on, seven-year-old boy who murdered his father and was last seen flying out the window. The second strand, "Horror," filmed in the lurid expressionist angles of an old black-and-white B movie horror film, concerns a scientist who has isolated the sex drive in liquid form. Drinking his potion by accident, he's transformed into a contagious, pustule-dripping fiend known as the Leper Sex Killer. Complicated camp, this section functions as a metaphor for AIDS — but it's also a commentary on the way in which AIDS has been sensationalized by the media. "Homo," in the mythopoetic rough-trade style of Genet, mixes artifice and brutality in its hothouse depiction of a prisoner's sexual obsession for a fellow inmate. In each of these contrapuntal stories about taboo breakers and outcasts, Haynes seems to be exploring the sadomasochistic patterns of society that become internalized and acted out in the individual. *Poison*'s rich layers of juxtaposed images can't be easily digested in one viewing. The acting is uneven, the lighting sometimes dim, the tone at times deliberately awkward. But this suggestive, discordant movie takes you places you haven't been.

Haynes, a thirty-year-old New York filmmaker who was raised in LA's San Fernando Valley and educated at Brown, made his name with his now legendary forty-three-minute *Superstar: The Karen Carpenter Story,* which used Barbie-size dolls (as well as newsreels and interviews) to dramatize the life and death of the anorexic singer. (Due to legal problems, the film has been withdrawn from circulation.) It was an audacious and surprisingly touching film that shares with *Poison* a similar fascination with the body and its relation to the body politic. There will probably never be a mass audience for the kind of heady, unclassifiable movies Haynes is committed to making — they demand an audience with a taste for cinematic deconstruction, not to mention a pretty bizarre sense of humor. *Poison* doesn't go down easy, and isn't meant to. But we should thank the NEA, not curse it, for helping the movie on its way.

Newsweek, April 29, 1991

POISON

Bruce Williamson

Thank the Reverend Donald Wildmon for bringing public attention to *Poison,* a not-so-shocking independent film made in 16mm for relatively small change. When *Poison* captured the grand prize at Park City, Utah's Sundance Film Festival this year, the Reverend Wildmon found out that writer-director Todd Haynes's meager financing had included a $25,000 grant from the National Endowment for the Arts. Visions of Mapplethorpe and immorality dancing in his head, Wildmon denounced the movie as a threat to his American Family Association. Had he cooled his jets or gone to see the movie, Wildmon might have discovered that *Poison* — though based on several stories by France's Jean Genet, who doted on depravity — runs the gamut from outrageous to downright dull.

In the trio of tall tales, there's a broad, amusing fantasy called "Hero," about a young boy whose mother insists he flew out a window after killing his father. The second piece, "Horror," is a fairly inept parody of a B movie shocker about a leprous sex maniac whose mottled skin keeps changing between attacks — probably because filmmaker Haynes couldn't afford better makeup effects. The controversial best tale is "Homo," projecting a typically Genet view of sadomasochistic sexual obsession in a men's prison. The sex acts, though unsettling, are never explicit. Even so, Wildmon went public with his charges and managed to put the movie on the map by opening everyone's eyes to Haynes's vices instead of his virtues. When the smoke clears, he may be seen as a filmmaker who is exciting, original, but not yet entirely accomplished.

Playboy, August 1991

BASIC INSTINCT

Peter Travers

Fade in: A man and a woman in bed. Both nude. A mirrored ceiling. No sound, except for heavy breathing. The woman, a blonde whose hair covers her face but not her centerfold body, straddles the man, who seems a nanosecond from the come of the century. His hands are tied to the headboard with a white silk scarf. Hermès. Class. Cut to the woman's hand, holding an ice pick. K Mart. Tacky. Close-up: Her hand slams down repeatedly. Blood gushes in orgasmic spurts.

Basic Instinct doesn't waste time establishing priorities. This is one charged-up erotic thriller — gory, lurid, brutally funny, and without a politically correct thought in its unapologetically empty head. Still, director Paul Verhoeven's cinematic wet dream delivers the goods, especially when Sharon Stone struts on with enough come-on carnality to singe the screen. Stone, a former model, is a knockout; she even got a rise out of Ah-nold in Verhoeven's *Total Recall.* But being the bright spot in too many dull movies (*He Said, She Said; Irreconcilable Differences*) stalled her career. Though *Basic Instinct* establishes Stone as a bombshell for the nineties, it also shows she can nail a laugh or shade an emotion with equal aplomb.

Stone plays Catherine Tramell, a bisexual heiress and mystery novelist. San Francisco cop Nick Curran (Michael Douglas) and his partner, Gus Moran (George Dzundza), arrive at Catherine's swank beach house — Jan De Bont's camera makes everything look deluxe — to question her about the ice-pick slaying of her graying rock-star lover, Johnny Boz (Bill Cable). It seems Boz's murder was copycatted from Catherine's latest novel. She insists it's a setup, but she goes downtown with the cops, stopping only to slip into heels and something short and clingy. She wears no underwear, a detail that doesn't escape her interrogators, who attend to each uncrossing of Catherine's legs like overzealous gynecologists.

The interrogation scene is the film's comic high point. The cops frown when Catherine lights a cigarette. "What are you going to do," she asks, "charge me with smoking?" When they try to establish whether Catherine liked Boz, she responds tersely, "I liked fucking him." It's a cheeky beginning for Stone and the film. Before the plot thickens — congeals is more like it — she and the bristling Douglas make flinty sparring partners. Curran, derisively nicknamed Shooter for accidentally killing two tourists while on duty, is a reformed boozer and cokehead. He drove his wife to suicide and has a shaky relationship with an improbably tarted-up police shrink, Beth Garner (Jeanne Tripplehorne). Catherine knows this because she's keeping a file on Curran for her next novel. The fact that the prototypes for Catherine's books wind up dead both frightens and excites Curran. He tries some roughhouse sex with Beth (he rips off her clothes; she sucks his fingers, à la *Cape Fear*), but nothing will do except Catherine herself. There's a complication: Catherine's lesbian lover, Roxy (Leilani Sarelle), is lethally jealous. But what does Curran care? After an all-night marathon with the object of his lust, the weary cop feels born-again. Catherine describes it as merely "a pretty good beginning." (The sex scene was trimmed by sixty-eight seconds to avoid an NC-17 rating, but enough sizzle remains to indicate that Stone did indeed work without a "crotch patch.")

Is Catherine the killer? Or is it Roxy? Or Beth, who had a fling with Catherine when they were at Berkeley? And why is Curran drawn to his own destruction? If this sounds familiar, it's no wonder. Screenwriter Joe Eszterhas has a thing for dangerous liaisons. In his *Jagged Edge*, a lawyer falls in love with a man she's defending on a murder charge. *Basic Instinct* is a virtual remake of *Edge*, from the ritual opening killing to its climactic reenactment. But Eszterhas isn't alone in cribbing. Verhoeven lifts from his superior 1984 Dutch thriller, *The Fourth Man*, about a bisexual author hung up on a three-times-widowed *femme fatale*. Douglas brings along countless allusions to *Fatal Attraction*. And Stone recently did *Scissors*, about another blonde slasher.

The hodgepodge wouldn't matter, of course, if *Basic Instinct* made a lick of sense. It doesn't, and neither does the ambiguous trick ending, which makes what preceded even more confounding. The insistently purple tone of the dialogue doesn't help either. Eszterhas got a whopping $3 million for his script, which leaves you computing the monetary value of such lines as "She's got that *magna cum laude* pussy on her that done fried up your brain." But don't look for logic in *Basic Instinct*. In that way lies madness. Protests from the gay community about the film's negative treatment of lesbians are also pointless, since no one in this kinky sex fantasy demonstrates anything resembling recognizable human behavior.

What makes *Basic Instinct* a guilty pleasure is the shameless and stylish way Verhoeven lets rip with his own basic instinct for disreputably alluring entertainment. The film is for horny pups of all ages who relish the memory of reading stroke books under the covers with a flashlight. Verhoeven has spent $49 million to reproduce that dirty little thrill on the big screen. You can practically hear him giggling behind the camera. His audacity makes you giggle along with him.

Rolling Stone, April 16, 1992

BASIC INSTINCT

Carrie Rickey

Call me a prude, but it's not sexy watching an erotic thriller in which every time a couple does it, one of them gets it with an ice pick. I don't care how many firmly toned tummies and tushes are bared.

Nor does it make a difference that two of the bods belong to Michael Douglas (as a killer cop) and Sharon Stone (as the suspected ice-pick murderess), whose flesh looks airbrushed with that bronzer you see slathered on centerfolds.

Basic Instinct quickly announces itself as a nineties-style experiment in psycho-terror. Every sexual coupling is accompanied by the threat of violence or pain. Much of the San Francisco action takes place in fabulously appointed Nob Hill mansions and beachfront estates that glow in the Pacific twilight. (Even the detective's apartment has a breathtaking view of the Transamerica pyramid.) Everyone wears designer duds, including a police psychiatrist whose miniskirts are more provocative than Barbra Streisand's in *The Prince of Tides.*

To heighten the plausibility factor in this movie populated with killer cops and cop killers, everyone leaves his/her front door un-locked.

The only way you can tell the difference between the psycho crimi-nals and the wacko crime solvers is that at least the psychos know they're sick.

Basic Instinct's basic premise is that heiress–mystery writer Cather-ine Tramell (Stone) is a prime suspect in a sex murder exactly like one described in her latest paperback best-seller. When Detective Nick Curran (Douglas) picks her up for questioning, he is aroused by this blonde ice — or is it ice-pick? — queen who talks so profanely about hot sex.

Further, Catherine knows secrets about Nick that the disturbed cop has never shared. Not even with his estranged girlfriend, Dr. Beth Garner (Jeanne Tripplehorne), a police psychiatrist assigned to help him. When Catherine throatily discloses that her latest novel is based on Nick — it's about a trigger-happy San Francisco cop who falls in love with the wrong woman and gets killed — the cop and sus-pect begin a game of psych-out that inevitably leads to the sack.

Since the plots of Catherine's murder mysteries have a way of being acted out in real life, Nick and his colleagues are stumped. Are the books a way for Catherine to premeditate and rehearse her crimes? Or is someone trying to frame the tawny blonde who never wears underwear beneath her creamy silk dresses?

Omnisexually voracious Catherine likes to provoke her lovers, so there are a tantalizing number of suspects with motive. One is Roxy (Leilani Sarelle), her jealous lesbian girlfriend. Another is Hazel (Dorothy Malone), a paroled mass murderess who Catherine claims is a "source" for her books. Add to these Nick, who enjoys competing with Roxy for some sheet time with Catherine.

Those concerned about the movie's purported negative stereotypes of lesbian and bisexual women should know that *Basic Instinct* isn't homophobic. It is misanthropic. Crossing preference lines, the film ascribes hateful characteristics to everyone, male and female, hetero- and homosexual. It's not a simple question of whether the hero is straight and the villain is gay: In this movie *everyone,* psychologically speaking, is crooked.

Because for filmgoers all movies cost six dollars, I normally don't mention the price tag of a screenplay or production. But considering that scriptwriter Joe Eszterhas received *$3 million* for this murder mystery that's confounding as to whodunit, you figure he's made the real killing.

Eszterhas, who here plagiarized his own screenplays for *Jagged Edge* (which I very much enjoyed) and *Music Box,* never before has written a thriller this preposterous. *Basic Instinct*'s characters lack psychology and therefore motive. Admittedly they possess pathology, but that's not enough to maintain suspense in a movie with plot holes big enough to drive a tank through.

The PQ—preposterous quotient—is further upped by Dutch director Paul Verhoeven, who was much more assured with the special effects of *RoboCop* and *Total Recall* than he is dealing with actors here. Although he was great with the performances in *Spetters* and *The Fourth Man,* the dialogue in *Basic Instinct* is hastily emoted with such overemphasis—"You're dealing with a devious mind!" the shrink shrieks to Nick—that it recalls a Grade Z horror flick. This cost $49 million?

Now, about those ice picks. A rather archaic bar tool to be so commonplace in these high-tech kitchens, no? Given the upscale suspects in this film, where even the cops wear Armani, isn't it odd that *not one character* possesses a freezer with an automatic ice maker or cube tray?

Philadelphia Inquirer, March 20, 1992

THE ZEITGEIST ZONE

Movies are our cultural seismograph. The films that register the spikiest readings often elicit the most contradictory yelps. Is *Fatal Attraction* a freaked-out fable about a proud, sexually liberated woman wronged? Or is it a viperish recasting of the single professional woman as harridan? Is *Thelma & Louise* feminist or rabidly antifeminist? These are message movies of a sort, but, as is often the case, the message is encoded, cross-wired, not fully thought out. Part op-ed piece, part Rorschach blot, these films, by the very nature of their confusions, work their commentators into a giddy lather. They give you a lot to kvell over, which is nirvana for a critic.

Starting with its inception as a script, a film generally takes years to reach the screen. From a sociological standpoint, this accounts for the time-lag fuzziness of most movies (and the comparative immediacy of television). By the time an "issue," a mood, makes it into the multiplex, we've usually moved on to the next fracas.

But the national mood swing can be mainlined, as evidenced by the films in this section. Whether by accident or design — or, more likely, a combo of both — these movies raided the zeitgeist. They became the films that everybody was talking about because they were about what everybody was talking about — or avoiding.

Movies reflect the political climate in which they are made, and the movies of the Reagan-Bush era often proffered a heartland sentimentalism. The pop impulse in these films was not only to go back to an earlier and simpler way of feeling, but also to evoke an earlier and simpler movie past. For some critics, *Places in the Heart* had the reassuring murmur of home truths; others regarded its haze and homilies as all of a piece with the Reagan re-election campaign's "It's Morning in America" TV ads. Kevin Costner, lithe and flat toned, became the zeitgeist's all-American poster boy. *Field of Dreams* was touted and torched for basically the same reason: It was deemed Capraesque. Costner, of course, was dubbed Cooperesque. His next hit film, *Dances with Wolves,* which he also directed, was honored by the Academy for its epic sympathies for the Sioux. Others scalped it for being the latest New Age variant on an old cowboys-and-Indians formula. Essential to the critical admiration for these films was the belief that the sentimentality, which was freely acknowledged, didn't matter; that it served a higher truth and so transcended sentimentality and became myth.

Some movies express the status quo, some subvert it. A film like *Batman* plugged into the same socket as many of the films mentioned above—and got high on the zap. As the flip side to all that agrarian idealism, it cartoonized and demonized urban life (the film's subtitle could have been *Rust Never Sleeps*). This subversive streak may also suggest why, in a feel-good era, movies have never been more violent. Roger Ebert, in an essay on the subject, puts on the gloves.

The messiness of modern male-female relationships doesn't fit any of the Hollywood formulas. The result: Buddy-o-ramas reign while "female-driven" movies are barely a blip on the radar. Hollywood has never been as dry a gulch for actresses as it is right now. An essay here tries to explain why.

Were you offended by the press-bashing in *Absence of Malice,* or did you see it as a reasonable and necessary tarnish to the Woodward-Bernstein halo? Were you prickly about what you believed to be the patronizing of the sixties in *The Big Chill?* Read on.

A decade later, the yuppie achievers in *The Big Chill* might have evolved into the recession-era sourpusses of films like *The Doctor* or *Regarding Henry.* An essay on the new genre of male weepies these movies has spawned rounds out the section.

ABSENCE OF MALICE

Kenneth Turan

Five years ago, in a one-shot apotheosis that took its beneficiaries totally by surprise, Hollywood raised newspapermen, once the lowliest of the low, to the right hand of God. Most reporters, being cynical types, knew it couldn't last, and they were right—for now, in a bit of poetic justice in its purest form, what *All the President's Men* gave, *Absence of Malice* has taken away.

If *All the President's Men* was largely a fantasy that glamorized the profession and its putative rewards, *Absence of Malice* is truer to the awkward realities. Kurt Luedtke has seen to that. A reporter and editor for close to twenty years, Luedtke knows where the bodies are buried, where ethical corners are cut, how reporters are used, and how they hide when they're found out. Luedtke's aware screenplay, combined with the slick, entertaining style of director Sydney Pollack and the star power of Paul Newman and Sally Field, has made *Absence of Malice* into a first-rate piece of informed, popular filmmaking, one of those infrequent motion pictures that engages an audience emotionally without shortchanging its moral concerns.

Those concerns center on the conundrum of what is true versus what is merely accurate, whether newspapers can tell the two apart, and, more cuttingly, if they really care to. As a matter of law, the attorney representing the *Miami Standard* tells reporter Megan Carter (Sally Field), "The truth of your story is irrelevant. We have no knowledge the story is false; therefore we are absent malice. We have been both reasonable and prudent; therefore we are not negligent. We may say what we like about Mr. Gallagher, and he is powerless to do us harm. Democracy is served."

To the Gallagher in question, Michael by name (Paul Newman), things are hardly so cynically simple. The son of an old-time bootlegger and the nephew of the local Mafia capo, Gallagher has been chosen by Elliott Rosen, the head of a Justice Department strike force, as the man to squeeze for information about the disappearance of a union leader. No one suspects that Gallagher is guilty of anything, but the best way Rosen can think of to put pressure on him is to leak a story to the susceptible Megan Carter to the effect that Gallagher is under investigation. The story runs in a prominent spot on page one, and Michael Gallagher's world starts to break into pieces.

One of the things *Absence of Malice* does especially well is contrast the haphazard way journalists often put stories together—how awfully vulnerable they are to manipulation—with how arrogantly they stand behind what they've written once it has been printed. Starting with a chance remark from a secretary, Carter uses subterfuge and little white lies to gain information, allows herself to be skillfully managed by Rosen to get even more, and, in a sadly realistic session with her editor, pumps up her opening paragraph, changing "under investigation" to "suspect" to "key suspect" to make things as punchy as the shaky facts allow.

It is a process that makes even Carter feel vaguely uncomfortable, but when Gallagher comes in to complain, all her doubts are replaced by the complacent "the paper is always right" smugness that comes with the habit of playing God. Carter has stopped perceiving the people she talks to as vulnerable human beings; they have all become types, to be handled in a variety of timeworn ways. She uses her surface charm to mask a chilling professional insensitivity. It is not the most appealing of roles, and it is a mark of Sally Field's continuing maturity as an actress that she involves us in Megan Carter's difficult trek from casual self-importance to a semblance of self-knowledge.

Paul Newman's role, that of the aggrieved innocent, is more sympathetic, but he does not take the easy way out in playing it, does not for a minute fall back on his wide, easy grin the way Jack Nicholson is forever doing. Newman has aged well, and having reached the stage where he knows enough to do more with less, he uses his presence, the back and forth flicker of his eyes, to establish his character's identity. Michael Gallagher is a distant man, one who does not give trust easily if at all. Though he can call on a gruff kind of sophistication if necessary, he is more naturally menacing, someone who knows how to take care of himself. Yet when faced with the faceless arrogance of the *Standard,* he too is, for a time, frustrated and helpless.

Yet only for a time, because, lest we forget, *Absence of Malice* was sired in Hollywood, and no hero is helpless there for long. Luedtke has given Gallagher some very pointed verbal ammunition, as when he tells Carter, "You say somebody's guilty, people believe it. You say they're not guilty, nobody's interested." She tries to tell him it's not the paper's fault but people's—"they believe what they want to believe"—but he comes back with a quiet "And who puts out the paper? Nobody?"

More than angry words, *Absence of Malice* gives Gallagher a fairly complex method of revenge, and the only place the film wavers a bit is in detailing how he sets it up. But the momentum is more than recovered with the appearance of Wilford Brimley as assistant attorney general James J. Wells, a folksy *deus ex machina* who uses words such as "horse puckey" and, in a bravura piece of character acting, wraps up the plot in terrific style. Even in a film noteworthy for its exceptional supporting roles — John Harkins as the lawyer Davidek and the legendary Luther Adler as Gallagher's Mafia uncle are the most obvious examples — Brimley stands out for the way he casually but surely owns the screen for the quarter hour he is on it.

Director Pollack, who does an expert job of clothing (but not suffocating) issues in the garb of melodrama, is, unfortunately, sure to be criticized for doing just that. People will grumble about the inevitable Gallagher-Carter romance, appropriately wary and subdued though it is; they will complain that what happens to Gallagher is a worst-possible-case scenario; they will wail that Pollack has made nonserious use of serious matters; and they will all be wrong. Film is not a narrow, precious way of looking at the world, it is a brawny, popular art that should be reaching the largest audience with as significant a message as possible. If crusty V. I. Lenin, who considered cinema a potent tool of revolution, could understand that, surely domestic churls can be made to see the point as well.

New West, December 1981

ABSENCE OF MALICE

Michael Wilmington

Always be wary of the Hollywood movie that advertises itself as "a film about ideas." That's the old Stanley Kramer tune — "thoughtful films for mature audiences." It usually means a plush production with big stars, where the director escorts the social issues in with stiff-necked gallantry and a fixed smile. Nobody could beat Kramer at this; he had the sincerity that killed.

Now Sydney Pollack seems to have picked up the baton. His *Absence of Malice* is a meretricious, contrived, empty melodrama in which everything is worked out mechanically, nothing is felt. This is "a film of ideas" that sets out (in the words of Columbia's loftily phrased press kit) to "explore the parameters of a complex and tenuous relationship: that of the journalist and subject . . . to explore and raise questions about the very real collision between individual and societal rights." In other words, it's melodrama with a purpose, melodrama that will teach us something.

Here are the visual aids in this lecture on journalistic ethics: Bright, bouncy *Miami Standard* reporter Megan Carter (Sally Field) stumbles onto a federal investigation into Michael Gallagher (Paul Newman), son of a deceased bootlegger, nephew of Miami's mob capo, and a possible suspect in the murder of a local longshoreman boss. She writes the story, and Gallagher's wholesale liquor business begins to suffer. Actually, Megan has been set up: Elliott Rosen (Bob Balaban), a tense little lizard of a federal investigator, leaked her the story to put pressure on Gallagher.

Gallagher has an alibi, but he won't use it. His motives are sterling: He was out of town arranging an abortion for a thirty-eight-year-old unmarried Catholic schoolteacher. So he calls on Megan, tries to reason with her. Megan wilts under his brilliant blue gaze, and they wind up in the sack. (This is how you make "ideas" palatable to the masses.) Afterward, the teacher, desperate to clear Mike, confides the truth to Megan—who, after a little soul-searching, prints the story of her abortion and precipitates a tragedy.

Gallagher is incensed: wrath incarnate. He manhandles the truth out of contrite, trembling Megan, and then teams up with his Mafia relative, jolly old Uncle Santos, to lay a trap for the feds. Everybody but Santos winds up in the courthouse, where a kindly, rustic (but hopping mad) old coot of a federal prosecutor neatly squares all the accounts. And at the movie's climax, we see Gallagher with Megan— now chastened, now a journalist with a heart—bidding goodbye, and Gallagher sailing off dreamily into the ocean, in search of cleaner ports, braver people. . . .

I ask you: Does this sound like a film of ideas? Do you think you're going to get any perceptions about "the parameters of complex and tenuous relationships" from watching this absurd story? The plot of *Absence of Malice* is so superficially complex—it takes so much babble and exposition just to keep it straight—that all its dopey incongruities, skin-deep situations, and characters tend to glide on by. Kurt Luedtke, who wrote it, was a journalist and editor in Miami and Detroit; presumably he knows about newspapers (although the newspaper scenes have no pith or conviction), and he claims to have based his script on real-life incidents.

In fact, there *is* a Miami mob boss named Santos—Santos Trafficante, described in the U.S. Congress Final Assassinations Report as "the Cosa Nostra leader in Florida," the man who controls the "violent narcotics trade" on the Gulf Coast and who "recruited Cuban nationals to help plan and execute the CIA's assignment to assassinate Fidel Castro." It was also Trafficante who—enraged at Robert Kennedy's pursuit of Jimmy Hoffa—told a federal informant in September 1962 that President Kennedy was going to "get what is coming to him," was "going to be hit."

Luedtke was a reporter for the *Miami Herald* in the early sixties; he knows all about Trafficante. So how in the world did he come up with jowly, jolly old Uncle Santos, a kindly old Saint Nick of a Mafia capo who whiles away his time at Little League games and looks as if he wouldn't crush a fly? And why does he portray the feds on Santos's tail as little worms who deserve to be stepped on? Why does the movie show Rosen, the most obnoxious worm of them all, with a very prominent photo of JFK on his office wall? Did Pollack—and fervent JFK supporter Paul Newman—think this was irony? Did they think they were showing ambivalent, tortuously human figures who were pursuing noble goals with shoddy methods?

If they did, they were kidding themselves: *Absence of Malice* has no irony or ambivalence. It's a cardboard melodrama, where the heroes and villains are recognizable the moment they walk on. Newman, of course, carries instant integrity; Bob Balaban, as Rosen, plays a neurotic creep who keeps snapping rubber bands like Queeg with his ball bearings. And Luther Adler gives no menace at all to Santos. He's just a foxy old grandpa, a hood with a heart of gold.

And what about the other obvious parallel—another real case where a union leader disappeared and a mob figure's son (with an Irish name) was pilloried in the newspapers? The labor leader was the man Trafficante was so worried over: Jimmy Hoffa. The suspect was Chuck O'Brien, son of Sam Scarardino and Sylvia Pagano—also Hoffa's mistress, and said to be his original contact with organized crime.

The newspapers probably wreaked as much havoc with O'Brien's life as the *Miami Standard* does with Gallagher's—but there was something more to the case than simple investigatorial malice or zeal: O'Brien was the last known man to see Hoffa alive, and Teamster historians like Dan Moldea are still convinced he drove Hoffa to his execution date. (Nor was there any real-life abortion alibi; you know you're confronting shameless hacks when they dream up tearjerkers like that to push across their "issues.") You may have forgotten the O'Brien story — but Luedtke was a reporter for the *Detroit Free Press,* in Hoffa's hometown. He's obviously drawing a parallel.

When you think over *Absence of Malice,* it becomes flabbergasting that Pollack, Newman, and Field wanted to do it in the first place. Luedtke's script is not only puerile in itself, it's a ridiculous perversion of the events he covered as reporter and editor.

What kind of "liberal" lesson is this? That Mafia bosses are lovable old pussycats, and that the people who investigate and write stories about them are heartless curs and dupes? Are Pollack and Newman proud of making a movie where a sympathetic character (that lovable old coot of a prosecutor) says "there ain't no such animal" as a reporter's First Amendment rights — and nobody raises a word of objection? And what about Sally Field's role — this fuzzy-cute little feminist, bright and chirpy, who does her job too well — and has to be screwed, be thrown on the floor, and have her blouse torn open (by the hero!) before she comes to her senses? This is a film about individual rights? The only ones it seems to value are Gallagher's right not to rat on his relatives and Uncle Santos's to kill people without excessive interference.

But even if you forget all the real-life parallels, it's impossible to swallow. The machinations in the *Standard*'s newsroom — the rationalizations beforehand, the wailing and gnashing of teeth afterward — are glib and pat beyond belief. And why is Gallagher so incensed at the feds — and not at all, apparently, at the *Standard*'s editors, who decided to print the abortion story in the first place? Why is there no sense that he's dealing with the devil when he pleads for Santos's help? *Absence of Malice* is loaded with outrage, but its sense of evil is highly selective.

I'm sure everybody who made *Absence of Malice* — except Luedtke himself, whose motivations I can't fathom — was sincere, decent, earnest. I'm sure they wanted to make something intelligent and adult, something they could be proud of. And, on a superficial level, it's well made: The acting is good, the locations attractive, the direction smooth and professional, though glib. Perhaps Pollack has gotten so proficient at selling ideas that he doesn't examine them much anymore. But he's dealing with adulterated stuff here: The passions, and the issues themselves, are in a desperate muddle. The whole trouble with *Absence of Malice* is that it has far too much malice, far too few ideas.

Isthmus, December 18, 1981

THE BIG CHILL

Richard Corliss

These Americans are in their thirties today, but back then they were the Now Generation. Right Now: Give me peace, give me justice, gimme good lovin'. For them, in the voluptuous bloom of youth, the sixties was a banner you could carry aloft or wrap yourself inside. A verdant anarchy of politics, sex, drugs, and style carpeted the landscape. And each impulse was scored to the rollick of the new music: folk, rock, pop, R&B. The armies of the night marched to Washington, but they boogied to Liverpool and Motown.

Now, in 1983, Harold & Sarah & Sam & Karen & Michael & Meg & Nick — classmates all from the University of Michigan at the end of our last interesting decade — have come to the funeral of a friend who has slashed his wrists. Alex was a charismatic prodigy of science and friendship and progressive hell-raising who opted out of academe to try social work, then manual labor, then suicide. He is presented as a victim of terminal depression from the orbital flight of his college years: a worst-case scenario his friends must ponder, probing themselves for symptoms of the disease.

Who are these friends, who "knew each other for a short period a long time ago" in a galaxy far, far away? Harold (Kevin Kline), the weekend's host, owns a burgeoning chain of stores that peddles overpriced sneakers to the jogging, today person. His wife Sarah (Glenn Close) is a physician who, five years ago, threw off the "disgusting curse of being a good girl" and had an affair with Alex. Sam (Tom Berenger), once a Movement rhetorician, went to Hollywood and became the macho private eye in a hit TV series, which one of his pals describes as "a sitcom with a machete." Karen (JoBeth Williams), who used to be a closet poet, is now the restless wife of an ad executive. Michael (Jeff Goldblum) made Alex famous by writing about him in the *Michigan Daily:* now he profiles fourteen-year-old blind baton twirlers for *People* and tries vainly to assign himself a story on the lost hope he sees around him this weekend. "You think everything's boring," he snarls to his editor over the phone. "You wouldn't say that if it was the Lost Hope Diet." Meg (Mary Kay Place), a lawyer, got tired of public-defending minority criminals who "were just so . . . *guilty*" and went to work for a posh law firm whose "clients were raping *only* the land." Nick (William Hurt) went to Vietnam and got his manhood blown off: Now, the impotent cynic, he does and deals drugs.

One of the nice things about this funny and ferociously smart movie is that it is not only about the sixties. Instead, it works from several assumptions about those times to create an impromptu dormitory of likable individuals who know each other well enough to can the sloganeering. Much more is expressed by the way people walk and sit, by the not-quite-facetious insult, by the silent, shared memory. This is a movie about getting through a weekend without being bored or driven to tears, about bull sessions that become psychodramas, about making do and making love and making breakfast the next morning. Like John Sayles's fine film *Return of the Secaucus 7, The Big Chill* is a house party of reconciliation.

The alien being here is Chloe (Meg Tilly), Alex's ex-girlfriend, a decade younger and more limber, monitoring the action with eyes that have seen it all and ain't telling. You have to make eye contact with this wonderful ensemble of actors; the pregnant or averted glances they exchange constitute a geometry of tangled passions. JoBeth Williams can say more by directing her big sad eyes offscreen than volumes of Emily Dickinson; in Mary Kay Place's squint is the weather-beaten humor of a career woman who wants an emergency jolt of motherhood; William Hurt's eyes move like restless laser beams; Tom Berenger's search the room in masked desperation, trying to crib emotions from his quicker, less guarded friends. No joke or gesture is forced in these performances. The eight star actors deserve one big Oscar.

☆

There is another invisible presence in *The Big Chill*: that of filmmaker Lawrence Kasdan (Michigan '70). Kasdan came to a kind of shadow prominence writing scripts for George Lucas: If *The Empire Strikes Back, Raiders of the Lost Ark,* and *Return of the Jedi* juggle craftiness with kid innocence, it is partly owing to Kasdan's easy wit and trove of B movie lore. His debut as a writer-director, *Body Heat,* updated the

Double Indemnity plot with equal measures of fire and ice. *The Big Chill* marks another sure step forward for Kasdan. This is a movie that can exist outside the confines of movie genres, with characters whose lives seep outside the screen frame, who persuade the viewer to care about their pasts and futures.

It also boasts a great Greatest Hits sound track, which finds just the right comic or dramatic settings for such fine sixties songs as "You Can't Always Get What You Want," "Good Lovin'," "Ain't Too Proud to Beg," and "A Natural Woman." Indeed, the entire film is a kind of sock-hop benefit for Approaching Middle Age. This maturing generation never played "Taps" with such glamour or good humor. Play the music and let the big chill — the knowledge that "we're all alone out there, and we're going out there tomorrow" — melt away in the warmth of the feel-good movie of eighty-three.

Time, September 12, 1983

THE BIG CHILL

David Denby

Lawrence Kasdan's *The Big Chill* is an uneasy experience. It's a movie about self-doubt and self-searching — highly tentative emotions — that has nevertheless been made with enough slick confidence and "pace" to propel a hit Broadway show. A genial, largely conventional house-party comedy passing itself off as a serious examination of a generation's values, *The Big Chill* is at war with itself, and it feels hollow and worked up. This movie about introspection is so tightly wound it doesn't *breathe.*

A sixties counterculture veteran, "too pure" to fit in anywhere but seemingly happy, has inexplicably killed himself. His closest friends from college days gather for the funeral and then stay on for the weekend at the beautiful South Carolina home of two of the friends. Most of the group — four men and three women in their midthirties — have become very successful, but in the wake of the suicide their doubts and self-disgust rise to the surface. They feel abashed by how far they've fallen away from old ideals, old passions and causes. From a number of hints, we assume they were once radicals — Kasdan and screenwriter Barbara Benedek don't risk alienating any of the audience by spelling out what they did. But Kasdan doesn't stint on the sixties music, which still gives off a powerful charge and certainly won't send anyone home angry. Throughout the weekend, the old friends revel in Aretha Franklin and the Stones and the Band; they eat, drink, get stoned, play football, jog, make love; they live communally, recreating their old warmth, and then, suddenly, they get very rueful and bitter. The movie is filled with regret, with glib resentment — a kind of plastic *Weltschmerz*. It's very cynical, almost voluptuously cynical, and after a while, as the self-recriminations and self-justifications pile up, it begins to feel like a crock. *The Big Chill* may be nostalgic for the late sixties, but it's been shrewdly designed for the Reagan eighties.

For a time we're captivated by the charm and high spirits of the ensemble, with its eight ambitious, moderately famous performers working at full pitch. Kevin Kline, so frantic and remote in his earlier screen appearances, has calmed down at last and become a wonderful movie actor. Kline, the host, plays a successful manufacturer of running shoes, a man who knows the value of his marriage, his property, his gracious, comfortable life. Perhaps Kline should always play normal men; he brings more variety and life to this happy bourgeois than he did to the psychotic in *Sophie's Choice*. Playful and generous and levelheaded, he makes happiness seem eminently reasonable.

Kline serves as a foil for the others, especially for William Hurt, who shows up with an earring in one lobe, his shabby Porsche loaded with drugs. Hurt is a dope dealer, highly intelligent but completely alienated from everything and everybody, a Vietnam vet whose wounds have left him impotent and who now must live with the humiliation of knowing how attractive women find him. This self-conscious actor puts quotation marks around everything he says, and I couldn't tell right away if he was giving a pretentious performance or effectively playing a pretentious man. Hurt may have become too private and eccentric to play well with anyone else, but when he shows us the vulnerable side of this arrogant hipster, we realize that he knows exactly what he's doing.

Tom Berenger is touching, too, as a well-meaning dolt — a former radical speechmaker turned actor who has achieved an amazing success on television as a Tom Selleck–type action hero. Grinning sheepishly under a thick mustache, Berenger makes the actor seem embarrassed by his own fame. His discomfort humanizes him; he's a nicer man than he thinks he is. Jeff Goldblum, on the other hand, plays a *People* magazine journalist who glories in being a creep. Tall and broad-shouldered, Goldblum walks with his head thrust forward and his shoulders bent, the complete urban neurotic weighted down by the sheer impossibility of getting out of bed in the morning. Goldblum's short haircut brings out the jut of his features; he looks, at times, like a Soviet poet of the twenties, at other times like an anxious shorebird searching for land. Goldblum's deadpan, furrowed-brow delivery of crass lines is explosively funny — he's like a great thirties character actor, stealing the movie from everyone else.

The men have careers, personalities, quirks. But Kasdan and Benedek haven't conceived the women in the same colorful terms. They are simply *women;* they have women's problems, and the problems define their characters. Glenn Close, as Kevin Kline's wife (she's supposed to be a doctor as well, though she hardly seems like one), positively glows with generosity and nurturing warmth. JoBeth Williams, miserably married to an unimaginative man, at least gets to show some desire and anger, but the character is just an outline, a type — a dissatisfied woman. Her face as rumpled as a washcloth, Mary Kay Place is even more dissatisfied. A lawyer who has given up defending indigent rapists and murderers (her new, wealthy clients, real-estate people, "only rape the *land*"), she's never been married, and she wants a child. So she spends the weekend trying to get one of her old friends — the best men she knows, she says — to impregnate her. Her quest, which is about the only active plot element, is mainly embarrassing, and pretty close to Broadway-comedy pathos.

As that terrific music floods the sound track, Kasdan sets up a whole system of nostalgic references, a network of unresolved love affairs, tense friendships, and so on — and then he doesn't do much with any of it. Except for one short, blood-clearing argument between Kline and Hurt, the tensions so carefully developed never explode. Kasdan is right to avoid standard drama, but the terrible thing is that what he's put in its place — the where-have-we-gone group-therapy scenes — doesn't add up to much. One character says something and then remains silent as another character speaks, and just as Kasdan, in this stiff way, is working up a little momentum, he cuts to something else. Terrified of boring the audience with talk, he wields too insistent a directorial hand, and the editing keeps jerking you away. Most of the scenes are short vignettes leading up to a reversal of expectations — an entertaining but shallow way of covering a lot of ground. There are repeated jogging scenes, and a meaningless use of montage to pick up speed — bundles of shots showing headlights going on and people unpacking their things or straggling in, at different hours, to breakfast. All this stuff is there to give the appearance of order and rhythm to potentially formless material. What's needed, however, is not punctuation but substantial ideas, not rhythmic recharging but more melody.

Lawrence Kasdan has contributed to the screenplays of *The Empire Strikes Back, Raiders of the Lost Ark,* and *The Return of the Jedi.* Apart from his collaborative work on these amazingly lucrative projects, everything he's done has been derivative. *Body Heat* was a frequently ludicrous pastiche of forties film noir attitudes and visual motifs; the screenplay for the unfortunate *Continental Divide* (Michael Apted directed) worked the Tracy-Hepburn formula, but without charm; and now Kasdan has made a slick, expensive version of John Sayles's 1980 house-party movie about veterans of the sixties, *The Return of the Secaucus 7.* Sayles's characters droned away in a jargon-ridden style that could make you wince, but you got the feeling that the social idealism of the sixties had changed them all irrevocably. For Kasdan, the sixties seem to be a time when people were nice to one another. At the end of *The Big Chill,* the bitter, frustrated William Hurt is softened by the kindness of the others, and Mary Kay Place becomes pregnant when one of the other women gives up her man for the night (an act that some of us may find more creepy than noble).

A few puffs of pot, a communal weekend, a friendly gesture of dubious sanity . . . As an epitaph for a generation, it's not much, is it? The characters in *The Big Chill* are first patted on the back for having had the ideals, and then teased for so easily giving them up. The movie is doubly patronizing, and it displays the infuriating, dumb cynicism of people who know nothing of life outside show business. Kasdan's point is clear: If you were touched by the spirit of the sixties, your fate must be a painful one — either you embrace the system uncritically or you become a suicide or a drug dealer. Actually, many people formed by the sixties continue to use what they learned (and I mean businessmen, lawyers, and doctors, as well as artists and writers) and still make a decent living. The pessimism of *The Big Chill* is fake, but it might be very appealing to the *Risky Business* crowd — the kids of the Reagan generation, who haven't any illusions to give up. Among other things, the movie tells them they can save time by not bothering with all that idealism crap.

New York, September 26, 1983

Places in the Heart

Richard T. Jameson

About two-thirds of the way into *Places in the Heart,* Edna Spalding (Sally Field), a widowed mother trying to hang on to home and family during the Depression, goes to see her banker. At the newly lowered market price, the cotton she planted on her back thirty acres won't quite bring in enough money to meet the next mortgage payment. Would the bank consent to take what she earns from the cotton crop and wait a while for the balance? Only the president of the bank can make that sort of decision, she is told. She watches as the officer with whom she normally deals crosses the main floor of the bank and mounts the stairs to the dim brown mezzanine.

It is in the nature of *Places in the Heart* that the outcome of the conversation on that mezzanine is not directly reported. While she is waiting, Edna Spalding, forced since the sudden death of her sheriff husband to take a crash course in survival, looks around the bank offices and seizes upon another possible solution to her immediate money problems. But before the film takes off on that course, one can't help pausing to savor the piercing evocativeness of this scene.

Not all of us have sat in a bank or loan office waiting for someone to make a life-or-death decision about our future. But I daresay each of us, as a child, had the experience of visiting an adult enclave like this bank and noticing, perhaps only inadvertently and some time after arriving, that there was a separate zone like the mezzanine in the film, above eye level and also somehow above the normal comings and goings of the public below. The very existence of such a zone was awesome. One dreaded to know, yet couldn't help being curious, exactly what went on there. Someday one might have to find out. That was what being a grown-up was all about.

Robert Benton was inspired to make *Places in the Heart* after taking his children to visit his hometown of Waxahachie, Texas, which he himself hadn't seen for decades. Although based on memories of his 1930s upbringing stimulated by this visit, the movie is not autobiographical in any slavish way. There is no reason to assume, for instance, that Edna Spalding's nine-year-old son Frank (Yankton Hatton) "is" Benton; the boy does not loom that large in the scenario or function as a point-of-view character. Yet the film is unmistakably imbued with the feeling that someone with intimate knowledge of a place, and the people who lived there, and the order of life they led, has somehow evoked not only that place but also his own early knowledge of it, and made that early knowledge almost tangible on screen.

"Places in the heart" emphatically should not be read as merely a sentimental formula. The phrase will be invoked henceforward as one of our most succinct indices of movie classicism, along with Orson Welles's "ribbon of dream" and Peter Bogdanovich's "pieces of time." It has chanced that Waxahachie, Texas, survives today as much the same physical entity Benton knew. That must have been handy for the filmmakers, but the documentary veracity of locations isn't the most important kind of cinematic truth. Place isn't just something you point a camera at, somewhere things happen. It's something you define by pointing a camera with feeling and comprehension. It's an event in its own right. A room can be a place, but so can the various corners and perspectives in that room. The space within the four sides of a motion picture frame is also a place. So is the complex of space and time defined within a traveling shot that begins at one point and ends at another, and measures the emotional and existential growth that takes place in between, in the very process of passing "in between." In this sense, in a film all "places" are essentially figures of style. In the best movies, all places are places in the heart.

Places in the Heart addresses itself to this notion from the outset, in its sublime credits sequence. As a small but fervent church congregation sings a Protestant hymn, we are vouchsafed glimpses of some of the people and some of the spaces we shall encounter in the film to follow: families at table; barns, fences, lanes; an itinerant black man receiving a plate of food at a woman's back door and bowing his head in prayer; a heartbreakingly beautiful long shot of several men in conversation in a field—a banker, it appears, and a couple of farmers. Benton has freely acknowledged that this sequence was conceived and executed by his film editor, Carol Littleton, who assembled it from outtakes and shot-tails. But it's fair to insist that Littleton's sensitive work represents the best kind of creative collaboration, a response to and extension of the writer-director's vision. "This is my story, this is my song," goes the hymn's gladsome refrain, and without a hint of hubris this is absolutely true. The sequence is brilliantly functional, establishing the existence of a community and preparing us to recognize the communal connections that form the fiber of the film. It is also a formal statement of individual artistic method and purpose, and an article of spiritual and aesthetic faith. The fusion is thrilling.

No single character dominates the action. Certainly Edna is the central figure, and Sally Field gives her a quiet strength and resolve that it would never occur to her to call heroism. But the story of Edna's sister Margaret (the estimable Lindsay Crouse) and Margaret's errant husband Wayne (Ed Harris) isn't so much a subplot as a minor theme, another look at a household that might be torn asunder. Margaret is supporting them, barely, by operating a beauty parlor out of her front room; Wayne, out of work like so many others, has drifted into an affair with her best friend — and his best friend's wife — Viola, the local schoolteacher (Amy Madigan). These characters are drawn with such unassuming tenderness and love, allowed to breathe so fully, and developed with such integrity by the performers — three of our best younger actors, none of whom can be caught repeating a move or inflection from a previous performance — that we should be willfully remiss in classifying them as supporting roles.

The same goes for the two men who become members of Edna's household. Moze (Danny Glover) is a wandering black who comes seeking work around the place, is turned away, but circles back into the story by way of an instinctive contract spontaneously struck between him and Edna. Likewise Mr. Will (John Malkovich), a sightless war veteran whose banker brother-in-law (Lane Smith) wants to be rid of him, becomes a boarder in circumstances neither he nor Edna would have chosen. Without recourse to handy epiphanies or sentimental calculation, without betraying Mr. Will's considerable sense of pride and independence or wishing away the racial and sociological fact of Moze's separateness in the American South of the thirties, Benton ineluctably persuades us that both men grow to be members of the family as well.

I shouldn't like to give the impression that *Places in the Heart* is an American fairy tale. It describes a world in which triumphs are small-scale in the general scheme of things, and pain, frustration, anger, and powerlessness before some terrible natural and sociopolitical forces are not to be wished away. It's even fair to say that the town lies in a kind of grief belt where, as Viola Kelsey cries in a desperation larger and more intimate than she can name, "There's always goin' to be tornados, people's always goin' to be poor." Life's like that, and with all the love in the world Robert Benton can't change it. But with his limpid, honest artistry, he achieves an order of metaphysical transcendence we normally associate with masters like Mizoguchi, Ford, and

Bresson. His final sequence is the most beautiful film passage we're likely to see for many a moon.

No, I'm not about to describe that one; it is to witness for oneself. But for a distinctive sampling of the uninsistent beauty and powerful emotional discretion of his style, consider another detail from early in the film. Royce Spalding (Ray Baker), Edna's husband, has got up from his Sunday dinner to answer a call for assistance, and been killed by appallingly casual mischance. Some townsmen bring his body home, his deputy trying, and failing, to prepare Edna beforehand. Behind the deputy, the townsmen carry Royce through the front door and into the dining room. As the body is lifted across the frame space, right to left, we perceive, almost subliminally, Edna's hands in the foreground of the shot as she backs out of the way, left to right. She holds the Sunday linen and silver, just gathered from the table that will now bear another charge.

The Weekly (Seattle), October 3, 1984

PLACES IN THE HEART

David Denby

At the beginning of *Places in the Heart,* the new film written and directed by Robert Benton (*Kramer vs. Kramer*), the sheriff of the small Texas town of Waxahachie is called away from his dinner table to pacify a black boy who has got himself wildly drunk. Down by the railroad tracks, the boy shoots his gun in the air; he's not vicious, or even particularly dangerous, he's just plastered, and wheeling around to the sheriff, he's ready to give himself up — when he pulls the trigger again, accidentally plugging the sheriff in the chest.

This brutal opening — violence bursting out of an overflow of high spirits — is convincingly crazy in the same way as the violence was in *Bonnie and Clyde* (1967), which Benton also wrote (with David Newman) and which was also set in Depression Texas. But after this scene, Benton puts away his surprises and starts exploiting familiar responses. Restrained, tasteful, almost pious in its celebration of hard times and togetherness in the Depression, *Places in the Heart* has the stiff dignity and liberal earnestness of a Pulitzer Prize–winning play of thirty years ago. Benton has drawn on memories and legends generated by his own family in Texas, and he seems paralyzed by respect. Parched and academic, the movie is too square for art — though it's perfectly designed for Oscars.

The sheriff's widow, Edna Spalding (Sally Field), hasn't any idea how to support her two children, and she's in danger of losing her house and land — the bank wants to foreclose on her mortgage. Desperate, Edna allows a black vagrant, Moze (Danny Glover), to live on her property. Earlier, he stole some of her silver, but she forgives him because he knows all about farming cotton, and he's hardworking and sweet tempered and polite. Against the advice of everyone, the white woman and the black hobo go into business together, planting, picking, negotiating with crooked cotton dealers, battling the long odds of the Depression, literally from their knees. The Spalding family, altered somewhat, survives and even grows larger. Edna takes in a boarder — Mr. Will (John Malkovich), who was blinded in the World War. Haughty and standoffish at first, he soon fits right in, becoming the family's defender and protector. At the same time, in an unconnected subplot, the husband (Ed Harris) of Edna's sister (Lindsay Crouse) has an affair with a married woman (Amy Madigan). I imagine that Benton is trying to get at the spiritual and moral life of the entire community, and that's why he doesn't bother to integrate the two stories. If his material were bolder, he might have pulled it off, but these characters, perfectly costumed as they are, speaking in the modest tones of plain country folk, refuse to come to life.

Who knows, for instance, what to make of Benton's heroine? Sally Field has the strong back and thighs of a working country woman; her face can crumple with exhaustion, and she looks right in her print dresses and frizzy hair. She's perfectly in period, but that's all you can say about her. Edna is indomitable and also charitable and kindly (she's always giving breakfast to someone), but she's so impersonally drawn that she could be a poster icon — the Depression mother as heroine and workhorse, eternally at the stove with her frying pan.

Almost everyone in the movie behaves extraordinarily well. Edna is without a man, yet neither of her boarders makes a pass at her; her little son, caught smoking at school, bravely bends over, volunteering his rump for a walloping; Ed Harris's adulterer, posing a threat to the peace of the community, stops pursuing the woman he loves when she momentarily pulls away. Benton doesn't get into the emotions that create adulterous passion; adultery in this movie exists only to be renounced. The dangers to these people come from *outside*—from a tornado, which is magnificently staged and filmed (the high point of the movie), and from the Ku Klux Klan, which Benton uses as a ready-made symbol of irrational hatred.

The level of craftsmanship in Robert Benton's films is always extraordinarily high, but in this case the handsomeness and restraint serve only to disguise how conventional the material is. Cinematographer Nestor Almendros captures the homely American classicism of the Depression—the light gleaming off the flat-topped thirties sedans; the heroism of the lonely clapboard house; the men and women at a dance standing tightly packed under reddish light. Benton, a discreet and gentlemanly director, never shoves the camera in the face of a suffering or humiliated character. The picture moves calmly, quietly, with extraordinary confidence in itself; yet after the opening scene it does something unexpected only once. John Malkovich, who has the suggestion of an overly punctilious school principal in his high forehead, pursed lips, and bowtie, comes charging angrily into Sally Field's kitchen one night, and even though he can't see her, he realizes quickly enough that she's sitting naked in the washtub. What Malkovich does then is complex and beautiful: Blind or not, he has invaded her privacy, and his anger gives way to discomfort and then to a kind of awed bashfulness before the fact of her nakedness; it is the homage that the lifetime bachelor pays to the woman he will never possess.

If the whole movie were composed of scenes as well imagined as that one, Benton's discretion would be masterly. But most of this movie is muffled. From time to time in *Places in the Heart,* Benton gives us the sounds of a church chorus and glimpses (from different angles) of the town's stone church, its imposing brown towers visible from every corner of the town. At the end, Benton makes his intention explicit: We have been watching the mishaps and glories of a Christian community, the struggles of men and women sanctified in the eyes of God. But wouldn't this assertion be far more moving if God's tolerance were tested a bit harder? Divine forgiveness is sublime only when pushed to its limits. Edna and the rest, it turns out, are in no need of God's grace; Robert Benton has already gathered them to his bosom.

New York, October 1, 1984

FATAL ATTRACTION

Owen Gleiberman

In movies, psychos on the rampage have become as unthreateningly predictable as the boy next door (in fact, most of them *are* the boys next door). Any cheapjack thriller can trot out a fiend with a kitchen knife. It's the part before the kitchen knife — Norman Bates in his study talking about how "we're all in our private traps," or Tom Noonan in *Manhunter* asking his blind coworker on a date, or Eric Roberts in *Star 80* playing Dorothy Stratten's killer-stud Svengali as an inferno of crisscrossed drives — that can titillate you with a mixture of fascination and raw fear and even sympathy. Ultimately, none of us (not even shrinks) truly understands psychotics, and that means we're never quite sure where they stand in relation to the "normal." The best psychological thrillers play off the notion that a psychotic may or may not turn violent, and that the ones who do are at once perilously close to us and perilously far away.

For a while, Adrian Lyne's erotic adultery thriller *Fatal Attraction* leads you into a creepy, seductive realm where the lines separating desire and passion and violent obsession have been quietly rubbed out. Dan Gallagher (Michael Douglas), a successful New York attorney and contented family man (he's got a young daughter and a beautiful wife he's still very much in love with), has a torrid weekend affair with a glamorous, unmarried publishing executive named Alex Forrest (Glenn Close). Why the tryst if he's so satisfied? His wife (Ann Archer) is away for the weekend, and beyond that the film is smart enough not to bother explaining. There's one brief scene in which Dan enters his bedroom and discovers that his daughter has elected to share the folks' bed (in other words, no hanky-panky tonight). But this sort of inconvenience hasn't really soured him on domestic life; it's a trifle, and he knows it. The real reason for the affair is that Alex, with her crooked come-hither smile and her aureole of frizzy blond hair, is sexy and exotic and up-front as hell — aggressive but not really pushy. Besides, these things (as we all know) just happen.

According to the publicity material, Dan sees the affair as "a diversion," and that, perhaps, is how it's meant to start. But the movie takes its erotic urgency from the hero's jumping into a relationship he thinks he can walk away from and then discovering he's entered a

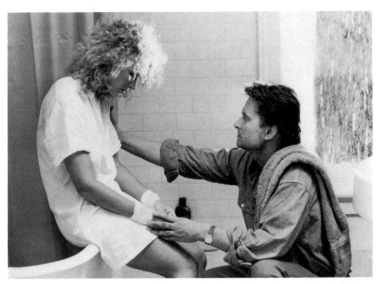

Dan (Michael Douglas) discovers that Alex (Glenn Close) has made him the subject of a pathological obsession in *Fatal Attraction*. (Photo by Andy Schwartz, courtesy of Paramount Pictures Corp.)

nightmare—and one that's not without its undertone of lurid temptation. Alex, the woman who's seduced him away from monogamy, turns out to be unstable beyond words. When the weekend ends, she won't let go of him—she can't. Gradually, her need shades into compulsion and psychotic treachery and finally violence, and what's fun about the movie is the way it lends her behavior a satirical double edge: Is this just craziness, or is it true passion—the naked beast itself—in a dispassionate age? Lyne stages Dan and Alex's first coupling as though he were trying to atone for that soft-core designer-kink fiasco *9½ Weeks.* As the two go at it in the kitchen, Alex, who's propped up on the sink, accidentally turns on the faucet and then scoops up some water to drench the front of her shirt (ah, the inspirations of love). You're reminded that a truly hot sex scene probably depends less on the usual "steaminess" than on exactly this sort of thrashing around. Lyne earns his erotic stripes: This scene cooks more than all ninety gauzy minutes of *9½ Weeks* did, and it tells you that if Dan has a reason for walking away from this affair (i.e., to save his marriage), he's also got a reason to stay (i.e., he probably wouldn't mind some more thrashing around).

We're hardly used to thinking of Glenn Close as sexy. And though *Fatal Attraction* may not make her a bigger star than *Jagged Edge* did, it could well make her a different kind of star: She's never given a performance that had you hanging on every line, every luxurious facial gesture, the way this one does. A friend of mine says that much of Close's sudden sexiness can be chalked up to her frizzed-out hair, and there's no doubt that it lends her angular features — the sharp nose, the downturned mouth, and especially that thrusting chin — an alluringly soft frame. But this is also a superb, magnetic performance. Close's Alex is seductive and frightening at the same time; a man's temptation to sleep with her is matched by the fear his genitals won't be there in the morning. This may just sound like the classic Hollywood man-eater in a new-style perm, or even a cheap castration fantasy (and that level is certainly there). Close, though, is playing a genuine character, perhaps a new screen type: the yuppie femme fatale. Although Alex is technically the home wrecker, she's also a victim; her obsession with Dan doesn't start out as destructive, and his unwillingness to live up to it comes to seem the movie's sly parody of contemporary commitment anxieties. What he's frightened of "committing" himself to is the intensity of their mutual attraction. And Close makes this work — that is, she lends some credence to the sanity, even the tragedy, of Alex's obsession by digging into the character with a smoldering purity. Her eyes give off adoring beams, and her smile is both witchy and motherly. It's a triumphant, impossible-to-read smile, like the mock-beatific grins on the faces of the Manson girls, and when Close flashes it she's radiant — her Alex isn't just mad, she's in *love*.

Well, OK, she's also nuts. *Fatal Attraction* is best when it stays on this level of Hitchcockian ambiguity and dread, the one you remember from *Psycho, Strangers on a Train,* and *Shadow of a Doubt.* But the (supposedly) sensation-starved masses must be served, and the film eventually turns into another thriller about . . . a fiend with a kitchen knife. I hardly mean to imply it would have been a masterpiece otherwise; there's a languid insubstantiality to the first half, too. It's a little difficult to say why. This isn't Adrian Lyne the phony of *9½ Weeks,* and it isn't Lyne the synth-pop-drunk happy droid of *Flashdance,* either. He's trying to be a director here, in a way he hasn't since his overlooked first film, *Foxes* (1980), about teenage girls in the Los Angeles fast lane. Despite its tawdry, sub–Harlequin Romance title, *Fatal Attraction* is a Hitchcockian thriller in a way most movies branded with the term aren't. It seduces you into the guilt and adventurousness of someone who has an extramarital fling just because he feels like it. Then, when the thrills seep in, they're like larger-than-life, roller-coaster projections of what he's feeling. And Douglas and Close have some terrific scenes together: a restaurant flirtation in which Dan thinks he's keeping the situation under control until Alex feeds him a come-on too obvious to miss, and Douglas's face grows almost stricken with longing; a morning-after scene with Alex throwing a tantrum because Dan won't stay (Close makes her need seem physical, and ditto for Douglas in the way he recoils); the first time Alex, standing there in her white bathrobe, does something truly shocking—for a few queasy-bloody moments, she seems on call to a higher power.

So why is the movie—with the exception of Close's performance—just borderline enjoyable? I think that's because Lyne, even when he's working "sincerely," is still a string puller, and his calibrated, up-from-television-commercials style only makes you more aware of the manipulativeness of the thriller genre. A director like Hitchcock, or Philip Kaufman in the 1978 *Invasion of the Body Snatchers,* doesn't just ease you into suspense; he does it *nimbly.* Lyne is one of the least spontaneous directors around, and because he brings the same naturalistic, cocktail-lounge atmosphere to every environment (it's the world viewed through a martini glass darkly), you can't take plea-sure in the sheer mechanics of what he's doing the way you can with Hitchcock. In his Americanized-Eurochic way, Adrian Lyne is like an art-film stylist searching for "truth"—he's at the (junky) end of the lineage that starts with Hitchcock and goes through Alain Resnais and Nicolas Roeg and Alan Parker. *Fatal Attraction* holds you, at least until the last third or so, when it grows a little monotonous (the film could easily have lost half an hour). It's consumable, though—a quicksilver exercise. Whatever draw it has comes from the efficiency of Lyne's technique (most audiences won't know he's ripped off the climactic bathtub stunt from the 1955 French thriller *Diabolique,* but there's no arguing with the chilling way it's been staged), and from the performances.

In the opening scenes, Michael Douglas looks so yuppie-ish it's funny—with his square-faced handsomeness set off by an immacu-late smile, he could be Michael J. Fox at forty-five. He's always been sinewy and intelligent, one of the few contemporary American actors who can project Eagle Scout virtue and still hold your interest. Here, as usual, he plays a man with "character" (in the old-fashioned sense), but he's also confident enough to let a few moldy cracks show. For Douglas, it's an intense, even raw performance. He puts everything he has into his increasingly maddening confrontations with Close, and also into the scenes with Anne Archer, who plays his wife as a soulful, deeply contented woman—and then, when his infidelity is revealed, as one who's grown powerful through sorrow. On some level, *Fatal Attraction* wants to be about the domestic complacency of these two. It's witty enough to suggest that the intensity of Alex's desire is what threatens this family, that her passion is partly crazy, partly something the placidity of yuppie life can't contain. But Lyne's style finally lacks the depth—the layers—to give this notion a threatening undertone. He isn't quite a director in *Fatal Attraction;* he just does a damn good impersonation.

Boston Phoenix, September 25, 1987

FATAL ATTRACTION

David Ansen

Glenn Close has changed her image with a vengeance. The noble, ethereal heroine who graced *The Big Chill* and *The Natural* is nowhere to be seen in *Fatal Attraction.* The "new" Glenn Close, playing a psychotic, highly sexed book editor named Alex, is a figure designed to send men rushing off to their shrinks, aquiver with sexual paranoia. Batting her eyes under a Medusa tangle of blond hair, Alex seduces married man Dan Gallagher (Michael Douglas) into a tempestuous one-night stand and then turns into a knife-wielding harpy when he shuts her out of his life. What Freddy or Jason is to horny teens, Alex may become to the yuppie male contemplating an extramarital fling.

Close makes a smashingly depraved villain, but *Fatal Attraction* is in no way worthy of her resonant perversity. As he showed in *Flashdance,* director Adrian Lyne is a slick technician who will sacrifice anything for an effect. A former commercials director in England, he knows how to sell a product, in this case fear and loathing. But in the course of getting an audience to squirm and writhe, he dispenses with whatever psychological nuance might have made James Dearden's story something more than mere exploitation.

Douglas plays a successful, happily married New York lawyer who slips into his fling one weekend while his beautiful wife (Anne

Archer) and doting six-year-old (Ellen Hamilton Latzen) are away. After a steamy night with Alex, he gets his first taste of her mental condition when she slashes her wrists in protest of his departure. She gets progressively more loony, badgering him with phone calls, meeting with his wife, sending him obscene tapes. What drives her over the edge is the discovery she's pregnant. Now the fun begins, as the initially sympathetic nut case turns into a full-scale movie monster out of *Nightmare on Madison Avenue.*

Fatal Attraction originally had a different, far less violent ending, which met with disapproval from preview audiences. Lowering their sights, Lyne and producers Stanley Jaffe and Sherry Lansing went for the jugular, borrowing every scare tactic from Polanski's *Repulsion* to the hoariest devices of *Friday the 13th.* You have to feel bad for Close and Douglas: Whatever work they've done to give *Fatal Attraction* a smattering of psychological veracity gets cynically chucked out the window for the sake of cheap thrills. What is this movie saying? Beware of single women with lust in their hearts? That infidelity will be punished with blood? One may giggle recalling the press clips that hailed Sherry Lansing, once chief of production at Twentieth Century Fox, as some sort of feminist. What she and her cohorts have made is the *Reefer Madness* of adultery.

Newsweek, September 28, 1987

BATMAN

Jay Carr

Tim Burton's new, dark *Batman* isn't a great action movie. It's something better — a great city movie. There's a lot to be said for Michael Keaton's brooding Batman; and as the white-faced, green-haired, leering Joker, Jack Nicholson slams home one of Hollywood's great demento numbers. The inescapably penile Batmobile suggests a cross between an armadillo and a vintage Corvette, and the Batwing is a dream toy, too. But the thing that's going to make you want to see *Batman* a second and third and fourth time is Gotham City as a brutal pile of dour, gothic, art deco menace. Girdered, buttressed, thrusting, crushing, it's architecture from hell, a nightmare projection of civilization in malignant, life-threatening retreat, a literally fantastic projection of the city as a huge dead battery.

In short, *Batman* will take its place alongside the small handful of film's visionary apocalyptic cityscapes. After *Metropolis* and *Blade Runner* and *Brazil* there haven't been many. Not that *Batman* hasn't got more going for it than doom-laden scenery. It's an inspired visual expression of a world in which art as well as heroes have fallen into disrepute. One of its best sequences involves a square-off between Batman and the Joker in a heavy metal mausoleum wickedly called the Flugelheim Museum, in which the Joker's vandalizing of paintings seems less barbarous than the so-called museum's display of them. There's something almost heroic about the Joker's way of manically raising the energy level in the soul-crushing world he wants to rule. Once he takes that acid bath that contorts his face into its permanent leer, he never lets up. There's nobody like Jack Nicholson if you want an over-the-top Jack Nicholson impersonation.

There's also an invigoratingly perverse wit in the Joker's crimes. First he rubs out Jack Palance, his double-crossing boss, in an art deco penthouse whose nocturnal beauty is stronger than the bloodshed. Then he makes his victims his collaborators in ways that would have aroused in Richard Widmark an envy greener than the Joker's hair. Then he gets to people through their vanity, lacing a factory batch of cosmetics with a poison that causes people to die laughing. Burton uses a TV anchor team to wicked effect to illustrate the poison-cosmetic murder wave. After an anchorwoman dies on the air after laughing at other victims, her coanchors keep showing up on TV with messier and messier complexions: They're afraid to use cosmetics. Later, when the Joker decides to decimate the population of Gotham City, he uses greed, riding a parade float through town, scattering money, then gassing the masses after he slaps on a respirator.

But any Batman movie in which the architecture and the Joker take over is, you will gather, a bit lopsided. What's wrong is that Batman is too muted, his conflicts too internalized. He's got a great Robocop look — his suit is black molded armor, not the comic-book gray — and he retains the vulnerability that always made him more appealing than Superman. Unlike the Man of Steel, who could fly through brick walls as long as they didn't contain kryptonite, Batman becomes admirable for his cleverness in inventing gadgets to extend the range of human activity. He's great with the utility belt, whether shooting a grappling hook onto a roof or radio-controlling the armored Batmobile. Keaton is just as fascinating as the Robin-less millionaire playboy, Bruce Wayne.

In civvies, his brooding works. He knows he's a guy with a problem, that his need to glide through life caped and masked stems from more than a need to avenge his parents' death at the hands of street thugs. His dilemma is captured wittily and wordlessly by Burton in a scene with Kim Basinger. After they've made love, she falls asleep, then awakens startled to find herself alone in bed. Peering through the murk, she finally spies Bruce Wayne on the other side of the room, hanging batlike by his feet from a gravity bar. The succinct visual wit here almost makes up for the lack of a revelation scene when she learns he's Batman. One minute she thinks he's Bruce Wayne; the next, she's in the Batcave, talking to Michael Gough's suave, warm Alfred, the butler and factotum. Batman, meanwhile, grows too internalized. There are a lot of scenes that seem not so much edited as abruptly truncated; this is the most glaring.

Not that Basinger is a major ingredient in *Batman*. She's pretty much just along for the ride, a distraction to take our minds off the fact that Robin has been broomed. In the film, she plays a photojournalist named Vicki Vale. But she's less than Batman's Lois Lane. Robert Wuhl, her snoopy reporter colleague at the wonderful retro newspaper named *The Gotham Globe,* with its yellowing clip file, marble columns, and fedora-hatted wiseguys, is more fun to have around. Others, such as Billy Dee Williams's district attorney and Pat Hingle's Police Commissioner Gordon, are restricted to brief window-dressing roles. We never even see Batman summoned by the Batsignal. But one of the film's most effective moments comes early on when Batman drops silently to a tenement rooftop in a swooping glide, then takes out a couple of muggers.

There's something spidery and eerie in Batman's first entrance that Burton and Keaton only intermittently recapture. To their credit, they don't beat into the ground the notion that Batman and the Joker need each other to define themselves. Instead, Burton displays their mutual dependency as a symptom of the spiritual corrosion (one of the film's visual metaphors is pervasive rust) in which Gotham City is steeped. Audiences expecting an action movie will find *Batman* insufficiently active and dramatic. Narrative isn't Burton's strong point. And *Batman* loses impact by not getting the Batman–Joker balance right, by not tipping the film more toward Batman. Terrific as Nicholson's bravura Joker is, he'd be even better if there were ten minutes less of him. Yet you wouldn't want to miss the showdown between Batman and the Joker atop an exfoliating gothic cathedral lifted from Fritz Lang's *Metropolis* by way of Antonio Gaudí.

If slack intrudes as the narrative thins out, and if Batman sometimes grows recessive, Burton gets the important thing right. Just as he did in very different ways in his first two films — *Pee-wee's Big Adventure* and *Beetlejuice* — Burton specifies a world that's vivid and very much unlike anything quite put on film before. He and his production designer, Anton Furst, fill their high visual style with weight and impact, and draw us into it with the undertow of the dreamlike. Burton further increases his film's unsettling sense of dislocation by blurring the year in which it takes place — it could be anywhere from the thirties to a retro twenty-first century. Burton is an original. His flawed but powerful *Batman* is a world apart from Hollywood's summer parade of play-it-safe sequels. It's the first Hollywood movie of 1989 I can't wait to see again.

Boston Globe, June 23, 1989

BATMAN

Richard Corliss

The familiar blue sky behind the Warner Brothers shield grows dark. The clouds gain some menacing heft. A cumulus of urban steam shrouds the camera as it goes cruising for trouble in Gotham City. Nighttime is the right time for . . . Batman.

Not *"Baat-maaaan!"* Not the bleating trumpets and pop-art facetiousness of the sixties TV series, which turned Bob Kane's superhero into a camp crusader. Director Tim Burton's approach is deadly serious. He renounces the bright palette, the easy thrills, to aim for a psychodrama with the force of myth. He creates a Gotham City that looms like a rube's nightmare of Manhattan. He strips the Bruce Wayne legend down to its chassis, dumping Robin and the goony rogues' gallery. This is a face-off between two men in weird masks: one in a leathery black item out of a dominatrix's pleasure chest, the other with a grin frozen into a rictus. One man obsessed with good, the other enthralled by evil: Batman (Michael Keaton) and the Joker (Jack Nicholson).

Ambitious goals, most of which are not realized. The film stints on narrative surprise. It prowls — slowly, so slowly — in search of grandeur, but it often finds murk. It permits a few inside jokes (a cartoon of a bat in a suit, drawn by Kane), but mines its main humor from the Joker's ribald misanthropy ("This town needs an enema"). *Batman*'s style is both daunting and lurching; it has trouble deciding which of its antagonists should set the tone. It can be as manic as the Joker, straining to hear the applause of outrage; it can be as implosive as Batman-Bruce, who seems crushed by the burden of his schizoid eminence. This tension nearly exhausts the viewer and the film.

Inconsistencies abound. The Joker falls into a vat of toxic slime that eats the skin of his body but doesn't damage his signature deck of cards; when he gaily vandalizes some classic paintings, the film spells the museum's name two different ways; and when he starts tossing $20 million in cash onto the street, the good people of Gotham don't go into a looting frenzy and attack his perch. More important, the picture's first hour poses one big question: How will ace photographer Vicki Vale (Kim Basinger) react when she learns that Bruce is Batman? We never find out; the revelation occurs offscreen.

Anyone can take pleasure in the matching of Keaton and Nicholson, their dueling eyebrows poised like crossed swords. And Keaton does locate the troubled human inside Batman's armature. He is amusingly awkward wrestling with the threat that Vicki's inquisitive love represents. He knows the world is not quite worth saving, and yet, "It's just something I have to do," he says, "because nobody else can." Same with Nicholson. Who else could play the Joker? He has a patent on satanic majesty. His performance is high, soaring, gamy. He is as good, and as evil, as the film allows him to be. Which, finally, is not enough.

Here's why. At the end, Batman and the Joker realize they must destroy each other because, in a way, they have created each other. It would be nice to say that the Joker is Batman's lost, twisted twin; then his clumsy antics could be seen as an expression of existential anguish. He could feel as much pain as he dishes out. He could be Hamlet dressed as a clown. But the Joker's malignancy is neither seductive nor poignant. His power never tempts Vicki or compromises Bruce. His soul must have been stripped away with his skin, and what's left is the spirit of anarchic violence, giggling at its own enormity.

What's left in *Batman* is the skeleton of a nifty film. Its heart got lost on Tim Burton's storyboard.

Time, June 19, 1989

FIELD OF DREAMS

Roger Ebert

The farmer is standing in the middle of a cornfield when he hears the voice for the first time: "If you build it, he will come." He looks around and doesn't see anybody. The voice speaks again, soft and confidential: "If you build it, he will come." Sometimes you can get too much sun, out there in a hot Iowa cornfield in the middle of the season. But this isn't a case of sunstroke.

Up until the farmer (Kevin Costner) starts hearing voices, *Field of Dreams* is a completely sensible film about a young couple who want to run a family farm in Iowa. Ray and Annie Kinsella (Costner and Amy Madigan) have tested the fast track and had enough of it, and they enjoy sitting on the porch and listening to the grass grow. When the voice speaks for the first time, the farmer is baffled, and so was I: Could this be one of those religious pictures where a voice tells the humble farmer where to build the cathedral?

It's a religious picture, all right, but the religion is baseball. And when he doesn't understand the spoken message, Ray Kinsella is granted a vision of a baseball diamond, right there in his cornfield. If he builds it, the voice seems to promise, Joe Jackson will come and play on it — "Shoeless Joe," who was a member of the infamous 1919 Black Sox team but protested until the day he died that he played the best he could.

As *Field of Dreams* developed this fantasy, I found myself being willingly drawn into it. Movies are often so timid these days, so afraid to take flights of the imagination, that there is something grand and brave about a movie where a voice tells a farmer to build a baseball diamond so that Shoeless Joe Jackson can materialize out of the corn-field and hit a few fly balls. This is the kind of movie Frank Capra might have directed and James Stewart might have starred in — a movie about dreams.

It is important not to tell too much about the plot. (I was grateful I knew nothing about the movie when I went to see it, but the ads gave away the Shoeless Joe angle.) Let it be said that Annie Kinsella supports her husband's vision, and that he finds it necessary to travel east to Boston so he can enlist the support of a famous writer (James Earl Jones) who has disappeared from sight, and north to Minnesota

Ray Kinsella (Kevin Costner), his wife Annie (Amy Madigan), and their daughter Karin (Gaby Hoffman) are greeted by a youthful John Kinsella (Dwier Brown), Ray's father, in *Field of Dreams*. (Photo courtesy of Universal Pictures.)

to talk to what remains of a doctor (Burt Lancaster) who never got the chance to play with the pros.

The movie sensibly never tries to make the slightest explanations for the strange events that happen after the diamond is constructed. There is, of course, the usual business about how the bank thinks the farmer has gone haywire and wants to foreclose on his mortgage (the Capra and Stewart movies always had evil bankers in them). But there is not a corny, stupid payoff at the end. Instead, the movie depends on a poetic vision to make its point.

The director, Phil Alden Robinson, and the writer, W. P. Kinsella, are dealing with stuff that's close to the heart (it can't be a coincidence that the author and the hero have the same last name). They love baseball, and they think it stands for an earlier, simpler time when professional sports were still games and not industries. There is a speech in this movie about baseball that is so simple and true that it is heartbreaking. And the whole attitude toward the players reflects that attitude. Why do they come back from the great beyond and materialize here in this cornfield? Not to make any kind of vast, earth-shattering statement, but simply to hit a few and field a few, and remind us of a good and innocent time.

It is very tricky to act in a movie like this; there is always the danger of seeming ridiculous. Kevin Costner and Amy Madigan create such a grounded, believable married couple that one of the themes of the movie is the way love means sharing your loved one's dreams. Jones and Lancaster create small, sharp character portraits — two older men who have taken the paths life offered them, but never forgotten what baseball represented to them in their youth.

Field of Dreams will not appeal to grinches and grouches and realists. It is a delicate movie, a fragile construction of one goofy fantasy after another. But it has the courage to be exactly what it promises. "If you build it, he will come." And he does.

Chicago Sun-Times, April 21, 1989

FIELD OF DREAMS

Julie Salamon

Kevin Costner is unquestionably a movie star, big and handsome and self-effacing in the Hollywood tradition. His status has been confirmed by the editors at *Vanity Fair* and the *New York Times Magazine,* who have devoted a great deal of space in recent issues to proclaiming Costner this generation's Gary Cooper.

These promotional pieces were pegged to Costner's latest vehicle, *Field of Dreams,* a baseball movie. This is not a sequel to the witty and sexy *Bull Durham,* Costner's previous baseball movie, though in this case a sequel would be welcome. *Field of Dreams* doesn't have brains or style, but it does have a baseball field carved out of an Iowa cornfield and enough gooey sentiment to drown the state.

Yet, inexplicably (to a person not automatically moved to tears by the advent of spring training), this mawkish nonsense has a great many fans. "This is a Zen baseball movie," explained one of them. "It's about how baseball is connected to all of life, to capturing your lost dreams and reconnecting with your father."

Oh. And I thought *Field of Dreams* was just another inarticulate picture in which the main character's response to plowing under his cornfield to build a baseball diamond when ordered to do so by a mystical voice is: "Isn't it cool?"

Costner, looking just great in jeans and a jacket, plays Ray Kinsella, a thirty-six-year-old former Brooklyn boy–Berkeley rebel now settled on a farm in Iowa with his wife (Amy Madigan) and little girl. He tells us he is afraid he's turning into his father, that he may never take a risk, and that is why he digs up his cornfield when this mysterious voice commands him to do so. The voice *is* a little Zenlike: "If you build it, he will come," it whispers to Ray. (This coy voice from beyond made me long for the old Bible movies when God very directly issued commandments in unequivocal terms.)

Ray builds the field and, sure enough, he comes, "he" being "Shoeless Joe" Jackson. You may recall, either from history or from the movies (John Sayles's *Eight Men Out*), that left fielder Joe Jackson was one of the eight Chicago White Sox players excommunicated from baseball for conspiring to lose the 1919 World Series.

The fine actor Ray Liotta plays Joe, but all he's been given to do is look saintly and intone religious utterances about baseball. Costner must react to this creature, which he does by affecting the expression of a guest at a funeral trying to look appropriately somber.

Other disgraced White Sox appear and throw baseballs around. You don't see them much because The Voice sends Ray elsewhere, to recruit other souls for salvation through baseball and bring them back to that patch of heaven in Iowa.

This leads Ray to Boston to pick up a retired radical writer (James Earl Jones), then to Minnesota to seek a doctor (Burt Lancaster) who gave up a professional baseball career to practice medicine. Ray's mission is to make everyone, including himself, realize that the choices they've made in life were the correct ones.

This theme, like everything else in this movie, is announced, not dramatized. Still, inevitably, the picture has been compared with Frank Capra's *It's a Wonderful Life,* in which Jimmy Stewart's small-town banker learns that handing out mortgages was a noble endeavor after all. But where's the wit, the style—excuse me for being old-fashioned—the story?

Not in this adaptation of W. P. Kinsella's book, *Shoeless Joe.* Writer-director Phil Alden Robinson substitutes sentimentality. When characters aren't declaring how magical and fine everything is, the music announces it for them with irritating insistence. At least Robinson's first movie, *In the Mood,* a World War II period piece, sneaked in a few laughs before Robinson started ladling on the extra-thick corn syrup.

There are no laughs here, just the sorry sight of some very good actors being ill-used, and winning plaudits for it. Even the closing credits are cloying: The actor playing "The Voice" is identified as "Himself."

Wall Street Journal, April 27, 1989

ON ACTRESSES

Peter Rainer

In *Pretty Woman,* Julia Roberts plays a minty-fresh hooker who finds true love with her wealthy john. In *Miami Blues,* Jennifer Jason Leigh's hooker is a perky, girl-next-door type who yearns for homespun married bliss with a psychopathic trick. In *Last Exit to Brooklyn,* Jason Leigh is a tough-tender streetwalker who lures unsuspecting galoots to their doom.

What does it say about Hollywood that, of all the roles being offered actresses right now, these three are probably the juiciest? Women are such an endangered species in the movies that the vamp has become high concept.

There have probably never been as many gifted actresses in America as there are right now, but their gifts have been allowed to flourish almost exclusively in the theater or on television. On stage, performers like Mercedes Ruehl (*Other People's Money*) and Joan Allen (*Burn This*) and Patti LuPone (*Evita*) are electrifying. On television, you watch Annette O'Toole in *The Kennedys of Massachusetts* in a state of rapt admiration. When these same actresses show up in films, it's likely to be in scrunched-up bit roles: Ruehl had a dismally straitlaced cameo as a sympathetic shrink in *Crazy People;* LuPone was shoe-horned into *Driving Miss Daisy;* Allen was an extended blip on the screen in such films as *Tucker* and *In Country.* O'Toole was harrowing as a distraught wife in *Love at Large* — for all of her ten (count 'em) minutes of screen time. [Editor's Note: Ruehl did better in 1991, winning the Best Supporting Actress Oscar for *The Fisher King.*]

Even the actresses well known — honored — for their past film work are likely nowadays to be playing blurry backups to male leads. In *Bird on a Wire,* Goldie Hawn appears to have entered a boodie-shaking contest with Mel Gibson. (Worse, she loses the contest.) Barbra Streisand and Bette Midler are the female stars with the greatest clout, but Streisand is just now about to begin filming her first film in three years, and Midler has turned into a weepy self-parody. Even her silly, wiggly walk lacks spring.

It's heartbreaking to scan the pool of great (or potentially great) actresses out there: not just the famous ones, like Jessica Lange and Debra Winger and Michelle Pfeiffer, but the scores of the less renowned—Maria Conchita Alonso, Bridget Fonda, Joan Cusack, Joan Chen, Pamela Reed, Lena Olin, Natasha Richardson, Anjelica Huston, Christine Lahti, Dianne Wiest, Laurie Metcalfe, Ellen Barkin, Blythe Danner—to mention only a handful. The embarrassment in this embarrassment of riches is that these actresses, all primed for major careers, are entombed in Hollywood's development-deal dungeons. An entire generation of female performers is being squelched by an industry that finds no percentage in accommodating their talents. And by repeatedly going buddy-buddy or solo, an entire generation of male performers is being squelched, too.

Things weren't always this bad. Until the past several decades, women were as integral to the movies as men; female stars were as hallowed as their male counterparts. Lillian Gish and Richard Barthelmess were equally revered. Greta Garbo hogged as much of the glory as John Gilbert. The goddesses, like Joan Crawford and Lana Turner, were, in their heyday, as big a box-office draw as the gods, like Gable and Bogart. Their salaries were commensurate, too; money is always a tip-off to what Hollywood thinks of you. The roles of Hollywood's Golden Age goddesses may not have been any more complex or advanced than the roles offered today's top stars (although many of them were), but at least there were far more of them, and the characterizations, because they were designed to fulfill people's fantasies, meant something special to audiences.

The old studio system was responsible for many travesties, but most of the memorable movie goddesses, from Garbo and Dietrich through Gardner and Monroe, were creations of that system. The studio's stable of writers and directors and cinematographers and costume designers were allowed to work up intensely creative partnerships with performers. The studio machinery was geared up for the long run of an actor's career. Aging beauties were eased into more "realistic" roles.

Today, an actress who has passed unrecognized into her thirties stands almost no chance of making it, because in that age bracket the roles just aren't there for her to be discovered. And even the actresses who do achieve success in their twenties and thirties often find they've been put out to pasture later on. The vital female stars of only a decade or so ago, like Jill Clayburgh and Ellen Burstyn and Cicely Tyson, are, for all intents and purposes, in a state of involuntary semi-retirement from the movies. Like their younger counterparts, the ones without movie work, they reserve their occasional successes these days for the stage or TV. It's as if their movie careers never happened.

The free agency of the current post-studio-system era has not been kind to the creation of movie stars. Left to their own devices, many stars choose projects that are almost comically wrong for them (like Jane Fonda's spinster *gringa* in *Old Gringo,* or Dustin Hoffman as Sean Connery's son in *Family Business*). But male stars at least have a surplus of decent roles to fight over, since virtually all of the "important" movies, and most of the unimportant ones, are written expressly for them. With women, what's left after Meryl Streep goes shopping?

The movie business is increasingly being driven by the blockbuster mentality, and blockbusters are almost always action epics in which women are relegated to a status position somewhere between the hardware and the special effects. The true partnership in these films is between man and machine. The production costs are rising — *Total Recall* and *Die Hard 2,* for example, both reportedly around $60 million. At a time when foreign markets are becoming almost as lucrative as domestic ones, it makes commercial sense to stock these films with American stars who have international appeal. And that invariably means male action heroes. Don't count on seeing *Batwoman* any time soon (particularly after the smashing success of *Supergirl*).

For women in the movies, their heroism is reserved almost entirely for the emotional arena, where the triumphs are less photogenic — i.e., less saleable. Occasionally you get something like Sigourney Weaver as an intergalactic Mother Courage battling aliens, but most female action heroines are simply women recast in standard male scenarios, like the lady cops of *Blue Steel* and *Impulse.*

The scant supply of meaningful roles for women isn't only a product of the blockbuster mentality; it's equally linked to Hollywood's avoidance of what is disparagingly referred to as "women's issues."

The conflicts of contemporary women don't fit neatly into the standard Hollywood story lines, and in today's Hollywood, neatness counts. The disarray of modern relationships is confusing and threatening—that is to say, uncommercial—to studio heads. And these days, with the demise of most of the small independent companies, the studios are practically the only game in town. Since the new conflicts are not readily marketable, and the old conflicts, in a contemporary setting at least, are moldy, the studio solution has been to can the conflicts altogether.

On television, where projects can move into production faster and where there is less at stake commercially than in the movies, one is much more likely to see honest depictions of women's emotional lives, even the messier aspects; one is also much more likely to see, especially in the never-never land of the soaps, the kind of old-fashioned romantic scenarios that thrived in the forties and fifties. There's something for everyone, and if the TV shows are no good, there's still the great old romantic movies on view on cable TV, a spectral reminder of what once was.

☆

It's no accident that virtually the only movies to offer full-scale roles for women these days are the ones either set in the past, like *Enemies, a Love Story* and *Dangerous Liaisons* and *Driving Miss Daisy,* or else in some dream-time present, like *The Fabulous Baker Boys,* which draws on our romantic notions about the past as filtered through the movies. The pastness of these movies functions as a kind of shield from contemporary concerns, and yet, because many of them feature a real avidity for sexual and emotional conflict, they seem more alive, more in the present tense, than many of the contemporary movies. (*Enemies,* set in 1949, is a lot more vital than, say, the modern-day *Stanley & Iris* or *Stella,* both of which might have emerged from the thirties.)

The truly contemporary movies that attempt to show off "modern" conflicts often end up schizzy and retrograde. *Baby Boom* proffered an impossible fantasy; it said women could be CEOs and homemakers and land Mr. Right, all at the same time. *Working Girl* featured a heroine, Melanie Griffith's Tess, who was both ditz and whiz; she reaches the top because of her business smarts but also, although the film doesn't point it up, because (unbeknown to her) she sleeps with the right guy.

Of course, the weirdest hybrid fantasy around is the aforementioned *Pretty Woman.* If you bother to take this retooled *Pygmalion* seriously, you might balk at the dubiousness of its dual protagonists: Julia Roberts's Vivian, the happy hooker with a heart of gold, and Richard Gere's corporate raider with a heart of gold. Clichés old and new, both crocks. The film is a smash hit, but it's also provoked more vehemence from moviegoers I've heard from than any other current film I can recall. It confirms a dirty little truth: Retrograde fantasies still hold sway.

Vivian could have been something else besides a prostitute and the film would still have fulfilled its fairy-tale aspirations. And yet, in the current movie climate, it makes perfect sense that she is one. The film solves the problem of how to create a modern romantic relationship by making it strictly cash and carry (at first). The film is like a reversal of those gold-digger comedies where Marilyn Monroe cajoled the Corporate Man into loving his millions—in order, of course, to lavish them on her. In *Pretty Woman,* Vivian shames her john into looking beyond his millions (while still reaping their benefits). *Pretty Woman* functions as a warped Prince Charming fantasy for women while, for upscale men, it offers the reassuring life lesson that women aren't just after them for their money.

I don't mean to imply that actresses should only play "politically correct" parts. As a matter of fact, most roles worth playing are politically *in*correct. Who would argue with Jane Fonda's performance in *Klute?* Or, for that matter, with Julia Roberts's enchanting work in *Pretty Woman,* or Jennifer Jason Leigh's in *her* two current films? But the sudden influx of these roles is, I think, part of a long-term industry-wide retreat from feminist concerns. At the root of these concerns is the old male bugaboo: Can women be trusted—as business associates, as sex partners, wives? As equals? The answer usually takes the form these days of a brutal put-down. The implication of a film like *Pretty Woman* is that Vivian is a hooker not because of degraded economic necessity but because she chooses to be one—because she *deserves* to be one.

☆

In the immediate post–World War II era, women who had entered the work force during the war found themselves cast out and replaced by returning veterans. Hollywood responded to the problem by concocting fantasy goddesses—the pneumatic, walking, talking pinups who reached their apotheosis in Marilyn Monroe. Their cheesecake glamour, totally without threat, was a kind of antidote to the anxieties of the times.

In today's sexually confused society, Hollywood's response to feminism can't be as blithely concocted as in those va-va-va-voom days. As a result, there are very few, if any, "pure" sex sirens on screen today, certainly none who are major stars (Madonna probably comes closest). Male stars, because their appeal is more simplified and comprehensible, have even taken over the pinup function from women. The latest films of Mel Gibson and Tom Cruise and Eddie Murphy practically dispense with female costars altogether. They're self-infatuated swoon-a-thons.

☆

The dynamism of many of Hollywood's legendary actresses, like Bette Davis and Katharine Hepburn and Barbara Stanwyck, often carried a threat even when their roles didn't. And it's often been the case in the past that men, more so than women, responded to these stars. Men don't usually go for the ladylike types; paradoxically, they seem to want more of a challenge from their female stars than do the women in the audience.

But the only dynamic, threatening women in the movies right now are the crazies. Their conflicts may develop from a realistic base, like Glenn Close's spurned avenger in *Fatal Attraction* or Kathleen Turner's miserably unhappy wife in *The War of the Roses,* but invariably these characters spin off into a self-immolating, horror-flick rage. Even a "role-model" heroine like Sigourney Weaver's Dian Fossey in *Gorillas in the Mist* is made to seem inhumanly obsessed with her mission. Her heroism comes across as lunacy.

☆

Everybody recognizes that the movies reflect shifting attitudes in society, but that doesn't mean that those attitudes automatically show up in the movies. At least not right away. There's a built-in time lag in the way Hollywood confronts social upheavals — look at how long it took to get Vietnam on the screen — and never more so than in these dog days of the bottom line. Hollywood's solution to the "woman problem" may yet result in a compensatory avalanche of strong, complex, smart, funny female portrayals. In the meantime, this waiting game is excruciating.

Los Angeles Times, June 3, 1990

ON VIOLENCE

Roger Ebert

More than anything else, the American movie audience loves violence. This is a fact of life. Comedies are fun and everybody approves of family films, but if a Hollywood studio wants to pull down a surefire $20-million weekend, what it takes is blood and gore, gunfire and car chases, and new twists on sadistic mayhem.

Some people consider the Fourth of July holiday the most typical of all American holidays (I prefer Thanksgiving, but realize I am hopelessly idealistic). In backyards and city parks and on beaches from coast to coast, we observe our national birthday with loud bangs and explosions and thunderous whistling rockets that send showers of fire floating through the sky. At the end of the day the nation is minus a few eyes and fingers, but what a small price to pay for so much noise!

Fireworks, alas, are only tolerated around the Fourth. The rest of the year, we indulge our passion for mayhem by going to the movies. In the summer of 1990, for example, millions of moviegoers thrilled to *RoboCop 2,* a mediocre movie distinguished by:

- A twelve-year-old boy who uses all of the usual four-letter words and kills people with machine guns.
- An operation in which a man's brain is taken from his skull in gory detail. First a saw is used to cut through the bone, then the top of the brain is popped off by a surgeon who stands holding it, so we can get a good look.
- The brain is installed in a killer robot, which engages in a fight to the death with the "good" RoboCop, who eventually can kill it only by tearing open the mechanical braincase, pulling out the living gray matter, and smashing it on the pavement.

RoboCop 2 is not one of the great violent movies, but it will do for the audiences who have worked their way through *Total Recall.* Then there is *Die Hard 2,* which is relatively restrained in its violence — apart from the villain who is squashed on a conveyor belt and another who is sucked into the jet engine of a Boeing 747 and sprayed all over the side of the plane. Another summer offering, *Dick Tracy,* did surprisingly well, considering it contained no four-letter words and no realistic violence. In the summer of 1990, *that* was risky filmmaking.

Critics such as myself, paid to evaluate the new movies, fall back on a generic approach. We are more likely to approve of movies that supply violence with humor and style. I enjoyed *Total Recall,* for example, for such reasons as the movie's visionary special effects, its cleverness, and the strength of Arnold Schwarzenegger's performance. I appreciated the good character performances and exciting story of *Die Hard 2.* I disliked *RoboCop 2* because of its messy plot, its stupid characters, and the truly shocking spectacle of that foul-mouthed little villain (is nothing sacred?).

Some violent movies can be exhilarating. I've enjoyed the *Lethal Weapon, Mad Max,* and *Indiana Jones* movies. When I get letters from readers protesting a movie I've recommended, however, it is almost never a mass-market Hollywood bloodbath. I doubt if I get a single letter questioning my recommendation of *Total Recall,* but there was a stack on the desk from people who were appalled by *The Cook, the Thief, His Wife and Her Lover.*

That's partly because the people going to see *The Cook* are mostly art-film lovers, not hardened to the conventional levels of violence on the screen. It's also because the violence in *The Cook* has a psychological realism that's lacking in mass-market gore. There's a certain lack of reality about what happens to the victims in *RoboCop 2.* They're ducks in a shooting gallery, and after they're dead the movie has no further interest in them.

The mainstream movie audience is not interested in movies like *The Cook,* which uses violence because it *wants* to disturb the audience. The big-time violent films work by making the violence abstract and human lives meaningless. Characters are introduced for no other reason than so they can experience sensational deaths. They're picked off as casually as the little computerized villains in Nintendo games. The *fact* of the loss of life, which used to be shocking in the movies, is now no longer even noted. It is the *manner* that counts.

It is routine for editorial writers to be pious about this bloodshed on the screen, and for citizens' groups to decry the violence. But nobody is listening. There is still a censorious lobby against sex in America, but violence is a lost cause. It provides the very building blocks of our national entertainment machine. The movies and television could not exist without relying on stories about people killing each other. Many teenagers will not sit still for anything else. Violent movies do not have to be as carefully written, as intelligently constructed, or as lovingly photographed as other kinds. They can be assembled out of elaborate stunt sequences, and in many cases the stunt and explosion and car chase experts are consulted on a shot-by-shot basis.

I see all the movies, and so I am a little hardened. Like the typical moviegoer, I can distance myself from this stuff. When the guy went into the jet engine, I wasn't particularly appalled; I could see it coming from the setup earlier in the scene. It was inevitable. When they pounded the living brain matter against the sidewalk in *RoboCop 2,* I was appalled, however. Hadn't seen *that* before.

And when they let the little kid use all those four-letter words, it seemed to me that they'd broken an unwritten rule. They'd violated a taste barrier that even the most cynical of Hollywood movies had respected up until then — the notion that kids are supposed to be protected from the vile ugliness of life. But what the heck! Kids see these movies on video anyway, don't they? Might as well give them someone to identify with.

When I was a teenager, we went to the movies to see how adults lived. Now kids go to the movies to see how they die. Is Hollywood creating this universe of blood and doom? No, it's supplying a product for which there is a great national affection. And our anarchy is being unleashed on the rest of the world. Is there an answer? Of course there is — an obvious one. We must gather the children and womenfolk and the wise books of our civilization, and go to the caves in the wilderness, and wait there for the coming of a gentler age.

Chicago Sun-Times, July 1, 1990

DANCES WITH WOLVES

Joseph Gelmis

Add *Dances with Wolves* to the list of major Hollywood westerns that have humanized the Native American. It's a very short list — consisting of John Ford's elegiac *Cheyenne Autumn,* Arthur Penn's satirical *Little Big Man,* and a handful of others we can argue about.

The Sioux tribe in *Dances with Wolves* is a sympathetic extended family, like yours or mine—but more idealized, less neurotic. They treat each other with affection and respect. They have a sense of humor. They cherish the land, honor tradition, are at peace with themselves—though not with their enemy, the Pawnees, a bloodthirsty people.

But times are changing. The South is about to lose the war and America is preparing to start west in earnest, to fulfill its Manifest Destiny. The Sioux medicine man—whose responsibility is to preserve the links with the tribe's past and contemplate its future—is justifiably concerned about white men: Will they come in great numbers, and what kind of people are they?

If all *Dances with Wolves* achieved was to allow us to take that leap of the imagination that puts us into a Native American's skin, it would be a commendable effort. But it's much more than good intentions: It's good moviemaking.

Dances with Wolves is an exhilarating adventure in a spectacular western landscape. Majestic vistas filmed on location in South Dakota play a featured role. The spiritual grandeur of the wilderness counterpoints and gives purpose to an intimate drama of a Union Army officer who turns Indian.

His conversion, accompanied by a rousing muscular-yet-melancholic John Barry score, takes place in the course of an exciting buffalo hunt and battles sufficiently ferocious to satisfy any lust for action—so don't assume it's boring, just because it's socially significant.

Another thing that makes *Dances with Wolves* satisfying is that it's a victory—not for the Sioux, who were eventually driven off their land, but for the handsome leading man who felt compelled to tell this story, who used his muscle as a star to get the movie made and then, as a first-time director, did a fine job of putting it on screen with the support of a splendid Native American cast, who speak the authentic Lakota language of the Sioux (translated in subtitles).

I've never been a Kevin Costner fan, until now. He seemed bland, even in his most popular roles, in *Field of Dreams, Bull Durham,* and *The Untouchables.* So far as I could see, he had been typecast as a virile, handsome, essentially virtuous kind of guy—a likable but uninspired corny throwback to the small-town hero of the pre–World War II era.

Now, in *Dances with Wolves,* that matter-of-fact underplaying, and that Middle American nondescriptness, has a dramatic weight I've never felt in him before. Costner plays Lt. John Dunbar, a hero of the

Civil War who asks to be posted to the frontier, where he hopes to find beauty and serenity in the wilderness. Because he is sensitive, as well as an honorable person, he discovers that he has more in common with the Sioux Indians than with white civilization.

Costner is outstanding. He speaks on the sound track the flat, matter-of-fact observations recorded by Dunbar in his journal. He does his own stunts, including bareback riding during the buffalo hunt. And he adds a gentle comic note by playing Dunbar as a slight klutz, as well as a mensch.

Dunbar is an ambiguous character — a Zen figure whose behavior is an unpremeditated act in response to circumstances. His heroic deed in Tennessee, which gets this movie moving, was actually a suicide attempt that had the unexpected effect of rallying the demoralized Union troops into winning a battle. He is monosyllabic, like Gary Cooper. He doesn't analyze. His reticence automatically irritates some people — such as the unhinged commanding officer (a memorable degenerate, created by Maury Chaykin) at the outpost, which is the jumping-off place for his trek into the wilderness.

Reporting to his post, Dunbar finds it deserted. And here we get the first evidence of where the star-director — and screenwriter Michael Blake — are taking us. The post is a filthy pigsty: The white men who couldn't cope left their piece of the wilderness a polluted junk heap.

Dunbar cleans it up, befriends a wolf, makes himself useful to the local Sioux tribe, saves a boy from being trampled by a buffalo, falls in love with a white woman who lives with the tribe and is the widow of a dead brave.

The role of this white woman in the tribe is vital to our feelings about the Sioux. In flashback, we see her as a child escaping a Pawnee attack on her homesteading family. Taken in by the humane Sioux, she is raised as a member of the medicine man's family. She gets involved with Dunbar, reluctantly, as an interpreter.

Mary McDonnell brings a pathos and, eventually, a believable passion to the film as this woman, Stands with a Fist. And Graham Greene, as Kicking Bird, the medicine man who is her adoptive father, gives a transcendent performance of one of nature's noblemen, a guy with power who uses it wisely.

Dances with Wolves is very long, at three hours, but not too long — it takes the time to tell its story properly. It makes the point, possibly too simplistically, that the Union Army couldn't distinguish between good and bad Indians and was barbarous and cruel. But that's just turning eighty-five years of cinema stereotypes inside out, and it's OK with me—as politics and as moviemaking.

Newsday, November 9, 1990

DANCES WITH WOLVES

Owen Gleiberman

If you're in the mood to see a leisurely, three-hour hippie western about a Union soldier who drops out of the Civil War, joins a tribe of noble and reverent Sioux, and comes to see that the Indians are In Touch With Life in a way that white men aren't, you could probably do worse than Kevin Costner's *Dances with Wolves.* Costner is the director, coproducer, and star of this beautiful and soft-headed frontier epic, which looks at Native Americans through New Age–colored glasses.

Stepping behind the camera for the first time, Costner proves a modest craftsman with a knack for expansive, calendar-art imagery. *Dances with Wolves* has some genuine visual treats: awesomely clear skies dotted with thick, almost tactile clouds; explosive purple sunsets; a scene in which the Indians spot a thundering mass of buffalo from afar (at first, it resembles a swarm of insects) and then, with arrows poised, cruise through the dusty stampede on horseback. This last scene has a fairy-tale grandeur: For a few moments, we seem to be entering the American frontier of our dreams, a setting at once splendid and terrifying, full of forces one can negotiate but never tame.

For all that, Costner isn't quite a filmmaker. Working from a script by Michael Blake, who adapted his own novel, he comes up with a ploddingly "mythic" story that never succeeds in portraying the Indians as full-fledged human beings. This is a dramatic shortcoming, to be sure, but it's also a case of too many good intentions gumming up the works.

Costner's character, Lt. John Dunbar, is a beatific oddball who is offered his military assignment of choice. He elects to man the most remote outpost possible, and when he gets there he discovers he's a garrison of one. But that's all right by him, since he's looking to *bond*—with the frontier, the animals, and, finally, the stern Sioux warriors who begin showing up at his cabin. Costner's smartest decision as a director was to let the Indian actors—many of them native Sioux—speak in their original Lakota and Pawnee tongues, with English subtitles. The languages are full of delicate, musical consonants that draw you directly to the speaker, and it's easy to understand why Dunbar is enchanted.

For the audience, though, it's not enough to watch Dunbar learn the Sioux languages, or get christened with one of the Indians' somberly descriptive names (they start calling him "Dances with Wolves" because of his fondness for cavorting happily with his pet wolf), or offer to join his new comrades on the warpath. We've got to understand his emotional relationships with these people. And that's what's missing from the movie. Aside from the tribe's wise and soulful religious leader (Floyd Red Crow Westerman), the only character with whom Dunbar forges a convincing friendship is Stands with a Fist (Mary McDonnell), a white woman who was abducted as a young girl and raised as an Indian.

When these two Caucasians fall in love, it has the unfortunate effect of dehumanizing the Sioux. The Indian actors are wonderful to look at, but couldn't some of them have played characters who were selfish, angry, egotistical? Couldn't they have had a few *complications?* Things seemed a lot more advanced during the late seventies, when Native American actors like Will Sampson and Chief Dan George played men with quirky depths. Essentially, *Dances with Wolves* is *Robinson Crusoe* with a tribeful of Fridays. The Indians come off as photogenic saints, which is almost as patronizing as the "we smokum peace pipe" clichés Costner is trying to undo.

What's more, the movie is very, very long. *Dances with Wolves* isn't exactly *Kevin's Gate,* but you feel every minute of the three hours. That's because there's no texture to the storytelling. Costner has made an earnest but hollow epic, a fable about brotherhood that stirs the eye and (occasionally) the mind, but never the soul.

Entertainment Weekly, November 16, 1990

THELMA & LOUISE

Richard Schickel

It is "the first movie I've ever seen which told the downright truth," says Mary Lucey, a lesbian activist in Los Angeles.

It is a "paean to transformative violence . . . an explicit fascist theme," writes social commentator John Leo, who went out prospecting for a column in *U.S. News and World Report* and discovered a mother lode of fool's gold.

It is, according to Cathy Bell, a Houston environmental communications specialist who was once married to "a redneck control freak" and found the courage to dump him after a liberating weekend trip with a girlfriend, "like seeing my life played before my eyes."

"It justifies armed robbery, manslaughter and chronic drunken driving as exercises in consciousness raising," charges New York *Daily News* columnist Richard Johnson, who also finds it "degrading to men, with pathetic stereotypes of testosterone-crazed behavior" and half-seriously proposes a ban on it.

It is, according to *Miami Herald* movie reviewer Bill Cosford, "a butt-kicking feminist manifesto . . . which sweeps you along for the ride." No, says Sheila Benson, a *Los Angeles Times* film critic, it is a betrayal of feminism, which, as she understands it, "has to do with responsibility, equality, sensitivity, understanding—not revenge, retribution or sadistic behavior."

Whole lot of heavy thinking going on out there. Some pretty heavy journalistic breathing too. Hard to believe that the occasion for this heated exercise in moral philosophy and sociological big-think is a modest and, at its most basic level, very enjoyable little movie called *Thelma & Louise,* which is so far a moderate commercial success. It has earned about $20 million in its first three and a half weeks of release—less than a muscular big-boy movie like *Robin Hood* or *Terminator 2: Judgment Day* could expect to make on its first weekend.

No matter. *Thelma & Louise* is a movie whose scenes and themes lend themselves to provocative discussions. What business it's doing is in all the right places—the big cities and college towns where opinion makers are ever on the alert for something to make an opinion about. For their purposes, this movie is a natural. In the most literal sense of the word. For the picture has a curiously unself-conscious manner about it, an air of not being completely aware of its own subtexts or largest intentions, of being innocently open to interpretation, appropriate and otherwise.

This, indeed, is its salient redeeming quality. If it were as certain — and as clumsy — about what it was up to as its more virulent critics think it is, it might easily have been as overbearing — and as deadly — as some of their interpretations are. It is not, though, and anyone with a sense of recent film history can see *Thelma & Louise* in the honorable line of movies whose makers, without quite knowing what they were doing, sank a drill into what appeared to be familiar American soil and found that they had somehow tapped into a wild-rushing subterranean stream of inchoate outrage and deranged violence. *Bonnie and Clyde* and *Easy Rider, Dirty Harry* and *Fatal Attraction* — all these movies began as attempts to vary and freshen traditional generic themes but ended up taking their creators, and their audiences, on trips much deeper, darker, more disturbing than anyone imagined they were going to make.

These are not the big-budget movies that solemnly announce the importance of their subject matter and often totter off into oblivion clutching a Best Picture Oscar — emotional irrelevancy's consolation prize. The true genre-bending films are less pretentious, less carefully calculated entertainments that may have only a hazy idea of their objectives. And (best thing about them, really) they have a way of driving some people — the ones who think movies ought to be a realistic medium or an ideologically correct one — crazy.

Consciously or not, these films tend to serve as expressions of the values or confusions jangling around in their society, or occasionally as springboards for earnest discussions of them. At a time when moral discourse has been reduced to the size of a sound bite and rapid social change has everyone on edge, the messages conveyed in even the most frolicking of these movies stir peculiar passions. Such films often have an astonishing afterlife, not only in popular memory but as artifacts that vividly define their times.

These times, in movies as in American society, seem defined by perilous, off-balance relationships between men and women. The year's two top box-office winners, *The Silence of the Lambs* and *Sleeping with the Enemy,* dramatize the judicious revenge that a woman takes on a brutalizing man. In another new film, Alan Rudolph's dour and inept *Mortal Thoughts,* two women (Demi Moore and Glenne Headly) kill a hateful husband (Bruce Willis, who lately can't seem to get a break). The trend straddles oceans too: Luc Besson's stylish French thriller, *La Femme Nikita,* is about a woman (Anne Parillaud) whose romantic life conflicts with her career as an espionage hit person.

The movie summer promises more women who take their life — and a gun — in their own hands. Kathleen Turner will play a tough private eye in *V. I. Warshawski.* Even the budget-bustin' action-adventure *Terminator 2* offers a strong female figure: Linda Hamilton as an embattled mother powerful enough to square off alongside Arnold Schwarzenegger.

The success of these films as popular entertainment and as clues to the zeitgeist remains to be determined. But they will have to go far to match *Thelma & Louise.* "Ten years from now it will be seen as a turning point," says Peter Keough, film editor of the *Boston Phoenix.*

He is more than likely right. Movies achieve this kind of historic stature not because they offer a particularly acute portrayal of the way we live now or because they summarize with nuanced accuracy the opposing positions in an often flatulent quasi-political debate. They work because somehow they worm their way into our collective dreamscape, retrieve the anxious images they find there, and then splash them across the big screen in dramatically heightened form.

That's why most of the questions raised about *Thelma & Louise* seem so weirdly inappropriate. Does it offer suitable "role models"? Is the "violence" its heroines mete out to their tormentors really "empowering" to women, or does it represent a feckless sacrifice of the high moral ground? Is its indiscriminate "male bashing" grossly unfair to an entire sex?

Should we care? As Barbara Bunker, who teaches psychology at the State University of New York, Buffalo, very sensibly notes, "It's a dramatic piece, not a [literal] description of what's going on in our society. It seems to me that drama is supposed to make things larger than life so you get the point." Agrees Regina Barreca, who teaches English at the University of Connecticut and is the author of *They Used to Call Me Snow White . . . but I Drifted,* a book about women and humor: "it has got to be seen not as a cultural representation but as a fairy tale." In other words, as a dream work, full of archetypes and exaggerations.

This does not mean that *Thelma & Louise* is or was ever meant to be a sweet dream, a comfortable, comforting movie like, say, *City Slickers.* "Screenplay idea," jotted Callie Khouri in her notebook one day in 1987: "Two women go on a crime spree." Khouri, whose first screenplay this is, had the notion that if a female couple were somehow forced by circumstances to take up the outlaw life, they would, under the suspenseful impress of life on the lam, undergo the same kind of bonding process—sweet, funny, appealing—that male protagonists customarily experience in this kind of movie. But she also seemed to sense that just because of its off-casting, it could have a jagged edginess that its models had long since lost.

Khouri's idea was, to borrow a term from old-time Hollywood writers, a nice little switcheroo—logical, easy to explain, and not too threatening in its originality. Moreover, the times were right for it. Everyone was complaining that there were too few good roles for women in American movies—especially roles that permitted their characters to make their own decisions, control their own destiny. In fact, according to Mimi Polk, *Thelma & Louise*'s producer, the movie did not "pitch well" to studio executives: "The script was full of subtlety that was lost in a two-sentence description." Polk feels, as well, that had she and her partner, Ridley Scott, proposed two male stars in the lead, they could have got a budget heftier than the $17.5 million they ultimately spent.

It is possible, of course, that the Suits were just as nervous about the story that Khouri developed as some of the film's latter-day critics have turned out to be. Hollywood is not, after all, the world capital of the new masculine sensibility.

Be that as it may, the movie, which Scott (*Alien, Blade Runner*) eventually decided to direct himself, starts out in a low, ingratiating gear. It looks like a "buddy romp," as Geena Davis, who plays Thelma, puts it. Thelma is married to a carpet salesman named Darryl, who represents everything stupid and stupefying about traditional masculinity, keeping Thelma in a state of near childish dependency. Her best pal, Louise (Susan Sarandon), lives with an oft traveling musician named Jimmy, who is nice but suffers from the other great modern male defect—a maddening inability to make permanent commitments. Both women feel more than entitled to shed their mates for a long weekend at a friend's vacation retreat.

On the way, they stop at a roadhouse for a drink. One of its resident lounge lizards mistakes Thelma's naive flirtatiousness for a come-on, follows her to the parking lot, and almost succeeds in raping her. Louise rescues her at gunpoint. Then, just as you are figuring that this is an unaccountably dark passage in an otherwise sunny film, Louise kills the would-be rapist. In cold blood. With malice aforethought, however briefly considered.

It is a remarkable mood swing, one of the few authentically daring narrative coups in the cautious recent history of American film. And it is by no means a carelessly considered one. "It was a goal to make that resonate throughout the film," according to Davis. It does, and it has a transforming effect on *Thelma & Louise*. It lifts it beyond the reach of gags like columnist Ellen Goodman's characterization of it as "a PMS movie, plain and simple." More important, it lifts it beyond the effective range of ideologically oriented criticism. "The violence I liked, in a way," says Sarandon, "because it is not premeditated. It is primal, and it doesn't solve anything."

It is also blessedly unexplained. In the aftermath of the killing, we do learn that something dreadful happened to Louise years ago. Obviously it was some kind of sexual assault, but she never reveals its exact nature. This, of course, runs counter to the conventions of popular culture. If this were the TV-rape-movie-of-the-month, a hysterical revelation of the exact nature of the abuse—especially if it were, say, gang rape or years of incest—would be obligatory in order to balance the moral scales.

Such an explanation would have quelled much of the "male bashing" criticism leveled at *Thelma & Louise.* But it would also have cheapened the movie in some measure, suggesting that some kinds of sexual violence grant their victims murderous entitlements while others do not. By leaving Louise's mystery intact, the film implies that all forms of sexual exploitation, great or small, are consequential and damaging.

Within the moral scheme of the movie, writer Khouri's choice of this particular crime as the motive for the women's "crime spree," instead of, say, grand theft—auto, has other advantages as well. For one thing, it ironically restores Thelma and Louise to equality with men—at least in one realm of action. Says Martha Nussbaum, a philosophy professor at Brown and an expert on women in antiquity: "I think the modern idea that women are gentle and sweet is parochial. Just look at Medea." The Greeks, Nussbaum suggests, understood that crimes are committed by those with the least access to power, which then, as now, included women. "As the ancients said, 'No force in nature is stronger than a woman wronged.'"

Or, perhaps, a woman who has had a taste of revenge and would like to gulp down more of it. Believing that no one is likely to accept their account of what happened in the parking lot, Thelma and Louise decide they have no choice but to make a run for the Mexican border. This long concluding passage of the film, rich in irony and ambiguities, is fueled dramatically by a slow, steady shift in their relationship. As Sarandon notes, Louise suffers "great remorse" about the murder.

"It doesn't change the world, and in the long run it doesn't serve to her advantage." Indeed, fear of her act's consequences slowly undoes her former take-charge capability. She gradually cedes leadership of their little expedition to Thelma — possibly because she sees that it can end only in tragedy, while Thelma can't see anything because she is having the time of her life.

It is Thelma who spots a really cute hitchhiker by the side of the road and decides she just has to have him. With him she has great sex for the first time in her life. To him — he's a convenience-store bandit — she loses all the getaway money that Louise had scraped together from her life savings. But what might have seemed yet another rape, this time of a more symbolic kind, turns out to be a fair exchange. The hitchhiker, using Thelma's hair dryer as a gun substitute, teaches her the tricks of his dubious trade; soon she is doing holdups. It is Thelma too who gets the drop on a cop who stops the two women for speeding, orders him into the trunk of his squad car, and gently warns him to be sweet to his wife, adding, "My husband wasn't sweet to me, and look how I turned out."

Literalists criticize Thelma's erotic awakening because, they say, it could not happen so soon after the trauma of near rape. Doubtless that would be true in circumstances less special than the ones the movie sets up. The point it's insisting on is that a sudden access of freedom is eroticizing as well as empowering.

By the same token, some representatives of the world's largest minority, the humor impaired, regard the women's response to an oil-tank trucker with whom they keep playing fender tag as excessive. Every time they encounter him, the guy proves by word, smirk, and obscene gesture that he's a chauvinist dinosaur. When he inquires if they're "ready to get serious," they reply encouragingly. What he doesn't know, of course, is that they're thinking metaphorically, with a little help from director Scott, with whose surrealistic reinvention of the West — one-third desert, one-third industrial wasteland, one-third unzoned strip development — this oil-truck rig fits right in. In Scott's eyes, and his heroines', it is a gigantic penis. And, yes, they are ready for that. Ready to blow it to smithereens with their little guns.

It is, as State University of New York, Buffalo's, psychologist Bunker says, "a fabulous movie dramatically, a catharsis for all those times you've taken something and couldn't give it back." But taken together with some of the women's other acts, does it represent an excessive response to the provocation? Sarandon insists not. She says the charge shows "what a straight, white male world movies traditionally occupy. This kind of scrutiny does not happen to *Raiders of the Lost Ark* or that Schwarzenegger thing [*Total Recall*] where he shoots a woman in the head and says, 'Consider that a divorce.'" Sarandon insists that all concerned spent a lot of time making sure *Thelma & Louise* didn't turn into "a bloodlust-revenge film." Certainly, compared with the typical male-action film, the violence here is spare and rather chastely staged.

But that's not really the issue. What people sense, particularly in Davis's performance, is that she is getting off on her newly discovered taste and talent for gun-slinging outlawry. It's a kick, not so very different from, maybe part and parcel of, her newly discovered pleasure in sex. This is something nice girls—nice people, nice movies— are not supposed to own up to, let alone speak of humorously. But as Bunker observes, violent assertiveness is "basically unrestrained expressiveness," and, let's be honest about it, we all enjoy our opportunities, all too rare in the real world, to partake of its pleasures.

The cost, though, is high. It is toward self-destruction that Thelma and Louise's road inevitably winds. For all the time they have been out there expressing themselves, a posse has been relentlessly closing in on them. By a pleasing irony, it is led by the only thoroughly nice guy in the picture, detective Hal Slocumbe (Harvey Keitel). A patient, sympathetic man, he is this myth's wise father figure. By the time Thelma and Louise finally see him, however, he is one of a small army of cops who have hemmed them in against the top of a sheer canyon wall. Hal advances toward them, arms outstretched, in a last-minute plea for reason.

Fat chance. The women eye him, eye the drop ahead of them, imagine a prison stretch, contemplate the last free choice available to them—life or death—and floor the accelerator, sailing off the cliff into the movie's concluding whiteout.

Unlike most of the plot points that have stirred debate, this one actually deserves it. Sure, everyone recognizes it as a straight steal from *Butch Cassidy and the Sundance Kid,* but what final meaning does it impose? Sarandon thinks it's "the least compromising ending. You built this whole film to have these people not settle anymore, and then you'd toss them back into the system?"

It's hard to find anyone who thinks the women should have turned themselves in. It is equally hard to find anyone who detects a note of triumph in their suicide. Novelist Alix Kates Shulman quotes La Pasionaria on this point: "It's better to die on your feet than live on your knees." But as Brooklyn Law School Professor Elizabeth Schneider points out, the message here is that "self-assertion and awakening lead to death." Or, as film scholar Annette Insdorf puts it, "When death is your only choice, how free are you?"

All of which is a way of saying, "Baby, you've still got a long way to go." As a way of saying that, seen in narrowly feminist terms, *Thelma & Louise* advances the women's movement only a few hesitant steps. But perhaps the film should not be looked at that way. Davis, for one, resents the connection: "Why, because it stars women, is this suddenly a feminist treatise, given the burden of representing all women?"

A good point. In its messy, likable way, *Thelma & Louise* is getting at even larger, more mysterious issues. Carol Clover, a film scholar at the University of California, Berkeley, says the movie is trying to study, among other topics, "the distance between men and women, the desire for each sex to separate itself." It also attempts to look at the opposite side of that coin: the increasingly dangerous ways in which the sexes come together. Novelist James Carroll wrote last week in the *New Republic* that "when men and women reduce each other to sexual objects, they take the first step toward beating each other up."

Since this movie demonstrates Clover's point, and since it places that point in a context that is satirically aware of the violent and depersonalizing traditions of our visual popular culture, it just may be that *Thelma & Louise* is in fact better than any of its exegetes have made it sound. It remains the most intriguing movie now in release. No other cheers one's argumentative spirit, stirs one's critical imagination, and awakens one's protective affection in quite the way *Thelma & Louise* does.

Time, June 24, 1991

THELMA & LOUISE

Sheila Benson

Call *Thelma & Louise* anything you want but please don't call it "feminism," as some writers are already doing. As I understand it, feminism has to do with responsibility, equality, sensitivity, understanding —

not revenge, retribution, or sadistic behavior. It's not *Butch Cassidy and the Sundance Kid* with women, either, although its actresses certainly exert an equal magnetism.

For all the sleekness of its production, for all the delicacy of the performances by Susan Sarandon (especially) and Geena Davis, for all of director Ridley Scott's visual improvements on Monument Valley, *Thelma & Louise* is high-toned *Smokey and the Bandit* with a downbeat ending and a woman at the wheel.

Heaven knows it aspires to more. Over and over, in the long-lens, supra-reality of its images, we're given hints that these women on the run are a modern-day Bonnie and Clyde. But see those weathered faces staring straight at the camera from behind a cracked and dusty window or a rotting door screen? Americana. Dorothea Lange. Outlaws on the run. As Susan Sarandon's Louise drives farther into the desert, the pioneer motif is unavoidable; her tied-down hat even suggests a covered-wagon bonnet.

I suspect there is a substantial audience that would welcome strong, smart women at the center of a movie. Sarandon and Davis have even played them, in *White Palace* and *The Accidental Tourist,* respectively. Those were stubborn women who held out for their own needs, not victims with no choice left but some specious idea of *freedom,* which in this case equals death.

You wouldn't even have to stack the deck, the way new screenwriter Callie Khouri has, and make all the men cartoons. As audiences have known from the days of Nick and Nora Charles, through Margo Channing and her Bill, Charlie Allnutt and his Rosie, and all the pictures Katharine Hepburn played with Spencer Tracy, sparks between equally matched characters are the best fireworks. But only the women are matched in *Thelma & Louise;* its men are pitiful.

Rather than being equals, the men are drawn for the express purpose of being toppled, fatally or otherwise, with the exception of Harvey Keitel, an Arkansas detective with a sometimes New York accent who's an absolute Greek chorus of empathy, and Michael Madsen, Louise's long-term boyfriend. Thelma's husband, a bullying, oppressive, philandering carpet salesman, is such a caricature, and so grotesquely overplayed, that audiences can't wait for him to get his. They don't have long to wait.

The rest reflect an awful contempt for all men. They're vile or sniveling, or, in the case of a rapist, both, and proud of it. There's a young stud-robber, with largely scatological small talk. A scuzzy, tongue-happy trucker, who may just be Red Sovine's Phantom 309, popping up mysteriously whenever the plot needs him. One FBI boss advises Thelma's husband: "Be nice to her on the phone . . . women love that shit." Incredulous looks all around.

So, they're impossible.

But they don't make it any easier for an audience with any conscience to fall in behind Thelma *or* Louise. Not Louise, whose secret past makes her shoot a man, not during an attempted rape, but just afterward, in his ugly moment of mouthy bravado. Or Thelma, whose eyes get all soft when the cute cowboy hitchhiker she's in bed with tells her he's a convenience-store bandit.

Thelma & Louise pushes bloody, sadistic, or explosive revenge for the evils men do: Shoot 'em, blow up their vehicle, or stuff them, whimpering, into the trunk of their car in the desert sun. Action like this is despicable: Why should it be any more acceptable when it's done by women? Because it's our "turn"?

No thank you.

Are we so starved for "strong" women's roles that this revenge, and the pell-mell, lunatic flight that follows, fits anyone's definition of strength, or even more peculiarly, of neofeminism? Louise coming unglued in the face of a problem like Lucy Ricardo, without Lucy's cunning?

Actually, *Thelma & Louise* has the same, simple good–evil equation as any Stallone movie. And as in those movies, nothing in *T&L* makes very good sense, emotionally or logically, or portrays how women would behave in these situations. How could Thelma—beaten and saved from a rape attempt by a murder at close range—beg to pick up a strange hitchhiker eighteen hours later because she likes the cut of his jeans? To write such perky bounce-back doesn't suggest resilience, it suggests that no one's home, emotionally. It's fine to have such characters, just don't be surprised if an audience resists seeing them as heroes.

And are we not supposed to notice that the crucial twist of the plot comes from screenwriter Khouri's bland acceptance of the oldest line in movies: that good sex validates a woman's life? Give her that—and today that means a room-wrecking sexual destruction derby—and she wakes up with a smile on her lips and her brain turned to cream of wheat.

Thelma, the moral midget who thinks of a package-store stick-up man as "an outlaw," is so blown away by her first orgasm that she leaves her outlaw in the same room with all the money Louise has in the world. (Louise has left it with her so that the movie won't end forty-five minutes sooner.) And, before she comes up with her terrific solution, to hold up a convenience store herself, Thelma wails, "I've *never* been lucky, not one time!" as though choice had nothing to do with her life. Must our heroines be unconscious as well as terminally dumb?

Well, nothing in *T&L* makes very much sense logically, either. If director Scott hadn't made it so highly stylized, so that the visuals of the movie revolved around a sole, turquoise convertible against the red sandstone of the desert, the story possibly could have been nudged into believability. They could have changed cars and gone to one of three sensible destinations: the cabin, back home, or the police station. It's understandable that the women might have panicked and left the scene of the murder, but flee to Mexico? The women outlaws escaping over the border? It doesn't seem quite to fit this day and age.

But *T&L* is not meant as a realistic film. It's Bigger Than That. You know that when each butte in the Monument Valley has its own concealed spotlight, or when, at night, Sarandon's vintage Thunderbird, lit from everywhere including its undercarriage, casts as warm a glow as a welcoming campfire. It's Ridley Scott's great visual images that made *Blade Runner* the most visually influential film of the 1980s, made *The Duellists* as irresistible as it was, and gave *Black Rain* its patent-leather gloss. None of these films, however, is noted for its personal stories or relationships.

So Scott is probably the ideal director for the last, supremely silly sequence, the women's leap "of faith." That whole, hyped-up chase sequence is the most bullying part of the movie. Having pushed its characters into a no-win situation, the filmmakers now cast their deaths as "freedom," when, in fact, their fate all along has been determined by men, not their own choice. Some feminism.

Los Angeles Times, May 31, 1991

THE DOCTOR

Kenneth Turan

If Giorgio Armani doesn't start making power suits out of camouflage material, he is missing a good bet, because successful professionals are fast becoming the most endangered on-screen species since Bambi's mother. First in *Regarding Henry,* now in *The Doctor,* we are invited to relish the spectacle of a hard-driving hotshot finding out that there is more to life than insensitively bludgeoning your way to the top.

Yet despite plot parallels that uncannily extend to even minor points, the surprisingly good news is that *The Doctor* is the opposite of *Regarding Henry* in almost every respect. More honest and more effectively acted and directed than its predecessor, it shows how far quality work can go in redeeming a plot that is as pat and predictable as they come.

Most of the credit for this must go to director Randa Haines and star William Hurt, who last collaborated on *Children of a Lesser God.* Clearly working in tandem here, they have made *The Doctor* a film that manages to be decent and sensitive for quite some time before finally succumbing to the inevitable dynamics of its plot and falling into the trough of sentimentality. After all, a film that accurately advertises itself as "A story about a surgeon who became an ordinary patient and then became an extraordinary doctor" can only escape its fate for so long.

When we first meet Dr. Jack MacKee (Hurt), fate is the last thing on his mind. A top heart and lung man, he is glimpsed in his glory, dominating his operating room like Daryl Gates dominates the LAPD. A brisk, no-nonsense workaholic who is prone to cracking wise and living by the tidy credo, "Get in, fix it, get out," he is filled with the inescapable knowledge of his own self-importance.

Palling around with an equally infantile practitioner (Mandy Patinkin) and openly mocking the only decent medical man he knows (Adam Arkin), Dr. MacKee is, in short, the classic Big Doctor, a picture of breezy macho arrogance who sees no danger on the horizon except the dread possibility of, perish the thought, personally caring about the condition of his patients.

Of course, the God of Fair Play, who seems to reside mainly in Hollywood, has quite another scenario in mind. After the most sinister cough this side of *Camille,* Dr. MacKee goes to visit a throat specialist (Wendy Crewson) who is if anything more implacable than he is. "Doctor," she says in a voice frigid enough to blight an entire orchard, "you have a growth."

Indeed he does, and you don't need any fancy diagnostic tools to guess (a) that it's malignant and (b) what will happen next. Dr. MacKee is about to take a radical change in status from being a lordly doctor to being a lowly patient, and the trip is going to change his view of both his life and his profession.

Schematic as this journey sounds (and in fact is), several factors combine to make it both involving and honorable. For one thing, unlike being shot in the head and not recognizing your wife, the experience of being a patient dehumanized by medical routine is a common one that most adults of a certain age can identify with, and that spine of reality is a crucial one.

Also, Robert Caswell's script (based on a nonfiction book by a doctor who had a similar experience, albeit at age seventy) makes the journey of redemption a fairly torturous one. Alienated from his sympathetic but frustrated wife (Christine Lahti) and resistant to the simplest acts of caring, Dr. MacKee fights to remain a colossal pain in the neck for a surprisingly long time, and that, too, adds some welcome grit to the proceedings.

And the filmmakers couldn't have made a better choice than William Hurt as the ever-abrasive Jack MacKee. Few actors are better at projecting distance and self-absorption than he is, and none of those can remain as likable while they're doing it. Though Hurt's Dr. MacKee has to crack rather too many jokes (courtesy, perhaps, of Disney executives worried about the film getting too serious for general audiences), he makes his character's change of heart as believable as circumstances allow.

Believability is also the keynote of the work of Randa Haines. In her hands, *The Doctor* becomes a study in evenhanded assurance, largely because by all appearances she has not only insisted on but achieved a high standard of believability from all her actors, not just Hurt. Scenes that would have come off as saccharine or pretentious in the hands of many another director have a welcome integrity because she would not have it any other way. There is a lot to forgive about the plotting of *The Doctor,* but acting and directing this satisfying make that absolution easier to do.

Los Angeles Times, July 24, 1991

ON MALE WEEPIES

Peter Rainer

The male weepie, a newly minted genre for the post-yuppie era, is in full flood.

Consider so far: In *Regarding Henry,* a crass, hotshot lawyer, played by Harrison Ford, is wounded in the head, suffers almost total amnesia, and, in his new life, realizes the error of his anything-for-success ways. He and his family end up making the supreme downwardly mobile sacrifice: They trade the Upper West Side for Greenwich Village.

William Hurt's crass, hotshot doctor in *The Doctor* literally gets a taste of his own medicine when he comes down with cancer of the larynx. His suffering is meant to tenderize him to the plight of others and make him a better healer.

In Mel Brooks's *Life Stinks,* a billionaire LA developer agrees on a bet to live as a moneyless vagrant for one month; in between clonking his fellow ne'er-do-wells, he gets a new lease on sensitivity. He drives off in his Rolls-Royce a wiser man.

In the current Michael J. Fox comedy *Doc Hollywood,* a hip Washington, D.C., surgical resident, on his way west to the nip-and-tuck Valhalla of Beverly Hills, detours in a small South Carolina town and learns to appreciate the corny pleasures of simple country life, as demonstrated by his repeatedly taking a huge porker out for a stroll.

In *Dying Young,* a well-to-do, highly educated cancer patient, played by Campbell Scott, finds true love in a seaside idyll with his down-to-earth, working-class nurse, played by Julia Roberts(!).

In *City Slickers,* three male friends led by Billy Crystal escape the upsets of their professional and personal lives and go on a cattle-drive vacation that turns into a consciousness-raiser on the prairie. Crystal even gets to deliver a calf.

Even the Terminator is weepy these days. In *Terminator 2: Judgment Day,* our Austrian-accented cyborg wonders why he can't cry and sacrifices himself so that others might live. The last words spoken about him have the ring of benediction: "If a terminator can learn the meaning of a human life, we can too."

☆

For a while, it looked as if the only men making a grand-scale impression in the movies were the psychos — the wiseguys in *GoodFellas* or Dr. Hannibal Lecter in *The Silence of the Lambs.* The men in the new male weepies are the reverse image of the psychos; they implode not from rage but from "sensitivity."

We've been primed for these guys for a while now. *Awakenings* was essentially a male weepie: a doctor–patient bonding movie between two afflicted men. *Dances with Wolves* was one too. It had many of the requisite requirements, including a martyred central male figure who chucks the cruelties of civilization for "the simpler life." Kevin Costner's Lieutenant Dunbar was a selfless sufferer — and we got to witness his selflessness in, by rough estimate, 469 adoring close-ups. Raging narcissism is the keystone of the male weepie.

The major precursor, however, is probably *Big,* where Tom Hanks played an eight-year-old in a grown-up's body. The film's measured, ungoofy style clued us in that it wasn't just a romp — it was a *parable.* It stumped for the spiritual benefits of being a child again. The new male weepies, keying into the current pop-psych-speak, are real big on "locating the child within yourself" — though most male execs don't seem to have any trouble locating that child. It's the humane adult they can't find.

In a male weepie like *Regarding Henry* or *T2,* the hero is led by a child to discover his innocence, and, in effect, becomes a child himself. This infantilization is basic to the genre, and inseparable from its narcissism. The alternative to the hard-driving, powermongering breadwinner is a kind of stunted, baffled, sexless creature. We've gone from Rambo to Rain Man.

Like most movie trends, the male weepie (the Meepie?) is a delayed reaction to long-term rumblings in society. It's actually a step behind: In popular culture now, the sort of male sensitivity training represented by these films has been muscled aside by the likes of Robert Bly (author of *Iron John*) and Sam Keen (*Fire in the Belly: On Being a Man*), patriarch worshipers who sponsor retreats where middle-class achievers huddle in tepees, grab their tom-toms, and get all atavistic.

Sometimes what's churning up the country never makes it into the movies at all; the studios, which thrive on formula, are scared off by anything they can't categorize. Hollywood conspicuously ignored feminist outrage in the seventies and eighties, in much the same way that Vietnam was ignored for many years. But in this age of the recession, the downturn of the well-to-do has a Depression-era sentimentality that Hollywood, and many film critics, find irresistible. These movies give everyone a chance to plump their virtuousness.

Hollywood is never so much Hollywood as when it's thumping for the simple, humane life — for everything it isn't. (May one presume that the producers of these films will follow the advice of their movies and devote the remainder of their lives to good works?) Since most of the big breadwinner roles still go to male stars, it makes sense that many of these actors would mainline the new sentimentality by sucking in their cheeks and looking bereft. (How aptly named is William Hurt!) It's the kind of socially conscious star trip that actors, and Oscar voters, adore.

The male weepie shares many of the same defining qualities as the female weepie, and it has the added commercial advantage these days of attracting a sizable female audience. Both genres are intimately keyed into middle-class values. Despair is usually recorded as a fall from affluence; the sanctity of home and hearth is nostalgically rendered; romantic transgressions are punished with a Puritan vigor. The tone of these films is often subdued and dewy, for that all-important "prestige" effect. Repeated close-ups of the trembling, suffering hero or heroine are stockpiled.

But there are also some important divergences between these two types of films. Unlike the female weepies, the male variants generally end on an upbeat. They push for change rather than a reconciliation to fate. They're *activist* weepies.

It should come as no great surprise that the women in these new movies are really no more invigorating or three-dimensional than in the usual Hollywood fare. Since the male weepie is essentially about the hero's narcissism, the wives and girlfriends appear primarily as helpers. They broker their men's newfound sensitivity. It's significant that very few of the male-female relationships in these films have a sexual edge. The women's ministrations are essentially motherly, as befitting their infantilized men. If the female weepie, with its cult of sacrifice, often reinforced the female audience's most masochistic side, the male weepie tells men not to worry if they fall from grace. Someone will still be there to tuck them in at night.

The dream of chucking it all for a simpler life is rampant right now among superannuated yuppies, but the simple life in these movies still looks pretty flashy. No one takes a real financial bath: That downgrade from West Side penthouse to Village townhouse in *Regarding Henry* is about as bad as it gets. This have-your-cake-and-eat-it-too fantasyland quality is typical of the male weepie: Just as what befalls the hero is often "accidental" (an unexpected affliction, an unplanned detour to South Carolina, and so on), so is the resolution equally fortuitous (the illness is stayed, the memory creeps back, justice prevails). The social background for these movies is rooted in Reagan-era, greed-is-good malfeasance, but the movies themselves have no social reality. Weepies rarely do. And so it's probably irrelevant to point out that, of course, fancy apartments in the Village cost a fortune, or that famous surgeons are not likely to get routine patient treatment in their own hospitals.

The hero's loss of traditional, career-related power in these films is accepted as a virtue. That's because power, as defined in movies like *The Doctor* and *Regarding Henry,* is perceived as a disease separating these men from their own best and most tender selves. It's a disease handed down from father to son: Both movies point up how the father's work ethic was instilled in the boy. (Hurt's character is the son of a doctor; the father of Ford's character cofounded his law firm.) The lawyer played by Harrison Ford is shown to be a conniving workaholic who chews out his daughter, carries on an affair, has gaudy, expensive tastes, and doesn't like showing affection in public (or, one presumes, in private). Why, he even *smokes.* The doctor drives around in a Mercedes, talks glibly to his patients on his car phone, and actively downplays the importance of a bedside manner. "A surgeon's job is to cut" is his credo.

The Doctor doesn't register how a surgeon's crassness, like a soldier's, might be his way of coping with all the bloodshed and lives lost. The lawyer in *Regarding Henry* is introduced to us chiseling a decrepit old man out of his medical benefits. What if instead we had been shown a crass, well-off, workaholic lawyer who was carrying on a fight for civil rights, or the homeless, or the environment? The implication in these movies is that, in the professional arena, absolute power corrupts absolutely. It's a convenient fantasy for a downwardly mobile era.

The psychosexual subtext of the greed-is-good eighties was that riches equaled virility. Lucre was the emollient of the soul. We passed through that decade as we might pass through a radioactive cloud, and now the most irradiated and soul-sick of its moneyed survivors—the shell-shocked, fallen-on-hard-times careerists—are starting to crowd our screens. In the new recessionary climate, the same Hollywood that used to glorify money and macho now glorifies their absence. In eighties terms, the men in these movies have been emasculated, but that's not how we're meant to view them. Instead, their weepiness is sugarcoated in moral superiority. In the guise of a new sensitivity, the male weepie is simply glamorizing the loss of power. Its heroes have the glossy, martyred look of sainthood.

Los Angeles Times, August 19, 1991

IN A FAMILY WAY

I n "prestige" movies, families are rarely just families. They symbolize everything that is rotting or wondrous about America. The Corleone family in the *Godfather* movies is a vast sprawl of corruption and retribution; the Jarretts in *Ordinary People* are clogged with the repressions of WASPdom; the knockabout mother-daughter duo in *Terms of Endearment,* set in the scrubbed suburban heartland, is a piece of nutbrain inspirationalism.

Whenever we *do* see traditional all-American homesteads in the movies now, the intended effect is usually savage-satiric (as in, for example, *The Stepfather*) or folksy-metaphysical (as in *Field of Dreams*). Television, particularly with its sitcoms, is the last bastion of unabashed "normalcy" for the American family. With its daisy chain of tell-all tabloid talk shows, television is also our national theater, our national fun house, of family catastrophe.

It comes as no surprise, then, that two of the films in this section, *Ordinary People* and *Terms of Endearment,* were accused of being tonier versions of television fare. (Along with *Kramer vs. Kramer,* they pioneered dysfunctional family chic.) To its detractors, *Ordinary People*'s problem-drama clichés about parents and their children were dipped in rosewater—Pachelbeled. The jokiness of *Terms of Endear-*

ment was regarded as new-style camouflage for old-style weepiness. To their supporters, these films brought out the grain and the varnish in those old TV problem-drama building blocks. They revealed the poignancy and the heartfelt nuttiness in the mundane.

The reception that greeted *The Godfather Part III* was particularly contentious because so many people had an emotional stake in the Corleones. They were our great mythological American family. For many of us who loved the first two *Godfather* movies, the Corleones may have felt as much a part of our lives as our own real families. And so the critical debate surrounding *The Godfather Part III* had the tang of a family quarrel. The movie's failures were regarded as blood betrayals; its successes were hailed as blessed events. Because the first two *Godfather* movies seemed to express all that was hallowed and horrible about the American family, and by extension the American dream, audiences for the new film thirsted for revelations. They craved some new clue to the national psyche, which the *Godfather* movies, more than any other American film epic, had convinced us was the twin of our own.

Whatever their scope or intentions, the family films in this chapter were employed by audiences on all sides as tribal therapy sessions.

Ordinary People

Richard Schickel

They *are* ordinary people, if by that one means that they enjoy conventional middle-class prosperity and adhere to traditional family values. If the problem that the Jarrett family faces — an adolescent son trying to recover from a mental breakdown signaled by a suicide attempt — is perhaps an extreme one, it is hardly unknown in bourgeois America. Nor are the tensions that have been moving for a long time beneath the surface of the Jarretts' existence — an inability to express genuine affection or even speak frankly — exactly exotic.

But let the catalog of what is ordinary about *Ordinary People* stop there. For the fact is that Robert Redford, directing his first film (based on Judith Guest's novel), has created an austere and delicate examination of the ways in which a likable family falters under pressure and struggles, with ambiguous results, to renew itself. This is not very show bizzy stuff, but for once, a movie star has used his power to create not light entertainment or a trendy political statement, but a work that addresses itself quietly and intelligently to issues everyone who attempts to raise children must face.

As this soberly paced film opens, a father and mother (Donald Sutherland and Mary Tyler Moore) are treading softly around their son Conrad (Timothy Hutton), full of false cheer and barely suppressed anxiety. He is excessively solicitous. She is too brisk. The boy is trying to take up the normal life that was broken off by the death of his brother in a boating accident for which he feels responsible, and by his subsequent stay in a mental hospital. School, the swimming team, girls — he would like to return to them all with a full heart. But he can only mime the old moves. His mind is clogged by guilts he cannot express to his family or, at first, to the psychiatrist (Judd Hirsch) to whom he reluctantly reports.

The film sounds like another earnest effort to popularize psychiatry. The power of *Ordinary People* does not lie in originality but in the way it observes behavior, its novelistic buildup of subtly characterizing details. One begins to see that the father's inarticulate patience represents a form of strength, that the mother's cheery orderliness is a mask for terror, that their son is fighting not just himself but an entire suburban society's reluctance to define, let alone accept, the responsibilities imposed by familial love. The deep desire to evade these responsibilities and the equally powerful imperative to fulfill them provide the movie's tension. They also supply the logic for a nuclear family's final explosion, which leaves one awash in powerful, and powerfully conflicting, emotions. No pat answers here.

☆

Redford's use of previously unexplored locations around Chicago gives the picture a fresh, honest look. He has also asked much of his actors, and they have all responded superbly, but it is within the Jarrett family that the biggest chances are taken. The dramatically risky stillness in Donald Sutherland's performance remains constant as he moves agonizingly from being a passive player to being an active force in reshaping his family's life. Mary Tyler Moore deserves some kind of award for her courage in exploring the coldness that can sometimes be found at the heart of those all-American girls she often plays. As for Timothy Hutton, son of the late Jim Hutton (*Walk, Don't Run*), he handles the sulks, rages, and panics of adolescence with a naturalness any parent will recognize. He is a nice boy, but there is a scary power in the emotional volatility of his age, and he shows how that can tyrannize the lives of those around him. There are no villains in Redford's work, only fallible human beings trying to work things out, failing and succeeding in touchingly recognizable ways. That is a rare enough viewpoint to find at the movies now, but coming from a man whose fame might have carried him far from the realm of *Ordinary People,* it seems little short of miraculous.

Time, September 22, 1980

ORDINARY PEOPLE

Stephen Schiff

You recognize the clean, buttoned-down world of *Ordinary People* at once. It's the world of Woody Allen's *Interiors,* a place where the love of life is smothered by repression and good taste, where well-heeled, well-meaning folk fall to pieces because they don't know how to feel. The ordinary people who reside there are ordinary only on the surface. What lies beneath the monotonous stability of their lives, of course, is emotion—*extra*ordinary, seething, and dangerous. And also, I'm afraid, poetic. Directing for the first time, Robert Redford begins his adaptation of Judith Guest's 1976 best-seller very poetically indeed: silent credits, white on black; then somber, sylvan autumn scenes. The music starts up: it's Pachelbel's "Canon in D"—a classical piece that everybody knows and likes. It used to be that if you wanted to be arty but weren't sure how, you'd put Beethoven's Fifth on the sound track. Nowadays, Beethoven is a movie joke; you use Pachelbel's "Canon" instead. As soon as we hear that plunky ostinato and see those shots of mournful trees shedding their colors, we know *we're* about to be smothered by repression and good taste along with the characters. Nothing's happened yet, and already the movie's trying to look like a masterpiece.

Judith Guest's novel had no such pretensions. Flat and clunky though it was, it worked: Once you got used to the strained psychology and the stiff "naturalism" of the dialogue, you could be swept along by the characters and their predicament. Guest was out to tell a story, not create a classic. Her setting is Lake Forest, Illinois, a prosperous suburb of Chicago, and her subject the disintegration of a very presentable WASP family. Cal Jarrett (played in the movie by Donald Sutherland) is a tax attorney; his wife, Beth (Mary Tyler Moore), a model citizen. There were once two sons—Buck, a likable, golden-haired athlete, and his younger brother, Conrad (Timothy Hutton)—but now there is only one. Buck was killed in a boating accident for which Conrad felt responsible, and shortly thereafter, the younger boy began to unravel: attempted suicide, hospitalization, electroshock therapy. When we first meet him, Conrad is struggling toward stability, fighting the turmoil aroused by his father's feigned cheeriness and his mother's inability to forgive him for his breakdown. And what fascinates Guest is that while Conrad yearns to be less singular—he's dying to be ordinary, invisible, a face in the crowd—his father, Cal, comes to hate being ordinary, comes to realize, in fact, that being ordinary means you don't allow yourself emotions or reflections or questions; it means you know who you aren't, not who you are. Guest has her earnest, poeticizing side, but at least she doesn't mess around with symbols or stylized comments on bourgeois life—or any of the other weighty devices that sink Alvin Sargent's screenplay.

Sargent, of course, is one of the contemporary cinema's great embalmers. If there's life or warmth or humanity wiggling around in a story, he'll inject it with rhetoric until it just lies there. Much of Guest's awkward dialogue has been transferred directly, or almost directly, to the screenplay, and it simply isn't movie dialogue. When it drips out of the actors' mouths, it sounds like those ghastly speeches in *Interiors,* the ones about how haunted by death everybody is. (It also sounds like the gruel Sargent cooked up for Al Pacino and Marthe Keller in *Bobby Deerfield*—remember Keller beckoning Pacino to "Come with the wind"?) In *Ordinary People,* Beth wants to get away from Conrad for a while. "Christmas in London would be like something out of Dickens," she flutters—is Beth trying to *sound* like Dickens? That's the sort of Guest dialogue that Sargent should have dropped; instead, he adds some solemn meaningfulness of his own. In one of Conrad's several attempts to break through and communicate with his mother (and these are among the film's best moments because you can feel the prickly tension between Timothy Hutton and Mary Tyler Moore), he starts babbling about a pigeon who used to perch on the family car. "That was the closest we ever came to having a pet," Conrad muses—yep, those mean-spirited Jarretts won't even buy their kid a dog. (In the novel, of course, the Jarretts would give Conrad anything.) And instead of dramatizing the sterility of suburban life, instead of letting it emerge through the characters and situations, Sargent fills the movie with—well, with sterility-of-suburban-life shots. In scene after scene, we watch poor Conrad blink and twitch and force himself to be affable while his mom and dad discuss the new mechanic at the garage and the sale at Marshall Field's. A cocktail-party scene that crackles with sexual tension in the novel is transformed into a series of peeps at middle-class emptiness, and it's edited in the most ponderous, unrevealing style imaginable: one meaningless social encounter per shot.

Does anybody need to be told yet again that bourgeois life mummifies people—or that madness can await those who fight the smugness and placidity? This was a favorite theme of the fifties, of course, and of the sixties, too—of the era of R. D. Laing and heiresses who became revolutionaries. Now it's hard to imagine what could make it seem worth exploring again, at least in the same old terms, with the same old lawyer husbands and pretty mommies and cocktail parties. Published in 1976, the novel doesn't feel dated because Guest is more interested in the psychology of its characters than in their milieu. But Redford's film could just as well take place twenty-five years ago, and even so, it's not half as trenchant as, say, *Rebel Without a Cause*. *Ordinary People* is utterly oblivious to rock 'n' roll, movies, drugs, politics, or even television. The only contemporary reference I can recall (apart from cars and clothes) is one made by Conrad in a session with his psychiatrist, Dr. Berger. Conrad says he'd like to be more like John-Boy Walton. But an eighteen-year-old whose idol—indeed, whose only contemporary cultural referent—is such a monument of youthful virtue is some kind of throwback, or else an idealization so dreamy as to beggar plausibility. In the old days, when a good, middle-class kid began to smother, he turned naughty and rebelled, and movies about rebellion could excite us, because the rebellion took such exhilarating forms—hot-rod races, rumbles, cross-country motorcycle trips, and the like. But the misunderstood kid of the eighties doesn't rebel, doesn't turn naughty. He remains a very, very good boy; he just slinks into the bathroom and slices his wrists. And so, instead of getting caught up in his liberating anger, all we can do is cluck over his plight—and raise our fists at that terrible middle class that could make such a sweet kid want to do himself in. Indeed, since the audience the film is intended for *is* that terrible middle class, the effect of *Ordinary People* is much the same as that of movies like *Guess*

Who's Coming to Dinner or *To Sir with Love*—it arouses white-liberal guilt.

The inhabitants of this movie—of this clean, expensive world—are WASPs. They live in their neat houses and wear their neat clothes and fill the gaps in their conversations with convivial small talk, lest emotion or pain seep in. But they're confused and benighted, poor things, and they don't know how to stop hurting one another. Fortunately, somewhere across town, there lives a wise Jew—the psychiatrist Berger (Judd Hirsch)—who can see into the WASPs' simple souls and dispense gnomic wisdom to them from his dilapidated office. Try as he may to impart a certain contemporary sizzle to his scenes with Timothy Hutton, and later with Donald Sutherland, Judd Hirsch can't defeat the hokiness of it all. His jaunty performance hints that sanity lies in the Jewish knack for taking things humorously, and that disaster awaits those who closet their feelings. But that hint should be enough, and when Sargent translates it into earnest, uplifting dialogue, and into scenes depicting big, curative breakthroughs, you feel as though you were peering through the cobwebs at some well-made *Playhouse 90* production.

Redford obviously likes these scenes—he's the WASP admiring Jewish warmth from afar—and on them he has lavished his most overt stylistic device. As Dr. Berger penetrates Conrad's pain, autumn passes into winter, the days grow shorter, and Berger's office gets darker and darker. By the time Conrad touches the source of his pain—and learns to like himself and even to win the heart of that cute new girl at school—Berger's office has become a shadow world where the phantoms of the subconscious can emerge and be recognized. This is a pretty touch, but elsewhere Redford's attempts to forge a style look tentative, half-baked. Much of the background is sketched in an oddly clipped manner; there are lots of short, choppily edited portraits of suburban *angst,* scenes that strain to be revealing but never show us anything new. Visually, Redford seems to be experimenting. Toward the beginning, he shows us all sorts of surfaces sliding by—trains, the sides of buses, walls—and you begin to think he's attempting some sort of statement on facades, or on superficiality, or maybe on walls—something. But it isn't long before he abandons the tactic. Like so many other things in this movie, it even begins to look like a mistake.

Redford may not yet know what he wants out of visual and narrative style, but he understands actors. And what gives *Ordinary People* the poignancy it has isn't Pachelbel or autumn leaves or truisms about showing your emotions — it's the performances of Timothy Hutton and Mary Tyler Moore. True, Donald Sutherland shows a lot of sensitivity toward Cal's weakness and passivity, but he doesn't give us anything else, and so we never see what it is that a tough, self-possessed woman like Beth sees in him — we never understand how their relationship might once have worked. Timothy Hutton, the son of the late Jim Hutton, handles sorrow and pain more convincingly. Although Redford has him doing an awful lot of neurasthenic shaking (and although his makeup during the first part of the film makes him look like a raccoon), Hutton has a sure, almost instinctual grasp of the ebbs and surges of adolescent despair — he plays Conrad with a lump in his throat.

Most remarkable of all, however, is Mary Tyler Moore, whose portrayal of a Lake Forest ice princess is so cool, brittle, and nasty that it borders on the perverse. By all rights, Beth should not seem a villain. Her inability to express emotion is a reflection of her son's, and because she's a hopeless case, the filmmakers would like us to pity her. But the ear-to-ear smile of Mary Tyler Moore is too familiar, too comfortable and practiced to seem the panoply of an Illinois housewife. It's a star's smile, intense and ferocious, and when we detect hatred or duplicity beneath it, it's so powerful that it comes to seem evil: the deceptive grin of a monster. This is a distortion, of course. Neither Guest nor Sargent and Redford ever meant Beth to be so remote and unsympathetic. But Moore's been telling interviewers recently that she wants to break out of the Mary Richards mold, wants to stop being America's sunshine girl. And that yearning has given her acting here a wicked vitality that you welcome, especially in so limp a film. The ironclad smile of a housewife — of an ordinary person — would surely crumble, or at best strain, under the pressure the Jarretts experience. But Mary Tyler Moore may smile, and smile, and be a villain.

Boston Phoenix, September 23, 1980

ON FAMILIES

Andrew Sarris

The weekly grind of movie reviewing sometimes prevents the reviewer from zeroing in on certain recurring themes and subtexts. I have been meaning to write something on the screen treatment of the family ever since *The Shining* came out to face very mixed critical and commercial reactions. Jack Nicholson's cartoonish villainy was singled out as particularly problematic in his ostensibly "loving" scenes with his son. I happened to be in Cannes when *The Shining* was released in New York, and when I finally saw the film I felt that many critics and viewers had missed the whole point. I am not suggesting that *The Shining* is completely successful. Tom Allen's genre-oriented review in the *Voice* was accurate as far as it went. *The Shining* is not truly scary in the conventional sense, and the truly minimal bloodletting is anticlimactic. Stanley Kubrick can be expected to undercut genre conventions whenever he can. Hence, he and his very talented scenarist Diane Johnson depart from Stephen King's source novel in order to kill off the handyman (Scatman Crothers), the only completely sympathetic character on the premises, and the only black character besides. This plot switch is a cool downer for most audiences, and typical of Kubrick's strategy of alienation.

But what I think really turns off audiences is the messy state of the family from the word go. Jack Nicholson and Shelley Duvall are so grotesquely mismatched as husband and wife that one would expect a child of this union to emerge monstrously as a matter of course. It can be argued that if one thinks too much about Nicholson and Duvall as husband and wife the credibility of the characters becomes suspect on any realistic level. As is so often the case with Kubrick, he seems to have lobotomized the pastness out of his personages so that the clinical laboriousness of the King novel has been supplanted by a cartoonlike lucidity, and psychology has been replaced by mythology.

Ultimately, *The Shining* makes no sense whatsoever except in terms of an Oedipal conflict to the death, putting a father of discernibly declining powers against a hateful wife and a hyperintuitive child. All the supernatural effects in the film serve as metaphors of the child's growing awareness of the father's murderous hatred. Kubrick's celebrated tracking shots pay off as they have never paid off before when we follow the child's exploration of the resort hotel's long corridors on an inexorably forward motion toward the two little girls murdered years ago by another maddened father. There it is. The son has come face to face with his father's hatred, and he can never turn back to an earlier innocence. He must continue moving forward into the labyrinth of his own magical powers until his father has been vanquished. Yet the very inevitability of the son's victory over the father destroys much of the suspense of the film as all that is left to watch is the intricate design of the triumph.

But I would be remiss at this late date if I did not marvel over one of the most brilliant sequences in the history of the cinema, and one that must be credited to Kubrick and Johnson, since it did not appear in the novel. It is the sequence in which Duvall comes upon the hundreds of pages typed up by Nicholson. The same line is repeated in many different typographical formations: "All work and no play makes Jack a dull boy." There is a double edge to the horror in this episode. On one side is the visual manifestation of every writer's nightmare about writer's block, and on the other is the enraging humiliation of being discovered in one's deception and perversion by a nagging authority figure. Between the banality of failure and maladjustment, and the horror of a hate-filled family, Kubrick and Johnson have challenged many comfortable assumptions about family feelings. Even people who make generation-gap jokes about the Andy Hardy family and Ozzie and Harriet and "Father Knows Best" still cling to the notions that deep down parents love their children and children love their parents, despite all the violent evidence to the contrary. In this context, *The Shining* would have been a more comforting horror film if the father-son conflict could have been blamed on the devil, or a mental illness, or a Freudian fury, or even a malignant invader from outer space. Instead, the family structure generates its own psychic poisons with just a little help from an exotic setting.

Actually, the family has been under siege on the screen for some time. No longer do the censors protect the alleged sanctity of the family with their strictures against filmic representations of painless divorce, joyful adultery, or even lustful marriage. For a long time, however, the commercial predominance of punk-and-kiddie movies tended to encourage scenarios with comparatively rootless protagonists suspended with romantic independence between childhood and parenthood. The most violent fantasies were endorsed as authentic expressions of a fashionably anarchic attitude. I have referred in previous columns to the divergence of taste between the cinema of gentility and the cinema of brutality, and I do not wish to pursue the implications of this divergence in the context of this column. I wish instead to place into context a group of films that seem to be finding favor with grown-up audiences at a time when the kiddies do not seem to have as many fivers in their jeans as they once did to see a *Jaws* or a *Star Wars* again and again and again.

What fascinates me about such "grown-up" films as *The Great Santini, Ordinary People, It's My Turn, Private Benjamin,* and *Resurrection* is the emotional response they can evoke by challenging the traditional sentiments of family life. I am fascinated also by the facility with which many critics can dismiss these films on supposedly aesthetic grounds. Even *Kramer vs. Kramer* gets sniped at on occasion by the cinema-as-energy crowd. It's just television, some people say. Well, I would answer, a lot of television is currently more interesting than a lot of cinema. As for the alleged inadequacies of the mise-en-scène in the "genteel" works, I would suggest that there is considerably more "miss" than "scene" in many of the "brutal" works. It is all a matter of balance. I like genre films as well as the next person, but not at the expense of intelligence. In the forties and fifties, genre films were closer to psychological and social reality than were the so-called significant films. In the seventies, however, genre films have lost a great deal of their sharpness by seeking to appeal to the increasingly jaded tastes of male adolescents. Consequently, a cultural vacuum has been created on the screen. I am not suggesting that the vacuum has been completely or even adequately filled by the genteel films I have mentioned. Nor am I, notorious romantic that I have always been, suddenly preaching the virtues of a New Naturalism. I am not even sure yet what is actually happening between movies and their audiences, but I would like to record some initial impressions for future reference.

There are very terrible relationships between daughters and fathers in *The Great Santini, Private Benjamin,* and *Resurrection,* but these relationships are obscured in each instance by the emotional domination of the screen by a star personality. Robert Duvall throws *The Great Santini* out of family focus by making his hawkish air-ace father and husband too explicit and uninhibited for Blythe Danner's warmly matriarchal mother. It is the Nicholson-Duvall problem in a more sentimental context. The Duvall-Danner marriage is too schematically dialectical to be believed, and the triumph of the mother's values in the son's personality is somewhat muddled by the guilt-ridden bathos over the father's death in action. Nonetheless, many people of my generation and beyond assured me that they were "wiped out" by *The Great Santini,* a film more for parents than for children.

The sequence everyone talks about in *Ordinary People* involves Mary Tyler Moore's disposal of her son's french toast down the garbage disposal. There is more genuine horror in that one gesture than in all the bloodletting in *Dressed to Kill.* But most audiences wait comfortably for the inevitable reconciliation between mother and son. It never comes. This alone makes *Ordinary People* one of the most audacious movies in recent years. The tragic headlines about Mary Tyler Moore's real-life son add a Pirandellian overcast to the proceedings, but there is no need for this morbid overkill. Every parent I encounter has been wiped out by *Ordinary People,* and almost every such parent has a similar horror story in his or her family. Much of *Ordinary People* is glib and simplistic, but the implacability of the alienation of Mary Tyler Moore's mother character from Timothy Hutton's suicidal son character is as commendably anti-cliché as anything I have seen on the screen in years. (I might add parenthetically that Robert Redford should not be disqualified as a director simply because his name does not end in a vowel, but then I have always felt that having garlic on one's breath is only incidental to the task of directing.)

What surprised me most about *Private Benjamin* is how ferociously antimale it is. Almost every critic quoted a Goldie Hawn line to the effect that she would have married Alan Bates in a second if she had been Jill Clayburgh in *An Unmarried Woman.* The implication of this line is that Hawn's character is a refreshingly antifeminist rebuke to the Jill Clayburgh character in both *An Unmarried Woman* and *It's My Turn.* But when I finally caught up with *Private Benjamin,* I was startled to discover that all the male characters in the film were overbearing, deceitful, unloving, uncaring, and thoroughly contemptible. Hawn, who has patterned her personality somewhat after that of the late Judy Holliday's, finds genuine rapport only with a few of her lower-class female buddies in the army. The men in her life are progressively disastrous to the point that she winds up at the altar socking her third-husband-to-be out of her life forever. The supposedly feminist Clayburgh is far more solicitous of the men in *her* life. Hence, whereas the Hawn character in *Private Benjamin* ends up hating and despising her father for his callous indifference, the Clayburgh character in *It's My Turn* ends up understanding her father's vulnerability and mortality. Yet the women in both films are united in their realization that they will have to make it through life without the support of their paterfamilias. Ellen Burstyn in *Resurrection* carries the discord between father and daughter to the grave and beyond before there is even a semblance of reconciliation.

A political commentator recently suggested that the American people in 1980 may be looking more for a mother figure than for a father figure in their choice for president. The signs on the screen indicate that the patriarchy may be crumbling even in the midst of an antifeminist backlash. In both politics and cinema it would seem that an unfulfilled need for nurturing is beginning to make itself felt as the myths of the family are dispelled on screen and off.

Village Voice, November 11, 1980

TERMS OF ENDEARMENT

Richard Schickel

The movie begins with anxious, ferocious Aurora Greenway (Shirley MacLaine) clambering up over the side of her baby's crib and hurling herself on the tot, hysterically convinced that she has only seconds to administer the kiss of life to her darling Emma and save her from crib death. Naturally, all she does is disturb a healthy infant's sleep. From this scene it is obvious that *Terms of Endearment* is a comedy.

The story ends, some three decades later, with the same mother and daughter (played from adolescence onward by Debra Winger) confronting the same issue, the possibility of the younger woman's premature death, this time a very realistic one, in a cancer ward. From this sequence it is clear that *Terms of Endearment* is a serious film that is trying to say something important about how people can triumph over the worst kinds of adversity.

Between that first intimation of mortality and the final acknowledgment of its certainty, Emma grows up to endure marriage with feckless, womanizing Flap Horton (Jeff Daniels) and have more children than they can afford on his itinerant teacher's pay. She manages to ignore the many opportunities life now offers to raise her feminist consciousness to that minimum daily level of awareness required for the modern woman's mental health (having an affair with the nice man down at the bank doesn't really count). This clearly means *Terms of Endearment* is a cautionary tract for the times, something Phil Donahue can really get behind.

But wait. What about uptight Aurora and that raffish former astronaut, Garrett Breedlove (Jack Nicholson, giving a joyously comic display of just the kind of wrong stuff that appalls and attracts her)? Merely thinking over the possibilities he presents takes some comical time. He has been living next door to Aurora for ten years before she hints that she might entertain a luncheon invitation from him. Five years later she actually accepts it. Thereupon a woman who once told an admirer not to worship her unless she deserved it plunges giddily into a relationship with a man she knows suffers that common cold of the male psyche, fear of commitment. This is, without question, the stuff of romantic comedy. Is that, finally, the way to describe this picture?

Well, no. And that, perhaps, spells trouble. According to Hollywood's favorite adage, it is impossible these days to sell a film successfully if it cannot be summarized in a single catchy line of ad copy. If this is true, then what are the guys over in marketing going to do with a movie that its own maker defines largely by negatives? "It was rarely 'Wouldn't it be great to do that?' but more often 'Better not do this,' " says director James L. Brooks, who shared creative credit for both "The Mary Tyler Moore Show" and "Taxi" on television and who spent four years adapting Larry McMurtry's novel to the screen. How, indeed, are they going to handle the writer–director's entirely accurate description of the way his film works: "There is never a moment in the picture that takes you to the next moment or the next place. You just arrive and it seems inevitable — I hope."

But not to worry. What may, at first, be a commercial inconvenience will surely, in the end, turn into an artistic coup. *Terms of Endearment* does work off the conventions that rule more ordinary movies, but only to enrich its own singular voice. Its quirky rhythms and veering emotional tones are very much its own, and they owe less to movie tradition than they do to a sense of how the law of unintended consequences pushes us ceaselessly through the years, permitting no pause for perspective. *Terms* comes to at least glancing terms with almost every problem a person is likely to encounter in life, but it really has only one important piece of business in hand: an examination and resolution, in comic terms, of the relationship between a mother and a daughter. Everything else is in effect a diversionary tactic, a way of placing this brilliantly devised and disguised core of concern within the context of lifelike randomness.

As Brooks sees them, his movie's mother and daughter are actually sisters under the skin, connected not just by kinship but by subtle parallels of emotions and experience. Aurora appears initially to be no more than that familiar figure of satire, the American Mom as American Nightmare, all coy snarls and fierce demureness, while Emma, protected only by a thin skin of perkiness, seems to be her victim. "You aren't special enough to overcome a bad marriage," Aurora snaps on the eve of Emma's wedding, voicing her own fears about what might happen if she ventured outside her perfectly tended Texas house and garden. "I am totally convinced that if you marry Flap Horton tomorrow you will ruin your life and make wretched your destiny," she adds. As always with Brooks, locution is character.

But when Emma moves out, Aurora discovers that her child has no corner on inappropriate males. After Flap takes a job in Des Moines ("You can't even fail locally," cries Aurora, whose contempt for her son-in-law is her one immutable, hilarious quality), a plaintive note creeps into her obsessive phone calls to her daughter. Parent is now becoming a dependent, in need of a confidante, especially with that astronaut orbiting around her.

This is a new role for Emma, but one that she is entirely up for. Her ability to cope with each new child and all of Flap's vagaries suggests that somehow even a so-so family life actually makes happy her destiny. If this were an ordinary comedy, that medium-size irony would have been enough to satisfy its creator and send the audience home happy. But Brooks has one more question in mind. Could these two find it in themselves to reverse this role reversal one more time and arrive at a balanced acceptance of each other? Emma's illness provides the occasion for that final adjustment. Inevitably her growing weakness draws the young woman back toward childish dependency, and the need to defend her daughter against suffering summons forth Aurora's old ferocity. Whether she is questioning empty medical pieties or keeping poor Flap shaped up ("One of the nicest qualities about you is that you always recognized your weaknesses; don't lose that quality when you need it most") or bullying the nurse into administering a delayed sedative, MacLaine achieves a kind of cracked greatness, climax to a brave, bravura performance. Winger has an uncanny instinct for inhabiting a role, for implying that she knows even more about the character than words permit.

But then there are no bad performances, no slack scenes, no inattention of any kind in *Terms of Endearment*. The impulse in praising a film for which there are almost no analogies is to define it by what it is not, but that is really not good enough. It deserves some blunt declaration of respect and unguarded affection. Therefore, these three: No film since Preston Sturges was a pup has so shrewdly appreciated the way the eccentric plays hide-and-seek with the respectable in the ordinary American landscape; no comedy since *Annie Hall* or *Manhattan* has so intelligently observed not just the way people live now but what's going on in the back of their minds; and finally, and in full knowledge that one may be doing the marketing department's job for them, it is the best movie of the year.

Time, November 28, 1983

TERMS OF ENDEARMENT

Pauline Kael

Sitting in the theatre where *Terms of Endearment* was being previewed, and listening to the sniffles and sobs of the audience that only a few minutes before had been laughing, I flashed back to *Penny Serenade* in 1941, the picture in which Irene Dunne and Cary Grant as a young married couple stood by helplessly as their little adopted daughter died. And I watched as, once again, the survivors overcame their pettiness and selfishness and showed the strength they had in them; they demonstrated their American middle-class (white) moral fiber. This is a real-life-tragedy movie that leaves you no choice but to find it irresistible. It's exactly the kind of bogus picture that will have people saying, "I saw myself in those characters." Of course they'll see themselves in *Terms of Endearment.* James L. Brooks, who directed it, guides the actors with both eyes on the audience.

He works this way in perfect sincerity. Brooks was one of the two collaborators who thought up "The Mary Tyler Moore Show," and he and three other fellows put "Taxi" together; as a writer-producer on those series (and others), he developed a sixth sense for what makes TV watchers laugh. An enthusiastic reviewer said of the characters in *Terms of Endearment,* "You would be happy to spend several more hours in their company." That's exactly how you feel about the best half-hour series shows. They're entertaining in a ran-

Aurora Greenway (Shirley Maclaine) and Emma Horton (Debra Winger) are a contentious mother-daughter duo in *Terms of Endearment*. (Photo courtesy of Paramount Pictures Corp.)

dom, eccentric way; you have no idea what will happen next. The acting has a comic-strip frame around it; it's stylized and comfy. The actors are out to please you and keep you coming back for more. And you want to like them. The characters they play represent our own notions of who or what we would be *if* (if we were snobs or buffoons, or whatever). Sometimes watching a character is like watching our alter ego going at a problem. Often the cleverest characters set themselves up for the line that demolishes them. (Of course, they're not really demolished: They continue to have lives after the commercial.)

In *Terms of Endearment,* which Brooks adapted from the 1975 Larry McMurtry novel, he keeps the audience giggling over the same kind of ramshackle comedy. Shirley MacLaine is all tics as Aurora Greenway, a snappish, compulsively neat widow tending her house and garden in the prosperous River Oaks section of Houston—a Southwestern Scarsdale. Aurora is a little dotty: In our first view of her, she's climbing into her sleeping infant's crib to make sure the baby hasn't died. Everything about her—her pert little expressions, her pinched-tight mouth and narrowed eyes, her standoffishness, and even the pair of devoted suitors who hang around for years—is quaint. This isn't meant as a putdown of Shirley MacLaine's performance; I don't know how else the role could be played. Aurora doesn't exist except as a pixie horror to string gags on. She's a cartoon: a rich skinflint with a blond dye job and pastel frills. Surely she's not meant to be believable? She's a TV-museum piece, like the characters in "Mary Hartman, Mary Hartman" or "Soap"; she's warped. And so is the pie-eyed lecher who's her next-door neighbor—a former astronaut named Garrett Breedlove, played by Jack Nicholson. (It's only in the world of TV comedy that characters *have* next-door neighbors.) Spanning thirty years in the lives of the cantankerous Aurora and her straightforward daughter, Emma—played from adolescence on by Debra Winger—the movie is one droll payoff after another, with Nicholson kept on the sidelines until Emma, married and with a child (and another on the way), moves to Iowa with her husband, and, after a time, Aurora and Garrett Breedlove have an affair.

It's a screwball, sitcom affair, but Brooks pulls some sleight of hand and "real feelings" come out of it. Aurora falls in love with Garrett the guzzler, but—in the psychiatric hand-me-down vernacular—he isn't ready to make a commitment. Aurora is, though, and the emotion she feels for him helps her become human; when tragic illness strikes her family, she shows her mettle. I think I hated *Terms of Endearment* the most when the grief-stricken Aurora embraces her longtime servant, Rosie (Betty R. King), who shares her misery. Greer Garson in her Mrs. Miniver drag was only a shade more noble. When

Aurora and Rosie hug each other—sisters under the skin—the audience is alerted that Aurora is really a good person, and from then on she becomes useful and considerate. As the Second World War movies taught us, the function of adversity is to build character.

All this retro-forties virtue piled on the cartoon underpinnings of TV comedy shows might seem utterly nuts if it weren't for Debra Winger. The movie is a Freudian story of role reversals between mother and daughter, told in a slaphappy style. Most of the time, Aurora is a vaudeville joke—she's the mother who's always phoning her daughter at the wrong moment. She refuses to attend her daughter's wedding, but phones her bright and very early the next morning. I didn't feel much love or any other connection between MacLaine's brittle Aurora and Winger's fluid Emma. They don't have the uncanny similarities—the vocal tricks, the syntax, the fleeting expressions—of real mothers and daughters. I'm not sure what Brooks meant to show us, but what comes across is Aurora as a parody of an anti-life monster and Emma as a natural woman—a life force. The two actresses might be playing in two different movies. Debra Winger—as she did in *Urban Cowboy* and *An Officer and a Gentleman*—gives you the feeling that she's completely realized on the screen. There's a capacity for delight that is always near the surface of her characters (and she never loses track of what turns them on). The adolescent Emma (in braces) has a husky, raucous voice and a low-down snorting laugh; this is not a standard ingenue. Winger heats up her traditional-woman role and makes it modern by her abandon. She floods the character. When Emma's two little sons give her a bad time and she fights with them, she's direct and all-out; she's totally involved in this power struggle with her kids, and they know it. While Aurora overgrooms even her backyard garden, and the flowering bushes look cramped and forced (they're as contorted as the little statues stuck among them), Emma lives in the disorder of three children, dilapidated houses, not enough money, and a college-English-teacher husband (Jeff Daniels) who's having an affair with a graduate student. The predictions that Aurora makes when she tries to talk Emma out of marrying the handsome lunkhead—he's like a big floppy stuffed animal—turn out to be accurate, but what Aurora doesn't foresee is that Emma will be fulfilled in the marriage and the kids. Emma thrives on the semicontrolled chaos of family life; she accepts messes—life is messes. All this is in Debra Winger's performance; she's incredibly vivid, and she has fresh details in her scenes—details like spotting a zit on her husband's shoulder while she's lying in bed next to him, talking to her mother on the phone. But Emma has been made too heartbreakingly wonderful. She's an earth mother, of course, with some sort of supernal understanding of Aurora, and when she has her third child she gives birth to her mother — her little girl is a tiny ringer for Aurora. The way that Emma is presented she's a glorified ordinary woman — a slob angel.

Brooks does some cramping and forcing of his own when he cross-cuts between Aurora's first date with the astronaut and Emma's extramarital romance with a timid bank officer (John Lithgow, as a jumbo-size shrinking violet). The two relationships may be vaguely parallel, but they take place in different time frames, and the film cuts back and forth between actions that are a few minutes apart and actions that are days or weeks apart. This is the clumsiest patch of the movie, although there are other sequences that don't come off — such as a trip to New York that Emma takes. And there are characters who don't come off — such as those perennial suitors, who seem to follow Aurora around just so she can be bossy with them, and Patsy, Emma's friend from her school days, who suggests the New York trip. (Patsy seems to be waiting around for her running gag to be given to her, and she never gets it.) But most of the time Brooks's TV-trained intuitions are more than adequate to what he's doing here — extending half-hour gag comedy to feature length by the use of superlative actors who can entertain us even when the material is arch and hopped-up.

The movie gains its only suspense from keeping Jack Nicholson waiting in the wings for almost half its running time. After eleven years of living next door, Garrett asks Aurora out to lunch; four more years pass before she accepts. By that time, you're so primed that his every kidding leer rocks the theatre. When he comes on to her in the Nicholson lewd, seductive manner and tells her that she brings out the devil in him, it may sound like the wittiest, most obscene thing you've ever heard. The years have given Nicholson an impressive, broader face, and his comedy has never been more alert, more polished. He isn't getting laughs because of his lines; he's getting them because of his insinuating delivery. He has one inspired nuance: When Aurora accepts his invitation to lunch, this flabby old astronaut glances up at the heavens as if to ask, "Why did you make me so sexy?" Whatever Nicholson does — lick his lips, roll back his eyes, stoop slightly, or just turn his head — he keeps the audience *up*. There's a charge of fun in his acting; he lets you see the bad boy inside him. When Garrett stands, stripped to his trunks, in Aurora's bedroom, it isn't just the flab hanging out that makes him funny—it's that he stands like a dirty-minded little kid who hasn't yet learned to suck in his gut, and an old sex warrior who can't be bothered.

There's nothing visually engaging in the movie except the actors. I liked the way Shirley MacLaine flung herself about in a hospital scene: Aurora has a tantrum because the nurses have failed to bring a suffering patient a scheduled painkiller, and you feel the emotions that Aurora has had to suppress suddenly exploding at the only target she can find. (This tour-de-force scene was the one time Aurora's rambunctiousness seemed to have any subtext.) I liked the desolate look on Lithgow's yearning face when Emma says good-bye to him. There are enjoyable bits all through this movie; a staggering amount of contrivance has gone into it, and when all else fails, Nicholson's sparse hair sticks out at the sides of his head, or something else is surprising and screwy. Brooks does perhaps his best directing with the two small boys (Troy Bishop and Huckleberry Fox) who play Emma's sons—Tommy, at about ten, and Teddy, at about six. The boys don't like a lot of what goes on between their parents, and they show it. On the other hand, Brooks is shameless about exploiting the children's emotions to jerk tears from the audience. The picture isn't boring; it's just fraudulent.

In this debut film, Brooks appears to be a genuinely clever fellow with an inspirational psychology. Aurora, who has tried to keep life out, finally welcomes it. And, of course, Garrett Breedlove, the potbellied satyr, has to become a responsible guy. Brooks was probably attracted to the McMurtry novel because McMurtry's people are eccentric in a way that's supposed to make them lovable and forgivable, and Brooks, who added the character of Garrett, has made him in the same mold. Garrett is like those wastrel British aristocrats in the pukka-sahib pictures: When the crisis comes, his fundamental decency rises to the surface; he straightens up and does the right thing. He and Aurora are good Americans.

Terms of Endearment is being compared to two high-prestige, award-winning pictures—*Ordinary People* and *Kramer vs. Kramer*—and though *Terms* is both tackier and livelier than they are, the comparison is apt: It, too, is pious. And the piousness is integral to the whole conception. If *Terms* had stayed a comedy, it might have been innocuous, but it had to be ratified by importance, and it uses cancer like a seal of approval. Cancer gives the movie its message: "Don't take people for granted; you never know when you're going to lose them." At the end, the picture says, "You can go home now—you've

laughed, you've cried." What's infuriating about it is its calculated
humanity.

The New Yorker, December 12, 1983

THE GODFATHER PART III

John Powers

Francis Ford Coppola (he's resumed his middle name for the occasion) has made a movie to argue about and dream on. Since I saw it,
I've talked about little else — finding echoes of the earlier films, recasting a few roles, reshooting scenes, speculating about the great stuff
that Coppola obviously had to cut to reach a commercially viable
running time. (I'd love to see the five-hour version.) This *Godfather*
doesn't equal either of the first two; there are fewer transcendent moments, more clinkers, and the pacing feels both sluggish and rushed.
Yet it's always absorbing, because Coppola's ambition is so grand
and his conviction so genuine — like Part II, this movie revises what's
come before. *The Godfather Part III* may be disappointing when you're
watching it, but in your head it's likely to start turning into a
masterpiece — the conception, anyway, is nothing short of magis-
terial.

This means that Coppola's done better than I expected. I entered
the theater dreading that he might betray two movies that are so
much part of my life, I almost feel I've lived them; it would be hard
for a 1990 sequel to live up to the originals, let alone people's memories of them. When *The Godfather* and *The Godfather Part II* came out,
during the Watergate years, they seemed to encapsulate a whole corrupt era when evil was done behind closed doors, politics and business appeared a higher species of gangsterism, and America was
stained with the blood of its victims. (Say what you will against
Nixon, he could get your adrenaline going.) Part III carries no such
cultural urgency. Yet the original characters remain so fresh that,
even sixteen years after Part II, this film can introduce a major new
character — Sonny Corleone's illegitimate son, Vincent Mancini —
without explaining who Sonny was or belaboring the ways Vincent
resembles his father. The *Godfather* films have entered our cultural life

as no movies have done since, in ways ranging from the most commercial (the Godfather's pizza chain) to the most frankly emotional — I know people who've said they wished they could have grown up in a family as *warm* as the Corleones. Merely to mention Fredo or Tom Hagen is to call up types so vivid, no further explanation is needed.

The Godfather Part III draws on our abiding dedication to these characters, and even when it goes wrong, it resonates far more than a stylistic tour de force like *GoodFellas*. Such is our loyalty to the original two films, which, taken together, come closer to being the great epic of twentieth-century America — or at least American manhood — than any other works of art I can name. At times, they seem greater than that. In a shot nearer to Shakespearean majesty than anything since Welles, *The Godfather Part II* ends with Michael Corleone (Al Pacino) sitting in a chair on his lawn, terribly still as leaves blow around him, the impassive corruption of his face partially eclipsed by the hand so often kissed by those who call him Godfather, a monster no less monstrous for being tragic.

Part III opens twenty years later, in 1979. Now in his sixties and still alone, Michael is writing a letter to his children — like Lear, he's calling his family to him. He asks them to attend a church ceremony in New York awarding him the Order of St. Sebastian for the charitable work that's his road to redemption. And so this film begins, as do the others, with a religious ritual that brings the family physically together and, inevitably, sends the Godfather to a shadowy back room to meet with those needing favors. This time the supplicants include his own family: his ex-wife, Kay (Diane Keaton), begs Michael to let their son quit law school and try to make it as a singer, while his bastard nephew Vincent (Andy Garcia), who's hot to join the family business, has a run-in with the dapper mobster Joey Zasa (an unnatural-seeming Joe Mantegna, who evidently thinks he's still starring in *American Buffalo*).

The opening half hour is enjoyable but unsettling. Not only has the story lost the period setting that was one key to the earlier films' alluring mood, but there's a lot of comedy, which led me to fear that the Corleones were about to be *Texasville*d. But the tone merely reflects the changes in Michael. Decked out in peculiar, rather imperial-looking regalia, he's less imposing than we remember. His thickened face has gone baggy eyed with a dour slackness to his lips, and his voice has grown more gravelly, its echo of his father's only making us more aware that he lacks Vito's potent dignity—he has not become a ceremonious old man. Though now a legitimate businessman and richer than ever (he's able to give $100 million for charity work in Sicily), Michael seems vacant, gutted. And Pacino plays him as a slow, at times shuffling, figure—almost comic, yet aching with a desire for forgiveness.

Ever dreaming of respectability, Michael is scheming to take over Immobiliare, a European conglomerate. Naturally, the other New York families want to wet their beaks, too. When Michael refuses, a flamboyant murder attempt is made against him (shades of the first *Godfather*), and the Corleones are plunged into conflict with the greatest and most treacherous mob in history: the back-room caesars at the Vatican, whose caves connect them to the great Sicilian mob families and to the most ruthless and legitimized centers of Italian power. (All this is based on the actual late-seventies scandal at the Vatican Bank, whose corrupt dealings, some say, led to the murder of the honest Pope John Paul I weeks after his election.) After decades of striving to be assimilated, the Corleones return to Sicily for the second half of Part III.

This plot's tortuous twists aren't easy to follow, but the difficulty is at least half deliberate. By Part II, the simple murders of Michael's youth had already become the stuff of nostalgia; the plots and counterplots of his business had grown so deadly elusive that many viewers got lost in Michael's dealings with Hyman Roth and Frankie Pantangeli. In Part III the conspiracies have grown even harder to unravel; they're as invisible as the helicopter that blasts away at Michael and New York's other family heads as they meet in the glass-walled penthouse of an Atlantic City hotel.

What has always made the *Godfather* movies thrilling is their willingness to tackle a subject most movies and books are scared by: the mysteries of power—its seductiveness, its spiritual cost, the way it actually works on the street and in the boardroom. As a man who used violence to gain mastery, Vito Corleone always dreamed that Michael would become not a criminal but a respectable power, "the one to hold the strings." Michael's whole career has been torn by the effort to simultaneously go straight and pull all the strings, which also meant manipulating the evil essential to his world. As Michael grows mired in increasingly obscure machinations—his enemies' and his own—he learns the futility of his attempts to keep power and be clean: "The higher up I go," he laments, "the crookeder it becomes."

In the past, Michael concentrated himself more fiercely as his world grew more diffuse, but now he's lost his killer instinct. Though he still talks about saving the family, he's reluctant to make war on his enemies, and his sister Connie (niftily played by Talia Shire as a cross between Lady Macbeth and Poe's Raven) keeps goading him to do something to win respect. But Michael is sick, tired, guilty, lost. An Italian Catholic, he naturally craves forgiveness and redemption, but he's also a burnt-out case—utterly self-absorbed, utterly decentered. In his heart, he knows he's ruined his own life and the lives he's touched—he plays home movies in his head—and he *still* can't understand why the world fears and despises him. He shambles through this picture, a grab bag of moods, now wry with his nephew, now raging at his enemies, now racked by remorse, now impishly donning a chauffeur's cap and offering the startled Kay a guided tour of Sicily.

From the beginning and even at his worst, Michael has always been the character the audience identifies with. But it's hard to connect to him here. We're not sure what he's thinking, and as often in Part III, it's difficult to know whether this is a muddle or a deliberate effect. For my part, I wound up thinking that Michael's lack of focus is one of the film's boldest and psychologically truest ideas—a harrowingly acute picture of an ambitious man whose inner life has been swallowed up.

Michael's feelings come to a head in the film's bravest, most perplexing scene. He goes to Cardinal Lamberto (Raf Vallone) for help in slowing the Vatican schemers, and in the presence of this saintly man, winds up confessing his sins face to face in a courtyard. (The real-life Cardinal Lamberto, later Pope John Paul I, was legendary for provoking just such responses.) Michael's confession is obviously a turning point, and watching it we may recall the earlier films, when Michael played a satanic inquisitor who, promising forgiveness, forced his brother-in-law Carlo and his brother Fredo to admit their perfidies—then had them murdered. Here he finally unburdens himself, and though Coppola and Pacino's technique falters—perhaps they lost courage shooting a scene of such gravity—Michael's admission that he killed Fredo is so freighted with meaning it's still deeply moving. Graham Greene once referred to "the appalling strangeness of the mercy of God," and Michael's confession leads to a moment of such strangeness: When Michael says he can confess but not repent, the Cardinal replies that he can be forgiven anyway. God's grace extends, it seems, even to monsters.

Not that Michael is monstrous here; he's pathetically human. Stricken by a diabetic seizure, he frantically begins guzzling orange juice and cramming candy bars into his mouth, bits of chocolate hanging off his lips and cheeks — his desperation so naked, it's frightening.

☆

While Michael has always been the center of the *Godfather* trilogy, the enduring unit has been the Corleone family. In fact, many people liked the earlier films partly because they caught the incredible complexity of family life. The Corleones embodied the myth of the family — the emotional warmth, lasting connection, and powerful father figure so many of us crave. But they also revealed the capacity for madness in these idealized patriarchies — in the name of the family, Michael can kill his own brother.

Despite their increased power, the Corleones waned over the first two films. Part III introduces a source of renewal — a man able to inject new blood into the family. Just as Michael took over when his father was shot, so his own physical and spiritual debilities make room for Vincent Mancini, who, as you'd expect of Sonny's child, just loves kicking ass and being a gangster. (He's like a nobler version of the GoodFellas.) "All my life I wanted out," Michael says to his successor, an old man's warning to impetuous youth. "But I don't want out," Vincent replies, "I want the power to preserve the family" — which in his case also means being granted the family name. In love with the Corleone glamour (for him, the family history has the allure of *The Godfather*), he even wants to marry Michael's daughter Mary (Sofia Coppola).

Part III sketches Vincent's rise and also marks Andy Garcia's arrival at stardom after years of circling the possibility (most recently in *Internal Affairs*). Slim and almost pretty, Garcia's a charismatic actor, and things never come more alive than when Vincent's wooing the ladies, jovially blasting people's brains out, wreaking vengeance on those who tried to kill Michael, biting Joey Zasa's ear bloody, and then giving a sly little smile as he walks off. When we first meet Vincent he's clad in a hood's leather sportcoat and walks with the same aggressive arm-swinging stride that James Caan gave Sonny. It's fun to watch this rude boy prepare to become the new godfather, receiving the same time-honored advice Sonny and Michael got from their father. "Never hate your enemies," Michael instructs him. "It affects your judgment."

Something must've affected Coppola's judgment in his handling of Vincent. Although his scenes are the liveliest in Part III, a lot of his story is missing. (You can almost hear the good footage rustling to the editing-room floor.) Now, I'm not sure this is a completely bad thing; Vincent's an inescapably glamorous figure—infinitely handsomer than any mobster you'll ever see on the news—and there's no point in reglamorizing gangsters at this point in the *Godfather* series. Still, it's hard not to feel gypped if a movie's most gripping character keeps receding when he should emerge. When Vincent pretends to defect to the enemy Lucchesi organization, we don't see how he pulls it off—the kind of gangstercraft that I eat up. We don't get to understand his calculations when Michael forces him to choose between being don and staying with his daughter. And the film ends without our knowing what kind of godfather Vincent's destined to become. Will he become another Michael, and, if not, *why* not? This question cuts to the heart of the whole series.

Vincent takes over just in time for the film's climax, set at Palermo's Teatro Massimo, where, conveniently enough, Michael's son Anthony (Franc D'Ambrosio) is debuting in Mascagni's one-act opera *Cavalleria Rusticana*. This sequence follows the series' familiar tack of crosscutting between a public ritual (here, the operatic performance) and a flurry of violence: Vatican skullduggery, a hit man significantly disguised as a priest coming after Michael, the Corleones' habitual elimination of their enemies in one glorious swoop. At the end of this teasingly long set piece, which may well run forty minutes (and should have been pruned), Coppola delivers a tragic finale that approaches the sublime strength of Greek tragedy. Michael's horror at himself and his life produces a great, lacerating silent scream of recognition worthy of Edvard Munch or Francis Bacon, Michael's distorted features and dark, empty mouth the very image of an annihilated soul. The whole trilogy builds to this black, pagan scream, which rides roughshod over any idea of Christian redemption.

☆

Leaving the theater moments after this breathtaking climax, an unmoved colleague raised an objection I've heard several times since: Coppola has stolen shamelessly from himself. Yet I don't think Part III is simply Coppola offering a "*Godfather*'s Greatest Hits" reel, despite his use of old clips, the reappearance of familiar lines ("Never let anybody know what you're thinking," Michael admonishes Vincent, as Vito had admonished Sonny), and the soaring crescendos of its operatic climax.

I'm still not sure that Coppola and (cowriter) Mario Puzo were right to literalize the series' opera metaphor in this final installment, but I can see why they wanted to. From *Finian's Rainbow* through *The Cotton Club,* Coppola has always been attracted by reading real life as musical theater. For the film's last hour, his characters have been inescapably linked to Sicilian art and architecture—Coppola's shown them dwarfed and invaded by expressions of a centuries-old culture, by vengeance-packed puppet shows, monumental buildings, the cruelly beautiful landscape where daily existence has always been a struggle. In filling this movie with obvious references to earlier films, and staging its climax at the quintessential Sicilian opera, Coppola is aiming to place the whole Corleone saga inside a cycle imbued with the force of myth—the eternal recurrence of the same ungodly events.

In the face of such a magnificent conception, I'd like to be able to proclaim *The Godfather Part III* a great film. But movies don't live by conceptions alone. Although sumptuously made—Gordon Willis's photography offers the usual masterful interplay of light and shadow—this third panel of *The Godfather* triptych lacks the commanding authority of its predecessors. Those films were dazzling in the novelistic richness that let Coppola and Puzo cram in scads of plot twists and grace notes, big performances and small epiphanies, without ever letting us feel that anything was being hurried. And everything seemed to count. When, in Part II, the dictator Batista passed around a solid gold telephone he'd been given by an American firm, the scene told you something about the corruptions of Cuba and multinational capitalism, but it also let us see how both Michael and Hyman Roth didn't pay the phone any mind—they were focused on power itself, not its gaudy trappings. There are few moments so radiant in Part III. Despite its slow pace, Coppola can't even find enough time for his most exciting character, Vincent, or to give his polemical plot about the Vatican the sharply observed villains we desire. The daringly diffuse story line never quite comes together, leaving you unsure about Coppola's intentions—and in a movie as ambitious as this one, that matters.

Nor does Coppola elicit the unforgettable performances of the earlier films. Good as Garcia is, he's lost in the shuffle; Coppola doesn't let him shine as memorably as Brando, Pacino, Robert De Niro, James Caan, John Cazale, Robert Duvall (whose solidity this film misses), or even Lee Strasberg. Except for Eli Wallach's Don Altobello, a Sicilian Uriah Heep, the bit players scarcely register.

Coppola's visual style is still wonderfully lucid, but his once-sure dramatic touch has faltered. He lolls through scenes whose details he once would have caressed, and he seems not to notice (or care) that his daughter Sofia's heartbreaking clumsiness mars every scene she's in, even the opera-house climax. (Nepotism is its own punishment.) Indeed, this young actress's only virtue is that she distracts us from Diane Keaton's continuing awfulness as Kay—not that anyone would shine given Kay's lines. (Michael: "I did all that I could to protect you from the horrors of this world." Kay: "You were my horror.")

It would be possible to keep piling up examples of how Part III could have been better. But my heart points in the other direction. I'm surprised by how well Coppola's done with a project that could easily have been a disaster. His achievement's all the more striking when you remember he was working from a position of weakness.

Coppola had been spurning this sequel for years, and I presume he finally agreed to do it to save his career—a career that, in the years since Part II, has paralleled Michael's tale of success and excess, of declining powers and the increasingly heavy weight of the past. I suspect Coppola could identify with Michael's words about the gangsters who won't let him go straight. "Just when I thought I was out," Michael cries, "they pull me back in." Paramount's execs have pulled Coppola back in for *The Godfather Part III,* and though they're probably grousing that it needs more box-office punch—after rushing it into the theaters—it's still the best and noblest movie that studio's put its name to since, maybe, *The Godfather Part II.*

Sartre said that the very greatest art is about the passing of time. This theme inspired Sergio Leone's great, wounded masterpiece *Once Upon a Time in America,* another diffuse gangster epic that does hold together—in the memory of Robert De Niro's character, Noodles. Time's angry handwriting is all over the *Godfather* series too, giving the whole a retrospective poignancy that this final installment doesn't always earn. It's there in the aging faces of the stars, reminding us that we too are growing older. (A friend says the trilogy's like an American version of *28 Up*.). It's there in Coppola's diminished artistry and in the steady decline of American filmmaking in the years since Part II. And, of course, it's there in the saga of the Corleone family.

Late in *The Godfather,* Vito laments that he hasn't done everything he hoped to for his family—he couldn't even keep Michael out of the mire. "There wasn't enough time," he says sadly, to which Michael responds: "We'll get there, Pop. We'll get there." *The Godfather Part III* shows the tragic innocence of those words spoken so long ago. After decades of death and American dreams, Michael winds up back in Sicily, sitting in a chair alone as ever, the casualty of an endless cycle of killing and revenge that reduces every individual life, even a godfather's, to the futile jerks of destiny's puppet.

LA Weekly, December 28, 1990–January 3, 1991

THE GODFATHER PART III

Julie Salamon

The Godfather Part III has been constructed as a formal ceremony, a reverential homage to its predecessors. The picture's elegiac mood, its rigorous adherence to the dictates of pomp and circumstance, make the entire enterprise seem not so much a movie as a religious service. Unfortunately, like many religious ceremonies, the content of this one falls far short of the somber beauty of its physical surroundings.

The first two movies in the *Godfather* series deservedly hold a special place in Hollywood film history. The pictures potently combined and altered two mainstays of popular American culture—the gangster film and the family melodrama. The director Francis Ford Coppola found in these stories of the evolution of the Corleone clan the perfect outlet for his emotional, operatic sensibility. He presented the Corleone saga as the darkest side of the classic American success story: the successful immigrants who made good by doing evil.

Now, sixteen years after *The Godfather Part II,* Coppola has tried to complete the story with a Shakespearean flourish. Michael Corleone, the idealistic child of the Mafia who ultimately became more ruthless than his father, is a man in his sixties. He's spent the past several years trying to reconstruct himself as a good man, to leave behind a false, noble legacy to his children. He's divorced himself from the underworld and channeled his money into legitimate businesses and charities. But he can't escape his past; the filmmakers punish him for his sins with stern Old Testament justice.

This scenario, devised by Coppola and his coscreenwriter, Mario Puzo, is exactly the right way to conclude the Corleone legend. And Al Pacino's haunted portrayal of Michael Corleone's confrontation with his past bristles with a raw honesty. He is a tragic figure, a great man who devoted his passion and energy to evil and hypocrisy. Looking haggard and tired, Pacino brings a powerful, quiet despair to this portrayal of a wicked person whose conscience has been re-awakened by closer proximity to death.

Unfortunately, the script betrays its idea and Pacino's performance with weak dialogue and ill-conceived scenes that either play too long or shouldn't have played at all. The picture feels bloated. Coppola lays out a series of lushly conceived settings whose richness only accentuates the hollowness of the words and actions that take place in them.

The beauty of *The Godfather Part II* lay in its originality. It was a continuation of *The Godfather,* but also a textured movie all on its own. This new *Godfather,* however, has all the weaknesses of the typical sequel. The characters frequently seem to be explaining what they're doing — and how what they're doing relates to the past. Characters from the earlier movies show up to lecture Michael or to haunt him. The occasional new and interesting character — Bridget Fonda as a reporter, Joe Mantegna as a publicity-hungry mobster — are dispensed with all too quickly.

The *Godfather* series has been particularly compelling because of the connecting dramas between the Corleone family and the other family, the Mafia. By the time Part III begins, the Corleone line has been severed because Michael's own son has disowned him. So the filmmakers brought in the illegitimate son of Sonny, Michael's dead brother, to serve as heir to the throne. As Vincent the bristly charmer, Andy Garcia injects some much-needed energy into the mix. However, even his part is diminished by the script, and, more critically, by a sad casting error.

Winona Ryder, the young actress who was supposed to play Michael's daughter Mary, dropped out of the movie and was replaced by Coppola's own daughter, Sofia Coppola. This substitution has a disastrous effect on a crucial moment in the film's final tragedy, which turns on Michael Corleone's disapproval of the romance between Mary and Vincent, her first cousin.

Sofia Coppola's awkwardness and lack of conventional beauty might have come off as a bit of charming realism if she were a gifted actress, or even a competent one. Unfortunately, she is so uncertain and clumsy that it is impossible to believe for an instant that a slick operator like Vincent would even notice her, much less be infatuated with her. When Mary Corleone looks at Michael and says, "Dad, how could you do this to me?" the line takes on an unintended note of comedy.

The picture is, nonetheless, an ambitious undertaking. Coppola and Puzo reshape the Banco Ambrosiano scandal to forge a link between the Corleone family and the Vatican in scenes that are satisfactorily portentous. But too often *The Godfather Part III* is labored and tedious and preachy, like an old man boring the relatives at a holiday gathering with his falsified version of his life story.

Wall Street Journal, December 27, 1990

ON THE CONTRARY

L egendary movie fiascoes give rise to legendary anecdotes. There's the story of how John Boorman flew in from London to Los Angeles, was limo'd directly to the all-media screening of his *Exorcist II: The Heretic,* endured an hour of the audience's raucous titters, then hightailed it back to the airport, back to London.

Legendary fiascoes also inspire rescue missions; they can bring out the savior in a critic's soul. Upon release, virtually all of the movies in this section were vilified by the public, and by most of the press.

Heaven's Gate, with a budget that ballooned from about $11 million to about $44 million, single-handedly upended United Artists. (A fuller discussion of the *Heaven's Gate* fracas can be found in John Powers's Michael Cimino piece in "Auteur/Hauteur.") *Ishtar,* extravagantly expensive, buried Elaine May's directing career in high drifts of hot sand. *Hudson Hawk,* with its multi-earringed star Bruce Willis, was dubbed the *Ishtar* of 1991. *The Adventures of Ford Fairlane* inspired legions to dish the Diceman.

The following reviews were all written in the heat of the moment. Would a little dust-settling revise these critics' views? Would arrant advocacy switch to plea bargaining, or perhaps even to a verdict of guilty? Or is there more to these films than their detractors first claimed? To suggest the possibilities, a contrasting pair of reviews written almost ten years apart by Sheila Benson on *One from the Heart* is included. For avid contrarians, this chapter also proffers Henry Sheehan's paddling of *It's a Wonderful Life* and Kenneth Turan's defense of colorization.

HUDSON HAWK

Hal Hinson

As Hudson Hawk, cat burglar extraordinaire, Bruce Willis is part James Bond, part Cary Grant, and part Buster Keaton — a one-of-a-kind combination for sure, and just the right sort of hero for this exhilarating, one-of-a-kind movie. Directed by Michael Lehmann, who showed a talent for smarty-pants irreverence in *Heathers,* the picture brings to mind a lot of other, older movies — and a lot of older movie pleasures — but its spirit is wholly modern and wholly new.

Lehmann has found his perfect star in Willis; they were both born with a smirking hint of mischief in their eyes. And what they and their screenwriters — Steven E. de Souza and Daniel Waters — have created here is a precision universe of wiseacre high jinks. It's an action picture packed dense with the wit of a screwball comedy. And while that may not be a first, it's so bizarrely inventive that being first seems not nearly as important as being best.

Basically, *Hudson Hawk* is a caper picture, with Willis buddied with Danny Aiello as Hawk's thieving partner, Tommy Five-Tone, but it's a caper film with a teasingly absurdist point of view and a love of high-blown outrageousness. The movie begins in the time of Leonardo da Vinci, with the master himself rushing from project to project as if his pants were on fire. After a doozy of a Mona Lisa joke, Leonardo is shown moving on to his greatest creation, a colossal machine built to convert lead into bronze. But even a genius makes mistakes, and instead of changing lead into bronze, the machine converts it into solid gold. Immediately realizing the importance — and the danger — of his creation, Leonardo decides to render it useless, hiding the essential components inside three other works.

Four centuries later, Hawk is just getting out of prison, and a pair of power-crazed billionaires named Darwin and Minerva Mayflower (Richard E. Grant and Sandra Bernhard), having nothing better to do, devise a scheme to steal the three precious works, re-create the gold machine, and devalue the world's monetary system. Clearly the Mayflowers need Hawk, but having spent the last ten years behind bars, the master criminal wants to walk the straight and narrow. Fat chance, though, especially with the CIA (represented here by James Coburn) and his partner in on the score.

Nothing that follows is predictable and nothing is played straight—not even the heists. But, oh, what blessed crookedness. Hawk and Tommy are thieves with a touch of Katzenjammer craziness about them. Their jobs require precise, down-to-the-second timing, and so, to keep themselves on schedule, they choreograph their break-ins to songs like "Swinging on a Star" and "Side by Side." They're musical heists, with each culprit crooning the sound track to his crime.

Lehmann's staging here is blissfully relaxed, and yet every sequence has a prankish charge. What's unique is how the film combines suavity with rude, almost punkish comedy. It's a crafty satire, but with a swashbuckling soul. At times it even veers into the surreal, especially in the scenes with Grant and Bernhard—the most naturally surrealistic actress of all time—who are the best Bondish villains since Goldfinger. But even the patter—not to mention the skin-of-your-teeth escapes and stunts—has a Dadaist twist to it. It's cerebral, but somehow still rooted in lowbrow tradition, as if the filmmakers were tapping into the natural connections between surrealism and slapstick.

The key to it all, though, is Willis, who brands the film with his own stamp of indelible cartoon cool. There's no one else in the movies who could bebop through this kind of camp nonsense without losing his star charisma. He gets the most out of the jokes and makes everyone around him look good—even Aiello and Andie MacDowell, who plays a Vatican art historian who falls for Hawk.

The movie keeps edging its heroes toward the blades of buzz saws, but the action never seems routine or mindlessly ugly. (There's very little real violence.) It's exciting, but not in a way that makes you feel as if your guts have been run through a blender. And it keeps pitching ingenious little jokes and sight gags at you, an incredibly high percentage of which are strikes. It's fun in a way that makes your brain tingle. This Hawk flies.

The Washington Post, May 24, 1991

ISHTAR

Sheila Benson

In the guise of a sort of liberal's rethinking of the Hope-Crosby Road movies, Elaine May has created a love letter to show biz dreamers and called it *Ishtar*. It is a smart, generous, genuinely funny affair. Sometimes, like the camel who almost ambles away with the picture, it's longish in the tooth, but it is based on an extremely astute vision of life.

Writer-director May suggests that passionate dedication to one's art in the face of no discernible talent is no sin. Instead, it's admirable and rather sweet. And certainly "no discernible talent" describes Rogers and Clarke (Warren Beatty and Dustin Hoffman, respectively), her pair of over-the-hill singer-songwriters, whose teaming together suggests a man with no life preserver clinging to a man who cannot swim.

As acting partners, however, Beatty and Hoffman are an unselfishly inspired pair, creating character, not shtick. In its first twenty-five minutes, the movie goes a long way toward cementing our goodwill, as May fills in with affectionate wit every detail we could want to know about this wildly disparate pair.

The image of the sexually assured Beatty vanishes inside the sweetly oafish Lyle Rogers, a Southern country boy completely in awe of Hoffman's seemingly assured Chuck Clarke. To Lyle, Chuck is Tom Jones and Barry Manilow rolled into one compact little bundle of talent. For his part, Chuck, who likes to call himself Hawk, is content to bask in Lyle's unquestioning vision of him as an inspired tunesmith, as well as a Manhattan ladies' man without peer.

Actually, these two shouldn't be let anywhere near each other: Lyle, who wrote "Hot Fudge Lover" while driving an ice-cream delivery truck, and Chuck, author of "There's a wardrobe of love in my eyes / Try it and see if there's something your size." They are already such kindred spirits it's frightening.

But, hey, how are you gonna stop the meeting of true artists? Soon Rogers and Clarke, spiffed out with bongos, bow ties, and natty, checked headbands, are hitting the free audition club circuit, semi-paralyzed with fright but unfortunately still able to play and sing. (On a par with their act are May's shots of its reception: a young audience, openmouthed in incredulous horror.)

It does get them an agent—of sorts—the splendidly seedy Jack Weston, and his offer of ten weeks' work in Morocco gets this Road movie on the road. The desert entanglements will include Arab revolutionaries, ancient maps, hovering vultures, a beautiful veiled guerrilla (Isabelle Adjani, impassioned but underemployed), and the omnipresent CIA (Charles Grodin)—the stuff that usually produces dumb-dumb comedy of contrivance.

Yet although the space between laughs—or appreciative chortles, which is closer to *Ishtar*'s consistent level—does get longer once we're out of sight of New York, May doesn't get rattled and blow it all. *Ishtar* may have trouble finding the exit signs, but it remains a deadpan comedy of character and observation.

Its stars are on their best behavior. Beatty fleshes out Lyle, that sweet, self-deprecating twenty-watt bulb, with a gangling lope and an amazed appreciation for his partner's quickness: "You can only do that with a small body," he says wonderingly.

And although May is never ungracious enough to betray Chuck in front of us in New York, Hoffman lets his edge of anxiety whine through like a dentist's drill. Chuck doesn't really come into his own until the desert. First, there's that matchless rush of approval when their nightclub act finally finds its audience. (Never mind that they're singing "That's Amore," not their own songs.) Next, there's Chuck's life-saving improvisations at an arms auction, a rapid-speed gibberish routine that reveals a Hoffman with a Danny Kaye–like dexterity and command.

After its superstars, *Ishtar*'s niftiest character is Charles Grodin's silkenly untrustworthy CIA chief. When properly used—his manic intensity set firmly in reality—the button-eyed Grodin is unparalleled, and this may be his finest hour.

Ishtar also remains doggedly endearing. Unlike in the 1940s Road movies where squabbles over the girl always threatened to split up Crosby and Hope, Lyle and Chuck have a passionate bond, their (heaven help us) *art*. And when both of them are deserted by the women in their lives, they really do have each other. You can get all mushy inside when Lyle rescues Chuck from self-destruction—until you realize that Lyle has said, admiringly, "You'd rather have nothing than settle for less." Logic notwithstanding, it is a tender moment, and that affection permeates the film.

May fills the edges of her screen with quirky filigree work while the plot, such as it is, unfolds center stage. At the American Embassy in Ishtar, an overwrought Beatty pounds the wall for emphasis, and his fist goes right through the cardboard-thin partition. The bureaucratic panic this creates becomes a kind of anthill counterpoint to the action.

Then there's the blind camel, who begins as a secret password and goes on to be the biggest scene-stealer since Baby Leroy. It might be argued that this witty detailing is sometimes at the expense of the big picture. Agreed. *Lawrence of Arabia* this is not. It's not even an epic spoof, *Lawrence of Astoria.* It's merely an entirely intelligent, drolly funny comedy with something on its mind. It has two exquisitely detailed characters, three lapidary performances, the cinematography of Vittorio Storaro, the costumes of Anthony Powell, and the damnedest, most memorably awful songs that Paul Williams and/or Elaine May could devise. And from where I sit, *that's* amore.

Los Angeles Times, May 15, 1987

HEAVEN'S GATE

Kevin Thomas

In its new two-and-a-half-hour version, Michael Cimino's *Heaven's Gate* is an experience that leaves you feeling you have witnessed a true screen epic.

But then to see it in its original three-hour forty-minute version — that's including a ten-minute intermission — is to understand why it invited the critical bloodbath it received in New York [in November 1979], a bloodbath that led to the immediate cancellation of further openings.

In the longer version, problems of clarity, especially in time elements, are compounded severely by an ending so miscalculated as to elicit derisive laughter. Virtually all of this, however, has been corrected by Cimino and his editing team headed by Oscar-winning veteran William Reynolds, who in the revision has been promoted from lead editor to an executive in charge of postproduction. Indeed, the restructured ending of *Heaven's Gate* is one of ineffable poignancy and one of the film's key strengths.

Now cut to the bone, the film is not only far clearer but free of other occasional risible moments. It is also considerably less violent. To be sure, you can't cut an hour out of a picture without losing some telling details and shading, but on the whole *Heaven's Gate* has suffered no crucial losses and has gained immeasurably in power and coherence in the process.

Remaining quite intact is Cimino's central theme, which is the betrayal of the American Dream for the common man by those in power. This was also the major concern of Cimino's Vietnam saga, *The Deer Hunter.* Once again Cimino confronts an ugly national tragedy, yet, nevertheless, is able to carry us through it to express a profound love of this country. The key difference is that the Johnson County, Wyoming, range war of 1890 is as obscured as our debacle in Southeast Asia is familiar.

But first, what is *Heaven's Gate* like? To begin with, it takes its time in establishing its people and their relationships to each other and their society and environment.

Photographed by the masterful Vilmos Zsigmond, *Heaven's Gate* begins with commencement at Harvard in 1870 — this sequence was actually filmed at Oxford — at which time a sober Joseph Cotten takes the lectern to admonish his increasingly boisterous graduates "to diffuse high learning and culture among the people" and to live up to "the high ideal of the education of a nation." Among those scorning his words are Kris Kristofferson and his friend John Hurt. We've already heard Kristofferson ask Hurt if he's still going with him to Wyoming. At last, the graduation ceremonies give way to a glorious waltz on the lawn, with the entire class of seventy whirling its pretty ladies.

Suddenly, it's twenty years later, and a bearded, graying Kristofferson is arriving by train in Casper, Wyoming, a bustling town thronged with immigrants. If you're listening intently, you'll hear the station master, through his thick Irish brogue and the noise of the train and the townspeople, address Kristofferson as "Marshal." (This information is too crucial for Cimino to have left it to chance, especially when he has taken such pains to clarify lesser matters.)

Meanwhile, we get our first glimpse of Christopher Walken through a gunshot hole in a sheet. He has killed an immigrant settler who had stolen cattle to feed his starving family. Walken works for the Stock Growers Association, headed by the coldly aristocratic Sam Waterston, who has declared war on such settlers, branding them "thieves, anarchists, and outlaws." Among them is the madam of nearby Sweetwater, a beautiful French émigré (Isabelle Huppert, the French actress in her American film debut) who is loved by both Kristofferson and Walken.

Cimino has thus set in motion the coming of a savage range war and the unfolding of the rivalry between Kristofferson and Walken for Huppert. These three gradually emerge as archetypal frontier figures—the Hero, the Good-Bad Guy (Walken eventually sees the light), and the Hooker. But not with the Heart of Gold: Huppert is capable of loving two men at the same time, but she's not sentimental. All three, however, are flesh-and-blood people.

The stars are splendid and are surrounded by some equally vivid presences. There's Hurt, now a reluctant member of the association, a hard-drinking, self-mocking weakling; Jeff Bridges, a saloon keeper and the proprietor of Heaven's Gate, a large, tented skating rink and assembly hall in Sweetwater; and Brad Dourif, the thickly accented president of the chamber of commerce who makes the shocking discovery that the state militia is an enemy, rather than a protector, of the people of Johnson County.

There are, at times, thousands of people in front of the camera; and there are certainly hundreds behind it. Composer David Mansfield's seductive, mandolin-tinged score and Tambi Larsen's incredibly meticulous production design contribute immensely to the film's varying moods and rich ethnic flavor. The level of craftsmanship could scarcely be higher.

Set against a vast backdrop of snow-covered mountains and endless expanses of cloudy skies, this is an essentially elegiac and formal film, though there were some humorous moments. (Some of the best are contributed by Geoffrey Lewis as a comical trapper.) There's a folksy celebration at the skating rink that echoes the elegant waltz sequence an hour earlier. And there are many wry observations that stick in the mind. Bridges to Kristofferson, for example: "It's a disgrace to be poor in this country, isn't it?" "It always was," replies Kristofferson. And finally, inevitably, there's the battle, when, led by Kristofferson, the settlers bravely fight back.

Making movies has always been an art-industry, a hyphenate in which the two elements have been at odds more often than not, especially in America. There have been reams of copy written about the problems of *Heaven's Gate,* its prohibitive cost—estimates range to $40 million—its disastrous initial opening, its dire implications for the motion picture industry, and on and on. Now it is time to sit back and enjoy all that Michael Cimino has wrought.

Los Angeles Times, April 25, 1980

THE EXORCIST II: THE HERETIC

Dave Kehr

Suddenly I find myself in the ridiculous position of sticking up for *The Exorcist II: The Heretic,* a film that has been almost universally despised, and not without some good reason. It's not a great film, God knows, and I'm not sure if I'd even recommend it as anything more than a curiosity. But John Boorman, the director, has put some genuine effort into it — it shows thought and care and more than a touch of originality. Boorman takes some interesting chances, and even if none of them really pay off, he deserves a little credit for trying to bring something other than mindless mimicry to a sequel.

Despite a few minor exceptions (*Magnum Force, The French Connection Part II*) and a single major one (*The Godfather Part II*), the sequel has remained one of the saddest and most cynical manifestations of an economically debased Hollywood. They have a simple formula in LA: A sequel is guaranteed to make at least half as much money as the original. You could put out two hours of black leader titled *The Sting '77* and expect a $35 million return. The only trick is not to offend the audience by giving it something too much different from what it expected. The expanded ambitions of *The Godfather Part II* were probably responsible for its disappointing gross rental of $28.9 million (only in today's Hollywood can 30 million bucks be disappointing) as opposed to the $86 million garnered by its predecessor. Coppola was trying to top himself; Boorman has only to beat William Friedkin, the director of the original *Exorcist,* which is a much easier task. But Boorman has committed the sin of overzealousness. He's improved on the original beyond the point of good taste — and even beyond the point of immediate comprehensibility. A confused audience is not a happy one. People are coming to see a rerun of Friedkin's crude suspense mechanisms — ten minutes of utter boredom followed by two minutes of green puke, followed by ten minutes of utter boredom, etc., etc. — but they're not getting it. Instead of William Friedkin, Boorman is serving up a blend of H. P. Lovecraft, Vincente Minnelli, and Luis Buñuel.

The secret of William Friedkin's success may be his lack of imagination. *The Exorcist* scored most of its points by being appallingly literal about the supernatural. Val Lewton, who pioneered most of the techniques of the modern-day horror film with the series of B pictures he produced for RKO in the forties (*I Walked with a Zombie, The Cat People*), learned to avoid the actual depiction of ghosts and monsters at all costs. A man in a rubber suit is, after all, a man in a rubber suit: Lewton let the horror grow in the viewer's mind, creating a sense of swelling uncertainty. The masterpiece of the Lewton style is probably *Curse of the Demon,* a 1958 film produced in England by a former Lewton collaborator, Jacques Tourneur. In it, Dana Andrews, an American scientist, tries to expose a fraudulent warlock only to discover that he's no fraud at all—a lurid plot toned down to insidious subtlety by Tourneur's restrained but infinitely suggestive direction (and marred only by a few shots of a slobbering demon inserted later by the studio). Friedkin learned one of Lewton's lessons well—that today's audiences won't be frightened by mere makeup—but he discarded Lewton's emphasis on atmosphere and implication in favor of an almost documentary-like approach, relying on the most literal of all human acts, extreme violence, rendered as realistically as possible. Everything in *The Exorcist,* from the flying furniture to the spinning heads, is depicted with the cool detachment of a short on strip mining. Friedkin's innovation is actually a retrenchment, a return to the nineteenth-century Grand Guignol and its popping eyeballs, splitting heads, and severed limbs.

So here's poor John Boorman, a switch-hitting art/genre director (*Leo the Last, Hell in the Pacific, Point Blank, Deliverance*), faced with the prospect of following up Friedkin's already excessive style. What to do? Making the film even more violent seems futile: There is such a thing as a law of diminishing returns in screen gore. Boorman, nobly enough, decided to remain true to himself. *The Heretic* looks like less of a sequel to *The Exorcist* than to Boorman's own last film, *Zardoz,* a thoroughly eccentric science fiction fantasy that went down in critical and commercial flames in 1974.

Boorman's most personal films share a single structure: The hero (Lee Marvin in *Point Blank,* Marcello Mastroianni in *Leo the Last,* Sean Connery in *Zardoz*) enters a foreign territory, struggles to learn its laws, and, failing, ends up by destroying the system he can't understand. *The Heretic* takes a similar tack, but there are two heroes this time—a priest (Richard Burton) and a psychiatrist (Louise Fletcher)—entering a territory of a different sort, the demon-ridden mind of a sixteen-year-old girl (Linda Blair).

One of Boorman's problems is that he doesn't seem to know the rules of the game. *The Heretic* switches between realism and fantasy with an abandon that becomes almost comic at times. A science fiction film audience will accept anything that comes down the line — the free play of imagination is part of the genre. But a horror movie audience has to be guided through what's come to be known as "suspension of disbelief" — things have to be built from a rational, or at least marginally plausible, base. Boorman ignores that requirement entirely, offhandedly introducing the film's most preposterous device — two strobe lights wired back to back that somehow link two minds in simultaneous hypnosis — before he's even finished the exposition. If you're not on the bus by then, you never will be: *The Heretic* seems to get wilder with every passing frame, as Burton and Fletcher tour Blair's subconscious, discovering links to Africa and locust gods, and finally face down the demon queen in an Armageddon set in Georgetown. All of this is backed by a bizarre metaphysic that has something to do with the elemental forces of good and evil struggling for possession of the "world mind" — a collective consciousness focused (ironically enough) on apple-cheeked Linda. As if that weren't enough, by the end of the film Blair seems to have become Christ him/herself.

Conventional narration — with scene following scene in logical order — can hardly support a plot line like that. Boorman has substituted a system of visual and aural motifs, an interesting artistic maneuver but one that's guaranteed to drive any thrill-seeking audience up the wall. The flashing lights of the strobe machine are first introduced in an expository sequence set in a Mexican church, where strings of twinkling Christmas lights cover the altar. They recur as traffic signals, headlights, light reflected in rain-covered glass, and so on, as Boorman shows tremendous ingenuity in introducing the visual theme smoothly and unobtrusively into the action. A cliff motif, with the appropriate overtones of a metaphysical drop, is also maintained, appearing first as the porch of Blair's penthouse apartment, again as a mountaintop church in Ethiopia, and finally as a scar in the earth during the climactic sequence. This tactic works on two counts: The film is pervaded by a sense of déjà vu, as the repeated images trigger subconscious associations, while the visual theme stands as a repressed metaphor for Boorman's elaborate metaphysical system. The world of *The Heretic* is pervaded by strange, unreadable signs: The flashing lights become messages from a separate, unknowable order, pushing its sinister way into the light of day.

Eventually, though, the enigmatic signs become readable, and that's the point where *The Heretic* begins to stumble. Hinting at "other worlds" is one thing; drawing them out in painful detail is another. Boorman is a victim of the overexplicitness that mars much of H. P. Lovecraft's late work: Once you've seen the Elder Ones playing space tennis, they're no longer frightening—they're just ridiculous. "Well, there's this locust god, see, and it's trying to take over the world mind, see, and . . . " Enough. Give me back my monster.

Still, the suspicion persists that Boorman really wasn't trying to make a horror movie. There are few shock effects in the film: Boorman is after oohs and aahs rather than shrieks, a subtler, less immediate kind of fear. The mise-en-scène often works brilliantly toward that end. Borrowing a sense of the baroque from Vincente Minnelli, Boorman overloads his frame with visual detail. Images are sliced by strong diagonal shafts of light; mirrored surfaces divide the characters into a thousand schizophrenic reflections; the bizarre angles of the sets create curious psychological tensions. The stability of the image is consistently undermined. Boorman's characters are divorced from their environment; the decor itself seems evil, threatening.

This sense of alienation, of being a stranger in a strange land, is a theme that Boorman has pursued in most of his films, and if *The Heretic* makes any ultimate sense, it's only when seen in the context of his career. As a sequel to *The Exorcist,* it's an obvious flop, but as a continuation of the concerns that have governed Boorman's art, *The Heretic* has to be counted as a quasi success. Some directors have the ability to fit their vision to almost every genre—musicals, westerns, comedies, thrillers, whatever—but Boorman hasn't quite been able to bring it off. He's trapped on two sides, by the requirements of the horror film and by the much more severe limitations of a sequel. Under those circumstances, it's a miracle that he's been able to achieve anything at all. But he has: *The Heretic* stands as an intriguing, if not memorable, experience.

Chicago Reader, June 24, 1977

THE ADVENTURES OF FORD FAIRLANE

Armond White

Critical consensus was obtuse, as usual, when *The Adventures of Ford Fairlane* opened. This genre spoof, starring crude humorist Andrew "Dice" Clay, was condemned as the most tasteless and inept film of the summer. That's actually a too-harsh judgment, considering the garbage most critics praise, but it's the result of a reactionary shock wave against Clay's individual show-biz project. He's being treated as an aberration when, in fact, he underscores the cultural norm.

Mainstream pundits have been campaigning against the bad taste in Clay's stand-up comedy routines on records, in concerts, and on TV with facile, moblike disdain. (The tide peaked when *Saturday Night Live* performer Nora Dunn self-righteously boycotted Clay's comedy over the other offensive humor the show is known for.) Talk about a crisis in leadership! Clay has been singled out as the enemy, but his critics don't acknowledge that he is among us, part of us, for us. Us being the United States of America and the social attitudes regularly expressed and promoted in our culture—which movie reviewers regularly acclaim.

To give *The Adventures of Ford Fairlane* a fair viewing: It is a not-uninteresting expansion on the Andrew "Dice" Clay persona, only less wholesomely domesticated than his surprisingly charming performance in the 1988 film *Casual Sex?* Clay's appearance there as The Vin Man, a fifties greaser retard trapped in eighties sexual panic, made a sensible effort at putting his comic act in a plausible dramatic context. *Ford Fairlane,* which wasn't originally written by or for Clay, was adapted and reconceived for him by producer Joel Silver and director Renny Harlin (the purveyors of crass taste responsible for *Die Hard 2*).

This "Diced" version of a detective parody is revealing. *Ford Fairlane* combines the retro-chic of hard-boiled film noir and "classic" rock 'n' roll. Now, conflated into Clay's act as the super tough, super cool, red-blooded American male—"the rock 'n' roll detective from Brooklyn to save the world"—that whole "hip" sensibility and its macho ideas are also *deflated.*

Clay, as Fairlane, adapts himself to the most widely accepted American mode; he is presented in terms of James M. Cain detective fiction and lust-driven rock music — two essentially sexist pop forms. The movie — set in the nightclub and beach house locales of Los Angeles, traversing the milieu of wealth and show biz, recording industry professionals and groupies — offers an authentically debased universe.

No, it isn't a critical view and it's only mildly satiric, but bad-boy Clay fits into the movie's very recognizable terrain as perfectly as Pee-wee Herman in his Playhouse. That's what the film's reviewers won't admit in their simplistic, moralizing analyses. Clay's jokes about women as disposable sex toys come out of the same rotten cynicism as the bimbo brain surgeon in *Days of Thunder,* a critically respected film. *Ford Fairlane* actually has better performances and a few good jokes. ("Is Sting really an asshole?" a groupie asks bon vivant Fairlane.)

Clay's crucifixion (last week, Twentieth Century Fox postponed the release of his concert movie) smacks of cultural hypocrisy. But this movie is rather fascinating because the world of *Ford Fairlane* isn't only an emotional projection. As in *Pee-wee's Big Adventure,* the hero's personal, juvenile vision is corroborated by what he experiences and we witness, but the effect is far from innocent wonder.

The self-conscious sleaziness with which Clay portrays Fairlane accurately depicts the benign aggression and jaded delight that America's proles feel when embracing and asserting their "normality." Privilege defines the way Fairlane disses women and gays or regales his penis (naming it Stanley), and it is consistent with the way he walks into a club and commandeers the stage for an extemporaneous R&B solo. (For Black viewers this scene sums up the wretched history of blue-eyed soul; Clay is as bad as, say, Taylor Dayne or Michael Bolton.)

As a comic, Clay's instinct is to expose this pathetic, misdirected need to be cool. (Any sensible person watching *Ford Fairlane* can see that Clay knows he is merely acting out white, male, heterosexual insecurities.) But he doesn't go any farther than this because he lacks the very intelligence and courage that reviewers debunked in Sandra Bernhard's *Without You, I'm Nothing.*

In that brave, underrated film, Bernhard challenged herself and her audience in the way of a politically conscious person who perceives herself as an outsider for how she was born and for what she loves and respects. Every moment was a feminist, gay breakthrough and, perhaps most of all, an ethnic breakthrough as Bernhard scrutinized the Jewish American's sense of displacement and compensatory dominance of show biz. That's what "Dice," born Andrew Clay Silver-stein, won't dare. Posing as a quasi-Italian Bensonhurst thug trying to get one up on everyone, he practices the illusion that Hollywood knows best, running with America's sexist, racist wolf pack. Still, he's not the problem, just a symptom.

Bernhard's insights left one exhilarated yet discomforted; Clay's movie is a funny-pathetic romance of empowerment. Neither should be dismissed without being understood. Besides, without America the way it is, Bernhard and Clay wouldn't matter.

City Sun, July 25–31, 1990

ONE FROM THE HEART

Sheila Benson

It's so easy to love *One from the Heart;* you just let yourself relax and float away with it. A work of constant astonishment, Francis Coppola's new film is so daring it takes away your breath while stagger-ing you visually.

At the same time, it is easy to understand the mixed-to-discour-aging words *One from the Heart* suffered in New York. Because, even though it is set in the no-roots insubstantiality of Las Vegas, *One from the Heart* in essence is an LA movie. Not Los Angeles, not Hollywood—LA, wrapped in neon and punctuated with palm trees, bungalow courts, Airstream trailers, and thirties Moderne.

The picture comes from the same artistic impulses that inspire air-brush art, three-dimensional pop-up greeting cards, and the delicately beautiful new neon that illuminates LA shops. It is post-Warhol, where everything is "pretty," all slickness and sleekness, and it cher-ishes its surfaces even more because of the hollowness they cover.

The story is the least of the film's preoccupations. The script, by Armyan Bernstein and Coppola, is about as substantial as a Necco wafer and equally sweet.

Lovers Frederic Forrest, now a strawberry blond and, in his girl-friend's disgusted description, "egg shaped," and Teri Garr celebrate their fifth anniversary on the Fourth of July. In O. Henry tradition, they exchange two "Gift of the Magi" presents. She, a travel agent,

Teri Garr walks the rain-slicked, manufactured streets of Las Vegas in Francis Coppola's *One from the Heart*. (Photo courtesy of Zoetrope Films.)

gives him escape in the form of two plane tickets to Bora-Bora. He, a junkyard owner whose life is surrounded by the impermanent, gives her solidity—the deed to the house they share.

But they are each a little wistful about the erosion of their romance. Singer-composer Tom Waits's emery-board voice sings for Forrest, and Crystal Gayle sings for Garr: "Is there any way out of this dream?" Even their lovemaking is now a kind of courtesy. The celebration turns into a real Independence Day when Garr picks a fight and they split up.

Both get themselves new partners: Forrest pursues this generation's Leslie Caron, Nastassja Kinski, a circus performer; Garr finds a sweetly romantic Latin lover (Raul Julia), who turns out to be a waiter as well as a songwriter. (He sings her one of his more arresting works, "Meet me tonight, it's raining Cuban cigars.") Both Garr and Forrest get ample advice from their respective cronies, Lainie Kazan and Harry Dean Stanton.

But as the two search frantically for fresh romance, their faces merge, recede, and fade in and out of each other's memories. They pass each other on the glittering street in a parody of the ballet convention of lovers who cross but do not notice one another. But if you know your fairy tales you can have faith in the ending of the film. What can't be anticipated is the *how* of it.

Coppola's leap into years-ahead technology is sure and dazzling. "It's artificial," he seems to say. "Isn't it gorgeous?"

Indeed it is — sumptuous, sensuous, stunning. At the same time, the wind that never quite leaves the sound track says something else: It may be hot and gaudy here but the desert can cover anything over any day now. Impermanence and emptiness crowd the film as densely as its hundreds of extras and dozens of writhing dancers.

Two kinds of audiences will accept *One from the Heart* easily: *naïfs* and sophisticates. Those in the middle will worry too much about the silhouette-thinness of the characters. They shouldn't. Musicals have been far emptier than this in terms of real emotion, and very few have dared this greatly. There are excesses, times when you feel the strokes, the wipes, the dissolves. But it is still a work in progress, and if it goes as every other Coppola film has gone it will be worked on up to and even after it opens in theatres.

It will be fascinating to see the differences that emerge and to write about the film at length in its final form. But there is a feeling of sureness this time that was not the underlying emotion in the last frantic previews of *Apocalypse Now.*

One from the Heart revels in the surfaces. We've lived among surfaces so long that we'd better find them exhilarating; they're what we have.

Los Angeles Times, January 22, 1982

POSTSCRIPT: Revisiting a work that seemed to be a high-water mark of freshness and astonishment even a short while ago can be a reassuring or a painful event. At a Richard Lester tribute earlier this year, a spot check of 1964's *A Hard Day's Night* showed that the Beatles still kept their own, cheeky magic, whereas the kookiness of *Petulia,* in which Lester's insights and innovations had seemed timeproof, felt infuriatingly self-conscious.

Looking again at Francis Ford Coppola's *One from the Heart,* the pain is all mine.

On that night eight years ago, carried along by the visual astonishment of Coppola's bittersweet love story, I thought the movie was enchanting. Its musical score still is, every ironic, revealing note of it. ("I told you before, I'll tell you again," Tom Waits's disgruntled lover growls to his imperfect sweetheart. "Don't defrost the icebox with a ballpoint pen.") The fact that this rich original score—sung to such great effect by composer Waits and Crystal Gayle—was passed over for a 1982 Academy Award seems as much of an outrage today as it did then.

At that time, *One from the Heart* seemed a film that reveled in its surfaces. Now, alas, it seems to be only those surfaces—and its music.

They are still prettily persuasive surfaces, however. The artificiality of the whole endeavor seems to be part of its point: a show-offy, "look at what we can do on a studio sound stage" boast, pulled off, on the whole, with extravagant success.

It still seems to be a film that's less about Las Vegas than it is about the bungalow courts and neon of Los Angeles and the crap shoot that is the movie business. And to us here in Los Angeles, the film's suggestion of impermanence is haunting: the threat that the wind that never quite leaves this sound track could cover over this place, too, at any time with the desert that lurks just a little offscreen.

The movie's visual effects can suddenly transport you or make you grin at their audacity: that amazing moment, for example, when that huge, plainly artificial airplane takes off directly over our heads; the light-bulb jungle of downtown Las Vegas; or the automobile junkyard garden, where a wire walker blossoms overhead.

It seemed a great challenge at the time; recently, with a movie like *Tucker,* you can see Coppola's further refinement of *One from the Heart*'s magical shifts in place and time, using light and scrims.

But ah, my foes, and oh, my friends, the stuff that sticks the marvelous bits together now seems, frankly, strained beyond the most passionate loyalty.

So what changed since 1982? Did a certain cynicism arrive, welcome as a death chill? I don't think so. The waves of affection I felt for *One from the Heart* don't embarrass me; I wish I could feel them again, but frankly I can't . . . only scattered ripples here and there.

The answer, I think, is not to try to love films less or with less enthusiasm, but to understand that love is not fixed forever, any more than taste is. I asked an astute friend once if she liked an outrageous hemline in a fashion magazine. "Not yet," she said, cheerfully.

From some of our past loves, we get a glimpse of who we were then, and an insight into why this or that persuaded us so. I can remember, for example, arguing that there was *nothing* neurotic in the behavior of *Jules and Jim*'s Catherine, so there is something to be said for a modicum of personal mileage. In the same way, each one of us could probably pick a book, a movie, or a bit of music that seems irreplaceable now and may only mortify us a decade later. Nuthin' to get hung about.

One from the Heart is still a landmark in the time line of Coppola's films, and a 70mm screening of it is rare enough to seek out and try for yourself. Who knows, it may become the love of *your* life.

Los Angeles Times, March 1, 1990

IT'S A WONDERFUL LIFE

Henry Sheehan

Only fifteen years ago Frank Capra's *It's a Wonderful Life* was still languishing in the obscurity that had been its apparent fate since its disastrous release in 1947. The film was the second feature produced by the fledgling Liberty Films, an independent production company formed by Capra and fellow directors William Wyler and George Stevens. The first release featuring the Liberty Bell trademark was Wyler's *The Best Years of Our Lives,* a sentimental drama of returning veterans that was received with critical and popular acclaim. Whatever goodwill and profits were reaped by *Years,* however, were soon dissipated by *Wonderful,* and the company was forced out of business before Stevens ever got to make his feature.

The hostility and indifference engendered by the film did more than put a company out of business, however. Wyler and Stevens picked up their careers more or less where they had left off, both continuing to work on big-budget, prestige projects for major studios. By his own autobiographical admission, however, Capra lost the wind from his creative sails. He directed the bitter *State of the Union* (the movie from which Ronald Reagan stole his "I'm paying for this microphone" line) the next year, but then completed only four pictures over the next decade. After a particularly bad experience on 1959's *Pocketful of Miracles,* during which he clashed repeatedly with the film's star, Glenn Ford, Capra retired permanently from filmmaking at the age of sixty-two. After three decades of popular success, Capra simply was overcome by his sudden lack of contact with the audience.

In retrospect, it is possible to surmise that Capra, though he had directed a number of wartime documentaries, had simply underestimated the impact the war had had on the American public. Whereas Wyler's film had in part tackled the difficulty demobilized soldiers had in readjusting to civilian life, Capra's film almost denied that the war had occurred. The war was present in the plot, of course—everyone knows how little brother Harry went to war and saved a shipload of troops by shooting down an enemy plane in a dogfight—but the film's general tone and thematic progression was exactly the same as in Capra's huge prewar successes. As in *Meet John Doe, Mr. Deeds Goes to Town, Mr. Smith Goes to Washington,* and others, a seemingly unexceptional young man, George Bailey (James Stewart), the son of a savings and loan owner, rises, through simple virtue, to extraordinary heights and saves his town and townfolk from vice, ruin, and the machinations of big-time capitalists.

Of course, the charm of the story is that George does not know that he has accomplished all this until, in a fit of despair, he is granted the divine opportunity to see what life would have been had he never been born. And we all know what turn that world would have taken: toward unmitigated hell. The snug little community of Bedford Falls would have been nothing less than the rundown, honky-tonk haven of Pottersville, a sin pit populated in the main by whores, madmen, and spinsters.

The virtues of *It's a Wonderful Life*—its humor, its warmth, Capra's meticulous storytelling skills, the vividly drawn secondary characters, the sinuous twists and turns of the plot, the exquisitely manipulated emotional orchestrations—are well enough known to bear skipping here. Consider them pronounced and appreciated. In fact, I have nothing like the space to even list them all. However, there are some dark undercurrents to the work, as there indeed are to all the Capra films commonly referred to as "populist."

Populism, after all, is not always democratic. For one thing, it embodies the notion of popular will, a force projected by, but somehow detached from, the vast masses. This will, in Capra's films, always starts off unheeded, often by the very institutions ostensibly constructed to obey it. The newspaper in *John Doe* attempts to twist, rather than respond to, the popular will. In *Mr. Smith,* it is the United States Senate that no longer conforms to popular demands. In each case, a leader, the famed, idealized Capraesque "common man," must emerge from the undifferentiated murk of the masses in order to smite the offending institution.

This is majority rule with a vengeance. The problem is, the very institutions that Capra sets up for destruction are meant to be checks on majority rule. The Senate was devised to allow sparsely populated regions the right to block bullying by more crowded neighbors. Newspapers, similarly, are supposed to represent a diversity of opinion, not a single blanketing consciousness. Populism, with its notions of moral as well as political righteousness, has no room for the democratic outcry of unpopular ideas.

Capra's heroes are a little frightening, too. For all the vividness of their personifications by stars like Stewart and Gary Cooper, they really have very few identifying characteristics. They are all as pure as Boy Scouts, and rather than faults, they have shortcomings—a stutter or a bad temper. Their anointing as leaders is nearly mystical (literally mystical in *Wonderful Life*), and the people—who, in Capra's films, always have the same opinions on the same subjects and are as malleable as clay—recognize them instantly through an emotional process that defies the intellect.

In other words, for such an avowed enemy of fascism—and Capra was a tireless and prodigious worker in the war effort—there are certainly an awful lot of protofascist heroes in Capra's films.

To one degree or another, George Bailey fits all the requisites of these sub-Nietzschean good guys. His divine recognition has already been noted; the angels themselves have picked out George for special assistance. But this recognition of extraordinary qualities also extends to those inarticulate spear carriers, "the people." Remember, George is given control of his bank by a board who just know that only George can keep it running in the face of assaults by the greedy banker Potter (Lionel Barrymore). But George is also the beneficiary of small tokens of obeisance, as when the town cop Bert (Ward Bond) and the town's sole apparent cabbie Ernie (Frank Faylen)—and has anyone else ever wondered whether these two are the inspiration for the like-named Muppet characters?—go to considerable lengths to fix up a wedding-night nest and croon a nuptial serenade.

And although all George can really do to fight Potter's financial speculations is to provide mortgage money that the old cuss refuses, somehow he exerts a moral force as well. The bartender (Sheldon Leonard) at Martini's actually has his financial status bettered in the otherwise bleak vision of a Georgeless world, since he now apparently owns the place (and is providing better music as well), but for some reason he has turned from a polite and protective provider of liquid refreshment to a surly, bullying whiskey slinger.

Yet, Capra has also reined in some of his more disturbing passions, as well. For one thing, George is tilting not at political windmills, but at a financial one. Although the Capra bad guys were always rich and often controlled corporations and banks, old man Potter is, I believe, the only Capra bad guy who is into banking exclusively. And, in the little Bailey Savings and Loan, Capra's populist impulse does merge with more democratic — in capitalist terms, at least — notions, since he makes it clear that the depositors' money functions as a kind of community investment service for the common good.

Also, the supporting cast amount to more than the merely colorful supernumeraries they often remain for Capra. In the most outstanding case, for instance, one practical reason George appeals to the savings and loan board as an attractive executive is that the immediate alternative is his crackpot Uncle Billy (Thomas Mitchell).

Yet, too often these common folk are shuffled on and off screen merely so they can praise, thank, or pay tribute to George. The film declares that its point is found in the moral that each life touches every other one, like the proverbial ripples that ebb out from a stone thrown into a lake. However, those ripples are decidedly one way in *It's a Wonderful Life.* Any number of the other characters could be erased from the book of life without unduly disturbing any of its chapters. What if the old druggist had never been born, or Bert, or Uncle Billy? True, all those famous men aboard the transport ship would have drowned if Harry had not been there to save them, but Harry's existence is properly caught in the flow of George's tides.

Really, only George reaches out to all the others, this aw-shucks natural leader, divinely anointed to do battle with the forces of monopoly capital and to uplift the moral life of his brethren. From out of the undifferentiated mass — "the people who do most of the living and dying in this town," as George protectively refers to them — comes the leader who will tear down the old and replace it with the new (in this case the suburban brightness of Bailey Park).

Well, the title does say that it is *a* wonderful life.

Los Angeles Reader, December 8, 1989

ON COLORIZATION

Kenneth Turan

It came out of nowhere, this tempest, this storm of storms, erupting from a situation so calm you could almost hear paint drying. Not just any paint, however, but the discreet computerized colors two different firms, Colorization Inc. and Color Systems Technology (CST), were quietly using to add hues to black-and-white war-horses. The first two colorized features, 1937's friendly-ghost story, *Topper,* and Laurel and Hardy's vintage *Way Out West,* were issued in 1985 and everybody smiled for the camera.

Stan Laurel's daughter pronounced herself "delighted, or perhaps I should say overjoyed" at the results, adding, "My father would surely have raised his derby" in tribute. Cary Grant, *Topper*'s star, said he trusted the Colorization folks "will continue to color other memorable films in the same manner." And from the White House, film buff Nancy Reagan wrote that she "didn't think *Topper* could ever be improved, but we were most impressed with the colorization of that fun movie. . . . A clever idea. The President joins me in sending best wishes for your continued success."

Presidential wishes apparently don't count for as much as they used to, because storm clouds soon began gathering, clouds shaped suspiciously like film directors with time on their hands. The venerable Fred Zinnemann, who hadn't worked since the somnolent *Five Days One Summer,* called the adding of color "a cultural crime of the first order" that was surely "against the national interest" and insisted that resisting its encroachment may soon turn out to be "the last stand before the entire art form is totally degraded and goes down the drain."

With a heavy hitter like Mr. Z. leading the way, no director worth his jodhpurs wanted to be left behind, and soon the attacks came pouring in like grapeshot from Captain Blood's cannon. Joe Dante likened it to a death knell, John Huston pronounced himself "astounded [at] the vulgarity of the whole idea," Woody Allen called it "an ugly practice, venal, anti-artistic." Then came the battle of the metaphors, as directors vied with one another for the most creative comparison. The winner: Milos Forman, whose "like putting aluminum siding on a seventeenth-century castle" narrowly edged out Peter Bogdanovich, who, in an unexpected burst of creativity he would've done well to save for his films, called the process "like putting pubic hair on *Venus de Milo.*"

Taking the brunt of this punishment was Color Systems Technology, the company with $24 million worth of contracts to color everything from the films of Shirley Temple to John Huston's *The Maltese Falcon* (released in November [1986]) and the venerable *Casablanca* (due out [in 1987]). CST vice-president Charles M. Powell, a rollicking Hollywood figure who'd been senior vice-president in charge of marketing for Columbia, Universal, and MGM, was feeling a little feisty. "People come in here with their stories already written. I know all the questions by heart: 'Why are you doing this?' 'Weren't these films meant to be shot and shown in black and white?' 'Is it true you ruin these pictures?' Give me a break!"

A break, however, was the last thing Charlie Powell was going to get. A blue-ribbon committee of the Directors' Guild of America, announcing that the issue was moral, not commercial, called the colorists "cultural butchers" and charged that "these fellows are lifting their legs on people's work." Not to be outdone, the Writers' Guild lashed out at "cultural vandalism," and the American Film Institute, whose chairman, George Stevens, Jr., had called the process "a plague on the history of American film," called a press conference at which spokespersons dressed only in black and white denounced the process as a malicious gimmick.

Earl Glick, the board chairman of Hal Roach Studios, the parent company of Colorization, was reduced to a dazed "I don't believe it" when asked for his response. Glick remembered the day when Frank Capra came to his office and *asked* to have his films colorized, but Capra has long since succumbed to peer-group pressure and withdrawn his support. And over at CST, the voluble Charlie Powell had been silenced. On the advice of its attorneys, a spokesperson said, the company was going to take a lower profile.

The colorization brouhaha is more than the usual Hollywood tempest in a teapot. It is a situation made to order to illustrate the duplicity and doublethink that make the movie business what it is and our films what they are. Truly, Hollywood is a Wonderland dizzier than anything Alice experienced.

First, though it very much goes against the grain of the situation, let's try to pin down a few facts. No one, Bogdanovich's heartfelt metaphor notwithstanding, is tampering with so much as a frame of an original negative of a black-and-white film. All coloring is being done on tape copies, a process much closer to collage than to desecra-

Reprinted with special permission of King Features Syndicate, Inc.

tion. Not to mention the fact that the whole concept of "creative rights" sounds awfully suspicious coming from directors who think nothing of ignoring and/or completely obliterating the artistic integrity of screenwriters when it suits their purposes. Now that their ox is being gored, however, it's suddenly become quite a different story.

The fuss also conveniently ignores the reality of the black-and-white print situation. Yes, it's true, seeing films in color is not seeing them as their makers intended, but on the other hand, seeing them on a tiny television screen, broken up by commercials and arbitrarily shortened to mesh with a network's time considerations, is, if anything, more of a desecration.

And the situation in revival theaters, places none of these protesters apparently frequent, is hardly any better. True, the prints are full size, but they are often eighty-third generation 16mm dupes that are so fuzzy and scratched, Jimmy Stewart comes out looking and sounding like Gabby Hayes. The idea that color is going to drive out gorgeous black-and-white prints ignores the fact that aside from archival showings those pristine originals are already scarcer than VW bugs at Mortons's parking lot. And to those fearful that color will force black-and-white tapes from the market, Earl Glick, whose company distributes *It's a Wonderful Life* in both versions, says absolutely not. "The boxes and the masters are already made. We will sell both as long as there is a demand."

Yet another bogus argument concerns the quality of the color. Much has been made of its lack of pizzazz, and sweater men Ebert and Siskel, pious as choirboys at a right-to-life rally, have protested such sacrileges as the mistaken brown coloring given Frank Sinatra's eyes in the 1954 picture *Suddenly.* Yes, it's true that the color is nothing to die for, and mistakes have been, and will continue to be, made. But the CST folks are expending a considerable amount of effort on color authenticity, and it's without question that the process will improve. And even if it doesn't, there are positive aspects to colorizing that have not been given their due.

For one thing, though it may be heretical to suggest it, color has the potential to increase audience interest in classic films. Like it or not, most moviegoers, especially younger ones, have little patience with black and white. "Our research told us that 85 percent of viewers prefer seeing movies in color," says Cheryl Lynne Gersch, marketing director for Hal Roach Studios. Isn't it at least conceivable that these films could function in the same way that Charles and Mary Ann Lamb's famous *Tales from Shakespeare* has for nearly two hundred years, as a way to introduce material to an audience that otherwise might choose to ignore it? If a choice needs to be made between people widening their horizons by seeing great films in color or not seeing them at all, it would seem only logical that the advantages to be gained, in whatever form, would offset any negatives.

And there is no doubt that people are responding to what's been done to these films. When *Miracle on 34th Street,* hardly the greatest picture ever made, was televised in a colorized version in 1985, the audience it drew was 600 percent greater than that of its previous black-and-white showings, making it the highest-rated syndicated film of the entire year.

It is this very area of audience response that provides the skeleton key that unlocks the secret of this death-before-dishonor fuss. Basically, all the colorists are saying is "no harm, no foul": If an audience decides this is what it wants to see, so be it. Should this argument sound familiar, it's because it's the very one the powers that be in Hollywood invariably use to justify not-so-tasty items like *Rambo, Cobra,* and *Friday the 13th, Part VI.* "Is it our fault if people like this stuff?" is their invariable, somewhat plaintive defense. Why, all of a sudden, has this reasoning been found lacking?

The answer is that—no surprise—appearance counts more than reality in Hollywood. This is an industry where a right-thinking but ponderous and predictable movie like *Gandhi* can win the Best Picture Oscar because voting for it allows the Academy pooh-bahs to feel a spiritual kinship with Mother Teresa as they luxuriate in front of their swimming pools. It is a way to take a stand and strike a pose without any risk or even the slightest discomfort, and that, like bashing colorization, is an opportunity too good to pass up.

Watching all these self-appointed guardians huffing and puffing about the death of an art form is a little like watching John Wayne riding in to rescue a bunch of besieged settlers. Because—in case you haven't noticed—the movie business is bedeviled by a whole bunch of problems far more serious than colorization. But have you heard of any organized institutional protests about the way films pandering to teenagers are strangling the adult audience? About the unconscionable multimillion-dollar cost of studio productions, a cost that has the most chilling effect possible on the chance for anything but lowest-common-denominator films being made?

Of course not, because those are pocketbook issues; they mean money both to individuals and, more important, to the studios that employ them. The truth of the matter is that despite the occasional lip service paid to the idea of quality films, most of Hollywood is living too good a life off bad films to really care if they get better or not. The fancy cars, the exclusive parties, the celebrity screenings, the big salaries—they all exist whether films are inferior or superior. If these ever-so-concerned directors really cared about whether the film business was in its death throes or not, they'd be suggesting things like salary caps for themselves and actors and everyone else involved in the business. But that would be threatening the goose that laid their golden life-styles, and no one in Hollywood wants to be an artist all that badly.

The saddest thing about this whole colorization business is how much filmmakers want to be thought of as artists and how little they are willing to sacrifice to gain that sort of recognition. The directors who made the films in Hollywood's heyday, men like John Ford and Alfred Hitchcock, by and large considered themselves craftsmen and popular entertainers; they were concerned with giving value for money, both to the audience and to the studio. But the auteur theory compounded by the adulation of generations of graduate students has given directors swelled heads: When a first-time director insists on "A Wile E. Coyote Film" credit, he really believes he deserves it.

Unfortunately for these people, when you open the movie section of any major newspaper and look at the ads for what's playing, "art" is the last word that comes to your mind. Too morally bankrupt to do battle with the real forces of evil, the solons of Hollywood have grasped the straw of colorization in a feeble attempt to convince the world at large that they are serious about what they do. This macho attempt to assert a dubious cultural manhood, however, is not likely to fool anybody, or solve any of the very real problems in the movie business. What everyone seems conveniently to forget is that what made *It's a Wonderful Life* a great film was not that it was shot in black and white but that it was the expression of a sensibility that has all but vanished from Hollywood. And it'll take more than bellyaching about colorization to bring it back.

GQ, January 1987

LIT CRIT

t's practically a truism that middling books stand a far better chance than great ones of becoming first-rate movies. The web and texture of a great writer's vision is so intimately joined to the language that any attempt to reproduce its marvels as a movie must seem like a violation. When William Faulkner describes a sunset as a "wan hemorrhage," it won't do to show a violet nightfall, no matter how beautifully shot and framed. Norman Mailer once remarked in an interview that "literature haunts our intellect, movies haunt our dreams."

And yet the greatest filmmakers are often drawn to the greatest fictions, and there are enough examples of improbable triumphs to spur the folly—for example, Josef Heifetz's *The Lady with the Little Dog* (Chekhov); Carol Reed's *Outcast of the Islands* (Conrad); Victor Sjostrom's *The Scarlet Letter* (Hawthorne); and David Lean's *Great Expectations* (Dickens). Even failed literary adaptations—like, inevitably, John Huston's *Moby Dick* or Renoir's *Madame Bovary*—often succeed in communicating the filmmaker's love for both literature and the movies. Their ardor becomes the film's true subject.

The three films covered in this section are all derived from books routinely described as notoriously unfilmable. For the directors in-

volved, Huston, Philip Kaufman, and David Cronenberg—all notorious mavericks—the challenge must have been irresistible. Traditionally the literary adaptations that often work the best with the
public, and with many critics, are the primped and plumped period
pieces: the deluxe Dickens and Austen adaptations of Hollywood's
so-called Golden Age, the Ivory-Merchant Forster adaptations of
our own. But how does one adapt the rhapsodic spritz of interior
monologue in Malcolm Lowry's *Under the Volcano?* How do you provide an equivalent to the narrator's self in *The Unbearable Lightness of
Being?* How do you animate Milan Kundera's intellectualisms? And
what is there to be done with the hallucinatory ejaculations of William Burroughs's *Naked Lunch?*

In attempting to answer these questions, the critics of the following
pieces are also implicitly addressing the key issue in any film adaptation: How faithful should a movie be to its literary source?

THE UNBEARABLE LIGHTNESS OF BEING

Terrence Rafferty

For long stretches of Philip Kaufman's *The Unbearable Lightness of Being,* we seem to be looking at nothing but the eyes of lovers: gazing
at each other as they lie in bed, searching for signs of infidelity;
watching themselves in mirrors as they make love, mediating their
intimacy with another—imagined—perspective, seeing themselves
as a voyeur or an artist might; staring at rooms left empty by a
vanished other and trying to gauge the finality of the departure; scan-
ning the face of a lover who has reappeared out of nowhere and trying
to judge the permanence of the return; looking through the lens of
a camera at the history that changes lives, as if their eyes had become
everyone's and everyone's theirs, as if the act of fixing and printing
a moment of vision were the most complex kind of personal intercourse, a way of restoring a shattered relationship with the world; or
alternating glances at each other with concentration on the road
ahead, their vision blurred by the rain on the windscreen and inter-
rupted by the rhythm of the wipers (regular as a metronome or a
pulse), but shared, for a few seconds, with each other and with us, in

the film's, and their, last image, before everything dissolves into a whiteness that hurts our eyes.

After nearly three hours of Kaufman's film, we sit staring at a white rectangle as if at the blank page at the end of a novel we've stayed up all night to read, and try to gather all we've taken in into that space, to project on the blank screen our own most personal imagery. Our impulse, on finishing a work we love, is to hold on to it for a while, and we strengthen our hold by means of unconscious, benign distortion of what the author has put before us — bending his point of view a few degrees until it becomes ours, freezing a handful of moments from the temporal flow of the narrative and merging them with our memories as if they were part of our own experience. The white screen at the end of *The Unbearable Lightness of Being* might stand for the moment when Philip Kaufman read the final words of Milan Kundera's novel and, not wanting to let it go, gave himself over to the reverie that became this film.

Kaufman's movie is an extraordinary adaptation of a difficult book. Just how remarkable it is may not be fully apparent on a single viewing, when readers of the novel may be distracted by what looks like Kaufman's simplification of the material and also by the peculiarly *American* tone of his treatment — which is unmistakable despite the European locations and omnipresent Czech accents, the all-European cast, the Janáček music on the sound track, and the participation of Pierre Guffroy as production designer, Sven Nykvist as cinematographer, and Jean-Claude Carrière as Kaufman's collaborator on the screenplay. This adaptation has a kind of fidelity to its source that's different from what we're used to: It's faithful to the novel as it exists in the mind of a reader, rather than to the novel considered as some sort of autonomous entity, or to a notion of the author's intent.

In interviews, Kaufman has said that the novel's most interesting character is Kundera himself, the discursive, digressive narrator who keeps interrupting the telling of his fairly simple story with long meditations on Nietzsche, Beethoven, Parmenides, kitsch, the history of Europe, the relationship between the body and the soul, and the very art of narration, and who makes clear that the story he relates in this fragmented way is just one part of his thought process, an instrument of speculation. "It would be senseless," he says at one point, "for the author to try to convince the reader that his characters once actually lived"; in his new book, *The Art of the Novel,* he repeatedly defines characters as "experimental selves."

Without Kundera's voice, the novel would be immeasurably diminished; paradoxically, Kaufman's elimination of it doesn't weaken the film. Kaufman seems to understand instinctively that it would be senseless for him to try to convince the audience that his film represents the mind of Milan Kundera; senseless for him to pretend that the film's characters are merely notional, speculative, since what we're watching are living, breathing actors on the screen; senseless for him to imagine the characters as someone else's experimental selves—even if such an act of projection were possible, it would drastically limit the filmmaker's ability to define his own relation to the characters, which is all that matters. The movie's most interesting character is Philip Kaufman.

Kundera's novel is overtly, determinedly self-reflective. Kaufman's presence in the movie is only implicit, but no less pervasive: Instead of introducing himself as a character, he simply makes self-reflection the dominant theme of the work. The staggering variety of looks the characters give each other and the world outside, with each of the film's innumerable close-ups seeming to register a fresh emotional nuance of these people's shifting, exploratory relationships, is, in a sense, a record of the filmmaker's own explorations—the gaze he levels at the text and the experience it represents, his attempts to penetrate, with the lens of a camera, an alien consciousness, a history that can't be his.

We never stop being aware that this movie is an American artist's effort to understand a profoundly European sense of life, because the film is at every moment reminding us of the heartbreaking distances that separate people's imaginations, of the enormous difficulty of seeing the world through another's eyes. The air of erotic melancholy that hangs over Kaufman's film is a reflection of the distances that persist even in the most intimate relationships, of the imperfections of all our projections. There's a section of Kundera's novel called "Words Misunderstood"; Kaufman's movie is about images misunderstood.

At one point, the film's heroine, the innocent Tereza (Juliette Binoche), is horrified to discover that photographs she has taken of the Russian invasion of Prague are being used by the Communist authorities to identify those who resisted the tanks: As her pictures are flashed before her, moments of her own experience, her eyes begin to blur and the images lose their definition. The sequence ends with an ominous close-up of the lens of the slide projector, its single eye beaming a blinding light. It's a shocking perversion of the powers of vision, and a metaphor, somehow, for the small personal betrayals that have made Tereza's marriage to the philandering Tomas (Daniel Day-Lewis) into a series of agonies for her. (She sees his acts of infidelity nightly in her dreams.) At this crucial point, about halfway through the film, we begin to sense how wide and how deep Kaufman's ambitions are: He has conceived his *Unbearable Lightness of Being* as an epic of cognition.

The story, reduced to its outlines, would seem too fragile to support that sort of undertaking. Tomas, a talented young neurosurgeon at a Prague hospital and an inveterate womanizer, meets an earnest country girl named Tereza who becomes, much to his surprise, the first woman ever to spend an entire night in his bed—he wakes up to find her hand tightly gripping his. They marry, but Tomas continues to see other women: His favorite, and longest-running, mistress is an artist named Sabina (Lena Olin), with whom he has a playful, ironic relationship defined by a fetish (a bowler hat) and an urge to watch themselves in mirrors when they make love.

After the Russian invasion in 1968, first Sabina and then Tomas and Tereza leave Czechoslovakia and settle in Switzerland, where they live, for a while, with the wary freedom of exiles until, one by one, they leave: Sabina flees to America when her earnest lover Franz (Derek de Lint) leaves his wife and announces his intention to move in with her; Tereza can't sell her photographs of Czechoslovakia and can't photograph what would sell (nudes and plants), so she returns to Prague; Tomas, the last one left, misses his wife and follows her back. Tomas can't get his old job back, because he had once, almost as a lark, written an article using Oedipus' blindness as a metaphor for totalitarianism; rather than recant, he works as a window cleaner, which gives him fresh opportunities for adultery.

Tereza, more tormented than ever by his unfaithfulness, tries to revenge herself on him (or perhaps simply to understand him) with a one-night stand of her own—but then fears that her affair was set up, engineered by authorities watching her with hidden cameras. They move again, this time to the country, where their beloved dog dies, but they feel happier together, free of scrutiny, closer. After they spend a blissful night of drinking, dancing, and making love in a country inn, their truck crashes on a slick road. Sabina gets a letter in California informing her of their deaths.

It sounds like little more than a soap opera with some political overtones, or, at best, one of those old-fashioned romances in which the lovers are "swept up in the tides of history" or some such. In the novel, Kundera's philosophical digressions and his fragmented, non-chronological narration keep us from getting that gooey *Zhivago* feeling. But Kaufman tells the story straight, from beginning to end, flirting with the Hollywood love story grand manner, almost daring us to find his film banal or sentimental. He makes us realize, though, that this is the way the story has rearranged itself in our heads after reading the novel — and also that its very plainness is a large part of what makes it so moving. Kaufman's directness in this respect links him to Tomas, the no-nonsense seducer who simply gazes at women and commands "Take off your clothes": he examines them and makes love to them at the same time. That, in a way, is what Kaufman does to Kundera's novel — he strips it so he can know and love it better.

☆

But that's not his only mode of knowing. Sabina is one of his experimental selves, too. Her restlessness and her uninhibited sense of play are qualities that Kaufman has demonstrated, not just here, but throughout his career. His films have been unusually diverse, each one radically different from the others and stylistically eclectic in itself. *The Great Northfield, Minnesota Raid* (1972) is an atmospheric, unsentimental western in which Jesse James is portrayed as, of all things, a religious fanatic. *The White Dawn* (1974), about a trio of New England whalers marooned among the Eskimo, is a historical film shot almost as a documentary: The loose narrative seems far less important than the anthropological investigation of the Eskimo's society. His 1978 remake of *Invasion of the Body Snatchers* is a surprisingly funny and lyrical science fiction satire, in which the target of the conformity-inducing pods is the free-thinking, anything-goes culture of San Francisco. *The Wanderers* (1979) is a rambunctious comedy about Bronx gangs in the early sixties, a much more serious movie than it initially appears: In its slapdash way, it actually tries to capture and define a key moment of cultural change. And *The Right Stuff,* his 1983 adaptation of the Tom Wolfe book about test pilots and astronauts, is a three-hour all-American jamboree, a movie that mixes styles and tones so promiscuously that it seems, finally, to express everything that is most beautiful, most heroic, and most irredeemably stupid about American life, all at once.

Sabina is this movie's primary wanderer: As an artist and as a woman, she shuns permanence with an instinctive horror. In Prague, her paintings are elegant, suggestive abstractions with an ominous sexuality reminiscent of Georgia O'Keeffe. In Geneva, her art is constructed of daggerlike shards of mirrors: Her apartment/studio is like an expressionist changing room, in which a visitor, undressing, is constantly surrounded by splintery images of himself. In California, Sabina spray-paints seascapes for elderly buyers: The paintings are blandly serene, as if the sea (as in Baudelaire) has become her mirror but she doesn't quite see herself in it.

Her sex scenes with Tomas are, thanks to the mirrors (she has one in Prague, too), dazzlingly complex, and all the more erotic for their formal complexity. The relationship of their bodies to each other keeps shifting in the frame, in unexpected configurations, and their (and our) angles of vision do, too. Nothing is fixed — heavy, in Kundera's terms — and their lovemaking sequences come to seem perhaps the movie's purest expression of the delights of irony: the exhilaration of seeing oneself, and others, always from a bit of a distance, of being able to observe, with amused dispassion, the infinite patterns our parts can arrange themselves in. When, on Sabina's last night in Geneva, Tomas visits her in a hotel room and they lie in bed together looking directly into each other's faces — without benefit of mirrors for the only time in the movie — it's one of the saddest moments in *The Unbearable Lightness of Being.* A terrible weight seems to have settled on them. Looking straight into each other's eyes, their self-reflective irony has deserted them. Their frank gazes have the desperate, commemorative urgency of last looks: They reflect nothing but the sudden, startling desire to fix a final image of something precious about to disappear forever.

In that scene, Tomas and Sabina find themselves looking at each other, for one surprised moment, in the way that Tereza *always* sees the world, and from that point on, Tereza's way of seeing begins to dominate the film. There's a brief scene in which the shift is made explicit. After Tereza has left Geneva, Tomas sits in their empty apartment and stares at a small potted cactus, a bleak little object that Tereza had spent hours contemplating, because a Swiss magazine editor suggested that this was the sort of photograph he might be interested in. Tereza has looked at this absurd thing with growing misery, unable to photograph it, unable, we feel, even to *see* it — an object that, like everything in Geneva, she is incapable of discovering her relation to, a sight she feels not the slightest impulse to commemorate.

As Tomas sits before the cactus, he — and we — are invaded by Tereza's vision, her frustration and despair at gazing always, in her exile, at things that remain so stubbornly outside her, things she can never truly feel are hers. As if possessed by Tereza's spirit, Tomas, too, goes back, and the film takes on a more somber tone. At first, we miss Sabina mightily: The sequences that follow Tomas's return to Prague (and precede the final, pastoral section) are the shakiest passages in the film. Even Kaufman seems a little dispirited: Deprived of the occasions to exercise his visual inventiveness that Sabina's scenes provided him, his moviemaking briefly loses a bit of its zest. But Tereza's worldview does finally take hold, because Kaufman has prepared us for it — it has always been one of the possible visions proposed by the movie — and because Tereza, too, is clearly an aspect of himself.

In the first section of the film, before the invasion, Tereza, though charmingly played by Binoche, is nearly as puzzling to us as she is to Tomas. She's unformed, compared to the other characters, and her simplicity and possessiveness seem out of place in the liberated atmosphere of Dubček-era Prague: She's an outsider among the sophisticates, an intent but slightly baffled observer. The exuberance of these early sequences suggests that this period in Czech history is, for Kaufman, the easiest part of the story to represent — a time when his characters live, in a sense, as Americans do, heedlessly and optimistically. He doesn't *need* to assume Tereza's perspective until the tanks roll in and he has to call on something that will take him far beyond the frame of his own experience.

The invasion sequence is Tereza's first big moment, and Kaufman does it full justice. It's a wrenching montage of stock footage and stills, mostly in black and white, intercut with shots of Tomas and Tereza rushing through the crowds (all shot as if they, too, were part of the grainy file film), as Tereza snaps more and more pictures: Finally, almost all of what we're seeing is imagery her camera has caught. Kaufman's treatment of the invasion is actually fuller and more emotionally intense than Kundera's, for a good reason: Kundera needs to distance himself from this pivotal event in his life, to gain perspective on it; Kaufman, who has experienced the invasion only through documentary footage, newspaper photos, and Kundera, needs to get closer.

And that's why Tereza becomes more important to Kaufman as the film goes on, why he treats her with greater tenderness than her creator does. Kundera sees her fierce attachment to home, her heavier passions, as weakness, and in doing so seems to be conducting an argument with himself — against whatever impulses he might feel to return to his native country. To Kaufman, however, she is the mystery that must be penetrated for him to make this film: the most rooted of the characters, the least "American" in spirit. And in the invasion sequence, we feel the excitement of his discovery of what connects him to her. Her picture taking brings everything into focus. He understands, because he's such an emotional image maker himself, her impulse to fix moments on film as a way of making sense of her own life: Her need to possess these images and her need to possess Tomas are essentially the same urge — an urge that can't be so unlike what impelled Philip Kaufman to put this book on film.

Between the invasion and Tomas's return to Prague, Tereza's point of view gathers force. In that section of the film, there's an extraordinary sequence in which Tereza and Sabina take turns photographing each other in the nude in Sabina's mirror-crammed studio. This is the scene in which the movie's experiments in vision come together, the give-and-take of the two women's examinations of each other complicated by the implicit presence of Tomas: Looking at each other unclothed, each is aware that she is seeing what Tomas has also seen. By the end of this superbly choreographed play of visions, some miraculous unity seems to have been achieved, a resolution of Tomas's and Sabina's and Tereza's points of view into a single, undifferentiated image of happiness as the two women lie naked and laughing on the floor. (This is, surely, just as Tomas would imagine it.) But that image is erased immediately by the arrival of Franz, which precipitates Sabina's flight from Geneva and thus begins the process of sending the characters again on their separate roads.

It's no wonder that Tereza's possessive spirit holds sway in the second half of the film. The moment of harmony dissolved so quickly, and nothing like it occurs again until the very end, during Tomas and Tereza's night at the inn and their drive home. Through the artifice of Kaufman's editing, Sabina seems to be present, too. The scene in which she receives the news of their deaths comes halfway through the dancing, so the rest of Tomas and Tereza's story might almost be happening in her imagination. Tomas turns to Tereza and says, "I'm thinking how happy I am," in the moment before the screen — their view of the road — begins to go white, another harmonious vision vanishing too soon. But in this movie Philip Kaufman has made such a vision appear before our eyes twice, with Tereza on screen both times, as if her dogged, heavy, loving spirit had led him to it once and then again, as she led Tomas back to Prague. She's the filmmaker's guide both because she's the farthest from him and because she's the nearest. She seems to have made him believe that the taking of images — the impulse to hold on to what we love — is the highest form of reading the world, and the truest guarantee of eternal return.

Sight and Sound, Summer 1988

THE UNBEARABLE LIGHTNESS OF BEING

J. Hoberman

Engineers of the text, Philip Kaufman and Jean-Claude Carrière have between them tackled sources as varied as Richard Price and Jacques Tati, *Invasion of the Body Snatchers* and *The Mahabharata.* But it required more than usual boldness to essay the winding byways and airy turrets of Czech émigré Milan Kundera's *The Unbearable Lightness of Being.* Kundera's characters are abstract and his plots elusive; he's not primarily a storyteller. More interested in narrative performance than in narrative per se, he structures his novels like fugues and filters his creatures through the prism of his authorial persona so that they seem incorporeal as angels. Kundera's people cast no shadows; they're a priori resistant to film.

But Kundera is destined for Nobelity and, from the leisurely credit sequence on, Kaufman and Carrière are determined to award his sardonic, convoluted parable of the womanizing surgeon Tomas (Daniel Day-Lewis), his dependent wife Tereza (Juliette Binoche), and sometime mistress Sabina (Lena Olin) the posh, epic treatment. *The Unbearable Lightness of Being* is nothing if not thoughtful — in everything from the philosophical bedroom scenes to the Janáček-scored comedy bits to the outer-Slovakia local color. Still, the popularization of Kundera seems foredoomed, not least because of the author's built-in injunction against that universalizing of emotion he calls kitsch: "Kitsch causes two tears to flow in quick succession. The first tear says: How nice to see children running on the grass. The second tear says: How nice to be moved, together with all mankind, by children running on the grass. It is the second tear that makes kitsch kitsch."

Transforming Kundera's meditation on love into a love story while skewing the book so that the 1968 Soviet invasion of Czechoslovakia becomes its centerpiece, Kaufman and Carrière can't avoid that second tear — although theirs is an intelligent adaptation that in some respects enriches its source. The movie makes explicit Kundera's affection for characters who can't handle exile or who refuse to leave their unhappy country, and it gives them an iconic, if chintzy, glamour. Daniel Day-Lewis is too callow and, initially, wound too tight to give Tomas much deadpan savoir faire — particularly in the more self-conscious sex scenes. Reserved and thin-lipped, he doesn't look like a sensualist and, paired with the ripely feline but inexpressive Olin, a member of Ingmar Bergman's theatrical company, he seems more panicked than smug. He eventually relaxes into his role, losing some of his edginess in his later scenes with Binoche, whose soft, indistinct features cling to the screen like cashmere.

The Unbearable Lightness of Being isn't dependent on its source, but the action is limned with voluptuous melancholy if you're familiar with the novel's ending. Of course, Kaufman suffers from a nervous apprehension that his audience doesn't know what Czechoslovakia is, or worse, doesn't care. Prague Spring is crudely sketched; the essence of '68ness is conveyed mainly by miniskirts and a rendition of "Hey Jude" in Czech (too bad the English version wasn't released until after the Russians entered Prague), and events grind to a halt for explicit explanations: "I think the Russians will interfere, remember Hungary!" one intellectual cautions. "The world wouldn't allow it," his friend replies. Kundera evoked the invasion with masterful indirection, one sentence here, a few paragraphs there. In the movie, it arrives like an earthquake and rocks the house — the stars cleverly matted into black-and-white footage of Soviet tanks and surging crowds (a feat less remarkable than the conversion of certain neighborhoods of Paris and Lyons into something like Prague).

Alternately droll, earnest, and aimlessly trashy, *The Unbearable Lightness* has no style to speak of — by the time the principals make their escape to tranquil Switzerland, it's begun to resemble a dubbed, denatured international copro. With the Anglo-Swedish-French cast madly rolling their *r*'s and *v*-ing their *w*'s in a parody of Czech-inflected English, it's David Lean for intellectuals, an egghead *Dr. Zhivago*. Not until the action returns irrevocably to the Gulag (a moody, hopeless shot of a provincial train station in the rain, signaling the final movement) does Kaufman hit the appropriate note of romantic fatalism. Before long, the neurosurgeon is reduced to cleaning windows — at the screening I attended, the audience visibly snapped to attention at the sight of so harshly rewarded integrity —

and the narrative picks up a spiraling momentum as Tomas and Tereza retreat into the countryside to meet their particular doom.

The Unbearable Lightness could have been so much worse that one might praise it out of proportion were the film itself not so inflated. Ideas are introduced with portentous pauses and bracketed by admiring reaction shots. Kaufman is never matter-of-fact when he might be picturesque; there's a surplus of postcard posing. (It's as though he's fearful of East European "grayness.") Still, the emphases on submission and skepticism, the iron rule of history, and the erotic mysteries of the organism are so foreign to most Hollywood movies that *The Unbearable Lightness* has a weird, almost enchanting novelty. It's an East European wannabe, the exact opposite of an "American"-style thriller like *Kojak in Budapest*. (If the Kaufman opus weren't three hours, it would be perfectly prefaced by one of the Philadelphia-born Quay brothers' pseudo-Czech puppetoons.)

Often flat-footed, Kaufman's direction lacks the ferocious irony that an Ivan Passer or Agnieszka Holland could have brought to the material, but, as if in recognition that there are some roles an outsider will never master, he produces a pair of actual East Europeans, Laszlo Szabo and Daniel Olbrychski, to play police interrogators. The latter gives a particularly witty performance, pirouetting around Day-Lewis in a blur of sidelong glances, bad teeth, and curdled charm: "Of course we can't allow a politically suspicious man to operate on brains." It's the combination of necessity and superfluity, self-awareness and self-deception, that gives Olbrychski's joke its kick. The least one can say for *The Unbearable Lightness* is that it leaves you with a sense of lives that are neither black nor white, but rather sumptuous in their shades of gray.

Village Voice, February 9, 1988

UNDER THE VOLCANO

Sheila Benson

"Come, amigo, throw away your mind," the courtly Mexican doctor tells his English drinking companion, Geoffrey Firmin, in *Under the Volcano.*

The Consul (Albert Finney) grabs a bottle and pushes through the dense foliage as he tries to escape himself and those around him in *Under the Volcano*. (Photo by François Duhamel–Mega, courtesy of Universal Pictures.)

It makes perfect sense, since Firmin (Albert Finney) lives almost entirely inside his head, but it's a phrase that also makes sense when addressed to the moviegoers. If we didn't already know from our own attempts to read the original Malcolm Lowry novel, we hear on every side how baroque, how challenging (*and* how infinitely rewarding) it is, and how impossible to translate to the screen.

But it has been done. In his bold, intelligent screenplay, twenty-seven-year-old Guy Gallo has given us the heart of the Lowry novel, and director John Huston has filled in its soul in a lean, immaculate, superbly crafted film. And, to see it, you do not need to live in your head. Although it is this year's treat for adults, *Under the Volcano* is both completely accessible and completely unpretentious – those Huston hallmarks.

In a remarkable compression of time, the action now takes place in almost twenty-four hours, in Cuernavaca, Mexico, in 1938, during the mystical Day of the Dead celebration; if you were to graph it, the action would be a downward progression.

In the film, we see that plunge represented by the careening progress of a little, rust-yellow Mexican country bus, beginning at the upper left of the screen and moving down and out of frame on the right. It carries the film's three central characters: the alcoholic Geoffrey Firmin (Albert Finney), called the Consul but actually the ex–British consul to Cuernavaca; his wife Yvonne (Jacqueline Bisset), who had left him but has only that morning returned; and Firmin's half-brother, Hugh (Anthony Andrews), who has briefly been Yvonne's lover.

Scaldingly aware of this past relationship, the Consul nevertheless takes Yvonne's return as an almost literal sign of faith. And, as all three walk from their thick-walled house out into a Day of the Dead fiesta, they see the film's reiterated theme, *No se puede vivir sin amor* (one cannot live without love), visualized touchingly in a father and son from the village.

Love seems *almost* a possibility again. A little later, after a scene at a country bullring that reinforces Hugh's physicality and his romantic flair for action, there is the film's most poignantly lyric scene. In a reckless, resolutely naive reaffirmation of their love, Yvonne and Geoffrey talk of a new life together, far away from Mexico. But the Consul's code does not allow him the comfort of forgiveness, and we know it as surely as he does.

Lowry's great feat in the novel was his ability to create a double world: the real Mexico in which the Consul lives, and the hallucinatory one that the Consul, who is seen as a magician, a priest, or an emerging saint, sees around him, a result of his epic drinking. The problem has always been how to let us see both those worlds, for although *Volcano* is an intensely visual book, it is not a visualizable one.

The filmmakers have faced this problem directly by admitting that you cannot reproduce this rich inner world without hopelessly confusing the audience. They have rendered the Consul's state via his occasional soliloquies, and it works surprisingly well. The reason, of course, is Albert Finney's towering portrayal of Geoffrey Firmin, who, although never once sober at any time we see him, remains a man of dignity, charm, courage, humor, and pervasive sadness.

Bisset and Andrews are simply fine as the two who love him yet must stand by helplessly as his plunge accelerates. In the book, Geoffrey is haunted continuously by the memory of his wife's "simplicity and comradeship . . . fundamental sanity . . . untidiness . . . equally excessive neatness — the sweet beginnings to our marriage." Bisset has created a woman with a hint of all of this, as well as a deep sense of what she and her husband once had together.

Andrews is particularly good when you examine his role and realize that, right causes and all that aside, Hugh is really a great booby. If, as he hints, he's bound for England and the coming war, he will probably get himself killed and it will be called a great sacrifice, not empty-headed gallantry.

The Mexico that is such a crucial part of all this (a country in 1938 not immune to the growing strength of Nazism) is amazingly re-created in a production whose every detail is superb. Mexican artist-painter Gunther Gerzso was the production designer, working with Tom Shaw (*Wise Blood*), production supervisor.

They are helped enormously by the soft, sad beauty of the photography by the great Gabriel Figueroa, Alex North's superb musical score, exceptionally sinuous and deft editing by Roberto Silvi, and a cast of fine Mexican actors including Ignacio Lopez Tarso as Dr. Vigil, actor-director Emilio Fernandez as the owner of the Farolito, Rene Ruiz as its malevolent dwarf pimp, and Katy Jurado as the cantina owner who cannot hear the truth in the Consul's meanderings.

If the film is an absolute triumph for Finney, it is also a notable one for Huston. The Consul clearly must refuse any easy compromises on his hideous path to salvation, but imagine what Huston must have had to resist, for almost forty years, before choosing this elegant path to the heart of a dark and difficult novel.

Los Angeles Times, July 6, 1984

UNDER THE VOLCANO

Peter Rainer

John Huston has wanted to make a movie out of Malcolm Lowry's rambling, visionary, expressionist novel *Under the Volcano* for thirty years, and now that he's finally made it, he still doesn't have a movie. Of all the major postwar novels (*Volcano* was begun in 1938 and finally published in 1947), Lowry's is probably the least likely candidate for a successful film. Set on the eve of World War II in Cuernavaca on the Mexican Day of the Dead, it's about the last twenty-four hours in the life of alcoholic British ex-Consul Geoffrey Firmin (played in the film by Albert Finney). In the course of the day, Geoffrey's errant wife Yvonne (Jacqueline Bisset), who has been separated from him for a year and filed for divorce, returns to him; unable to bear the weight of this long-sought gift, Geoffrey spirals even further into self-destruction.

The semiautobiographical novel takes place almost entirely inside Geoffrey's mind, and his whole life pours through the prose: his fears and philosophies and evasions and longings. His tragedy is both a specialized case — a boozer's apotheosis — and a symptom of a death-rattled, valueless world on the verge of a Fascist apocalypse. The reason this novel has been so difficult to adapt to the screen is that, if you eliminate its dense exfoliation of ideas and emotion and just stick to the story, you're left with a rather paltry plot. And that's exactly what John Huston and his screenwriter Guy Gallo are left with. They've reduced Lowry's novel to a maundering movie about a portentous drunk.

The film doesn't even function as an explanatory slide show of the book. How could it? The movie medium is capable of a great many miracles, but explicating interior states of consciousness isn't one of them. To those unfamiliar with Lowry's novel, Huston's film will probably seem puzzling and a bit blank: There's obviously something "important" happening, but the movie rarely lets on what that might be. Guy Gallo's fidelity to the bare bones of the plot may seem like an intelligent choice, but it's also a classy form of uninspiration. (Probably the only way to make the novel work on film would be to completely rethink it — in the manner of, say, Robert Altman's *The*

Long Goodbye.) But even if one accepts the film's surface fidelity, Huston's film skimps on the available opportunities.

He doesn't, for example, try to find a cinematic equivalent for Geoffrey's rich, subterranean moods; Gabriel Figueroa's cinematography is disappointingly glossy, and the Mexican symbology — such as the skeleton's Dance of Death that opens the movie — hits you over the head. (Anyone who has ever seen Eisenstein's documentary *Que Viva Mexico,* or even seen stills from it, will feel a distinct visual comedown in this film.) Huston's straight-ahead, unadorned style is temperamentally unsuited to Lowry's material; he can't — or doesn't want to — bring out the resonances in the landscapes, and the Mexican peasants look posed. Even though Yvonne's return to Cuernavaca is made memorable by Albert Finney's acting in the scene (he has to look at her four times before he believes it's really her), Huston subsequently does nothing to make her wondrous: Jacqueline Bisset's beauty is supposed to be enough for us (her wan performance certainly doesn't help).

The third major character in the film, Geoffrey's half-brother Hugh (Anthony Andrews), who was Yvonne's lover and is staying temporarily with Geoffrey, registers even less; there's almost no sexual tension between Hugh and Yvonne. Hugh, who spent time with the Republicans in the Spanish Civil War and wears a cowboy hat most of the time, is supposed to represent the man-of-action pose that Geoffrey rejects. (At one point in the film Hugh shows off by jumping into a bullring and playing the matador.) But Hugh comes off as such a ninny that he's no match for Geoffrey even at his most sozzled. Despite Huston's long-term preoccupation with this project, there's no urgency in his filmmaking; his imagery doesn't have the force of obsession. Lowry's novel, paradoxically, is a much more cinematic experience than the film.

The Consul's self-destructive, self-dramatizing despair has many roots in the novel. In the movie, his despair seems primarily the result of a failed marriage; in other words, in its own quietly efficient way, Huston's *Under the Volcano* is a Hollywoodization of the story. (The movie's ad line reads: "One cannot live without love.") But the lost-love scenario doesn't explain why, when Yvonne returns (inexplicably) to Cuernavaca, eager to rehabilitate Geoffrey and take him out of Mexico, Geoffrey deliberately trashes their hopes. His action only makes sense if you understand Geoffrey's demons, and his demons are too expansive and nightmarish for the narrow confines of this movie. Huston shows us scenes from the book, such as Geoffrey's loop-the-loop ride at a local fair, where everything falls out of his pockets, but it doesn't mean anything special to us. Here's how Lowry described the same scene: "Everything was falling out of his pockets, was being wrested from him, torn away, a fresh article at each whirligig, sickening, plunging, retreatable circuit, his notecase, pipe, keys, his dark glasses he had taken off. . . . " Later on: "There was a kind of fierce delight in this final acceptance. Let everything go! Everything particularly that provided the means of ingress or egress, went bond for, gave meaning or character, or purpose or identity to that frightful bloody nightmare he was forced to carry around with him everywhere on his back, that went by the name of Geoffrey Firmin." In the movie, this episode comes across as little more than a funny-sad lark.

Huston has, however, done one shrewd thing: He's hewed the movie to Albert Finney's performance, hoping, perhaps, that his acting would provide the passion that the rest of the film lacks. And Finney comes through, or at least as much as any actor could under the circumstances. We *do* get a sense of something larger — something more fearful and ominous and ruined — in his Consul; Finney's performance gives the movie a heavy, ambiguous weight. Strapped into his tux, with his dark sunglasses blanking out his eyes, his arms bent at his side like broken wings, Finney's Consul seems perpetually aghast, and yet he's a tough old lush. He may fall down stuporous in the street, but, when a British motorist drives by and inquires if he's all right, Geoffrey snaps to groggy attention — he even uses the occasion to satirize the motorist's upper-crust accent. Geoffrey's drinking is presented (as it also was in the novel) as a form of heroism. He never slobbers disgustedly over anyone, never throws up, never gets the DTs. He even frequents a whorehouse — he's surprisingly potent. But Geoffrey's spiritual impotence — his unwillingness to break out of his fantasies into the world of action — is what gnaws at him. And yet he prizes the way he is; he regards the world as too blighted to be worth his sobriety. He's proud to be among the damned.

It's amazing how much of this comes through in Finney's performance, considering how little he had to work with. Jacqueline Bisset and Anthony Andrews offer such slim support that he's practically doing a solo. Finney knows how to portray the various moods and levels of drunkenness; he knows how to use his voice so that it's a cracked quaver one moment and a booming instrument the next. He can slide imperceptibly into the sloughs. In Finney's most remarkable scene, he jabbers good-naturedly with Hugh and Yvonne and then, in a flash, almost apologetically, confronts them about their affair and then flees to his doom. We can see in this confrontation how Geoffrey's anger has fermented into self-hatred; in an earlier sequence, he and Yvonne talked of a paradisiacal future together, and now, with these belated accusations, he's junking that future — the future he cannot face.

Huston has made a career out of challenges, and he's often won. *Under the Volcano* was probably the biggest challenge of them all — even bigger than *Moby-Dick.* He's made extraordinary movies out of books as disparate as the Bible and *The Red Badge of Courage* and *Reflections in a Golden Eye,* and, a few years ago, he entered into Flannery O'Connor's Southern Gothic nightmare world in *Wise Blood.* But *Under the Volcano* might have meant more to Huston thirty years ago, when he first wanted to make it. The movie needs the touch of a cracked, crazed visionary — a Werner Herzog or an Orson Welles or a Luis Buñuel (who once wanted to adapt the book and then rejected the idea). At seventy-eight, age has transformed Huston's style into something which, at its late best, as in the 1975 *The Man Who Would Be King,* is contemplative and serene. (That's what Buñuel's last films were like, too.) In *Under the Volcano,* that serenity sometimes gives the film a fated, deliberate pull but, for the most part, it comes across as perfunctory. Huston can no longer connect with Geoffrey's cry: "Hell is my natural habitat." The best he can manage in *Under the Volcano* is purgatory.

Los Angeles Herald Examiner, July 5, 1984

NAKED LUNCH

Hal Hinson

Naked Lunch, William S. Burroughs's controversial 1959 novel, was a masterpiece about what he called "The Algebra of Need." Its subject was heroin, and addiction in general, and no other author, before or since, has had greater firsthand knowledge of his material or used it to re-create in such vivid, ant-crawling detail the plunge into the hungry abyss of drugs.

The movie *Naked Lunch* is a different sort of masterpiece altogether.

It's not about drugs, per se, though it euphemistically dives into the universe of mind-altering substances as deeply and lustily as any movie in history. Drugs serve as the film's background, its world, but not its substance. Adapted by David Cronenberg, the Canadian director of, among others, *Dead Ringers* and *The Fly,* the film isn't a literal transcription of the novel at all; it's more a fictional essay on Burroughs and the anxious birth of the novel. It's a movie about a writer's relationship to his work—and, as such, perhaps one of the most penetrating examinations of a writer's processes ever made. Certainly it's one of the strangest and most disturbing.

For Cronenberg, Burroughs's *Naked Lunch* served only as a jumping-off point. Sprinkled throughout are bits from other Burroughs books, particularly *Junky* and *Exterminator!* all of which are folded in with incidents from Burroughs's life. The film's biographical details are more metaphorical than literal, too, including Burroughs's relationships with Jack Kerouac and Allen Ginsberg, his accidental fatal shooting of his wife, Joan, and his encounters with Paul and Jane Bowles. When Cronenberg introduces his hero, Bill Lee (Peter Weller), it's 1953 and Lee's an exterminator slaughtering roaches and centipedes in New York with a pump canister of yellow bug powder. At this point Lee is not a writer, at least not like his friends Hank and Martin (Nicholas Campbell and Michael Zelniker), who are modeled on Kerouac and Ginsberg and struggling to get into print. He is, however, a pungent rhetorician. "Exterminate all rational thought," he says, adding his two cents to the literary babble between his friends.

The line is not idly dropped, either by the character or the director; it points the way for what is to come. When Lee returns home, he finds his wife, Joan Lee (Judy Davis), with a hypodermic stuck in her breast—a hypo filled with bug powder. Yes, she admits, looking at him with coal-circled eyes, she has something of a habit, which also explains why he's been coming up short on his jobs.

Afraid of losing his gig, Lee visits a mysterious Dr. Benway (Roy Scheider), who says Joan can kick the bug stuff if Lee cuts it first with a vile-smelling black powder he's extracted from the giant aquatic Brazilian centipede. But before Lee can test the effectiveness of Benway's concoction on Joan, he tries it on himself and, still woozy from his injection, informs his wife that it's about time for them to show Martin their "William Tell routine." Obligingly, Joan puts a drinking glass on her head and Lee blithely pulls out a revolver and shoots, leaving a ruby red dot on her forehead.

Joan's death puts the cops on Lee's tail, forcing him to travel as a spy to a kind of fantastical Casablanca called Interzone. Burroughs has said that his wife's death was a pivotal moment in his life, and Cronenberg takes him at his word. He uses the incident as the event that catalyzes Lee's metamorphosis into a full-fledged addict and a writer. Following the instructions of a bony, greenish reptile called a Mugwump, he begins filing reports from Interzone on his trusty Clark Nova, a portable typewriter that, while Lee is working, transforms into a buggy creature that talks out of a sphincterlike opening beneath its wings.

There is, of course, no such place as Interzone; it, the Mugwumps, and the pestilent writing machines are all figments of Lee's drug-fevered imagination. And the dispatches he files from this hallucinatory nether realm are actually the raw stuff of what would eventually become *Naked Lunch*. In his novel, Burroughs showed that he was both a descendant of Swift and the paterfamilias to cyber-punk futurists such as William Gibson. And Cronenberg manages to capture the paranoid social satirist and the science fiction writer in Burroughs. Visually, the director has tilted the balance more toward the latter, though it's the grungy future-of-the-past we see, some surrealistic dimension where deranged junkie fantasy and emotional reality intersect. The way Cronenberg presents it, the story seems to slide out of some mutant polyp of roach brain in Lee's skull. It's a movie full of perverse longings, oozing fluids, and raunchy physical detail—a film constructed out of a genuine revulsion for the body, where the simple sight of human flesh is nearly enough to turn your stomach. It's a truly excremental movie, in the purest Freudian sense.

What's amazing, though, is that we feel as comfortable with the terrain as we do. The reason for this, I think, is that we remain connected to the sane part of the Lee character, the part that realizes that his hallucinated alternate reality is a product of his drug-induced virus and that stays detached enough to take notes on the experience. This is the result of both the cool clinicism of Cronenberg's direction and Weller's droll, atonal performance. Dressed in his proper, antihipster suits and ties, he gives a perfect approximation of Burroughs's secret-agent style; he's an invisible man, without definite gender or sexual inclination, and so bland that he fades instantly into the squalid woodwork, so suavely somatized that his reactions seem to register only after an eternity, as if they've made their way to the surface in slow motion from the bottom of the sea. Weller's comatose portrayal is stocked with hilarious detail; it's a wonderfully deadpan piece of acting, tense, precise, and painfully still. And Cronenberg positions it beautifully in counterpoint to the outrageousness of the imagined world around him.

Cronenberg hasn't always been as skilled with his actors; in past films they've often seemed lost, overshadowed by the graphic design of the work. Everyone in the cast here, though, is superb, particularly Davis in the dual role of Lee's wife, Joan, and Joan Frost, another writer and Mugwump-juice junkie (a character based on Jane Bowles) whom he meets in Interzone. Davis shows a different side of her cyclonic talent here; she's a burnout, with a world-weary sag to her features, and whenever she's in front of the camera a gaping, wounded hole seems to open up on the screen. She's not around much, but she leaves you wishing there were more of her character.

There's a synergistic overlap here between Cronenberg's own particular brand of weirdness and Burroughs's; they're both twisted in ways that complement each other nicely. If the movie has a flaw, it's that the aspects of Burroughs's work many believed unfilmable still resist visualization. What had seemed unthinkably subversive on the page seems slightly literal minded, and somehow tamer, on screen. Still, it's a dank, genuinely sick trip into the dark, rancid basement of the writer's mind — a fitting homage to the labors of a true original.

The Washington Post, January 10, 1992

NAKED LUNCH

Jay Carr

Nothing dates quicker than outrage. A generation ago, William S. Burroughs's *Naked Lunch* was on trial in Boston, accused of being obscene, eloquently defended by Norman Mailer as a religious novel depicting hell as the culmination of the scientific revolution, hailed by Allen Ginsberg for its extension of the theory of addiction to a materialistic society rampant with control addicts. Its hallucinatory scenes, its homoerotic intensity, and its druggy interior rant made it, by common agreement, unfilmable. So now, of course, it's art and there's a film of it. But David Cronenberg's *Naked Lunch* is an embalming kind of film, reminding us that Hollywood is the roach motel of art—where it checks in, but doesn't check out.

Large roaches are only one of the devices Cronenberg has added to Burroughs's own Mugwumps to bring *Naked Lunch* to the screen in a resourceful but compromised treatment that turns Burroughs's deviance and satiric riffs into a bug-ridden (and bug-written, as Burroughs's typewriters have a way of turning into roaches that bark orders at him) view of the writer's life. It looks dark and slimy and outrageous, until you realize that the creatures wouldn't draw a second glance at Toys "R" Us. Cronenberg hasn't so much filmed *Naked Lunch* as tamed it, turned it into entertainment, with oozy rubber bugs, big and little, that look left over from David Lynch's movie of *Dune,* or the intergalactic dive from *Star Wars.*

Except for the wonderfully ravaged air Judy Davis brings to the role of Burroughs's wife—who used to shoot up with the bug powder he stole from his exterminator's job, and who herself was shot dead by Burroughs in a William Tell episode after he saw her in bed with one of his writer friends—Cronenberg's *Naked Lunch* is utterly without the raw, unflinching urgency of Burroughs's prose, despite Davis's almost-as-good reprise as Jane Bowles when the story moves to Tangier, where Burroughs has a highly unlikely affair with her. The book is filled with a desperate lyricism. The film seems smugly content with de-emphasizing the book's homosexuality and turning Burroughs's buggy hallucinations into rubbery special effects—a Burroughs World theme park. The difference between the book and the film is the difference between Hieronymus Bosch and Walt Disney.

Cronenberg is at once too wholesome at heart and too glibly given over to hanging the film on his take on Burroughs's writing processes. The funniest thing is the way Peter Weller apes Burroughs's buttoned-down straight look, projecting muffled dread. Otherwise, though, there's nothing much coming out of him, certainly none of the raspy authority and back-from-hell insouciance that makes Burroughs Burroughs. And the cockroachy typewriters are so slimily cute that they obscure the real charge of paranoia that made Burroughs's writings on mind control so vivid. Weller, in short, is a Burroughs mannequin, not a reincarnation of Burroughs, with his slightly superior air of hipster cool. And Weller is symptomatic of the film's just-visiting air. Ian Holm, as Paul Bowles's stand-in, and Julian Sands, as a Swiss idler, elude the wax-museum quality that traps Weller, especially Holm, who reaches an interesting edge of prissy challenge. Michael Zelniker and Nicholas Campbell, as the Allen Ginsberg and Jack Kerouac figures, though, are bland.

The uncertainties of the Gulf War meant that Cronenberg had to film *Naked Lunch* on studio sets and forget going to Tangier (referred to by Burroughs as the Interzone). It was probably better that way, since stylized artifice is the currency in which this film is dealing, not wild emotions — although Ornette Coleman's saxophone solos conjure up the book's lunging disjointedness. Peter Suschitzky's cinematography is a plus, too. Like *Barton Fink,* this film conjures up an oily netherworld, the kind into which any addict could cheerfully vanish. But not a Burroughs addict. You'd think the man behind the deliquescence of *The Fly* and the clinical horrors of *Dead Ringers* would be just the one to take on the heightened nightmarishness of Burroughs's polymorphic world. But only a generation reared on TV sitcoms could find this film charged with any real edge. With its Smithsonian tableau quality, Cronenberg's *Naked Lunch* amounts to little more than "The Addams Family" for lit freaks.

Boston Globe, January 10, 1992

AUTEUR/HAUTER

At a time when most movies seem to be traffic-managed rather than directed, the concept of the auteur — so hallowed in the critic's lexicon — seems particularly tinny. In a machine-tooled, bottom-line movie era, the true auteur of a film is much more likely to be a studio production chief, or the head of a powerful talent agency, or the president of a powerful bank. Even most good directors nowadays aren't hoping to achieve a vision — they're hoping to achieve a job.

It makes sense, then, that a director who *does* come up with a startling style, even if it's at the service of the Terminator, is likely to be hailed as a visionary. It's not the quality of the vision that counts so much as the fact that there's any vision at all.

The directors in this section connect up with a more respectable tradition. They have all been acclaimed or derided as auteurs not just for their way of seeing but for their whole approach to experience. To critics, they function as benchmarks: How you define these directors is central to how you define yourself. Bertrand Blier's dreamy, gallivanting sex farces, for example, bring you up against your own erotic assumptions. The rage in Sam Peckinpah's movies comes out of a complete philosophy of life. If you reject a movie of his like *Straw Dogs,* as Judith Crist does here, you are also rejecting that philosophy.

Is Rainer Werner Fassbinder's work spiritual or soul-deadening? Is Jean-Luc Godard's gamesmanship the height of mountebankery? (But, in the movies, aren't mountebankery and genius sometimes joined at the hip?) Should we blame Steven Spielberg and George Lucas for turning our movies into theme parks? Was the violence in Spielberg's *Indiana Jones and the Temple of Doom,* which prompted a public outcry that led to the new parents' advisory rating of PG-13, a betrayal or a hoot? Is The Force pop transcendence or just popped corn?

For some critics, the Coen brothers' inky, hermetic universe is cluttery with clues, keys, portents. Others, agreeing with Gary Arnold's review of *Barton Fink,* may think it's about time for the Coens to get a life. The natteriness of John Cassavetes's movies may drive you up the wall. Or you may find them indispensable in scaling the same walls that other filmmakers can only hit their heads against. How much of Terry Gilliam or Michael Cimino is overlord and how much is overload? Can the high art of Peter Greenaway (*The Cook, the Thief, His Wife and Her Lover*) and the low camp of John Waters (*Pink Flamingos*) be reduced to scatology high and low?

Critics also define themselves by the ways in which they respond to the shifts in a director's career—Woody Allen's, for example, or Robert Altman's. Carrie Rickey's feature on the new black film directors closes the chapter by setting the stage for a new wave of auteurs. Many of these filmmakers are primed to jolt our movies with a new and fresh sensibility. Can they break through? Or will the directors riding this new wave end up beached and gasping for air? Their fates will say much about the fate of American filmmaking in the nineties.

SAM PECKINPAH: THE WILD BUNCH

Michael Sragow

When the heroes in Sam Peckinpah's movies died, it was often in circumstances too violent to permit a formal commemoration. But Peckinpah marked their passing in some of the most eloquent, piercing imagery ever committed to celluloid. I know of no more haunting sequence in all of cinema than the final ten minutes of *The Wild Bunch.*

After the gang led by Pike Bishop (William Holden) is killed while annihilating a Mexican army, bounty hunters led by Deke Thornton (Robert Ryan) arrive to gather up their booty. The old rider walks over to where his friend lies fallen, pauses, and in a gesture full of significance draws Pike's pistol from its holster. Sobered by the sight of the slaughter, Thornton refuses to return to Texas with his men, instead staying on in town. He watches his pack of "gutter trash" leave, Pike's men slung like meal sacks across their saddles. The mass evacuation of the town becomes a funeral procession for the Bunch. The legend has begun. Minutes pass. Shots are heard in the faint distance. Thornton, slouched against the town gate, smiles. The bounty hunters, too, have met their fate. Even in death, Pike's bunch are not caught; their bodies are retrieved by a former member who has taken up with Mexican freedom fighters. He invites Thornton to join him, and the two old comrades laugh, perhaps for what they consider Pike's bitter folly, or perhaps for the new bitterness of their own lives. As they ride off, the screen fills with images of the Bunch as they once were.

Peckinpah was attracted to eulogies and funerals because they permitted him, in the right old phrase, to take the full measure of a man. That's what his best movies were all about: defining heroes not by psychological profiles or sociological explanations but by the way they attacked the world.

To discover *The Wild Bunch* in the summer of 1969 was to be shocked, riveted, moved, pummeled, and finally reduced to awe. It was as if for two hours and twenty-three minutes (or two hours and fifteen minutes, if you saw the studio's cut version two weeks later) Peckinpah had managed to juggle and tap dance over a mine field. He transformed the western landscape beloved by directors as a "pure" canvas for morality plays. Peckinpah's south Texas and Mexico still have a parched visual grandeur, but they are filled with impurities. The Wild Bunch, an outlaw gang operating on both sides of the Rio Grande right before World War I, are unrepentant thieves and killers looking for one last big score. The "law" is just as bad or worse. The pursuing bounty hunters are ragged mercenaries working for the railroad. The Mexican overlord Mapache, who ropes the Bunch into stealing guns for his troops, is the worst of all, ravaging his country as he rules it. And society is no more responsible or cultivated than its sleazy citizenry: The south Texas civilians are unable to fight for their own interest, and the soldiers in their army (which ends up pursuing both the bounty hunters and the Bunch) are shown as peach-fuzzed bumblers. You feel that even if the Bunch were on the "right" side of the law, they would choose not to remain there, because their hunger is insatiable. The only community toward which they feel any sympathy is a group of Mexican revolutionaries.

The most innocent member of the Bunch is a Mexican named Angel. It is Angel who appreciates the wild beauty of his Mexican homeland; it is Angel who serenades the children and weeps for their rape and destruction. When he steals guns for his embattled revolutionaries, he goes beyond the pagan self-interest of the Bunch. When Mapache seizes Angel, Pike and his three remaining followers redeem their entire misspent existence by avenging him. By the end of the film we see these men as heroes.

Technically, the movie is superb. The gunfights are among the most amazing action sequences ever filmed. By combining slow-motion photography with rapid cutting, Peckinpah achieved powerful physical imagery while furthering the narrative's developing tensions. When a townsman is caught in the opening battle's cross fire, he punctuates the scene by framing two young children hiding by the side of a building, their initial horror at the bloodshed turning to overwhelming fascination. The conventional wisdom says that the grisliness of these scenes makes voyeurs of us all: As the camera records its subject, a man is shot full in the face, or a throat is slit. But Peckinpah's techniques *objectify* the violence by first catching us up in its surging emotions and them impelling us to grasp the viciousness of slaughter.

In any case, *The Wild Bunch* has a power that goes beyond its technical brilliance and impassioned ambivalence. Part of this has to do with our seeing a piece of history told straight out for the first time. According to Jay Robert Nash's *Bloodletters and Bad Men,* in the last decade of their existence the real Wild Bunch "left hundreds killed, wounded, and crippled." The response of proper citizens matched the Bunch's savagery. When a sheriff killed Bunch member George L. "Flat Nose" Curry, Nash recounts, the townspeople "took out hunting knives and stripped away his flesh from his chest. One ambitious townsman made a pair of shoes from the flesh. Another swatch wound up as a good-luck charm and was carried from vest to vest through generations of outlaw *aficionados."*

Peckinpah's emotional commitment to his work prompted Dan Yergin, in a 1971 profile, to quote Saul Bellow on those people "who take on themselves to represent or interpret the old savagery, tribalism, the primal fierceness of the fierce, lest we forget prehistory, savagery, animal origins." Yet that primordialism doesn't fully encompass his power, either; this director's art is more than a mere volcanic outburst. When an instinctive artist like Peckinpah works all out, he touches on eternal mysteries. He brings us such a full understanding of tragedy that we feel both purged by pity and terror and haunted by the question, "What was it all for?" *The Wild Bunch* is Peckinpah's answer.

[The preceding is excerpted from a career appreciation of Sam Peckinpah written on the occasion of his death.]

Boston Phoenix, January 8, 1985

SAM PECKINPAH: STRAW DOGS

Judith Crist

If the first month of the year has contributed anything to our movie experience, it is at least proof positive of the moronic aspects of the rating system. Anyone under eighteen is forbidden to see the best film of 1971, Stanley Kubrick's masterly *A Clockwork Orange,* X-rated because there is nudity and a murder (although we do not see the actual deed or the corpse) by a blow with a large erotic sculpture. But you may take your young to the worst film of 1971, Sam Peckinpah's R-rated *Straw Dogs.* After all, they won't see pubic hair—just a gang of mental defectives slaughtering each other and raping a very rapable girl in a vast variety of blood-soaked sadistic and perverse ways, without pause and without purpose.

The Kubrick film, let us fear, might get a message across to the intelligent and perceptive young by way of its darkly imaginative and wry fairy tale that if we continue in our social fecklessness, we will face a tomorrow of ultraviolence; that the cure is not in mind-tampering by conditioning and drugs but in the re-establishment of the moral choices that differentiate the human from the inhuman animals. But shucks, the Peckinpah film, like his *The Wild Bunch,* is pure inspiration, telling us, wonder of wonders, that evil lurks in the hearts of men—as de Shadow done know from way back—and proceeding to show it by way of an incredible and unoriginal "realism" (three parts a Hardy-country version of *Tobacco Road,* one part *Of Mice and Men,* six parts pure de Sade). It is one of the trash series of films we've endured (all parts pure von Sacher-Masoch) in recent years that tell us that violence and/or war are not nice and wallow in the unniceties for hours.

We hasten to note that a certain school of young critics, dedicated to discovering a masterpiece a week, has deemed the Peckinpah spew a masterpiece. Consider what they have to swallow whole. Dustin Hoffman, exuding a catatonic sweetness, is presented to us as a brilliant American "astro-mathematician" given a grant of some sort to spend time in the English countryside working on a book. Frankly, this could set the Fulbright or Guggenheim grant programs back a century, considering the cretinous social and intellectual level on which our American scholar functions. He seems along the way to have married the campus whore, a teenybopper sprung from the British branch of the Kallikaks family as embodied by Susan George, who strolls around stark nekkid (especially so when wearing sweaters) popping her gum, walking into his study with a cheery "Hi! Thinking?" and either changing a plus to a minus in one of the many formulae spattered across hubby's blackboard (to indicate he's a latter-day Einstein) or parking her gum thereon.

For reasons unknown they've returned to wifey's homestead, where all the drooling young blades seemingly have "known" her and several are employed in building a garage. They're full of narsty tricks, like hanging the family cat in the bedroom closet ("To prove to you they can get into your bedroom," wifey explains) and taking hubby on a snipe hunt so their chums can rape wifey at leisure, but Hoffman doesn't lose his cool. It's only when the village idiot (portrayed with such style by David Warner as to make Hoffman seem merely a city idiot) kills a Jukes-family Lolita Lenny-fashion (he's got a loving brother but they don't talk from rabbit raising in this one) and takes refuge in Hoffman's house after Hoffman, who obviously couldn't operate a tricycle, runs him over in the blighty fog and the neighborhood Jukeses besiege the house, that Hoffman gets irritated. "This is where I live — this is me — I will not allow violence against this house," says he — and the blood fiesta is on, with folks getting their feet shot off and their necks massaged by broken glass as they pop through windows, rapers after wifey upstairs and murderers mayhemming with hubby below, with the *pièce de résistance* one villain getting his neck into an antique bear trap, which wifey, an ardent antiquer, collected at the film's opening and the two of them lovingly hung over the mantel—just to set the film's tone. Finally everybody's dead except the never-lovin' couple and the idiot. Hoffman sets out to drive him to town (only an idiot would consent to getting into a car with Dusty, his erstwhile runnerover). "I don't know my way home," says the idiot. "That's OK," says Dusty, "I don't either." And there's the metaphor safe home.

Written by Peckinpah and David Z. Goodman, the film is just aglow with similarly pithy dialogue. The rodent exterminator, a local yokel, says to Dusty, "Tell your wife I feel closer to rats than people. Their dying is my living. Rats is life"—and that old debbil metaphor gets another poke.

Peckinpah's contempt for intelligence (in his hero as well as his audience) and his obvious preference for the fighter-fornicator (as in *The Wild Bunch*) is the director's hang-up. What is truly contemptible is the suggestion by his admirers that non-machismo-minded men will get a vicarious release from the desperation of their own days by seeing the bookish worm turn! (All anyone with an IQ of 70-plus can get out of this film is a case of the heaves.)

New York, January 24, 1972

JEAN-LUC GODARD: FIRST NAME: CARMEN

J. Hoberman

"I'm the girl who shouldn't be called Carmen," a woman murmurs under a suavely baffling montage of nighttime traffic, surf breaking on the beach, and a string quartet rehearsing Beethoven. The voice belongs to Maruschka Detmers, eponymous heroine of Jean-Luc Godard's *First Name: Carmen.* Detmers plays, or rather embodies, the role like a fact of nature, and her protestation could be seen as a plea by Godard to forget Bizet, forget Carlos Saura, forget every film noir ever made and imagine the story again. "I think that the cinema should show things before they receive a name," Godard told a recent interviewer. "What comes before one's name?" his Carmen X wants to know.

Fun but thin, *First Name: Carmen* is filled with the things Godard does best—abrupt bits of music, sudden contretemps, droll set pieces, playful alienation effects. There's even a turn by the master himself. ("Care to know why I'm here?" Detmers asks Godard when she comes to visit him in a sanitarium for washed-up filmmakers. "Sure," he replies. "Makes for dialogue.") Scored with wall-to-wall Beethoven, *First Name: Carmen* is nearly as culturally insistent as *Passion*. What's more, it's almost linear — "a Godard film for people who don't like Godard," according to one serious fan of long-standing devotion. I'm not sure I agree — if anything, *First Name: Carmen* is quintessential Godard — but there's no denying that the film is more immediately likable, spare, and cornball than either the uneven *Every Man for Himself* or the problematic *Passion* (which, having also been shot by Raoul Coutard, is similarly concerned with the beauty of nondescript gas stations and incidental light).

Those who found *Passion* cold won't feel deprived of human interest here. Traffic, the ocean, and the rehearsal punctuate the action throughout, but, like *Numéro Deux,* the still insufficiently recognized masterpiece of Godard's middle period, *First Name: Carmen* flirts with pornography. The proceedings are eerily spiritualized by the Beethoven; still, the subject is sex, violence, *l'amour fou,* the fear of women, and the desire for one. Maybe it's a Bresson film for people who don't like Bresson, although I doubt a Bresson hero would ever be so blunt as to gaze at a woman's sex (with which he was sharing the screen composition) and mournfully remark, "Now I know why they call prison the hole."

As one might expect, Godard takes a free hand with *Carmen.* He virtually erases Bizet by citing Prosper Mérimée's novel as the source for Anne-Marie Miéville's screenplay. (In a rude sort of joke, however, snatches of "La Habañera" are twice whistled by random passersby.) What's really surprising about *First Name: Carmen* is how closely Godard hews to the original plot line. Or rather, how he turns it into a remake of *Pierrot le fou.*

Carmen X is part of a criminal gang. She meets the gendarme Joseph (Jacques Bonnaffé) during an elaborately choreographed and somewhat silly bank robbery. He falls for her (literally) — all of a sudden they're grappling on the floor like the lovers in *L'Age d'Or* — and they immediately go off together to her uncle's apartment by the sea. ("He's really nuts," says Carmen of her uncle. "There's a tape recorder in the fridge.") Full lipped, tousle haired, and totally lissome, Detmers is well complemented by Bonnaffé, a wiry big-jawed palooka with an orange pompadour — the two inescapably suggesting Anna Karina and Jean-Paul Belmondo, with the balance of power tilted decisively toward the former. There's no way Bonnaffé can have Belmondo's strength, since the role of Pierrot is here split in two: The uncle, whom Carmen has previously visited in a sanitarium, is played by Godard himself.

Detmers's delectations aside, the most crowd-pleasing aspect of *First Name: Carmen* is Godard's wonderfully disheveled presence. Wandering unshaven into a café, carrying a biography of Buster Keaton (another onetime has-been), and gnawing on a spent cigar, the maestro absentmindedly slates the scene and begins quoting Mao, concluding with a blunt aphorism of his own: "Kids today are scum." As if to prove him right, Carmen and her accomplices have the idea to use making a film—ostensibly a documentary on luxury hotels—as a cover for a kidnaping. (Is this Godard's metaphor for filmmaking in general—the production of fantasy masking a scam involving terror and abduction?) Indeed, Carmen—or, rather, Detmers—is something like the muse of cinema herself. "Don't you want to go back to making movies?" she tempts Uncle Jean, even offering to let him use his video equipment on her project. "Don't you want to make lots of money?" "We should close our eyes, not open them," Uncle Jean sniffs, in one of his more cantankerous aphorisms.

In the current issue of *Film Quarterly,* Godard tells Gideon Bachmann that he acted in *First Name: Carmen* because of future plans to play a lead "like Jerry Lewis." But his performance is also a link to the movie-crazed features of his first decade. It was part of Godard's particular genius that he was the first director to perceive film history as a text available for quotation. Here, he uses himself as a totem in precisely the same way he used Fritz Lang in *Contempt* or Sam Fuller in *Pierrot le fou.* There's a sense in which *First Name: Carmen* is actually a bitter, confessional parody—and commercial repetition—of Godard's first films. While the ultraromantic *Pierrot le fou* is the film it most closely resembles in plot, performers, and even specific details, there are references to *Le Petit Soldat* and *Bande à part,* stylistic leitmotifs taken from *A Married Woman, Alphaville,* and *One Plus One.*

"What do I want in life?" asks Detmers, answering herself with a statement that could just as well have come from the heroine of *Breathless.* "To show people what a woman does to a man." The fatal woman has been as constant a Godardian theme as the philosophical prostitute, but there may be a more practical reason behind his attraction to the eternal femme fatale, Carmen. *Passion* was a terrible flop, and Isabelle Adjani, France's reigning box-office queen, suggested an adaptation of Bizet's opera with herself in the title role. Once the shooting began, however, Adjani reportedly walked off the set in a rage when she saw how much nudity Godard required. (The director, of course, has another explanation. In his interview with Bachmann, Godard views Adjani's fear of exposure more pragmatically. The actress, he says, was frightened by his and Coutard's propensity for natural light: "Adjani thought, like all stars, that a lot of lighting, a lot of spots, is a guarantee for their appearing beautifully on the screen. She could not accept that daylight, slightly corrected, could be a much better guarantee for her beauty.")

Although the representation of women has been a recurring and unresolved issue in Godard's oeuvre at least since *A Married Woman,* the films of Godard's third period have been distinguished by a combination of frank sex and blunt autobiography. (Here again, *Numéro Deux* is the key precursor.) In *Every Man for Himself,* the movie widely hailed as Godard's commercial comeback, the male protagonist (one Paul Godard, TV producer) regales his twelve-year-old daughter with his sexual fantasies about her, while the film's set piece has an officious tiger of the business world engineering a Rube Goldberg daisy chain (complete with sound effects) involving himself, two bored prostitutes, and an eager-to-please junior executive. Although sexually more reticent, *Passion* features copious female nudity, and a film director hero who is transparently Godard's alter ego.

First Name: Carmen, however, is notable for the director's unabashed obsession with Detmers's body and even bodily functions. Escaping from the robbery, Joseph binds Carmen's wrist to his to make it look real. "Untie me, I have to piss," she says as they drive into a gas station. "So do I," Joseph agrees, and there's a wonderful sight gag in which they set off in opposite directions for their respective toilets. Ultimately, however, Joseph exercises his power, dragging Carmen off to the men's room. She's forced to relieve herself in the urinal and, with sheer force of personality, turns this into a triumph. "Why do women exist?" Joseph wonders after opening Carmen's blouse — the sort of existential query that could only occur to a Godard hero. The question is reprised, after a fashion, late in the movie. When Carmen tells Joseph their affair is over, he symbolically — and impotently — rapes her in the shower, holding her with one hand and brandishing his flaccid penis in the other, furiously trying to give himself an erection. When he fails, he grabs his whole genitalia in painful frustration as Carmen wriggles free, crawling across the floor and hissing, "You revolt me." "Me, too," Joseph sadly agrees. But Carmen is not done. "Why do men exist?" she asks.

Why indeed? After *First Name: Carmen* it should come as no great surprise that Godard is now preparing a contemporary version of the gospels with the working title *Je vous salue Marie* (Hail Mary), the same characters as Joseph and Carmen, and a lot of Bach. Puritanical as Godard is, one wonders if this is penance for having succeeded, as Nietzsche said of *Carmen,* in showing — all too well — "love as *fatum,* as fatality, cynical, innocent, cruel, and precisely in this a piece of nature."

Village Voice, August 14, 1984

JEAN-LUC GODARD: HAIL MARY

Owen Gleiberman

Since the subject of sacrilege is at hand, let me offer a blasphemous confession of my own: I have never been able to sit through one of Jean-Luc Godard's movies without wanting to throw something (preferably something heavy) at the screen. This aversion has always nagged me, since the critics I respect most all cherish the guy — or at least his undeniably innovative work of the sixties. Then again, Godard's output, including *Hail Mary* (which I'll get to in a minute, and which I consider a forgettable but morally inoffensive film), has always found its natural audience in critics, who like to sit in the dark analyzing everything they see. And don't his films sound enticing when you read about them! Here's the man who reinvented cinema for the contemporary age: the French visionary who created the jump cut, who scrambled sixties pop culture and revolution and his love of American B movies, who gave us "the children of Marx and Coca-Cola" in *Masculin/féminin* and the children of capitalism eating their own kind in *Weekend,* who seemed to swallow the history of Western culture whole (everything from Dante to Bogart to graffiti to Kierkegaard) and then spew it out in a heady comic-strip blur — a chaotic/beautiful essayist for a chaotic/beautiful age. Like I said, sounds great on paper.

But then you go to the movies (and I mean the "good" Godard movies), and what you get, in a word, is obscurity: fractured thoughts, fractured feelings, fractured dialogue and characters and

Jean-Luc Godard incurred the wrath of the Catholic church right up to the pope when he recast the story of the Virgin Birth among the present-day Swiss in *Hail Mary*. Pictured here as Mary is Myriem Roussel. (Photo courtesy of New Yorker Films.)

actions—everything so fractured that it yields no more meaning than a pile of shattered eggshells spread across the floor. Godard is cerebral to the point of craziness. His films aren't just chilly and intellectualized; they're psychotic—mosaics of alienation devices designed to keep throwing you out of whatever reality has just been established, so that pretty soon there's no reality left, nothing but the clink of dialogue that has no connection to the sound of people talking and every connection to the hyperactive voices Godard must hear in his dreams. Godard has always claimed that he doesn't "trust" language, yet has there ever been a filmmaker who assaulted you with more of it? Watching a Godard film can be like reading the endnotes to "The Waste Land"—and skipping the poem. With their quotations from random literary sources, their words flashing across the screen in subliminal bursts, their mock-absurdist happenstance, his movies allow you no continuous involvement; all you can do is ingest the flow of ideas and analyze. Some people, I guess, find this stimulating, but to me it's always seemed the soul—the definition—of creative decadence. A work whose effect is to carve away all emotional response may be a valid artistic artifact for an overly brain-quick era (and Godard's films are nothing if not artifacts). But even if you take away a few fleeting impressions, the experience can't enter your bloodstream.

Do Godard's celebrants ever wonder why his films, with the exception of *Breathless,* are rarely revived, and why audiences today greet them with little more than shrugs of baffled indifference? Perhaps it was easier to respond to them in the heated experimental climate of the sixties, when their raw, stripped-down rhythms were new, and when Godard's ideas (prostitution as a metaphor for capitalism and all that) were considered a hip revelation; certainly, it's easy to see that a *Bonnie and Clyde* or a *Mean Streets* is unthinkable without his influence. But influence may not be everything. A movie worth its salt must last — if not till the end of time, then surely twenty years? And what reasonable, halfway intelligent young person today could make heads or tails of *Pierrot le fou* or *Two or Three Things I Know about Her* or *La Chinoise?* A great many people once flocked to Jean-Luc Godard's movies and found them "interesting" (and a great many filmmakers assimilated the freedom of his audiovisual techniques — though not, it's worth pointing out, a fraction of his radical worldview). Today, Godard isn't a creator of any importance, and he isn't "interesting." If only the pope had bothered to sit through *Hail Mary* before issuing his statement of condemnation: He'd have been so confused he might never have bothered to damn the thing.

In *Hail Mary,* Godard is trying to work in a more rhapsodic vein than before. The photography is hypnotically clear and dark toned, and there are many beautiful images of the sun and the moon and ponds and fields; on the sound track, in nearly every scene, one hears the tumultuous strains of the Dvořák Cello Concerto. In Godard's previous film, *First Name: Carmen* (also based on a famous old story), it was Beethoven's string quartets; in his own fluky way, the arch-modernist director is trying to become a classicist. Yet even the music is shattered: Godard (purposefully) jumps in at the center of climaxes and then cuts away just as jarringly, so that you seem to be listening to the Dvořák in the middle of an acid trip. There's the usual array of Godardian baffle-the-audience flourishes (a shot of a young woman sitting by a window fondling a Rubik's cube; titles reading "At that time"; dislocating shots of a women's basketball team). And as always, the fragmentation of sound and image works on you viscerally, physically: It becomes a denial of pleasure, of the ebb and flow of human response. That's why all the hoopla about blasphemy is such a joke: To be blasphemous, this movie would have to be *about* something.

Godard has given us a contemporary version of the Virgin birth, but except for a few names it's hardly "the story of Mary and Joseph"—this is the director who couldn't stick to a story line for thirty-five seconds if someone held a gun to his head. (And you thought MTV was jittery.) Instead, Godard uses his gimmick for some light comedy and then plunges into a feverish visual poem centering on the enigma of pregnancy itself. Mary (Myriem Roussel) is a quiet and attractive dark-haired Swiss girl who works at her father's gas station and plays basketball; Joseph (Thierry Lacoste), a grouchy cab driver, is her boyfriend—but not her lover. At first, when the self-effacing virgin finds herself mysteriously pregnant, Joseph complains that she must have gone to bed with another guy (not an unreasonable assumption). We're supposed to chortle and think, "No, fella—it was the big guy upstairs." It's only half a joke, though, since the notion that these two good-looking modern people are entwined in a relationship without having slept together is just a makeshift conceit.

But Mary is innocent, and Joseph, bitter and suspicious, must stand by as she withdraws into a private world of eroticism, spirituality, grace. In *First Name: Carmen,* Godard returned to using the sort of fresh-faced young actors he'd featured throughout the sixties (occasionally casting his own tart, pretty girlfriends in lead roles), only he seemed to have no connection left to anything they were thinking or feeling. In *Hail Mary,* the stylized impersonality is complete: You can barely remember what the performers look like from scene to scene. There's another couple in the film, a more conventional pair who sleep together (and are therefore denied heavenly miracles), and for a while I was wondering whether the blond-haired Anne Gauthier was Mary, or whether Myriem Roussel was Mary, or whether they were both supposed to be Mary. How can we tell when there's no true conversation (just snippets of ideas), no interactions? The children of Marx and Coca-Cola have given way to the children of IBM and Thorazine, and you watch them in vain, staring into their ironically blank expressions, searching for the barest sign of character behind the beautiful masks.

What Godard hasn't lost is his frank adoration of the female form. Having now married a grudging Joseph, Mary doesn't so much accept her special fate as revel in it. Naked, lying alone in bed, her room bathed in shafts of icy blue light, she writhes in soulful abandon, experiencing her miraculous conception as a kind of chaste substitute for erotic fulfillment. Godard is saying that pregnancy and birth are inherently erotic (hardly a revolutionary notion). And it's obviously the nude photography that has so upset the Catholic authorities — for them, the portrayal of the Holy Virgin as even a tastefully erotic figure is far more sinful than, say, the lapsed-Catholic ravings of Ken Russell's *The Devils* (a film that truly is blasphemous). Yet what I found nearly as unfathomable are the critics who've turned around and hailed *Mary* a profoundly "religious" film. The shots of Mary unveiled do have a surging imagistic power; like many avant-garde movies that feature nudity with no pornographic intent, these expressive visions ask us to sit back and contemplate the sheer beauty of skin, hair, breasts. The more you stare at Mary's body, the less familiar it looks, the more enchanting and unique. And her pregnant belly, of course, does seem a miracle — as does any pregnant belly, though if the movie hadn't been called *Hail Mary* I'm not sure anyone would be nattering on about the presence of the divine. Certainly, one reason religion has lost some of its sway is that people today have little trouble accepting the natural world (and even sex) as sacred without invoking the image of an all-powerful being. The world *Hail Mary* unveils doesn't strike me as especially blessed: It's sensually charged, yes, but also disjointed and obtuse — less a world of mystery than an unsolvable puzzle.

There's a masochistic undercurrent to the movie, as there was to *First Name: Carmen.* Both have their brooding male protagonists brusquely shunted aside by unreachable young lovelies; in both, consummation becomes an impossible dream. *Hail Mary* isn't as tortured a vision as *Carmen,* where the hero was rejected, over and over, by the blasé tease of a heroine (even as the camera drank in her body) and then found himself impotent when he tried to make love to her in the shower. But here, once again, Godard spends most of the time fawning over a body that no one can have. It's that old-time religion: grace tinged with denial. And it's definitely a body that's being revered, not a character. You leave *Hail Mary* with images flowing through the brain, because Godard photographs Myriem Roussel rapturously, obsessively. Yet she remains, to the end, an object — not a sleazy or a sacrilegious one, but an object nonetheless. It strikes me that part of Godard's aesthetic has always been to objectify everything on screen — actors, words, ideas, images — and then to bamboozle us with his big message: that the reality of cinema is a false one, and that what he's doing is making us aware of the illusion. He gives himself too much credit. Reality isn't an illusion in Godard's films — it's a nonentity. The director fears it, twists it, strangles it.

Boston Phoenix, November 26, 1985

JOHN WATERS: PINK FLAMINGOS

Kevin Thomas

The self–X–rated *Pink Flamingos,* made by undergrounder John Waters, creator of *Multiple Maniacs* and *Mondo Trasho,* is subtitled *An Exercise in Poor Taste* — which doesn't even remotely begin to suggest the extremes to which it goes. It makes as total an assault on conventional sensibilities as is imaginable without becoming downright morbid.

That's because it is as funny as it is outrageous. And as we're being liberated by our laughter we're made aware how much more easily we can be offended by actually quite harmless scatological excesses than by the realistic depictions of bloodshed and brutality that are routine — and that are markedly absent from his movie.

Still and all, *Pink Flamingos* is strictly for the very open-minded and is best left to those who've been able to go along to the outermost limits of filmmakers like Andy Warhol and Robert Downey.

In comparison to *Pink Flamingos, Blazing Saddles* is the proverbial Sunday school picnic.

So much for the warning (which can't be underscored strongly enough). *Pink Flamingos* takes its title from some cheap statuary in front of a house trailer — also predominantly pink — parked somewhere in the Maryland countryside.

It is the home of Divine (played by a hefty drag queen who goes by that name); her even fatter mother, Edie (Edith Massey), who is mentally retarded and, dressed only in a girdle and bra, spends all her time in a playpen gobbling eggs; her "son" Crackers (Danny Mills), a sort of sex fiend; and Cotton (Mary Vivian Pearce), a vague blonde dressed and coiffed thirties style.

With her forehead shaved high and made up like a clown, Divine favors Fredericks of Hollywood–style fifties finery — tight capris, spring-o-lators, cheap lamé and furs. (On one level, *Pink Flamingos* is a satire on nostalgia kitsch.)

It seems that Divine has been named the Filthiest Person Alive by a sensational tabloid — that does not mean she doesn't bathe: It refers rather to her seemingly infinite capacity for committing acts of grossness.

Her title incites the jealousy of Connie Marble (Mink Stole) and her husband, Raymond (David Lochary), who sell the babies produced by the girls they kidnap and imprison in their farmhouse cellar. (Their transvestite chauffeur fathers the babies — via artificial insemination!)

Connie is a skinny, harshly dyed redhead with rhinestoned glasses; Raymond, a flasher, dyes his hair blue green. Anyway, the Battle of Filth is quickly under way.

Now there's much foul language and uninhibited sex, all of it hilarious as it is kinky, and all manner of shenanigans that can't even be hinted at, let alone described, in a family paper. To be sure, Divine keeps her title — and celebrates it in an appropriately revolting way.

Los Angeles Times, December 13, 1974

JOHN CASSAVETES:
A WOMAN UNDER THE INFLUENCE

Judith Crist

There's the contrast of grim reality from John Cassavetes's *A Woman Under the Influence,* his first film since *Minnie and Moskowitz* in 1972. Once again the writer-director is exploring man-woman relationships, this time in what is painfully the diary of a mad, working-class housewife, concentrating on a woman without identity, lost in love and housewifery. The value of this intense story of husband and wife, unable to communicate beyond the constant iteration of love and the outbursts of violence and doomed to the hysteria of their relationship, is that it leaves itself in large part to the eye of the beholder and the heart of his experience. See it as the story of a faceless woman — while marveling at the physical loveliness Gena Rowlands sustains in her most agonized contortions — who seeks refuge from the emptiness of her life in childishness, in meeting her children on their level, in resorting to the face making and splutters and arrested gestures of aggression for repressing the angers and frustrations of her life, in demanding that her husband tell her "what" to be. See it too as the story of the ultimate *macho* — Peter Falk is adept at the "nice" ego-stud image — a man who cannot face his wife, whether it is after her disappointment in his having had to work late or after her confinement in a mental hospital, without a houseful of visitors to give him the illusion of "good times" and well-being.

There is nothing here of the intellectual probing of the emotions and intelligence of two educated, civilized people that one finds in Bergman's *Scenes from a Marriage.* That is neither Cassavetes's style nor his intent as his characters improvise their way through inarticulation, slashing and hugging and shouting and coming to untidy and temporary truces, making it through the night and leaving tomorrow to its turmoils. This is at once the writer-director's talent and his weakness, for once again we get bogged down in self-indulgent meanderings.

The 150-minute film is a half hour too long, but it is worth all your attention for Rowlands's remarkable performance that brings us to the very core of the mind in retreat, the woman withdrawn with no place of refuge beyond the body rhythm. And Falk, in his explosive hard-hat sense of propriety, his helplessness in the face of misbehavior, his tough affection for his children (there is a delicious sequence in which he and a coworker take the children to the beach for determined camaraderie, with his best communication the sharing of a can of beer). The children are remarkably natural, as are Katherine Cassavetes and Lady Rowlands, mothers of the husband-and-wife director and actress, who negate nepotism by their performances. Fred Draper and O. G. Dunn are very good, and only a few of the nonactors on hand can be faulted. Cassavetes's improvised atmosphere is at its most controlled to date, but he still lacks the discipline that would give the work as a whole the intense power of so many of its parts.

New York, November 25, 1974

JOHN CASSAVETES:
A WOMAN UNDER THE INFLUENCE

Pauline Kael

The theories of R. D. Laing, the poet of schizophrenic despair, have such theatrical flash that they must have hit John Cassavetes smack in the eye. His new film, *A Woman Under the Influence,* is the work of a disciple: It's a didactic illustration of Laing's vision of insanity, with Gena Rowlands as Mabel Longhetti, the scapegoat of a repressive society that defines itself as normal. The core of the film is a romanticized conception of insanity, allied with the ancient sentimental mythology of madness centering on the holy fool and with the mythology about why Christ was crucified. The picture is based on the idea that the crazy person is endowed with a clarity of vision that the warped society can't tolerate, and so is persecuted. Laing's approach is a natural for movies at this time, since the view that society is insane has so much to recommend it that people may easily fall for the next reversal that those whom this society judges insane are the truly sane. Possibly it can be a healing step for some people to let themselves go, but Laing—in some ways a super-smooth snake-oil salesman—toys with the rakish notion that going crazy is a sign of health.

Laing has given modern weight to a persistent, emotionally appealing myth, and his books, such as the campus favorite *The Politics of Experience,* tell counterculture readers what they are already disposed to believe. For those who feel blocked or ineffectual, the view that the good are the victims of the family and of society's other authoritarian structures can be wonderfully satisfying. It's the furthest extension of the line taken by William Inge and Elia Kazan in the 1961 *Splendor in the Grass.* In that simplistic Freudian film, the adults, who had lost the ability to love, frustrated their children; the adolescents (Warren Beatty and Natalie Wood) weren't allowed to consummate their passion, and as a result she lost him and went crazy. By the end of the sixties, the division of the world into bullies and victims had become an article of faith for much of the counterculture, with its emblematic figure James Dean, the misunderstood kid.

Whether or not Laing is right in seeing the irrational pressures of family and society as the cause of schizophrenia, his poetic myth that the mad are the pure ones — the ones with true vision — is a piece of seductive nonsense. It's this nonsense that has made Laing a messiah to the drug culture; some acolytes have felt they had to take acid to go fearlessly mad and be worthy of him. In *A Woman Under the Influence* the schizophrenic heroine is the misunderstood kid as the ultimate Friendless One. Mabel Longhetti is basically spontaneous and joyful, but only children respond to her on her own terms. Every impulse she has is denied, and she's stampeded into madness by her violently irascible husband, Nick (Peter Falk). Mabel is as helplessly wronged as a battered baby. This frantic, wilted heroine is a Los Angeles housewife and the mother of three; a big, beautiful blonde in bright, short chemises, she darts about like an anxious speed freak, her manic gestures dissociated and jerky, her face changing rapidly from foolish smiles to uncontrollable punch-drunk agonies. After her husband and his harpy mother (Katherine Cassavetes) have had her locked away for six months of shock therapy, Mabel returns, chastened, a fearful, hurt-animal look on her face, and, in case we missed the point of the process by which society drove her mad, Cassavetes now provides a quick recapitulation by having the key people in her life gather to welcome her home, prepared to do her in all over again.

It's never suggested that there's something wrong with Mabel for not getting herself together. Others reduce her to pulp; she's not a participant in her own destruction. The romantic view of insanity is a perfect subject for Cassavetes to muck around with. Yet even in this season when victimization is the hottest thing in the movie market this scapegoat heroine doesn't do a damn thing for him. He's always on the verge of hitting the big time, but his writing and directing are grueling, and he swathes his popular ideas in so many wet blankets that he is taken seriously — and flops. In *Faces* and *Husbands* Cassavetes might almost have been working his way up to Laing; his people were already desolate, hanging on to marriages that made no sense to them because nothing else did, either. And his last film, *Minnie and Moskowitz,* a screwball comedy about maimed lovers — a loudmouth parking-lot attendant (Seymour Cassel), irrepressibly life loving, and a bruised, beautiful woman (Gena Rowlands) — could almost have been a garbled sketch for *A Woman Under the Influence.*

Mabel, however, is more (and less) than a character, since she's a totally sympathetic character: She's a symbolic victim, and a marriage victim especially. Cassavetes has hooked Laing on to his own specialty — the miseries of sexual union. The Laingian schizophrenic scapegoat is, typically, one who suffers the irrationality of the mother and father, and this was the pattern in the English film *Family Life* — called *Wednesday's Child* here — which was directed by Kenneth Loach from a screenplay by David Mercer. Its heroine is a passive, weak-willed young girl who can't defend herself against her inhibited, respectability-centered parents and becomes schizophrenic. Sent to a hospital, she is at first treated in a relaxed, informal experimental ward run by a Laingian, and it appears that she needs to learn to stand up to her family — a wondrously simple cure for schizophrenia. But the Laingian is dismissed, and she is given shock treatment and is left, at the end, a vegetable. The Loach film was a far more obvious case of special pleading for Laing than *A Woman Under the Influence* is, but it was also simpler and made better sense. In the Cassavetes film, the husband, Nick, seems to be taking a bum rap, since it's hard to believe that Mabel would be so easy to cut down if she weren't already shattered. (A child can be without recourse, but a wife?) Both pictures suffer from a single-level, one-sided approach: The authoritarians who do the damage are despicable, comic-strip conformists; the good people are liberal, open, natural. It's generation-gap psychology.

Like all Cassavetes's films, *A Woman Under the Influence* is a tribute to the depth of feelings that people can't express. As a filmmaker, he himself has a muffled quality: His scenes are often unshaped and so rudderless that the meanings don't emerge. This time, he abandons his handsome, grainy simulated *cinéma-vérité* style. The shots are planned to make visual points that bear out the thesis (though there are also arbitrary, ornamental angles, and vistas that make a working-man's cramped house big as a palace). But once again he has made a murky, ragmop movie. Actually, he doesn't know how to dramatize, and one can try to make a virtue of this for only so long. When the actors in his films strike off each other, there are tentative, flickering moods that one doesn't get in other kinds of movies, but these godsends are widely spaced, and it's a desert in between. He still prolongs shots to the point of embarrassment (and beyond). He does it deliberately, all right, but to what purpose? Acute discomfort sets in, and though some in the audience will once again accept what is going on as raw, anguishing truth, most people will — rightly, I think — take their embarrassment as evidence of Cassavetes's self-righteous ineptitude.

His special talent — it links his work to Pinter's — is for showing intense suffering from nameless causes; Cassavetes and Pinter both give us an actor's view of human misery. It comes out as metaphysical realism: We see the tensions and the power plays but never know the why of anything. Laing provides Cassavetes with an answer. However, his taking over Laing's views has cost him something: He didn't have comic-strip villains — or villains at all — before he swallowed Laing. In his earlier films, he commiserated with those who couldn't make contact except by brutalizing each other. Their drunken hostilities and blighted, repetitious conversations weren't held against them; their insensitivities were proof of the emptiness they felt. He used to love violent characters and outbursts of rage. Now the actors, no longer given their heads, are merely figures in a diagram. When Nick yells, the picture's only concern is the effect on Mabel. Cassavetes has gone so far over to the most literal-minded Laing position that the society he shows us is implausible — a society of boorish people with such limited awareness that they're barely human. Since they are principally blue-collar workers, it looks as if he thought that hard hats were retarded.

Mabel Longhetti is bombed out because she has always wanted to please everyone, so she can be considered one more victim-heroine for "women's liberation" — but only by women's liberationists who are willing to accept textbook spinoffs as art. The Junoesque Gena Rowlands (Mrs. Cassavetes) is a prodigious actress, and she never lets go of the character. Now at an indeterminate age when her beauty has deepened beyond ingenue roles, Rowlands can look old or young, and shades of expression transform Mabel Longhetti from a radiantly flirtatious beauty into a sad, sagging neighborhood drunk. Rowlands externalizes schizophrenic dissolution. Mabel fragments before our eyes: A three-ring circus might be taking place in her face. Rowlands's performance is enough for half a dozen tours de force, a whole row of Oscars — it's exhausting. Conceivably, she's a great actress, but nothing she does is memorable, because she does so much. It's the most transient big performance I've ever seen.

Mabel tries to slash her wrist, and Nick puts a Band-Aid on the cut: The idiot symbolism may make you want to hoot, but this two-hour-and-thirty-five-minute film leaves you too groggy to do more than moan. Details that are meant to establish the pathological nature of the people around Mabel, and so show her isolation, become instead limp, false moments. We often can't tell whether the characters are meant to be unconscious of what they're doing or whether it's Cassavetes who's unconscious. Mabel's children keep murmuring that they love her, and there are no clues to how to decipher this refrain. Are the children coddling her — reversing roles and treating her like a child in need of reassurance? Or are they meant to be as unashamedly loving as she is? And what are we to make of Nick the pulper's constant assertions of love? The movie is entirely tendentious; it's all planned, yet it isn't thought out. I get the sense that Cassavetes has incorporated Laing, undigested, into his own morose view of the human condition, and that he somehow thinks that Nick and Mabel really love each other and that *A Woman Under the Influence* is a tragic love story.

The New Yorker, December 9, 1974

RAINER WERNER FASSBINDER: THE MARRIAGE OF MARIA BRAUN

☆

Andrew Sarris

If the New York Film Festival gave out awards, Hanna Schygulla would be an odds-on favorite for best actress in her vibrantly distanced portrayal of a soldier's wife, whose melodramatic life story parallels Germany's postwar economic miracle, in Rainer Werner Fassbinder's *The Marriage of Maria Braun.* Fassbinder himself appears on screen as a peddler with a taste for Kleist, but the beating heart of the film is all Schygulla's in the guise of Maria Braun. Klaus Lowitsch as her steadfast, passive, and self-sacrificial husband, Ivan Desny as her rich patron, and Gottfried John as her culturally trendy friend all evolve with Schygulla's Maria as a historical expression of a Germany of which Fassbinder deeply disapproves.

A German journalist once complained to me that Fassbinder helped create a climate for leftist terrorism with his nihilistic attitudes and that we, his American admirers, only encouraged him to continue in the same vein. On the other hand, many American leftists find Fassbinder not ideologically pointed enough. Gay rights advocates are made somewhat uneasy by the dismal flatness of his avowed homosexual sensibility.

One would have to stretch a point to describe any of Fassbinder's films as erotic, apart from the sensual suggestiveness of an actress like Schygulla. Camp specialists are put off by Fassbinder's elaborately antidynamic mannerisms that mock the absurdities of most of his plots. I have noted all these objections, and still Fassbinder continues to surmount them as far as I am concerned. *Maria Braun, Effi Briest,* and *The Merchant of Four Seasons* are his three masterpieces, and it is perhaps no accident that Hanna Schygulla is in all of them.

Village Voice, October 22, 1979

RAINER WERNER FASSBINDER: VERONIKA VOSS

David Denby

The floors are white, the walls and ceilings are white, and the imitation Greek statue, a nude but demure lady, is white, too. It's a doctor's office, though it looks like the boudoir of a very rich woman with terrible taste. The camera prowls up and down the corridors, peering through the interior walls, which are made of glass, taking in the innumerable shafts of light reflected by a mirrored ball hanging from the ceiling. The inhabitants of this milky hell are a large, elegantly dressed female doctor; her look-alike assistant; a black GI happily filling up ampules with morphine; and an aging female movie star, a morphine addict, who is their prisoner. When the star attempts to kill herself with sleeping pills, the doctor, in sinister, caressing tones, tells her, "You can't die until I let you." At this, they all break into laughter — gales and gales of laugher.

Thus the principal setting of *Veronika Voss,* one of the last works completed by Rainer Werner Fassbinder before his death, last spring, at the age of thirty-six. The atmosphere is unmistakable: No one else has staged these drenched-in-despair melodramatics in such brazenly kitschy interiors. Heavy spirited and bizarre, fanciful but solemn, *Veronika Voss* is the kind of movie in which pairs of evil women loom into close-up like horror-film zombies. In a word, it's dreadful. Yet it's pure Fassbinder, and for many people that's enough. The Fassbinder cult has grown into a sizable and steady art-house audience. Both *Lola* and *Veronika Voss* are flourishing, and a local Fassbinder retrospective will soon be getting under way. In the universities, Marxists and structuralists rejoice: Fassbinder's work, with its infinite number of variations on a small range of themes — class oppression, victimization, sadomasochism—is a treasure trove, a quarry, an inexhaustible oil well. The quarterlies have already begun their special issues.

A few years ago, having greatly enjoyed such "middle" works as *The Bitter Tears of Petra Von Kant, Ali—Fear Eats the Soul,* and *Fox and His Friends,* I became a moderate booster myself. In the increasingly vapid and cautious foreign-film scene of the seventies, these movies, with their acrid jokes, their cruelty and comic dismalness, offered the peculiar stimulation of a cold rain taken directly in the face. And the *idea* of Fassbinder was satisfying. A director who worked with incredible speed, he used the same crew and a stable group of actors over and over, turning out three or four movies a year. He was a workshop director, committed to filmmaking as a continuous activity rather than as a search for ultimate expression, and if you were willing to accept, in a tentative, anticipatory spirit, a series of streamlined fables, you could appreciate his experiments in tone and style—the scandalous bluntness, the freezing eroticism, the mixture of intentional banality and *outré* aestheticism.

Fassbinder was something new—a surly camp, a put-on artist with no particular desire to give pleasure. Of course, those who admire him deeply don't talk of him that way. Instead, they speak of his profoundly despairing view of life, his revolutionary attitude toward form, his greatness as a satirist. Vincent Canby has even tried to make him out as one of the great directors in film history, right up there with Godard and Buñuel. Hoping to offer help to the uninitiated, Canby has divided Fassbinder's work into amiably eccentric categories like "Masterpieces Probably," "Quintessential Fassbinder," and so on. In so impersonally authoritative a place as the *Times,* a statement of one man's taste is always welcome, but really, come *on.* People who go to such movies as *In a Year of 13 Moons* and *Despair* expecting greatness are going to come out with the taste of ash on their tongues.

By the late seventies, some of us wanted more from Fassbinder than the ironic teasing of banality and Thorazine-style acting; we wanted him to be more than "interesting." And we couldn't help noticing that he was repeating himself—not once or twice but again and again. His extraordinary productivity, once the subject of awe, began to look a little strange. Didn't he ever stop to read, think, or live a little between films? It's a naive question, normally irrelevant, but his work, which had never exhibited the range of interests or sympathies that the great directors have all had, compelled it. Weariness and dismay settled into our reaction to his new films. His surly wit, experienced for the eighteenth time, was no longer bracing; it was all but indistinguishable from misanthropy. Dividing the world into winners and losers, he showed little interest in his characters except as players in the eternal struggle between rich and poor, strong and weak — the power game that, for him, was a system of sadomasochism writ large.

In *Veronika Voss,* set in 1955, Fassbinder has offered his sour comment on *Sunset Boulevard.* Billy Wilder's movie is widely considered one of the most sardonic works in American film history, but Fassbinder must have found it sentimental, for in this gloss on it he makes his aging star not a magnificent (though undeniably grotesque) relic like Gloria Swanson's Norma Desmond but a pathetic mediocrity, a favorite of Goebbels's, whose career has foundered after the war. Now a drug addict, Veronika Voss (Rosel Zech) is finished when we first meet her, and she sinks lower and lower, literally falling to the floor in agonizing fits. If Fassbinder cared for her, her disintegration might be painful. But he stages it as a camp spectacle — there she is carrying on about her comeback at a party in her gruesome house, with its candelabra and shrouded furniture. When Norma Desmond did the same thing, you felt the grandeur and craziness of her will — the woman was still *dangerous.* Fassbinder's heroine is just a loser.

A rather stolid sportswriter (Hilmar Thate), the equivalent of the William Holden figure in *Sunset Boulevard,* makes a feeble attempt to save her. I won't reveal what happens. Not that it matters. In a Fassbinder film, the game is always rigged; the denouement invariably arrives as a confirmation of the power relations the movie has already demonstrated with crushing bluntness. Working with two screenwriters, Fassbinder has relied on the kind of melodramatic contrivance and sinister dragon-lady characterizations that were dropped from Hollywood movies two decades ago. If *Veronika Voss* were only funny, one might be able to accept this stuff as parody or even "satire" (Canby's word). But the movie is repellently grim.

Veronika Voss can be enjoyed only as an extended essay on the possibilities of black-and-white cinematography. As always, Fassbinder does some stunning things visually. When the sportswriter picks up Veronika Voss in a rainy park and then rides with her in a trolley, the gleaming headlights striking the windows of the trolley car are brilliant and icy cold against the black, freezing night. Fassbinder, a minor baroque stylist of great skill, never lost the ability to put some sting into conventional romantic imagery. That so tirelessly perverse an artist could be turned overnight into an academic classic is an irony that I don't think he would have enjoyed. With luck, his best films will survive the flattening-out effect of adulation, and future generations will rediscover what was once so exciting in his work.

New York, November 1, 1982

STEVEN SPIELBERG AND GEORGE LUCAS: ON PETER PANAVISION

Morris Dickstein

Return of the Jedi is not only the third installment of George Lucas's *Star Wars* saga but the latest chapter in Hollywood's fabulously lucrative love affair with kids and adolescents who make up an ever-larger share of the movie audience. Long before the *E.T.* bonanza, studios found that youngsters would keep going back to movies they liked, spread the word and form cults around them, and gobble up millions of dollars' worth of tie-in products from bubble gum and T-shirts to high-priced toys and video games. The toys in turn would make them want to see the movie again.

This was no great novelty except for the size of the take. The Disney studios had made money for decades by hooking up their moviemaking with a television series, comic books, theme parks, toys, and momentary fads (like Davy Crockett's coonskin caps). The images of Disney's cartoon characters belonged to the permanent pantheon of pop culture, like Chaplin's tramp and Groucho's mustache and cigar. Yet for Disney the culture of childhood was still a separate realm of wishful fantasy, a never-never land of the kind J. M. Barrie had conjured up in *Peter Pan.*

In the seventies, though, American moviemakers discovered they could lure grown-ups to these movies as well, just as potheads had turned out for revivals of Disney's *Fantasia.* At a time of economic troubles and international reversals, when many of our problems began to seem intractable, the audience was getting a little tired of sex and violence and bleak negative visions. Realism was out; sentimentality was in. Fantasy, adventure, and fairy tales all suited this new escapist mood. The more hopeful, more trusting myths of childhood were alive but dormant in the minds of adults, waiting only to be tapped by the right formula. Even TV zombies could be brought back to the movies by something clean, wholesome, and upbeat—just the kind of positive thinking the old Hollywood had specialized in. Hadn't Frank Capra himself acclaimed *Rocky* for bringing heart back into moviemaking?

☆

In the successful movies of the late sixties the young were shown as rebels or outlaws—gently unconventional in movies like *The Graduate* or *Alice's Restaurant,* or directly at war with society in *Bonnie and Clyde* and *Easy Rider.* But the youth movies cloned from *Easy Rider* failed at the box office, and so did several remarkably silly movies about campus revolutionaries. By the early seventies it became clear that the young themselves were less rebellious and audiences were ready for a less trouble-making image of them.

Into this breach stepped George Lucas, a protégé of Francis Ford Coppola who had grown up racing cars and chasing girls in Modesto, California—far from Berkeley or Columbia, and before psychedelic drugs, unbuttoned sex, and the Vietnam draft changed the very meaning of youth for many Americans. In *American Graffiti,* a surprise hit of 1973, Lucas turned his own nostalgia into a new staple of American pop culture. "Where were you in '62?" the ad campaign kept asking, and soon TV spin-offs like *Happy Days* began giving their own dumb answers. Even the rock 'n' roll of the period, featured on the movie's sound track, enjoyed a new vogue and became a spearhead of the fifties revival.

The following year an even younger director, Steven Spielberg, released his first theatrical feature, *The Sugarland Express,* which contains in embryo nearly every movie he's made since. It looked like a couple-on-the-lam movie in the darkly fascinating tradition of *You Only Live Once, They Live By Night, Gun Crazy, Bonnie and Clyde,* and *The Getaway.* But *The Sugarland Express* introduced touches that took it far away from the mood of a film noir. Significantly, the whole plot revolved around a child. The pair of petty criminals (played by Goldie Hawn and William Atherton) who abduct a Texas state trooper are not so much trying to get away as to recover their baby from a foster family. Soon the tension of their battle with the police is deflated by countless bits of silly comedy, including auto pileups that foreshadow Spielberg's biggest flop, *1941.* Their hostage, a green kid like themselves, gradually comes to identify with them. Along the way they become folk heroes and people start pressing food and flowers on them. The police betray them and one of them is finally killed, yet the film has something of a happy ending: The mother and child will be reunited.

Though made with a self-assurance remarkable for a twenty-six-year-old filmmaker, *The Sugarland Express* never caught on with audiences. Its little jokes and asides retard the pace of the narrative. Its protagonists are too strident and unattractive; they lack emotional nuance and are hard to identify with. Perhaps the movie still had too much of a sixties kids-against-the-world theme. Yet at the same time it lacked grit and tension; Spielberg's vision was far too benign for the grimly romantic genre he was working in. In *Jaws,* a year later, he let his kids get chewed up and showed us much of the carnage from the angle of the monster. But it was not until 1977 that Spielberg's and Lucas's kind of movie really came into its own and drastically changed the direction of Hollywood.

When Lucas's *Star Wars* and Spielberg's *Close Encounters of the Third Kind* came out that year, they seemed to herald a big revival of science fiction, as *Jaws* and *The Exorcist* had pumped new life into the classic horror film. George Lucas was more precise in calling his movie a "space fantasy." Far from relying exclusively on sci fi, he had borrowed freely from westerns, war movies, animated films, adventure serials, and fairy tales, plundering the high spots and action bits from each of them.

"I researched kids' movies," he later said, "and how they work and how myths work." His homework done, he built his archetypal plot around the call and initiation of the young hero. The callow protagonist, Luke Skywalker, the spunky heroine, Princess Leia, the sage old Jedi knight, Obi-wan Kenobi, and his dark antagonist, Darth Vader, all come trailing clouds of Arthurian romance. Only a stunted juvenile mind would have taken Luke and Leia for credible imitations of full-fledged human beings (though *Jedi* concludes with a confrontation between Luke and his father, a rare moment of strong human interest). They were ciphers of chivalric legend and Hollywood cliché in futuristic drag. The mystical mythology of The Force, that tells Luke to "let go your conscious self," "act on instinct," and "stretch out your feelings," reeks of the wooliest self-help nostrums of the sixties. Yet kids everywhere loved the kind of imagination and humor that went into the 'droids (R2-D2, C-3PO), Wookies (Chewbacca), and other fantastic creatures. (Like the computer HAL in Kubrick's *2001,* they had more personality than the people.)

Perhaps Lucas's imagination was nostalgic for feudalism and a servant class, but he also knew how to mobilize the money and technology that made the special effects so striking. When the mercenary adventurer Han Solo's ship goes into "hyperspace," or overdrive, the kid in all of us goes zooming through the meteor fields.

With its endless astral dogfights (made possible by computer-guided cameras), *Star Wars* was a triumph of special effects over human effects. It had a more salutary impact on the toy business and on video games than on Hollywood movies. Kids playing Asteroids and Space Invaders were living out the *Star Wars* experience. Despite its inventiveness, charm, and excitement, *Star Wars* ushered in a puerile era of overblown epics for underfed minds. (These included many straight Arthurian romances, such as *Excalibur, Dragonslayer,* and *The Sword and the Sorcerer,* that paralleled the Dungeons and Dragons craze.) Kids' stuff became so expensive and so profitable that it was hard to get any other kind of movie made. At a time when Hollywood had just begun to feel the influence of the European New Wave — with directors gingerly trying out more difficult styles and subjects — the new vogue of high-tech fantasy made adult moviemaking seem irrelevant. Small, cheap movies with real scripts were a luxury the studios could no longer afford.

☆

This was confirmed when Spielberg's *Close Encounters* came close to duplicating the success of *Star Wars* and later when Lucas's *The Empire Strikes Back* worked some improvements on its predecessor, including more advanced visual effects and a far less clunky script. Meanwhile, with *Superman* in 1978 and *Popeye* in 1980, the studios rediscovered comic-strip heroes as source material for cartoony extravaganzas. There was something irresistibly amusing about these movies' ingenious attempts to stylize flesh-and-blood actors into pieces of pop iconography. The tongue-in-cheek humor of Margot Kidder's wide-eyed exchanges with Christopher Reeve in *Superman* was a way of twitting the myths while paying tribute to them.

Robert Altman was less fortunate when he assembled a townful of oafish clowns, clumsy acrobats, and witless vaudevillians to represent the world of Popeye's Sweethaven. With creepy intuition, he cast the principal players almost too well, like animated figurines, and set them down in a shantytown in Malta that is too picturesque for words. Perhaps the most playful director not working today, Altman was simply too clever at thinking through the problem of doing a live-action animated cartoon, even holding back sure-fire touches like Popeye's spinach and the music of "I'm Popeye the Sailor Man" until the grand finale. After an unbearably mannered first half, *Popeye* gradually discovers the kind of simplicity and story emphasis that such a movie needs.

No one would ever accuse Lucas or Spielberg of such an excess of sophistication. But Spielberg's advantage over his friend is that his movies are partly set in the real world, not in some extragalactic fairyland. Between *The Sugarland Express* and *Close Encounters* he obviously learned how to work the humorous and human touches into the story itself to make it more credible. *Close Encounters* remains the most convincing and densely detailed movie Spielberg has made; it was certainly the mother ship for *E.T.* and *Poltergeist,* which also deal with alien beings in ordinary suburban settings and center on the children (like Cary Guffy in *Close Encounters*) who make first contact with these creatures. Spielberg has been praised for his gentle social satire, but the suburban worlds of these movies strike me as dim, stereotyped, and pretty much interchangeable. He loves suburbia too much to examine it closely and, despite broken homes and other modern problems, his vision of the nuclear family, presided over by loving guardians, is not far removed from "Father Knows Best."

☆

Still, Spielberg extracts stupendous performances from children and good ones from their parents as well. The funny yet believable acting of the mother and father, played by JoBeth Williams and Craig T. Nelson, does much to hold *Poltergeist* together, just as the natural behavior of the kids, Henry Thomas and Drew Barrymore, anchors *E.T.* But the character Spielberg identifies with most is Roy Neary in *Close Encounters,* another grown-up kid whose increasing obsession with UFOs disrupts his family and makes him break away to something beyond. Here Spielberg may be commenting on a certain compulsive perfectionism in his own relation to movies that may make it difficult for him to live out the family life he eulogizes.

Whether this is the case or not, there's no doubt that the hyperactive Richard Dreyfuss, who played Roy Neary, was the perfect vehicle for Spielberg's brand of kinetic moviemaking. It sometimes seems like sheer busyness—an attempt to hook the audience by loading up the action and increasing the tempo, as in the first ten minutes of *Close*

Encounters or *Raiders of the Lost Ark.* But Dreyfuss's performance — his gradual breakdown, for example — takes on an emotional shading and a depth of anguish extremely rare in Spielberg's rosy universe, where almost everything can be externalized or resolved by good will and strenuous effort. Even the aliens in *Close Encounters* and *E.T.* turn out to be friendly if not furry creatures, blending in perfectly with the stuffed toys in a middle-class child's big, crowded closet. Spielberg directs these machines with the same close attention he lavishes on the children.

For a science fiction movie deeply indebted to the paranoid classics of the fifties, *Close Encounters* (like *E.T.*) is an astonishingly benign work. *Star Wars* is all about Good and Evil: Darth Vader and the Empire don't hesitate to blow up a whole planet to show they mean business. In *Close Encounters* no one gets hurt. The men who disappeared decades ago return from space without having aged — a cardinal wish of all juvenile fantasy. (*Peter Pan* is subtitled *The Boy Who Would Not Grow Up.*) Instead, they have had some kind of religious experience, reflected throughout the movie in the rapt expressions of all who have come into contact with the UFOs — Spielberg's version of The Force.

François Truffaut, who played the French scientist Lacombe, described afterward how difficult it was for the actors to be constantly gazing in wonderment at a blank spot just beyond the camera. Yet Spielberg has made this shot practically his signature; it's certainly the weakest element in *Close Encounters* and it leads directly to the feeble ending that undercuts the whole movie.

☆

In the "special edition" Spielberg recut in 1981, we actually see the inside of the alien mother ship that will transport Roy Neary on his pilgrimage into space, and it looks like a garish Hyatt Hotel lobby, complete with oversized chandelier. As a blissed-out idiotic grin spreads across the actor's face, we hear the melting strains of "When You Wish upon a Star" on John Williams's sound track (a ludicrous touch that set early preview audiences tittering). The Disney side of Spielberg's sensibility tugs the movie into dreamy wish-fulfillment, abolishing the emotional complexity that preceded it.

It would surely be a mistake to see any real religiosity in Spielberg's imagination, though this was supposedly a key feature of Paul Schrader's discarded script for *Close Encounters.* And the divine intervention at the end of *Raiders of the Lost Ark* is straight out of Cecil B.

DeMille, that live-action forerunner of Disney who pioneered in transposing the Divine Word onto celluloid.

Like George Lucas, Spielberg has the kind of sixties sensibility that makes it a virtue to be credulous, innocent, and gullible. This is at the root of his feeling for children and his rapport with audiences. People love to be taken for a ride, even when they sense the shameless manipulation at work—the sentimentality, the coy humor, the echoes of other movies, the technical tricks, and the hyperbole that turns every scene into the perfect essence of whatever it's supposed to be. There's not a dry eye in the house as Elliott tells the dying E.T., "I'll believe in you all my life, every day. I love you, E.T.," or at his departure when he points his long, crooked finger at Elliott's head—or is it his heart?—and says, "I'll be right here."

☆

After the moon shots and the space walks, it was probably inevitable that our imagination of outer space would begin to be domesticated. Spielberg and Lucas mitigate the deep-seated anxieties projected in earlier science fiction by assimilating it to fairy tales and adventure stories. Setting in motion the vast apparatus that goes into their movies, Spielberg and Lucas are like computer-age children playing games with state-of-the-art technology. In their work the trash culture of the fifties, which they grew up on, gets recycled through the Munchkin sensibility of the sixties by way of the big budgets and high-tech machinery of the seventies.

An important key to Spielberg's success is his acute visual sense, even if his facility with images sometimes works at cross-purposes to his generally benevolent vision. This was clear as early as *Duel,* his 1971 TV movie about a killer truck that, for no apparent reason, stalks a car driven by a hapless Everyman, played by Dennis Weaver. Without ever showing us the driver of the truck, Spielberg uses an extraordinary range of tilted shots to make the vehicle seem demonically alive. He builds up a powerful sense of menace without stopping to explain. Eventually we feel he's cheating on us, coasting on his visual virtuosity to manipulate us.

Something similar happens in the opening scenes of *E.T.* when we get a series of terrifying waist-high views of the men who are hunting E.T., faceless behind their bobbing flashlights and jangling keys. Spielberg is already showing us the world from E.T.'s (and Elliott's) point of view, but the sense of menace is just for kicks; it has nothing to do with the movie. The false sense of danger recurs when men in space suits break in on all sides of Elliott's mother's house; they also turn out to be well intentioned, as are nearly all figures of authority in Spielberg's world. Sometimes Spielberg's stylized imagery works well. His warm backlighting makes us feel the security of Elliott's nest and lends a luminous glow to his communion with E.T.

Spielberg's kind of visceral filmmaking proceeds in terms of isolated scenes and effects. His visual shorthand, borrowed from older movies but accomplished through careful storyboarding, often plays havoc with story and continuity. In movies like *Raiders of the Lost Ark,* Spielberg aims directly at the gut in every scene. In a sense this is also a comic-strip movie, stuffed full of astonishing action bits, with two-dimensional characters larger than life but smaller than real. The same can be said of its explosive Australian counterpart, George Miller's *The Road Warrior,* with its blank-faced, laconic, Clint Eastwood–style hero, heart-stopping action sequences, and cartoonlike cast of supporting characters. After looking into books like Joseph Campbell's *The Hero with a Thousand Faces,* the director seems determined to give every arbitrary twist of plot an archetypal resonance. Even more than *Star Wars* and *Raiders,* this supercharged movie is like an illustrated lecture on heroes, villains, and the mythology of adventure. *The Road Warrior* is staggeringly inept on any human level, but it may be the best action movie of recent years. Miller's self-consciousness, which can be fatal with pop material, doesn't paralyze him; his trashy sensibility feeds on it.

Not all the movies produced by the youth cult avoid credible human beings or center exclusively on a child's viewpoint. Many teenage pictures are simply raunchy and exploitative, but a few like last year's *Tex* and *Fast Times at Ridgemont High* take us right back to *American Graffiti.* These films have their poignancy and humor, but their soft-centered characters can be hazy and shallow. (Or else, like Matt Dillon in *Tex,* they look too pretty in a movie-star way.) And their problems are usually less than earthshaking, even by the standards of adolescence. Occasionally a movie like *Diner* will appear, an American *I Vitelloni,* to measure the distance between what we remember and who we are, between the aches of adolescence and the bittersweet discoveries of growing older. But what a rarity this is, when escapist fantasies are so much in demand that small-scale humor or honest recollection seems like self-indulgence.

Lucas and Spielberg have taught the movie studios how to give young audiences exactly what they want, and this has made the new Hollywood, with its slick production values, look more and more like the old one. By lovingly updating old movies — and even, in the case of *Raiders,* improving on them — they have re-created the split between European and American movies, between worldly sophistication and pop mythmaking, between art movies about grown-ups and popcorn fantasies about kids and muppets. Thanks to them Hollywood has undergone a collective regression, which should soon be flooding the market with *E.T.* and *Jedi* imitations. The fountain of youth has regenerated Hollywood commercially, but it will take a stronger elixir to revive its artistic conscience.

In These Times, June 15–28, 1983

STEVEN SPIELBERG: INDIANA JONES AND THE TEMPLE OF DOOM

Richard T. Jameson

Have people become so consciousness raised they can't have a good time at the movies anymore? When I caught the opening-day matinee of *Indiana Jones and the Temple of Doom* during a visit back home, I had a swell afternoon. My brother, who's fifty-one, not the least bit consciousness raised, and hadn't been out to a movie in years, said it "made him feel like a kid again." I told him about *Raiders of the Lost Ark,* the first picture to feature globe-trotting archaeologist hero Indiana Jones, and urged him to see it sometime: "You'll enjoy it too — although this new film is even better."

I never imagined that was going to be a minority opinion, at least insofar as published commentary is concerned. Nor did I anticipate (though I suppose I should have) that this latest fun machine from the Lucas-Spielberg factory was going to stimulate not the usual cascade of cover-story raves, but a spate of grave editorials on the "excesses" and "intensity" of its action and violence. Yet there they were, boxed and encapsulated on the front page of the *USA Today* my cousin passed me before dinner the next evening. Even the film's director, Steven Spielberg, was quoted to the effect that he wouldn't take children under ten to visit *The Temple of Doom;* it might give them nightmares.

That struck a chord. How many times over the past several decades had I heard people, anywhere from their teen years to comfortable middle age, say, "I had nightmares over that for weeks" while reminiscing about some movie from their youth? The cinematic sources of those remembered nightmares were various: King Kong shaking the sailors off the log span and into the valley of spiders; a tribe of arctic zealots proposing to lower a red-hot iron pot over a friendly explorer's head in the 1935 *She;* a party of scientists and Air Force officers, their breaths steamy in the freezing corridor, opening a laboratory door to discover The Thing standing just on the other side. Perhaps closest to the immediate point, there was *Gunga Din,* with the mad, firelit scowl of guru Eduardo Ciannelli, the flicking tongues of his pet cobras, the windblown cries of *"Kaaaa-eee-leeeee . . . "* echoing from the cliffs as the Thuggee murder cult prepared to do its thing. What never varied in these reminiscences was the tone in which "I had nightmares for weeks after" was pronounced: fond, nostalgic, I-wouldn't-have-missed-it-for-the-world.

I'm pretty sure today's kids will be talking the same way about *Indiana Jones and the Temple of Doom* in decades hence. But of course it's not the kids who are fretting even now. And what the editorial writers want to save them (or themselves) from isn't so much the "horror" or "violence" of specific passages—for one instance, the high priest of Thuggee plucking a sacrificial victim's heart right out of his chest. The anti-*Indy* rap is subtler than that. The watchword here is not "violence" but "intensity." Spielberg's breathless roller-coaster ride—much more assured than that of the widely loved *Raiders*—is in fact *too* assured for some tastes. One comes out of *Temple of Doom* keyed up by the relentlessness of the energy, the one-damn-thing-after-another eventfulness, the breathtaking expertise of the filmmaking—and some folks would rather not *be* keyed up, thanks just the same.

Spielberg has run into resistance of this sort before, though the argument was couched differently. In 1979, his film *1941* was generally held to be an aesthetic, and certainly a commercial, catastrophe. Oh yes, I panned *1941* myself, and rather complacently, too. It seemed so obvious that Spielberg had got carried away by the machinery involved in making a multimillion-dollar comic extravaganza, and that, in adding screwball set piece after set piece, he'd wound up with a raucous, mindless, monotonous, and almost entirely unfunny movie. I still think *1941* has big problems; but over the years Spielberg's quiet "I never thought of it as being especially *funny*" nagged at me: What if we reviewers had been watching the wrong movie?

When I finally checked out *1941* again, on cable TV, I found much of it eerily compelling — a cinematic ballet of mass hysteria that, however dubious as a picture of the United States at the outbreak of World War II, makes personal and honorable aesthetic sense as an expression of the flip side of Spielberg's sunny *Close Encounters-E.T.* sensibility.

This fascination with the machineries of mayhem rather than the machineries of joy finds happier, and more salable, expression in Spielberg's Indiana Jones adventures — for they *are* adventures; they *do* deliver the generic thrills. As it happens, *Indiana Jones and the Temple of Doom* also delivers considerable comic exhilaration in much the same way.

Consider the opening, as inventive and dazzling as the encyclopedically perilous intro to *Raiders* in an underground Peruvian shrine — Indiana's confrontation with some nefarious Chinese in a Shanghai night spot. The essential situation is simple enough: Indiana has a rare archaeological find to trade for a fabulous gem. The Chinese want the treasure, but would prefer not to part with the diamond. They would also prefer that Indiana Jones not walk out of the Obi Wan Night Club alive.

Spielberg has introduced this sequence with a multileveled movie in-joke, a production number that begins with the striking of a great gong (compare the opening credits of *Gunga Din*), has songstress Willie Scott (Kate Capshaw) emerging from a red-smoking dragon's mouth that looks as if it ought to be decorating a Temple of Doom somewhere, and then lurches into the kind of Busby Berkeley song-and-dance extravaganza no nightclub stage could ever accommodate. Having scrambled levels of cinematic artifice for us ("Anything Goes" is the song being performed — entirely in Chinese except for the title phrase), Spielberg proceeds to compound the gamesmanship by making punny jokes at every level of visual, aural, and pop-cultural association.

The Chinese, for instance, are pidgin-English Mr. Moto villains (just as the villains of *Raiders* were cheerful throwbacks to the stock Germanic villains of prewar movies), and they and Indy swap treasure and diamond, and conduct a running liars'-poker duel by means of a lazy-Susan tabletop — a preposterous vehicle for suspense, and an apparatus we chiefly associate with Chinese restaurants. Indiana discovers he has just swallowed a poisoned drink; he staggers to his feet, and his drugged movements seem uncannily choreographed to merge with the dance number continuing in the background. The antidote to the poison is by now clattering to and fro on the nightclub floor, along with the diamond, likewise gone astray; and just as Willie Scott, a thirties gold digger par excellence, lunges after the stone, a champagne bucket is spilled and the "ice" is lost in a wash of ice. It's a mad, giddy whirl, but as intricately designed and balanced as the works of a fine watch whose every tick inspires glee.

One would have to be very poor in spirit to disdain such beauties as merely "mechanical." Not only is Spielberg a supremely accomplished filmmaker, he also conspicuously delights in what he's doing, and the sense of play is eminently communicable. His lust for cinematic storytelling is prodigal. At a later point in the film, as Indiana and his street-urchin companion Short Round stand talking on a night horizon in India, a meteor streaks through the sky behind them; only the audience sees it and Spielberg makes nothing of it explicitly, but this vagrant grace note, evoking the cosmic splendors of *Close Encounters* and *E.T.,* brushes across the viewers' sensibilities like a testimony of the wondrousness of the imagination: Anything goes; anything's possible when stories are being told. Such tokens of the wondrous punctuate the action at its more intensely adventurous moments: a magical, and masterful, play of shadow work and shrewd art direction that allows a strangler to step seemingly out of midair behind Indy in a palace bedchamber; a sword-toting skeleton that rises from the floor of a dungeon — an inexplicable manifestation until we perceive the rational, and much more terrifying, explanation of why the dead should seem to rise. Mechanical? Spielberg strews such frissons like cinematic bonbons.

Temple of Doom does have its shortcomings. The titular Temple of Doom sequence is not excessively horrific — it just goes on too long, with too little in the way of fresh discovery, and the gambit of teasing us as to whether Indy has lost his soul after being force-fed a goblet (skull, actually) of ceremonial blood falls flat. Likewise the Lucas-style insistence (George Lucas again exec-produces, as in *Raiders*) that the pragmatic Indy learn to believe in the Force behind a stolen sacred stone. Spielberg's Forces aren't rhetorical; they don't derive from comic-book conceits. They're vivid, immediate, lucid; not invoked platitudinously but measured by the perfection of fluid camera movements, the inevitability of an exactly judged cut. Even when he's only making movies for fun and games, they're beautiful to behold.

The Weekly (Seattle), June 6, 1984

STEVEN SPIELBERG: INDIANA JONES AND THE TEMPLE OF DOOM

Peter Rainer

For its first twenty minutes or so, I was convinced that *Indiana Jones and the Temple of Doom* was going to be deliriously enjoyable entertainment. (It's set in 1935, a year before *Raiders of the Lost Ark,* so I suppose it's a "prequel.") We initially see Harrison Ford's Indiana in a white dinner jacket, in a fancy Shanghai nightclub, as he barters with three Chinese meanies — they'll give him the antidote to the poison he just drank in exchange for the walnut-size diamond in his coat pocket. In the ensuing tussle, both the diamond and the antidote vial go skittering across the floor, along with practically everyone else in the nightclub. Bales of balloons and spilled ice cubes confound the search; so does a gold-digger chanteuse named Willie (Kate Capshaw), who opens the film in a sequin-encrusted gown warbling Cole Porter's "Anything Goes" in Mandarin against a chintzy musical-production-number backdrop. The action swivels and swirls with such breakneck finesse that it's both great action–adventure filmmaking and a great satire of action–adventure movies. We laugh at the majestically facile pyrotechnics. Steven Spielberg, who directed this George Lucas production from a script by Willard Huyck and Gloria Katz, knows how to make an action scene snap, crackle, and pop, with each shot lasting not a millisecond longer than necessary. (His editor here is the peerless Michael Kahn.) When Indy and Willie tumble out of the nightclub and into the jitney of Indy's sidekick, a twelve-year-old Chinese orphan nicknamed Short Round (Ke Huy Quan), the chase is on, and it speeds along for ten minutes in an unbroken arc with the help of a pilotless plane, an inflatable river raft, raging rapids, and steep cliffs, before finally setting down in an impoverished Indian village.

That's when the movie gets into trouble. Up until this point, the movie has a breathless ease; the filmmakers have crammed a half dozen classic perilous escape–and–chase scenes into such a short time span that we giggle at the sheer improbability of the feat. The opening number — "Anything Goes" — is certainly appropriate to the action, and we look forward to more of it. We look forward to seeing how Spielberg will top himself. But the action bogs down fairly early on;

except for a roller-coaster-ride scene in a mine shaft near the end, Spielberg never does equal his opening. But he certainly tries to, and the way he goes about it is perversely wrongheaded. Instead of the whiz-bang free-spiritedness of the intro, Spielberg settles into a story that's replete with crushings, whippings, maimings, torchings, and gougings. And he *lingers* on this material. It's as if all of his filmmaker's energy had turned mean spirited and bilious.

This movie is not a "darker" version of *Raiders of the Lost Ark;* it does not, as some have been saying, bear the same relationship to *Raiders* that *The Empire Strikes Back* had to *Star Wars. Empire,* directed by Irvin Kerschner, was a glorious engorgement of rich, sinister compositions, and it had a fullness of feeling that raised emotion to almost mythic heights. It was a great piece of magical filmmaking. But *Indiana Jones* is simply another piffle: Only it's a poisonous piffle. There's less concentration on Indiana Jones's character quirks, less humor, and even less romantic spirit than in *Raiders*—that is to say, there's hardly any romance at all. That lack of spirit made the first film exhausting after a while; watching it was like watching a feature-length trailer. But at least *Raiders moved;* it covered a dizzying number of locations. *Indiana* stays put in the Temple of Doom for most of the movie and, after a while, you don't really care whether Mola Ram or Chattar Lal or the other Kali cult villains get offed or not. You don't even care whether the Indian children who have been beaten and imprisoned in the temple are saved. You just want *out.*

The liberation of these children, who have been stolen by the malevolent neighboring denizens of the Palace of Pankot from that impoverished Indian village, is ostensibly the movie's driving force. Even though Indiana claims he's only interested in recovering the village's sacred stone from the palace's temple, it's the recovery of the children that fuels his mission. Before he sets out on elephants to the palace, along with the reluctant, pampered Willie and the feisty Short Round, there's a scene that clinches Indiana's resolve. At night, the withered potentates of the village tell him that ever since their sacred stone and their children were stolen, nothing grows in the soil anymore. The place is like an Indian, death-rattled version of Hamelin after the Pied Piper lured all the children away. And then a starving Indian boy—an escapee, apparently, from the Temple of Doom—staggers onto the scene and collapses in Indy's arms. It's a strong sequence, but I also couldn't help wondering: How did they make that poor boy look so convincingly emaciated? Was he starved for the role, or was he already starving? It's indicative of the movie's numbing, literal-minded horrors that such a question is even raised.

Even if one accepts this movie's percussive, brutal techniques, it really doesn't work on its own terms. Indiana Jones wasn't exactly a hero for the ages in *Raiders,* but here he's not given much more to do than scowl and look raggedy (except for that white-suited entrance in Shanghai, where he out-debonairs 007). Harrison Ford, like Spielberg, seems to have channeled his energies into something sourish and nasty this time out — maybe that was the only way he could troop through yet another of these kiddie escapades and still keep his self-respect. Ford must realize that this movie really isn't designed for actors, and he's too good (and too unrecognized) an actor not to feel the constraint. So he plays Indiana sullen and nasty. With his battered, dusty fedora and ripped brown leather jacket, Indy is a bit like Fred C. Dobbs in *The Treasure of Sierra Madre,* right down to the sneaky glint of psychopathology in the eyes. With a little limbering up, Clint Eastwood could have played this role.

Raymond Chandler once said that he had a foolproof prescription for holding his readers' attention: Whenever the story flagged, he'd throw in a dead body. In a way, the Chandler principle is at work in *Indiana Jones.* When Indiana and his cohorts have dinner in the palace, which is presided over by a boy rajah, the feast is live snakes, eyeball soup, chilled monkey brains. When Indiana finds a hidden passageway into the Temple of Doom, it's not unsurprising that Spielberg festoons the darkness with spikes and skeletons and every imaginable variety of creepy crawler. When Indiana observes from afar a sacrificial rite in the Temple of Doom, we get close-ups of a man's heart being ripped out by the hands of a high priest; then the man, still alive, is pinioned inside a mechanical cage and slowly lowered into a molten vortex. Later on, there are scenes of the chained Indian children being flogged; when Willie and Indiana are captured, we get to go through the heart-wrenching, charbroiled stuff all over again.

The "light" touches in this film are so infrequent that they almost feel like sops to the audience: Indiana whisking his beloved fedora at the last second out from under a descending wall of spikes; a contentious bedroom bartering scene between Indiana and Willie, as close as this film comes to romantic high spirits (they sleep in separate bedrooms in the palace, and, in her silk pj's, she bets him that it won't be five minutes before he's knocking down her door); a few moments between Indiana and Short Round (marvelously played by little Ke Huy Quan), whose New York Giants cap is as indispensable to him as Indy's fedora. (Short Round, incidentally, is a homage to the boy of the same name in Samuel Fuller's *Steel Helmet*.) These moments aren't necessarily any better executed than the brutal material, but at least they have a whiff of human emotion to them. They freshen up the fetid air inside the palace.

As fairy tales go, *Indiana Jones* isn't necessarily much more brutal than some of the great Grimm stories, or even parts of Disney's *Bambi* and *Dumbo,* for that matter. And I don't doubt that some teenagers will gulp down the violence with the same thirst that they, and older audiences, display for slash-and-splatter movies. But that doesn't necessarily justify what the filmmakers have perpetrated here. Aside from the fact that most of the under-ten crowd will probably (as the movie ads warn) find this PG-rated film "too intense," it is, I think, irresponsible to cook up such a caldron of violence for young audiences — or old audiences, for that matter. (I gather adults aren't supposed to find hearts being pulled out of chests "too intense.") If you argue that fairy tales are inherently violent (as they often are), and that, as long as things end happily, violence in fairy tales can actually be cathartic (as some child psychologists do argue), then what is there to prevent filmmakers like Spielberg and Lucas from perpetrating even more vicious movies with a clean conscience? They are using the fairy-tale trappings of *Indiana Jones* as a license to kill — so to speak.

And *Indiana Jones* isn't even a good fairy tale. Its imagery and terrors don't have the force of the unconscious behind them; they're machine tooled, which makes them seem even more calculatedly sadistic, since they don't appear to issue from human anguish. (The violence in this movie isn't so much scary as disgusting; as a comparison of *E.T.* and *Poltergeist* also bears out, Spielberg is much better at childhood wonderment than childhood fright.) In a good fairy tale, villainy has its attractions, goodness has its luster; but in *Indiana Jones,* Indy is a disgruntled misfit and Kate Capshaw, with her goldilocked resemblance to Mariette Hartley and Cathy Lee Crosby, is TV-bland and too eighties for this thirties setting. The villains aren't attractive, they're just bald-pated ogres. A classic fairy tale, as Bruno Bettelheim has written, is structured so as to give a child a way of understanding himself through the painful progress of the story. A child looks to a fairy tale, however subconsciously, for a clue to the meaning of life. In *Indiana Jones,* Short Round is in the movie to give kids someone to identify with, but it's not his movie — it's not his story. The best that can be said for Short Round, in fairy-tale terms, is that he ultimately survives because of his love for Indiana. But a child looking at this film for more than fun-house carnage is going to be very disappointed. Has Steven Spielberg joined the dark side of the Force?

Los Angeles Herald Examiner, May 23, 1984

BERTRAND BLIER

Pauline Kael

The French writer-director Bertrand Blier has an authentic, lyrical impudence in *Get Out Your Handkerchiefs.* This is the third in his series of male erotic fantasies. Blier, who is a novelist and the son of the well-known plump character comedian Bernard Blier, started to direct movies in the sixties, and then in 1974 made *Going Places* (the original title is *Les Valseuses,* French slang for testicles), and in 1976 *Calmos* (it turned up, without publicity, in New York last year under the title *Femmes Fatales* and disappeared almost immediately). Perhaps *Handkerchiefs,* a more subdued, deeper variation on the themes of those two films, will make it easier for audiences to respond to what he's about and to look at his earlier work without becoming incensed. When *Going Places* was released here, in 1974, it was variously described as "sordid," "loathsome," and "disgusting," and just this past March it was taken off the Home Box Office schedule because of complaints from affiliate stations. What is the picture's crime? Probably that viewers find themselves laughing at things that shock them. At one point, the two young roughneck protagonists (Gérard Depardieu and Patrick Dewaere) board a train and observe a beautiful, pure-looking young mother (Brigitte Fossey) nursing her baby in an otherwise empty car. They offer this madonna money to give them a sip and, apparently terrified of refusing, she accedes. When she gets off the train, her husband, a scrawny, pasty-faced soldier on furlough, is waiting, and as she walks to join him she has a silly, happy grin on her flushed face. Audiences have come to accept the dirty joking in Buñuel films; the years, the honors, the press have given it a pedigree. But Blier's joking is so un-self-conscious that it makes Buñuel's seem preconceived, almost pedantically outrageous. Blier gives us the kind of joke that can't be done by implication or symbolically—that has to be absolutely literal. This kind of joke has found only verbal form before, yet Blier visualizes it—as if that were the most natural thing in the world to do. The two roughnecks act out their sex reveries—in which, no matter what a woman says, she's really begging for it, so they're doing her a favor if they force themselves on her. And people watching this may be so fussed about the disreputability of what excites them that they can't accept the humor of their own situation. *Going Places* is an explosively funny erotic farce—both a celebration and a satire of men's daydreams—and some people find its gusto revolting in much the same way that the bursting comic force of the sexual hyperbole in Henry Miller's *Tropic of Cancer* was thought revolting.

Going Places shakes you up and doesn't seem to leave you with anything to hang on to. It's easy to find it upsetting and degrading. But that's part of what makes it funny. The two men's crude energy is overwhelming, grungy, joyous. Life to them is like a big meal: They go at it like hungry workmen tearing at a carcass of beef, with greasy fingers. They aren't hippies rejecting middle-class materialism; they have none of the sanctimonious counterculture glamour of the pals in *Easy Rider*. They're closer to the joyriding lowlifers in *The Wild One*. These two pals talk in rough lower-class accents and don't fit into modern urban France, with its homogeneous middle-class culture. They're outsiders without jobs or money who want to live the life of the rich and satisfy their appetites. So they help themselves to things: They snatch purses, steal cars, pilfer shops, and make passes at almost every woman they get near. They're not professional criminals; they just rip people off. They harass shopkeepers and work them up into a rage, but, in terms of the film, this is the only excitement the smug, bored shopkeepers get, and it's way in excess of any damage that the boys actually do. The atmosphere is that of classic farce, as in Ben Jonson: These two are no worse than the respected members of the bourgeoisie, they're just less skillful in their methods. It takes a half hour or so before a viewer grasps that the two pals (one is twenty-five, the other twenty-three) are guileless raw innocents and that almost everything they do backfires on them.

The tone of *Going Places* is startling, both brutal and lyrical. The men are barnyard characters with the kind of natural magic that the kids have in Vigo's *Zero for Conduct* and that Jean Renoir's *Boudu* has; there's a poetic logic in what they do. They pick up a compliant scraggly-blond waif, a beautician (Miou-Miou), who is so used to being treated as something inanimate—as garbage—that she thinks she is garbage. The two guys beat her up and abuse her. Yet they also like her, and they take turns trying to bring her to orgasm—one of them even encouraging and coaching the other. But she remains sad and frigid, and they become furious with her. In between their heterosexual episodes, Depardieu jumps Dewaere (he yelps); he has also suffered the indignity of being shot in the groin, sustaining what the doctor calls "an abrasion of the left testicle." After the failure with Miou-Miou, the two go off to find an experienced older woman who will feel something; they wait outside a women's prison, confident that discharged prisoners will be sex starved, and a middle-age woman (Jeanne Moreau) who has spent ten years inside emerges. They treat her royally, with food and attention, and she gives them a great night of sexual maternal passion. But in the morning she kisses them both as they sleep and commits suicide by putting a gun to her vagina. Shocked by this first encounter with real madness and pain, they go back to their frigid little beautician; they weep and she comforts them, and then, out of a sense of responsibility to the dead woman, the three of them travel to another jail to await the release of her son. He turns out to be physically unappealing and not quite right in the head, but when the four of them are off in the country at a hideaway and the two pals are fishing they hear their frigid girlfriend, who is in bed with the crazy jailbird, making cries of sexual arousal, and in a minute she rushes out, radiant, to tell them the happy news of her first orgasm. (They pick her up and dunk her in the river.) Once aroused, she is always eager, and the two pals keep swapping places in the back seats of stolen cars.

The social comedy in Blier's work is essentially sexual comedy: Sex screws us up, we get nicked in the groin or jumped from behind, idiots make out better than we do, and some people are so twisted that no matter what we try to do for them they wreck everything. And sex between men and women is insanely mixed up with men's infantile longings and women's maternal passions. Sexually, life is a Keystone comedy, and completely amoral—we have no control over who or what excites us.

Going Places was perhaps the first film from Europe since *Breathless* and *Weekend* and *Last Tango in Paris* to speak to us in a new, firsthand way about sex and sex fantasies; it did it in a terse, cool, assured style influenced by Godard, yet with a dreamy sort of displacement. (Godard achieved something similar in the postcards sequence of *Les Carabiniers*—also a two-pals movie.) When Blier's two pals are not in movement, they're disconsolate; they can't think of what to do with themselves from day to day. The landscapes without other people, the deserted places they go to, suggest a sex-obsessed dream world. These are cavemen who give women what in their exuberant male fantasies women want. The dialogue is slangy, the mood buoyant—flagrantly funny in a special, unpredictable way. You have no idea what may be coming. The distinctive aspect of Blier's method of work is that although his scripts are completely written in advance of the shooting—and he doesn't improvise—he writes in an improvisational manner. Most scenarists, like dramatists, think out their structure in terms of the development of a situation—with conflict and resolution. They instinctively plan it out and know where they're going. Blier writes psychological picaresques: He begins with a group of characters and a certain tone, and then he may veer off and go wherever his subconscious takes him. Where he ends up probably surprises and partly mystifies him, as it does us. But generally he's right to trust his impulses, because they take him somewhere we might not have got to in any other way. Crazy connections get made—things unexpectedly tie together. And there is, finally, an underlying set of themes that emerges, and it's much richer than if he'd stuck to a conscious plan. The limitation—if one chooses to regard it as that—of Blier's go-with-your-subconscious method is that, naturally, his films all have the same themes. But he has the wit to treat his own subconscious as a slapstick fantasy land.

☆

Blier's method worked in *Going Places,* and it works in *Handkerchiefs,* but something went wrong in his sexual extravaganza *Calmos* (and the picture failed, even in France). The first half hour or so of *Calmos* is a hilariously scandalous dirty-boy romp. Blier has such economy that he goes right into the comedy; there are no preliminaries, no waste—you're laughing before you've settled into your seat. There are two pals again, but now they're forty-year-old boulevardiers who look like wax grooms on a stale wedding cake. One is a gynecologist (Jean-Pierre Marielle), and the other a baby-blue-eyed pimp (Jean Rochefort). The doctor can't bear to look at women's genitals anymore; the pimp is exhausted by women's sexual demands—he feels women are chasing him even in his sleep. When the doctor's wife (Brigitte Fossey), hoping to tantalize him, offers herself for bondage—tells him she's ready for *anything*—he asks for foie gras. It's a dumb joke, but her nudity and his uncontrollable disgust make it lewdly, visually funny. The comedy is derived partly from a banal premise, a reversal of women's saying they have a headache. But the men's satiation—their demonstration of revulsion against sex—has real comic conviction. The two men run away together into the country-side, to a village where they eat and drink and wear old clothes and begin to stink. Calm, that's what they want. Eating is the only thing they can get excited about. They sit at a Rabelaisian feast, along with the local curé (Bernard Blier) and his helper, in an old house, and the cinematographer, Claude Renoir, makes the house, the food, the landscape sinfully beautiful. This opening is an inspired exploitation porno fantasy, with Renoir's images (and the music, by Georges Delerue) providing a feeling of grandeur and folly. But then the story enlarges and takes a science fiction turn. It shifts from the lunacy and regressions of these two men to the sexual revulsion of men en masse. Blier and his coscriptwriter, Philippe Dumarcay (who also worked on *Going Places*), lose the flavor and the characters, and the picture falls back on the stored-up debris of mass culture. The two men are joined by other escaping men; women demanding gratification come after them with guns, and it's a full-scale tedious war of the sexes until, finally, the two pals, old men now and shriveled in size, are dropped out of a cloud onto an island, where they walk through the pubic hair of a giant black woman and slip into her vagina just as her giant black lover arrives to deflower her, and crush them. *Calmos* is an overscaled back-to-the-womb satiric fantasy—a male daydream about the im-possibility of escape from the sexual wars.

How much distance does Blier have from his characters' foolish-ness? Well, at least enough to make us laugh at them. In a sense, *Calmos* is about sex rather than about women. A couple of guys com-ing out of a bar late at night might talk like this—about wanting to go home just to sleep but knowing that there's a woman waiting up for them, and not being able to face it. It's about the demands of sex on men who spent their youth chasing women and now—jaded—want a break from it. There's no macho in the male bonding of the Marielle and Rochefort characters; they just want to be left alone for a while—they want to go off and live like pigs. It's a funny idea, and though *Calmos* abandons it, there are still things to look at all through the picture. It was a stroke of genius to use Renoir and Panavision: The images have clarity, depth, richness, sweep, and the color is deeper even than Decae's. Early on, there's a streetcar full of avid women—a not-too-bright idea that is given a redemptive comic in-tensity by Renoir's lighting. Throughout, the women are made repel-lently beautiful—they have a neon voraciousness. Brigitte Fossey, a blonde cat with a perfect tiny mouth, is like sensual porcelain. The light on her is so metallic and cold that her makeup seems to be dry ice. Any man would fear to come to her: Who could live up to the glittering desire in her cat eyes? And even the idea of the giantess (shot on a beach in Guadeloupe) is almost redeemed by Renoir's use of Eastman color and Panavision. No one but Blier has matched such raunchiness and such visual beauty; you have to have a true respect for raunchiness to do that.

☆

The title *Get Out Your Handkerchiefs* suggests a mockery of such movies as *Love Story,* but it also carries another suggestion — that we *should* be prepared to weep at the perplexities of love. It's a gentler, more refined comedy than either of the others; our laughter is never raucous. The wildness of *Going Places* hasn't disappeared, though — now it's underneath. The impression that the film gives is of freshness and originality, and of an unusual serenity. Feelings are expressed that haven't come out in movies before, and in a personal voice of a kind we think of as novelistic, yet nothing is wasted in the shots. Everything is to the point, and so we sit trustingly as things drift along and work themselves out. Here, as in the two other pictures, we never know where the story is going, and there's a considerable shift of direction midway, but this time it's all reassuringly quiet. The music is by Mozart, by Delerue (writing in the spirit of Mozart), and by Schubert, and this has an additional modulating, controlling effect. The style is almost chaste.

The two protagonists are played by the stars of *Going Places,* Depardieu and Dewaere (it was written with them in mind), but they're not the boors they were before — there's no violence in them. They're polite, harmless workingmen — Depardieu a driving-school instructor, Dewaere a playground supervisor. The picture opens at Sunday lunch in a Paris café. Jug-faced and serious, the powerfully built Depardieu is eating robustly while his lovely dark wife (Carole Laure) pecks at her food. Suddenly, he begins expostulating; he explains to her that she doesn't eat because she's sick of his face. He says that he loves her and wants to make her happy, so he'll bring her the man sitting opposite her whom she's been staring at and wants to go to bed with. There's something Neanderthal about his clumsiness; he's telling her of his consideration for her while making a public spectacle of her misery and their sexual failure. He goes over, introduces himself to the bearded stranger (Dewaere), propositions him, and says, "If you get her to smile, you'll be my pal." From this first scene—which is as deft and quick and funny as scenes in Sacha Guitry's comedies, such as *Lovers and Thieves*—Blier is playing with his characters and with us. The wife certainly looks bored and depressed, but we don't see her eying Dewaere—who wears glasses, and looks rather vague and self-absorbed. He accepts the invitation, though, and becomes the wife's lover, and the men then take turns trying to impregnate her—it being their theory that she is silent and morose because a woman needs a child. What we do see once the two men become pals (without Dewaere's getting her to smile) is that neither one makes any emotional contact with her. Dewaere has the complacency of a literate simpleton. He owns five thousand of the Livre de Poche paperback classics; reading them and listening to Mozart are his life. And he proselytizes, and converts Depardieu to his interests, while the wife scrubs and knits. When a neighbor (Michel Serrault, the star of *Lovers and Thieves*) bangs on their door at night to complain of the sound of a Mozart record, Depardieu sits him down and converts *him*.

So far, it's an enchantingly quirky sex comedy. The situation of the sterile wife and the rattled husband has its classic-farce overtones; the cuckolded husband is generally rich and decrepit, of course, but this is a classic farce in modern slang, with a barrel-chested, virile young husband who cuckolds himself with complete casualness, on the spur of the moment. Yet the film's texture is soft and sensual; there's a velvety underlayer to the scenes. Jean Penzer's cinematography suggests another world—like something shot from a diving bell. Because of Blier's method, nothing is ever explained. It's clear the two men are chumps. But if they don't have any idea what's going on in the wife's mind, neither do we. And the secret of the film—its essence—is that Blier doesn't, either. Carole Laure, with her neat little choirboy head and her slender, sinuous body, is treated as an object throughout. But never with contempt. And Carole Laure is a wonderful reactor. Her elusive, doleful shades of feeling delight us, even though we can't be sure what they mean; we can't tell if her knitting is a way of escaping the men's idiocy or if her mind is blank, or both, but we enjoy entertaining the possibilities. Are the men right to think she will be happy only if she has a child? Maybe so, but they go about trying to give her one without ever getting through to her. Their obtuseness—their clumsiness—may be the reason they can't reach her, but then perhaps it's her unreachability that makes them so clumsy. She has the natural, yielding grace of a sapling.

In the second half, the classical elements vanish, and the picture becomes more mysterious, leisurely, and meditative. In all three of these films, the movement is from the city to the country — to the primeval wilderness — and it's always the men's propulsion. This time, the two men decide that the wife they've been sharing needs country air, and the three of them go off to be counselors at a summer camp for the underprivileged. The camp has one wealthy child, a thirteen-year-old boy (the child who plays the part is billed only by his nickname, Riton, to protect him from notoriety); he has been sent there by his parents to obtain experience of the underprivileged, whom he will be dealing with when he takes over the family's industrial enterprises. He's a smart brat, with a genius IQ, though he looks unformed; there is no suggestion of horniness about him, and the first time we see him, when the other children are picking on him, we might easily take him for a girl. But he's far more clever than the two pals, and he hasn't had any reason to feel that he's clumsy; he has his child's guile and seductiveness. He says and does the shrewd things that thirteen-year-olds must want to say and do but don't have the courage for, or the knowledge, except in their dreams. He uses entreaties drawn from Cherubino in *The Marriage of Figaro*. And he gets through to the wife. The men were right: She wanted a child.

The woman takes this little boy to her bed, and can't live without him, even if that means he must be kidnapped. When he has been sent away from her to boarding school, and is in the dorm at night telling his awed fellow students the story of his conquest, and the woman herself tiptoes in and, in full view of all those boys, kisses him, we're watching a mythological romance. There are all the obstacles, such as the boy's parents, to be taken care of, but the two men (who turn into her clown attendants) help her, though it lands them in jail. How can they not help? The boy prodigy is like their Mozart. The film goes off in this weird direction, yet it all seems uncannily logical and prepared for. At the end, the woman has her child lover and is pregnant as well.

It's bewildering yet mysteriously right, satisfying, down to the pensive sounds of Schubert at the end. There's a gravity to this film — to Blier's generous, amused giving in to a sense of defeat. At some level, he has the feeling that what women want men for is to perpetuate the species — that they really want a child. And he has compounded this fantasy by having a child father the child, thus eliminating the need for men altogether. *Handkerchiefs* is a farce that turns into a fable. Now we recognize why everything about the young wife is so ambiguous — that melting look in her eyes, her shimmering beauty. Now we can understand Dewaere's double take when he was spending a night with her and said he wondered what her husband was doing, and she said "Who?" This is a sleeping-beauty fable, but told from the point of view of a man's erotic fears. This woman is to be awakened not by a prince but by a princeling. At the moment that her child lover is seducing her, in the sleeping quarters at the summer camp, the two chumps come down the hallway, pause outside her door, and discuss whether to go in. They decide that there's no reason to worry — the boy is too young. It's a funny moment, yet there's poetic tension in it, and the hallway has a palpable sensual beauty. They're losing out forever.

All three of these films are about two pals who don't really understand women — and their not understanding women is part of their bond. The teamwork of the actors is the true marriage. Depardieu, with his beautiful long jaw and his loping walk, and Dewaere, with his nearsighted vagueness (he's like a more delicate Timothy Bottoms), move together rhythmically. Marielle and Rochefort twitch and grimace and drop their eyelids in perfect counterpoint; their show of revulsion at women is the flirtation dance of impotent roués. The pal teams in these movies have intuitive rapport. They hang loose when they're together.

In *Handkerchiefs,* Blier's fantasy themes seem to turn against the male fantasist. There's pain along with the humor. The thirteen-year-old who arouses the wife is a variation of the jailbird who aroused the beautician, but, once aroused, the lovely wife does not want the men — she wants only the child. The two men who were so happy with the mother figure played by Moreau, and who wanted to be suckled on the train, are now rejected by the mother. Marielle and Rochefort at least found their way back to the womb, but Depardieu and Dewaere seem to be locked out. All they've got is each other, and at the end they're going off together, maybe to live happily like pigs. But that's not how it looks. Discharged from jail and carrying their belongings, Depardieu and Dewaere peer through an iron gate into the window of the solid, rich home where the wife they have lost sits contentedly knitting baby clothes, and then disappear down the road.

Blier's poetic logic is so coolly, lyrically sustained in *Get Out Your Handkerchiefs* that nothing that happens seems shocking. You feel you understand everything that's going on. But only while it's happening — not afterward. Afterward, you're exhilarated by the wit, and by your own amusement at how little you understand. What does the woman respond to in the child? His need? His foxiness? His strength? His childishness? It's a mystery. Sex is emotional anarchy.

Blier doesn't attempt to present a woman's point of view; he stays with the man's view of women, and that gives his films a special ambience. For a woman viewer, seeing *Handkerchiefs* is like a vacation in a country you've always wanted to visit. Reading a book such as *From Here to Eternity,* a woman enters an area of experience from which she has been excluded; seeing a Blier film, a woman enters a man's fantasy universe stripped of hypocrisy. Blier's films have no meanness about women; the wife in *Handkerchiefs* isn't neurotic — just elusive. Women are simply seen as different. A man friend of mine used to say, "If the first Martian who lands on earth is a male, I'll have more in common with him than I do with all the women on earth." Blier's is an art of exaggeration: He takes emotions and blows them up so big that we can see the things people don't speak about — and laugh at them. *Get Out Your Handkerchiefs* makes you feel unreasonably happy.

The New Yorker, October 16, 1978

MICHAEL CIMINO: YEAR OF THE DRAGON

John Powers

Outside MGM's Cary Grant Theater the advance word was positive on *Year of the Dragon.* True, no one you met had actually seen it, but the rumors were encouraging ("New York was amazed") and the name Cimino still tickles local psyches. The preview audience was uncommonly excited, which is to say they were marginally less blasé than usual. Why not? An almost biblical event might be in the offing, a resurrection at best (or worst, depending on your allegiance), and people were glad to be there.

For about ten minutes, as David Mansfield's score bounded over the credits and Alex Thomson's pictures splashed the screen with Chinatown colors, Lazarus seemed to be cracking an eyelid, critics rehearsed their revisionism ("the misappreciated *Heaven's Gate*"), and one thought *maybe, just maybe.* Then, the characters began to talk (for want of a better term), the pleasure began to fade, and with the well-oiled inevitability of a hot rod screaming toward a cliff, the movie roared toward the thin air of pretension, hovered a moment, and cracked up, scattering bile and bushwah all over the screen.

Los Angeles, too, was amazed.

Though faster and viler than its notorious predecessor, *Year of the Dragon* did drag on for what seemed like a year, and even in this city without memory or generosity, a generous watcher couldn't help remembering an earlier movie. The theater exits beckoned like the very gates of heaven, for up on the screen it was all blood, fear, hatred, muddle, grandiosity, and dullness. If dementia has a name, it must be Michael Cimino.

For all his vanity and ambition, Cimino is a bad filmmaker and a terrible storyteller. Yet he himself is a terrific story, one of the most revealing that movie culture has to offer. In only four films he has fashioned a career exploding with the contradictions of Hollywood, its shotgun wedding of commerce and "creativity" (which term has a special meaning when spoken by a producer), its inbreeding of talent, its worship of success, its blindness to merit, its fluttering dreams, and its fear of that box-office death which smells even sourer in a sanitized high-rise boardroom.

No film in history has proved more noisome than 1980's *Heaven's Gate,* the state of the art in debacle and hubris, a $44 million western that earned back a little over $1 million in ticket sales. Long before it was released (no false humility here), I had decided only fools would entrust Cimino with all those millions. Now, five years later, one of the fools has spoken and proves himself brighter than one had imagined, or at least foolish in a more dignified way.

Stephen Bach, then senior vice-president and head of world production for United Artists, has taken up pen to give us his anatomy of the fiasco in *Final Cut: Dreams and Disaster in the Making of "Heaven's Gate"* (Morrow, $19.95). Wry, self-effacing, and as sensible as nannies' shoes, Bach's account depicts, both consciously and otherwise, the true horror of the corporate mind, especially when confronted with anything so wayward as artistic ambition or popular taste. *Final Cut*'s blow-by-blow chronicle gives detail to a cultural free-for-all whose contours are already well known.

Even in summary, the story is remarkable. In early 1979 UA hired Michael Cimino to make a film, *The Johnson County War,* originally estimated to cost $7.5 million and budgeted for just over $11 million. With money in hand, Cimino went artsy bananas and donned his Napoleon hat for the slow, slow, *slow* march to masterpiece Moscow. In his first six days of shooting, he fell five days behind schedule. Like mad royalty adding rooms to the palace (to nudge the metaphor with Pauline Kael's regal simile), Cimino shot take after take and printed them all at outlandish expense. As he pursued the phantom of perfection, even ordinary things became difficult—he did fifty-three takes of Kris Kristofferson brandishing a bullwhip—and while the budget doubled, tripled, and begged to quadruple he amassed more than *220* hours of printed footage, a *Guinness Book* feat to set alongside record-setting flagpole habitations.

Now gaudy excess is not unknown in an industry that spawned von Stroheim, Welles, and Coppola, but UA's reaction might well have been: They let it happen . . . and happen . . . and happen. Although they fretted and bitched, Bach, David Field (co-head of production), and UA President Andy Albeck never really *did* anything. They were too decent to be good at their jobs. As *Final Cut* reveals, they continually believed Cimino's latest assurances (lies?), they cowered when he threatened to take *Heaven's Gate* to Warner's, they tolerated (miserably) his refusal to speak to them, they pondered various options (abandonment, containment, firing the bastard), joked of killing Cimino, hid behind other projects, and, even after they cracked the legal whip, still didn't assert control. UA executives never saw the finished *Heaven's Gate* until its calamitous premiere in November 1980.

☆

The immediate origins for this comedy of errors came in January 1978. After a decade of battling the parent Transamerica Corporation, UA Chairman Arthur Krim resigned, moved to Orion, and publicly blasted Transamerica for its commercialism and contempt for creative endeavor. One imagines that his words weren't wholly disinterested, but no matter, for Krim was arguably the most respected figure in Hollywood, and UA immediately took on a bad rep: In an industry dependent upon "the creative community," UA had been labeled the land of the money-flunkies.

For Albeck, Bach, Field, and the others concerned with production, it became imperative for UA to establish artistic credibility, partly by holding onto its talent (Bach describes the failed efforts to keep Woody Allen), partly by starting new creative projects. In keeping with post-*Jaws* Hollywood's search for blockbusters (what Albeck called "locomotives"), UA was looking for the hot talent who could offer them the big score.

Enter Michael Cimino in a dazzle of lights. He was perfect, the doctor's prescription for a studio with creative anemia. He had a good background (Yale M.F.A., commercials), had worked successfully with Clint Eastwood on *Thunderbolt and Lightfoot,* and, most important, had completed *The Deer Hunter,* an "epic" that Bach and Field knew would make him a commercial and critical success. (Indeed, it won the Oscar for Best Film and Best Director.) If that weren't enough, Cimino even had the proper ethnic pedigree: He was another of those East Coast Italians with operatic styles, vaulting ambition, and inspiration coming out their ears, a group Hollywood never tired of worshipping in the late seventies.

Although money is generally thought to be the soul of Hollywood, one should never underestimate the role of seduction in deal making. Bach may have had a few reservations (what did *The Deer Hunter*'s script actually *look* like?), but he and his fellow UA execs were enthralled by Cimino's "creative" glamour. And then, Cimino was very persuasive — even his arrogance contributed to his artistic cachet. Like ingenues touring Rome, they were prepared to believe the romantic words whispered in their ear by the Italian who would later screw them. And screw them Cimino did, time and again, in what Bach terms the "two-year Cimino cure for auteur worship."

If you want to know why UA didn't cure itself sooner, one answer lies in the studio's eagerness to prove itself to the "creative community." Firing the newest Oscar-winning director would be reckoned negative proof, especially as Cimino's excesses would confirm his genius in a city that equates expenditure with inspiration. Another answer lies in the simple bad judgment of production bosses Bach and Field, who by temperament and education allied themselves with creation and artistry — no financial louts they! — yet overlooked the pathological jumble of *The Deer Hunter* and were bowled over by the few handsome feet of *Heaven's Gate* that Cimino condescended to show them.

Then, of course, they were weak. Trapped between the impersonal lockstep of corporate life and the laser-eyed fanaticism of the Napoleonic auteur, they froze in their deepest being — stood still — before retreating to the camouflage of communal decisions, the snickering solace of meetings, the impotent rage of memos and hopeful delusions. Their timidity was complemented by UA's scattered authority (power in New York, power in LA, Cimino in Kalispell, Montana), in which decisions were taken thousands of miles apart by people who, like Bach and Field themselves, were jockeying for position against one another.

Shorn of passion, but not cold-blooded — such is the mediocrity of the corporate ethos, especially the Hollywood ethos that sleeps with art yet is wedded to business. *Final Cut* makes sure we don't forget about that marriage, for it opens with Transamerica Chairman John Beckett assuring Bach that UA "is not for sale," and it ends with him selling it to MGM one year later. In this large duplicity, caused at least partly by the *Heaven's Gate* episode, one finds a fitting end to a book brimming with comic futility and bad faith. MGM's owner, Kirk Kerkorian, was so keen to acquire UA that Transamerica cleared a profit, despite the $40-odd-million loss brought by cinema's greatest white elephant.

☆

With its access to the trade-paper dullness of industry meeting rooms, Bach's book provides a handy view of the Hollywood mind at work. It has been widely praised for its efforts to be fair — even to Cimino, whom he obviously hates (under "Cimino" the Index lists "megalomania," "narcissism," "sulks and silences," etc.). But as one who plunked down his $19.95, I must confess that Bach's "balance" is more admirable than enjoyable. The great god Fair Play might be smiling, but I'd hoped for something spryer and more venomous, more charged with invective against all those folks who turned Bach's stomach to acid and eventually got him fired. Though occasionally waspish and sharply critical of Cimino, the book is nice. Too nice.

And not sufficiently incisive. Bach's "ordinary, decent chap" manner has its virtues — he makes sensible observations on the nature of artistic discipline — but it suffuses *Final Cut* with a pervasive sense of sensitive mediocrity. Bach freely admits his errors of judgment, yet he stops short of illuminating self-knowledge or self-revelation. Even his mea culpas come with a willing ease that smacks of the higher defensiveness.

Had he taken a hard, gutsy look at his own deepest motives ("Die, Field, die!"), or had he questioned the presuppositions of his job and his values (his first thought about *The Deer Hunter* was that, ho-hum, "it was impressive"), he might have painted a penetrating, memorable portrait of himself and, by extension, of the Hollywood executive of the eighties. He might have described life where it's actually lived. Instead, after four hundred pages, he remains middling and nondescript. With his bland, serviceable, occasionally maladroit prose ("In spite of disappointments like Sellers' death . . . ") Bach tells the truth as he knows it. But it remains the plain, flat truth of the literate businessman.

It follows, then, that Bach would be less than revelatory about Michael Cimino. He has the nice man's blankness in the face of something "other," a problem made worse by Cimino's refusal to talk to him. And so, addressed only from without, Cimino remains *Final Cut*'s hollow, enigmatic center, like one of Conrad's tortured romantics (Kurtz or Lord Jim) known only through his behavior.

☆

Who then, one might ask, is Michael Cimino? This question is not asked without risk, for to plumb any heart, much less such a dark one, could take an honest man forever and threaten to turn him into Michael Cimino himself. Since I can think of few more dismal prospects (being Stephen Bach might be one), let me be rather brief and messy at the edges.

In the photos I've seen, Michael Cimino has the no-neck squatness of the Roman peasant, but a peasant who's won the lottery and can afford patrician curls and the expensively informal garb (do I remember a gold necklace?) of Beverly Hills royalty. This contradictory mingling of the plebe and the toff is simply one aspect of a cubist personality, one facet driven artist (who claims "I have no personal life"), one facet grifter (who *does* have personal property and gets it improved on the *Heaven's Gate* tab), one facet Jay Gatsby (sweetening his past), and one facet the con man who has bought his own hustle and now sees himself as Howard Roark. Yes, Howard Roark, architectural mastermind and hero of *The Fountainhead,* the Ayn Rand novel that Cimino — voluminous detail — proposed as a project before settling on *Heaven's Gate.* (To his credit, Bach nixed the idea; too late did he discover what Cimino's desire to film *The Fountainhead* actually revealed.)

In Rand's jejune novel, Roark is invariably, indisputably right. He's misunderstood, yes, beleaguered, you betcha, but in the end he's cosmically vindicated in his work, in his life, in the hay. That's why fourteen-year-olds identify with him. Out in the world, however, things aren't so simple. If Howard Roark isn't a genius, wouldn't his rampaging self-assurance be simple megalomania? What if Howard Roark turned out to be Captain Queeg? Nimrod? Rasputin? Wile E. Coyote?

Or Michael Cimino. It's not that Cimino's talentless—he has (or had) some striking cinematic skills—but none of his work could justify either the praise he has received or the grandiosity with which he touts his own artistic mission. He's a minor, psychologically racked talent, and this has been clear all along.

After a successful career making commercials in New York, Cimino moved west and began to sell scripts, including such dogs as *Magnum Force* for Clint Eastwood. This, in turn, led to his promising directorial debut in *Thunderbolt and Lightfoot* (1974), a superior genre picture made quirky and affecting by the performances of Eastwood and Jeff Bridges, our two great screen-acting naturals.

Visually nifty and reasonably brisk, *Thunderbolt and Lightfoot* remains Cimino's most controlled piece of storytelling, largely (one suspects) because Eastwood had the real power on the set. Yet beneath the formal control, one senses the very real psychological pressure of the film's homoerotic theme—the love between Eastwood and Bridges (who, at one point, dresses up as a woman and looks dishier than you'd expect).

By the time of the much-vaunted *The Deer Hunter* four years later, Cimino's control was waning and his unconscious was running amok. Genre conventions were replaced by a freewheeling fantasy about machismo that confronts myth with experience yet leaves the myth untouched. (In the John Wayne role, Robert De Niro plays a character named, ahem, Michael.) Because Cimino clearly believes this "real man" stuff, the movie has a pulpy vitality and conviction. But it takes its heat from the fast-burning fuel of lies. *The Deer Hunter* mixes a fraudulent naturalism that glamorizes mill-town Pennsylvania with a racist surrealism that makes the Vietnam War even worse than it was.

It's a nasty, meandering bit of work whose narrative weakness is all too apparent. Once past the lovely sweeping camera movements and the cleverly deployed motifs (blast furnace/napalm, deer hunting/war), one finds inept dramatic construction that depends upon Russian roulette sequences to give the story kick. If these episodes weren't so sick they'd be laughable, especially the final one, when the androgynous-looking Christopher Walken dies in De Niro's arms.

More damning still, Cimino never thinks through what he's saying—he just spills his guts—so that the cast's final chorus of "God

Bless America" makes no statement, passes no judgment, has no meaning. It's all sound and fury.

By comparison, *Heaven's Gate* is far less personal. Despite the lunacy of the undertaking, it's driven more by Cimino's desire to make Art than to exorcise the demons in his skull. Watching it again recently (let no one envy me my job), I was struck that it almost seems a kind of apologia, evidence that Cimino isn't a racist (he's on the immigrants' side) or a reactionary (he makes the ranchers wicked) and proof that he doesn't depend upon cheap melodrama (hence the story's pace — it moves like a snail dragging its shell across a flypaper prairie).

Because it's less filled with hatred than *The Deer Hunter,* I hate it less than most viewers do. True, I've never actually made it through the long version in one day, much less one sitting — all the dust makes me thirsty — but taken in snatches, the film works a peculiar magic, especially David Mansfield's lovely score and the astonishing glow of the images.

At the same time, it's a corrupt, empty work that, like *The Deer Hunter,* betrays the absence of humane judgment. In the world of *Heaven's Gate,* proportion vanishes: A railway conductor meeting a train has equal weight with a bloody murder. Cimino's pursuit of Art leads him to a heartless kitsch that makes misery *pretty,* that turns a trudging immigrant family into the stuff of a prize-winning calendar photo. By demanding those fifty-three takes of Kristofferson cracking his whip, Cimino was not making simply a financial blunder, but a human one. To give such care to the inessential reveals a blindness to what really matters.

Although these three works have many of the formal qualities I customarily admire, including a mastery of mise-en-scène, these virtues become almost death-eating when used to portray his view of the world: an unearned — nay, an *unconsidered* — nihilism. Cimino's work has the commercial maker's moral stupidity. It tries to sell us an image of truth by playing on our worst instincts.

George Orwell once remarked that Salvador Dali was a genius "from the wrist down"; one might say that Cimino is a genius from the retina out. But in *Year of the Dragon* his moral myopia has begun to attack his cinematic eye. His once-flowing technique has become almost a parody of visual style (he uses relentless tracking shots to jack up excitement, and sets up almost every scene with the same fishhook-shaped camera movement). It's the ugliest film he's ever made, the kind of work that invites psychotherapy, not criticism.

Merely to summarize the story is to condemn it. Mickey Rourke plays Stanley White, a designer-haired supercop who's sent to New York's Chinatown precinct to help combat gang violence. Since White (clever name) is still angry about losing the Vietnam War, this assignment gives him a chance to vent his rage on various yellow-skinned people ("Chink" this, "Chink" that, "Fuck *you,* Chink") and to declare war on the Chinese Mafia, which—in this film anyway—runs Chinatown like a sadistic theme park. Quicker than you can say My Lai, the Chinese start dying, most of them killed by other Chinese at the cunning instigation of Joey Tai, a GQ Fu Manchu played with smarmy, epicene brilliance by John Lone. (Lone does for his character what the script doesn't do: gives him some life.)

As if cleaning up millennia of Chinese corruption weren't job enough for any man, much less a self-proclaimed Polack, White must confront an angry wife ("you missed my ovulation"), battle the usual assortment of bureaucratic namby-pambies, listen to a chum tell him to eat better (now *that's* friendship), and chase Chinese-American anchorwoman Tracy Tzu (played with utter obliviousness by some actress named Ariane). A "real man," Stanley won't be denied. After she refuses his advances, he rips off her clothes and forces her to screw him. Like any real woman, Tracy loves him for it—though everything about White suggests that he'd come too soon.

Year of the Dragon has the psychological rawness of pulp but none of the pleasures one gets in, say, *Dirty Harry* or Jim Thompson's novels. Although scattered bits of meaning litter the screen (Joey and White are doubles, of sorts), the whole thing is a mess of fragments, as if Cimino had simply smacked his head open like a piñata and filmed the things that fell out. To be fair, some of this rubbish fell from the head of cowriter and cobigot Oliver Stone (*Midnight Express, Scarface*). And they're not the only ones. At the Cary Grant screening, many people laughed every time White made a racial slur.

Leaving aside its dictionary-of-clichés aspect (trust me on this and I'll spare you a list), *Year of the Dragon* can be read on several levels, none of them coherent or satisfying. What's most annoying is that Cimino's direction never finds an attitude toward Stanley White. In Mickey Rourke's unlikable performance, White seems like a walking Polish sphincter, but the scenes (and compositions) are structured to make him heroic.

As a piece of literal storytelling, it's totally haywire, violating plot plausibility and character motivation in its pursuit of aimless sensation. It's no more effective as the allegorical reprise of the Vietnam War it sometimes seems to be. Despite some feints toward meaning (White: "This is a fucking war and I'm not going to lose it — not *this one*"), the film doesn't explore White's rage about Vietnam, doesn't show the sickness of his feelings (or their validity). It just exploits a chain of associations many Americans feel about Vietnam and, in a nasty, Yellow Peril twist, hangs them on the Chinese.

The movie makes more sense as a metaphor for Cimino's own career, which, like White's (and Howard Roark's), is one of supercompetence in the face of social mediocrity and personal cowardice. When White cries angrily, "How can anybody care too much?" one can almost see Cimino berating a UA executive as he set up that fifty-fourth shot of Kris Kristofferson and his bullwhip. One can see why the film continues to like and justify White's behavior long after the crowd wishes he'd choke on his own arrogant spleen.

Year of the Dragon makes equal sense as a psychodrama inhabited by Cimino's specific (and often hateful) quirks, his brainless machismo, his virulent racism (more unsavory here than in *The Deer Hunter*), his ambivalent homoeroticism (clear in the fascinated depiction of Joey Tai), and the misogyny that violates women, has them like it, and strips them naked for the camera when the action gets slow. Some will praise Cimino for his capacity to impress an audience — to make an impact — and others will applaud his willingness to expose his psyche for all to see. But to do this is really to do nothing at all. The genuine film artist, as opposed to the madman with a camera, gives a meaningful shape to his or her experience so that others might understand it.

No one has exposed his neuroses more insistently than Woody Allen — his psychic shambles is the fertile soil of his art — but Allen has become one of our great contemporary filmmakers by finding a *public form* in which his personal anxieties, lusts, and rages can be shared. *Annie Hall* and *Manhattan* may lack some of the "visceral" wallop of *Year of the Dragon,* but they offer more than just guts, which, even when they smack our faces, remain mute.

Yet as I said earlier, Michael Cimino is a Hollywood phenomenon, and the trashiness of *Year of the Dragon* is merely the latest chapter in a darkly comic story. No matter what I say, Cimino will emerge from this movie with an improved reputation. Not of course because he's made something good, heavens no, even his mom would hate this one, but because he's answered the greatest single doubt about his career. As the movie's press kit explains (in something resembling English):

"Michael Cimino and his team wrapped their film in the style guaranteed to bring a smile to any producer's face — on time and on budget. In fact, however, Cimino even exceeded his own optimistic prediction by completing principal photography seven days ahead of schedule."

"On time and on budget." For Cimino, these words mean he can be trusted again, and in the blockbuster-mad city of Hollywood, there are many who will trust him and, sad to say, even think him a brilliant filmmaker. The *Heaven's Gate* disaster will be reckoned an aberration, and though some decent execs were disgraced by it, Cimino will thrive, free to follow that credo that encapsulates so well the thoughtfulness and humanity of his career:

"You follow an obsession . . . and it leads you somewhere."

Where that somewhere is, I don't want to be.

LA Weekly, August 16–22, 1985

TERRY GILLIAM: BRAZIL

Kenneth Turan

On those increasingly infrequent occasions when a Hollywood studio is in possession of the kind of serious, provocative film it assumes intelligent adults will like (as opposed to what are euphemistically known as "audience pictures"), the powers that be usually don't place obstacles in the way of getting the word out. Phone calls are made, screenings are set up at convenient times and locations, one's attendance is earnestly importuned. However, in the case of the brilliant, darkly fantastic *Brazil,* the most potent piece of satiric political cinema since *Dr. Strangelove,* more than a drive to a nearby screening room was required. To see *Brazil,* I had to go all the way to Paris.

True, it didn't have to be Paris. I could have gone to Belgium, Austria, Germany, Italy, Spain or England, Scandinavia or Latin America, even Australia or New Zealand. And soon, I could have gone to the Orient as well. Because America, first in war, first in peace, first in the hearts of its countrymen though it still may be, is just about dead last in getting to see this exceptional film. That situation so frustrated Terry Gilliam, the picture's director, that he recently took out a full-page ad in *Variety* that read, "Dear Sid Sheinberg, When are you going to release my film, 'BRAZIL'?"

Sid Sheinberg, as readers of *Variety* know, is the all-powerful president and chief operations officer of MCA, the parent company of Universal, the studio which holds the American rights to *Brazil*. The film has been on and off Universal's schedule since January of this year, promised and then withdrawn, promised and then withdrawn, like some out-of-control carrot-and-stick mechanism. "This thing has been dragging on for so long," Gilliam said by phone from London, "I've been going slightly crazy."

Universal is doing more than sitting on *Brazil*. Using as an excuse the film's two-hour-and-twenty-two-minute length, seventeen minutes over what Gilliam contracted for, the studio has, in two separate stages, attempted violence to *Brazil*'s structure. The first series of changes got it down to two hours and eleven minutes; Gilliam reluctantly made those cuts himself out of consideration for his producer, Arnon Milchan, and the $4.5 million Universal owed the project but was withholding. Now, however, Universal is tinkering still more with *Brazil* ("We're going to do further work on the movie, then examine which version to release," Sheinberg told the *Los Angeles Times*), and Gilliam is outraged.

"The reaction in Europe has been fantastic, but this supposedly isn't enough for America, they work on the principle that Americans are subnormal humans, not as sophisticated as Europeans, and that's just rubbish," he says. "They're not just shortening the film now, they're changing the actual concept; Sid is, in fact, making his cut of the film, which I think is a very brave and exciting thing as far as art is concerned. He's doing what a man has got to do, and I'm thinking of coming out to Hollywood to give him support for his bravery, to let the American public be party to the rare and exciting experiment that is going on. All I ask is that he put his name on the film, call it Sid Sheinberg's *Brazil*."

Certainly no one is ever going to confuse *Brazil* with *E.T.*, *Jaws*, *Back to the Future*, or any other of Universal's major money-makers. Gilliam himself has accurately described it as "Walter Mitty meets Franz Kafka," with an added nod to what he calls "*real* fairy tales, not the bowdlerized, aseptic versions often presented. Real fantasies have danger in them; they're threatening and grisly," and so — very much so — is *Brazil*.

Brazil is named not for the Latin American country but rather in reference to that seductive, syncopated 1939 song whose familiar, caressing samba beat is the leitmotif of its sound track. But more than the song itself, *Brazil* is named for the mood of escape that its music creates: exotic, fanciful, carefree, and the polar opposite of the bleak, harrowing images Gilliam and cinematographer Roger Pratt have put on the screen.

Breathtakingly production-designed by Norman Garwood, *Brazil*'s world is sometime in the future but with half a mind in the past. All the men dress alike in slouch hats and the kind of three-piece tweed suits 1940s films were rife with, and the women are costumed to match. Much of the decor is tattered and tacky, and the all-controlling, unseen government that runs things is bumbling, incompetent, and absolutely drowning in useless paperwork. Yet that absence of efficiency only serves to underline the only thing the government does slick as you please, and that is torture and terminate its citizens. If *Brazil*'s world seems at first a parody of totalitarianism, we soon realize that that's precisely the point screenwriters Gilliam, Tom Stoppard, and Charles McKeown want to make. To live under that kind of system is to feel it can't possibly be real, to conclude that this much incomprehensible terror must be some kind of awful, insupportable joke.

In this cold, boggling *1984* world where fancy restaurants serve piles of premasticated mush and billboards for vacation sites read "Luxury Without Fear, Fun Without Suspicion," only Sam Lowry (Jonathan Pryce of *The Doctor and the Devils* and *Something Wicked This Way Comes*) emerges as a recognizable human being. Contentedly ensconced in a dead-end job in a backwater department of the omnipotent Ministry of Information, Sam insists, despite his youth-obsessed mother's attempts to get him more status, that he is a man with "no hopes, no wishes, no dreams." Or so he says. In fact, Sam has been having these dreams, wonderful romantic fantasy dreams about a beautiful girl whom he heroically rescues from a number of numbing situations. The dreams are more real to him than his drab life, providing exactly the kind of escape the ever-present *Brazil* music symbolizes.

Sam's problems begin when he becomes reluctantly involved in the sad case of Archibald Buttle, a harmless fellow who, in *Brazil*'s typically unsettling opening, is abruptly abducted from the bosom of his family by a team of black-suited, hooded commandos whose leader calmly intones, "You are invited to assist the Ministry of Information with certain inquiries," as they zip the poor man into a body bag. Though this kind of thing happens all the time in *Brazil,* the difference here is that the state is not after Buttle at all but rather renegade heating repairman Archibald Tuttle. For in a society paralyzed by bureaucracy, Tuttle is a dangerous kind of hero: a swashbuckling freelance repairman, the Errol Flynn of maintenance engineers, who arrives and departs à la Spiderman and lives only for the challenge of fixing faulty cooling systems before inept but authorized Central Services personnel (like the vindictive, demented Spoor) can arrive on the scene. In trying to untangle the Buttle-Tuttle imbroglio, Sam comes across his dream girl in the flesh, and his normal, healthy impulses toward love inevitably lead to agony and destruction.

Brazil's universe is so exactingly conceived that, demented and abhorrent though it is, its reality is never in doubt. Gilliam's totally original, bravura imagination, evident in the animation work he did as the only American member of the Monty Python troupe and in his last film, the exciting, inventive *Time Bandits,* rises to an entirely new level here. Scenes like a battle with a monstrous samurai, who catches fire instead of bleeding, and a dead-on quote from the Odessa Steps sequence of Eisenstein's *Potemkin,* with a vacuum cleaner standing in for the baby carriage, reveal a flair and a daring that is enviable.

Most striking of all of *Brazil*'s accomplishments is the room for humor Gilliam and his cowriters have found in this hermetic, harrowing society. We're not talking "Three's Company" here: A considerable portion of *Brazil*'s jokes come out of situations so horrid the laughter almost literally chokes in your throat, but it is that very audacity, that willingness to seek amusement in the most god-awful places, to interweave broad farce with unspeakable horror, that sets *Brazil* apart from almost any film you can name. Jonathan Pryce is exactly right as Sam, the solid center of the film, but most of the fun comes from a memorable cast of supporting actors: Bob Hoskins as Spoor, the sadistic heating engineer; Gilliam's fellow Pythoner Michael Palin as Jack Lint, the happy-go-lucky torturer; and Robert De Niro (yes, Robert De Niro), in a throwback to the kind of deadpan stuff he did for Brian De Palma in *Greetings* and *Hi, Mom!* as the heroic Archibald Tuttle, the Lone Ranger of repairmen.

Given its tone and objectives, there is a sense in which the qualms *Brazil* causes in the Universal hierarchy are perfectly understandable; there is no way a film this unapologetically black is going to break box-office safes across America. Still, this is no script angling for development funding, this is a finished film, and a brilliant one at that.

If even a fraction of the lip service studio executives pay to quality is sincere, they ought to be ashamed, and deeply so, for sitting on this picture for so long, let alone baldly attempting to emasculate its message. "They're trying to reduce something extraordinary to something ordinary, playing it safe in the hopes of guaranteeing something at the box office," says a distraught Gilliam. "What they don't want to do is let people think, let them have an experience they're not normally allowed to have in the cinema. This division between popular cinema, which is lightweight, and art cinema, where you're allowed to think, is something I hate.

"I didn't make this film to be a cause to fight over. People are saying to me I shouldn't be doing this, I shouldn't be this committed to my work," Gilliam says, the static from London punctuating his words. "People say, 'You'll never work in Hollywood again.'" A pause. "You know, a lot of people are making careers out there, but only a few people are making films." Truer words . . .

California Magazine, December 1985

TERRY GILLIAM: BRAZIL

John Powers

Brazil is a visual steamroller that flattens everything in its path, including (it seems) critical judgment. Caught up in the much-publicized game of chicken between director Terry Gilliam and Universal boss Sidney Sheinberg (who reportedly wanted a "happy ending"), the Los Angeles Film Critics Association snuck into secret screenings, clutched their noggins in art-struck awe, and named *Brazil* the Best Picture of 1985, even before its release. Inspired by all this free publicity, Sheinberg knuckled under and Gilliam's "cut" has opened to booming business. [Editor's Note: In the end, *Brazil* was not a commercial hit.]

This is OK by me, for *Brazil* is better than most movies. Every frame offers something fun to look at and expresses the personality of its creator. If you watch 10 minutes at random, you might even think *Brazil* a masterpiece. Watch all 131 minutes, however, and you may well find it tiresome, contradictory, and superficial—every 10 minutes is the same 10 minutes. It's certainly worth seeing, but like bargain sushi (or the Reagan presidency), it goes down much more easily if you don't let yourself think about what you're swallowing.

Brazil emulates and parodies *1984*'s vision of repression and failed romantic rebellion. It follows Sam Lowry (Jonathan Pryce), a well-born petty bureaucrat whose longing for a truck driver named Jill (Kim Greist) leads him to flout society's rules and act on his dreams. Such giddy individualism doesn't exactly fly in the film's nightmarish mock present, an affectless alternative world ("somewhere in the twentieth century"). In this society, the Ministry of Information tortures innocents in the name of "security," Central Services electricians bully the citizenry (but can't keep things functioning), and terrorist bombings punctuate the aimless consumption.

Brazil is itself something of a consumerist movie, a garish shop window full of gags (many mistimed), tricks, and visual knick-knacks. Rather than implicate you emotionally or intellectually, it gives you a lot to gawk at in nearly every shot. It's a tour de force of visual style, highlighted by extraordinarily brilliant production design and governed by an intoxicated logic. (In a key image, a bottle-waving derelict looms like a dipso King Kong over a scaled-down replica of a housing project called Shangri-La, a utopian environment that's grown ramshackle and dingy.)

Creating a world of rotting high rises and proto-fascist architectural pomp, Gilliam and designer Norman Garwood achieve a witty density of detail that recalls our own world, yet seems utterly alien. Posters blare advice from the walls: "Trust in Haste, Repent in Leisure"; "Suspicion Breeds Confidence." Familiar objects recombine to make quirky contraptions: computer terminals blooming from old typewriters, surveillance cameras sidling along on stick-insect bodies, glassy elevators running horizontally. And everywhere are the Central Services ducts, ungainly conduits of water, power, and sewage that run through the middle of rooms, providing visible reminders of social channeling and power.

Except for an odd (and revealing) lack of people on the streets, this fictional world is jam-packed with invention. No one will forget the image of Lowry's mother (Katherine Helmond) having her face stretched like taffy, or the camera skating along an endless office corridor aswirl with gray-clad bureaucrats, or the one-legged woman standing on the Metro as healthy men sit, or the two malicious Central Services workers (including the incomparable Bob Hoskins) performing Pat-and-Mike vaudeville patter beneath caps with foot-long bills. Each of these moments is memorable, but they are preeminently *moments* — funny, creepy, or violent, they all add up to far less than one would wish.

From time to time, isolated bits do cohere and sustain themselves, as when Sam visits the office of his friend Jack Lint (Michael Palin), a torturer for the Ministry of Information. In the waiting room, a dippy old mum of a secretary transcribes a torture victim's shrieks; inside, Jack stands in a blood-spattered white uniform while his young daughter plays with a ball in a cozy parlor area across the room. Absurd, funny, and bleakly touching (Palin's work here is impeccable), this marvelous scene suggests all the film might have been — and is not.

In *Brazil*, the inessential is king, and while almost all the tangential elements are wonderful, the story itself is woefully thin, a pretext for mere cleverness and visual brio. No doubt aware of this problem, Gilliam brought in two other writers (Tom Stoppard and Charles McKeown) to starch up the narrative, to give it a texture and flourish equal to the film's baroque imagery. Despite their efforts, however, the story lacks force. It functions like a thread that leads Gilliam through an elaborate labyrinth whose architecture and decor interest him far more than *Brazil*'s characters.

At the heart of this labyrinth, one finds a set of ideas that have grown senile since the clocks first struck thirteen in the opening sentence of *1984*. Nothing is more firmly entrenched in popular mythology than Big Brother's watchful eye or the beleaguered individual who dreams of escaping this oppressive reality. In 1986, these are modern clichés, aspects of a two-dimensional social vision that has lost its power to clarify the world or bum out the most angst-riddled of sophomores. Modern life may be bad, but it's still richer and deeper than this.

Brazil's mushrooming details are scarcely more original or trenchant than the overall conception. The damsel-in-distress dreams that express Sam's romantic selfhood are embarrassing in their psychological simplicity and lack of individuality. They look like an excuse for neat-o special effects. Much of the social satire is either ham-fisted (a group called Consumers for Christ) or passé. Jokes about processed food goop have been on the sci-fi menu for years. Plastic surgery has been a target of black comedy since Thomas Pynchon's 1963 *V.,* with its hilariously harrowing nose job.

Several of my friends concede these objections but praise *Brazil* for its uncompromising social negativity, for its resolute refusal to be uplifting in the era of *Rocky* and refried Spielbergers. Such an argument overlooks how the mistrust, even hatred, of society runs through dozens of current movies—it's the flip side of brainless exhilaration. *Brazil* may seem daringly dark, but there's nothing threatening about it, nothing that attacks anyone's prejudices or special interests. It is as friction-proof as *The Color Purple.*

Politically, its vision is blurry. True, *Brazil* attacks repressive state machinery and refuses to moralize about terrorism. Still, we never learn who runs the society it depicts; we never learn who's bombing whom—or why. Given this ambiguity—an absence of real politics—people of any persuasion could find it equally to their liking. (Indeed, Gilliam's interviews make him sound leftish, while coauthor Stoppard is a staunch Thatcherite.)

If anything, the film recalls the nastiness of *A Clockwork Orange.* Both dehumanize characters so we can *enjoy* their pain (here, they drown in crap, liquify, get blasted in the head). Both delight in making cruelty and tyranny into a visual feast. Both want to overpower the viewer with their imaginative energy. In all these ways, *Brazil's* cinematic onslaught comes closer to what it is ostensibly criticizing than to any values it might wish to defend.

The wan love story is symptomatic. Given the film's violent and entropic world, viewers readily identify with Sam and Jill. But not very deeply. Although Sam's love for Jill is the plot's motor and emotional core, Gilliam won't take time to build the scenes that would make it persuasive. He can't resist the unnecessary joke; he's hooked on goosing the viewer, and this predilection ultimately denies us the resonance that might compensate for *Brazil's* intellectual shallowness. But though it keeps hitting you with sharp images—jab, jab, jab—you never feel fear, pity, compassion, or love. Everything has the same weight. Compared to the emotionally polyphonic *Blade Runner* (another visually brilliant film), *Brazil* has all the tonal variation of a kazoo.

If any emotion seems dominant, it's the nostalgic wistfulness typical of dystopian fantasies. On several different levels, *Brazil* aches with the desire to turn back the clock, whether in the face renewals of its aging female characters, in its fondness for *Casablanca,* the Marx Brothers, and film noir saxophone, or in the thirties popular song that gives the film its title and whose lyrics comment ironically on the story's guttering passion: "Recalling thrills of our love / There's one thing I'm sure of / Return I will / To Old Brazil."

When it comes to bloodier passions, *Brazil* runs dry. In fact, just as the fictional world thwarts its inhabitants' hopes and desires, Gilliam unnecessarily frustrates ours, incessantly diverting our attention from his story's human meaning. Even the terrible loses its terror. Scenes of police-state cruelty become no more than a visual motif and horrify us less than a child's bang-bang game in *The Official Story,* a film about a real police state.

It's possible that Gilliam fears the emotions his work might summon up, and deflects or displaces them whenever he can; then again, he may simply prize his imaginative doodles over everything else. Whatever the reason, *Brazil* hides feeling beneath a familiar veneer of cleverness. You have the I-went-to-college allusions to Freudianism (Sam's refurbished mother looks like Jill) and *Heart of Darkness* (a Mr. Kurtzmann in the bowels of the Ministry of Information). You have the insignificant pun: The prominently displayed initials of the Ministry of Information spell the French word for "me," but *Brazil* doesn't make the connection relevant. And, of course, you have the inevitable nods to (and borrowings from) other films: *Battleship Potemkin, Alphaville, Playtime, The Road Warrior,* and so on.

Like everything in the Monty Python tradition (except *Fawlty Towers*), *Brazil* can't keep its story afloat for more than twenty minutes. This didn't matter on television, whose fractured, ephemeral nature lends itself to the Pythons' narrative anarchy. They deliberately opted for raggedness to subvert the conventions of "well-made" entertainment, wallowing in bad taste, cutting off skits in midplot, or belaboring sophomoric jokes. But what liberated them on the box has confined them on the screen, where their anti-aesthetic aesthetic has kept them from making a wholly successful movie. Theirs is the cinema of inspired potluck.

In a sense, Gilliam has never outgrown the Flying Circus. Although *Jabberwocky, Time Bandits* (which I love), and *Brazil* each mark an enormous technical advance over his clip-and-move animation on the Python show, he still composes his shots the same way, using his actors, props, and sets like the big feet and Karl Marx busts that stomped and soared across his TV efforts. For all its increased visual richness, Gilliam's work hasn't gained proportionally in wisdom and emotional truth. His characters are still flat as can be, and they live on very flat worlds.

LA Weekly, January 17–23, 1986

WOODY ALLEN: HANNAH AND HER SISTERS

Jay Carr

"God, she's beautiful," Michael Caine says in a voice-over at a party, staring at his sister-in-law, Barbara Hershey. In that opening moment of Woody Allen's *Hannah and Her Sisters,* we feel instinctively that the film is special, has wings. We sense the beginnings of Caine's obsessive, illicit fixation. We're drawn into the gravitational field of Hershey's allure. And here's how we know we're in for a treat, even before the laughs begin: We see Mia Farrow, as the model wife (Caine's) and Thanksgiving dinner–cooking earth mother to the whole clan, and can feel the way her generosity and perfection drive her sisters and errant husband up the wall.

For the next hour and forty minutes, as the film moves through two years and three Thanksgiving dinners cooked by Farrow, *Hannah and Her Sisters* keeps expanding in fresh, funny, rueful, honest, touching ways. It's one of the best films of the new year, and one of Allen's best as well. With love and fluency, it zeroes in on the fragmented lives of the sisters and their angst-ridden men. But it isn't cold and solemn, like *Interiors.* Allen even kids his former need to make a Bergman movie by having Max Von Sydow show up as the dour, stifling, condescending Scandinavian lover Hershey knows she must ditch. And what sets its amorous scamperings apart from those of the much darker *Manhattan* is the fact that its characters aren't as isolated. For better or worse, they're all connected, and Allen makes us feel it's better.

Hannah and Her Sisters is, in short, as funny as any Allen film and more openly compassionate. It's as if he's reconciled himself to human imperfection and limits, and, like a latter-day Candide, is content to make his own garden grow. Also, Allen for the first time has cast himself in a supporting role. In his last film, *The Purple Rose of Cairo,* he didn't appear at all. Obviously, he's been thinking about how best to incorporate himself into his films. He couldn't go on playing the schlep who backs into heroism and gets the girl. There was no way to reconcile that person with the high opinion of himself that began to surface in such films as *Sleeper* and even *Annie Hall.* *Hannah and Her Sisters* is more modest, generous, relaxed, true to life than his previous movies.

Here, Allen divides in two the role he played in the past. Caine plays the man agonizing over an impossible love, courting his sister-in-law with e. e. cummings, gassing on about volcanic love while fearing that his wife will learn of his infidelity. Caine handles both pursuit and guilt lightly, his best work in years. Amazingly, he even begins resembling Allen physically as the film proceeds. Allen, meanwhile, shows up as Farrow's ex-husband, a fretful TV producer who imagines a headache into a brain tumor, and briefly, hysterically, converts from Judaism to Catholicism. Mostly, he's comic relief, but at the end he's the one who voices the up-front benevolence in the new Woody Allen.

While Farrow's present husband is involved with one sister, her ex takes up with the other one, Dianne Wiest, the definitive arty neurotic whose blurry, about-to-dissolve face has never been better deployed. Gabby, vulnerable, brittle, a shade self-destructive, she's a cinch for a best supporting actress nomination in next year's Oscars. Allen stops playing the fool long enough to realize that if there is no immediately discernible God, then the Marx Brothers in *Duck Soup* will do. Having found salvation in comedy, he and Wiest, whose compulsive coke-snorting hilariously wrecks their first date, are able to lighten up. They're more than nut cases who have found each other. She's becoming saner; he's becoming more accepting. He reminds her that "the heart is a resilient little muscle," to say nothing of a wayward one. That's the film's message, insofar as it has one. It's coming from a mellower Woody Allen than the one who gave us *Interiors* and *Manhattan.*

In fact, you need the fingers of both hands to count the delights in *Hannah.* Let's start with Allen's insouciant nose thumbing at assertions that he's a novelist who wandered into the wrong art form. Stylistically, he uses literary devices as metaphors for the characters' fragmented lives; he gives them equal weight by dividing his film into chapters with title cards. Voice-overs feed the film's novelistic sensibility, too.

The acting, far from being capsized by the film's short takes, is perfection. In their different ways, Hershey, Wiest, and Farrow shine as the latter-day Chekhovian sisters, especially in a classic tension-ridden lunch scene. Maureen O'Sullivan (Farrow's real mother) plays her fictional mother here, an aging actress given to drink and married to another show-biz vet, the late Lloyd Nolan. He plays a crabby character, but Allen's familial, reconciling impulse is too strong to allow any souring (the film uses seven of Farrow's eight real-life children, also her rambling West Side apartment). *Hannah and Her Sisters* is a valentine, not only to New York and its great buildings and old show tunes—Allen has done a number of those—but to the people who keep it, and him, humming. It's the film in which everything seems to come together for Woody Allen.

Boston Globe, February 7, 1986

WOODY ALLEN: HANNAH AND HER SISTERS

Michael Sragow

When it comes to Woody Allen films, I feel like the extraterrestrials in *Stardust Memories*—the ones who said they liked his early, funny movies best. I respect his artistic ambition as well as his impulse toward profundity. I just think he's never more artistic and serious than when he's also being funny.

The good news about *Hannah and Her Sisters* is that it contains some of his most humorous, least precious material since the first half of *Annie Hall.*

This new comedy-drama covers the same ground as his 1979 *Manhattan*—courtship and marriage, infidelity and flirtation, East Side, West Side, all around the town—but it does so in a better mood. This time, with only one or two exceptions, you don't feel that the characters are about to pop an artery rather than crack a smile.

The bad news is part of the good news. Allen is in such a happy frame of mind, he's intent on spreading the word that even a known depressive can learn how to live life to the fullest. Do we really need Woody Allen, the man who's done the most to introduce downbeat neurotic content into stand-up comedy, telling us that we should experience each day as if it's our last? This movie purports to be about the getting of wisdom; it's really about the getting of homilies.

Hannah and Her Sisters has been compared to Chekhov, but it plays more like Allen's homage to Bergman's *Fanny and Alexander,* another maddeningly erratic work that didn't live up to its masterpiece billing. *Hannah* opens with Thanksgiving dinner just as *F&A* opened with Christmas dinner, and it celebrates the same virtues of familial love and creativity (both artistic and biological).

If Allen's film doesn't revolve around a little boy and girl as Bergman's did, it does revolve around adults who sometimes behave like little boys and girls — and who also belong to a large theatrical family. At the epicenter is Hannah (Mia Farrow), the actress-wife of an accountant named Elliot (Michael Caine), and the daughter of ex-actors played by Lloyd Nolan and Maureen O'Sullivan (identified only as Hannah's father and mother).

Hannah, who's just scored a triumph as Nora in *A Doll's House,* is the sister of an *aspiring* actress named Holly (Dianne Wiest), who's prone to excessive cocaine use. There's only one nonactor in the family: Lee (Barbara Hershey), a reformed alcoholic (unlike her unreformed mother) who's been living with an autocratic, eccentric painter named Frederick (Max Von Sydow), but is about to enter into an affair with Hannah's husband, Elliot.

Just when you think you've sorted out all the characters and interrelationships, Allen himself enters the picture as an anxiety-ridden TV comedy producer, Mickey, Hannah's ex-husband. Mickey is enough of a misfit to serve as the black sheep for the whole extended family. His major characteristic is hypochondria. But there's something fearless about his paranoia. While the other characters are busily diddling or "creating," Mickey drops out of TV in order to have a full-scale midlife crisis.

As a piece of acting, writing, and directing, Mickey is one of Allen's finest creations. Sorry, Mel Brooks — watching Mickey push his doctor into giving him a terminal diagnosis is to experience high anxiety at its fullest. And when he plays off of Dianne Wiest's dizzy, love-starved Holly, the two of them create a brilliant, hilarious duet for emotional cannibals. You've heard of bee-stung lips; Wiest has a bee-stung *face.*

It's easy to see that Mickey and Holly are supposed to be naked personalities who can't help but express the rest of the characters' root dilemmas — confronting loneliness and the meaning of life. In the movie's funniest sequences, Mickey considers converting to Catholicism (Hail Woody!), while Holly tries to create order out of emotional chaos by writing a couple of ripped-from-real-life plays.

In *Hannah and Her Sisters,* Allen as director tries to prove that his own concerns about Love and Death even affect people who care only about Love and Life. Allen punches home that thought when the supposedly self-sufficient Hannah screams out, near hysterically, that she, too, has "enormous needs."

The problem is that Elliot et al. seem to be acting out a postpsychoanalytic version of a Noël Coward play (with contemporary New York cultural credentials), while Mickey and Holly are both echt Woody Allen.

The Allenesque characters have resonances. But for all the cunning of Michael Caine, the vibrant beauty of Barbara Hershey, and the solid sweetness of Mia Farrow, their characters are almost as weightless as the old-movie caricatures in *The Purple Rose of Cairo*.

Allen hopes to knit his intimate, but sprawling, story together with the film equivalent of chapter headings — key topics taken from scraps of dialogue — and with a sound track full of pop standards like "Bewitched." In many of his group scenes, he succeeds in expressing how a tight-knit group can play telephone with emotions, passing a message around a table and having it end up in a totally different form.

But Allen rarely succeeds at giving this movie the kind of emotional unity it needs. And I think the happy ending he devises, with Mickey regaining faith in simple, family pleasures, is nothing less than bogus.

In the past, my problem with Allen's unhappy endings (even in *Annie Hall*) has been that they were gloomier than the characters deserved. The happy ending in *Hannah and Her Sisters* is equally uncalled for. When Mickey undergoes a change of heart simply by watching *Duck Soup*, it's as if he's engaging in Norman Cousins's laugh therapy.

Allen wants to give his movie the emotional roundness of a nineteenth-century novel. But he doesn't have the breadth, or perhaps the patience, to build characters step by step so that their fluctuations seem inevitable.

Elliot, Hannah, and Lee aren't abstractions like the characters in *Interiors*, but as people, they're too shallow to convey this movie's daring range of feelings. Perhaps their fickleness and their self-forgiveness are what strike a contemporary chord.

But to make an old-fashioned sense of affirmation work in a modern setting, you still have to do it the old-fashioned way. As John Houseman would say, you must *earn* it.

San Francisco Examiner, February 7, 1986

WOODY ALLEN: CRIMES AND MISDEMEANORS

Gary Arnold

An ingenious and absorbing feat of hypothetical, didactic storytelling, Woody Allen's *Crimes and Misdemeanors* consists of two cleverly balanced and counterpointed scenarios on the theme of moral cowardice. It emerges as a surprising and gratifying comeback effort for Allen as humorist, stylist, and would-be moralist, pulling him out of the ludicrous tailspin that began with *September* and worsened with *Another Woman.*

Those lulus had threatened to turn him into an incorrigible laughingstock. In many respects, *Crimes and Misdemeanors* is as self-consciously formal and verbally ornate as its immediate predecessors, but Allen is nimble enough to steer clear of their stilted pitfalls. He has also struck an effective balance between serious and humorous tendencies.

The principal characters are middle-age professional men—a respected physician played by Martin Landau and a struggling, kvetching documentary filmmaker played by Allen himself—who are weak enough to blunder into compromising situations.

They are introduced to us at a testimonial dinner, following which they go their separate misguided ways, one ominously serious in nature and the other disarmingly comic. Their stories follow along parallel lines through most of the movie until they cross again at the finale, when they meet at another festive occasion and share a brief conversation that serves as ironic summary for us.

Their stories are designed to illustrate the commonplace observation that some people can get away with murder—literally in one case, figuratively in the other.

In the predominantly serious tale, Landau brings his wonderful new aura of pensive gravity and authority to the role of Dr. Judah Rosenthal.

Dr. Rosenthal is an eminent ophthalmologist who takes desperate measures to protect his marriage and reputation from scandal when pressured by a panicky, trouble-making mistress.

(Allen seems to be poking fun at himself when he blithely inserts the title of one of his fiascoes into a line of dialogue: "I've done a stupid thing," confesses Martin Landau at one point. "Foolish, vain, dumb. *Another woman . . .* " Say no more.)

As the foolhardy mistress, Dolores, Anjelica Huston is a neurotic sensation, blending pathetic and alienating attributes so effectively that Dr. Rosenthal's eventual crime never lacks a compelling and even sympathetic motive. Dolores is clearly a wrecker and her own worst enemy. The moral question is, How will Dr. Rosenthal deal with her threats to his security?

He decides that he would prefer to conspire in the death of this suddenly demanding and threatening lover rather than risk the consequences of a full, humbling confession to his unsuspecting wife, Miriam (a shortchanged minor role that wastes Claire Bloom). Agonizing and rationalizing all the way, the good doctor finally reconciles himself to murder as a form of self-defense.

In the humorous counterpart to this grimly compromising fable, Allen plays a patsy named Cliff Stern. He is a documentary filmmaker who suffers a rude awakening after agreeing to a no-win Faustian pact.

Financially strapped, professionally obscure, and still unable to say no to his wife, Wendy, despite the icy drift of their marriage, Cliff interrupts a cherished project of his own to shoot a celebrity profile for network television of his detested brother-in-law, Lester (Alan Alda), a comedian so unspeakably successful that he's become a household nuisance throughout America.

In the course of recording this blowhard's celebration of himself (and Alda seems wittily right for the role of overbearing egomaniac), Cliff discovers that he's deluded himself about how and where to find consolation and self-esteem. The comic victim of a guy who can get away with murder, in a relatively harmless manner of speaking, Cliff tries to outfox the dreaded Lester, only to come up a multiple loser.

The crowning joke is the sight of Woody Allen in a yarmulke and utterly bewildered expression, nominally attending a wedding ceremony but still stunned into a self-pitying trance by the realization that fate has been playing by Lester's rules.

Cliff serves as a kind of displaced Sancho Panza to Dr. Rosenthal's mortally sinning Quixote, and it's doubtful if either narrative would play as effectively without the other. Rosenthal the sorrowful victimizer needs Stern the absurd victim, and vice versa, to prevent the film from going overboard on either the solemn or humorous side.

Cliff's follies are put in proper small-scale perspective in Allen's ethical fable, as if they were meant to echo his self-disparaging remark about an award won at the Cincinnati Film Festival: "Everyone got honorable mention who showed up."

If Dr. Rosenthal qualifies as a prize-winning, premeditating sinner, Cliff represents the vastly larger group that tends to mess up in less drastic but still humiliating ways in the course of simply showing up for life.

Their mutual blindness is underlined perhaps a bit too obviously by Dr. Rosenthal's work as an eye doctor and a linking character played by Sam Waterston—a sweet-natured rabbi who happens to be going blind.

Rosenthal's patient and Cliff's second, *unoffending* brother-in-law, the rabbi is something of a fake-out. In Allen's most adroit resorts to fantasy, Dr. Rosenthal appears to be airing out his conscience with the rabbi, but it's evidently a phantom rabbi, conjured up in his imagination in order to make the outcome of the debate a foregone conclusion.

There are enough expedient and debatable touches along the way to require a similar fix on behalf of *Crimes and Misdemeanors* itself.

Though never particularly convincing as a more or less realistic chronicle, the film does insinuate itself as a dramatically effective pretext for discussion. It's that oddity: a thesis movie that wins you over. It seems rewarding, in a modestly thought-provoking way, to play along with *Crimes and Misdemeanors for the sake of argument.*

The argument would be even more persuasive if Allen hadn't shortchanged a number of amusing devices. In particular, I think he miscalculates by showing Cliff defiantly screening an unflattering assembly of Lester footage for Lester himself.

This is a brainstorm that ought to be offered as a furtive labor of love to Halley (Mia Farrow), an associate Cliff falls in love with while making the picture. The kicker would then be her inability to accept it in exactly the spirit he intended—and thought they would share.

It seems to improve things immeasurably that Allen has shifted his focus to male characters and rediscovered a New York Jewish idiom. *Crimes and Misdemeanors* doesn't labor under the handicaps of the compassionate condescension and constipated diction that distinguished his "serious" movies set among genteel but suffering examples of upper-crust WASP femininity.

Perhaps the funniest submerged joke in the conception is the apparently profound fear of wives shared by Cliff and Dr. Rosenthal, who could avoid a great deal of grief if they simply dared to confront their mates with distressing news.

Beneath the surface of Allen's intriguing new movie one detects the venerable henpecked husband, so loath to disturb domestic tranquillity in Dr. Rosenthal's case that he'd rather commit murder than jeopardize his status with the Little Woman.

To Mr. Allen's credit, he doesn't try to deflect blame onto the women. If his protagonists are henpecked, it's because they've found it a convenient excuse for failing to do the right thing.

The Washington Times, October 13, 1989

WOODY ALLEN: CRIMES AND MISDEMEANORS

Bruce Williamson

Judging by some of his recent films, Woody Allen has a not-so-secret longing to be dour and Swedish rather than droll and Jewish. Allen's latest, *Crimes and Misdemeanors,* is partly a somber, melodramatic film noir about the indiscretions of a wealthy New York ophthalmologist (Martin Landau). The panicked doctor gets his gangster brother (Jerry Orbach) to hire a hit man to murder his mistress (Anjelica Huston), because *that* angry, vindictive lady has been threatening to confess everything to his wife (Claire Bloom) and blow his entire life sky-high. Linked to this, but very tenuously, is a seriocomic subplot starring Woody as a filmmaker with his own marital problems. He'd like to trade his shrewish wife (Joanna Gleason) for Mia Farrow, the pert divorcee assisting him on a movie about his famous, obnoxious brother-in-law (Alan Alda), a big wheel in television. Yet another brother-in-law (Sam Waterston) is a rabbi who's going blind and consulting Landau about his eyes. It is either God or justice that's blind, according to *Crimes and Misdemeanors,* which has some Allenesque one-liners ("The last time I was inside a woman was when I visited the Statue of Liberty") uneasily mixed—clearly for comic relief—with Ingmar Bergmanesque flashbacks and fantasies related to Landau's private ordeal. The message written large is that bad people get away with murder, or the girl, while good guys get the shaft, and that's life. Probably true. But Allen is better company when he doesn't take his nihilism quite so seriously.

Playboy, January 1990

PETER GREENAWAY: THE COOK, THE THIEF, HIS WIFE AND HER LOVER

Michael Wilmington

Elegance inside; filth in the alleys. Frans Hals paintings and ornate red decor in the dining room; bustle and steaming caldrons in the kitchen. Civility at the tables; wild screwing in the ladies' room. Pheasants and succulent creams on the plates; dog shit and maggot-ridden trash out back. Manners above, murder below.

These are among the many dichotomies of Peter Greenaway's brilliant, savage morality play, *The Cook, the Thief, His Wife and Her Lover*—in which we are told, not for the first time, that within humankind's allegedly civilized breast beats sometimes the heart of a predatory beast or swine. Few films ever have served up humanity and its foibles with such infernal relish and poisonous panache. It's a feast for the eyes, a purge for the belly, and a scourge for the soul.

The beast here is a Thief (Michael Gambon, of the BBC's "Singing Detective"), who also acts as the financial "angel" for an impossibly posh gourmet restaurant, eating there free with his retinue of greasy hoods and his slightly haughty but sensitive Wife (Helen Mirren). The Thief is a bullyboy and a boor, who belches, swears, and intimidates everyone; yet he's a bully with style. It's clear he relishes the sophistication of the place, clear also that he revels in the power of trampling on it, of behaving badly and getting away with it. He's like the Mafiosi who take pride in knowing the best *ristorante*. Taste is his weapon and his joke; consumption is his only culture.

Culture of a different kind is represented by the Wife's Lover (Alan Howard), whom she spots at another table, quietly reading books—and it is this introverted intellect to whom she gravitates, exchanging eye signals, arranging an assignation in the ladies' room under the very eye of the Thief and, later, carrying on with this stranger night after night—always with the Thief and his mob ostentatiously present—and with the cooperation of the Thief's apparent lackey, the Cook (Richard Bohringer)—the culinary artist who has sold him his soul.

Now, the Cook is another story entirely. He, after all, is the false king of this palace—the Thief is the true monarch, the man with clout—and he has the face of a dreamy-eyed romantic, pasted over with layers of survivor's cunning. The Wife and her Lover are mad with passion; the Thief is mad with gluttony; the Cook is mad for art: the twin arts of appeasing lust and gluttony. Food is his religion—a blond kitchen boy constantly sings hymns as he works—and to practice his religion and art, he needs the Thief. To demonstrate his power, the Thief needs him—while the Thief's Wife lives upon her husband and betrays him. Her Lover, in the end, is exploited and victimized by them all.

Such is life, Greenaway says dryly, and he connects all of it through stately lateral tracking shots that take in huge gulps of decor and move freely through all levels, smashing the fourth wall as they slide along. As in *The Draughtsman's Contract,* he presents a world where the most exquisite, rarefied, or pretentious art depends upon the patronage of morally repulsive exploiters and dandified pigs. Here, however, in a slightly overwrought but satisfying finale, art turns against its tyrants, uses the very tools of gluttony and murder to conquer them.

Despite the demonstrably brilliant settings, camera work (Sacha Vierny), writing, and acting—particularly by Gambon, with his virtuoso loathsomeness, and Mirren, with her farcical mastery of sudden lust—it will be a hard film for some to take—ironically, not because it is more extreme than dozens of movies that safely pass the ratings boards, but because Greenaway's juxtapositions are so extreme. He shows the seemingly vilest and highest appetites in such close proximity that he makes our gorge rise.

It's not an empty giddiness, though. The film, at its darkest root, is about exploitation. Greenaway's corrosive allegory has many applications—one of them, of course, to the movies themselves. Surely the Thief can represent the crass studio executive and producer, making a mockery of taste and consumption—as much as the Cook can represent the motion picture artist, Greenaway himself.

But that's only a limited view; Greenaway's joke is more cosmic. Beneath all our art, all our pretension, all our civilization, the film suggests, lies a wormy layer of evil and lust and blood and shit. The soaring strains of a magnificat are only a tracking shot away from the howls of a maddened dog, battening on garbage.

Greenaway's Jacobean climax—*Titus Andronicus* under glass—is perhaps a touch too forced and pat; the one time in the film where, paradoxically, I felt he had not gone far enough. But this gifted, unique film artist goes far enough often enough: all the way from dung to glory, all the way from artifice to slaughter, all the way from hideous exploitation to exquisite revolt.

Isthmus, May 4, 1990

PETER GREENAWAY: THE COOK, THE THIEF, HIS WIFE AND HER LOVER

Terrence Rafferty

Peter Greenaway's *The Cook, the Thief, His Wife and Her Lover* is a movie about a crude British thug whose favorite method of terrorizing people is ramming things down their throats. It begins with a scene in which the bully, Albert Spica (Michael Gambon), and his henchmen smear dog shit all over the body of a naked man and then make him eat some. Later victims are force-fed shirt and trouser buttons and pages from old books. Albert eats only haute cuisine; he and his wife, Georgina (Helen Mirren), and his low-life entourage dine every night at a posh establishment called Le Hollandais. (The name of the restaurant is a dry joke: In the dining room, there's a large painting by Frans Hals of a group of officers seated around a banquet table; the arrangement of Albert's unseemly aggregation is meant to echo and parody this composition.) He fancies himself a gourmet, but he scarfs up the exquisite dishes prepared by the chef, a Frenchman (Richard Bohringer), as if they were fast-food burgers; his instinct, apparently, is to eat with his hands and save his cutlery for threatening his dinner companions. (In one scene, he sticks a fork through a woman's cheek.) Albert's vulgarity—his lack of respect for the highest achievements of European culture—is made to seem his real sin, because this is an Art Movie, refined and terribly formal; Greenaway places the barbarian smack in the middle of his "painterly" compositions and encourages us to see him as a steaming hunk of offal desecrating the beauty of an artist's creation.

American movies about gangsters have traditionally shown at least some grudging admiration for their heroes' reckless vitality and huge material appetites—perhaps because our movies are fueled by similar qualities. Peter Greenaway not only lacks sympathy for his protagonist's animal nature but seems offended by it. Albert is loathsome through and through, an evil lout who just does one evil, loutish thing after another for two solid hours. As a rule, bullies aren't very interesting: Their dramatic functions are simple, and their appearances are brief—they barge into scenes when a quick shock or a gruesome joke is needed to jolt the audience awake, and then are hustled off until their specialized services are required again. Greenaway's camera *lingers* on Albert, feasts on his awfulness, eats him up, and the static intensity of its regard is baffling. The movie isn't probing the character's soul; as far as the filmmaker is concerned, this beast doesn't have one. And Greenaway's relentlessness isn't an indication of passion, either; we never have the sense that he's implicating himself in the horrors he shows, acknowledging a perverse attraction to his monster. His gaze is lordly, imperial — the disdainful stare that the pukka sahib directs at a servant who has inconvenienced him.

The care that Greenaway lavishes on the structure and the imagery of his films is fantastic, obsessive. But it's all manner — obsession without an object. His previous features (*The Draughtsman's Contract, A Zed and Two Noughts, The Belly of an Architect,* and *Drowning by Numbers*) were self-consciously empty — meticulous elaborations of arid little reality-and-artifice paradoxes. Greenaway seemed to be making movies with the monotonous dedication of a hobbyist, and the products of his labors were immaculate and pointless, like ships in bottles. The pictures didn't bother much with narrative, and barely even pretended to refer to anything outside themselves. *The Cook, the Thief, His Wife and Her Lover* is no different. It gives an impression of greater consequence only because its imagery is more violent than usual and thus evokes fear and disgust — not the most enlightening emotions a movie can produce, but two more than Greenaway generally allows us to feel. The notion, suggested by several reviewers, that this movie is some kind of political allegory is absurd. Greenaway is an aesthete, and that's all he is. *The Cook, the Thief, His Wife and Her Lover* isn't about oppression, or capitalist greed, or Margaret Thatcher; it's about the superiority of its maker's sensibility. He gives us pretty pictures to look at, and they're color coded: the dining-room scenes are red; scenes in the restaurant's kitchen are green; scenes in the parking lot are blue; and so on. And he creates a central character whose only function is to be unworthy of the high-art splendor of his surroundings. As a critique of contemporary society, this leaves quite a bit to be desired.

Greenaway has a lot more in common with his protagonist than he thinks. He obviously regards himself as a pure artist, a virtuoso — like the haughty chef in this picture — but he's really just a cultural omnivore. (He eats for taste, not for sustenance.) His manners are no better than Albert's; he chews with his mouth open — we can identify almost every piece of art that has fed his imagination. And, for the benefit of those who are too uneducated to pick up all the references and allusions, he's willing to supply them afterward: In his interviews and writings about the film Greenaway has linked himself to Hals, Jonathan Swift, the Brothers Grimm, and Jacobean dramatists. (He doesn't mention Buñuel, whom he borrows from constantly, but perhaps he doesn't want to sully himself with a comparison to a mere filmmaker.) As a conspicuous consumer, Albert has nothing on the man who invented him.

There are many ways of being a bully; physical violence is only the most direct. Greenaway doesn't seem at all averse to other forms of power tripping, such as intellectual intimidation. His attitude toward his characters and toward his audience is one of professorial condescension. Watching this picture is like being trapped in a nightmare art-history seminar: We sit there, cowed and miserable, as the teacher spews high-toned abstractions and dares us, smirkingly, to raise a common-sense objection — we know we'll be ridiculed if we do. In Greenaway's view, what's so unspeakable about Albert has to do less with the thug's desire to hurt and humiliate people than with the way he expresses it; his *physicality* is the crime he's convicted of (and executed for). The only thing in this movie's tidy, hermetic universe that Greenaway is unable to control, or disguise with fancy brushwork, is his loathing of the body. The beatings and the killings aren't really any uglier than the eating scenes. And the depictions of sex are pointedly grotesque. In the course of the film, Georgina takes a lover, a gentle, bookish patron of Le Hollandais named Michael (Alan Howard); he is, of course, the civilized antithesis of Albert, and the affair is clearly meant to be Georgina's chance to save herself from the everyday barbarity of her marriage. But Greenaway can't bring himself to present their romance as an idyll, even though his story's structure demands it. The lovers couple in the most degrading settings — in a lavatory stall; among plucked chickens and skinned rabbits in the kitchen — and at one point we see them huddled together, naked and filthy and shivering, in a meat van where bloody animal carcasses hang.

Despite the ornateness of the design, *The Cook, the Thief, His Wife and Her Lover* has a very simple message: that nature — one's own appetites or other people's — is abominable, because it threatens the purity of the artist. I saw this picture in London a few months ago, and I didn't bother to review it when it opened in this country last month, because I assumed that American audiences wouldn't be any more interested in Greenaway's latest art-for-art's-sake exercise than they had been in his four previous ones. However, the Motion Picture Association of America did the movie the enormous favor of giving it an X rating (the distributors released it without a rating), and thus made Greenaway seem a kind of martyr, like Robert Mapplethorpe—a victim of repressive philistinism. (It must be a role he relishes.) Some prominent critics, flashing their anticensorship credentials, proclaimed the movie a masterpiece, and a lot of filmgoers must feel compelled to buy a ticket as a protest against attempts to muzzle artistic expression. Also, because everyone knows by now that the movie features several gross-out scenes, including a climactic act of cannibalism, it is, in a sense, a perfect date movie for a certain audience—the intellectual's equivalent of a *Friday the 13th* picture. To sit through it with a worldly, unshockable air and then deliver a lengthy opinion about it is to display, irrefutably, one's liberal *cojones.* The movie is doing big business at the art houses.

You can hate *The Cook, the Thief, His Wife and Her Lover,* or even ignore it completely, without lining up alongside the MPAA and Jesse Helms. What's offensive about Greenaway's picture isn't its violence or its visceral shocks but the patrician arrogance, the smug aestheticism, the snobbishness that suffuse every frame. The film's success is a ghastly joke. Greenaway probably sees this as a vindication, a delicious irony: The vulgarians who meant to torment him have instead helped him achieve a box-office hit. He has made a movie whose object is to push us to the ground and kick art in our faces. We may not feel that it's right to take revenge on him for this rude treatment. It seems sort of abject to thank him for it, though.

The New Yorker, May 7, 1990

JOEL AND ETHAN COEN: BARTON FINK

Peter Travers

Wrapped in plain brown paper and no bigger than a typically swelled Hollywood head, the box looks ordinary. It's not, of course. This is a movie from the Coen brothers, and as you may have gleaned from their earlier work (*Blood Simple, Raising Arizona,* and *Miller's Crossing*), the Coens do not traffic in the mundane. The box figures prominently in the climax of *Barton Fink,* the partly hilarious, partly horrific, totally mesmerizing new film from these Hardy Boys from hell.

Charlie Meadows (John Goodman), a good-natured slob of a traveling salesman, has entrusted the mystery parcel to Barton Fink (John Turturro), a creatively blocked screenwriter who lives next door to him in a shabby Los Angeles hotel, circa 1942. With perverse glee, the Coens never let us see what's in the box. But they drop dark hints — *Barton Fink* is the most chilling Hollywood comedy since *Sunset Boulevard.* What starts as a slyly ambitious send-up of Faust — Fink is a serious New York playwright tempted to sell his soul for success in movies — ends as an apocalyptic vision of a world ablaze with hypocrisy. Though Fink rarely leaves his room, the Coens have fashioned a tale that encompasses betrayal, murder, genocide, world war, and figures as diverse as Louis B. Mayer and Adolf Hitler.

Sometimes enigmatic to the point of exasperation, *Barton Fink* is not summer fun on the order of *City Slickers.* But the attention the film demands of its audience is richly rewarded. At the Cannes Film Festival in May, *Barton Fink* walked off with the top prizes for film, director, and actor (Turturro) — the first such hat trick in the festival's forty-four-year history. But even that victory could backfire by branding the film as art-house material. Despite raves, *Blood Simple* (1984) and *Raising Arizona* (1987) never went beyond cult status. And the ticket buyers for last year's acclaimed *Miller's Crossing* could all gather comfortably in Fink's tiny hotel room. This public indifference to two of the most gifted filmmakers in the business is mystifying.

The Minnesota-born Coens are most frequently hoisted on the petard of their own curriculum vitae. Joel Coen, thirty-six, is a graduate of New York University's film school. Ethan Coen, thirty-four, has a degree in philosophy from Princeton but shares his brother's lifelong obsession with genre movies. *Blood Simple* was their take on film noir, *Raising Arizona* the screwball comedy, and *Miller's Crossing* the gangster epic. Coen bashers consider this raiding of Hollywood's past to be grounds for dismissing the brothers as clever show-offs trying to hide the emotional emptiness of their films.

It's a facile charge, easily disproved when you consider the depth of feeling in the characters played by Frances McDormand in *Blood Simple,* Holly Hunter in *Raising Arizona,* and Gabriel Byrne in *Miller's Crossing.* What is true is that these characters are unsympathetic (a cheating wife, a kidnapper, a hood) and don't wear their hearts on their sleeves. The Coens make you dig to discover someone's true nature. That used to be called characterization. These days, with one-note movies like *Regarding Henry, Dying Young,* and *The Doctor* ladling out sentiment like butter on popcorn, complexity is regarded as a failure to communicate.

A more disturbing charge against the Coens — in that it has some validity — is their tendency to put style ahead of substance. In their first two films, the Coens did everything but swing the camera from the ceiling to call attention to their technical prowess. *Miller's Crossing* took a more subdued approach, and *Barton Fink* continues in that vein. Except for two look-at-me-Ma dolly shots (one into a trombone at a USO dance, the other down a hotel drain), this is the Coens' most adventurously low-key film.

The brothers conceived *Barton Fink* while suffering a severe case of writer's block during the writing of *Miller's Crossing.* The Fink story was both a distraction and a way to wrestle with their demons. They imagined the title character as a driven playwright, an up-from-poverty New York Jew enjoying his first success on Broadway with *Bare Ruined Choirs,* a paean to the common man. As Fink, Turturro sports glasses and wiry hair that recall the socially conscious dramatist Clifford Odets (*Golden Boy*).

Hollywood calls on the boy wonder. Fink resists; he's on a mission for the little guy. But his agent, Garland Stanford (an elegantly sleazy David Warrilow), persuades him that it's time to make a buck, saying, "The common man will be here when you get back."

Initially, Fink clings to his proletarian roots by staying at the rundown Hotel Earle. But Fink caves in almost immediately when studio chief Jack Lipnick — a vibrant monster in the expert hands of Michael Lerner — gives him a week to write a wrestling picture. Lipnick and his flunky Lou Breeze (the great Jon Polito) flatter him into agreeing. "We need that Barton Fink feeling," says Lipnick, who knows as much about Fink as Fink knows about wrestling — namely, nothing.

Lipnick will literally kiss a writer's feet to get what he craves: art that makes money. That's why he has also hired the great southern novelist W. P. Mayhew (John Mahoney), a character meant to recall William Faulkner, whose work for movies included *The Big Sleep.* On a drunken tear in a park, Mayhew lambastes the pretentious Fink, then sings "Old Black Joe," pisses on a tree, and smacks around his southern lady friend, Audrey Taylor, beautifully acted by Judy Davis. Fink is appalled by his idol's behavior but smitten with Audrey, who is rumored to have written the great man's last two books. Fink wants to get closer to this mother-protector, but the studio's production supervisor, Ben Geisler (an inspired turn by Tony Shalhoub), rides him to start writing.

All of Fink's anxieties come into play at the Hotel Earle, shot by Roger Deakins (*Sid and Nancy*) with a poet's eye for glory in decay. Thanks to Dennis Glassner's evocative production design, you can almost smell the banana trees rotting in the empty hallways. Fink's room, containing a bed, a dressing table, and a typewriter, seems even more claustrophobic when Fink realizes after days of work that he can't get any further into the script than setting the opening scene in a tenement on the Lower East Side. A picture of a bathing beauty, which Fink hangs above the typewriter, provides the only color.

That is, until Charlie Meadows makes his entrance. On his first night at the hotel, Fink complained to the desk about moans coming from next door. Now Meadows wants to see who did the complaining. Miffed at first, this good-time Charlie soon warms to his neighbor. Meadows helpfully demonstrates a few wrestling holds and offers to tell Fink about life on the road and "the misery of the planet."

Meadows is the common man incarnate — he even resembles the burly actor Wallace Beery, for whom Fink is supposed to be tailoring his script. Fink is grateful for Meadows's sympathetic ear but pays him little mind. Even when Fink becomes so desperate that he drops his standards and begs Audrey to finish his script, the writer fails to see the source of inspiration in front of his face. In trying to live a "life of the mind," Fink has lost touch with reality. Turturro brings a startling originality to Fink, finding the humor and the terror in a man who learns the hard way that he's a charlatan sliding by on borrowed ideas. Somehow Turturro makes the pompous, platitudinous, self-deluding, socially inept Fink both understandable and human. Goodman has perhaps an even trickier role as the salesman whose snappy patter can't disguise his loneliness. His talents are well known from TV's "Roseanne" and such films as *True Stories, The Big Easy,* and the Coens' *Raising Arizona.* But Goodman has never had a role like Charlie Meadows; he's a flat-out marvel. Turturro and Goodman deliver spectacular performances, and the film needs all their power and finesse when the Coens switch moods dramatically at midpoint.

There's a murder, bloody and cataclysmic. Fink is implicated by the police, and Meadows comes to his aid before heading back on the road and leaving his friend with the box for safekeeping. Fink doesn't look inside. But he keeps the box near his typewriter, writing for the first time in a fever of conviction. Later, when Charlie returns, a fire breaks out in the hotel. Fink manages to save the box and the script, which the studio harshly rejects. "We don't put Wallace Beery in a family movie about suffering," says Lipnick in a rage.

The story ends with a surprising coda in which Fink walks on the beach carrying the box. Like the box, the film is an enigma that elicits strong feelings. Though the Coens have clearly shared with Fink the temptation to betray their ideals in order to get the next word on paper, they are still more interested in provoking audiences than pandering to them. *Barton Fink* is stimulating entertainment, as rigorously challenging and painfully funny as anything the Coens have done. But it's necessary to meet the Coens halfway. If you don't, *Barton Fink* is an empty exercise that will bore you breathless. If you do, it's a comic nightmare that will stir your imagination like no film in years.

Rolling Stone, August 22, 1991

JOEL AND ETHAN COEN: BARTON FINK

Gary Arnold

Barton Fink is the third consecutive decadent oddity from the United States to win the grand prize at the Cannes Film Festival. It's difficult to know whether this streak — it began with *sex, lies, and videotape* and continued with *Wild at Heart* — is getting to be a national embarrassment or an inspired running gag.

Despite cleaning up at Cannes — not only the grand prize but also the best actor award for John Turturro and the best director award for Joel Coen — *Barton Fink* leaves one with a distinctly hollow, defeatist sensation. It's a brilliantly stylized turnoff and flameout, a nightmarish fable about the costs of creative isolation and inertia that ultimately seems too vain about its own diabolical-sadistic showmanship and too detached from genuine, inconsolable suffering to earn Profundity Points for emotional integrity or illumination.

The fraternal team of writer-director Joel and writer-producer Ethan Coen possesses an eerie, imaginative flair for filmmaking. At its most arresting and effective, *Barton Fink* is a witty showcase for predatory decor from designer Dennis Glassner and virtuoso weirdness from Turturro and John Goodman, who demonstrate phenomenal control of starkly contrasted states of dementia — one meek and oblivious, the other robust and explosive.

However, back-to-back "originals" as peculiarly hermetic, derivative, and defensive as *Miller's Crossing* and *Barton Fink* suggest — with a kind of silent, echoing shriek — that it's time for the Coen brothers to get a life. A life, that is, apart from the cultivation of their precocious cinematic creativity, which has painted them into redundantly freakish, alienating corners. Having carried arty pulp allegory to extremes in *Crossing,* they now carry it to extremes again in *Barton Fink.*

Turturro plays the title character, a scared-mouse Broadway playwright with fatuous populist pretensions. His new play, *Bare Ruined Choirs,* has supposedly made him the toast of Broadway, circa 1941. He's persuaded, none too plausibly, of the benefits of a Hollywood screenwriting contract and holes up in a limbo hotel called the Earle, whose splendidly cavernous lobby is supplied by the ornate old Wiltern Theater in Los Angeles.

Assigned a B movie quickie, a wrestling yarn for Wallace Beery, Fink feels so intimidated by the domineering boss of Capitol Pictures, Jack Lipnick — Michael Lerner in an overstuffed caricature of Harry Cohn, Louis B. Mayer, and Jack Warner at their most notorious — that he remains in an impotent daze. The paper stares back blankly at Fink from his Underwood portable. He hasn't a clue about how to get unblocked for a strictly formulaic hack-work scenario.

The filmmakers heap contempt on Fink by stressing his inability to comprehend that his neighbor in an adjoining room, Goodman as a suspiciously fuming but also cordial and solicitous salesman called Charlie Meadows, is a potentially colossal life study. The writer is too self-centered and self-pitying to pick up on any of Charlie's clues, from simple pointers about wrestling to infernal intimations of distress. Fink would rather babble about an idealized Common Man than observe the overpowering, ominous reality of the one next door.

Ultimately, the folly of his blindness is revealed to Fink in terrifying, bloodcurdling, flamboyant terms. His sleepwalking appears to have contributed to at least two grisly murders and maybe more. Though spared from a wrathful convulsion that recalls Carrie's revenge on the prom, Fink doesn't seem to be much the wiser for being granted a private audience with death incarnate.

Turturro's spellbinding performance is assembled from spare vocal parts of Sterling Holloway and Everett Sloane, George S. Kaufman's haircut, and a painfully funny look of bewilderment, but the conception reflects a contemptuous view of Clifford Odets that the material never begins to justify. Fink's situation in Hollywood bears little resemblance to Odets's. The time frame should obviously be cranked back five or six years to secure a sounder historical and show-business setting.

Fragments of at least two of Odets's plays, *The Country Girl* and *The Big Knife,* drift in and out of the continuity. Since Wallace Beery wasn't playing wrestlers at this period — he was playing garrulous old outlaws or salts at MGM — the Capitol quickie functions only as a derisive allusion to Odets's greatest success, the boxing melodrama *Golden Boy.* John Mahoney and Judy Davis are inserted as fleeting caricatures of William Faulkner and his Hollywood consort Meta Carpenter, called W. P. Mayhew and Audrey Taylor. They're exploited with a facetious brutality that makes one rather grateful the Coens aren't looking after literary reputations and old-age pensions.

What accounts for this exaggerated spitefulness at the expense of famous writers? The only ready psychological explanation would seem to be the Coens' own apprehensions about being perceived as Hollywood hacks and sellouts. In *Miller's Crossing* they identified with the foxy survivor who outsmarted all the beasts in a New Orleans mob jungle. In *Barton Fink* they seem to identify despite themselves with the jittery little writer who fears that he'll be swallowed alive by Hollywood monsters.

Unless what? He acquires a tragic understanding of life, theoretically. Worked out as luridly and expediently as it is, the theme doesn't carry tragic resonance. It only persuades you that the Coen brothers need some remedial mopping of their fevered young brows. They're trying to protect their artistic purity by making stylish monstrosities.

The Washington Times, August 21, 1991

ROBERT ALTMAN: VINCENT & THEO

Roger Ebert

How to portray the artist at work? Directors through the years have shown them sporadically applying paint to canvas, but for the most part the artist's task in the movies is to drink wine, argue by candle-light, and spend a good deal of time in unheated studios with undressed models. The big dramatic scenes involve confrontations with those who do not understand his genius: His dealers, his lovers, his public, and his creditors.

Only occasionally does a film come along where we get the sensation that actual creation is taking place before our eyes. That happens when the filmmakers are also in the art of creating, and transfer their inspiration to the characters in a sort of artistic ventriloquism. *Camille Claudel* (1989) had that feeling, as Isabelle Adjani grubbed about in a ditch, digging up clay for her sculptures. And now here is Robert Altman's *Vincent & Theo,* another film that generates the feeling that we are in the presence of a man in the act of creation.

True art is made as if God were a lot of little cottage industries. Artists take up shapeless raw material — paint or clay, or a blank sheet of paper — and transform it into something wonderful that never existed before. This is such a joyous activity that I am at a loss to understand how an artist could ever be unhappy, and yet so many are. Perhaps, like God, they grieve when man ignores their handiwork.

Vincent van Gogh was one of the unhappiest of artists. Some medical experts now believe it was because he suffered from a maddening ear disease. *Vincent & Theo* does not attempt a diagnosis. It simply regards the fact that van Gogh, whose paintings most people today instinctively love from the first moment they see them, suffered all of his life from overwhelming rejection. He did not paint because he wanted to; he painted because he had to. He did not develop a style; he painted in the only way he could. During his lifetime he sold only one painting. How would you feel, if you worked a lifetime to create beautiful things for people to look at, and they turned their backs and chose to look at ugly things instead? And if you saw your brother sacrifice himself to support your lonely work?

Altman's approach in *Vincent & Theo* is a very immediate, intimate one. He would rather show us things happening than provide themes and explanations. He is most concerned with the relationship that made the art possible, the way in which Theo, the younger brother, essentially became Vincent's parent and patron. We meet van Gogh (Tim Roth) and his brother (Paul Rhys) in the middle of their relationship, we hear them fight and see them through the thickets of exasperation, and at the end we realize that it took two obsessives to create the work of Vincent van Gogh: The brother who painted it, and the brother who believed that to support the painting was the most important thing he could possibly do with his lifetime.

The movie takes place inside and outside the claustrophobic art world of Paris in the late nineteenth century, where the two Dutch brothers try to make their mark. Theo is a passable art dealer, skilled at selling safe paintings to cautious people, and he is lucky in finding employers who sympathize with his more radical tastes and eventually give him the opportunity to strike out on his own. Even then, given free rein, he is unable to sell his brother's work. And Vincent lives in a series of barren rooms and small houses, writing continuously to his brother (the apparent subject is art, but the buried subject is usually money).

There is the sense that Vincent had no knowledge of the way people normally behave toward one another. At some point in his childhood, he failed to decipher that code. Consider the scene where the prostitute (Jip Wijngaarden) comes to pose for him. She is cold and hungry, and the only support of her daughter. Vincent asks her to come and live with him. She explains her needs. He agrees to them. His need is to have someone to paint, and everything else—the expense, the distraction, the responsibility, and certainly the subject of sex—never occurs to him.

His painting is such a direct expression of his mood, indeed, that ordinary human speech often seems unnecessary. He is the rare artist who truly does speak through his work, and Altman dramatizes that in a remarkable scene in a field of sunflowers, where, as van Gogh paints, Altman's camera darts restlessly, aggressively, at the flowers, turning them from passive subjects into an alien hostile environment. The film is able to see the sunflowers as Altman believed van Gogh saw them. To make a sunflower stand for anything other than itself is a neat trick, and Altman accomplishes it in his own way, as van Gogh did in his.

The details of van Gogh's life are here. The infamous ear episode. The fights with Theo. The death. *Vincent & Theo* follows the trajectory of a biopic more faithfully than we might have expected, given Altman as the director. This is a more classically constructed film than much of his work, and although Altman says it's that way because he had to follow the chronology of a man's life, I think the reason is more complex: that van Gogh's personality was so fractured and tortured that the movie needed to be stable and secure, as a frame for it.

Chicago Sun-Times, November 16, 1990

ROBERT ALTMAN: VINCENT & THEO

Dave Kehr

After Peter Bogdanovich and his dispiriting *Texasville,* here is another seventies idol fallen on hard times. It isn't easy to recognize the iconoclastic touch of Robert Altman—the director of *Nashville, Brewster McCloud,* and *McCabe and Mrs. Miller*—in the sodden heap of *Vincent & Theo,* a "cultural project" in the PBS style almost completely devoid of sensibility and interest.

Altman was never a filmmaker of particular technique or formal assurance, but he did possess an attitude—an engaging post-hippie blend of innocence and cynicism, of revolutionary longings and real-world despair.

Those longings now seem to have deserted him, and even his despair no longer carries much conviction. *Vincent & Theo* is a by-the-numbers art biography that barely succeeds in recapping the best-known events in the life of its subject, Vincent van Gogh. There is something almost chilling in the degree of the director's evident disengagement from his material and the complete lack of craft with which he has filmed it.

The screenplay, by Julian Mitchell (*Another Country*), seems once to have possessed a point of view. By intertwining the story of Vincent (Tim Roth, a gaunt figure with blackened teeth) with that of his art-dealer brother, Theo (Paul Rhys, a worried smile frozen on his face), Mitchell is constructing a topical fable of art and commerce, referring directly and pointedly to the absurd prices van Gogh's paintings have recently achieved at auction.

The film, in fact, begins by flashing back from videotape of the record-breaking Christie's sale of *Sunflowers* in 1987 to the glum spectacle of the artist shivering in a filthy room. The ironies are obvious (van Gogh sold only one painting during his life), but Mitchell seems prepared to go beyond them. His real hero is the unsung Theo, engaged in a desperate struggle to put across the new art of his brother and the other postimpressionists in the face of academic hostility and ridicule. Creating a market is also a kind of self-expression, and by no means a facile one. Mitchell even suggests that Theo's suffering may have transcended Vincent's, unprotected as he was by genius, obsession, or psychosis.

Altman, however, puts his emphasis on a conventional notion of the artist as a romantic figure engaged in a gallant struggle against the bourgeoisie, an approach that begs the question of the considerable support van Gogh received from middle-class sources (notably the sympathetic psychiatrist played here, apparently phonetically, by French actor Jean-Pierre Cassel) and the cruelty with which he was treated by his fellow artists (notably the Paul Gauguin here bearishly interpreted by Wladimir Yordanoff).

The international casting — which casually mixes British, French, and Dutch performers — leads to a hopeless muddle of styles that Altman does little to alleviate. The scenes between the driven, self-sacrificing Theo and his uncomprehending wife, Jo (Johanna Ter Steege), which should be among the movie's most wrenching, instead seem faintly ridiculous: Why should Theo have a British accent and his wife a Dutch one, when they both come from the same city in Holland?

Clearly, there is no attention to detail in *Vincent & Theo,* or to much of anything else. Most of the scenes are staged as if before a painted flat: The actors enter awkwardly from the sides, stand nervously to deliver their lines, and then are left to make their own hesitant ways off, as if Altman hadn't even bothered to lay out the blocking. Meanwhile, the camera, wielded by Jean Lepine, zooms idly in and out, with no regard for the rhythm of the sequence or its dramatic focus. The movie grinds on in its glum, enervated manner, until all of the obligatory scenes (cutting off the ear, cracking up in the wheat field) have been dully, dutifully checked off.

Chicago Tribune, November 16, 1990

ON NEW BLACK DIRECTORS

☆

Carrie Rickey

Warrington Hudlin calls it the Renaissance. Its artists are not Donatello, Leonardo, Michelangelo, and Raphael, but Mario, Matty, Reginald, and Spike.

They are painters of celluloid, and their artworks have titles like *New Jack City, Straight Out of Brooklyn, House Party,* and *Jungle Fever.*

Taken together, their films, by turns confrontational and confessional, fun and furious, are a heroic fresco of urban life. They depict the crack houses that divide communities, and also the architects who want to rebuild the inner city but who must start by rebuilding their own lives. They chronicle the teenagers who grow up prisoners of the projects, and those contemplating the broader horizons of college and career.

"There will be more movies by African-American filmmakers released in 1991 than in the whole prior decade," observes Hudlin, thirty-eight, producer of *House Party* and president of the Black Filmmakers Foundation.

Indeed, the explosion of new-black cinema, nineteen films this year alone, has yielded a handful more films than the number released in the last fifteen years. And though mathematically nineteen films represents an insignificant 5 percent of the four hundred plus movies produced annually in the United States, it is a significant number emotionally.

For African-Americans, who constitute 12 percent of the population but, by Motion Picture Association of America estimates, 23 percent of all movie ticket buyers, it means this is a first: the opportunity to see different aspects of black life on screen created by black filmmakers. For those directors (and for tomorrow's Spike Lees), it means doors slammed shut for twenty years have finally swung open in Hollywood.

Consider the list. So far in 1991, the Philadelphia market has seen *Boyz N the Hood* (directed by John Singleton), *New Jack City* (Mario Van Peebles), *Jungle Fever* (Spike Lee), *A Rage in Harlem* (Bill Duke), *Straight Out of Brooklyn* (Matty Rich), *The Five Heartbeats* (Robert Townsend), *Chameleon Street* (Wendell B. Harris, Jr.), and *Up against the Wall* (Ron O'Neal).

Still to come are *Hangin' with the Homeboys* (Joseph Vasquez), *Livin' Large!* (Michael Schultz), *True Identity* (Charles Lane), *Talkin' Dirty After Dark* (Topper Carew), *Juice* (Ernest Dickerson), *Strictly Business* (Kevin Hooks), *House Party 2* (George Jackson and Doug McHenry), *Daughters of the Dust* (Julie Dash), *Street Wars* (Jamaa Fanaka), and *Perfume* (Roland Jefferson).

As Warrington Hudlin says, "Spike Lee made a film for $175,000 (*She's Gotta Have It*, 1986) that made $7 million."

Hudlin and his brother Reginald made 1989's *House Party* for $2.5 million—and, Warrington says, it "generated a $27 million box

Spike Lee, shown here as Mookie in his film *Do the Right Thing,* is the most outspoken and controversial black director of his generation. (Photo courtesy of Universal Pictures.)

office. It's simply good business for Hollywood to be in business with black filmmakers."

Confesses one top-ranking studio executive: "Every studio wants its own Spike Lee."

Despite a popular illusion that Hollywood moguls are hanging around film schools scouting potentially hot black directors (such as twenty-three-year-old Singleton, whose *Boyz N the Hood* earned a whopping $10 million last weekend), not everyone shares Warrington Hudlin's exhilaration about this historic moment. As a younger generation of black filmmakers basks in the euphoria of Hollywood courtship, veterans are more cautious. African-American filmmakers have been pursued before, during the seventies, and then unceremoniously jilted when "blaxploitation" movies ceased to enjoy box-office success.

Between 1972 and 1976, more than one hundred films were built around black characters, ranging from the prestige *Sounder* to the exploitation *Boss Nigger.* Prestige pictures were assigned to white directors; black directors were given low-end fare.

"Because of what happened during the seventies, there is some cynicism now that . . . no matter how well our films perform, it's only a matter of time before the rug is going to be pulled out from under us," says Bill Duke, forty-eight, who began directing TV in the eighties and made the recent *A Rage in Harlem.* "Our fear is that this is some flavor-of-the-month thing and that we'll be allowed to make some money for the studios for a year or two, but that there will be no basic changes in business-as-usual."

Duke isn't willing to call this the Renaissance because, "in the context of the entire industry, what's happening now is only a small step. In Hollywood, there are still no African-American executives who can greenlight a project. In the realm of distribution, there is no African-American–controlled entity. In marketing, there is no one. And in exhibition, there is only one first-run theater in the entire country, the Baldwin (in Los Angeles), that is African-American owned."

Changing these conditions would alter what many, Duke included, perceive as a Hollywood double standard working against black filmmakers.

"If a white director like Michael Cimino or Francis Ford Coppola or Woody Allen makes a movie that fails or performs moderately, it's not believed that white directors can't make blockbusters," Duke says. "White directors are allowed to fail. You can't grow unless you're allowed to fail."

Although he doesn't name names, Duke could be alluding to Robert Townsend's *The Five Heartbeats,* a $10 million period musical released in March that failed to recoup its costs. Some, but not Townsend, believe that Twentieth Century Fox effectively sabotaged *The Five Heartbeats* with a lackluster ad campaign and insufficient production budget.

"There seems to be a ceiling on how much Hollywood is willing to budget a black-directed movie," says Warrington Hudlin. "The industry feels that they have one of two options: to budget $4 million on a black filmmaker and generate $25 million, or budget $50 million on a white filmmaker in the hopes of making $250 million. The return on the investment is the same. But black directors are locked out of the $50 million league—the ceiling seems to be $15 million."

Duke likewise worries that the industry courts African-American filmmakers because they will work on the cheap. "If you're black, you constantly have to prove that you can make your films for lower budgets than white directors and that they will gross bigger returns."

Wonders Duke, "When are we going to get the gravy instead of the scraps?"

Another factor that could potentially wither the romance between African-American filmmakers and the industry is that two recent gang-themed movies by black directors, Mario Van Peebles's *New Jack City* and John Singleton's *Boyz N the Hood,* have sparked violence in or near some movie theaters where they have been shown.

Several African-American filmmakers note that this is yet another double standard: The same controversy does not shroud films by white directors, such as Francis Ford Coppola's *The Godfather Part III,* which triggered violence when it was released in December.

The more mature generation of black directors in Hollywood knows, as George Santayana warned, that "those who cannot remember the past are condemned to repeat it." A filmmaker such as Michael Schultz (*Cooley High, Car Wash,* and the still-to-come *Livin' Large!*) has enjoyed a comparatively long and prolific career, despite the reality that "the history of black filmmakers is a history of fits and starts," as Schultz, fifty-two, reminds you. "Each new wave showed great promise—and then there were years of nonrepresentation."

In the years after World War II, Schultz says, "Hollywood's whole dealing with black Americans has always been about the color line. When Harry Belafonte and Dorothy Dandridge were on screen, none of the dark-skinned actors could get work. When Sidney Poitier came along, none of the lighter-skinned actors got hired." The directors of these films starring Belafonte, Dandridge, and Poitier were inevitably white.

"Melvin Van Peebles's *Sweet Sweetback's Baadasssss Song* (1971) was the groundbreaker that opened Hollywood's eyes to the fact that there was a black audience and that we would come out to see a picture by a black director," recalls Schultz. Along with Gordon Parks's *Shaft* (1971), *Sweet Sweetback*—produced, directed, written by, starring, and distributed by Van Peebles, father of *New Jack* director Mario—spawned the blaxploitation cycle.

At the time, Schultz, director of the PBS drama "To Be Young, Gifted and Black," thought the time was ripe for African-Americans in Hollywood. "I got my foot in the door right before it closed. I came to Hollywood at a time when there was a lot of social pressure to open the unions to minorities and women. Then I realized Hollywood would hire me and think it had done its job."

When Bill Duke came to Hollywood as an actor in 1973, "the industry was opening itself up to the possibility of black producers and directors. There were Ivan Dixon, Stan Lathan, Gordon Parks, and Michael Schultz. But the door closed as fast as it opened."

Says Schultz, "The black audience got fed up with the steady stream of negative images accompanying blaxploitation, the pimps and prostitutes. There was a social backlash. And instead of making a different kind of black movie, Hollywood said, 'If you don't like these movies, we'll stop making them. Period.'"

However prolific and talented, Schultz is emblematic of the limited range permitted black filmmakers by Hollywood. "The initial success of *Cooley High* (1974) and *Car Wash* (1976) made me very popular," he says. *Cooley High,* a nostalgic high school comedy-drama in the manner of *American Graffiti,* and *Car Wash,* a comic look at a depressing workplace, typed Schultz a director of light fare.

"I tried to get the studios interested in serious subject matter, in historical material. But they were only interested in me for comedies or anything with pop music in it. Even though I've had a blessed career, the offers to do even comedy or music stuff thinned out in 1980."

Committed to "making films with positive images targeted to black audiences," Schultz worked independently of the studios to make the enormously profitable movies *The Last Dragon* and *Krush Groove.*

Schultz concurs with Warrington Hudlin and Duke that financial restrictions remain the greatest problems black directors face: "We don't want to be handicapped with budget limitations that are lower than the norm and be expected to perform far greater than the norm, even though we often do." He points out that "when a big-budget [black-themed] picture like *The Color Purple* or *The Golden Child* came along, they never thought of hiring a black director."

According to Schultz, "it's only when Spike hit the scene [working] outside the system on the art-house circuit that Hollywood started getting interested in black directors again.

"But *She's Gotta Have It* was a comedy, and it wasn't until *Do the Right Thing* that a major studio handled a black-themed film properly and it was serious subject matter. *Do the Right Thing* was the key that unlocked the door again in Hollywood. For the first time, they looked at a black director and said, 'Hm-m-m-m, maybe it's not all just singin' and dancin',' " Schultz says. "And now there's a mad scramble for each studio to find the next Spike Lee."

Disney's Touchstone division may have found its Spike Lee in the thirtyish Charles Lane, the talented director and star of the Chaplinesque *Sidewalk Stories,* whose film *True Identity* is due next month. Not yet battle scarred by Hollywood, Lane is optimistic that the black-director phenomenon indeed is a Renaissance.

"I equate this with the breaking down of the Berlin Wall. Unlike the sixties and seventies, in the nineties we have African-Americans writing the material, behind the camera as well as in front of it. It's an entirely different situation than in the 1970s, when so often you saw black faces on what were essentially white stories. Now you're getting the experiences of African-Americans on screen."

Asked if he is troubled by the lower budgets imposed on black directors, Lane says, "*True Identity* cost over $16 million and Eddie Murphy's *Harlem Nights* was budgeted at $30 million. The signs are that black filmmakers can get bigger budgets for their projects, that we won't be ghettoized by lack of funds." Lane is optimistic that Spike Lee will get within striking distance of the $35 million budget he wants to make his biography of Malcolm X. [Editor's Note: Budgeted at $28 million, the film ended up costing around $32 million.]

While Charles Lane and Warrington Hudlin are more likely to call this the Renaissance than are Bill Duke and Michael Schultz, all agree that the new opportunities in Hollywood are for black men only. Where are the African-American women directors and stars?

"I find it a paradox," Schultz says, "because historically black women move faster and further than black men because they're less feared." Duke is less puzzled: "Just look how Hollywood looks at women."

Warrington Hudlin predicts that vanguard filmmaker Julie Dash will make the leap to mainstream production. He also thinks TV directors Debbie Allen and Neema Barnett, known for their work on "A Different World" and "The Cosby Show," will jump to big-screen projects.

But the absence of women in the Renaissance rankles Hudlin. "It proves that Hollywood is one industry where sexism is still a bigger obstacle than racism," he says. "In literature, black women provide profound vision and voice, and that they are unable to do this on screen means that the audience is being deprived."

Philadelphia Inquirer, July 21, 1991

PLAYERS

I n the bygone years when most movie actors were under exclusive long-term contract to the studios, their careers were often subject to the cast-iron whims of the production chiefs. Groomed, molded, traded, cast aside, even the most popular performers lacked the autonomy that might have led to more challenging and offbeat roles.

This may not have been an entirely bad thing. It may have spared us Marilyn Monroe as Ophelia, Henry Fonda as Hamlet. One big reason many of the studio-contract movie stars remain stellar in our memories is that the studio heads, whatever else they may have been guilty of, recognized, and exploited, the popular essence of their stable of luminaries.

Still, it's inconceivable that the current explosion of good acting in our movies could have been duplicated back in those straitened times. What the new generation of performers may lack in iconographic power is more than made up for in artistic reach. For those actors with box-office clout, their comparative, though by no means complete, freedom to choose their own roles has added an extra dimension to film criticism: A Meryl Streep performance, for example, is often discussed not merely on its own merits but also in terms of Streep's perceptions of how she should be cast. (Why does she keep trying out those accents? Why doesn't she do more comedy?)

The three actors discussed in this chapter are also three of the biggest stars. The underlying questions each piece poses are: In what ways do these performers represent something new? Is their stardom subversive or retrograde? Or both?

As one of the very few black superstars in the history of movies, what has Eddie Murphy accomplished with his vaunted power? (Both Murphy pieces also lead inevitably into discussions about Richard Pryor.) How, asks Dave Kehr, is Julia Roberts a star in ways that, say, Barbra Streisand, Goldie Hawn, and Jane Fonda are not?

Michelle Pfeiffer seems an especially apt candidate for this section. With her versatility and her soulful, surfer-chick look, she's the perfect amalgam of old-style and new-style star. For some critics, Pfeiffer's beauty, in combination with her talent, is a formidable gift. Because we enjoy watching her, she is licensed to play an almost limitless variety of roles. For others, her beauty is caked with a repressive ideology. Audiences who admired Kathy Bates as the romantically alienated waitress in the Broadway production of *Frankie and Johnny in the Clair de Lune* denigrated Pfeiffer's casting in the movie version as a flagrant example of "looksism." Armond White, in his provocative piece on the actress, argues that the Pfeiffer-worship of an adoring press is really a form of white worship.

Movie stars are ready-made objects of adoration. For critics, the knottiness, and the fun, in writing about them is tempering the analytic impulse with the impulse to go gaga.

EDDIE MURPHY

Owen Gleiberman

Early on in his punchy, exhilarating new concert movie, Eddie Murphy does an amazing impression of Richard Pryor. He recalls how he used to entertain the neighborhood by doing a Pryor-style monologue on one of the few topics that, at fifteen, he knew much about: taking a shit. Then he does the monologue, and it's hilarious in the *exact* way it would be if Pryor did it. Murphy doesn't just get Pryor's madman-evangelical mannerisms — the screamingly high voice, the look of suppressed pain. He gets the poetic outrageousness, the sense of a man engaged in a love/hate dialogue with his own body. This homage to Pryor's genius is so superb that, ironically, it outclasses most of the rest of Murphy's material — but then, perhaps the only one who could pay such brilliant tribute to Pryor is somebody with a touch of genius himself.

Has there ever been a stand-up comic with the *confidence* of Eddie Murphy? Most comics use their humor as a defense mechanism, but Murphy, with his sexy, liquid stare, his awesome control, his lickety-split verbal aggressiveness, might be a man who'd never felt a tremor of anxiety or doubt. In *Eddie Murphy Raw,* he's the comedian as rock star, as master of the universe. He gets all kinds of laughs in this movie — cheap ones, honest ones, and, at his best, what *Newsweek*'s Jack Kroll called "not laughs but *laughter,*" the sound an audience makes when it isn't just cracking up on cue but is riding the waves of a routine, cresting on the absurdity and humanity of it. This movie offers Murphy at a crossroads. He's already the most popular comic of his generation, and he's shown that he wants to be more than a comic, that he'll reach for success on any terms the culture offers. In his stand-up act, his parodies of singers like Michael Jackson are there, in part, to demonstrate how good a singer *he* is; when that wasn't enough, he went out and made an album. (It scored a hit single, but with the assistance of sideman Rick James, so now Eddie says he's going to do an album without help — he's going to prove he can be a pop star all by himself.) His last two movies, *The Golden Child* and *Beverly Hills Cop II,* were shoddy and insulting, but in odd, telling ways. *Cop II,* in particular, was less a comedy than a mindless gloss on contemporary action movies, with Murphy playing Axel Foley as a synthesis of Murphy the comic, Dirty Harry, and James Bond. The film seemed designed to show that he could be a straight hero, that he could score a monster hit with only a smattering of jokes — and, sure enough, he did.

But where is all this box-office omnipotence getting him? In *Raw,* Murphy makes a welcome return to the slash-and-burn comedy his stardom rests on. It's a damned good show, at times an inspired one. Eddie spins routines out of his celebrity, his near-marriage, his undisguised love affair with himself. He does bits on whites, blacks, Italians; on Pryor, Bill Cosby, Michael Jackson; on sex (lots of good stuff on sex); on childhood. Part of what's arresting about the movie is seeing the two Murphys — the superstar and the artist — duke it out, and hoping the one doesn't KO the other. Eddie Murphy is the MTV-generation heir to Richard Pryor and Lenny Bruce: At this point, he's part genius, part box-office whore, and the two parts are inseparable. He draws his comedy from an impulse—a need—to shock, and what's cleansing about this need is that it has its roots in something deeper. I'm tempted to call it a truth-telling reflex, only that makes it sound pretentious. Let's put it this way: Like Pryor or Bruce, the shocks Murphy elicits are really shocks of recognition—the giddy recognition that our lusts, our prejudices, our whole selfish, mangy, beautiful *lowness* as human beings is something we spend too much time covering up. The laughter these comics provoke has something to do with why rock and roll exists: What they give us isn't merely funny, it's essential, a way of cutting to the core of an overcivilized world. Yet Murphy is in a different position from that of Pryor and Bruce. A superstar by his early twenties, he hasn't had to take the risks they did. The threat of arrest or legal censorship is history—he can say whatever he likes. And because Pryor, his mentor, detonated so many taboos, Murphy struggles to match him. He knows he's adding new rooms to the house Richard built.

And so he's upped the ante, or tried to. He's doing a punkier version of Pryor, telling jokes tailor-made to piss people off. And he's succeeded. Gays are pissed, women are pissed, Bill Cosby is pissed. And the more they get pissed, the more Eddie flashes his horsey grin. There's calculation in all this—too much calculation. For Eddie Murphy, shock-the-audience has become a commodity: pure show biz. And I have mixed feelings about his compulsive nastiness. He's funny when he's rude, and I think it's fundamentally priggish to circumscribe what a comic should or shouldn't be making jokes about. Yet if you believe, as I do, that Murphy has the talent to become as great a comic as Pryor (that is, as great a comic as this country has ever produced), you may feel the relentless, teasing fuck-youness of his routines is ultimately something he has to outgrow. Murphy isn't bitter the way Pryor is; his racial humor doesn't have the same righteous edge. He's still young, and *Raw* is a young man's show-off movie—an I-can-get-away-with-anything movie. When he isn't flaunting his nastiness, though, he does some bits here that can rival anybody's. Beneath his imperiousness, Eddie Murphy has the gift of empathy. He *understands* people, how they act and where they live, and that, more than anything, is the source of his humor.

The gay stuff is a good example. In *Raw,* Murphy does what can only be described as a swish routine (Robin Williams, it should be pointed out, gets just as much mileage out of the same thing), but to slip into his homo persona, it's not as though he has to joke about tight buns: All he has to do is stand there and . . . pop his eyes. It's like a special effect. Murphy is satirizing a quality some homosexuals are actually quite proud of (a hyperawareness, a glittery-eyed sensitivity), and he's doing it with such dead-on understanding that there's no way you can simply write it off as a homophobic potshot. Of course, part of what seems cutting about this is that he makes such a big deal of pushing his own machismo. He gets off a couple of great lines about what would happen if he escorted Brooke Shields to the Oscars, and his routines on sexual relationships are ruthlessly honest. They're cynical bits, and very up-to-the-minute, especially concerning the new, mythical eighties woman, whom Murphy (in a nifty repeated gag) posits as living by the Janet Jackson song "What Have You Done for Me Lately?" When he debunks inflated romantic notions of "making love" versus "fucking," it's hilarious, and there are some great lines about men and women cheating on their partners — although Murphy is mostly interested in what happens when men do it. But he also spends far too much time talking about his pet dilemma, the fear that a woman is going to marry him for his millions and then walk off with "half." Are we all supposed to *relate* to this, to giggle in sympathy? At times, you can't tell whether he's flaunting his celebrity or whether he's just stopped registering anything outside it.

Murphy is terrific at ballooning his satirical notions into paranoid comic fantasy. He gets in a few standard Italian-street-punk jokes and then comes up with a priceless scene in which a shrimpy Italian saunters up to a concession counter and orders a six-foot-five "moolie" (black guy) to pay for his candy. In a routine like this, you can tell that Murphy didn't just learn how to cuss from Pryor; he absorbed Pryor's gift for lyrical hyperbole. And perhaps the highlight of the movie is his wonderfully innocent story about having to eat one of his mother's elaborate home-cooked hamburgers instead of one at McDonald's. There's horror in Murphy's voice as he recalls fetching green pepper and onion for the recipe ("But there aren't any green peppers at McDonald's!") and then watching the dreaded green-pepper burger being cooked up. When it turns out that all the other neighborhood kids got to eat at McDonald's, he turns their singsong chant ("We got McDonald's! Weeee got McDaaah-nowld's!") into a prepubescent epiphany.

Raw is uneven. For every wonderful bit, such as the McDonald's routine or Murphy's sublimely dorky impression of white people dancing, there's a forced, rambling one, like the closing story about how his father's family were so poor they had to eat toys. Still, this bold concert movie has more belly laughs — more *laughter* — than any mainstream comedy in months. As an entertainer, Murphy embodies the slick imperiousness of the Lucas/Spielberg era. There's a special kind of self-awareness built into his act — an awareness of how big he is, and a bottom-line desire to stay there. Luckily, his talent transcends his worst impulses.

Boston Phoenix, December 24, 1987

EDDIE MURPHY

Peter Rainer

Harlem Nights is the first movie to costar Eddie Murphy and Richard Pryor. Watching the sorry, unfunny mess that has resulted is like witnessing a highly touted heavyweight title bout that inexplicably turns into a pat-a-cake session between cruiserweights. Even those of us who have just about given up on Murphy hoped the pairing with Pryor would snap him to attention. But it's been a long stretch since either Murphy *or* Pryor has thrilled audiences with anything more than their star power.

There was a time — say, seven or eight years ago — when such a confab would have raised the rafters. Murphy began his four-year stint at "Saturday Night Live" during the 1980–1981 season, and his appearances on that show, with his impersonations of pimps, jailbirds, Gumby, Buckwheat, and Bill Cosby, are still his comic high point. Pryor, of course, had a thriving if uneven movie career in the early eighties. His glory, however, was his stand-up comedy films, particularly the 1978 *Richard Pryor Live in Concert* and the 1982 *Richard Pryor Live on the Sunset Strip.* They were the movies in which Richard Pryor could be Richard Pryor.

In the intervening years, Murphy has become a major movie star largely at the expense of what made him a TV star. He's moved away from the quicksilver, revue-sketch humor and the edgy playfulness of his "Saturday Night Live" days and turned himself into a commodity. His comic facetiousness has turned stone-cold. Whereas he once professed his idol to be Richard Pryor, his movies suggest another deity: Sylvester Stallone.

Murphy is a movie star because his films make fortunes, but is there anything stellar about his work as a thirties nightclub dandy in *Harlem Nights,* a movie in which his character's homicidal streak is played for cheap laughs? Is there anything anointed about his work in films like *Beverly Hills Cop II* (a movie originally intended for Stallone) or *The Golden Child* or *Coming to America?* His reprehensible 1986 stand-up comedy film *Raw,* which begins when, leather-suited, he strides on stage amid hoopla more appropriate to the Second Coming, represents his "purest" expression to date; in it, his free-floating hostilities descend on women, gays, whites, blacks—take your pick. *Raw* was a real potpourri of hate. To review it was to leave the domain of criticism for psychiatry.

Stardom can sometimes enlarge an actor's possibilities and bring out what was nascent, and best, in his talents. The reverse seems to have happened to Murphy. In "Saturday Night Live," he was part of an ensemble; he was challenged by the other performers. In his movies, starting with his first (and still best) film, *48 Hrs.,* where he costarred with Nick Nolte, Murphy has essentially been performing solo. He works with such crackerjack precision that sometimes he doesn't need anybody else around; he can be his own most appreciative audience.

But Murphy desperately needs to be challenged in the movies. Yet, given the fact that he controls them so completely—he is writer, director, and executive producer of *Harlem Nights*—how will that ever happen? His clout has allowed his worst instincts to come through.

Richard Pryor is playing his surrogate father in his new film, but there's an element of condescension in the casting. Pryor is positioned as Murphy's wise and cautious mentor, an elder statesman. It's the kind of "tribute" that's indistinguishable from neutering.

If Eddie Murphy's star power has allowed him all too successfully to tincture his films with the poison of his stand-up-comedy attitudes, then Richard Pryor has the opposite problem. His box-office clout has allowed him the opportunity to make a series of marginal movies with virtually no connection to his great stand-up persona. In films ranging from *The Toy* to *Bustin' Loose* to *Brewster's Millions,* Pryor has opted for the cushiony comforts of family entertainment. With his pick of writers, directors, and costars, he has willingly led himself into creative oblivion. It's as if Lenny Bruce walked into a movie career playing a Muppet.

It's never been easy for a volatile talent to score in the movies; the commercial demands of the business are invariably at odds with true subversiveness. But Pryor has the kind of control that might have preserved his rawness on film, not only in his concert movies, but in his dramatic films, too. The cuddliness of his screen image is a sick joke; it might seem like a put-on if only Pryor showed some sign that he was in on the con. But he's resignedly bland in his movies; anything malign or threatening has been bleached out.

With an artist as troubled and complicated as Pryor, it's difficult to assign motivation. Does a film like *Bustin' Loose,* where he plays a good-natured grump to a busload of kids, represent what Pryor thinks the movies deserve? Does he think such movies represent what *he* deserves? He has never quite given up entirely. Bad as it was, his 1986 autobiographical film *Jo Jo Dancer, Your Life Is Calling,* which he also directed, was at least an attempt to scour the treacle from his image. In a film like the 1972 *Lady Sings the Blues,* where he played Piano Man to Diana Ross's Billie Holiday, the 1978 *Blue Collar,* where he played an autoworker, and the 1981 *Some Kind of Hero,* where he played a POW returning from Vietnam, he gave indications of wanting to do more as an actor than just make nice. For years there was talk that he was preparing a film biography of Charlie Parker.

The problem may be that Pryor believes that, in order to quell his demons, he can't draw on anything in his life that means anything to him. In *Live on the Sunset Strip,* talking about his recuperation after his free-basing accident, he says, "Maybe I ain't funny anymore. Maybe I ain't angry at nothing for real in my heart." But the triumph of that performance was that Pryor demonstrated he *could* be an artist without working up a fount of rage. Pryor has been funnier than he was in that film, but he was never as mysteriously moving, or as fragile.

Actually, Pryor has always been mischaracterized as an incendiary comic. He was never really a social-activist crusader; his stand-up riffs exposed racism, but his humor was deeply personal, screwed up, aloof. The Get Whitey agenda of the early seventies never quite played for Pryor as it did for other black comics and actors because Pryor was after private demons, not white demons. His landscape was ultimately interior. He could split himself into an entire gallery of characters: winos, junkies, hustlers, movie executives, ex-wives. He could animate inanimate objects, like, most memorably, his cocaine pipe in *Live on the Sunset Strip.* The only thing Pryor can't play is normal, and that, ironically, is what he's set out to be in movie after movie.

The history of black performers in the movie business is such a trail of waste and despair that the ascension of Eddie Murphy and Richard Pryor has symbolic value out of all proportion to their actual achievement. With few exceptions, black actors have only been accepted as stars when they were comics.

This must explain some of Eddie Murphy's rage. Deprived in his early movies of any love interest with his white female costars, straitened into situations where he played the black sidekick joker to white actors, he has overcompensated by shunting his creative energies into a makeover that probably means a lot more to him than it does to audiences. His attempts to promote himself as a stud action-hero with a curdling cruel humor must function as a kind of retribution for him. For some of us, it's a punishment.

Los Angeles Times, November 24, 1989

MICHELLE PFEIFFER

Michael Sragow

Pfeiffer is *the* movie-acting phenomenon of the late eighties and early nineties. She's provided an unbroken chain of varied, sensitive, and imaginative performances in *Married to the Mob, Tequila Sunrise, Dangerous Liaisons, The Fabulous Baker Boys, The Russia House,* and *Frankie & Johnny.* Pfeiffer has often described her impersonation of a restaurant manager in *Sunrise* as one of her least favorite experiences. But under Robert Towne's direction, the deliberate professionalism of her delivery imbues the role with a comic charge. Her softspokenness is appealing; she doesn't seem to know her own strength.

In *Baker Boys,* Pfeiffer works a different type of show biz wizardry as aspiring singer Susie Diamond. When she sings her audition piece, "More Than You Know," she taps the psychic pipeline that can send passions rushing into the ear of the receptive listener. She's telling her auditioners (played by Jeff and Beau Bridges) that they need her more than they know. And in *The Russia House,* Pfeiffer takes another giant leap, mastering a Russian accent so un-self-conscious that it puts most of Meryl Streep's dialect work to shame. What's remarkable about Pfeiffer here is her Russian soulfulness. In this movie, Pfeiffer has gravity. She's formidable enough to create her own emotional free world.

In its variety and accomplishment, Pfeiffer's résumé is more than an arc of triumph. It testifies to her exploratory acting spirit—her willingness to take roles less traveled by, and to bring what she learns to bear on each successive project. Playing a sexually careworn waitress in the slim yet charming *Frankie & Johnny,* Pfeiffer is pragmatic *and* spiritual, lyrical *and* low-down-funny. Kathy Bates enjoyed a stage sensation in Terrence McNally's original theater piece, *Frankie and Johnny in the Clair de Lune.* Substituting Pfeiffer for Bates aroused controversy; she was supposed to be too innately alluring and erotic to convey the character's alienation from romance. Pfeiffer's artistry in *Frankie & Johnny* does more than silence her critics. It leaves even her fans dumbstruck.

Image, November 17, 1991

MICHELLE PFEIFFER

Armond White

Even before *The Fabulous Baker Boys,* Michelle Pfeiffer had been the object of film reviewers' adoration. She seemed to inspire the most shameless declarations of sexual preference, whether or not it was germane to the roles she played and, most remarkably, as if the appreciation of her beauty were universal and indisputable.

Baker Boys has brought this insanity to a head. One could shrug off Pfeiffer's acclaim in *Married to the Mob* (where she was neither convincingly likable nor Italian) and her victim role in *Dangerous Liaisons* (an inadequate performance of a sympathetic role that anyone — saint, whore, CPA, or canine — would have done to equal effect). But starting with *Tequila Sunrise,* the critical confusion of her California cheerleader's essence with acting became problematic. Plainly, Pfeiffer's praise is racist — that is, it's for her blond whiteness (say, a classy version of Ellen Barkin or Daryl Hannah).

Now, following her appearance in *Baker Boys,* Pfeiffer is being

Michelle Pfeiffer is the seductive, blues-singing Susie Diamond in *The Fabulous Baker Boys*. (Photo courtesy of Gladden Entertainment Corp.)

called both a great actress and a great singer. It's the movie equivalent of the Elvis phenomenon in which the white press is so thrilled with a version of itself that they promote it out of proportion to its worth.

The fact is, *Baker Boys* falls flat precisely because Pfeiffer lacks both the humor and the singing ability to put across this white romantic fantasy of sex and show business. In the plot, about a team of brother musicians, Frank and Jack (Beau and Jeff Bridges), who make their living playing at motor inn lounges and cheap nightclubs, Pfeiffer is the feminine element who disturbs the uneasy camaraderie of male bonding. A sexual catalyst, she makes the Baker brothers understand their unhealthy dependence upon each other. But the film's writer-director, Steve Kloves (*Racing with the Moon*), is shy of investigating masculine defensiveness. The Bakers are utter clichés. Frank is dull and business minded; Jack is a cynical would-be artist wasting his gifts on drinking, smoking, and womanizing.

Kloves doesn't animate or innovate a new, modernist romanticism as seen in the chic, attitudinizing, lovelorn characters of Alan Rudolph's marvelous *Choose Me* or *Trouble in Mind*. Like the latter film, *Baker Boys* is set primarily in Seattle, Washington, but Kloves can't make imaginative use of what Rudolph characterized as "Rain City." *Baker Boys* is a drab rehash of old-fashioned romance. Kloves, significantly, uses Pfeiffer as a goddess by nature. Her stage performance scenes and the "toughness" of her character (a former "escort" whose natural musical ability helps boost the Baker boys' faltering careers) make sense only as references to past backstage musical gimmicks and the all-pervasive charm of Hollywood deities. But if one does not buy into the WASP whimsy or shiksa worship, if one has another idea of "desirability" or of romance, Pfeiffer's casting, and her praise, seem fraudulent.

To paraphrase Robert DoQui to Gwen Welles in *Nashville:* Pfeiffer *can't sing.* It's impossible to believe her rescue effect on the Baker brothers' careers. This fundamentally dishonest film doesn't even acknowledge its crassest impulse—that its plot hinges on Pfeiffer's white sexuality. When she does an uninspired, barely sustained, and poorly choreographed version of "Makin' Whoopee" or "Ten Cents a Dance," the on-screen audience reacts to her brazen, sexual come-on, not to the "power" of her singing.

It's OK for Hollywood filmmakers like Kloves and his producer, Sydney Pollack, to be big-screen pimps, selling poontang (it's part of a long-practiced tradition). But to pretend that this film is something else—a meditation on contemporary malaise or the poignance of pop art—is offensive.

One can easily see through the lies of *Baker Boys* to the white exclusivity and segregation that have helped loosen Hollywood's hold on at least a part of the national consciousness. Filmmakers like Kloves and Pollack still are refusing to let people of color in on the national fantasy trip—and reviewers all are going along with their racism.

In the current social climate, *Baker Boys* would have made a great movie fantasy—the kind of film *The Cotton Club* or *Tap* was supposed to be—only with the right, talented actors. Would the filmmakers have had to look hard to cast this story Black? Lonette McKee, a proven, radiant film presence—a vivid, sensual actress who really can sing—could have hooked into our sanity and unleashed our fantasies. Pfeiffer's substitution for the kind of talent the role requires is a rebuke to our common sense. It says "only a white woman will do." This racially cautious way of making popular fiction—according to the literal methods of Hollywood's past—is stagnant, decadent. Was it naïveté that made Hollywood think only white people could be interesting on film? Or something more pernicious—a continuation of Western art's legacy that, in fact, denies the democratic potential of a mass medium like movies?

Whites no longer can stand as the only embodiment of our culture's artistic values or literary (cinematic) themes. One of the reasons watching music videos has been so rewarding this decade is it's the only motion picture medium in which people of color consistently are allowed to be witty, glamorous, and fantastic.

It isn't Pfeiffer's fault that she's become an icon of white supremacy, but when does this problem stop? In *Scarface,* she was stunningly effective as Elvira, a Third World gangster's idea of a prestige possession (the idea August Darnell satirizes with Kid Creole's Coconuts). De Palma exposed the unpleasant truth of that idea, but *Baker Boys* wants us all supplicating on Tony Montana's level, pathetically unenlightened about our subjugation (through the media) to the persuasion of white ideas and idols. Even Madison Avenue is more responsible about the ideas and products it sells—after the social revolution of the fifties and sixties, advertisers court buyers through flattery. In the eighties, Hollywood has the tacky arrogance to still foist off its ideas of white superiority knowing people will buy them out of habit. *Tequila Sunrise* was regressive in its determination to address the social phenomenon of eighties drug culture through the metaphors of attractive white protagonists. That's as much a social sickness as drugs.

Pop glamour needn't be defined by white skin, blond hair, and blue eyes any longer. It's a joke to see Pfeiffer described as "stunning," "incendiary," "thrilling" in the year of Neneh Cherry's hot, cosmopolitan, and *musical* music video debut. *Baker Boys* might have worked—trite melodrama and all—if we could believe in the performers. Kloves resorts to forties mnemonics to make his big lie; he even revives the old canard of a soulful white jazz musician. Jeff Bridges grimaces when he performs in a Black jazz club to show that he *feels* the music and, of course, the Blacks who hear him (including Albert Hall, a *Trouble in Mind* refugee) are impressed.

I'm not impressed. Movie fantasy is not harmless when it is this conceited and mendacious. It's in the oppressive glorification of white drama and white beauty that so much social depression (the sense of inferiority people can't put their fingers on) begins. Nonwhites get nothing substantive from this picture, and the whites who praise it and flock to it just add one more layer of dishonesty to their political cocoon.

Hollywood used to be better than this. When Rita Hayworth did the famous mock striptease to "Put the Blame on Mame" in the 1946 *Gilda,* the filmmakers knew how to contextualize her sexiness, and they dubbed her singing to preserve the fabulous illusion. *Baker Boys* tells us to worship Pfeiffer simply because she's there; the only possible value we can place on her is the value we place on her sociopolitical being, that is, her whiteness. Hayworth's Gilda and Pfeiffer's own Elvira in *Scarface* understood their sexual exploitation in the underworld class wars, and they fought against it — warning us. But in *Baker Boys,* Pfeiffer's character is reduced to race, sex, ego, and greed and, in true Reagan–Bush spirit, is justified as such. Her character's name — Susie Diamond — is the most hilariously venal moniker since Whoopi Goldberg, but one suspects Kloves is catering to, rather than commenting on, ethnic conceit. Susie-Pfeiffer is an ideological tool of the race that rules Hollywood. *Baker Boys* is a white exploitation movie.

City Sun, October 25–31, 1989

JULIA ROBERTS

Dave Kehr

A few weeks ago, film history was made when a modest thriller, Joseph Ruben's *Sleeping with the Enemy,* opened to a $13.7 million weekend — a figure that made it the most popular film ever to open in February as well as the biggest hit a female star has ever been able to spark entirely on her own.

The female star is, of course, Julia Roberts, the twenty-three-year-old little sister of actor Eric Roberts, who first came to attention in the unexpected independent hit of 1988, *Mystic Pizza.*

Since then, she has artfully tossed her long brown mane, flashed her big bright eyes, and unfurled her impossibly wide smile in *Steel Magnolias, Flatliners,* and *Pretty Woman,* the last becoming the second-highest-grossing film of 1990, largely on the strength of her delighted, startled expression on opening a jewel box.

Even at the peak of their popularity, such major female stars of the recent past as Barbra Streisand, Jane Fonda, and Goldie Hawn generated nothing like the warm, widespread affection that Roberts has coaxed from the American public. Roberts has even been nominated for an Oscar for her performance in *Pretty Woman,* an acknowledgment almost unheard of for a traditional star turn in an unabashedly commercial film.

As the French critic Yann Tobin has pointed out, there has been nothing like the Roberts phenomenon since 1953, when another coltish young performer, Audrey Hepburn, made her lead debut in *Roman Holiday,* and the world fell in love with her. "Upon seeing the film," Tobin writes, "every spectator — man and woman, young and old — succumbed exactly as the camera did to the mobile face, the ravishing smile and the spontaneous charisma of a young actress."

"To succumb" seems exactly the right verb, because Roberts's charm is one not of persuasion or slow insinuation but of immediate conquest. It is, for men, either love at first sight or eternal indifference; for women, a sense of instant identification or profound annoyance. It's clear, however, that for the vast majority of Americans, as we step gingerly into a new decade, Julia Roberts is the woman we want either to be or be with — the defining figure of a new femininity.

At this point in her career, Roberts is not a great actress. She has an extremely limited range of expression — beaming delight on the one hand, trembling anxiety on the other — and practically no depth of personality to back up her small effects. Next to an Anjelica Huston or a Debra Winger, she barely seems to exist.

But performing ability and stardom have never been closely related (though it's nice when it happens). We pick our movie stars on the basis of what we can immediately read in them — in their faces, voices, bearings, and bodies — rather than on the characters they self-consciously create for us. Meryl Streep and Robert De Niro will always be great performers, but they will never be great stars, precisely because they disguise themselves so well.

For Roberts, the Audrey Hepburn analogy is a useful one. Like *Pretty Woman, Roman Holiday* was a romantic comedy that took the form of an updated fairy tale (with Hepburn as a princess in disguise), and both films cast their fresh young female leads against established, stolid male stars not known for their senses of humor (Richard Gere and Gregory Peck). And not only was Hepburn nominated for an Oscar for her work in what was, for all practical purposes, her screen debut, but she won it, too.

Self-consciously or not, both films frame their young stars with a mythology of discovery and invention — *Roman Holiday* with a variation on the *Cinderella* tale (though this time it is the princess who descends among the commoners), *Pretty Woman* with a combination of *Cinderella* and *Pygmalion* (a role Hepburn would return to with *My*

Fair Lady). These are heroines who come along, seemingly out of nowhere, to redeem jaded, impassive, and considerably older men. They are living signs of rejuvenation and revitalization — of new beginnings.

Roberts, of course, possesses none of Hepburn's European polish and sophistication. She remains a rough-hewn, native American, and audiences love her in direct proportion to her uncertainty, awkwardness, and innocence. The opposite of the urbane, civilized Hepburn, Roberts attracts metaphors of nature and wildlife — she is not only coltish but skittish, frisky, gawky, frolicsome. Perhaps her real antecedent isn't Hepburn, but Bambi.

In matters of dress, Roberts favors floppy hats, print dresses, and oversized men's shirts. *Sleeping with the Enemy* even makes a plot point out of her taste in shapeless clothing: Her evil, controlling husband (Patrick Bergin) forces her to wear a tight, sexy cocktail dress to a party, while her new gentle lover (Kevin Anderson) treats her to a romp through the Victorian costumes in the local theatre's collection. Roberts still seems uneasy and uncomfortable with her body, as though she were astonished to find herself so suddenly an adult.

But for all of Roberts's sweetness and light, her films consistently place her in contexts that project anything but. So far she has been a Hollywood hooker, a victim of fatal illness, a medical student experimenting with suicide, a girl from the wrong side of the tracks looking for a rich boy, and now a battered wife. Her next project will be a Joel Schumacher film called *Dying Young*. One thinks of the career of Ingrid Bergman, who arrived from Sweden hailed as a glowingly healthy, farm-fresh young star and was promptly cast as an adulteress (*Intermezzo* and *Casablanca*), a nymphomaniac (*Notorious*), and a prostitute (*Dr. Jekyll and Mr. Hyde* and *Arch of Triumph*).

But the specter haunting Roberts is not sex, but death. At a time when there are no studios to guide the careers and shape the images of their contract players, it's amazing that Roberts's dramatic identity has acquired such consistency and resonance from film to film. She has become that central allegorical image of high romantic painting and poetry: the white-robed virgin menaced by the hooded figure of Death, youth and innocence threatened by mortality and experience.

It's intriguing that innocence should become such a priority with the American public at this point in time. After spending the eighties flirting with decadence — with the comic-book kinkiness of Madonna and the sadistic violence of the Stallone and Schwarzenegger films — here is an image of amazing purity and virtue, a return to the standards of Victorian innocence epitomized in the cinema by the Gish sisters (whom Roberts, with her huge eyes and mouth, eerily resembles).

If Roberts herself represents a rebirth—a return to first principles and fresh chances—her films place her in a context of finality and morbidity, of endings rather than beginnings. Roberts may embody our best hopes for a new, vital, self-confident America, but she brings with her the unspoken certainty of defeat.

The poignancy of Julia Roberts is the same poignancy inherent in our national desperation to convince ourselves that victory in the Gulf has somehow redeemed the disaster of Vietnam, or returned America to its former power and prestige, when deep inside we aren't so sure.

In *Sleeping with the Enemy,* she is allowed to triumph over death (represented by her creepily Euro-styled husband) by taking refuge in a dream of American small-town life, a flag-waving vision straight out of *Andy Hardy.* Yet it is a dream that the film itself acknowledges to be shopworn and unreal, through the visual exaggerations and ironies introduced by director Ruben.

Thus, even in victory, Julia Roberts allows us to shed a tear for our own demise. Beautiful but doomed, she is all-American to the last.

Chicago Tribune, March 24, 1991

RACE WARS

I n the critical arena, the heftiest knock-down-drag-out fights of
the past few years have been prompted by movies like *The Color
Purple* and *Mississippi Burning* and *Do the Right Thing.* The principled treatment of race relations, specifically the relations between black and white, has never been a Hollywood hallmark; the
standard dramatic approach wavers between exploitation and ten-
derization.

Not a few critics believe these approaches still hold sway. Steven
Spielberg's *The Color Purple,* for example, was attacked for being a
white man's zippadee-doo-dah vision of the Alice Walker novel.
Driving Miss Daisy was knocked for supposedly glossing over the
problems of race with a twinkle and a chuckle. Some feared Spike
Lee's *Do the Right Thing* would spark — was intended to spark, even —
real-life conflagrations equal to the one that closes the film.

As with so many of the most provocative films of our era, the matter of historical accuracy also became politicized. The revisionism of
a film like *Mississippi Burning,* which favorably highlights the role of
the FBI in the civil rights struggle, was attacked as a dangerous, racist
polemic. Others felt the historical make-over was made irrelevant by
the film's emotional power.

The dominant figure in this section is writer-director Spike Lee, but it should not be forgotten that, in 1991, there were approximately twenty films by black directors in release, including perhaps the most acclaimed one of them all, John Singleton's *Boyz N the Hood.* (Carrie Rickey details this movement in the chapter "Auteur/Hauteur.") When there were virtually no black directors in Hollywood, the issue was academic, but now one continually hears, from Lee and from others, the rhetorical question: Are black artists alone equipped to give us the truth of the black experience? And Hollywood, its gimlet eye ever on the buck, is asking itself how it can attract big interracial audiences with these movies at a time of rampant racial polarization.

The violence that attended the opening weekend of a film like *Boyz N the Hood,* where two died and thirty-three were wounded in theatres playing the film across the nation, points up another dilemma. Gang-oriented movies, even though their "message" be overtly non-violent, can bring the violence of the streets into the theater. They are also the films that tend to make lots of money. These new films have generally been more substantial and deeply felt than the so-called black exploitation cycle of the early seventies with its *Shaft*s and *Slaughter*s and *Superfly*s. Still, then and now, the question remains the same: Can Hollywood be entrusted to market rage?

THE COLOR PURPLE

Armond White

The Color Purple is the best movie of 1985 — and the strangest. Steven Spielberg adapts Alice Walker's popular tear-jerking novel with gleeful effervescence. He doesn't pretend to identify with the sorrowful story of southern Black women's struggle in the first third of this century; we might be intrinsically skeptical if he did. Instead, Spielberg shows the same simple, optimistic, childlike perspective of his other films. He brings out the feminist fairy-tale essence of Walker's novel, more than ever confounding and expanding one's view of pop art.

Spielberg's movie recalls a pop tradition so vast, it includes D. W. Griffith silents, Lana Turner soap operas, Picasso sculptures,

Ntozake Shange plays, rhythm and blues and gospel records, Charles Dickens serials, faux naïf Black musicals, liberal-social melodramas, and John Ford westerns. The film constantly shifts moods and effects and suggests other movies as Spielberg re-creates Walker's fiction out of his own pop culture syntheses.

Arguably this is the only measure of life that he knows, thus it's also an honest approach. Such a synthesis happens to bring Hollywood further up to date on feminist and racial issues than the critical establishment may be ready to admit or accept. For better or worse, *The Color Purple* is a genuine state-of-pop-consciousness movie. Its deft, undeniably effective emotional displays amid frequent, heavy-handed manipulations force a viewer to understand the artifice of which movie fiction is made and the visual, poetic codes from which Black people and Black experiences have been almost permanently segregated but that Spielberg now restores.

☆

Due to Walker's feminist preoccupation that places racial discrimination second to the oppression of women, the filmmakers (including Dutch screenwriter Menno Meyjes) don't get hung up on the same old fairness bug that prescribed all previous movies about Blacks. Watching this film is like returning to your own reflection in a mirror — you don't notice what others may see, you recognize traits distinctly familiar to yourself, perhaps marveling at their form and substance.

The Color Purple feels like the first insider's movie about Black Americans because the characters aren't defined by their relation to the white world nor created through a white artist's sympathetic condescension. These are new Black archetypes; as fictional creations they are so free of political justification that the whole issue of "correctness" is zapped. The actors are simply wonderful to behold (in part because of Spielberg and cinematographer Allen Daviau's determined prettiness). Here, at last, is a vivid panoply of Black faces, well lit and without exoticism, treated as natural screen images just as white faces always have been.

Because of Spielberg's famous sci-fi benevolence, you could call this "loving the alien" (he automatically transcends those do-good racial allegories *The Brother from Another Planet* and *Enemy Mine*). He has made the real advance of treating Black people (characters) as any other. Spielberg's consciousness here is so heightened, it's giddy; he floats above the earthbound particulars that snag other filmmakers who emphasize conventional Black dialects and ghetto atmosphere. Like Walker, who freely accepted these things (she knew that Black and southern didn't always mean impoverished), he works to convey a spiritual, emotional quality instead.

Not only have reviewers who have compared *The Color Purple* to Disney's *Song of the South* misunderstood Spielberg's ingenuousness, they've read it wrong. The film's characters are not carefree, inhuman, or dimensionless. The struggle toward self-respect by the protagonist Celie may be predetermined but it is neither shallow nor simplistic. Spielberg and Meyjes string together the most telling events of Celie's sojourn: from her submissive self-deception (Celie's advising a man to beat his wife may be the most succinct, multileveled illustration of Uncle Tomism on film) to her developing wiles in a round of pathetic-comic-ironic-then-defiant servant scenes. Each increment of her emotional climb is fleet and dramatically potent.

Profundity has only possessed Spielberg in relation to toys (*E.T.*, *Close Encounters,* or the climax of *Sugarland Express,* where a teddy bear bounces along a road). He's shown amazing depth in ways other "mature" filmmakers could not, such as the moment in *Sugarland* that wove a man's despair into a few stolen seconds of a Road Runner cartoon. Spielberg's snappy, head-on visual style is risky and arch for drama. It's what always kept people from taking him seriously, and *The Color Purple* often veers into the stylized hyperbole of Frank Tashlin farces and Byron Haskin adventure films.

But this cartoonlike zest may be the only way Spielberg knew to sustain the progression of radical feminist thought upon which the plot is constructed. He doesn't reduce those thoughts, he makes them *pop!* The novel was a veiled diatribe — Walker's accusation and castration of domineering men. Spielberg retains the best of the book's insights into oppression; the cogent feminist ideas allow him to be admirably subtle and elliptical about racism.

But his cartoon sensibility is not subtle enough for the few scenes of Black–white interaction — as when Miss Milly (Dana Ivey), a victim of white male supremacy, vents her helplessness in paranoid hysterics. Yet the problem may actually be that Ivey, an expert stage comedienne, lacks the emotional resonance of the Black actors. But it is nonsense to complain about Spielberg's facility. The precision of any one scene, such as a young widow admitting that her husband died "on top of me," packs an ideological wallop greater than Jill Clayburgh's whole bra-burning career.

The most common dispute with the film regards Spielberg working in broad, inappropriate slapstick for fear of alienating his audience. This has invited a backlash long brewing since such loud, blunt, even racist Spielberg productions as *Gremlins, Indiana Jones and the Temple of Doom,* and *Goonies.* It's unfortunate that this rancor has erupted with *The Color Purple,* because this film should redeem Spielberg's "genius." His instinct for the entertaining effect here transforms Hollywood's entire racist legacy.

☆

Racism in Hollywood films was usually subtle and select — the industry regularly chose not to give fictional validation to the Black experience or to include it only when comically expedient. Post–World War II filmmakers were stumped by the need for revision, and in the civil rights era it was necessary for filmmakers to depict Black characters solely in terms of social transition. The filmmakers could not relax their view, and audiences have been tense ever since. Today the only Black performer regularly involved in recognizable moral dilemmas is a human cartoon (Mr. T.); Broadway maintains the minstrel-show facade of Black life through pastiche shows like *Sophisticated Ladies, Ain't Misbehavin', Grind,* and *Dreamgirls,* and the highest-rated TV show in the land is Bill Cosby's pallid Black retread of *Make Room for Daddy.* In this context the need for large-scale Black mythical figures — a distilled essence of human experience in Black — is greater than ever.

The first half hour of *The Color Purple* forms the basis of Spielberg's vision of childhood desire and euphoria — a precious but genuine humanist link — and it's miraculous: In a series of classic vignettes Celie is sexually abused by her "Pa," gives birth to two children who are taken from her, and is married off to Mr. (Danny Glover), who finally separates her from her sister Nettie (Akosua Busia). As the young Celie, Desreta Jackson gives the most lucid, affecting child performance since Henry Thomas in *E.T.* She has the emotional transparency of legendary film actresses and, when paired with pert, doll-like Busia, they recall Lillian and Dorothy Gish in *Orphans of the Storm,* D. W. Griffith's 1922 epic about two lost sisters reunited after the French Revolution. Spielberg stages the scene of Celie and Nettie's separation with a raw, mythic power equal to Griffith's. And if his audacity has the old master, who also directed the Ku Klux Klan romance, *Birth of a Nation,* spinning in his racist grave, it's just! This is the birth of effective Black screen fantasy — not a story of Black people who behave like whites or who finally inherit the kingdom of heaven, as in Marc Connelly's scandalous yet popular insult, *Green Pastures* (1936). It's a vision of Black life that answers strictly emotional imperatives and is the first since King Vidor's unjustly neglected *Hallelujah* in 1929.

Spielberg's art fills in the gap that has existed between the invention of film fiction and acceptable Black screen portraiture. The narrative here is heroically simple because, as the film's Griffith and Dickens parallels suggest, the political implications don't need to be spelled out; we can intuit them, and in the remarkable teaching scene between Celie and Nettie, Spielberg adds his own sweet structuralist-linguistic flourishes.

Whoopi Goldberg as the adult Celie brings a crucial shrewdness to the film, acting out the character's secret intelligence and at the same time a demonstration of the Black survivalist's bag of tricks. Her childlike playfulness makes the performance more than clever. When Celie blooms under the loving attention of the bisexual blues singer Shug (Margaret Avery), her joyfulness betrays a perfect emotional empathy between actress and director. There is no movie scene this decade better performed and directed than the discovery and reading of letters between Celie and Shug.

The actors carry us through Spielberg's Black remake of pop and movie history — from Shug's Bessie Smith–style dress and singing to the politicization of the Big Mama myth by Oprah Winfrey as Sofia. It also places Walker's tale properly in the tradition of popular women's fiction. We see how *The Color Purple* answers the specific needs of modern women to shape their own triumphant fantasies as once provided by the books of Edna Ferber and Fannie Hurst and not just For Colored Girls . . . either. In *The Color Purple* one feels a continuity between such early feminist–race relations classics as Ferber's *Show Boat* and Hurst's *Imitation of Life* that also provided the staples of Hollywood melodramas about women who struggled free of dependency on men.

Spielberg somehow manages both the exuberance of *Show Boat* and the emotional punch of *Imitation of Life*. *The Color Purple* should prove as endurably enjoyable as both.

The film fails in one aspect only: It doesn't sufficiently rectify Walker's hatred of men. Spielberg almost gets out of this because Danny Glover — who suddenly and terrifically has become the most important Black male actor since Poitier — has a charming, intelligent presence that enriches the hard-hearted character of Mr., but the script neglects his turnabout. It's stupid to take this as a critique of

Black men in particular; the scenes between Glover and Adolph Cae-
sar as his father and Willard Pugh as his son construct a system of oppression that explains machismo as a tradition outside race. Anything
more would have significantly changed the material, which was conceived in terms of how women sustain each other — exaggerated to
the point of idealizing sisterhood as lesbianism (and at the other end,
projecting machismo into incestuous rape). Spielberg isn't up to
rethinking these kinds of literary tricks. He tries expanding himself
by crosscutting between Celie in Georgia and her sister in Africa;
Shug at the juke joint and her father in church. He does a technically
superb shuffle and condensation of various ideological and plot information but not much more (Quincy Jones's overripe score blends
themes more effectively).

All this means is that there are limits to Spielberg's artistry and that
The Color Purple often goes off track, even blank. But in such instances
it's on ground that no other mainstream filmmaker has finessed or
even dared. There's much to think about, to feel, much that matters
in *The Color Purple*. It's a flawed movie but possibly a great one because it's so vital.

City Sun, January 15–21, 1986

THE COLOR PURPLE

Julie Salamon

The ads for *The Color Purple* describe the movie version of Alice
Walker's novel like this: "It's about life. It's about love. It's about
us. . . . Share the joy."

What director Steven Spielberg apparently didn't want us to
"share" was the pain, the bitterness, and the anger that gave Walker's
book its power. From the moment this movie opens, with the pretty
picture of young black women frolicking in a sunlit field of purple
flowers, you get the sense that we are in for the *Sound of Music* approach of making it through hard times. Suffer a little, sing a little.

That isn't entirely fair. There are many scenes in *The Color Purple*
that are strong and affecting. They do not, however, compensate for
the often hackneyed vision of domestic humor, the overreaching for

artsiness, the rambling final twenty minutes or so in which Spielberg subjects us to the sight of hordes of blacks leaving the sinful confines of a jazz club and heading off to church, having already been overcome by a joyous fit of gospel singing. These hosannas, which are not in the book, are the silliest kind of stereotyping, as though any black movie—even a nonmusical—requires a climactic bout of rapturous singing with a lot of hand waving and foot stomping.

No one—at least no one who is black—is unredeemable in this picture, which is not the impression Walker's book left me. The author told her horrifying—and eventually redemptive—story about a black woman's difficult lot in the first half of this century through the tortured, innocent eyes of Celie, whose stepfather raped her and whose husband abused her. Whatever degrading circumstances may have helped create the two men's behavior, from Celie's point of view—the only one we have in the book—they are subhuman and cruel. Eventually, this beaten soul finds the strength to liberate herself after she falls passionately in love with a strong woman.

The best moments in the film are those in which Spielberg is in sync with the dreamy casualness of the folk language Celie uses in the book to write her letters to God, and to her sister Nettie. In one of these scenes we see—and mostly hear—a terrified young girl giving birth, we hear the ominous thud of approaching boots. The boots belong to the man she thinks is both her father and the father of her child, there to take her baby away. He is the fearful sum of his cruel voice and heavy footsteps, not a human. Later, the strongest sense we have of the way she feels about her husband, whom she calls, impersonally, Mr., again comes from the threatening sound of feet.

Yet the ferocity of Mr. (Danny Glover) is greatly diminished when the glamorous and independent Shug Avery arrives on the scene. This alternately dissipated and vibrant blues singer is the woman Mr. has always loved. Celie falls in love with her too.

Before Shug's arrival we see Mr. only as a tyrant who barks orders at Celie (Whoopi Goldberg), who tremulously obeys. When he leaves to fetch Shug, however, he becomes just another befuddled guy. He runs around the house in traditional movie male bafflement, forgetting cuff links and the like. Each time the (now endearing) Mr. runs back up the stairs, Celie is waiting with a patient smile, as though she's thinking, "Isn't he cute?" Not much earlier, she seemed ready to slice his throat with a straight razor.

Other, subsidiary, male roles, such as Mr.'s father, are built up to no apparent purpose. Still others, such as the part of Shug's preacher father, are created almost entirely of whole cloth, apparently to show that even a tough cookie like Shug Avery had some man whose approval she needed.

No one would dispute Spielberg's great abilities as a director. He knows how to put vivid images on the screen that heighten and transform reality. He can paint pretty pictures, too, like the flickering shadow paintings through which we watch Celie and her sister play hand-clapping games. But he can get too caught up in his own games. We find out Shug Avery's coming to town when the camera's eye is fixed on a pink piece of paper that twirls and spins and flies through the country air, Tinkerbell style, until it plasters itself right up against the screen door. The paper, it turns out, is a handbill announcing Shug's club date.

And Spielberg, who invested a make-believe creature like E.T. with unforgettable humanity, hits and misses when he's working with creatures that didn't come out of the nursery of his brain.

For example, one of the movie's best-realized characters is Sofia, who is portrayed with great gumption and sympathy by TV talk-show hostess Oprah Winfrey in her movie debut. Sofia, who marries Celie's stepson, is everything Celie isn't. She's fat, opinionated, and contemptuous of anyone who tries to walk on her. In the terrible moment when she lets a white person see that contempt — she socks the white mayor in the jaw — a crowd of yammering townsfolk descends on her. Even in this powerful scene, Sofia's fear of this descending horde doesn't come across anywhere near as starkly as the terror E.T. felt when the scientists converged on him.

Goldberg does, however, do a fine job with the difficult task of putting us in touch with Celie, whose voice we hear mostly in the narration of her letters. Until she consummates (off camera) her desire for Shug Avery, she is cowed, her thin shoulders bent forward, her eyes nervous as a rabbit's. When the full weight of the awful trick her husband has been playing on her for years finally sinks in, her murderous rage is all the more powerful because she's been so tightly reined in until that moment.

Yet Spielberg pulls back from developing Celie's charged, sexual feeling for Shug that is at the heart of the book. When Shug, played by the sultry Margaret Avery, breaks her wild, shimmying nightclub act at a local "juke joint" to sing a loving ballad to mousy Celie, great warmth but no charge passes between the two women. Later, in a lovely moment, Shug forces Celie, who's always been called ugly, to remove her hand from her mouth and look in the mirror at the bright smile she's kept hidden.

There are many bright moments like this one submerged in all the earnest goodwill, but not enough to make me feel great about this "feel-good" movie.

Wall Street Journal, December 19, 1985

MISSISSIPPI BURNING

Richard Schickel

Why does FBI agent Anderson (Gene Hackman) like baseball? Because, as he keeps telling people in *Mississippi Burning*, "it's the only game where a black man can wave a stick at a white man without starting a riot."

Were there in 1964 (or for that matter, have there ever been) FBI men like Anderson, who does not seem to own a black suit or a snap-brim fedora, who talks like a human being instead of a prerecorded announcement and shuffles slyly rather than striding officiously through an investigation? Were there, have there been, agents like his immediate superior Ward (Willem Dafoe), hiding a passionate moral (as opposed to a merely legalistic) commitment to the civil rights movement behind a prim manner and a pair of half horn-rims?

Who knows? And, finally, does it matter? For the business of these two agents in Mississippi, who are never referred to by their first names, is not to typify realistically an institution, but to represent two basic, conflicting human responses to being cast by chance in a tragic historical drama. Anderson and Ward are investigating the disappearance of three civil rights workers, two northern college students and a local black—a fictional case obviously inspired by the murders of James Chaney, Andrew Goodman, and Michael Schwerner, working in the 1964 drive to register black voters in the Deep South.

But the aim of this movie is not purely, or even primarily, documentary. The truth of its testimony is not so much literal as gospel, using that term in its revivalist sense. *Mississippi Burning* is a cry of anguish turned into a hymn of desperate hope, a glory shout in which remembered indignities mingle with moral inspiration.

Ward, the idealistic agent, understands and relishes the symbolic significance of his case. If the bodies of the missing youths can be recovered and it can be proved that they were murdered by organized racism, then their deaths will be redeemed by martyrdom and justice. The movie argues that Ward's confrontational tactics, which include bringing in a huge investigative task force and attracting excessive national media attention, not only delay progress on the case but also stir more violent crimes in response: beatings, church burning, even a lynching.

Anderson, who was once a sheriff in a county like this one, is much more the compassionate pragmatist. He wants a quiet investigation, conducted through sidelong glances, little toe-scuffing chats with the locals, and the free play of his instincts. He can kick into angry overdrive with a grin still on his face, and is not above conducting a shy, country-boy courtship of a key witness (Frances McDormand) to get on with his job, which, as he sees it, is simply to find the criminals, not to change the world.

Hackman is probably the subtlest screen player of his generation. He is a genius at hiding his true feelings under humor, letting them show with a seemingly unconscious flicker of expression or an unfinished gesture. Dafoe stands up to him with the kind of flat-voiced certainty mastered only by men of few, but unshakable, principles. Though each learns something from the other, their relationship retains its pure scratchiness from beginning to end. These guys are never going to be buddies.

Alan Parker (*Midnight Express, Angel Heart*) will never be a better director. He has always had a taste and talent for sudden violence, for making it explode out of ordinary contexts. That talent is well employed in *Mississippi Burning:* A scene in which a black congregation emerges from an evening prayer meeting to confront a silent group of hooded Klansmen, clubs at the ready, is a little masterpiece of terror.

But what truly distinguishes this film is Parker's acute reimaging of a time and place. The frightened silence of the black community (and the astonishing courage of some of its members); the sullen resentment of "outsiders" from the white community; the alternately bland, sneering, and self-righteous denials by the local lawmen that any crime was committed at all; the steadily mounting campaign of violence intended to terrorize everyone into complicity in this lie—all of this is handled with a deft and compulsive power.

That power finally sweeps away one's resistance to the film's improbability. It asks us to believe that the FBI, in those days still under J. Edgar Hoover's dictatorship, would have mounted an elaborate sting operation to bring the murderers at last to some rough justice under federal anticonspiracy statutes. That seems unlikely, especially given Hoover's hatred of Martin Luther King, Jr., and his allies. Still, narrow historical criticism somehow seems irrelevant to a movie that so powerfully reanimates the past for the best of reasons: to inform the spirit of today and possibly tomorrow.

Time, December 5, 1988

MISSISSIPPI BURNING

Jonathan Rosenbaum

The time in my youth when I was most physically afraid was a period of six weeks during the summer of 1961, when I was eighteen. I was attending an interracial, coed camp at Highlander Folk School in Monteagle, Tennessee — the place where the Montgomery bus boycott, the proper beginning of the civil rights movement, was planned by Martin Luther King, Jr., and Rosa Parks in the midfifties. As a white native of Alabama, I had never before experienced the everyday dangers faced by southern blacks, much less those faced by activists who participated in Freedom Rides and similar demonstrations. But that summer, my coed camp was beset by people armed with rocks and guns.

I believe that we were the first group of people who ever sang an old hymn called "We Shall Overcome" as a civil rights anthem, thanks to the efforts of the camp's musical director, Guy Carawan. But the songs, powerful as they were, weren't the main thing that kept us together; it was the fear of dying. When a local white cracker turned up on the grounds and fired a shotgun at campers who were swimming in the lake; or, on a drive back from Chattanooga, when a group of kids threw bricks and bottles at our cars; or when a midnight raid by several carloads of local rednecks who were ready to beat us up (or worse) was called off only because of a rainstorm, the question that always came up was whom we could turn to in a pinch for protection.

The answer was no one. Certainly not the local police or the FBI, as I quickly learned from the more experienced campers and counselors; the most we could expect from them was that they'd look the other way—or laugh in our faces. (I had already been warned by several white friends in Alabama that the FBI considered Highlander a communist training school, which meant that if I went there I'd never be able to get a job in government—or so they claimed.) In fact, the best that one could hope for in a tight situation in the Deep South was the presence of a *New York Times* reporter, and this was only because a white racist was less likely to bash in your skull if he thought it might get written up in a big Yankee paper.

Three summers after my stay at Highlander, three activists working to register black voters were killed by the Ku Klux Klan. With the complicity of a local sheriff and deputy, James Chaney, who was black, and Andrew Goodman and Michael Schwerner, who were white, were murdered in Neshoba County, Mississippi. Luckily, I was safe at home that summer; but my uncle, Arthur Lelyveld, a rabbi from Cleveland involved in the civil rights struggle, was bashed in the head with a piece of heavy pipe in Hattiesburg, Mississippi, a month later; and he delivered Goodman's funeral eulogy two months after that, when the bodies were finally found by the FBI. (His son Joseph—a *New York Times* reporter, as it happens—wound up interviewing former deputy Cecil Ray Price, who participated in the cover-ups, in 1977.) My own limited civil rights activities in Tennessee and Alabama never took me to Mississippi, an even more fearful place.

Given this background, it would be foolish to claim that I can approach *Mississippi Burning*, which deals with those three killings, impartially. But it would be equally foolish to claim that the movie elicits impartiality from anyone, or that impartiality of any kind informs its contents. It is, after all, a movie by Alan Parker, a stylish English director who got his start in TV commercials, and whose most popular features (*Midnight Express, Fame, Shoot the Moon, Pink Floyd—The Wall*, and *Angel Heart*) all reek of advertising's overheated style, where, regardless of truth or meaning, anything goes if it produces the desired hyped-up effect.

It's emblematic of the entire approach of Parker and screenwriter Chris Gerolmo that the movie focuses almost exclusively on the investigation of the murders by two FBI agents, fictional characters named Ward (Willem Dafoe) and Anderson (Gene Hackman), and that they're the only good guys in sight. Much of the drama, in fact, concentrates on the conflict between them: prim, moralistic, and zealous Ward, who antagonizes the local white community, and loose, ambling Anderson, who prefers to mingle with the locals, objecting that Ward's blunt methods might attract the northern press. Both are represented as moral spokesmen without a trace of prejudice—unlike every other white person in town—although the movie clearly favors Anderson's methods over Ward's. Broadly speaking, their positions might be called federal (Ward) and local (Anderson) ways of handling civil rights problems in the South, although needless to say the blacks themselves are given no voice at all in the debate; they're essentially treated like children, and emotionally speaking Ward and Anderson are the parents who have to decide what's best for them.

For most of its history, including the sixties, the FBI has been a racist organization. This isn't simply a matter of hearsay or folk wisdom; it's amply demonstrated in such places as I. F. Stone's 1961 article, "The Negro, the FBI and Police Brutality," James Farmer's *Lay Bare the Heart,* and any Martin Luther King, Jr., biography you care to pick. (The protracted persecution of King by J. Edgar Hoover is now part of the public record.) It's even come to light recently, when a black FBI agent brought charges of racial harassment against his colleagues. In 1964, of course, there was no such thing as a black FBI agent anywhere in the United States.

Unfortunately, the central narrative premise of *Mississippi Burning* sets up the FBI as the sole heroic defender of the victims of southern racism in 1964, which is more than a little disgusting. Embracing the premise unconditionally—unless one counts a single fleeting remark from a redneck to a journalist, that "J. Edgar Hoover said Martin Luther King was a communist," which the film neither confirms nor privileges—the film tampers more than a little with historical facts: It subverts the history of the civil rights movement itself.

It's true that the FBI did conduct a detailed and extensive investigation, file name "Mississippi Burning," in the summer of 1964, before the bodies of Chaney, Goodman, and Schwerner were finally found under more than ten tons of earth. But a look at the context of this investigation, which the movie can't be bothered with, tells us a lot more. Two of the three missing civil rights workers came from well-to-do white families. After the 1963 assassination of John F. Kennedy, the FBI's prestige was conceivably at an all-time low; Lyndon Johnson had signed the 1964 Civil Rights Act into law on the same day that Hoover finally announced his intention to open an FBI office in Jackson, Mississippi; and apparently Johnson had to twist Hoover's arm in the bargain. (As I. F. Stone wrote in 1961, "Mr. Hoover has made it clear that the FBI acts in civil rights cases only because ordered to.")

"1964 . . . Not Forgotten" is the final message of the movie—the words appear on the chipped, defaced tombstone of one of the slain activists—but it's hard to forget something that isn't known in the first place, much less remembered. The movie purports to re-create the past and to tell us what it meant, but the ignorance of *Mississippi Burning* is so studied that it only can be accounted for as a bulwark *against* knowledge, a denial of history for the sake of striking a glib and simple and easily digestible attitude against injustice.

It's not enough to counter that any Hollywood movie entails a certain amount of distortion. When Phil Karlson brought his actors and camera crew to Alabama in the fifties to shoot his low-budget "exploitation" docudrama *The Phenix City Story* (1955), which dealt with crime and racism in a similarly corrupt and terrorized community, he showed an attentiveness to the sound and look of his milieu, and the facts of his story, that even his own taste for lurid melodrama didn't falsify. Although it's shot on location in Mississippi and Alabama, *Mississippi Burning* doesn't try for even a fraction of the same authenticity; an undistorted depiction couldn't be further from its agenda. Parker's *Midnight Express* contrived to horrify audiences with the experience of an American teenager in a Turkish prison, while blithely ignoring what happened to Turks in the same place. *Mississippi Burning* shows a comparable indifference to the inhabitants and everyday life of its small southern town.

The film's two major characters are fictional, but both are analogous to real agents who worked on "Mississippi Burning" in 1964. Anderson is partially based on John Proctor, an agent from Alabama who worked in the North before he was assigned to Meridian, Mississippi, and who was friendly with two of the conspirators, Sheriff Lawrence Rainey and Deputy Cecil Ray Price. But the differences between the real agent and character are glaring. In the film, Anderson is a Mississippian who has worked both in the North and as a sheriff in Mississippi; he is untarnished by his friendly relations with the murderous villains. Joseph Sullivan—Proctor's superior, and the partial model for Ward (Dafoe)—hailed from the Midwest. In their recent book *We Are Not Afraid: The Story of Goodman, Schwerner, and Chaney and the Civil Rights Campaign for Mississippi*, Seth Cagin and Philip Dray describe him as follows: "A rugged six-two and known for his thoroughness and efficiency, Sullivan was the very personification of the qualities that epitomized the public image of Hoover's FBI."

Given the script that they have to work with, Dafoe and Hackman can't be blamed if their characters come across as dedicated liberals surrounded by evil rednecks. The only exception to this polarity is the deputy's wife (Frances McDormand), with whom Anderson flirts until she reveals the location of the activists' bodies. (In real life, the location of the bodies was found by bribing an undisclosed Neshoba citizen with thirty thousand dollars.) But properly speaking, Ward, Anderson, and the deputy's wife are the only figures with any density in the plot. The nameless murder victims, seen only in the opening sequence, are never allowed to exist as characters, and the local blacks — noble, suffering icons without any depth or personality — hardly fare better.

In fact, Ward and Anderson are practically the only people in the movie, apart from a barber or two, who are ever shown working. Their ninety-eight coworkers are mainly shown shuffling papers; the sheriff (Gailard Sartain), deputy, and other local racists seem to devote their hours exclusively to holding Klan or White Citizens' Council meetings, firebombing black homes and churches, and beating up blacks. (Even more improbably, despite placing the local blacks throughout the film in small, ramshackle, easy-to-burn houses and churches, Parker sets a black funeral near the end in a palatial sanctuary that's the film's biggest and most expensive interior — a good example of his preference for splashy effect over logic or continuity.)

I wouldn't expect a docudrama of this sort to deal with the literal truth. Even Parker admits in his production notes that "Our film cannot be the definitive film of the black Civil Rights struggle. Our heroes are still white. And in truth, the film would probably never have been made if they weren't. This is a reflection of our society, not the Film Industry." But Parker has stuck so exclusively to his white heroes that he has drained all complexity out of everyone else, blacks and racists alike, and he passes over many real-life details that would have made even his simple melodramatic approach stronger.

Cagin and Dray cite five local whites in Philadelphia, Mississippi, who stood against the community's conspiracy of silence, "all of whom were threatened and ostracized" and none of whom seems to bear any resemblance to the deputy's wife in the movie. Apparently, Parker and Gerolmo don't want to complicate their scenario with such people, or any other southern whites who showed courage, such as James W. Silver (whose remarkable and chilling *Mississippi: The Closed Society* was published the same year) or William Bradford Huie, a Philadelphia journalist who compared the race murders in Mississippi and Alabama with those of Auschwitz. They could have gotten a lot of mileage out of Buford Pusey, one of the local white dissidents, who joined the Mississippi NAACP in 1946 at age twenty-one because he thought that black World War veterans had a right to vote, challenged the local newspaper editor (who repeatedly called him a communist) to a duel in the late fifties, and as a consequence was himself denied the right to vote. (He also proved to be one of the few locals who assisted the FBI.)

Alternatively, if Parker and Gerolmo didn't want to deal with local eccentrics — which would have complicated their premise that the community consisted entirely of ignorant, bigoted, and interchangeable poor white trash — they could have dealt with certain aspects of the FBI investigation that are even more horrifying than anything they show. To cite Cagin and Dray again: "To the horror and disgust of southern blacks and movement people, several black corpses were found in Mississippi by authorities searching for Goodman, Schwerner, and Chaney. They were the routine victims of the Mississippi police/Klan juggernaut — found and identified this particular summer only as an unintended consequence of the national attention drawn to the state."

But fires are more photogenic than decomposing corpses. Since more than twenty black churches were firebombed in Mississippi that summer, *Mississippi Burning* opts for an endless spectacle of fires and beatings instead, taking care not to individuate too many of the black victims for fear of alienating "our society" (as opposed to the "Film Industry"). And what about the civil rights movement? What about the visits of King, James Farmer, John Lewis, Dick Gregory, relatives of the slain victims, and countless others to that part of Mississippi while the investigations were taking place? The movie can't begin to acknowledge any of these people as presences or voices, because, in terms of its own deranged emotional-ideological agenda, the FBI *is* the civil rights movement.

Parker's basic procedure is to stage as many dramatic confrontations as possible — between Ward and Anderson, between either or both of them and the townspeople, between the Klan and the blacks, or between an imaginary black FBI agent (Badja Djola) and the racist mayor (R. Lee Ermey) — without regard for the basic historical facts.

One of the first confrontations between Ward and Anderson occurs when they enter a luncheonette and Ward insists on joining the black men seated at a segregated counter (all of whom fearfully refuse to speak to him) despite Anderson's objections that this will cause an unnecessary commotion.

In order to stage such a scene, the filmmakers had to ignore the fact that, thanks to Jim Crow laws, no such seating arrangement was possible in Mississippi in 1964, even after the signing of the civil rights bill. Blacks were simply not allowed as customers in white restaurants; at best they could order take-out food from the back of some establishments, waiting outside near the kitchen. The film's indifference to the truth of the situation is indicative of where its real interest lies: with the good or evil intentions of whites, not with the everyday experiences of blacks.

But the movie's distortions go even further than that. Seth Cagin's article about the film in the December *Vogue* suggests that the movie's defamation (through neglect) of the civil rights movement is matched by its cockeyed distortion of the FBI's methods. An honest depiction might have pointed out, for instance, that their infiltration of the Klan was facilitated by agents who were themselves southern segregationists. But Parker's integrationist FBI, which even includes a couple of black agents whimsically known as Bird and Monk, opts instead for abduction and threats of violence (which, Cagin argues, fits directly into the Klan's cherished paranoid fantasies about the FBI).

This leads to one of the movie's most ludicrous scenes, when agent Monk, initially garbed in a Klan outfit, abducts the mayor to extract information. Threatening him with a razor, Monk proceeds to tell the (true) story of Judge Edward Aaron (called Homer Wilkes in the film), a black man selected at random, who was castrated with a razor by a white Alabama Klansman in 1957. That the movie occasionally makes use of actual historical occurrences — such as the horrifying crime against Aaron — can't really excuse its compulsion to use them to erect its own lurid fantasy scenarios.

I believe it was James Agee who remarked that some of the best art can grow out of moral simplification. It's a point that has some merit, but I would defy anyone who knows or cares about the civil rights struggle in any way to find much merit or art in the pile-driver simplifications of *Mississippi Burning* or the feast for the self-righteous that it makes possible. Ward makes a fancy speech (written by Parker himself) near the end of the movie, after the mayor has hanged himself (another clumsy invention), that argues that even though he wasn't a member of the Klan and didn't participate in the killings, the mayor is guilty—"maybe we all are"—because he stood by and allowed the murders and cover-ups to happen.

If Ward has a point, it's one that could also be made about this movie. The extravagant praise that's already been heaped on it by several national critics is apparently motivated by the sentiment that *any* treatment of the subject that is unsympathetic to the Klan has got to be an important step forward for mankind, regardless of how much obfuscation is perpetrated. Or perhaps some of these critics are too far removed from the historical facts to realize just how far the movie's distortions go.

But whether or not they realize what they're endorsing, critics and other spectators who celebrate this perversion of the past, this racism posing as humanism, this murder and cover-up of the historical record, this insult to the memory and legacy of Chaney, Goodman, and Schwerner, are as guilty in a way as Parker and Gerolmo, because they stand by and allow it to happen. Or maybe, better yet, we're all guilty—a nifty little formula that lets everyone off the hook.

Chicago Reader, December 16, 1988

DO THE RIGHT THING

Jonathan Rosenbaum

It's readily apparent by now that Spike Lee's *Do the Right Thing* is something of a Rorschach test as well as an ideological litmus test, and not only for the critics. It's hard to think of another movie from the past several years that has elicited as much heated debate about what it says and what it means, and it's heartening as well as significant that the picture stirring up all this talk is not a standard Hollywood feature. Because the arguments that are currently being waged about the film are in many ways as important as the film itself, and a lot more important than the issues being raised by other current releases, it seems worth looking at them again in closer detail. Ultimately most of these questions have something to do with language and the way we're accustomed to talking about certain things—race relations and violence as well as movies in general.

We all tend to assume that no matter how imprecise or impure our language may be, it still enables us to tell the truth if we use it carefully. Yet the discourse surrounding *Do the Right Thing* suggests that at times this assumption may be overly optimistic—that in fact our everyday language has become encrusted with so many assumptions that it may now be inadequate for describing or explaining what is right in front of us.

Consider, just for starters, the use of the word *violence* in connection with Lee's film. Some people have argued that the movie espouses violence, celebrates violence, treats violence as inevitable, or shows violence as therapeutic. (At one of the first local preview screenings of the movie, in Hyde Park, a paddy wagon was parked in front of the theater before the movie even started.) All these statements refer to instances of violence that occur toward the end of the movie, but none of them appear to be referring to all of these instances, which include the smashing of a radio with a baseball bat by the pizza parlor proprietor, Sal (Danny Aiello); a fight between Sal and the owner of the radio, Radio Raheem (Bill Nunn); the killing of Radio Raheem by white policemen who arrive on the scene to break up the fight; the throwing of a garbage can through the front window of the pizzeria by Mookie (Spike Lee), a black delivery boy who works for Sal; the subsequent looting and burning of the pizzeria by several nonwhites in the neighborhood; and the putting out of the fire by firemen, who knock down some people with the force of the water hoses. To make this list complete, one might also include the incident that sets off all the subsequent violent events: Radio Raheem entering the pizzeria after it's officially closed for the day with his ghetto blaster turned up to full volume, accompanied by two angry blacks who have previously been turned away from Sal's establishment for making disturbances—Buggin' Out (Giancarlo Esposito) and Smiley (Roger Guenveur Smith).

No one appears to be arguing that the movie treats *all* of these events positively, so there must be an underlying assumption that not all of these events are equally violent. The "real" violence, according to this discourse, turns out to be the destruction of white property (the throwing of the garbage can, the looting, and the burning)—not the creation of a disturbance (the blasting of the boom box), the destruction of black property (the smashing of the boom box), the fight between the two characters (Sal and Radio Raheem), or the destruction of a human life (the killing of Radio Raheem).

I don't think that the people making these arguments automatically or necessarily assume that a pizzeria is worth more than a human life, but I do think that our everyday use of the word *violence* tends to foster such an impression. There are times when our language becomes so overloaded with ideological assumptions that, however we use certain terms, they wind up speaking more than we do.

☆

Stepping outside the immediate context of the film for a minute, consider the appropriateness of terms like *black* and *white* — terms that we've somehow managed to arrive at by default rather than through any sharpening precision in our use of language. The evidence that our senses give us is that so-called white people aren't white at all, but varying gradations of brown and pink, while most so-called black people in the United States are varying gradations of brown and tan. Thus the skin tones in question aren't nearly as oppositional as the words that we use make them out to be. (It could be argued that capitalizing *black* only increases the confusion by further validating the concept behind the term as opposed to the visual reality.) A major reason that *Negro* ceased to be an acceptable word during the sixties was the belief that it was a "white" word and concept; unfortunately, *black* is a term that makes sense in a racial context only in relation to *white,* and if *white* is itself a questionable term, *black* or *Black* only compounds the muddle. (Consider also the consequences of this metaphysical mischief when one adds to the discussion Hispanics and Orientals, who are commonly regarded as neither white nor black, and Native Americans, who are arbitrarily designated in our mythology as red.)

I'm not arguing that we should go back to terms like *Negroes* and *Caucasians,* or that an arcane term like *colored people* is any better than *blacks* (it's often been pointed out that "whites" are "colored," too). The point is that we've reached an impasse in the language, and it ensures a certain amount of metaphysical and ideological confusion regardless of what we say.

☆

So far I've been speaking exclusively of verbal language. When it comes to the conventions of film language and what's known as the cinematic apparatus as a whole—the institution that regulates the production, distribution, exhibition, consumption, and discussion of movies—we may be in even deeper trouble, because the movie-related conventions that we take for granted aren't nearly as self-evident.

To start with one very general example of this, consider the way that most TV critics talk about movies. If the movies released this year were ten times better than they actually are, *or* if they were ten times worse, the discourse of these critics would be more or less the same, because the critics' functions in relation to this output would be identical. A major effect of this kind of reviewing is to keep the movie market flowing and to make the offerings of every given week seem important—a process that usually entails forgetting that last week's offerings were made to seem equally important. The critics' mission is not to educate us about the movies but to guide us toward some and warn us off others. Movies are either worth seeing or not worth seeing, and every week there are a couple of each.

Another example, this one more to the point: Many critics have commented that the expression "do the right thing" means something different to every character in Spike Lee's movie, but not very many have agreed about whether the movie itself presents its own version of what "the right thing" is or might be. Many people believe that Mookie's throwing of a garbage can through the pizzeria window is Spike Lee's version of "the right thing," but they arrive at this belief through a passive acceptance of certain movie conventions.

Spike Lee plays Mookie himself, and even though everyone knows that Lee doesn't deliver pizza for a living there's an understandable impulse to interpret his role as that of the hero or protagonist, according to the usual conventions governing writer-directors who double as actors (Woody Allen, for instance). In addition, there's a temptation to interpret the filmmaker's presence in the role metaphorically and autobiographically; for example, Mookie works for a white boss, and one could argue that Lee depends on "white"-run studios for the distribution of his movies (even though he insists on retaining "final cut," which gives Lee an autonomy that Mookie lacks). An even more basic assumption is that all commercial movies have heroes and villains and therefore take relatively unambiguous stands about what's "the right thing" and what's "the wrong thing" in any given conflict.

But what if *Do the Right Thing* doesn't have any heroes or villains? What if it doesn't propose any particular action as being the right thing? What if, in fact, it postulates — as I believe it does — that given the divisions that already exist in the social situation that the film depicts, it's not even possible for any character to "do the right thing" in relation to every other character? If the language that we speak is such that it can only express relative truths rather than absolute truths, it isn't difficult to extrapolate from this that the cinematic apparatus that we take for granted is similarly tainted.

☆

Even some of the most intelligent commentary about the movie suffers from certain built-in assumptions about it, which stem from unacknowledged assumptions about movies in general. Terrence Rafferty's review in the July 24 issue of *The New Yorker,* for example, which manages to avoid or refute much of the nonsense that has been circulating about the film elsewhere, still falls into the trap of imputing certain motives to Spike Lee that exist outside the film's own frame of reference.

"Raheem certainly doesn't deserve his fate," Rafferty argues, "but without [Sal's] inflammatory racial epithet" — Sal calls Raheem a "nigger" at the peak of his rage — "Lee would have a tough time convincing any audience that Sal deserves his." Rafferty is assuming here that Lee *wants* to convince the audience that Sal "deserves" to have his pizzeria burn down — an inflammatory accusation whose truth seems less than self-evident to me.

Rafferty continues with a string of rhetorical questions:

> Does Lee really believe that . . . any white person, pushed hard enough, will betray his contempt for blacks? Does he believe, for that matter, the tired notion that anger brings out people's *true* feelings? And does he also think that lashing out at Sal because he's white and owns a business and is therefore a representative of the racist structure of the American economy is a legitimate image of "fighting the power"? If you can buy all these axioms smuggled in from outside the lively and particular world this movie creates, then *Do the Right Thing* is the great movie that so many reviewers have claimed it is. But if you think — as I do — that not every individual is a racist, that angry words are no more revealing than any other kind, and that trashing a small business is a woefully imprecise image of fighting the power, then you have to conclude that Spike Lee has taken a wild shot and missed the target.

This sounds like impeccable reasoning, *if* one accepts the either/or premise and believes that Lee is smuggling these dubious axioms into his movie. But in fact the axioms and the smuggling both belong exclusively to Rafferty. The movie shows certain events happening and certain steps leading up to them; these events include one supposedly levelheaded pizzeria owner blowing his cool and a group of angry blacks trashing his establishment. At no point does the movie either show or argue any of the three axioms cited by Rafferty; at most, one might intuit that some of the film's angry black characters associate their trashing of the pizzeria with "fighting the power," but there's nothing in the film that suggests that they're right about this; nor does the film say that Sal is exposing his "true feelings" or that Sal is the equivalent of "any white person." Indeed, the movie takes great pains to show that the characters who tend to talk the most about "fighting the power" in less hysterical situations — Radio Raheem, Buggin' Out, and Smiley — are relatively myopic and misguided, and are seen as such by their neighbors; it also takes pains to establish Sal as a complex, multifaceted character who can't easily be reduced to platitudes.

Rafferty claims that one must accept questionable axioms to find *Do the Right Thing* a great movie. I would argue, on the contrary, that the film's distinction rests largely on its freedom from such axioms — a freedom that is part and parcel of Lee's pluralistic view of all his characters. This view simultaneously implies that every character has his or her reasons and that none of them is simply and unequivocally right. To seize upon any of these characters or reasons and to privilege them over the others is to return us to the paradigm of cowboys and Indians, heroes and villains. We've lived with this either/or grid for so long, it's probably inevitable that some spectators will apply it even on that rare occasion, such as this one, when a filmmaker has the courage and insight to do without it.

In place of either/or, Lee gives us both/and — epitomized by the two quotations that close the movie from Martin Luther King, Jr. (condemning violence), and from Malcolm X (describing situations when self-defense may be necessary). Some people have argued that Lee's refusal to choose between these statements proves that he's confused, but this argument only demonstrates how reductive either/or thinking usually turns out to be. The film's closing image is a photograph of King and Malcolm in friendly accord, not in opposition, and if the past of the civil rights movement teaches us anything at all about its future, then surely this future has a sizable stake in the legacies of both men. To view those legacies as complementary rather than oppositional is part of what Spike Lee's project is all about.

☆

Let's look at Lee's pluralism at the point when it becomes most radical — when the character who is the closest thing in the movie to a villain (without actually being a villain) is placed in a position where the audience is likeliest to agree with him. The character in question is Sal's son Pino (John Turturro), an unabashed racist who despises working in a mainly black neighborhood, which he refers to as "Planet of the Apes." ("I'm sick of niggers. . . . I don't like being around them; they're animals.") The moment in question is at the height of the pizzeria trashing, when the rioters are tearing Sal's establishment to shreds and raiding the cash register in a manic frenzy (certainly a far cry from anything one might call a heroic image). At this point the film cuts to a shot of Sal with his two sons watching from outside; Sal is screaming, "That's my place! That's my fucking place!" Then there's a cut to Pino watching the orgy of destruction with disgust and saying, "Fuckin' niggers."

It's easy enough to interpret this shot as the stock response of a mainly one-note character. But if one were to assume the vantage point of Pino and then select a single instant in the movie when his viewpoint came closest to being emotionally vindicated, or at least partially illustrated, for most people in the audience this would conceivably be the precise instant that Lee has chosen. For about two seconds, Pino is allotted the privilege — a relative privilege, not an absolute one — of saying the right thing.

☆

Just as Pino is the closest thing in the movie to a villain, Mookie is the closest thing to a hero. He occupies the space and the relative prominence in the film that would normally be accorded to a hero, but in spite of his overall charisma, his actions and attitudes are far from heroic. As Lee himself remarked to Patrick McGavin and myself in an interview earlier this summer, "He wants to have a little bit of money in his pocket [and] do as little work as possible." (Some viewers have complained that few of the characters in the movie are shown working, apart from the cops, the Korean grocers, and the workers at the pizzeria; these viewers seem to have overlooked the fact that the film takes place on a Saturday.) Mookie's sister Jade (Joie Lee), who helps to support him, and his Latino girlfriend Tina (Rosie

Perez), who feels neglected by him, both deride him constantly through the film for not living up to his responsibilities, which include concern and care for his infant son Hector.

Mookie's two major interests appear to be money and baseball; and while he is the only character in the film who serves as a link between the black and white people in the neighborhood, no one in the movie seems to regard him as a role model—with the partial exception of Vito (Richard Edson), Sal's younger son, a relatively sweet-tempered but not especially strong character who regards Mookie somewhat as an older brother in preference to Pino (which further intensifies Pino's racial enmity). In comparison to his sister, Mookie seems utterly lacking in ambition, and while most of the people on the block seem to like him—Sal says that he regards him as a son, and both Da Mayor (Ossie Davis) and Mother Sister (Ruby Dee) show a parental concern for him—no one apart from Vito can be said to look up to him, and there's certainly no hint that Vito's support extends to Mookie's eventual act of violence.

The only decisive moment in the film when Mookie appears to act on behalf of the local residents rather than in his own private interests—discounting the interests of Sal and his sons and the local policemen, none of whom live in the neighborhood—is when he sparks the riot by throwing the garbage can. But while Mookie clearly sets off the violence that follows, he doesn't participate in it, and there's no indication that he revels in the destruction either (which means the loss of his own job); near the end of the sequence, he can be seen sitting with his sister on the curb in front of the charred ruins, looking disconsolate rather than triumphant about what's happened. Nor can it be said that he is suddenly made into a hero by his one violent act; when Mookie is seen with Sal the following day haggling about money, there is nothing to suggest that he has grown or been changed by the experience of the previous night—his behavior is exactly the same as it was before the riot.

The two most insightful remarks I've encountered so far about *Do the Right Thing* haven't appeared in print; they've come from phone conversations with two friends and fellow critics who happen to be, respectively, the Los Angeles and New York correspondents for *Cahiers du Cinéma,* Bill Krohn and Bérénice Reynaud. Krohn views the film itself as a conflict between discourses, an approach that he traces back to Jean-Luc Godard in films of the sixties like *La Chinoise* and

One Plus One (the latter known in the United States as *Sympathy for the Devil*), films that were similarly misunderstood twenty years ago because people assumed that the violent discourses they contained — from French Maoists in *La Chinoise* and from black radicals in *One Plus One* — were necessarily and unambiguously the views of Godard, rather than simply discourses that he was provocatively juxtaposing with other discourses. (Whether Lee has been directly influenced by Godard is a secondary issue, but it's worth noting that two unorthodox uses of editing in Lee's film are distinctly Godardian: Mookie's initial greeting of Tina with a kiss is shown twice in succession, and there's a similar doubling of the action, from two separate angles, when the garbage can goes through the pizzeria window.)

Bérénice Reynaud believes that the basic conflicts in the film are ethical rather than psychological — particularly the conflict experienced by Mookie that leads to his throwing of the garbage can. The shot that precedes this action is probably the most widely misunderstood in the film; people who think that Mookie's action seems to come out of nowhere may be thinking this because they're misreading what's happening in the shot. Immediately after the police cars leave the scene, carrying away Buggin' Out (who is visibly clubbed by a policeman as the car drives away) and the dead body of Radio Raheem, the camera pans slowly from right to left past a crowd of onlookers in front of Sal's pizzeria. The people in the street are horrified and enraged by what's just happened, and most of them — in fact, all of them who are speaking — are addressing Mookie, who is standing offscreen, in front of the pizzeria with Sal and his two sons.

In part because of the unrealistic and highly stylized nature of the shot — each character delivers a pithy comment in turn as the camera moves past him, rather like the TV interview with combat soldiers in *Full Metal Jacket* — it's possible to misread the shot as a group of angry blacks who are simply addressing the camera. To be perfectly honest, I misread the shot in this way myself the first time I saw the film, although what the characters are saying is clearly addressed to Mookie: "Mookie, they killed him!"; "It's murder!"; and so on. The police are no longer around, and implicitly these characters are all asking Mookie what he's doing standing with the only white people in sight. Ethically speaking, they're all asking Mookie to do the right thing, and he responds accordingly.

But according to what has already been established in the film, there is no absolute or absolutely correct choice available to Mookie; whatever move he makes will at best be "right" for some of the film's characters and wrong for some of the others. He has been forced, in short, into an either/or position that falsely divides the world into heroes and villains — the world, in short, that most moviegoers seem to prefer.

If the audience members cannot think or feel their way into Mookie's position, and can't experience the challenge of those taunts about whom Mookie stands with, then Mookie's act of violence will seem rhetorical and contrived — an act that the film is imposing on the situation from outside to make a polemical point. But for any spectator who agrees to identify with Mookie and his ethical crisis, the moment assumes a certain tragedy — not a tragic inevitability, because Mookie could simply quit his job at this point rather than pick up the garbage can, but a tragic ethical impasse.

It's been reported that a major reason why *Do the Right Thing* failed to win any prizes at the last Cannes film festival was the objection of Wim Wenders, the president of the jury, that Mookie didn't behave more like a hero. Wenders's implied critique is that Lee should have made Mookie into a role model, superior to every other character in the film — a character who would exalt the either/or principle, which would imply, in turn, that the world is as simple a place as most movies pretend that it is, where simple and unambiguous choices are possible. The world of Rambo, in short — a world that is, curiously enough, not normally accused of fostering and encouraging violence to the degree that Lee's film has been.

Ironically, it is the moment at which Mookie throws the garbage can that he comes closest to functioning as a Rambolike hero — and closest to demonstrating how false and reductive the notion of such simpleminded heroism can be in a world as cluttered, splintered, and confused as ours. If role models are needed, Martin Luther King, Jr., and Malcolm X seem much better choices — not to mention Mister Senor Love Daddy (Sam Jackson), the local disc jockey whose patter periodically serves as narration; his most important message on a very hot day is for all of the characters to cool off.

Chicago Reader, August 4, 1989

DO THE RIGHT THING

Terrence Rafferty

In his first scene in *Do the Right Thing,* Spike Lee wears a Chicago Bulls jersey with a big *23* on it—Michael Jordan's number. Mookie, the character Lee plays, is no superstar: He's an ordinary young man who lives with his sister in a Bedford-Stuyvesant apartment, works—just hard enough to hang on to his job—at the pizzeria at the end of his block, and gets along pretty well with everybody. Amiable Mookie as the divinely inspired Jordan—who plays basketball so brilliantly that it sometimes looks as if he didn't need his teammates at all—is a bit of a joke. It's Spike Lee who's the one-man team here: He's also the writer, the producer, and the director of *Do the Right Thing,* and, as the most prominent black director in the American movie industry, he probably feels as if he were sprinting downcourt with no one to pass to and about five hundred towering white guys between him and the basket. Lee has all the moves. Since graduating from New York University's film school, in 1983, he has managed to get off three improbable shots, all lofted over the outstretched arms of the movie establishment—three movies, made and distributed, about black experience in America. The first, the buoyant and imaginative sex comedy *She's Gotta Have It,* seemed to come out of nowhere: Made independently, speedily, and on the cheap, it just streaked past all the obstacles, scored big commercially, and earned Lee the chance, almost unprecedented for a black filmmaker, to make entirely personal movies with major-studio backing. On the evidence of *Do the Right Thing,* Lee is all too conscious of both the responsibility and the power of his position. (Later in the movie, Mookie changes into a Dodgers shirt with Jackie Robinson's number on it.) He seems willing to do anything—to take on huge themes and assume the burden of carrying them both in front of and behind the camera. He just won't accept being ignored. He turns himself into the whole show, acting like Superman because he refuses, absolutely, to be an Invisible Man.

In *Do the Right Thing* this apparently fearless young moviemaker has, in Hollywood terms, cut to the chase. His two previous films (or three if we count—and we should—his splendid hour-long New York University thesis film, *Joe's Bed-Stuy Barbershop: We Cut Heads*) tried to dramatize what American movies weren't showing us about the real lives of black people in this grueling, reactionary decade; to find, if possible, a visual style specific to that experience, not borrowed from Hollywood or Europe; and to make it all so funny and vivid that everyone would have to pay attention. That's more than enough ambition to sustain a filmmaker through an entire career, but Spike Lee's no ordinary artist. Eager to keep things moving, to force the tempo of the game, he has decided to go for it right now, to catch us off guard — again — by rushing head on at the biggest, most dauntingly complex subject imaginable: racism itself. Who's to stop him? He's got the talent, the passion, the crew, the cast, and the money. But he stops himself: The gigantic theme ultimately exposes his weaknesses, overshadows his strengths. In the end, he takes what looks like a big risk, goes for the killer shot, and blows it.

By now, everyone must know that *Do the Right Thing* is about racial tensions in a black neighborhood on a punishingly hot day; that the focus of the action is the pizzeria where Mookie works, Sal's Famous, which is apparently the last white-owned business on the block (there's a Korean market across the street); and that the movie's climax is a full-scale riot sparked by a monstrous act of police brutality. The film's tortured message has been debated in the pages of the *Times* and *Newsweek* and the *Village Voice,* and on "Nightline" and "Oprah"; the movie has become, by virtue of both its explosive subject and its rather slippery point of view, a real cultural event, and if you haven't seen it yet you might almost feel that you no longer need to. Despite the interpretive deluge in the media, you *do* need to see it for yourself. It's a very unusual movie experience — two hours of bombardment with New York–style stimuli. You feel your senses alternately sharpened and dulled, as on a sweltering midsummer day, when the sights and sounds of the city are dazzlingly clear individually yet somehow unassimilable as a whole, overwhelming, brain fogging, oppressive. Lee is nimble witted, and he's always on the offensive; he stays in your face until you're too exhausted to resist. You have to watch your reactions closely or he'll speed right past you, get you to nod assent to an argument you haven't fully realized he was making. Most American movies just want to knock you senseless immediately and get it over with; *Do the Right Thing* tries to wear you down, and its strategies are fascinating.

In form, *Do the Right Thing* is a multicharacter, portrait-of-a-community movie. When this sort of picture is done skillfully, it can be exhilarating: Renoir's *The Crime of Monsieur Lange,* Altman's

McCabe and Mrs. Miller, and Scorsese's *Mean Streets* come to mind. The pleasure of community movies is their open-endedness, the (relative) freedom they allow us to observe the particulars of relationships in small, self-contained social units; they seem unusually responsive to the ambiguity and variety of experience. For long stretches, Lee's movie is enjoyable in this way. Characters are introduced, and while we wait to find out what they'll have to do with each other we can take in an abundance of atmospheric details—the lack of air-conditioning in the apartments, the way the sunlight looks sort of hopeful at the beginning of the day and then turns mean, the street wardrobe of T-shirts, bicycle shorts, and pristine Nikes—and listen to the casual speech of the neighborhood's residents, learn to hear in its varied rhythms how people who have lived too close for too long express their irritation and their affection. As we get our bearings, the movie has an easy, colloquial vivacity, and a sensational look. The superb cinematographer Ernest Dickerson (who has worked on all Lee's movies) gives the images a daring, Hawaiian-shirt glare: If the light were just a touch brighter, the colors a shade bolder, we'd have to turn away, but Dickerson somehow makes these clashing sensations seem harmonious. Lee's script seems to be trying to do something similar, but, despite its ingenuity, it doesn't succeed. As the long, sticky day goes on and the exchanges between the characters get edgier, nastier, more elaborately insulting, we begin to feel something ominous creeping in, which at the time we may take to be our realization that racial violence is inevitable, but which later on we may identify as our intuition of a different kind of disharmony—the jarring incongruity of Lee's "open" manner and his open-and-shut argument.

When the smoke clears—from the screen and from the insides of our heads—there are only two characters who really matter in *Do the Right Thing:* Mookie and his boss, Sal (Danny Aiello), who go one-on-one at the end. The rest of the characters are there to represent something or to move the plot along. There's an old drunk known as Da Mayor (Ossie Davis), who gets no respect from the younger people on the block but retains a certain wobbly dignity, and the sharp-tongued, independent-minded Mother Sister (Ruby Dee); they stand for the older generation, whose cynical "realistic" attitude toward living in a white society may have kept them from finding ways out of their poverty but may also have helped keep them alive. The next generation is represented by a trio of middle-aged gents who sit on the corner in kitchen chairs and provide, for anyone who wants to listen (only themselves, as it turns out), a running commentary on everything from neighborhood events to the melting of the polar ice caps. They're completely useless—their major occupations are drinking beer, boasting about sex, and coming up with new ways of calling each other "fool"—but their confident, vigorous inanity is very winning. Lee lets their routines run a little longer than they need to, just because the three actors (Paul Benjamin, Frankie Faison, and the wonderful Robin Harris, who plays the one called Sweet Dick Willie) get such sizzling comic rhythms going; these are the movie's loosest scenes. As examples of younger women, Lee supplies a responsible one, Mookie's sister Jade (played by Lee's sister Joie Lee), and a wilder one, his girlfriend Tina (Rosie Perez), who also gets to stand for unwed mothers and Hispanics. The young men consist of three mad-prophet figures: Smiley (Roger Guenveur Smith), a stuttering weirdo, who hawks photos of Martin Luther King, Jr., and Malcolm X shaking hands; Radio Raheem (Bill Nunn), a rap fan, who walks the streets with a mammoth boom box (it takes twenty D batteries), playing Public Enemy's "Fight the Power" over and over; and Buggin' Out (Giancarlo Esposito), a loud-mouthed "political" type, who wants to boycott Sal's because the pictures on its "Wall of Fame" are all of Italians. The whites are Sal's sons: Pino (the overbearing John Turturro), who's a virulent racist, and Vito (Richard Edson), who isn't. (Vito just looks passive and dim, actually.)

The thinness of the characterization isn't a big problem for the first hour or so, while the tone is still mostly light and comic. Lee is showing us types, but at least he gives us a lot of different ones (Hollywood movies rarely seem aware of any diversity in the black community), and their encounters are often funny. It's only later, when the whole crowded movie reduces itself to the symbolic confrontation between Mookie and Sal, that his approach lets the audience down. At its most basic, Lee's intention in *Do the Right Thing* is to demonstrate how in the context of a racially polarized society the slow accumulation of small irritations—the heat, some casual slights, bits of anger left over from old injuries, the constant mild abrasions of different cultural perspectives rubbing against each other—can swell to something huge and ugly and lethal. It's a solid idea for a movie—to show us the everyday texture of racial misunderstanding. But Lee wants to go further, to prove the inevitability of race conflict in America, and he can't do it, because no filmmaker could: Movies aren't very good at proving things. The obvious inspiration for the story is the appalling incident in Howard Beach, Queens, in 1986: Three young black men, stranded by car trouble in that very white neighborhood, were attacked outside a pizzeria by a bunch of youths armed with baseball bats; one of the victims, Michael Griffith, ran in front of a car while trying to escape and was killed. From this tragic event Lee has retained the charged iconography—the pizza parlor and the baseball bat—and changed everything else, with a view to making its significance larger, more general. He wants to create an event that can't be explained away as an isolated incident. And he's not about to let us believe that racism comes only in the form of teenage thugs.

So in *Do the Right Thing* it isn't Sal's vicious son who precipitates the violence but Sal himself—a man who, despite a fairly limited imagination, isn't an obvious racist. For most of the movie, Sal is a sympathetic figure: He's proud of the place he owns and proud of having fed the people of the neighborhood for twenty-five years, and he won't listen to Pino's suggestion that he sell the pizzeria and get out of Bed-Stuy. ("I've never had no trouble with these people," Sal says.) But in the end he becomes the enemy, and Mookie—the most easygoing and most rounded of the young black characters— becomes his adversary. By pitching his battle between the two most likable characters in the piece, Lee makes room in his story for the big statement: that in this society blacks and whites, even the best of us, are ultimately going to find ourselves on opposite sides. It's like a political rationalization of his aesthetic practice: Eventually, everyone reverts to type. The final conflict begins at the very end of this long, hot day, as Mookie and Sal are trying to close the pizzeria for the night. They stay open a few minutes longer to serve slices to a group of neighborhood kids, and in walk Buggin' Out and Radio Raheem; Buggin' Out starts yelling at Sal again about the absence of black faces on the wall, and Raheem's radio, turned up to earsplitting volume, is playing "Fight the Power" (which is also the movie's theme song). After the day he's had, Sal can't take it anymore, and goes berserk; he launches into a tirade, during which the word "nigger" slips out; he smashes Raheem's radio with a bat, and a fight breaks out. When half a dozen cops (all but one of them white) arrive, they go straight for Raheem, and subdue this large, strong-looking man with a choke hold, which kills him. The cops drive away, and the neighborhood people are all gathered outside Sal's, stunned by the tragedy. Mookie, who has been standing next to his boss, crosses the street to join his neighbors, picks up a garbage can, hurls it through the pizzeria's window, and the riot begins. Sal's is destroyed, as retribution for the death of Raheem.

In part, this powerful climax — and it *is* powerful — seems to come from Lee's sense, as a filmmaker, that he needs a conflagration at the end, a visually and emotionally compelling release for the steam that has been building up through the film. His model is clearly the Scorsese of *Mean Streets* and *Taxi Driver,* but in Scorsese's film the final bursts of violence are generated entirely from within, from the complex internal dynamics of the communities and individuals we've been watching. Lee's climax only seems to have that sort of terrible inevitability. In order to believe it, and to find the characters' behavior in these disturbing scenes wholly comprehensible, we have to accept a proposition that's external to the terms of the movie, an abstract notion of the kind that no movie can truly demonstrate: that we're all bigots under the skin. Lee prepares us for this with a sequence in which various characters — Italian, Korean, Hispanic, and black (Mookie) — shout racial and ethnic slurs directly into the camera. Sal's exasperation with Buggin' Out and Raheem, after he has spent twelve hours standing next to pizza ovens on a ninety-eight-degree day, doesn't seem a particularly racist response — until he says "nigger." (Being driven out of your mind by blaring rap music doesn't have to have anything to do with race. At that volume, Def Leppard or Philip Glass would have the same effect.) Raheem certainly doesn't deserve his fate, but without that inflammatory racial epithet Lee would have a tough time convincing any audience that Sal deserves his.

Does Lee really believe that, as he says in his published production diary, "sooner or later it comes out" — that any white person, pushed hard enough, will betray his contempt for blacks? Does he believe, for that matter, the tired notion that anger brings out people's *true* feelings? And does he also think that lashing out at Sal because he's white and owns a business and is therefore a representative of the racist power structure of the American economy is a legitimate image of "fighting the power"? If you can buy all these axioms smuggled in from outside the lively and particular world this movie creates, then *Do the Right Thing* is the great movie that so many reviewers have claimed it is. But if you think — as I do — that not every individual is a racist, that angry words are no more revealing than any other kind, and that trashing a small business is a woefully imprecise image of fighting the power, then you have to conclude that Spike Lee has taken a wild shot and missed the target. He ends his movie with a pair of apparently contradictory quotations — one from Dr. King, advocating peaceful change, and one from Malcolm, advocating violence (in self-defense). The juxtaposition suggests an admission that he doesn't know all the answers, but the movie, perhaps inadvertently, gives the lie to this confession of ambivalence. The imagery of the riot overwhelms the more incidental truths about human relations in the rest of the film, and Lee pays the price of all the little feints and evasions necessary to give his movie a socko ending: The half-truths add up, too. By the end, when Sal and Mookie are standing toe to toe in front of the burned-out shell of the pizzeria, and Mookie accepts his back wages, and more, from his employer, Lee actually seems to be saying that although Sal may not be the worst oppressor around, *someone*'s got to pay; the implicit message to the small businessman is "Too bad it had to be you, but what did you expect?" I think audiences, black and white, have the right to expect something more thoughtful than this from one of our best young filmmakers.

The "power" isn't guys like Sal, even though they benefit, modestly, from the biases of the economic system; they're just guilty by association, responsible for the deaths of young blacks like Raheem only in the most theoretical, distanced way. Although Lee must know this, he's clearly willing to sacrifice some political clarity for the sake of movie-style power. In order to make himself heard, he has chosen to adopt the belligerent, in-your-face mode of discourse that has been the characteristic voice of New York City in the Koch years. Spike Lee's movie isn't likely to cause riots (as some freaked-out commentators have suggested), but it winds up bullying the audience — shouting at us rather than speaking to us. It is, both at its best and at its worst, very much a movie of these times.

The New Yorker, July 24, 1989

DRIVING MISS DAISY

David Ansen

Is it possible that Jessica Tandy, at the age of eighty, is still reaching her peak as an actress? Can it be that Morgan Freeman, who was so terrifyingly brilliant as the pimp in *Street Smart,* is equally convincing as a soft-spoken, quietly dignified old southern chauffeur? Watching these two superb performers light up *Driving Miss Daisy* is an experience no student of great acting — and no moviegoer in search of a satisfying tug at the heart—will want to miss. Freeman originated the role of Hoke in Alfred Uhry's Pulitzer Prize–winning play. Tandy is new to the role of Miss Daisy Werthan, the stubborn, bossy, Jewish Atlanta widow who—at the insistence of her son Boolie (Dan Aykroyd)—begrudgingly takes on Hoke as her chauffeur after she's crashed her new 1948 Packard into a hedge. Over the course of the next twenty-five years, as she ages from seventy-two to ninety-seven, Hoke and Miss Daisy progress from a strained master-servant relationship into an enduring—but never informal—friendship. Tandy may not be the most Jewish of Daisys, but in every other way, she is definitive. It's an incandescent performance: sharp, droll, and deeply moving.

Uhry should be a happy man: Bruce Beresford's movie of his delicate, slight play is a model of stage-to-screen adaptation. Uhry has added new characters and settings to his three-character play—we get to meet Boolie's socially ambitious wife Florine (Patti LuPone) and Idella (the terrific Esther Rolle), Miss Daisy's longtime housekeeper—without sacrificing any of the intimacy. The added flesh is becoming: The movie actually strikes richer emotional chords.

Beresford, the Australian director, has had plenty of experience in stage-to-screen adaptations (*Breaker Morant, Crimes of the Heart*) but his touch has never before been this sure. He resists the many easy temptations a more insecure director would jump at—never going for the mawkish, never overplaying the themes of anti-Semitism and black-white racial relations that Uhry discreetly but resonantly leaves in the background. He knows that what remains unsaid between Hoke and Miss Daisy is as important as what is stated, and that much of the play's pathos is in the always proper distance across which they must communicate their true feelings. This lovely, quietly powerful movie would be worth seeing for the final image alone: The childlike, beatific expression on Tandy's face will haunt you forever.

Newsweek, December 18, 1989

DRIVING MISS DAISY

Armond White

As a stage play, *Driving Miss Daisy* was an acceptable little acting exercise that also made an interesting point about the irony of master-servant roles being played out in the American South between two "minority" types, an old Jewish woman and an elderly Black man. By transferring this sentimental sketch to film as a realistic chronicle of a platonic friendship, the delicate minor work becomes specious, distasteful, and offensive.

Bruce Beresford's genteel, picturesque direction turns Alfred Uhry's theater piece into a sentimental reverie on racism and classism as benign social circumstances. The film longs for the period when Black people knew their "correct" place as servants to whites; when Jews didn't have to think about committing the political sins they abhor in others.

Making this film was not a progressive thing to do; its critical acclaim is sad evidence of the backward social sense that is typical of current American movie culture. *Driving Miss Daisy* gives the nonthreatening treatment of U.S. race relations that people who hated *Do the Right Thing* longed for.

The kindliness of this story — how a retired handyman, Hoke Colburn (Morgan Freeman), becomes the chauffeur for an aging schoolteacher, Daisy Werthan (Jessica Tandy), but first has to win her affection — doesn't work in the "opened-up," realistic setting.

The real world that is lavishly presented in the film's period recreation (set in Georgia from 1947 to the early 1970s) imposes a political perception. This is not satisfied by such details as a movie marquee advertising *Gentleman's Agreement,* or the sound of Martin Luther King, Jr. (offscreen), delivering a speech. Hoke and Miss Daisy are unrealistic, cartoon figures — moral anachronisms.

And if one compares them to the master-servant characters of even such 1947 films as *Intruder in the Dust* and *The Reckless Moment, Driving Miss Daisy* still falls short of conveying the different worlds and worldviews that conceivably would mix as Hoke and Miss Daisy chatter on their road to nowhere.

Even forty years ago Hollywood filmmakers seemed to have a better grasp of the distance between races. *Driving Miss Daisy* suggests that the common sense of class and race perceptions needs to be learned all over again.

Beresford and Uhry's greatest failure is in keeping the characters stiff and one-dimensional. There is no room for subtlety in these characterizations — the roles have so many feints and so much circumspect behavior written into them that the actors cannot portray anything subversive or "deep." The only way to improve these roles for film is to reconceive them and bring the clash of temperaments to the fore.

Unable to add a note of militant truth that might challenge Uhry and Beresford's sweet-natured conception, Morgan Freeman seems stuck in superficiality. It isn't a bad performance but Freeman is sucked into repeating a stage triumph while forfeiting the control of the audience that originally gave the play its only justification. One could sense political forthrightness in watching Freeman match tempers with his white costar. In a spare, abstract setting, *Driving Miss Daisy* offered an egalitarian, theatrical coup.

Now that the control of the drama is taken away from the actors, the play only illustrates the complacency of Hollywood's dominant ideology. Uhry's title no longer has (vague) political resonance; it is just literal, banal. And with the status quo on Miss Daisy's side the film becomes a showcase for her crotchets and punctiliousness, thus an opportunity for the actress Jessica Tandy to dominate through her usual combination of opacity and skill that only occasionally gives a superficial role the breath of life.

Still, nothing said or done in *Driving Miss Daisy* causes one to question an unequal social situation. It's a breeding ground for horribly condescending attitudes such as in *The New Yorker*'s description of the maid's (Esther Rolle's) death and funeral scene featuring a gospel choir: "It must be worth dying to have singing like that." This movie is comforting for whites who feel that their own pleasure and convenience is the reason Black folks exist.

City Sun, January 10–16, 1990

JUNGLE FEVER

Stuart Klawans

Spike Lee's new film, *Jungle Fever,* begins on Strivers' Row in Harlem, in the sort of radiance that is a specialty of cinematographer Ernest Dickerson—a greenish yellow morning light, as fresh and tart as an apple. The camera creeps into a window to discover a couple making love; their daughter, listening in the next room, giggles in delight. Two hours later and a couple of blocks away, *Jungle Fever* concludes with Dickerson's camera rocketing forward into a bleached-out wasteland; a man is screaming in despair at the proposal of a street-corner blow job, offered by a prostitute who's addicted to crack.

If you were to reduce *Jungle Fever* to its dialogue, you might say that its core episode, the love affair between Flipper Purify (Wesley Snipes) and Angie Tucci (Annabella Sciorra), takes place in the context of racial and sexual stereotypes. As the late jazz master Art Blakey used to put it, opinions are like assholes—everybody's got one; and that's especially true in a Spike Lee film, in which people such as Flipper and Angie might well have been born just to give the other characters something to talk about. But if you watch the movie as well as listen to it, you might say that Flipper and Angie conduct their affair in an emotional space midway between the moods of the opening and closing scenes.

On the one side, you have the pleasure of everyday sights and sounds: the way a little girl's shoes slap the pavement as she walks to school, the timbre of Stevie Wonder's voice on the sound track, the textures of take-out food eaten late at night, under the glow of just a few lights in a darkened office. On the other side, you have the agony of losing contact with these simple things. Maybe, like Flipper, the afflicted person has messed up his marriage; maybe he's become an addict, like Flipper's brother, Gator (Samuel L. Jackson). Or maybe, as with Angie and her old boyfriend Paulie (John Turturro), stupid routine has made everyday life start to feel like a trap. For whatever reason, all these people have become deaf and blind to the riches with which Lee and Dickerson and production designer Wynn Thomas have surrounded them. They've turned inward, focusing on a single need or a fixed idea. In the case of Flipper and Angie, the hor-

Angie (Annabella Sciorra) and Flipper (Wesley Snipes) are involved in an affair that ignites their families and friends in Spike Lee's *Jungle Fever*. (Photo by David Lee, courtesy of Universal Pictures.)

rible irony is that they have limited themselves in the very act of trying to expand their lives.

As played by Sciorra, Angie is open-faced and easy in her posture. She comes from Bensonhurst—a notoriously self-enclosed neighborhood—and feels its atmosphere is stifling her, but she doesn't seem limited by her background. From the way she introduces herself to Flipper, when she appears as a temporary secretary at his architectural office, you get the feeling she would have walked up the same way to Haile Selassie himself, stuck out her hand, and said, "Hi." Flipper, for all his superiority to her in terms of education and experience, doesn't seem to feel half so much at home in the world. Snipes, who is a naturally strong actor, plays him against type, giving Flipper a suspicious glare that alternates with wide-eyed, pained bewilderment. Even when he's asserting himself against his bosses, Flipper seems held in; his voice is loud, but his arms stay close to the body, protecting him. To Flipper, Angie is a temporary refuge from the frustrations of his job, of his overbearing, puritanical father and impossible brother—perhaps as well from the constraints of maintaining a perfect marriage. To Angie, Flipper is nothing less than her ticket out of Bensonhurst—which means he's as big as the world itself. It's all the more hurtful, then, to hear Flipper tell her toward the end that she never really loved him, that she was "just curious about black." By withdrawing like that, reducing shared experience to a slogan, he insults not only Angie but himself.

A deeply sorrowful film with lots of funny moments, *Jungle Fever* lacks the visual jazz that animated *She's Gotta Have It* and the anger that sparked *Do the Right Thing*. It's less vivid than either of those pictures but also more firmly controlled. This time, Lee shows his directorial command largely through the way he works with the actors. You can see how he's let the principals collaborate with him in creating the characters; he also allows the actors enough latitude to improvise, most memorably in a rap session among Flipper's wife, Drew (Lonette McKee), and her friends. (An efficient response to the complaint that his female characters are weak: Lee invites a bunch of black women onto the set and turns the movie over to them for a while.) For in-your-face images, though, you will have to watch Lee's Air Jordan commercials. *Jungle Fever* does have one big set piece — Flipper's foray into a crack house in search of his brother — but I think Mario Van Peebles outdid that scene in his rather underrated *New Jack City,* and besides, the sequence leads nowhere in terms of the drama. It's mere scenery.

The other major complaint you might hear about *Jungle Fever* is that Flipper and Angie appear together too infrequently on the screen. Rubbish. If their encounter seems perfunctory, that's because it might have been, barring the effects of racism. First, social pressures turn a fling into a big-time affair; then the same pressures prevent the lovers from truly knowing each other. That's not schematic, allegorical, simpleminded, or anything else that Spike Lee's harsher critics have charged him with. It's complicated and heartbreaking. It's how a film that begins with the murmurs of love concludes with a howl of agony.

The Nation, July 8, 1991

JUNGLE FEVER

David Denby

In our time, all events turn into media events. Such brutal crimes as the assault on the Central Park jogger and the murder of Yusuf

Hawkins in Bensonhurst quickly lose their reality as horrifying acts with actual perpetrators and victims and are superseded by a more potent and (for many people) more useful symbolic version of themselves in the media — as if the crimes were the mere pretext for the real event, an endless media bash in which warring communities, using the crimes as clubs, attack one another in the press and on radio and television.

Spike Lee's new movie, *Jungle Fever* — the story of a love affair between a married black architect from Harlem and his white secretary from Bensonhurst — is itself an example of this dinning media furor, this public festival of racial acrimony. The movie is words, words, words. Some of the words are entertaining, but *Jungle Fever* is also raucous, tendentious, shallow, self-canceling, and finally senseless. Spike Lee carefully sets up an interracial love affair and then buries it in the predictably enraged opinions everyone has about it. Nothing is dramatized; everything is *said*. Spike Lee has many talents, but it's no longer clear that directing movies is one of them. On the other hand, he certainly knows how to pummel sore spots. He's become the cinematic equivalent of Morton Downey, Jr.

The two lovers are ciphers. Flipper Purify (Wesley Snipes) lives in a Strivers' Row brownstone with his elegant and successful wife, Drew (Lonette McKee), a Bloomingdale's buyer, and their little daughter. An apparently contented husband and father, Flipper strays because . . . well, who knows? There's a woefully tentative quality to Lee's conception of Flipper. At times, he hints that Flipper is a sellout to white values, but then he pulls back from that, leaving the character nowhere, a black Mr. Bland. Flipper's new secretary, a temp, Angie Tucci (Annabella Sciorra), is sweet and quiet; she has nothing much to say, but she has integrity, a modest but firm sense of herself. They work late together and after a few rather awkward conversations make love. The beginnings of this affair are weak and wispy, but I was expecting more — some explosive intimacy, some development and tension. The oddity of the movie is that nothing like a powerful passion develops between Flipper and Angie, nothing like defiance and desire in the face of adversity. Spike Lee has something besides love in mind.

Once the affair begins, Spike the inflammatory talk-show host takes over. Like teenagers thrilled to be making out, both Flipper and Angie immediately blab to their close friends about the affair, and then the friends blab, and within hours the families on both sides are going crazy, and soon whole neighborhoods are embroiled. Apparently dozens of people in the city of New York have nothing to do but talk about this tepid office affair. In Bensonhurst, the local layabouts wasting their days at a candy store pour out their hatred of blacks; in Harlem, the women gather and compare notes on the perfidy of black men and white women. It is the profane folk wisdom of neighborhood conversation, laced with race hatred and arranged into choral groupings. If only candor were the same as art.

In the Italian scenes, Lee is attempting to demonstrate the moral haplessness, the degree of suspicion, paranoia, and loathing that combined to produce the murder of Yusuf Hawkins. The working-class Italian-Americans in this movie come out of a patriarchal culture that has collapsed into hysteria. The older men may be pious about the dead wives who long scrubbed their backs, but they treat everyone else like dirt. The young men—Angie's brothers, for instance, who scream obscenities at each other and at her—are already damned. Like Martin Scorsese, Lee has realized that almost all speech is self-justifying, that virtually no one sees anything straight or gets anything right. Some of this losers' rant is funny, but it's funny only at the level of caricature. What Lee hasn't understood about Scorsese is the methodical way he builds his great verbal sparring matches, the way the climaxes come out of slow beginnings and rooted obsessions. In *Jungle Fever,* the Italian men scream right from the beginning of a conversation, and they hit women. For Lee, Italianness is mostly a disgrace. These people have no class.

The one exception is Angie's longtime neighborhood boyfriend, Paulie (John Turturro), who suffers the taunts of the candy-store wits when his girl takes up with a black man. Like Danny Aiello's pizza-store owner in *Do the Right Thing,* Paulie wants peace; he wants to treat people as individuals rather than as members of a group. Paulie is meant to embody the hope of a nonracist future; he falls for a black woman himself. Though it's a relief to see John Turturro in a gentle role, Paulie doesn't quite come to life. His natural impulses seem stifled, and I couldn't help wondering if Lee had not set him up as the one fully human person so that he could indulge his love of cartooning in the rest of the movie.

Spike Lee doesn't spare black people; he never has. On the other hand, I'm not convinced that he has gone deeper than caricature with any of his black characters. His treatment of ravaged black neighborhoods, for instance, is touristy and sensational. The worst thing in the movie: a huge Harlem crack house that is lighted like an atmospheric opera set, with human wrecks gathering in the sepulchral gloom. The scene is part of a subplot chronicling the final days of Flipper's crack-head older brother, Gator (Samuel L. Jackson). Hostile yet pathetic, trancelike in his crack highs, vicious and funny when he's sober, Jackson conveys the anguish of a talented man in a state of futility. What happens to Gator is the most sustained and emotionally commanding thing in the movie. But what is it doing there? *Flipper* should be the center of the movie. Spike Lee has captured the surface characteristics of many black Americans, but when he has the chance to go deeper, say with Flipper or with the jazz musician in *Mo' Better Blues,* he comes up with nothing. Why not? A guess: Lee's impassioned treatment of Gator suggests that he hollows out his successful, middle-class characters because he feels they are compromised by their success and the only reality of black life is the street. Some sort of complex self-hatred may be inhibiting his dramatic instincts.

Rather than dig in, he spreads out. Is it likely that a woman who discovers her husband is cheating on her would do what Drew does — immediately assemble her friends into a kind of group-therapy session? The scene is unbelievable, but it gives Lee the oppor-tunity to travel around a room of women and get their spicy remarks on sex and race. Black men want status, so they go out with white women. White women are fascinated with black men's genitals. Wow! Great stuff! Oprah, move over; Spike has come to town. *Jungle Fever,* it turns out, is not about adultery, or marriage, or love, or sex, or even sex and race together, that most explosive of combinations. The movie touches on all these things, but it's really about what in-terests Lee the most, race hatred and *color.*

Lonette McKee has to go through an excruciating scene in which she screams how humiliated she is because she's light skinned and she's lost her man to someone still lighter — a white woman. Flipper's dad (Ossie Davis), a fraudulent former preacher, gives a solemn speech, in a booming voice, about the sex life of a plantation and the octoroons who came out of it. Color is the only reality. But is Spike Lee perhaps a bit . . . overwrought? I know a few interracial couples, and I see a lot more walking around the city. They don't seem pursued by howling furies every minute of the day. Perhaps it is Spike Lee who is obsessed with color, an obsession he then projects onto the rest of us.

As in *Do the Right Thing,* extreme views are expressed, but Lee doesn't take the responsibility for any of them. He's an ideologue without an ideology, a demagogue with no program except to put himself at the center of things. The film technique he's evolved with his great cinematographer, Ernest Dickerson, is fluent and expressive, but it's a technique of kaleidoscopic glancing rather than dramatic involvement; the camera glides and circles, and everything it sees is vital, but nothing holds its attention very long.

The affair, it turns out, is truly skin deep. Angie may have been in love, but Flipper was just fascinated by skin color. At least, I *think* that's it; Lee is too indifferent to work out the motivation of the characters. *Jungle Fever* is emotionally vacuous and cynical. The movie is not about impassioned lovers pulled apart by social tensions, a tragic theme that would have given the picture some dignity. Instead, the lovers, who are just fooling around, get into much more trouble than they should. This is an ironic subject—but in that case, the movie should have been played as comedy, without all the violence and tumult and beatings, and without the pretense of explaining the social background of the murder of Yusuf Hawkins. In *Jungle Fever,* the foreground and background don't match up. The love affair is just a construct Lee uses to push people's buttons. And people will respond, no doubt about it. Geraldo, you're on.

New York, June 17, 1991

BOYZ N THE HOOD

David Denby

Boyz N the Hood, John Singleton's movie about the life and death of young black men in Los Angeles, is solidly constructed, honestly written, and funny and sad in equal measure. Singleton, twenty-three, a University of Southern California graduate, grew up in south-central Los Angeles and puts a lot of what he knows about this neighborhood in *Boyz N the Hood.* All day, jets heading for LAX (airport) come in low over the small tract houses; at night, police helicopters join in the din, training down their lights. The sun shines regularly, but the little boys play football near a corpse, and a teenage girl tries to read through the rattling of gunfire. The mothers are left without sons, the children without brothers.

The movie is a coming-of-age story. In 1984, when the hero, Tre, is about ten, his divorced mom hands him over to her ex, Furious

Styles (Larry Fishburne), who, she believes, can teach Tre to be a man. An ex-Army type who has begun a local home-mortgage firm, Styles has a very sure sense of himself, and big Larry Fishburne brings an even-tempered, unforced authority to the role. We've heard a lot about the missing father in the black community. Styles is a found father—a man with a genius for fatherhood.

If blacks are "brothers," Styles asks, why are they slaughtering one another? He tells his son that whites want black men to kill one another in order to reduce the black population. It's impossible to say whether Singleton endorses this Farrakhanite nonsense, but the movie suggests that such ideas, true or false, can help pull young black men back from violence. And the movie insists on the necessity of male authority: Only fathers can keep boys out of the streets.

Tre (Cuba Gooding, Jr.), who is seventeen during the main part of the story, and his friend Ricky (Morris Chestnut) are college-bound boys, but they are pulled by ties of loyalty and friendship into the neighborhood craziness. Ricky's half-brother Doughboy (the rap singer Ice Cube) and three friends, sitting on the steps of Doughboy's mother's house, do nothing all day, their talk a mass of self-justifying myths and infantile complaints. Singleton shows a lot of affection for these wasters. But the volatile social vacuum they have stepped into allows them few ways to assert themselves except in violence. Singleton brings out the insane combustibility in ordinary encounters—the jostling among teenagers that ends with guns blazing. He gets the heat and sass of young women, the despair of the older ones. He presents a coherent picture of a tragic way of life. At the end of *Boyz N the Hood,* you feel you've learned something about a whole community trapped in a malaise. It's a stirring and candid movie.

New York, July 22, 1991

POSTSCRIPT: On the opening night of *Boyz N the Hood,* young black gang members in roughly 20 of the 829 theatres in which the movie was playing shot off their guns, wounding thirty-three and killing two. The rest of the weekend was calmer. The movie, as I reported last week, is a sorrowful but finally upbeat portrait of a young man's coming of age in south-central Los Angeles; the sense of *Boyz N the Hood* is that gang warfare is inestimably tragic and stupid and that only a strong male presence in the household—a father—can prevent it. The movie is nothing if not responsible. John Singleton, the writer-director, cannot be held accountable for the violence. And though Columbia Pictures' trailers may have had an inflammatory effect, they were only standard movie ads.

Some of the gunfire (usually between rival gangs) began as soon as the lights dimmed; some took place outside the theatres, some inside. What the gunshots mean is that a number of young men are so excited by the presence of images of gang warfare that they cannot see what the images or the context around them is actually supposed to mean. They react as viscerally as did the early movie audiences who ducked under the seats to avoid shots of the ocean rolling in. They may not even find it necessary to *see* the images. Part of the response to *Boyz N the Hood,* in other words, confirms Singleton's view of south-central Los Angeles. Fights between gangs spring up out of nothing. Life is just fighting. The rest is waiting.

Young men like the ones shooting in the theatres must decide whether they want to live or die. The rest of us are generally sure that we do not want to die, particularly at the movies. I can understand why anyone might want to wait until *Boyz N the Hood* comes out in video. Nevertheless, assuming that things stay calm, I would hope that audiences will see the film in a theatre. Movies are already in danger of being stifled by the demand for "positive" images. *Boyz N the Hood* is both "positive" and "negative"—it's an honest movie. If the kids shooting off guns kill the movie commercially, it will be harder and harder for black artists to represent urban life honestly.

Seeing this decent movie is one way of supporting freedom for filmmakers. Beyond that, we have to decide whether we are satisfied with leadership that has allowed the urban environment to collapse to the point of chaos, cities in which guns are procurable by anyone. Yes, that sounds like a liberal editorial. What of it?

New York, July 29, 1991

BOYZ N THE HOOD

Dave Kehr

In the movies, attitudes shift very slowly. Change often occurs through the one-step-forward, two-steps-back formula, in which a progressive social theme is softened and made acceptable by a fiercely reactionary subtext.

That was the case recently with *The Silence of the Lambs,* in which the presence of a strong, independent female protagonist (Jodie Foster) was excused by the glorification of the film's ostensible villain — a domineering, literally devouring, male serial killer (Anthony Hopkins).

It's the case again in *Boyz N the Hood,* a debut feature by twenty-three-year-old University of Southern California grad John Singleton, in which a cry for racial justice is all but drowned out by some of the most shrill and violent misogynist attitudes ever seen in an American film.

Singleton's film compares the fates of two friends raised in a violent, desperately impoverished south-central Los Angeles neighborhood. One, a hefty, streetwise eighteen-year-old nicknamed Doughboy (played by rap artist Ice Cube), has been raised by a weak-willed, self-indulgent single mother (Tyra Ferrell), who is almost always seen wearing hair curlers and pulling on a cigarette.

The other, Tre (Cuba Gooding, Jr.), is a model of civic and academic responsibility, having been raised by Furious Styles (Larry Fishburne), a swaggeringly macho, firmly disciplinarian father, who keeps a gun in the house and launches into lectures on self-determination at the drop of a hat. Tre's mother (Angela Bassett) has abandoned the family to pursue a professional career in the white world and is subjected to a steady stream of abuse.

The film's other female characters, generally referred to as "bitches" or "whores," consist largely of predatory teenage girls who use sex as a way of trapping the boys into marriage. Occasionally, a vacant-eyed crack mother wanders through the scene, begging for drugs while her neglected baby crawls out into the middle of the street.

While Tre plans for a brilliant, prosperous future, Doughboy sinks farther and farther into the world of gangs and violence. Singleton's message is clear, and is unambiguously stated: Black women are too weak to raise black children — it takes a man to make a man.

It's a sentiment that flies so firmly in the face of reality that it gives *Boyz N the Hood* a distinctly neurotic cast: The more the film proclaims itself as pure, unadulterated social reality, the more it seems a purely subjective fantasy, a public dramatization of private demons. (Is it a coincidence that *Boyz* was produced by Steve Nicolaides, the producer of the equally antifemale *Misery?*)

For all his questionable beliefs, Singleton is not an unpersuasive filmmaker. Though the relentless parallelism of his screenplay smells a little too much of film-school technique, he has an excellent ear for dialogue and, in the surly, charismatic Ice Cube, a convincing mouthpiece.

Boyz N the Hood is, in every respect, a far more assured and polished film than its recently released East Coast analogue, Matty Rich's *Straight Out of Brooklyn.* But Rich's film had a roughness and sincerity that Singleton's work never achieves. Instead of speaking in the first person, as Rich did, Singleton seems to be approaching his subject through a whole system of established cultural models, including the politics-as-melodrama of the TV movie and the false, highly selective "immediacy" of the TV newscast.

There is also something a little disingenuous in Singleton's dual structure (a third leading character, Morris Chestnut's Ricky, is on hand mainly for plot purposes). With Tre on hand to provide "positive images" and Doughboy to deal in the traditional "blaxploitation" themes, Singleton is able to play the two main currents of African-American filmmaking against each other: the inspirational against the confessional, the sacred against the profane, the gospel against the blues. *Boyz N the Hood* wants to be *The Learning Tree* and *Superfly* at once, an ambition that doesn't seem quite honest.

Chicago Tribune, July 12, 1991

HISTORY LESSONS

Whenever a moviemaker alights on some loamy chunk of history, there's bound to be an uproar from the watchdogs and the schoolmarms. The controversy confronting the historical movie mirrors the one that attends the documentary. There may be something cobwebby, not to mention impossible, about the notion that filmmakers of historical projects should be sworn to tell the truth, the whole truth, and nothing but the truth. Still, if you are going to Mixmaster facts, or even factoids, with fiction, how much dramatic license is allowable?

Questions like these are often asked of recent historical films on the mistaken assumption that filmmakers should behave "objectively." In truth, most of the classic Hollywood historyfests — the war epics and royalty bio-pics and so on — were not nearly as objective as people like to remember. They just seemed that way because they were so dull.

The inflammatory debates in the historical film arena have been ignited by precisely those movies that didn't pretend evenhandedness. Oliver Stone's *JFK* was a long-standing personal project. So was Warren Beatty's three-hour-twenty-minute John Reed film *Reds* and Martin Scorsese's *The Last Temptation of Christ. JFK,* a veritable cottage industry of controversy, provoked more op-ed pieces than most of the campaigning presidential hopefuls. *Reds* was hailed as revolutionary by some, pooh-poohed by others as a piece of glamourpuss agitprop. *The Last Temptation of Christ,* which is perhaps less historical revisionism than messianical revisionism, brought on the wrath of Christian fundamentalist picketers and boycotters.

Sometimes the battles were about what *wasn't* on the screen. Richard Attenborough's South Africa epic *Cry Freedom* was scored for elevating the story of a white man, Donald Woods, above that of a black man, Stephen Biko. *Under Fire* was knocked not only for its supposed (and supposedly unethical) endorsement of the faked photograph of the rebel leader but also for its failure to explicitly link the Sandinistas with Communist powers.

The champions of these films have their own countercharge: How many movies even dare to tackle these kinds of subjects? And look at what riches *are* there. The Russian Revolution, the story of Christ, the murder of a president are fitted to the epic power of film. In what other medium can we be so completely enfolded inside the horrors and exaltations of history?

REDS

Michael Sragow

No other movie star in history has used power with such daring and wisdom as Warren Beatty with *Reds.* This vivid heroic saga—which Beatty not only acted in but also produced, directed, and cowrote—brings to life the tumultuous global upheaval that surrounded the First World War. Marxism, feminism, free love: These subjects might have assured box-office success in the late sixties, when Beatty first considered filming the life of activist reporter John Reed. Releasing this movie in the Reagan eighties would seem to be professional suicide. But the drama, romance, humor, and spectacle of *Reds* should transcend the conservative miasma of the moment.

Not since *Lawrence of Arabia* has there been a serious historical movie of this sweep, complexity, and intelligence. The events—the violent attempts to organize American labor, the early days of Bohemian Greenwich Village, the Russian Revolution — and the characters, including Reed, Louise Bryant (his wife), Eugene O'Neill, and Emma Goldman, are so well integrated that it is impossible to separate the personal from the political.

In a sense, Reed and Bryant starred in the social-sexual revolutions of their day. Reed's coverage of Pancho Villa's army earned him the title of the American Kipling even before he wrote *Ten Days That Shook the World,* his flashing account of the Bolshevik uprising. Though Louise Bryant eventually became a recognized journalist as well, history remembers her as a woman of mystery who captivated men of genius, including Eugene O'Neill. It is Beatty's inspiration to treat these two people as stars in the constellations of their culture.

Beatty punctuates that point with a unique device. Thirty-two "witnesses" are interviewed about the life and times of the Reeds, who strove mightily to capture a place in history. But the testimony poignantly illustrates how time had faded the meaning of their existence. These casual, beautifully filmed monologues float in and out of the narrative like poetic commentaries, and they enable the most uninformed viewer to compose an impressionistic picture of early twentieth-century America.

The key to the film's success is that Reed and Bryant are bigger than anything anyone says about them. This movie is about people who embody the conflicting drives of an era and are torn apart both by their unresolved personalities and by history. It feels right that these cultural stars of an earlier day should be played by Warren Beatty and Diane Keaton, whose most famous roles (in *Shampoo* and *Annie Hall*) epitomize the dynamic uncertainties of our own time.

Judged simply as a solo directorial debut (Beatty's fluffy *Heaven Can Wait* was codirected with Buck Henry), *Reds* is phenomenally ambitious — and extraordinarily executed. Though *Reds* does not have the originality to put it in a class with *Citizen Kane,* it rates very high. As a director, Beatty makes staging and shooting choices that are smart, tasteful, even impassioned. As a producer, however, he displays a flair and imagination comparable to Orson Welles's in his Mercury Theatre days. Like *Kane* or *The Magnificent Ambersons, Reds* boasts distinguished teamwork:

- Coscreenwriter Trevor Griffiths. Though Griffiths shares script credit with Beatty (and others are reported to have contributed), the biggest political speeches have the bristling rhetorical stamp that caused theater critics to deem Griffiths the most fiery English dramatic talent since John Osborne. In Griffiths's 1970 play, *Occupations,* a forthright, eloquent political drama, he pitted the tactics and principles of Italian socialist Gramsci, a leader of the factory takeovers in the workers' uprising of 1920, against a Soviet bureaucrat named Kabak, who was willing to sacrifice Italian workers for the good of the Russian state. Again, in *Reds,* Griffiths clarifies the differences between the idealistic socialists and Soviet bureaucrats, who ruthlessly protect the power achieved by the Bolsheviks in Russia. More important, this movie gives Griffiths his biggest opportunity yet to develop drama *dialectically.* The movie's structure is built on points and counterpoints that shift our perceptions of the characters as they change and grow. Beatty and Griffiths give the film's stirring images sturdy metaphoric underpinnings. The two key shots in the entire film—Reed climbing on a Mexican gun wagon near the beginning and trying to board a Soviet gun wagon near the end—crystallize Reed as a man forever chasing revolution.

■ Cinematographer Vittorio Storaro. In *Reds,* Storaro confirms his standing as the image master of the movies. His sometimes hard-edged, sometimes idyllic, and sometimes throwaway style helps express the characters' oscillations between old-fashioned elegance and rampaging modernity. Some of the cityscapes have the rainy erotic suggestiveness of Steichen's Flatiron Building photograph, while scenes in Cape Cod, where Reed, Bryant, and O'Neill lived and worked with the Provincetown Players, are shot through with the warm sunlight and slate shadows that marked Winslow Homer's paintings of sea and sand. When the Bolshevik revolt explodes, Storaro responds with great lyrical bursts. We see the "masses" as an inexorable historical force able to stop a streetcar in its tracks or topple Kerensky's compromise government in its Winter Palace.

■ Editors Dede Allen (coexecutive producer) and Craig McKay. Allen, who first gained fame by editing the Beatty-produced *Bonnie and Clyde,* and McKay, who edited *Melvin, and Howard,* imbue the whole three hours and twenty minutes with a bracing impatience.

Entire sequences use sound and image contrapuntally (just as

Russian masters Eisenstein and Pudovkin ordered). Songs as different as the wistful ballad "I Don't Want to Play in Your Yard" and "The Internationale" cut through scenes of the writers working, protesting, or making love, juxtaposing the incongruities of their lives. In one inspired, mystical moment, an old Russian woman chants a dirge before her icon while a silvery drinking cup—it's a common man's chalice—falls to the floor, marking John Reed's life slipping away at the Christ-like age of thirty-three.

- Production designer Richard Sylbert and costume designer Shirley Russell. The film is studded with small masterpieces of trompe l'oeil and period-costume re-creation. One of the great virtues of the production is that the physical splendor never swamps the intellectual topography.

What holds this monumental movie together is the intelligence of Warren Beatty. His problems would seem insurmountable: to anchor an epic production with a character who was an admitted adventurer. "It is only by drifting in the wind," Reed once wrote, "that I have found myself, and plunged joyously into a new role." Louise Bryant, too, was a bit of the will-o'-the-wisp; her ambitions were alternately unformed, formed, and dashed. But Beatty attacks the problem head-on by seeing his hero and heroine in a compassionate perspective that is as free of illusion as it is flush with sympathy.

For a long time—perhaps too long—we have to wonder whether Louise Bryant is committed to free love, radical writing, and Reed, or whether she does everything for effect. Reed, too, often appears as a mere romanticist and even a power-mad politico rather than an idealistic journalist. But the peculiar triumph of the film—and what makes it such an *American* movie—is that it persuades us that they both grew into the roles they carved out for themselves. They may come from privileged backgrounds, but they're self-made.

Right from the start, when Bryant meets Reed at the Portland, Oregon, Liberal Club, Beatty and Griffiths clue us in that modern times are bustin' out all over. Bryant soon propositions Reed with a startling comic directness. In the morning, when Reed asks Bryant to go to New York with him, she demands to know "as what?" She's got to be taken as an equal, not just as a concubine. All throughout the movie and their lives together, Reed and Bryant feel the pull of contradictory directions: forward to new social-sexual frontiers and back again to old-fashioned stability.

For northwestern innocents like Bryant and Reed, living together in Greenwich Village is like learning to swim in a maelstrom. It's a floating avant-garde salon, presided over by the unsinkable Emma Goldman (Maureen Stapleton, in a hearty, funny performance). Goldman is a grande dame for the twentieth century—a woman who holds sway over others by being more modern and liberated than anyone else. Every question she poses to Louise Bryant is an intellectual challenge that the Portland girl can't yet meet. Goldman seems to be saying, "You can't get by on charm alone with me, dearie."

Warren Beatty doesn't have the oratorical equipment to play Reed as a spellbinder, but he gets around this by selecting his scenes shrewdly and instead projects, without self-consciousness, the boyishness central to Reed's character. No one can do sheepishness, befuddlement, or defensive blowhardiness better than Beatty. His Reed is as tongue-tied in love and domesticity as he's cocksure in politics and adventure. Beatty makes us see the journalist's eternal dilemma: As an observer, he is always overshadowed by creative artists like O'Neill and radical activists like Goldman. Paradoxically, once Reed gets imbued with a religious brand of Marxism, he loses his boyish flexibility and kills off his own *élan vital.*

Diane Keaton, as Louise Bryant, shows an uncanny ability to express vulnerability when she's being aggressive and belligerent. Indeed, her outbursts are usually signs that she's been cut to the quick. Bryant constantly challenges herself to experiences and achievements that do not come easily to her personality. Her biggest test is Eugene O'Neill. Their affair exposes her ambivalence about romantic commitment.

O'Neill, played brilliantly by Jack Nicholson, functions as Bohemia's devil's advocate. He's in rebellion against *all* orthodoxies, whether "reactionary" or "progressive." And if his own view of human possibilities is limited, he does have the cleansing honesty that makes real progress possible. Nicholson looks relieved at having sharp, astringent dialogue for a change; he doesn't seem as hyped for a "big" performance as he did in *The Shining* and *The Postman Always Rings Twice.* He's relaxed and slithery, a charming serpent to Louise Bryant's brave-new-world Eve.

Working with Beatty must make actors (and nonactors like George Plimpton) deliriously happy. Keaton convinces us, as she never has before, that she can play a woman of backbone, and Beatty's self-effacement is itself almost an act of love. In a cameo as a hard-nosed editor, Gene Hackman stops the show with his joyous, barking bonhomie. Others, like Edward Herrmann's Max Eastman and Max Wright's Floyd Dell, register mostly as mysteriously "right" presences, as they might in a good Altman film. Plimpton, as a lecherous magazine editor, carries on with a faintly sepulchral wryness, like the Ghost of Café Society Past.

It's when the utopian revolution turns ugly that *Reds*'s themes come into focus. The Soviets strive to effect massive change through force of will alone. Shackling together disparate countries in chaotic Comintern committees, forsaking the immediate needs of their people to shore up the State, their liberations turn to tyranny. But as the revolution of the Soviets breaks down, the revolution of Jack and Louise's relationship—their attempt to be a marriage of equals—finally comes to fruition. At the end, they're comrades.

It's not incidental to the politics of the film that John Reed and Louise Bryant are American journalists. Free speech and the right to dissent are at the heart of this movie. In this century, social change in America hasn't happened because oppressed people altered the means of production, but because they manipulated the means of *communication.* This movie articulates the search for social progress when most of the nation is hiding behind patriotic platitudes. In this context, *Reds* might even be called a revolutionary film.

Rolling Stone, January 21, 1982

REDS

Stephen Schiff

In *Reds,* which is probably the most expensive and eagerly awaited of this year's Christmas pictures, Diane Keaton gets to wear lots of billowy blouses, pin-striped suits, pouchy sweaters, and sleek leather boots. And her hats look as if they were bent on world domination—they're huge, beretlike creatures that keep growing from one scene to the next, until they threaten to devour her whole head. The men

Radical journalist John Reed (Warren Beatty) speaks to a Communist rally in Moscow in *Reds*. (Photo by David Appleby, courtesy of Paramount Pictures Corp.)

are awfully fashionable too. Warren Beatty as the American revolutionary John Reed, Edward Herrmann as his editor Max Eastman, Jack Nicholson as Eugene O'Neill — they all wear crisp, pleated pants and huggy-looking sweaters, and, in the scenes set during the Bolshevik revolution, tall, fuzzy hats. I've been seeing this sort of stuff in places like the *New York Times Magazine* for months now

(What is it? The Russian look? The fellow traveler look? The Wobbly look?), and I expect to see more of it after *Reds* opens. Like *Annie Hall,* this movie is a valentine to Diane Keaton — and also a Diane Keaton fashion show. The clothes don't look quite appropriate to the era (1915–1920); they're a mite too chic. But *Reds* gets by with them anyway, because so much of it is set in a sort of boho never-never land, an aestheticized world of radicals and dilettantes and poets who whirl from Greenwich Village to Provincetown and then over to Petrograd for a spot of revolution, and back. The fashions — like Richard Sylbert's wonderfully detailed sets and Vittorio Storaro's deep-hued photography — are part of the come-on, the sugar coating. How else are you going to get people to see a three-and-a-quarter-hour movie about left-wing intellectuals of the early twentieth century?

Produced, directed, and cowritten by Warren Beatty, *Reds* is undeniably entertaining. It may have cost $33 million, but it's no *Heaven's Gate.* It's a little balancing trick, teetering between love story and hard-headed history, intimacy and spectacle, junk food and food for thought. And because it will satisfy nearly everybody in small ways, it winds up not giving anybody the deep, sonorous satisfaction of art. *Reds* is the grandest invention of Beatty's career. It's the fourth picture he's produced (the others were *Bonnie and Clyde, Shampoo,* and *Heaven Can Wait*), the third he's cowritten (*Shampoo* and *Heaven Can Wait*), and the very first he's directed all by himself. If you look to it for a glimpse of Beatty's soul, what you will see is a very careful, very calculating man — a man capable of polishing off a movie's rough edges until the thing suffocates in its own sawdust.

Reds is about leftist intellectuals, but they don't act like leftist intellectuals. They act like movie stars. Watching their glamorous lives, you feel as if you were flipping through a special bohemian edition of *People* magazine. Look, there's Emma Goldman (Maureen Stapleton), and here's Eugene O'Neill, and over there the Bolshie boys, Lenin and Trotsky. The movie begins in 1915, in Portland, where eminent journalist John Reed meets Louise Bryant (Keaton), the rebellious wife of a local dentist, and asks her to come to New York with him. There, in Greenwich Village, Reed shouts about how America shouldn't enter World War I because it's a war for the benefit of profiteers, not people. Goldman argues. Big Bill Haywood and Lincoln Steffens and Edna St. Vincent Millay are mentioned. It's a movable feast. And it moves to Provincetown, for parties, plays, and beach scenes, and an affair between Louise and O'Neill. To Croton-on-Hudson, where John and Louise marry, argue over extramarital hanky-panky, and split up. To the Eastern front, and then to Russia, where the revolution becomes the occasion for John and Louise's reunion. George Plimpton, the dapper editor of the *Paris Review,* shows up as Horace Whigham, the dapper editor of *Metropolitan* magazine. Gene Hackman suddenly bursts into the movie as a crusty newspaper editor, and for a few minutes, *Reds* shivers and smokes. The saturnine novelist Jerzy Kosinski appears as the saturnine Bolshevik Grigory Zinoviev. This is a movie for autograph hounds and rubberneckers; it makes austere eggheads like Goldman palatable by telling us that they were the Beautiful People of their day.

And in what turns out to be a master stroke, Beatty has decorated the outlines of his picture with a slew of real-life lefties — elders whom he calls the Witnesses and who show up intermittently, like a Greek chorus, to comment on the action. We glimpse them one at a time, their heads artfully posed against a black background, telling us they remember John Reed, or don't, or do but only vaguely. Some of them have died since the filming began — Henry Miller, for instance, and George Jessel — and since none of them is identified, the Witness sequences turn into a sort of highbrow guessing game. Perhaps one recognizes Adela Rogers St. John as the old woman whose face has become so intricately wrinkled that it actually looks quilted. Perhaps we recognize tart-tongued Rebecca West. But which one of these ancients is Will Durant? Or Hamilton Fish? Name that Commie.

At first, the movie's timing seems way off. When in recent American history have intellectuals been less popular — let alone Communists? *Reds* often seems as if it were trying to be a *Doctor Zhivago* for smart people, but *Zhivago,* which was about the loves of a poet, was made in 1965, when America was in a very poetic mood. And times have changed. Then, America was wealthy, booming, a nation of liberals, a nation that could afford to be generous, contemplative, abstract. We thought about things. We thought we might soon eradicate poverty. We thought we might soon unite the races. We thought we might soon fly to the moon — and we did. But in times of scarcity and recession, the airy play of thoughts is always the first luxury to go. We still have our intellectual heroes, but they're not the visionaries and philosophers and poets of the sixties. They're hardheads, fact compilers, analysts. Where once we looked to Buckminster Fuller, Marshall McLuhan, and, I suppose, Bob Dylan, now we look to economists, TV producers, diet doctors — Blondie. Now the air has hardened, and revolution seems a fondly remembered pipe dream.

It was in the days of the pipe dream that Warren Beatty began working on the idea of a movie about John Reed, the radical journalist who witnessed the Russian revolution, wrote *Ten Days That Shook the World,* helped found the Communist Labor party, and died in Moscow at the age of thirty-three. Had Beatty managed to make *Reds* then, it might have been a tale of triumph. Now, a decade later, it's a story for lapsed liberals and disillusioned hippies, for the flower children who became the fern-bar children. *Reds* is about nice, presentable intellectuals who are engaged in a Great Mistake. It pretends to celebrate Reed, but it doesn't celebrate anything he believed in; his passion for revolution is seen as a form of naive adventurousness. He's always off getting into some tussle over workers' rights or something, when he should be at home, tending to his stormy marriage. Leftist politics turns him into a fool, ruins his poetry, blinds him. We watch him splinter the American Communist party into weak, disorganized factions. We watch him become the dupe of double-talking Bolshevik leaders like Zinoviev. And gradually, we watch him become disillusioned with the Soviet cause. But these developments are so wispy, and the movie comments on them so vaguely, that we come away tutting indulgently. Oh, the poor, handsome, lovable fool. At least in the end, he admits he's been wrong. Lying on his deathbed in Moscow, he tells Louise that he wants to go home—he's like a pinko Dorothy longing for Kansas. All of which makes it clear that *Reds*'s appeal may be a lot broader than you'd think. For American liberals, curled up in unsavory corners licking their wounds, this movie says, "Yes, the sixties revolution, like the Russian revolution, was a dream, but it was a noble dream, dreamt by noble, good-looking—and remarkably well-dressed—people. So don't feel so bad." And for supply-siders, trickle-downers, and other assorted Reaganites, *Reds* offers a conciliatory message. These hoity-toity intellectuals were never as smart as they thought they were, but now they know they were wrong, and they're sorry, and it's time to forgive and forget. *Reds* may be set seventy-five years ago, but it's got the temper of the eighties down cold.

It's been beautifully edited—by Dede Allen and Craig McKay—and so it zips along like a sleigh ride. And Storaro's cinematography is magnificent. There's a kind of dusty, interior light in some of the crowd scenes that seems peculiarly American, like the thick browns in a painting by George Bellows or Thomas Hart Benton. In the Russian scenes, the colors turn to pewter and iron, and in a gorgeous but confused sequence set in embattled Baku (in southern Russia), there's an explosion of desert light, of dark Arabian faces under white turbans and wildly colorful effigies of John Bull and Uncle Sam. Here we see the first actual fighting of the revolution: Cannons fire and a pair of horses tumble like twin pinwheels. And amid the smoke, you catch the glints of blades and buckles and White Russian uniforms. In the Baku sequence, Reed leaves his comrades to chase after a cannon cart, and we don't know what's happening to him or why, but Storaro somehow makes the burst of colors speak for his disillusionment; it's as though he were suddenly seeing the subtle, in-between shades that his dogmatism had hidden from him.

And yet, for all that, *Reds* has no style. Beatty skips glancingly over everything—heated political dialogues, strikes, even the revolution itself—and when he wants to build, he doesn't intensify, he repeats. In the Greenwich Village sequences, he and cowriter Trevor Griffiths ought to give us a big, rich pirouetting scene that penetrates the leftist milieu. Instead, we get snippets: a snatch or two from a party, shots of dancing, a line or two in a bar, more dancing, a brief look at a rally, more dancing. Love is signified by lots of beach scenes, revolution by parades, a long night by lots of shots of coffee being poured. The movie is a succession of flurries, and Reed's life never acquires any weight. You feel as though you were watching one of those tricks from a thirties movie, where the pages from a calendar blow by to signify the passage of time.

Listening to the screenplay, you can hear how daunted Beatty and Griffiths must have been by their subject. Reed's life was so huge, so complicated, the characters come at us in shorthand. Everybody gets a characteristic line. People ask Louise what she does, and she always says, "I write," and from that we're meant to envision the spectrum of her ambitions, her pretensions, her insecurities. Reed's line is, "The taxi's waiting," because he's, you know, always on the go. O'Neill is less subtle; when he enters a room, he invariably mutters, "Where's the whiskey?" Sometimes the code comes from other movies; in fact, *Reds* putters down so many familiar roads, you may want Dramamine. I couldn't believe it when Reed was about to head back to Russia and Louise blinked back the tears and sputtered, "If you go, I'm not sure I'll be here when you get back." No one can bring off an old croak like that one. The lines are stuffed, and their cadences are too long because the screenwriters are trying to cram too much information into them. Only Jack Nicholson, wearing a thin, nasty mustache, plays them right, because for once he underplays. Slithering into each scene as if he intended to wind himself around someone's leg, he makes O'Neill such a tense, insinuating viper that every word has an extra twist. In *Reds,* O'Neill seems a man who could never find enough words for all the shades of meaning in his head.

In Beatty's performance, there are no shades. He's always been best at playing a heedless beauty, a troubled, inarticulate soul who's blind to the harm he does and sensitive only to his own pain. He's perfect for the scenes of Reed's disillusionment in Russia, but there are times when the movie wants him to seem heroic, decisive, and deeply committed, and Beatty's hurt, blinking eyes and halting gestures never convey determination or strength of will. This movie needs a strong John Reed the way the bits of a collage need glue, and it doesn't have one. What it has is Diane Keaton. Her Louise is smart, sexy, and a bit of a poseur, an early prototype of the flapper who likes to shock and yet wants to be taken seriously — and can't see why the one should interfere with the other. Keaton has never been an actorish actress. Her technique may flag or even disappear, but she burbles along on an amateur's energy. It's a great approach to comedy, because she's so limpid you can see right through her; you get two incongruous performances at once, the inner one and the outer one. But in drama, Keaton's been pallid and strained. This is the first time she's harnessed that self-consciousness and vitality of hers to a dramatic role, and it works because Louise herself is a self-conscious amateur: a pretender with something real beneath the pretense. In *Reds,* Keaton looks bunny-cute at one moment and ravaged and wrinkly the next, and when Reed is trapped in a Finnish prison and Louise decides to rescue him, her courage comes shooting out from beneath her flapper airs like fireworks.

That attempted rescue, which is one of the few parts of *Reds* invented from whole cloth, is the center of the movie. It's Lara running toward Zhivago across the snowy wastes, and it reeks of dramatic contrivance. *Reds* may need its love story (it needs *something* to pull you in), but you can't help wincing at the way the romance trivializes Reed's life and thoughts — and, conveniently, his leftist leanings. Here we are in the midst of the Russian revolution; the Winter Palace is in disarray; crowds march through the streets; history is being wrenched from its path — and what we're worried about is whether Louise will let Reed sleep with her that night. You understand why there have to be cuddly little scenes with John making a mess in the kitchen and Louise outside the door yelling the day's political news — but you can't help wishing these intimate little nothings would just go away, because they're such transparent "touches," and even if you've never seen them before, they feel like clichés.

Still, *Reds* never strikes one as being quite so superficial as it is, because Beatty and Griffiths have enough time to flash *everything* at us: Reed's views on the war, the complexities of the power struggle within the Socialist party — everything. There are details here that the story doesn't require — Reed's kidney operation, for instance — and they're there for a very simple reason: because they really happened. All of which gives *Reds* a special texture, the texture of an educational experience. Those Witnesses we see have the sort of faces and voices we associate with documentaries like *The Wobblies* or *Free Voice of Labor: The Jewish Anarchists,* and even if some of them had very little to do with Reed and his circumstances, they make you hang onto this movie in an unusual way — you feel as though there were something to learn from them. But in the end, their authenticity is like a reproach; it exposes Beatty's glibness. Somehow, even if all the facts about Reed are in place, we can see that he hasn't given us the truth in *Reds,* that amid the glitzy fashions and dazzling stars, his art has become tarnished. Someone, someday, could make a great movie about John Reed. But you can't make a great movie about anything if you aren't willing to risk your place in the pages of *People* magazine for it.

Boston Phoenix, December 1, 1981

UNDER FIRE

Pauline Kael

In the opening scenes of *Under Fire,* rebel soldiers in Chad are trying to move a caravan of elephants carrying crates of weapons across a patch of open field, and Nick Nolte, as Russell Price, a photojournalist, trots alongside, snapping pictures of the ponderous beasts and the drivers sitting way on top of them and their freight. Suddenly, a helicopter gunship appears, blasting, and the scene turns into a horrifying shambles of elephants running and men shot down as they scurry for the bush. Wherever he is, the big, blond Russell Price goes on taking pictures. He is covered with cameras; they're his only luggage, and they swing as he moves. He switches from one to the other, and with each small click of the shutter we see — in a freeze-frame that is held for just an instant — what he has shot. The director, Roger Spottiswoode, a Canadian-born Englishman who's thirty-eight now, began working in London studios at nineteen and already had several years of experience, including work as an editor on Sam Peckinpah's *Straw Dogs,* when he came to live in this country, in 1971. He edited two more Peckinpah films and Walter Hill's *Hard Times,* worked with Karel Reisz, first as editor, then as second-unit director and associate producer, and also wrote the first draft of *48 Hrs.* before he got a chance to direct (with *Terror Train* and *The Pursuit of D. B. Cooper*). He was ready — maybe more than ready — for *Under Fire.* It has been made with breathtaking skill. Price's photographs — those freeze-frames, most of them in black-and-white, some in color, and each with its small, staccato click — fix the faces, the actions, the calamities in our memories, and the film is so cleanly constructed that they have a percussive effect. They're what *Under Fire* is about.

When Price hitches a ride on a truck carrying rebel troops out of the area, he's not the only American (or the only blond) among the black men. Oates (Ed Harris), a mercenary with the grin of a happy psychopath, sits among the rebels thinking he's among the soldiers of the government that's paying him. Price sets him straight, and he chuckles; he doesn't care who he kills anyway — it's his sport. When Price gets back to his hotel, the foreign press corps — which includes Claire (Joanna Cassidy), a radio reporter who is just breaking up with her lover, Alex (Gene Hackman), and Alex himself, a celebrated war correspondent and Price's closest friend — is preparing to move on to the next big trouble spot, Nicaragua. And we realize that what we have seen is, essentially, the prologue. But we have already grasped the most important thing about Price, who risks his carcass as a matter of course: He's an image man. And, seeing through his eyes as he clicks the shutter, we intuitively recognize how good he is at what he does. There's a purity about his total absorption in images. Price doesn't even have to do the kind of interpretation that the reporters do; he doesn't have to try to make sense of things. Nolte's loping, athletic grace as he moves alongside fighting men adds to the feeling we get that Price is an artist and an automaton, too. His whole body is tuned up for those clicks. He couldn't explain why he shoots when he does; he simply *knows.* And Nolte has what is perhaps an accidental asset for the role: His eyes are narrowed, as if by a lifetime of squinting through cameras, and his eyelids look callused.

It doesn't take long to grasp that Price and Claire and Alex regard their lack of involvement in what they cover as part of being professionals. They are observers, not participants, and they're proud of it. It's the essence of their personal dash and style—the international form of the swaggering cynicism of *The Front Page.* They all risk their lives with a becoming carelessness. But that's almost the only thing they have in common with the heroes and heroines of old Hollywood movies. One conspicuous difference is that they're grown-up people in their forties; Alex may even be fifty.

The movie is set in 1979, during the last days of the rule of General Anastasio Somoza, the dictator-president whose family was put in power and kept there by the United States. And in a sense the Sandinist revolution—the imagery of it—is the star. This is trompe-l'oeil moviemaking, with Mexican locations in Oaxaca and Chiapas dressed up in the shantytown building material of Nicaragua (uncut beer-can sheets), and the political graffiti and the pulsing, hot colors—turquoise and flaming pink. The young Sandinistas who dart through the streets in striped T-shirts, with bright handkerchiefs masking their faces, have the street-theatre look that is so startling in the book *Nicaragua,* Susan Meiselas's 1981 collection of photographs of the insurrection. Spottiswoode knows not to make realism drab; there's dust and anger everywhere, but the country is airy and alive with color. Produced at a cost of $8.5 million (Nolte and Hackman worked for much less than their usual fees) and with only fifty-seven shooting days, the film is a beautiful piece of new-style classical moviemaking; everything is thought out and prepared, but it isn't explicit, it isn't labored, and it certainly isn't overcomposed. No doubt the cinematographer John Alcott, whose speed is turning him into a legend—he's the man who doesn't bother with light meters, he just looks at the back of his hand—gave it its tingling visual quality. The dialogue is exciting, too. The script, by Ron Shelton, working from a first draft by Clayton Frohman, is often edgy and maliciously smart. Terry Southern at his peak did no better than the lines Shelton has written for Richard Masur as Somoza's American publicity expert—the man trying to improve Somoza's "image"—as he offers condolences to the lover of a correspondent murdered by Somoza's troops: "Jesus Christ, a human tragedy. What can I say?" (Shelton was a professional baseball player for some time; he has been writing scripts for three or four years, but except for some rewrite work he did on *D. B. Cooper,* this is the first to be filmed.) What gives the movie its distinction is that the articulate, sophisticated characters don't altogether dominate the imagery. The Nicaraguans (some of them played by Mexicans, others by Nicaraguan refugees in Mexico) aren't there just to supply backgrounds for the stars.

With its concentration on the journalists — the outsiders — *Under Fire* is a little like Peter Weir's *The Year of Living Dangerously,* but visually and in its romantic revolutionary spirit it's more like the Cuban scenes in *The Godfather Part II* and Gillo Pontecorvo's *The Battle of Algiers* and *Burn!* Spottiswoode isn't inflammatory in the way that Pontecorvo is, but in his more subdued impassioned manner he presents the case for the 1979 revolution — the one that the United States government has been trying to undo by backing the insurgents known as contras or anti-Sandinistas. (I assume that the title of the film comes from the words of Augusto César Sandino, the leader of a peasant army, who was murdered in 1934: "It is better to die as rebels under fire than to live as slaves.")

The revolutionaries, with their poetic peasant faces, are presented in a grand, naive, idealized movie tradition. Anger doesn't make the Sandinistas mean or violent, and there's no dissension among them. (It's how we want to think revolutionaries are.) They don't have any visible connections to the Communist powers, either. Even so, this is one of the most intelligently constructed political movies I've ever seen. Its fictional inventions serve a clear purpose. Although the Sandinistas have always been led by a group, the story posits a single leader — Rafael — who gives the people hope. Rafael is featured in the graffiti — his face is the emblem of the revolution — but he has never been photographed, and the story involves the attempt of Price and Claire to find him, and the various forces that manipulate them before and after their search. One of these forces is a wily Frenchman, Jazy, who works for the CIA, and, as played by Jean-Louis Trintignant, he's a suave, lecherous imp. You know he's a dangerous little sleazo (he says he works for everybody, and he probably does), but he's also knowledgeable and witty. And when Somoza's men throw Price in the clink "for taking too many pictures" and kick him around, it's Jazy — a pal of Somoza's — who gets him released. Jazy is the kind of pal of Somoza's who amuses himself with Somoza's leggy young mistress, Miss Panama (Jenny Gago). The General himself is played by René Enriquez (of "Hill Street Blues"), who in fact is a Nicaraguan and was acquainted with Somoza. His performance is a finely nuanced caricature: This teddy-bear Somoza deludes himself that he's an aristocrat with thousands of years of tradition behind him. He has perfected a form of infantilism — he sees only what he wants to see and hears only what he wants to hear. He's so locked in himself he's like a product of inbreeding — a genetic idiot who thinks he's a grandee.

The corrupt environment creates tensions in the gentle, affable Price: anger at the way Somoza's bullies treated him, and a deeper anger at the way they brutalized the priest he shared a cell with. And something happens that upsets him so much that, photogenic as it is, he momentarily forgets to take a picture. When he and Claire are on one of their trips trying to find Rafael and are being escorted by Sandinistas, he sees the mercenary Oates hiding. Oates is out of his skull; he's an obscenity. (He stands in for all the mercenaries running loose in Third World countries.) But Price, being a journalist and regarding himself as "neutral," doesn't reveal Oates's presence. Then, as he and Claire are walking along and talking to their young Sandinista guide — who wears a Baltimore Orioles cap, because the Nicaraguan Dennis Martinez is on the team — Oates kills the kid. It's a spiteful, show-offy murder, and Price knows he could have prevented it. He's sickened; he's full of grief and disgust. It's Claire (whom he loves) who points out to him that he didn't take a picture; the artist-automaton broke down and behaved humanly, and that night is their first together.

When Price and Claire reach Rafael's hiding place and Price is asked to perform a crucial service for the rebels, he is emotionally prepared. He is asked to fake a photograph for them, and he does it, though this is a betrayal of his art and, if it becomes known, will almost inevitably wreck his reputation. Events then move very quickly. Shortly afterward, Price discovers that a whole series of photographs he took (just for himself) of the unmasked Sandinistas at Rafael's headquarters have been stolen and are being used by the demented mercenary Oates — a one-man hit squad — to identify the rebel leaders. Even Price's pure images are being polluted; they're being used every which way. They're marking his subjects for extinction.

Before Price came to Nicaragua, he was an overgrown small boy playing with what he loved to do: take pictures. (And this is why Nolte is a perfect choice for the role. He can be dumb, unthinking, oxlike, yet with a controlling intelligence and a central sweetness and decency.) In Nicaragua, where somebody's using you all the time, Price is in a new situation. Detachment can have hideous results, as he saw when the Orioles lover was killed. Whatever Price's misgivings as a professional photojournalist with a reputation for integrity, and whatever the effects of the action on his future, when he fakes the picture to help the Sandinistas he isn't destroyed by doing it — he's humanized. He is letting himself be governed by his own core of generosity. These are the terms of the movie, in which Price the photojournalist is a metaphor for the movie director. Making movies, this picture says, isn't about purity. It's about trying to suggest the living texture in which people make choices that may — from an academic point of view — appear unethical, crazy, wrong.

The movie fills our heads with images of people under fire. There are terrified peasants and Somoza's equally terrified national guardsmen — probably peasant boys who signed up because they were hungry. At one point, Price and Claire are in a car in a provincial town, and the driver panics when guardsmen direct him to stop; he backs up, and, with guardsmen firing at them, Price and Claire jump out into the street and try to hide. There's not much sense to anything that happens during the insurrection. Peasants in dirt streets stare at a shiny big automobile in flames. Refugees in the provincial city of León mill in the streets trying to escape the national guardsmen who are shooting at them, and they're simultaneously attacked by planes. In some neighborhoods of Managua, guardsmen fire into the flimsy beer-can shacks, and shoot everything in the streets that moves — even squealing pigs. It's in this sequence that the movie reenacts the 1979 killing of Bill Stewart, the ABC correspondent, at a national-guard checkpoint in Managua. After kneeling and holding his hands out, to show that he had no weapons, Stewart was told to lie down, with his arms over his head, and was then — for no particular reason — shot, while his cameraman went on photographing the scene. I hadn't been aware of how that footage had stayed in the back of my head for four years, but at the movie, as soon as I saw the guardsmen standing there in the street, and saw one of the characters mosey up to them to ask directions, I knew what was coming; Stewart's death was still so vivid that this reenactment almost seemed to be in slow motion, and, with Price's shutter-click frozen frames, in a sense it was. The killing has an eerie inevitability about it. *Under Fire* isn't just reproducing a famous incident here, it's making us conscious of the images we've got stored up. It brings the Nicaragua of countless news stories right to the center of our consciousness. We knew more about the place than we thought we did. And Jerry Goldsmith's spare, melodic score (one of the best movie scores I've ever heard) features a bamboo flute from the Andes with a barely perceptible electronic shadow effect — a melancholy sound that takes you back. It tugs at your memories.

There's a good reason, I think, for the use of grown-up people as the principal characters. These grown-ups aren't surprised or scandalized by what they see, and their lack of surprise is part of the unusual quality of *Under Fire*. There's no gee-whizz acting. After Hackman's Alex—who has been "hanging in there" with Claire, hoping she'll change her mind about wanting her freedom—decides to head back to the States and take the anchorman's job he has been offered, Claire says good-bye to him and watches as he goes off in the taxi that's taking him to the airport. Partway down the street, Alex sees Price walking up; he jumps out, and they hug each other. As he goes off again in the cab, Claire and Price both stand watching as it becomes smaller down the street and heads toward the hill in the distance. It's a beautiful shot, and expressive, too, because nobody (the audience least of all) wants Hackman to go. He's totally believable as a network's choice for anchorman—it's the quality in him that makes him so valuable to the movie (and picks up its energy level when he returns). Hackman seems leaner here than in his last films, and he's faster—he's on the balls of his feet. As the famous Alex, he maintains a surface jauntiness—he's professionally likable. But Alex has ideas ricocheting in his head, and whether he's sitting down at the piano in a Managua night club and singing or just basking in his celebrity he's never unaware of what's going on around him. He's always sizing things up—taking mental notes. He has an expansiveness about him; he's full of life (the way Jack Warden was in *Shampoo*). The three major characters have to be people who have been around, because outrage is not the motivating emotion of *Under Fire,* as it was in, say, Costa-Gavras's *Missing.* Spottiswoode and Shelton may be appalled, but they're not shocked. And they're not interested in presenting characters going through the usual virgin indignation. The United States has been setting up or knocking down Nicaraguan governments since 1909; the movie can hardly pretend to be showing us things we don't—at some level—already know. *Under Fire* is about how you live with what you know.

Joanna Cassidy, who has the pivotal role, is a stunning woman with a real face, and as Claire she has a direct look—the kind of look that Claire Bloom's characters have sometimes turned on people, and that Jane Fonda has had in her best roles. Joanna Cassidy is tall (Trintignant looks really petite when he's next to her), and as Claire she has the strength of a woman who's had to set her jaw and keep her smile for long stretches. Claire has had to be tough, and toughness deeply offends her. She has been struggling to keep some softness. The film catches her at a key time in her physical development. Running through the streets, she moves with extraordinary grace, and you certainly know why Price takes pictures of her sleeping nude. But her job has yielded her everything that it's going to. She has an almost grown-up daughter, whom she talks to on the phone and on tapes—she would like to be with her. This is a time in her life when doubts have settled in. The foreign press corps, like the mercenaries, jump from one chaos to the next; they go where the armaments shipments are going. They keep the people at home "informed," but to the people they descend on they must seem like powerful celebrities who could change things if they would just tell "the truth." Claire is doing her job almost automatically now, and her mind has a roving eye. When Price's automatic-response system fails him—when he doesn't take a picture of the dead kid right next to him—it's a change in him she can respond to. None of this is spelled out for us; it's all there in Joanna Cassidy's performance and in Nolte's response to her physical presence. As Price, he doesn't use the low, growling voice that he had in *48 Hrs.,* and his beefiness is all sensitivity. Nolte never lets you see how he gets his effects. His big, rawboned body suggests an American workingman jock, but he uses his solid flesh the way Jean Gabin did: he inhabits his characters. He's such a damned good actor that he hides inside them. That's *his* sport.

I have been wondering why some members of the press show so little enthusiasm for this picture. (It certainly couldn't be more timely.) Possibly the movie ladles too much guilt on journalists. (The mercenary who has been poisoning Price's life bids him a cheery farewell—"See you in Thailand.") But I can think of only a few scenes that aren't brought off and only one that's clumsily staged: the last appearance of Trintignant's fascinatingly crisscrossed Jazy. Three frightened young Sandinistas who have come to his house to kill him wait around while he explains his political rationale to Price—his fear of the future Communist takeover. I think there's something in *Under Fire* that's bugging the press the way it was bugged a couple of years ago by *Absence of Malice.* Price's faking the photograph and accepting the penalties that will follow may be bewildering to the run of journalists who make decisions about what to report on the basis of their own convenience and advantage all the time. Since they do it unconsciously, they can easily be aroused to indignation at Price's conscious act. Maybe they know that they wouldn't do what he does, and they think that that means he's morally inferior to them. And maybe, like other professional groups, they don't like movies about them that don't glorify them.

Spottiswoode could be a trace too sane; the actors go as far as they can with what they've got to work with, but possibly he doesn't go quite far enough (and neither, possibly, does the script). Spottiswoode doesn't have the wild, low cunning that the great scenes in Peckinpah's films have — he doesn't spook us. But he does everything short of that. In its sheer intelligence and craft this is a brilliant movie.

The New Yorker, October 31, 1983

UNDER FIRE

Richard Schickel

A freelance photographer is covering a revolutionary war in the Third World. Among his many expectations of discomfort, danger, and the constant threat of death, he dares harbor only one decent hope: that in some unlikely 250th or 500th of a second his shutter will open and shut and almost by accident freeze an image that will make some human sense out of the anguish to which he is the world's paid witness.

A post-Hemingway adventurer like Russell Price (Nick Nolte) does not, of course, permit himself to articulate such aspiring thoughts. With his thick voice, his beefy former jock's build, and his wary-passive manner, Nolte plays Price (very authentically) as a man who is all reflexes of the single-lens variety. The big picture in Nicaragua, as the Somoza regime yields to the Sandinistas in 1979, means little to Price, who is portrayed as being on assignment for *Time;* he is more concerned with the succession of little money-makers he must try to capture as they flee past his viewfinder. It is the business of the film to arrange a not entirely persuasive series of events that shatter Price's illusions about the power of objectivity to defend itself when political passion is afire. The rebels want him to fake a picture that will aid their cause; the government points him toward their secret base hoping some of his other pictures will help it identify the state's enemies.

To its credit, *Under Fire* does advance sensible arguments for letting history, not the correspondents on the scene, judge the ultimate meaning and morality of political events. But ironically it is the senseless death of the newsman who expresses these sentiments (Gene Hackman in a well-judged performance, not too cynical, not too idealistic) that turns Price into a Sandinista sympathizer. He takes with him into the rebel camp the newswoman both men love. And since Joanna Cassidy brings such attractive intelligence to her role, one's first impulse is to accept without protest the film's ambiguous climax.

But *Under Fire* is as duplicitous as it is busy. It has been sneaking in this direction from the beginning, showing all government figures as almost comically dumb and decadent, all rebels as rather decent sorts. One wishes it would state its sympathies openly, and perhaps allow Price to assert his craftsman's integrity and his disgust with everybody who wants to turn his camera into a deadly weapon. But that assertion requires an ability to make fine judgments and take a long view that no one, except the actors, has brought to the enterprise. Without a sufficient measure of authority, *Under Fire* ends up as a movie too pleased with its own intellectual bravado.

Time, November 7, 1983

CRY FREEDOM

Kathleen Carroll

In his celebrated epic, *Gandhi,* Richard Attenborough explored the life of Mohandas Gandhi, who developed his philosophy of nonviolence while living in South Africa. In *Cry Freedom,* his bold anti-apartheid movie, the Academy Award–winning director returns to the country that first aroused Gandhi's political conscience. And his hero is again a real-life political martyr, Bantu Stephen Biko, a moderate young leader of the Black Consciousness Movement, who died in prison in 1977 following a brutal interrogation by South Africa's Security Police.

The true story of Biko's death would not have been known had it not been for a white liberal named Donald Woods. A well-to-do newspaper editor, he lived in a tranquil suburb, in a luxurious home, his contact with black South Africa mainly limited to conversations with his maid. Then he met Biko and their subsequent friendship so alarmed the Pretoria government that Woods was eventually declared a banned person, a form of house arrest that is meant to silence opponents of apartheid. Despite the ever-watchful police, Woods escaped, and chose a life of exile so that he could tell the world what had happened.

Like *The Killing Fields, Cry Freedom* traces the political awakening of a journalist forced to confront government-sponsored terrorism. The movie begins with a horrifying, brilliantly edited montage that plunges you right into the middle of Crossroads, a black shanty settlement, as police—with their attack dogs and their raised clubs—charge into the shacks, and black men are shoved into vans, while a newscaster reports that "the illegals voluntarily presented themselves to the police." The movie ends just as powerfully with a replay of the Soweto children's march, which turned into a massacre, followed by a terse list of all those who have died in South African jails under mysterious circumstances.

The main body of the movie is, by contrast, somewhat talky and sluggish. The script tends to oversimplify the political situation. Denzel Washington is touchingly dignified as the articulate Biko, but the movie fails to show his human side. The white South Africans generally behave like thugs, while the head of the security police is a devious villain who—and this actually happened—confides to the press that "Biko's death leaves me cold." The last half of the movie, which deals with Woods's escape, is riveting. Kevin Kline is extremely engaging as Woods, whose family is subjected to vicious harassment. It's also impossible to resist the African music, which stirs the heart while this potent film succeeds in swaying the mind.

New York Daily News, November 6, 1987

CRY FREEDOM

Stephen Schiff

You can sense it when a director makes up his mind to manufacture an Oscar winner—an unsightly swelling sets in. His vehicle is generally a fat literary adaptation or a Broadway smash or the biography of a martyr. The budget is obscene, the production lengthy and embattled. When audiences come, they come dutifully, and when the Oscars come, they are greeted the way Richard Attenborough greeted his 1982 Best Picture accolade for *Gandhi:* "It's not me . . . you truly honor," he told the yawning zillions. "You honor Mahatma Gandhi and his plea to all of us to live in peace."

The nauseating truth is that he was right. Five years later, no one is reviving *Gandhi;* no one rents the videotape; no critic calls a new movie the best goldarn such and such since *Gandhi. Gandhi* is remembered, if at all, as a good cause, not a good film. And when bad movies happen to good causes, where does that leave the good causes? In the case of *Gandhi* or John Sayles's tedious *Matewan* or a dozen others, it doesn't matter much: Those movies genuflect in the general direction of sweetness and light without rubbing against anything very urgent. But Attenborough's new two-and-a-half-hour epic is different. *Cry Freedom,* for which the appropriate Oscars are already being dusted off, is about the South African crisis. The events it chronicles—the death of the black-consciousness leader Stephen Biko and the flight from South Africa of the white newspaper editor Donald Woods— are only a decade old and the horrors they emblemize still very much with us. We badly need an incendiary, high-profile movie about South Africa, but will audiences line up for more than one? Polished and suspenseful though it is, *Cry Freedom* is a flaccid piece of filmmaking; it ruins a great movie subject for everybody.

Biko alone would have made for a terrific movie: the charismatic black student leader who became an anti-apartheid martyr when, at the age of thirty, he was imprisoned, beaten until comatose, and then trucked seven hundred miles to the police hospital in Pretoria, where he died. (The Ministry of Police blamed his demise on a hunger strike.) The superb American actor Denzel Washington does for Biko a bit of what Ben Kingsley did for Gandhi. He conveys something charged and mysterious behind the eyes, as though some inner factory were crackling away back there, converting reservoirs of violence and rage into the magnetic virtue of the crusader. Wearing a goatee and straggly shreds of sideburn, Washington has somehow managed to make his squarish face look heart shaped, the way Biko's was; his teeth are fetchingly choppy, and the voice that emerges from between them has a low, musical tang. Like Kingsley's performance before it, Washington's has its own private rhythm; if this were really a movie about Stephen Biko, he might have saved it. But it's not.

It's about Donald Woods (played by Kevin Kline), who met Biko in 1975, was radicalized by him, and, from his powerful position as editor of the *Daily Dispatch,* set about antagonizing the South African government. Shortly after Biko's death, Woods was banned—that is, legally isolated. A banned South African (Biko was one from 1973 until his death in 1977) is not permitted to be in a room with more than one other person at a time, is forbidden to write, to be quoted, to leave the district in which he resides, to enter printing or publishing premises or factories or schools. He is under the surveillance of the South African Security Police, and if he is still deemed a menace after the usual five-year sentence, he may be banned again. Cut off from his job, Woods secretly began writing a book about Biko, and when he realized what trouble its publication would get him in, he determined to leave the country. On New Year's Eve 1977, he disguised himself as a priest and fled to Lesotho; his wife and five children followed the next day. They now live in England, where *Biko* was published in 1978.

☆

Woods was an active part of the South African struggle for about two years; Biko lived that struggle for the better part of his life, and is still remembered as one of its central figures. The movie treats Woods's evacuation as an act of sacrifice and heroism tantamount to Biko's own. Actually, it was one of many such escapes in the wake of Biko's death—escapes that played into the hands of the Afrikaner Nationalist government, leaving the anti-apartheid movement hobbled and in disarray for years. Woods cannot be accused of cowardice, but his is the tale of an observer, not a major participant. Attenborough's decision to focus on a white newspaperman comes to seem a failure of imagination and nerve: It's as though he couldn't rely on us to swallow Biko straight, as though he couldn't trust our compassion to encompass black anguish. He needed a honkie hero.

This tactic looks particularly grotesque in light of the movie's own rhetoric. "I just think," Biko tells Woods, "that a white liberal who clings to all the advantages of his white world—jobs, housing, education, and Mercedes—is perhaps not the person best qualified to tell blacks how they should react to apartheid." Nor, one might add, is he the person best qualified to represent South Africa's victims; *Cry Freedom* reminds me of the argument that everybody should start caring about AIDS sufferers because heterosexuals are getting it too. The movie's rhetoric comes at you in gushes, in cataracts, in big, foamy waves. Scene after scene finds Biko walking Woods through black townships and community clinics, spouting deep truths—"The only history we read was made by the white man, written by the white man"; "I just expect to be treated like you expect to be treated"; "We are in the struggle to kill the idea that one kind of man is superior to another kind of man" — while Woods nods piously or stares thunderstruck: Jeez, why didn't he think of that before? We Americans are luckier, of course — we already know all this stuff from Peter, Paul, and Mary albums. In *Cry Freedom,* you'll find only the wispiest hints of the real complexities in the South African struggle — of the government's perfidious use of the "homelands," of the conflict within the Black Nationalist movement, of the friction between the country's 1.5 million English inhabitants and its 3 million Afrikaners. Nothing is dramatized when it can be preached at us, and most of the preaching is done by Biko. He isn't a character, he's a mouthpiece.

☆

As Woods, Kevin Kline gives a restrained, earnest performance; he seems terribly awed. On the stage, he can be an enthralling actor, but on screen he's never found a role where he can do what he does best: leap and swashbuckle and make like Errol Flynn. So the movie dies about halfway through, when Biko does; the screenplay, however, gasses on. Its last fifty minutes busy themselves with Woods's escape, which is propelled by so much false suspense and trumped-up emotion that you can almost hear the wind being puffed into its ragged sails. There are at least five good-bye scenes, replete with quivering chins and bravely quelled tears. The screenwriter, John Briley (he won his Oscar for *Gandhi*), throws every conceivable obstacle in Woods's path — a recalcitrant wife (the real Wendy Woods was more fiercely radical than her husband), goats in the road, noisy music on the sound track — only to be undercut by Lesley Walker's messy editing, by flashbacks to Biko telling a white magistrate that Caucasians aren't really white, they're pink (did Pete Seeger sing that one?), and by the audience's dead certainty that Woods will live to tell the tale. Then, as our hero triumphs, Attenborough seems to have second thoughts; he can't end the movie on a note of uplift, can he? — not with millions still bleeding in South Africa. So we dolly in on Woods's face while he flashes back to the Soweto massacre of 1976. Students are beaten. Tiny children are shot. And we're left with the quintessential white-liberal sensation — we feel safe, but guilty about it.

It might be argued that when bad movies happen to good causes, not much harm is done. Simplistic rhetoric is preferable to silence, after all, and even a clumsy outcry against injustice is better than none.

But I'm not so sure. Consumers of daily newspapers and network news already have a more sophisticated view of the South African situation than the one this movie proffers, and for those who know nothing about such things, gulping down *Cry Freedom*'s blend of primer-grade history and white man's burden is like taking a little poison with your vitamin. The pill is awfully pretty. The cinematographer, *Gandhi*'s Ronnie Taylor (he won his Oscar, too), has lighted every shanty perfectly, every ravaged child just so. When the movie started, I gazed at the ramshackle Crossroads settlement it depicted, at the symmetry of the establishing shot and the subtlety of the blue grays in the hilly background, and I found myself sighing at the loveliness of it all. *Cry Freedom* has a kind of neocolonial enthusiasm for the picturesqueness of squalor. It's a postcard of misery, a snapshot from a tourist bus. Come April, I'd hate to see Richard Attenborough up there again, thanking suffering South Africa for getting him his Oscar.

Vanity Fair, December 1987

THE LAST TEMPTATION OF CHRIST

Michael Wilmington

Jesus Christ is the Lamb of Nazareth, the young Lion of Judea, the sufferer of Gethsemane, and the hero of Calvary. He begins a selfless crusade with a tiny band of devoted followers: Peter the rock, Thomas the doubter, Mary Magdalene the ex-whore, Judas the redheaded firebrand. He rages, suffers, laments, wars with the devil and his temptations, and finally clasps himself to God and ecstatically accepts his destiny as the savior of mankind.

This is the story Martin Scorsese tells in his film of the Nikos Kazantzakis novel *The Last Temptation of Christ.* In some ways, it's typical Scorsese material. He has often portrayed innocent or idealistic outsiders moving through a corrupt or menacing world, and here he shows the ultimate innocent, Christ (Willem Dafoe), moving through a bewildering maze of corruption, death, suffering, and seduction—to emerge, at the last, pure and triumphant.

Scorsese obviously loves Kazantzakis's novel and its subject, just as Kazantzakis obviously adored Christ. He's handled both book and subject with true reverence, keeping the form, translating the visual poetry, and preserving the tour-de-force trick philosophical ending: the last startling satanic temptation. His film is an act of devotion, both to Christianity and to Kazantzakis's special vision of it: one of the most intense and moving religious pictures made in America.

It's not an assault upon Christian values or beliefs, as its detractors claim, but an attempt to reconcile them with the attitudes and anxieties felt most keenly by unbelievers. The film—clearly labeled as a work of fiction and not an actual historical representation or adaptation of the Gospels—is an effort to make Christ real to audiences who might normally reject religious pictures out of hand.

People who go to this movie expecting a wild, sexy, blasphemous show will be disappointed; maybe they'll want their money back. Christ's divinity, virginity, purity, and Godhood are never questioned in *The Last Temptation*. The movie is not about any imagined sins of Jesus, but about his struggle and salvation.

The film is Martin Scorsese's supreme cinematic labor of love, an attempt at a poetic vision of Christ's passion aimed primarily at unbelievers: a mix of sophisticates, moralistic outsiders, and hip skeptics. All Scorsese's films have a religious underpinning, usually recognizably Catholic—although his gamy subject matter (outcasts, hoods, boxers, loners, rockers, outlaw groups) sometimes obscures this. And obviously, part of what fascinated him here was the possible similarities between Christ's apostles and the rootless urban loners of his other movies. But he's never before tapped a theme with such tragic or luminous dimensions, or worked with literary material as magnificent as Kazantzakis's.

For Kazantzakis—who wrote *The Last Temptation* in his late sixties at the end of an adventurous and tormented life—the crucial element in the story was the battle between flesh and spirit, between the two halves of Christ's dual nature: man and God. And unlike most writers who approach the Gospels, often assuming a spirit of sickly or pompous reverence, Kazantzakis imagined Christ's human side and the world around him with overpowering richness and intensity.

To make the spirit's triumph more meaningful, Kazantzakis hauntingly evoked the flesh: a world of blood and scorching sand, sweat and pungent tastes and odors, stark dreams and visions, lush fruits and stinging salt seas, dusty temples, odorous streets, hillsides aflame with flowers, terrifying violence, and wild, untrammeled sexuality. This is the quality Scorsese obviously loves: this fierce engagement with life, mingling with soaring spirituality.

And that's what he duplicates in his visual style: the raw, surging conflict between a savage world and a distant, pure ideal. It's the intensity that probably caught his imagination: The Judea and Galilee he shows here — shot in Morocco — have more immediacy, more boiling energy than practically any other biblical picture, including Pasolini's neorealist *The Gospel According to Saint Matthew*.

Against the primitive, jagged pulse of Peter Gabriel's score, the heat in this film seems almost cauterizing, the wind withering. When Scorsese shows nails driven into flesh, or depicts Christ's final agony, he doesn't use the distanced, fake-Renaissance awe of the usual movie crucifixion. Instead, his shots suggest the raw, hideous pain in a painting by Grünewald or Bosch.

The melancholy of Gethsemane has a redoubled force here. So does the awesome grandeur of Christ's last moments on the cross, as Kazantzakis reimagined them: when, in the twinkling of an eye, Satan tempts him one last time, deluding him with the vision of a normal married life, children, work, lassitude, old age. For Kazantzakis and Scorsese, the world is a place of such vibrant life and dangerous splendor that Christ's final victory is doubly awe-inspiring.

In the film, as in the novel, Judas Iscariot (Harvey Keitel) is the second key character: Jesus' flagellator, gadfly, and foil. He's a fiery rebel, an outlaw and Jewish guerrilla — raging against Jesus for not choosing violent revolution against their Roman oppressors. Judas, the man of action and ferocious hatred, the deadly idealist, may stand for another part of Kazantzakis's personality: the youthful attraction to Marxism and revolutionary politics that preceded his immersion in Buddhism, Nietzsche, the Greek classics, and finally Christianity.

It's here — not in the Christ–Mary Magdalene scene — that the film and book might rightly be accused of heresy. Kazantzakis cannot make Judas a villain. Instead he paints Jesus and Judas as conscious collaborators in Christ's final betrayal. Judas becomes Christ's dark emissary, and in the end his most faithful and self-sacrificing disciple, damning himself to trigger the machinery of salvation.

It's a key to the story's philosophical core: In the duality of man, everything has its place. Good and evil, dark and light, human and spiritual. Both sides are important; both sides feed each other. The bad, violent Judas is as vital to Christ as the sturdy Peter; the doubter Thomas as necessary as the dreamer Philip. Kazantzakis, a lover of all life, was no exclusivist or elitist, which is one reason he might be anathema to some Fundamentalists.

Keitel gives Judas a burry, smoky-eyed mean intensity: something like a Brooklyn Jewish zealot. But this anachronistic performance fits the movie. There's a social stylization here. The apostles all have lower-class American urban characteristics, while Pontius Pilate is played by David Bowie with the clipped, icy cuts of a British snob. Keitel is the most streetwise of them all. When he works with Dafoe's Jesus, his eyes have a wolfish, keen, fascinated glitter.

Dafoe's facial features, conversely, evoke the heartland: He's a native of Appleton, Wisconsin. Sometimes he vaguely suggests a more gnarled cousin of the American cinema's great unconscious Christ figure, James Dean, though he's more of a specialist in brooding villains. (Scorsese cast him after seeing his murderous counterfeiter in *To Live and Die in L.A.*) But Dafoe doesn't put any sinister glower into his role. He plays Jesus quietly, carefully, almost hesitantly. Goodness and spiritual anguish shine out of his eyes throughout, even in his most feverish, abandoned moments.

But the movie's most revolutionary performance — and its best — is Barbara Hershey's voluptuous, sad, desperate Mary Magdalene. It's fitting. Hershey was the film's original inspiration: She brought *The Last Temptation of Christ,* her favorite novel, to Scorsese in 1972, when she was twenty-four and they were making *Boxcar Bertha* together.

It's probably right that they waited. In 1972, Hershey was a sexy, rebellious teen queen; now she's coming off two successive Cannes Film Festival Best Actress awards. Her Magdalene is an incandescent performance, seething with the contradictions the book builds on: overpowering sensuality that yields to overpowering spirituality and self-abnegation.

The film has one major flaw: its language. Kazantzakis tried to translate Christ into his own terms — to portray experiences so scarring, visions so feverishly real, that the reader is drawn irresistibly into Christ's dilemma. And he described them in a rich, demotic Greek, drawing on the language of the peasantry: full of earthy, everyday metaphors, rather than the high-flown pseudo-poetic tropes of the academy.

Screenwriter Paul Schrader never gets a good equivalent for that demotic Greek, that peasant lyricism. He structures the script beautifully, but the dialogue is in a prosaic, flattened-out, modern urban vernacular: full of colloquialisms like "Give me a break" and "Beats me." Schrader's blunt words often rub abrasively against the impassioned, lovely images Scorsese has created; you almost wish he'd kept the lyrical dialogue in P. A. Bien's English translation instead of creating his own.

For Kazantzakis and Scorsese, it was necessary to make Christ real, to communicate the beauty and grandeur of his sacrifice: to experience the true exaltation of the idea of God-in-man and the redemption of man's sins by God. If Kazantzakis excelled, more than any other Christian writer, in the portrayal of that sin, that agony — if, in reading him, or in watching the film, we feel the joys and anguish of the flesh with a special intensity — it is a talent for which he, and now the film, pays bitterly.

There's a terrible irony here. Few American films in the last decade have argued so exquisitely and so powerfully for the vitality of Christ's principles in the modern world. Few have tried so heroically to construct a bridge between religion and the audience that usually rejects it. Few have been more suffused with a genuine, deep love of Christ. And none has been more completely misunderstood and despicably treated by the very people — allegedly devout Christians — who should have been, above all, sympathetic to its aims.

The charges leveled at this movie by its major detractors are monstrous and unfair; their tactics are childish and reprehensible. One wishes they would see the movie before screaming wildly for its destruction. And one wishes they would examine more closely their own motives and hearts and souls — spotted and impure as anyone's, perhaps inwardly as carnal as Magdalene's, greedy as Zebedee's, haughty as Pilate's, bloody as Judas's — before casting the first stone.

Isthmus, September 16, 1988

THE LAST TEMPTATION OF CHRIST

Gary Arnold

Martin Scorsese's film version of *The Last Temptation of Christ* arrived earlier than expected, riding what appears to be a lucrative, albeit unwelcome and somewhat ugly, wave of controversy to socko box office in its opening weekend.

If, like me, you find yourself keenly dissatisfied by the movie itself and short on tolerance for the Fundamentalist groups who've demonstrated how to elevate an object of indignation into an instant,

Willem Dafoe plays Jesus in Martin Scorsese's *Last Temptation of Christ.* (Photo courtesy of Universal Pictures.)

serendipitous commercial sensation, partly by heaping anti-Semitic abuse on executives at MCA and Universal Pictures, the whole uproar is supremely disenchanting.

Devout and thoughtful Christians do indeed have a legitimate quarrel to pick with Scorsese's obsessively unorthodox approach to the Passion of Christ, inspired not by Holy Writ but by a tendentious work of fiction, a 1960 novel by the Greek author Nikos Kazantzakis, best known as the creator of *Zorba the Greek*.

Not that Scorsese's fundamentally egocentric need to reinterpret the Passion threatens Christian orthodoxy in the slightest. Seeing the movie *before* condemning it might help to clarify the point. Scorsese's conception of Jesus proves so unsatisfactory both dramatically and spiritually that only the most defensive of believers could regard it as more than a transitory nuisance. The astute reaction would be to take pity on the poor boy for preferring such a lackluster and self-defeating conception of Christ.

The maddening irony of the current controversy is that Scorsese would have been on firmer ground as a dramatic artist by anticipating some of the problems and recognizing that Kazantzakis's Jesus left a great deal to be desired as a protagonist.

Religious sentiments and convictions aside, there's simply more character to conjure with in the scriptural Jesus, for the phenomenally simple reason that he talks and acts as if he knew his own mind and possessed the fortitude to accept a painfully sacrificial destiny.

The Jesus portrayed so dismally by Willem Dafoe in *The Last Temptation* is a bundle of doubts, confusions, and self-loathings: a veritable Jesus Christ identity crisis. With emphatic grunginess he's introduced as one very mixed-up and masochistic collaborationist, doing the Romans' dirty work by building the crosses used to crucify seditious fellow Jews.

He even practices for his own ordeal by lugging the crosses up to the execution sites. "You're a disgrace!" he's told by Harvey Keitel as Judas, eccentrically reconceived as a Zealot who treats Jesus with long-suffering exasperation, like a Big Brother trying to shake some sense into a delinquent Kid Brother.

What does the misguided carpenter have to say in his defense? Well, not exactly words to live by: "God loves me. I want him to hate me. I want to crucify every one of his Messiahs."

Nothing if not modern to a grievous, neuroticized fault, the Jesus derived from Kazantzakis by Scorsese and screenwriter Paul Schrader also begs for an emotional pummeling in the early rounds from Barbara Hershey as Mary Magdalene, now presented as a disillusioned childhood sweetheart who turned to prostitution. Pretty exotic merchandise she is too, in baubles, bangles, frillies, and intricate tattoos. She spits at Jesus in their first encounter, then gets to sneer at him when he slinks in after work hours (the filmmakers let us play voyeur while Magdalene is servicing her long line of clients) to ask her forgiveness for being such a wretch. Evidently not in a forgiving mood after another hard day's grind, she replies on the tart side: "You're pitiful! I hate you! You never had the courage to be a man!"

If the tone of all this early-blooming hostility and spitefulness sounds a trifle coarse and anachronistic, as well as excessive, it may be because Scorsese can't help echoing the idiom of *Mean Streets* in a Biblical setting. Obviously, we're also being set up for big reversals, once Jesus begins pursuing a more appropriate career and numbers Judas and Magdalene among his followers.

The guiding misconception is that Jesus resists his messianic fate almost to the last breath. The weakling collaborationist phase gives way to an overcompensating militant phase after Jesus starts his ministry.

If my eyes didn't deceive me, there was an astonishing moment when Jesus returns from meditative retreat to dazzle the disciples by reaching in and extracting his own heart for them to stare at.

Despite such virtuoso accomplishments, the Jesus of *The Last Temptation* remains a psychological cripple. Quivering, vacillating, and weak-minded, he seems to bring out the worst in Willem Dafoe, who perpetuates the tradition of sickly sanctimonious and conspicuously non-Semitic movie saviors. After two demented yet tedious hours in his uninspiring company, the plot leaves Jesus literally hanging on the cross in order to indulge a prolonged fanciful digression.

In the course of this presumably delirious fantasy, which does indeed seem delirious in another respect, because it reminds you of *It's a Wonderful Life* in a time warp, Jesus is released from his agony by an angelic girl. She continues to hover around while he lives out a "normal" life as loving husband to Magdalene, Mary, and Martha and doting paterfamilias to a swarming happy brood.

The last temptation, it transpires, is choosing to settle down and have a family.

Once the Scorsese-Schrader-Kazantzakis Jesus recognizes that these pleasures are also the work of Satan, he is freed at last to accept the destiny of the cross. Their Jesus expires with the words, "It is accomplished," but the quality of illusion falls so lamentably short of spiritual exaltation or mere emotional coherence that Scorsese himself might as well pop into view and announce, "That's a wrap!"

The filmmakers are struggling to rationalize a Jesus who reflects their own self-conscious anxieties and pretensions. They want him to be more human, more culpable, more *like them.*

But this prescription has little relevance for the vast majority of believers, who simply accept Jesus as the Messiah he claimed to be and feel no impulse to confirm their faith by reinventing a Savior to modern, clichéd, and ultimately self-pitying psychological specifications. This may come as a terrible shock to Martin Scorsese and Paul Schrader, but most Christians really aren't in the market for renovated or alternative Messiahs.

Latecomers like Kazantzakis and now Scorsese and Schrader are merely stroking their egos by reimagining Jesus as a fallible soulmate or alter ego.

Yes, Scorsese makes crucifixion look vividly barbarous and painful, but did anyone ever imagine otherwise? The Moroccan locations have some evocative power, and it was admirably resourceful to make a biblical drama on a $6 million budget, but in most respects *Last Temptation* suffers from all the ludicrous and solemn tendencies that habitually plague biblical movies. The curse of wishy-washy holiness makes Dafoe look like a downright stupid performer much of the time, and surely the filmmakers are flirting with burlesque when they show Jesus doing things like blowing his first sermon, a "love" message that ends up putting his audience in a fighting mood.

Confirmed moviegoers will find it all too easy to associate Dafoe's Jesus with the anguished, wayward protagonists of earlier films directed by Scorsese and written by Schrader, notably *Taxi Driver* and *Raging Bull.* In each case the filmmakers seem to be indulging psychodramatic motives, nominally "purging" their own tangled feelings of aggression and guilt by dwelling on heroes with time-bomb mentalities.

Despite that opening week bonanza, I would venture to guess that notoriety can carry a messianic formula this hapless only so far. At the first showing I attended there was a smattering of applause. It must have lasted at least three seconds.

The Connection, August 17, 1988

JFK

David Denby

Although you're not much given to mysticism, and perhaps possess no more than a New Yorker's normal dose of paranoia, you have had, I would bet, the following weird experience:

Walking down a busy street, you are suddenly overcome by the alarming notion that the random flux around you — the people going to work or walking dogs, the guy selling franks on the corner, the buildings, the garbage cans — are all part of some sinister and portentous design. The life around you is not casual, discontinuous, and inert but unified by a single purpose. You dismiss the mood with a laugh; nevertheless, you're haunted for an instant by the possibilities of connection among the many moving and still parts of what you experience — haunted by what this glance or that open window might mean. Usually it means nothing.

But not always. This intimation of the uncanny — the design in the seeming randomness of life — is what Oliver Stone has captured so brilliantly in *JFK.* The movie is appalling and fascinating — unreliable, no doubt, but an amazing visual and spiritual experience nonetheless, an experience of dread in the flux of life. Stone, recounting the questionable investigations of Jim Garrison (Kevin Costner), the New Orleans district attorney in the sixties, fleshes out Garrison's belief in a vast conspiracy of forces to kill John F. Kennedy; he traces the movements of Lee Harvey Oswald and a variety of other figures. The movie is an amalgam of facts and speculations, but at its core — a core that no amount of ridicule in the *Times* can convince me is less than great — Stone re-creates, from many points of view, what might have happened in Dealey Plaza in Dallas on November 22, 1963.

Stone displays the assassination of John F. Kennedy in the cataclysmic home movie of Abraham Zapruder, dissects it, shows the event again in simulated form from the vantage point of different witnesses and possible participants. He gives alternate versions, works out suppositions — demonstrating, for instance, what Oswald would have done on that day if the Warren Commission were right about him. As witnesses describe a variety of odd occurrences — the phony Secret Service men, the "man with the umbrella" — we see them, and their implications are explored and tied together. After strategically placing these many pieces of visual information within the story of Garrison's investigation, Stone gathers them at the end so that they link up and comment on one another. Once again the motorcade rounds the corner of Dealey Plaza; only this time, we see a concerted plot involving three teams of trained shooters. The effect of this reconstructed assassination is emotionally devastating.

But, you ask, is the reconstruction *true?* Let's say that Stone has pushed certain fragmentary bits of information to their limits: The movie is a projection of what *might* have happened. Other people, including the British producers of a recent series on the A&E network, have offered different theories. I'm not convinced, as Stone apparently is, that the assassination was a coup d'état backed by Lyndon Johnson and executed by the upper levels of the Defense Department, the CIA, and the FBI. All these men, according to Stone and co-scenarist Zachary Sklar (who have based their speculations on Garrison's *On the Trail of the Assassins* and Jim Marrs's *Crossfire*), wanted to stop Kennedy from winding down America's commitment to fight Communism in Vietnam. Two problems with this: On the subject of Vietnam, Kennedy was highly ambivalent, leaning this way and that in the weeks before his death; and such a conspiracy, if it existed, would necessarily have involved hundreds of important people, some of whom, overcome by remorse at what the assassination of Kennedy and the ascension of LBJ eventually led to in Vietnam, would surely have come forward by now. Even unremorseful Americans don't keep secrets very well.

I understand the initial hostility to the subject that many of you must feel: The CIA, the Cuban exiles, the Dallas police force . . . Oh, God, *that* stuff again? *JFK* is a monomaniac's treasure trove. In its ceaseless piling up of detail, it will give the untiring "conspiracy community"—American nuts of the highest salt!—enough to argue over for years. But saying that *JFK* isn't always convincing is hardly to dismiss it, as many overly literal types, blind to the powers of film, have already done. Stone has established a dense web of contingency, "coincidence," and design. He has made, if you insist, a fiction of the assassination, a countermyth, though I hasten to add that his version, at least as an account of the events in Dealey Plaza, is a lot more convincing in its physical details than the Warren Commission's. There was, I believe, *some* sort of conspiracy to kill the president.

Perhaps Stone would have seemed more convincing in general if he had shown Garrison as he was, a figure of uncertain temperament and doubtful method. But instead, Stone the moral realist gave way to Stone the Capraesque hero-worshiper. This Garrison is a true-blue American patriot, a mild-mannered man of conscience victimized by many forces both large and small, including his nagging, petty-minded wife (Sissy Spacek). At the end, standing virtually alone in his beliefs, Garrison makes an endless grandstanding speech about patriotism, the Constitution, and what it means to be an American. Throbbing at the temples, the movie congratulates itself on its own moral commitment, as if no one but Jim Garrison and Oliver Stone *cared* who shot Kennedy. Costner, wearing a remarkably ugly pair of horn-rimmed glasses, gives an uninventive, monochromatic performance that leaves us with the awkward question of how such a dull man could entertain so many extreme ideas.

Yet if Garrison is a bore, the bunch of New Orleans citizens he investigates are as lively as water bugs. In the months after the assassination, Garrison grabs wildly at the frayed corners of the event. There are Cuban exiles and embittered ex–FBI agents; David Ferrie (Joe Pesci), a manic bewigged homosexual who hangs out with the Cubans and who may have driven Oswald around; and Clay Shaw (Tommy Lee Jones), a wealthy gay businessman with a possible CIA connection. As Oswald, Gary Oldman, speaking in an odd, halting way, as if his brain short-circuited between words, passes in and out of the movie, a shadow of a shadow. Re-creating this obscure, hapless stuff—a corner of oblivion that just may have meant something—Stone relaxes for a change, allowing Tommy Lee Jones, for instance, to hold the camera long enough to savor Clay Shaw's elegant intonations.

A streak of mournful love for the president softens *JFK*. At the same time, Stone has restored the shock of the assassination—the autopsy photographs, for instance, strike us like stab wounds. What Stone is saying is that this event has been taken away from us, that the government is using our discomfort as fake justification for locking up evidence well into the twenty-first century.

This is undoubtedly true, but high-level conspiracy, as a movie subject, is very difficult to bring to life. Donald Sutherland shows up as a Deep Throat type (a character based on L. Fletcher Prouty, former aide to the joint chiefs of staff), and as Sutherland outlines the plot against Kennedy, *JFK* collapses into shadowy narrated scenes of powerful old men pursing their lips evilly. The movie becomes vague and self-important. The assassinations of Dr. Martin Luther King, Jr., and Robert Kennedy are thrown into the pot as further proof that "they" are controlling everything.

Yet all is not lost: Stone returns to the nuts and bolts of Dealey Plaza. Robert Richardson's cinematography is a miracle of spontaneous-seeming chaos and fleeting glimpses of trouble, and the editing by Joe Hutshing and Pietro Scalia stitches everything together brilliantly. As the new version of the assassination came together at the end, I felt a sickening thrill of dismay and fear, an intimation of mortal design in the flux, malignity revealed. Even God would be frightened.

JFK is a true adventure for the viewer. So plunge in, and for heaven's sake ignore such warnings as Tom Wicker's stuffy *New York Times* piece. Wicker sounds like a Victorian policeman in a whorehouse: He's shocked that a *movie star* and *film techniques* were used to deal with reality. He implies that you can't make a movie about an actual event unless you know the absolute truth. But that is nonsense. Whatever its flaws, *JFK* is a haunting and powerful piece of work, just possibly the jolt that a jaded and cynical American public needs.

New York, January 6, 1992

JFK

J. Hoberman

JFK may not prove the most important movie of the year but, as much intervention as entertainment, it's certainly the most self-important. "I feel like a presidential candidate," director Oliver Stone complained to one reporter during production, wondering aloud to another whether her piece was going to "assassinate" him. Stone may have a bigger ego than D. W. Griffith but even paranoids have enemies, as the hysterical prerelease response to *JFK* demonstrates.

Stone takes his history personally. Ostensibly the story of New Orleans DA Jim Garrison's quixotic investigation into the murder of John F. Kennedy, *JFK* seems to have been made to further illuminate Stone's trip to Vietnam. Opening with a kinescope of Ike's farewell warning on the dangers of the military-industrial complex, *JFK* is hardly a seamless period piece. It skitters back and forth in time, mixing documentary footage with pseudo newsreels, flashbacks shot as if through surveillance cameras with staged events. (The first: A hooker dumped from a car on a two-lane blacktop warns the audience, "They're going to kill Kennedy!") The visuals are violently unmatched — the image shifts from black and white to color to a sort of diseased sepia — and the structure is obsessive. *JFK* returns again and again to the primal scene at Dealey Plaza. The fatal motorcade is scored to portentous drumbeats — and everywhere else the montage longs to reproduce that six-second burst of fire.

Self-righteous and humorless as he navigates Stone's conspiratorial *Walpurgisnacht,* Kevin Costner plays Garrison as a speechifying version of Eliot Ness. Costner can't showboat the role but he can't be self-effacing either. If the actual Garrison was a roguish con artist (in a bizarre bit of hubris, Stone gives him a cameo as a pop-eyed Earl Warren), *JFK* makes him a sober family man. With Sissy Spacek surpassing even Meg Ryan's hippie concubine (*The Doors*) in the mandatory role of the great man's nagging wife, Garrison's life is set in contrast not only to Kennedy's but to the orgiastic masquerades and candlelight seductions of the film's homosexual villains, David Ferrie (Joe Pesci) and Clay Shaw (Tommy Lee Jones).

As a historian, Stone is a sub-Carlyle romantic for whom heroic individuals like Kennedy, Garrison, and himself are called to perform sublime missions. You can accuse him of muddying the well, but the waters he churns weren't exactly pristine. Stone at his most simpleminded is at least as credible as the Warren Commission. So here, once more, are the grassy knoll, the litany of dead witnesses, the multiple Oswalds. *JFK* is a movie that has been made several times before — albeit never for $40 million. The 1967 Mark Lane and Emile De Antonio documentary *Rush to Judgment,* which opened to respectful reviews soon after Garrison's investigation went public, was the first film to critique the Warren report; Lane was also involved in the fictional *Executive Action,* released on the tenth anniversary of the Kennedy assassination and at least as vilified as *JFK.*

Like *JFK,* if far more clumsily, *Executive Action* used an assortment of TV footage and faked newsreels to posit a conspiracy of right-wing industrialists who decided to remove Kennedy because he wanted to end the Cold War and "lead a black revolution" — a reading of presidential intentions only marginally more believable than the single-bullet theory cooked up for the Warren Commission by eager beaver Arlen Specter. Midway through *JFK,* the whole scenario is laid out by a former military intelligence officer (Donald Sutherland, who once owned the rights to *Executive Action*'s screenplay). Calling the Warren Report a fiction, this X tells Garrison that JFK sealed his death warrant when he decided to break up the CIA and order the troops home from Vietnam. "It's as old as the crucifixion." (Nothing if not maximalist, *JFK* invokes Shakespeare and Jesus at every opportunity.)

Stone isn't big on dialectics: after all, without Vietnam there would have been no *Platoon* for him to make. Still, the attacks launched by establishment journalists on him and even Costner (who probably got involved with the project thinking he was going to play Kennedy) only dispose me to support *JFK*. There is nothing more disturbing about the Kennedy assassination than the idea that, in a paroxysm of confusion, America's leading citizens (including, of course, responsible journalists) gratefully seized upon the lone-nut theory and, having swept the inconvenient details under the rug, are forever stuck in the historical equivalent of an alternate universe.

To prove a political motivation behind Kennedy's murder would be to unravel the events of the past twenty-eight years and leave us as vulnerable as a nation of newborns without blankets. Among other things, Stone illustrates the powerful idea that, on November 22, Kennedy himself was left uncovered and exposed—not unlike the moment in *The Godfather* when Michael Corleone discovers his father alone in the hospital.

Critics of the Warren Commission report delight in pointing out instances of doctored evidence. Of course, in introducing composite characters, ascribing fictional dialogue to historical figures, and integrating (even as he improves) a number of photographic actualities, Stone is scarcely less creative. *JFK* is as filled with simulacra as a dissertation on Baudrillard. The movie doesn't have the faintest embarrassment in flashing a photograph of Gary Oldman posed as Lee Harvey Oswald posing with his rifle and asking us to notice how the shadows show that this picture of "Oswald" has obviously been retouched.

One reason *JFK* inspires such fear is that it is of a piece with the canned show biz and controlled reportage that passes for our nightly news. As art, Stone's opus is far cruder than Don DeLillo's masterful *Libra*—a novel that uses Oswald's life to meditate on the ways in which fiction contaminates so-called reality. As spectacle, however, *JFK* has access to the first and greatest of Kennedy death films, the 8mm home movie that was shot by Abraham Zapruder and immediately turned over to *Life* magazine.

Indeed, Garrison's single greatest achievement may have been subpoenaing the Zapruder film—something Time-Life went to the Supreme Court to prevent. (That Time-Life is now Time Warner, producer of *JFK,* only shows that what goes around comes around.) The Zapruder footage is the basis for virtually all assassination research, the "clock" by which the Dealey Plaza drama is played out, and a challenge to the ontology of the medium itself. Not just an amazing snuff film and the vulgar modernist antecedent for the "structural" cinema of the late sixties, it was made to be blown up, slowed down, computer enhanced, and overinterpreted until not just the notion of documentary investigation but the laws of physics are subsumed in its seething grain.

To study the Zapruder footage is to enter a world of subatomic particles somewhere beyond the outer limits of photographic representation. As in response, *JFK* engages in a frenzy of articulation. The film has so much overlapping dialogue that it's virtually a radio play. Everyone's some sort of mouthpiece, and the most vivid turns — Oldman's Oswald, John Candy as a pumpkin-faced hipster — are the vocally most distinguished. (By contrast, Pesci — who plays Ferrie in a historically accurate orange fright wig — seems to have wandered out of Brooklyn.)

Moreover, while Garrison's investigation began in 1967 and continued into 1969, *JFK* seems to cram everything into the apocalyptic spring of 1968 so that the assassinations of Martin Luther King, Jr., and Robert Kennedy seem a response to Garrison's discoveries. (All that's missing is a bit of "Light My Fire" on the car radio. Someday, some discotheque or museum will give us a true Stone Soul Picnic — evoking the madness of the sixties by projecting alternate reels of *Platoon, Born on the Fourth of July, The Doors,* and *JFK* on the walls, floors, and ceiling.)

JFK's climactic trial sequence — a forty-five-minute tour de force — hammers the Zapruder footage into your skull like a pop song refrain, while adding a backbeat of gruesome autopsy photos to the mix. As Garrison stuns the courtroom, Stone probes the wound, restaging Oswald's capture (in a Dallas moviehouse prophetically showing *War Is Hell*). Liberally using the words *fascism* and *coup d'état,* citing Vietnam and calling LBJ an "accessory after the fact," invoking (once again) Shakespeare and tremulously quoting martyred presidents Kennedy and Lincoln, Stone's version of Garrison's summation makes more impressive use of *Mr. Smith Goes to Washington* than any event since the first Oliver North hearing.

As a fetish-ridden pop-culture assemblage, *JFK* is unusually rich. It's almost as dense as Kenneth Anger's *Scorpio Rising* (which had its theatrical premiere the month before Kennedy was shot) and nearly as steeped in magical thinking. Stone calls *JFK* a countermyth: "Hopefully, it will replace the Warren Commission as *Gone with the Wind* replaced *Uncle Tom's Cabin* and was in turn replaced by *Roots* and *The Civil War.*" Oliver Stone may be the quintessential post-Reagan filmmaker. For him, history is the nightmare from which we never can awake—except when somebody changes the channel.

Village Voice, December 31, 1991

VIETNAM HOT DAMN

Vietnam didn't just tear the country apart. It also tore up the movies. At first, the war was present in our films only indirectly; in the early to mid seventies, the high, almost giddy level of violence and despair in the cop thrillers and westerns and action pictures was like Vietnam's spreading stain. With the exception of John Wayne's *The Green Berets,* Hollywood pretty much steered clear of Vietnam until the floodgates opened in the late seventies. The flood has been gushing ever since.

Unlike the standard pre-Vietnam Hollywood war movie, with its patriotic core and comprehensible politics, the Vietnam movie has often been a species of horror film: It hoists high the derangement of our national self-image. Moviemakers like Francis Coppola (*Apocalypse Now*), Michael Cimino (*The Deer Hunter*), Oliver Stone (*Platoon, Born on the Fourth of July*), and Brian De Palma (*Casualties of War*) attempted to make films that would not simply reproduce the war but, in a sense, *be* the war. Stylistically, no other genre of war film in the history of movies has been so frenzied, so hallucinatory. Transposed to Vietnam, the traditional macho myths of the all-American action film were raided, exalted, exploded. The demonization of the enemy turned in on ourselves. Many of these films had the spooked, furious atmosphere of exorcisms.

The controversies connected to these films mirrored the controversy of the war itself. Were many of these filmmakers justified in depicting Vietnam in almost apolitical terms as America's "elemental" battle? Did the jungle fever of *Apocalypse Now* belong to its subject or its director? Was De Palma, both celebrated and reviled for his previous films' baroque psychosexual violence, exactly the wrong director to make a movie centering on the rape of a Vietnamese girl by U.S. soldiers? Were Stone's over-the-top stylistics too much? Or is there no such thing as too much in a Vietnam movie? And what *did* Cimino mean when he closed *The Deer Hunter* with a chorus of "God Bless America"?

The arguments raised by these Vietnam movies burst the bounds of traditional film criticism. What many of the critics of the following pieces are really asking is: How shall we regard this war? How shall we heal?

APOCALYPSE NOW

Joseph Gelmis

Two years behind schedule and, at $31 million, more than double its original budget, *Apocalypse Now* opened today in Manhattan. Put aside the ancillary issues. Judged simply as serious and stimulating entertainment, *Apocalypse Now* is one of the very few must-see movies of 1979. It's brilliant, beautiful, thought provoking, and superbly acted, a horror movie and an adventure story, an important Vietnam War document.

Inspired by Joseph Conrad's *Heart of Darkness,* a nineteenth-century novella of colonialism and atavism, *Apocalypse Now* has been updated by authors John Milius and Francis Coppola to the Vietnam War, circa 1967. Martin Sheen plays an American captain assigned by headquarters in Saigon to motor upriver, cross into Cambodia, and find and kill a renegade Green Beret colonel (Marlon Brando).

Setting the tone at the start and finish of the film is The Doors' recording of "The End"—a trancelike flow of fatalistic imagery and rhythms, with evocative lyrics such as "lost in a wilderness of pain

. . . all her children are insane." As leading character and narrator, Captain Willard (Sheen) encounters nothing but insanity in his journey.

Apocalypse Now pictures Vietnam as a nightmare that drove Americans crazy. For nearly all of its two-hour-and-twenty-six-minute playing time—uninterrupted by intermission—*Apocalypse Now* is a veritable acid trip, an LSD vision of Vietnam combat.

For instance, Sheen's patrol boat has to be assisted in entering the river that will take him to Brando. Robert Duvall, in black stetson and dark aviator glasses, as an air cavalry colonel and surfing fanatic, picks a Vietcong-controlled waterfront village for Sheen's entry point. He massacres civilians along with guerrillas, sacrifices helicopters and troops—just to seize some chancy moments of first-rate surfing at the village's beach that boasts six-foot waves. The battle scenes—with Duvall's helicopter cavalry blaring Wagner's "Ride of the Valkyries" on loudspeakers to scare the enemy—are extraordinary.

Each episode en route upriver adds to the hallucinatory nightmare that has a logic of its own. American patrol boats play "chicken"—daring each other to swerve out of the way; one sailor even firebombs another U.S. boat. Playboy bunnies, flown in to bump and grind for troops, incite a riot and have to be evacuated when mobbed by GIs. Nerves that have been frazzled by relentless carnage explode during a routine search of a sampan's cargo, and innocent civilians are massacred. A boat crewman (Sam Bottoms) drops acid the night of a Vietcong bombardment of a U.S.-held bridge, fascinatedly sees the mushrooming flames, drifting colored smoke, rockets, flares, tracers as a light show and hears the moans, shrieks, wails, rat-a-tat-tats as infernal music.

Cinematographer Vittorio Storaro and sound editor Walter Murch contribute exquisite sights and sounds to the hellish odyssey of *Apocalypse Now*.

Coppola's epic about atavism—regression to barbarity—falters only when Sheen reaches the stronghold of Colonel Kurtz, in the final minutes of the drama. A professional soldier with an iron will and a holy-war sense of mission, Kurtz has become a god to primitive Montagnard tribesmen whom he leads on head-hunting raids against the Vietcong. Sheen's confrontation with the shaved-headed Kurtz—filmed in the dark to camouflage Brando's eighty pounds of overweight—and Dennis Hopper's idolatrous groupie jabbering in behalf of Brando/Kurtz are incoherent compared to the vivid clarity of the rest of the film.

Ironically, Duvall plays a more godlike character than Brando. His own sense of immortality on the battlefield renders Brando's morbid, mystical spouting of poetry in the shadows of his Ankor Wat–like temple hideout superfluous and anticlimactic.

No matter that the film is marred by an inconclusive dramatic and emotional payoff to its incomparable combat footage and vision of moral vertigo. *Apocalypse Now* is exciting, ambitious, a near-great film.

Newsday, August 15, 1979

APOCALYPSE NOW

Richard T. Jameson

It was like another art altogether. That sombre theme had to be given a sinister resonance, a tonality of its own, a continued vibration that, I hoped, would hang in the air and dwell on the ear after the last note had been struck.

—Joseph Conrad

Apocalypse Now is a dumb movie that could have been made only by an intelligent and talented man. It pushes its egregiousness with such conviction and technical sophistication that, upon first viewing, I immediately resolved to withhold firm judgment until I'd seen the film again: Perhaps I'd missed some crucial irony, some ingenious framework that, properly understood, would convert apparent asininity to audacity. I didn't find it. It isn't there. What is there is the evidence of a reasonably talented filmmaker having spectacularly overextended himself—Francis Ford Coppola, who, having had a tony pop epic widely accepted as great cinema, felt he was ready to make *Citizen Kurtz.*

How poetically apposite it must have seemed, that the property Orson Welles nearly undertook to film before making history with *Citizen Kane* was Joseph Conrad's *Heart of Darkness.* How artful of

Destiny to have stayed his hand, so that around the end of the 1960s John Milius could show Coppola, his fellow film-school alumnus, a script transposing the 1898 novella from deepest imperial Africa to the morass of the Vietnam War. Kurtz, the scholarly representative of the ivory trade turned savage demigod, would become a Special Forces officer who had started fighting both sides of the war with a private native army based upriver in Cambodia; Marlow, Conrad's conscientious truth seeker and narrator, was to be transmuted into a hit man for the generals and an interested civilian agency.

It's easy to see what appeal this held for Milius, with his unabashed enthusiasm for superheroes and "man's inherent bestiality" (he has been involved subsequently with *Dirty Harry, Jeremiah Johnson, The Wind and the Lion, Hardcore,* and *1941,* among other films). Easy to see, too, how he would have made a more directly action-oriented film out of it (the best sequence in the film, the Air Cav raid on a Vietnamese village, is pure Milius in concept, as is Robert Duvall's surfing and napalm freak Colonel Kilgore, the only full-blooded characterization).

Coppola kept Milius's action set pieces but elected to frame them within a narrative structure that engenders a hallucinatory suspension, rather as the opening deathdream of Xanadu in *Kane* casts a spell that pervades the most dramatically vivid scenes in that film. He called his particular brand of hallucination "film opera," and relied on it "to create a film experience that would give its audience a sense of the horror, the madness, the sensuousness, and the moral dilemma of the Vietnam War." It was a bold stroke, inspired, and fatally ill-advised.

A sense of narrative suspension is entirely appropriate to an adaptation of the Conrad novella, in which Marlow's very telling of the tale is the definitive act over and above the events narrated. But Coppola's Marlow character is unqualified to provide the ethical and emotional referent so crucial to the drama. Captain Willard (Martin Sheen) begins the film in such a moral, physical, and spiritual funk that it's impossible to conceive how he could be further undone by a journey into any heart of darkness; nor have we reason to impute to him any capacity for illumination. There is no room for him to fall into any knowledge, no way for the journey upriver into the jungle to develop its proper resonance: the snake of civilization swallowing its pre-evolutionary tail. Willard is one of Coppola's affectless monsters—like Micheal Corleone at the end of the *Godfather* saga, but without the preceding six hours of film to explain how he got that way.

Captain Willard (Martin Sheen), in camouflage paint, cuts an eerie figure in the steaming jungle of Vietnam in *Apocalypse Now*. (Photo courtesy of Zoetrope Films.)

Everything is foregone. And it may be protested, of course, that that is How It Is. Mankind fell a long time ago; Vietnam was only the flowering of a corruption intrinsic to our national identity; "This is the end," the Doors sing at the beginning. That's profound — or sophomoric doodoo, depending on how it's put across. "Rosebud" is dollarbook Freud, as Welles called it, if you take it in isolation; but if you believe that the true Rosebud is not a sled, not a snow globe, but the whole intricate up/down, in/out, past/present, light/dark, living/dead construct, that Citizen Kane is *Citizen Kane,* not a man but a movie, the sum of all the contradictory jigsaw pieces of evidence, of identity — then Rosebud is brilliant, a cinematic stab at, say, William Faulkner's goal of writing the history of the world "between one cap and a period."

So foregone can be good. But it takes a stylist of considerable range and power to sustain that kind of narrative suspension. Conrad was such a stylist; Welles, too. It just may be that Francis Ford Coppola is not a stylist at all. He has a good eye, he composes his frames and shot sequences with intelligent purpose, and certainly he inspires a steely concentration in his actors (he needs more from them than most directors do); but he is a one-thing-at-a-time director. A given shot makes a single, clear statement. There is no resonance — although there is sometimes a built-in interpretation of the statement that is foregrounded so deliberately it *can't* resonate.

This is true even of his American art film *The Conversation,* a movie that seems to explore the ambiguity of media (as *Kane* does in spades). But whatever ambiguity it possesses is a function of the screenplay, not the direction. The central set piece — the conversation recorded by several microphones, played back a dozen times, filtered, synthesized, and also revisualized (presumably in the mind's eye) from a multiplicity of camera angles till it yields sinister, contradictory meanings — is fine as suspense stuff, but it's ambiguity-by-the-numbers: "I could have shot this scene all these different ways" instead of "I shot it right the first time and locked everything in." (Indeed, Coppola did go back and reshoot the scene when his editors called for additional footage to tinker with.)

Coppola is an excellent screenwriter (recall his achievement polishing Mario Puzo's *The Godfather* for the screen) and he has actually received more honors for his screenplays than for his direction. But he knows that the cinema is a director's medium, that the director is superstar. Pretty clearly, he determined that *Apocalypse Now* would be taken first and foremost as a director's movie (as *Kane,* for all the brilliance and detail of its script, is a director's movie). And, the miscalculations about the Marlow figure aside, it is as a director's movie that *Apocalypse Now* most resoundingly flops.

A lot of people who can see the problem with the film's scenario logic and characterizations nevertheless manage to come out cheering because of the "visual power." May I propose that "visual" is the most abused term in the filmcrit lexicon? It is not enough for a film to be full of moving subjects and moving camera, flaring lights and inky shadows, towering compositions and tricky dissolves. That can add up to arrant pictorialism, a miscellaneous light show, or meretricious folderol. It isn't "visual" unless it's informed by an organic intelligence. There is organization in Coppola's film, but organicity it's not. His motifs don't grow — they merely recur. His images, even when technically impressive, don't reverberate with possibility — they freeze up with literalness. They don't suggest — they denote.

To take a central image in both Conrad's novella and Welles's film, "darkness" becomes infinitely suggestive: of corruption, and the sacred privacy of the soul; the terror of the unknown, and the bliss of unconsciousness; unanswerable Nothingness, and uncreated worlds waiting to be intuited by an artist-god. To Coppola, it means that when you get to Kurtz's compound you turn out the lights and let Marlon Brando mumble in the dark.

Style isn't decoration. It isn't something an artist imposes on content. It's the life-energy of the work of art. It's life itself. The best artists feel awe toward their medium. It doesn't seem to hold any terror for Coppola. He's not a stylist—he's a technologist who confuses art with state of the art. Harry Caul in *The Conversation* could get emotionally involved only with the phantoms created through his sophisticated sound system; the centrality of technology to the method of that film prefigures the creative formula of *Apocalypse Now*. Coppola can buy better technology than anyone who's made movies before. He knows that 70mm cinematography is capable of incredible richness and texture, and that Walter Murch can mix more levels on a sound track than you can even identify. This produces a kind of depth, geophysically speaking, but other sorts are missing. Coppola's film is "operatic" because it's heightened—and thin.

In thrall to the kinesthetic firepower available to him, apparently confident that it will lift anything to new levels of expressiveness, Coppola perpetrates some of the most astonishing banalities in the history of prestige pictures. A phantasmagoric USO show in a Vietnam lagoon is a zapper for about as long as it takes Willard's river patrol boat to round the bend and afford a good look at it; after that, it's endless fascination with a Hugh Hefner Playmate rubbing an M-16 between her thighs, which seems to have something to do with sex and violence. A sun- and drug-zonked surfer in the boat crew paints his face like military camouflage and basks in the constant flickering of a meaningless night battle; Kurtz later appears similarly daubed, and of course there are all those primitive Cambodians painted head to toe: Who is civilized and who is savage?! The man who once orchestrated the stunning juxtaposition of a Corleone baptism and the nationwide elimination of the family's enemies here has Kurtz's natives slaughtering a ceremonial bullock while (can you dig it?) Willard swims through some handy primeval slime to assassinate Kurtz. It's as if Coppola were making an audiovisual aid for people who had never been introduced to any of these concepts before.

And yet he reaches the nadir when straining for the most intellectual—and silliest—signification. Both Kurtz and a spacey disciple of his (Dennis Hopper) quote T. S. Eliot—and not only Eliot, but "The

Hollow Men," a poem that bears an epigraph from Conrad's *Heart of Darkness!* And then the camera tips portentously to discover copies of *From Ritual to Romance* and *The Golden Bough* — Eliot's key mythic source material in composing "The Waste Land" — lying in Kurtz's quarters. I mean, what the *hell* does the man think he is doing? Are we to understand that Brando's Kurtz knows there was an earlier, fictional Kurtz whose footsteps he is retracing? Is this the ultimate form of narrative suspension? Is Coppola indicating his own serene acceptance of the inevitability with which *Apocalypse Now* will be subsumed in the racial consciousness?

Apocalypse Now is nothing if not an attempt to make a serious and important work of art. One must admire Coppola's crazy courage in laying fortune, career, even his home on the line to get the film made. And if he reached beyond his range as an artist, well, that is an honorable failing. But one thing is unforgivable. Francis Ford Coppola based his film on Joseph Conrad's *Heart of Darkness;* he even went back to Conrad to restore material omitted from that first John Milius screenplay. Almost everything that is any good in the film, that has lasting power to disturb, is based on Conrad's original vision. A seaman from the Polish Ukraine, who learned to use the English language with a majesty and subtlety few have equaled, created one of the definitive works of — and on — the Western imagination. There are no credits on Coppola's film, but the program book has columns of them. Joseph Conrad's name is never mentioned, although a photo caption reverently notes: "September 3, 1976. Marlon Brando arrives. He reads *Heart of Darkness* and shaves his head for the Colonel Kurtz role."

The Weekly (Seattle), October 17, 1979

THE DEER HUNTER

Stephen Schiff

In *The Deer Hunter,* director Michael Cimino has found a style that's at once elegiac and frighteningly aggressive. It's an overwhelming style, calculated to pin audiences to their seat backs, and the way Cimino sustains it makes his three-hour Vietnam saga inexorably powerful — surely one of the most powerful films of the seventies. Of course, raw force isn't the same as greatness — even the mealiest hack-'em-up can grab you by the throat. But *The Deer Hunter* doesn't revel in its power; it harnesses it, converts it into the electricity of myth. The result is wrenching and vivid and epic in scope: an utterly satisfying look at how traditional American heroism was consumed by the war it created — Vietnam.

Cimino, who has made only one other movie (the Clint Eastwood adventure *Thunderbolt and Lightfoot*), is nothing if not ambitious. During the film's first third, his portrait of a bleak, Russian-American steel town nestled in Pennsylvania's Allegheny Mountains strives for the sweeping scale of a Tolstoy novel. It's 1968, and we watch the heroes — Michael (Robert De Niro), Nick (Christopher Walken), and Steven (John Savage) — at work on the blazing floor of the steel mill's blast furnace. They wisecrack, booze, and gamble together at the local bar, girding themselves for the adventure they expect in Nam. Steven is getting married before their departure, and the splendid ceremony in the big Eastern Orthodox Church is punctuated with signs of the men's unspoken affection for one another — winks; gleeful, ill-contained grins; practical jokes. These men are comrades in the boys'-book tradition, the tradition of James Fenimore Cooper and Ernest Hemingway, of *Gunga Din* and *Only Angels Have Wings*. In their world, women are trifled with or excluded; one saves one's precious energies for battle.

This opening section is too long, but it has a rooted, documentary tone, and watching it is like leafing through old family photographs. Cinematographer Vilmos Zsigmond (*Deliverance, Close Encounters*) has shot the town in sooty grays and browns, but the clarity of the light he uses makes everything look strangely enchanting. He's showing us this desolate hamlet the way its inhabitants see it: as a warm, lovely, even majestic place, an entire universe. Without resorting to tricky angles or pretty camera movement, Zsigmond turns the black smokestacks of the steel mill into an arresting, Barnett Newman–like monument; the sludgy river becomes idyllic. And in the reception scene that follows the wedding, Zsigmond creates textures unlike anything this side of *The Godfather*. We sense that a hundred lives, a hundred impulses are passing before our eyes. True, screenwriter Deric Washburn's dialogue is often excruciatingly banal — in fact, there's not a memorable line in the whole movie — and we certainly don't need the portentous appearance of a gloomy, lizard-eyed Green Beret who answers De Niro's eager questions about Vietnam with a sullen "fuck it." But most of the playful, drunken gestures and clumsy flirtations you glimpse are fleeting and authentic enough to make you ache for these people. And so the film takes on an ominous tone. You feel the way Thornton Wilder's Emily must feel at the end of *Our Town* as she watches family and friends stumble through an ordinary day, blissfully, tragically unaware of their mortality.

Then the men embark on one final buddy-buddy ritual — a deer hunt in the misty mountains — and the film's tone turns hushed, mystical, exalted; a choir chants holy music on the sound track (another touch I think we could survive without). De Niro's Michael, who has emerged as the leader of the bunch and also as a man apart, oddly uninterested in women, pursues a magnificent buck and fells it with one clean shot. That shot is his communion with the gods, his purest prayer, his orgasm. And it's not hard to recognize in him Fenimore Cooper's Deerslayer, the sexless, heroic woodsman whom D. H. Lawrence described as "the essential American soul . . . hard, isolate, stoic and a killer." Michael's squirrelly friend Stan (played with a fine mixture of vanity and sorrow by the late John Cazale) calls him a "control freak," and so he is. He's the disciplined, unsullied warrior, the man we've always sent overseas to wipe out the barbarous enemy — with one clean shot.

☆

Things are different in Vietnam, however. There, somehow, evil overpowers discipline. Zsigmond films the Vietnam sequences in lush greens and reds, colors that blaze. And when the forest erupts in explosions and flame, you feel you're seeing a distorted-mirror image of the blast furnace back in Pennsylvania. The episode that follows is the centerpiece of the film and, I think, one of the greatest, most harrowing action sequences in movie history. Michael, Nick, and Steven have been taken prisoner. Standing in tiger cages suspended in murky green water, they await an atrocious fate: They're forced to compete against one another in games of Russian roulette, while their demonic captors slap them, taunt them, and gamble over which one will blow his brains out. With Steven convulsed in terror and Nick's nerves screaming, it's left to Michael to hatch a do-or-die plan that will save them. To face that single shot and live, that's the trick, and when Michael and Nick square off at the Russian roulette table, Cimino and his extraordinary editor Peter Zinner create a supercharged atmosphere of anticipatory terror — and excitement — that's like nothing you've ever experienced.

This incident changes the characters' lives, and Russian roulette reappears often throughout the rest of the film. No wonder several critics have thrown up their hands: This is so insistently a Grand Metaphor, yet its implications are elusive, shimmery, like the outline of something submerged in water. Is it a prize catch or just an old boot? Well, big conceits are always chancy devices in movies — they tend to crush the life out of the narrative — but for my money, this one works spectacularly. Russian roulette is a perversion of the woodsman's one-shot philosophy, an apt symbol of the way America's let's-go-in-there-and-clean-out-the-vermin heroism turned into mad, suicidal gambling in Vietnam. Back home, when Michael tries to revive the old bonds by embarking on another deer hunt with his buddies, he faces a buck on a lonely ridge only to find he can't bring himself to kill it. There's no honor left in the chase. In that Vietnamese prison camp, Michael has discovered something: To pursue one clean shot is to pursue madness. Indeed, we soon learn that when he and Nick faced off at the Russian roulette table, a grisly exchange had taken place. Michael's Deer-Hunter creed became his friend's crazy addiction. Later, Nick resurfaces, as a sort of nightmare reflection of the hunter-hero. He now plays Russian roulette for sport and money in the vice dens of chaotic, collapsing Saigon, where high-rolling Vietnamese bet on "the American" in a topsy-turvy version of the way our allies have always bet on the magic of the American warrior.

☆

I suppose a lot of people are going to criticize this movie for refusing to take a political stand on Vietnam. Of course, it portrays the war as being awful, but *The Deer Hunter* never condemns our role there, never points fingers or demands repentance. In the early Vietnam scenes, the Vietcong are shown to be unimaginably vicious (indeed, the film has a racist edge; the VC are as inscrutably evil as Fu Manchu). But in the sequence set during the evacuation of Saigon, brutal American soldiers slam our embassy's iron gates on the helpless Vietnamese they'd ostensibly come to defend. I find the film's refusal to take sides very easy to forgive. Audiences don't need more movies that pat them on the backs for harboring the right attitudes toward the war. Nor does anyone need another movie that pretends sympathy with the victimized American soldier while portraying him as a psychotic returning to wreak havoc on the homeland. Antiwar liberals who feel guilty — and scared — for having jeered at innocent GIs in the sixties must have purged themselves sufficiently by now in movies like *Coming Home, Rolling Thunder, Heroes, Tracks,* and *Black Sunday.* Cimino is after something much bigger — and, to my mind, much more profound. His film is an evolutionary step in the central American mythology: The lone hunter creates Vietnam, is twisted by it, and finally is destroyed by it so that a new hero can rise from his ashes. Ugh, you're probably saying, don't tell me that this is another ponderous foray into the jungles of American legend, another debunking, another genre piece, another Clint Eastwood–Charles Bronson–Paul Schrader–John Milius man-of-action picture. No, luckily it isn't. Cimino is the most intelligent mythmaker since the younger Norman Mailer (whose *Why Are We in Vietnam?* was a similar but less far-reaching attempt), and his film manages to reconcile two images of the American male that have been battling it out on the screen for years: the new, romantic "man who can cry" and the samurai who saves the imperiled heroine but never wins her.

☆

Michael is both. In the prewar segment, he stands apart from his friends, and, after the wedding, we see him tear off his tuxedo — the ceremonial uniform that affirms community — to break away and run naked through the streets. But in Vietnam he watches his brand of heroism go rancid. And when he returns to walk through the streets of his home town, greeting old friends, his efforts to shed the tough Deer Hunter's panoply have an almost unbearable poignancy. Empty and demoralized, the town needs him, and suddenly his aloofness no longer seems so heroic. Nick has not returned, and, battling his sexual reticence, Michael falls in love with his buddy's saddened girlfriend, Linda, a simple, inarticulate woman played with uncanny radiance by Meryl Streep. And finally, in one quiet, utterly heartbreaking scene, he goes to the hospital to visit Steven, who has lost both legs. As Michael approaches, his old pal watches him with trepidation. "My wife didn't send you, did she?" Steven asks. "I don't want to go home." "I know that," Michael replies, and the boyish camaraderie is re-established. Then suddenly, with a tremendous effort, Michael grabs Steven's wheelchair and begins rolling him out of the hospital. The buddyhood days are over. It's time to join the community.

I make great claims for *The Deer Hunter,* but perfection isn't among them. There are moments of hyped-up vainglory that make you gnash your teeth, especially during the sequence when Nick goes underground in a fiery, corroding Saigon. It's a pity, too, because the lurid tone and ludicrous dialogue—"When a man says no to champagne, he says no to life" and the like—obscure Christopher Walken's dreamy, sometimes feverish performance. As for De Niro's Michael, there's something impenetrable about him, and again I blame Deric Washburn's script. His jes'-folks dialogue exposes mannerisms, not emotions. Still, I don't think Michael's opacity will bother anyone while he's watching the film, because Cimino's command of narrative rhythm is completely disarming. He hits you, drops back while you're still reeling, and then, just when you come to your senses, bowls you over again. And De Niro himself is so generous, so regal, so pure and ferocious, that he rinses the entire film in a sort of nobility. Playing with gestures of self-effacement, irony, contempt, steely restraint, and even bloodlust, De Niro accomplishes something unexpected and marvelous: He gets you rooting not just for a hero, but for American heroism in the abstract. I haven't felt so patriotic since I was about seven. Yet, this is tempered, sadder-but-wiser patriotism. It's patriotism without flag waving.

Moviegoers are so used to films aimed at peabrains and adolescents that I'm not sure we're ready for *The Deer Hunter.* I know some critics aren't; they take the picture's graceful acceptance of the old heroism as well as the new to be a bewildering contradiction. They want the picture to plump for something, to tell someone off. But *The Deer Hunter* is beyond self-righteous breast-beating. It's a grown-up film directed at a nation groping for maturity. When the people of the little Pennsylvania town bury Nick and raise a last toast to him, they're saying farewell to the way of life that gave their country energy and purpose and then grew decadent—and finally had to be relinquished. According to *The Deer Hunter,* it's time to move on.

Boston Phoenix, February 13, 1979

THE DEER HUNTER

Jonathan Rosenbaum

Try to imagine a boneless elephant sitting in your lap for three hours while you're trying to think. It's flabby beyond belief, convinced not only of its importance but of its relevance to Americans (i.e., human beings) everywhere, and even winds up bleating a mournful rendition of "God Bless America" in your ear, hoping that you'll join in or at least have sympathy for its plight. Waving its snout in your face, it asks you to suspend whatever precious intelligence you have in exchange for a good cry about what nasty old Vietnam has done to poor beleaguered America. And in order for this to sing through your sinuses, you have to be stirred by its tear-jerker premises, which derive from yet another unconsummated, macho, all-male love story that puts more faith and value in violence than in women.

If only we could send this heavy gray lump off to school, or at least get it a respectable job in the circus. Unfortunately, it comes into our lives and neighborhood theatres with all the right social connections and credentials—a nod from the new-boy network of Francis Ford Coppola, John Milius, Paul Schrader, Martin Scorsese, and Steven Spielberg—which means that even some colleagues of mine who dislike the film are capitulating to marketplace pressures and assigning it an aesthetic importance they wouldn't dream of doling out to a Dreyer or a Visconti.

You think I'm exaggerating? During the same period that *The Deer Hunter* was being press-shown in New York—before opening for a limited run in New York and Los Angeles, in order to qualify for the Oscars it is so nakedly salivating to reap—I happened to hear that all the U.S. prints of Dreyer's *Gertrud* were being junked. Are we to conclude from this that a dull clinker in the national poet laureate sweepstakes is infinitely more important and meaningful to all of us? That's what the magazines keep telling us. And now that the most challenging European films are being virtually banned from and by the media, the expensive American art movie is being given the sweep of the market. (Is it any coincidence that *Interiors, Days of Heaven,* and *The Deer Hunter* are all "heroic" movies about cripples?) Thus Pauline Kael is perfectly right in a way when she calls *The Deer Hunter* an "epic that is scaled to the spaciousness of America itself." If we read "America"

Robert De Niro plays Michael Vronsky, a young Pennsylvania steelworker who likes to hunt with his buddies and ends up in Vietnam in *The Deer Hunter*. (Photo courtesy of Universal Pictures.)

as a code word for our shrinking film consciousness, I'd estimate that that's currently about two inches wide — at least in the preening mirror that media use to represent our collective face.

A personal confession seems in order. As someone who regards Coppola, Milius, and company as talented men without a good solid pound of genius between them, I'm not likely to be awed by the high school diploma of one of their greener disciples. From the moment that Michael Cimino's dull heroes (Robert De Niro, John Savage, and

Christopher Walken) make their exit from the steel factory in an imaginary Pennsylvania town, and De Niro starts laying on some jock mysticism about those "sun dogs" in the clouds — "old Indian things" that are supposed to portend dire events, apparently in the manner of Tolstoy — we already know that we're in for amateur night.

And when the director proceeds to lumber us through a Russian Orthodox wedding and a Vietnam send-off party for the heroes modeled on the *Godfather* bashes, the "richness of novelistic detail" usually adds up to about one simple idea per sagging shot, while the main instruction to actors and extras appears to have been "Look typical," perhaps in order to maintain this purity of intention. A folksy festive crowd gets dubbed by an all-male Dolby Russian choir, and after most of the beer-spraying chums drive off to the mountain to pursue their *Big Wednesday* capers, Cimino abruptly shifts to the style of a baby Leni Riefenstahl (or Daniel Schmidt) filming a remake of *Bambi* from the hunters' viewpoint. The heavenly male chorus resumes as De Niro sights his deer — which he kills in one shot, according to his profound mystic code. (Taking a second shot would be "pussy.")

Back in the bar, we're treated to a piano performance of Chopin (art, get it?) by one of the boys, and the camera pans interminably around the other guys' thoughtful faces — a stab at monumentality recalling Stalinist movies about Stalin, with Coppola again as the guide. Kael, who considers this movie "a small-minded film with greatness in it" — apparently believing in the greatness of small minds — proposes that if one of the men "had only fallen asleep the scene might have been as great as it wants to be." Mail-order recipes for greatness seem to be selling like hotcakes this season; it's too bad that dudes like Dreyer and Visconti still aren't to benefit from this sort of kindly advice.

Cut to Vietnam. It seems that what was so awful about this experience for Americans was principally a Russian roulette game that Cimino himself apparently invented, although the movie credits it to the Vietcong. It consists of taking two prisoners and giving each one in turn a revolver with one bullet and five empty chambers, and slapping each prisoner until he points the gun at his head and fires (giving De Niro a chance to redo his *Taxi Driver* epiphany). To make things more sporting, cash bets are placed by the Vietcong on whether somebody does or doesn't splatter his brains on the table. If he does, the Vietcong laughs, like Ming the Merciless. It's a cute game all right, and Cimino is clearly so enamored with it as a suspense mechanism that he trots it out like a vaudeville routine whenever the action flags, knowing it'll be a showstopper each time. ("One of the most frightening, unbearably tense sequences ever filmed," writes Jack Kroll, "and the most violent excoriation of violence in screen history"—real stuff for the troops.)

After trying this act out in the Vietnam provinces—where all three heroes have magically materialized, to be taken as prisoners and forced to play it—Cimino triumphantly takes it on the road and stages it for greasy foreign civilians in Saigon. Then back on the Pennsylvania mountain, after missing a second deer with the authority of a Zen master, De Niro, in a subsequent fit of pique, tries the game out on his buddy, played by John Cazale—regrettably wasted in his last screen performance. Then, for the grand finale, De Niro flies back to Saigon to retrieve Walken; he has to fork out a few thousand bucks in order to discover that his friend, crazed by his earlier experience of the game, now plays it for a living. (Three shows nightly?)

In an outrageously implausible maneuver designed to bring the house down, De Niro is forced to play the game with Walken in order to express his love for him. You think that's enough for an Oscar? Walken obediently splatters his brains out to give us our money's worth—and incidentally justify Stephen Saban's description of *The Deer Hunter* as "the cinematic equivalent of a Russian novel, a film more Russian than *Dr. Zhivago* . . . possibly one of the best films ever made." Considering that it's Russian roulette and that De Niro plays a character named Vronsky, how could it possibly be otherwise?

Take One, March 1979

PLATOON

Michael Wilmington

Oliver Stone's *Platoon* is a Vietnam War film that hits you like a rolling wave from a long-ago battle zone: a blood tide of rage and pain. It's a furious, blistering film. Like Arthur Penn's *Bonnie and Clyde* and Sam Peckinpah's *The Wild Bunch* in their day, it's a movie that sums up a whole national mood, that seethes with bitterness and bloody poetry, that shows such explosive anger and roaring impact you can't dodge it, can't look away from it, can't evade the blows.

Stone was a decorated Vietnam War veteran before he became a Hollywood screenwriter (*Midnight Express, Scarface*) and director (*Salvador*) — and here he's re-creating his own experience as a fresh-faced young American recruit in the sixties. (His surrogate, Chris, is played by Charlie Sheen — who brings in overtones of Coppola's *Apocalypse Now* and the central role played there by his dad, Martin Sheen.) But it's not a simple memoir; Stone magnifies the incidents, universalizes them into an epic-romance. He creates a morality play about the war between good and evil raging in his own guts, in Chris's — and, by extension, in their country's. *Platoon* is such an ambitious movie, it's amazing that it succeeds as well as it does. It comes across like a great howl, something Stone is tearing out of himself. But it's also slickly surfaced and hard as nails: a mixture of classic action movie and soaring confessional.

In the movie, Sheen's Chris gets the same kind of baptism in blood and fire that Stephen Crane's scared recruit, Henry Fleming, received in *The Red Badge of Courage.* But his agony doesn't stop there. After becoming a soldier, he's forced to choose between two father figures: Tom Berenger's scarred killing machine, Sergeant Barnes, and Willem Dafoe's compassionate and principled pro, Sergeant Elias. Barnes and Elias are equally good soldiers, but they're also fundamentally at odds. They represent two attitudes toward war, society, and their buddies. Barnes (like Sergeant Croft in Norman Mailer's *The Naked and the Dead*) is the man whose spiritual home is a battlefield, who takes pleasure in killing, joy in affirming his own seeming indestructibility. Elias is simply the professional who's adapted, who does his job well, knows how to survive, and takes care of his friends and men. In a clever twist Stone has cast, as Barnes (the Neville Brand–Aldo Ray part), an actor who has a stunning, movie-star profile (Berenger played the young Paul Newman in Richard Lester's prequel to *Butch Cassidy and the Sundance Kid*), and then seared over his glacial, Grecian good looks with a huge facial scar, like a volcanic seam. And the good soldier, Elias, is played by an actor, Dafoe, who has hitherto specialized almost exclusively in psychopathic villains (*Streets of Fire, To Live and Die in L.A.*). Appearances are deceiving, and on the battlefield, Barnes and Elias (and everyone else) are stripped bare, illumined by shrapnel fire and the moment of truth.

If Barnes and Elias represent two poles in the platoon, the men also

cluster around them in separate groups. Elias's buddies are multiracial, pot smoking: They carouse together in a tent fumy with smoke
and Motown. Barnes's bunch swigs booze and trades insults in a tent
decorated with *Playboy* centerfolds: Their number includes one cer-
tifiable psychopath, Bunny (Matt Dillon's younger brother Kevin).
The division is schematic — and it also identifies *Platoon* as a movie of
the more simplistic eighties, however much it may swim against the
mainstream. The villains here are craven or black-hearted, the heroes
sympathetic. There's very little crossover or ambivalence. Yet this
rock-hard certainty also helps the movie work, as does Stone's trademark dialogue — furiously profane, salty, hellish, almost comically
loaded with obscenity. (Stone's scatology is stylized: blank verse in
four-letter words.)

Stone captures, with amazing convincingness, two sides of war:
the fury and the pathological heat of the battles, and the intense, sim-
mering languorousness and fatigue in between. It's a tribute to the
film that, after watching it (however exaggerated the moral fable at
its center), you feel you may understand what combat soldiers must
have gone through. (This verisimilitude was deliberately sought after: Stone put his entire cast through two weeks of jungle drill and
boot camp before shooting. If they look sapped, draggy, desperately
exhausted, full of jumpy nerves, it's partially real-life transference.)
And the entire cast is fine. Even though the roles owe a great deal to
many other offbeat or antitraditional American war movies (Anthony Mann's *Men in War,* Sam Fuller's *Merrill's Marauders,* and Don
Siegel's *Hell Is for Heroes* spring instantly to mind), they all play with
rare conviction and intensity: Sheen, Dafoe, Berenger, Dillon, Forest
Whitaker as Big Harold, Francesco Quinn as Rhah, John C. McGin-
ley as the perfidious Sergeant O'Neill, Reggie Johnson as the screwup
Junior, Richard Edson as Sal. Watching *Platoon,* you are always aware
of several levels of meaning: what war has always meant to Americans as filtered through the movies, what it meant to the American
psyche and politics during the Vietnam years, and what, beneath it
all, it actually must have been. Stone shifts back and forth between
the levels: He never seems to be inhabiting any one zone completely,
though at the end he seems to revert to fable, poem, and symbolism
(and a climactic summing-up narration he probably should have cut).
Yet such is his passion here (he wrote *Platoon* ten years ago, and has
been working to film it ever since) that the movie never seems
strained; it grabs most of what it goes after.

If *Salvador* showed Stone as one of the gutsiest new directors in

Hollywood — a macho moralist in the Robert Aldrich–John Huston–Sam Peckinpah mold with his own special dose of scabrous full-throttle intensity — *Platoon* also shows him (and cinematographer Robert Richardson) as action moviemakers of the first water. The movie may have flaws, but it drives so hard, reaches so far, and churns up so much emotion that it seems niggling to recall them. Its weird intensity, perhaps, comes from contradictions in its creator. Like Peckinpah, Stone loves the macho irreverence and raw guts of his characters, and he's able to communicate the exhilaration of combat in a believable way. But he's also someone who looks straight at the dark side: the brutalities visited upon the villagers, the psychopathology given free rein in the heat of battle, the killer soul that Vietnam revealed in some. You get it all here, or most of it, and it's enough to leave you limp. Like warfare, *Platoon* leaves you exhausted, drained, exhilarated, sorrowful. The guilt is there, and so is the excitement: the remorse and the fever pitch. To dredge up an old critical cliché (which, here, is fully appropriate), it's a powerhouse of a movie. At its best, it's a grenade blast that cuts you to the heart.

Isthmus, January 16, 1987

PLATOON

Pauline Kael

Oliver Stone, who wrote and directed *Platoon,* based on his own experiences, dropped out of Yale at nineteen, taught Chinese students in Vietnam, did a stint in the merchant marine, and finished a novel (in Mexico), which he couldn't get published. Feeling, he says, that he needed to atone for his life of privilege and his individuality — that he had to be an anonymous common soldier — he enlisted in the army, and on his twenty-first birthday, in September 1967, he was on his way back to Vietnam, where he saw action with the Twenty-fifth Infantry along the Cambodian border. In the next fifteen months, he was wounded twice and decorated twice. He came home, he acknowledges, a freaked-out pothead; at one point, his stockbroker father paid off some people to get him out of jail for marijuana possession. In 1969, he enrolled at New York University film school, where he had Martin Scorsese as a teacher and pulled himself together. "Scorsese gave me film as a way to use my energies," he said to Peter Blauner in a recent interview in *New York*. We can surmise that Stone became a grunt in Vietnam to "become a man" and to become a writer. As *Platoon,* a coming-of-age film, demonstrates, he went through his rite of passage, but, as *Platoon* also demonstrates, he became a very bad writer—a hype artist. Actually, he had already proved this in his crude scripts for *Midnight Express* and *Scarface*. (He was also cowriter of *Conan the Barbarian, Year of the Dragon,* and *8 Million Ways to Die.*) Stone has an action writer's special, dubious flair: His scripts have drive—they ram their way forward, jacking up the melodrama to an insane pitch. Luckily, he's a better director than writer.

Salvador, the early-in-1986 film that Stone directed and cowrote, had a sensationalistic propulsiveness, and a hero (James Woods) whose hipster hostility was integral to the film's whole jittery, bad-trip tone. I don't think *Platoon* is nearly as good a movie. Although Stone was born in 1946, this is like a young man's first, autobiographical—and inflated—work. Written in 1976, eight years after his war experiences, the script is swamped by his divided intentions: He's trying to give us an account of what it was like to be an infantryman in Vietnam in 1967–1968, and to present this in all its immediacy and craziness, but he's also trying to compose a requiem for that war. The results are overwrought, with too much filtered light, too much poetic license, and too damn much romanticized insanity.

The picture begins with an epigraph from Ecclesiastes ("Rejoice, O young man, in thy youth!"), and then the music, Samuel Barber's "Adagio for Strings" (which was used so chastely in *The Elephant Man*), comes on in a soupy orchestration by Georges Delerue—and the movie is grandiloquent before it even gets rolling. The first images draw us in, though: Charlie Sheen's twenty-one-year-old Chris Taylor—the Oliver Stone character—arrives in the confusion of Vietnam, and the plane that brought him is loaded with body bags for the return trip. Just about everything to do with Chris's initial disorientation, his getting to know the men in the platoon, and the predawn jungle ambush in which he sees the enemy advancing but is paralyzed with fear and can't warn the other men, and then is wounded, has dramatic life in it. So does the small talk. There's a good, if perhaps too eloquent, sequence with the men in a hooch, drinking and doping, listening to rock 'n' roll and dancing; in a psychedelic, homoerotic bit, an older soldier blows pot smoke through a rifle and Chris inhales it—it's like the seductive smoke-through-the-prison-wall in Jean Genet's *Un Chant d'Amour*. And there's a fine, scary scene in which the men are attacked in their fox-holes and the bursts of fire are like a light show in the middle of a nightmare.

There are scenes unlike any I've seen before, in which we can see the soldiers' frustration, and how they're caught in a revenge fever. Then, when they take a small village suspected of aiding the Viet-cong, their rage against the villagers builds in waves and finds release in violence against animals, a helpless grinning idiot, women, children. The film shows Chris taking part in the cruelty and then gaining control of himself, and grasping at first hand what many of us at home watching TV grasped—that whether the Vietnamese won or lost in the fight it was what we were doing to them that was destroying us. The film is about victimizing ourselves as well as others; it's about shame. That's the only way in which it's political; it doesn't deal with what the war was about—it's conceived strictly in terms of what these American infantrymen go through.

Platoon has many things to recommend it, but its major characters aren't among them. Chris is a pleasant-faced blank—not the actor, the character—and, regrettably, he narrates the movie by reading aloud the letters he writes home to his grandmother. You might think that Stone would be too hip to add the explanatory emotions this way—particularly after Sheen's father, Martin, recited the tor-mented, purploid prose that Michael Herr wrote for the narration of *Apocalypse Now*. The voice-overs here are even more stupefying, since they're easier to comprehend. They're populist sentiments reminis-cent of the Joad family conversations in *The Grapes of Wrath*.

Well here I am—anonymous alright, with guys nobody really cares about—they come from the end of the line, most of 'em small towns you never heard of—Pulaski, Tennessee; Brandon, Mississippi; Pork Bend, Utah; Wampum, Pennsylvania. Two years high school's about it, maybe if they're lucky, a job wait-ing for 'em back in a factory, but most of 'em got nothing, they're poor, they're the unwanted. . . . They're the best I've ever seen grandma, the heart and soul—maybe I've finally found it way down here in the mud—maybe from down here I can start up again and be something I can be proud of, without having to fake it, be a fake human being. Maybe I can see some-thing I don't yet see, learn something I don't yet know.

It's like some terrible regression. Stone's gone back to being a literary preppy.

He's thinking like a preppy, too. Chris finds two authority figures in the platoon: the two sergeants, who were once friends, and are personifications of good and evil. Willem Dafoe's Sergeant Elias is a supersensitive hippie pothead, who cares about the men—he's a veteran fighter who's kept his soul. Tom Berenger's Sergeant Barnes is a kickass boozer—a psycho, whose scarred, dead-eyed face suggests the spirit of war, or the figure of Death in a medieval morality play. The movie is about the miseries of Nam, but it's also about the tensions that develop between the factions in the platoon who line up with one or the other—Love or Hate, Life or Death, Christ or the Devil. And it's about Chris's learning—and, worse, telling us—that "we weren't fighting the enemy; we were fighting ourselves," and, yes, that he feels "like the child of Barnes and Elias."

This melodramatic shortcut—and Stone's reduction of all the issues of the war to make them fit the tags "good" and "evil"—may make you wonder if he is using filmmaking as a substitute for drugs. (The picture itself, in representing the heads as the good guys, makes a case for the socializing, humanizing qualities of dope; God Himself seems to be on the side of the dopers.) Stone is in such a hurry to get a reaction out of us that he can't bother to create characters with different sides. The two sergeants are posed and photographed to be larger than life, but the roles are underwritten. Dafoe's tough, courageous Elias is like a young Klaus Kinski playing innocent miss, and Berenger's glamorous, scarred-up Barnes, who has been shot seven times but can't be finished off until he wills it, looks as if he were a killing machine carved out of jagged rock, though he moves with a slithering grace. The two are mythic figures out of nowhere—Elias who's high only on drugs and goodness, Barnes who's high on war. The men in the platoon may suddenly be trashed by a line. Round-faced Forest Whitaker, who plays gentle Big Harold, is going along all right until after the atrocities against the villagers, when he has to say, "I'm hurtin' real bad inside." That's the end of his performance.

Stone tries for bigger effects than he earns. When he doesn't destroy things with the voice-over banalities or a square line of dialogue, he may do it with a florid gesture, such as having the Christus, Sergeant Elias, run away from the Vietcong who are firing at him, run toward a departing helicopter, which is his only chance for life, and lift his arms to heaven. There are too many scenes where you think, It's a bit much. The movie crowds you; it doesn't give you room to have an honest emotion.

You knew you were getting pulp in *Salvador* because it was grungy; here the pulp is presented pedagogically, and it's made classy and meditative, but it's laid on thick—that idiot gets his head bashed in by Americans trying to wipe the grin off his face. Is it powerful? Sure it is. (This kind of routine played well in the twenties and thirties, too, when the bad guys in westerns did it, and it wasn't as graphic then.) Stone has talent: He shot this epic in the Philippines on a tight budget—roughly $6.5 million. He's a filmmaker, all right, but he lacks judgment. Just about everything in *Platoon* is too explicit, and is so heightened that it can numb you and make you feel jaded. You may suspect that at some low-down level Stone (he appears as the major blown up in his bunker at the end of the film) is against judgment. Elias is supposed to represent true manliness, but if Stone's other films tell us anything—if this film tells us anything—it's that he's temperamentally more on the side of the crazy stud Barnes. The preppy narration extolling the nobility of the common man is worse than a "privileged" boy's guilt—it's a grown man's con.

Stone's moviemaking doesn't suggest that he was a young, idealistic Chris Taylor going to war to find himself in the comradeship of the anonymous but, rather, that he was a romantic loner who sought his manhood in the excitement of violent fantasy. Stone seems to want to get high on war, like Barnes. The key scene in the movie is directed so that it passes like a dream. In a remote area, Chris calmly, deliberately shoots a fellow soldier. There is no suggestion that Chris is an innocent corrupted by having got used to violence. The murder is presented as an unambiguous, justified execution. This oddly weightless pulp revenge fantasy is floating around in Stone's requiem, along with a lot of old-movie tricks.

I know that *Platoon* is being acclaimed for its realism, and I expect to be chastised for being a woman finding fault with a war film. But I've probably seen as much combat as most of the men saying, "This is how war is."

The New Yorker, January 12, 1987

CASUALTIES OF WAR

Hal Hinson

Even at their most disturbing, Brian De Palma's films have always seemed like brilliant abstractions, sinister theorems from a bloody virtuoso. But *Casualties of War,* the director's rigorous, unflinching, masterly new film, is something else altogether. It is a film of great emotional power and great seriousness in which all of the filmmaker's talents and interests are in balance. It is a breakthrough work, a signal of an artist's blossoming maturity, and one of the most punishing, morally complex movies about men at war ever made.

Casualties of War takes place out in the world, not up in its creator's head. It's no less a consciously created work than De Palma's previous films, and no less spectacular stylistically, but there is a deeper involvement in his subject here, a new respect for his material. The sly theatricality has given way to a vivid realism. There is blood and violence, as there always is in a De Palma film, but when blood spills here, it is at body temperature, fresh from living, suffering people.

What De Palma gives us, essentially, is the anatomy of an atrocity. He shows us in detail the unraveling of the moral fabric, how the descent into barbarism is a journey of steps. The film's script was written by the playwright David Rabe, but its origins are in an actual incident, reported first in 1969 in *The New Yorker* by Daniel Lang, in which a five-soldier squad on a long-range reconnaissance mission kidnapped a South Vietnamese girl and took her miles away from her village, where four of the five men raped, brutalized, and eventually murdered her.

In the film the participants are heartland-bred American boys whose most remarkable quality is their averageness. Their leader is a sergeant named Meserve (Sean Penn), a short-timer who wants simply to live through the last few weeks of his stint and head back to the world. Chewing up his words in a thick Jersey accent, Meserve is tough in the way that comic-book soldiers are tough; he's all cigar butts and whorehouse bluster. In the field, though, he knows what's what, and the other men look up to him as a model of survival. They hang on his every word, even imitate his bantam strut, because they believe their lives depend on it.

The soldier with the most to learn is a fresh-faced kid named Eriksson (Michael J. Fox), who's been in the jungle for only three weeks and still can't quite get it into his head that he's signed up for a war and not a Boy Scout camporee. Early on, this bland kid's sunny naïveté provides us with a couple of endearing comic moments, especially when he risks taking a potentially lethal gift from a villager rather than act "rude." And in another scene, when he's helping an old man plow a rice paddy, his openness seems almost gallant, and we want to accept his vision of the world—even the world at war—as benign and forgiving.

We know from past De Palma films, though, that moments of peace are followed inevitably by violence. This eruption, in which Brown (Erik King), the squad's radioman, is cut off in midsentence by a sniper, may be the most devastating sequence De Palma has ever filmed. He gets something here that has never been captured before: that horrible instant at which time itself seems to explode from the pressure of some calamity and, simultaneously, somewhere in the deep center of the chaos, an almost surreal quiet prevails.

Like Meserve, Brown had only a short time left to serve, and his death seeps into the atmosphere like a poison. In the shower, the GIs talk about how much they hate the Vietnamese, who they feel have betrayed them in return for their help. Of all the men, Meserve is the most affected, and when his leave is canceled because "Charlie" is in town visiting the whores that are, by rights, supposed to be his, something in him snaps.

At first, when he outlines his plan to obtain "a little portable R and R," the other members of the squad—except for Clark (Don Harvey), the sadist—don't know how to react. But before dawn they have reached their destination, and Meserve and Clark have snatched their victim, Oahn (Thuy Thu Le), from her sleep and carried her off to the hysterical screams of her family. As they leave, the girl's mother runs after them and tries to hand a scarf to her daughter—a futile, illogical gesture that makes the whole scene unbearably believable.

Every move that De Palma makes here carries moral weight, right down to his choice of lens. Watching the movie, you feel that every frame is crucial. Perhaps only a director who is used to taking chances and used to controversy could film the scene in which Meserve, Clark, the dim-witted Hatcher (John C. Reilly), and the weak-willed Diaz (John Leguizamo) take turns with Oahn in the hut. There is nothing explicit or garish in the way De Palma has captured the horror of what is being done, but at the same time he doesn't turn away, and the tastefulness he shows in pulling his camera back, so that we see it from the point of view of Eriksson, the sole dissenter, makes the sequence all the more painful.

Fox is marvelous throughout the film, but especially here, when he is forced to stand his ground. By stages, we see the transformations in this optimistic kid; we watch him close down emotionally and grow disillusioned. Fox makes Eriksson's struggle to hold onto himself palpable; he makes us feel that his soul is caving in. At the opposite moral pole, Penn's Meserve is just as tormented, perhaps even more so for having completely regressed. Meserve isn't a likable character, but as Penn plays him we do have empathy for him. There are problems, though: Striving for big effects, Penn plays him too boldly. Where the other actors are restrained and forceful (especially Erik King as Brown), Penn at times seems mannered and cartoonish. He gives more where less would have been ideal.

On one level, De Palma's films have always been about complicity; in his pictures, everyone is implicated; no one is innocent, least of all the audience. In this sense, Eriksson acts as our surrogate, and he is not let off the hook simply by not participating. His horror is not enough, and neither is his determination to bring the incident to light. To demonstrate the burden of this memory, the film is presented as Eriksson's reverie as he sits on the BART train in San Francisco, haunted by the incident and going over the details, again and again, torturing himself for not knowing what action to take. And to cleanse him of his guilt, the filmmakers have provided a phony resolution, one set to the swelling of an angel chorus. The moment doesn't work, but it doesn't really matter. It — and one atrocious speech by Fox at the center of the film — are the only faltering steps in a movie that refuses to make facile choices. *Casualties of War* is the kind of culminating work that brings the rest of an artist's career into razor-sharp focus. De Palma has created a movie that is intensely personal and at the same time transcends the limitations of the personal. It is great in the ways that the best De Palma films have been great, but with something more — something like soul.

Washington Post, August 18, 1989

CASUALTIES OF WAR

Richard Schickel

Why are we in Vietnam? Again. At this late date. In the case of *Casualties of War,* there can be only one answer: for further diagnostic tests on the national conscience. For the story it tells, based on an incident first reported in *The New Yorker* by Daniel Lang two decades ago, is too brutally horrific to contemplate unless we can derive some moral edification, some guide to the larger enigmas of human conduct, from it.

The story, recounted in a grinding, realistic style that is unlike Brian De Palma's usual manner of playing fast and loose with death, is simple to describe. A small unit under the command of a Sergeant Meserve (Sean Penn, in an uncompromising performance) sets off on a long-range reconnaissance mission. On Meserve's orders, it stops at a peasant village, where it abducts a young girl and sadistically binds and gags her for the many awful hours of their trek. The girl, who is heartbreakingly played by a delicate newcomer named Thuy Thu Le, will serve as "portable R and R." In order words, Meserve intends that he and his men will gang-rape her. This they eventually do, with only one among them, Eriksson (Michael J. Fox), refusing to participate and trying to rescue the girl. She is murdered in a firefight, and ultimately Eriksson, despite threats to his own life and the indifference of his commanding officers, succeeds in bringing charges against his sometime buddies. They receive, at last, stern punishment from a court-martial.

Its surface realism notwithstanding, this movie must be read symbolically, especially since it is presented as a dream that overtakes Eriksson years later, when he encounters a young Oriental woman on a train who reminds him of the long-ago victim. In the dream, Meserve—arrogant, competent, headlong (in other words a born American leader)—is an archetype of the worst in the national character. Eriksson—frail looking but articulate and morally alert—is the beleaguered best. The remainder of the unit is, of course, the hulking, muddled majority, all too willing to be conned by anyone who seems to be sure of his goals, however perverse. Their victim represents all of the innocents who, by accident, find themselves in the path of Yankee imperialism.

The script, by playwright David Rabe (*Streamers, Hurlyburly*) introduces some complexities into this schematic story. Eriksson owes his life to Meserve's military skills. The sergeant, who is not presented as a psychopath, and the other men are in a furor because a buddy has been killed in an ambush at a supposedly pacified village. Eriksson has an interesting speech in which he argues that the standard rationale for bad wartime behavior ("we might at any second be blown away") is exactly wrong. It is precisely because soldiers live inches from death that they should be "extra careful about what we do." The ending, in which Eriksson is awakened from his nightmare and, in effect, offered absolution by his trainmate, seems to propose that decent Americans may, at last, enjoy sleep untroubled by the naggings of historical conscience. It is, at least in popular-cultural terms, novel.

But still the movie does not work. Its true story is too singular to serve as the basis for moral generalizations. The ideas advanced by the film are, in any case, not significantly different from the ones put forward by opponents of the war while it was going on. But it is a distant and curiously monotonous tone that finally betrays *Casualties of War*. It numbs the conscience instead of awakening it.

Time, August 21, 1989

BORN ON THE FOURTH OF JULY

Stuart Klawans

Most movies never reach an emotional simmer; a rare few boil over. And then there's *Born on the Fourth of July*, which shoots off the screen like pressurized steam. Directed with furious, relentless energy by Oliver Stone, the film keeps hitting moments that feel like climaxes and then pushes them further. Stone doesn't seem to think that it's enough to strand a pair of Vietnam veterans in the Mexican desert, as if they were Vladimir and Estragon in fatigues and wheelchairs. Whereas other directors might cut on that image, Stone has to go on, making the vets get into a fight over primacy in being damned. (The prize goes to the one who killed more babies.) And still the scene won't end. In case the audience should be insufficiently appalled,

Stone doesn't quit until the vets have knocked each other out of their wheelchairs and lie sprawled in the sand.

It's about time, too. *Born on the Fourth of July* has the urgency of a truth told — or screamed — against a deafening Muzak of lies. Based on the memoir of the same name by Ron Kovic (who collaborated on the screenplay), the film wants to shout down the sentimentalization of the Vietnam War, the sweet talk about national healing, most of all the current pieties about the war's veterans. This is perhaps the first I-was-there picture (including Stone's own *Platoon*) to vent full blast the self-doubt and self-pity and justifiable rage so many veterans have felt.

In outline, its story is simple. Kovic came from a working-class Catholic family on Long Island, enlisted in the marines, and served two tours in Vietnam. Wounded in battle, he returned home in a wheelchair, paralyzed from the chest down but still convinced he had done his duty, still certain that anybody who opposed the war should move to Russia. Then he started to think. He despaired; he drank; after a long, messy period, he turned to literature and activism. His memoir won him respect as a writer; his work with Vietnam Veterans Against the War made him a public figure.

But this is like summarizing *Il Trovatore* by calling it a story about mistaken identity. What makes *Born on the Fourth of July* so remarkable is the way it inflates Kovic's testimony to epic proportions. For the price of your ticket, you get a grand-scale re-creation of American life, 1956–1976; a psychohistory of the Vietnam War; a drama about Everyvet. The action stays tightly focused on Kovic (portrayed by Tom Cruise with more grit and self-abandon than I'd thought him capable of). The focus is so tight, in fact, that some of the close-ups threaten to burst the frame. The camera generally stays right on the surface of Cruise's eyes or else substitutes for them; with Stone's non-stop dollies and pans and tilts, you might come out of the theater feeling as if you had been fighting battles personally, rolling around drunkenly in a wheelchair, and getting hit on the head by cops. And yet, for all the hyperkinetic, subjective camera movement, the unrelenting focus on one character, the film probably tells you more about American society and politics than all previous Vietnam movies combined, with *Easy Rider* thrown in for good measure.

In particular, it dramatizes Kovic's notion that he received a military education just by living in Massapequa, New York. The first time we see this all-American boy, in a sequence that looks unnervingly like a conventional war movie, he is ten years old and playing soldier with his friends. "We couldn't wait to be men," Cruise says on the sound track. And then we see what a man's upbringing entailed: admiring the veterans in Independence Day parades, listening raptly to John Kennedy talk of sacrifice, attending to the bloodthirsty rantings of the high-school wrestling coach. It also meant a fear of women. In a remarkable extended sequence, with a 1960s mise en scène so thickly layered that the actors almost have to wade through the period detail, we see Kovic fumble his chance for a date, all because he's so caught up in getting out of Long Island and into the marines. He quakes at asking his sweetheart to the prom, as if she were the very incarnation of those impure thoughts he's been warned against. The best he can do is talk modestly about the job he's got to do in Vietnam, hoping she'll be impressed. Then, in his final moral conflict before leaving for boot camp, he gets down on his knees on prom night and prays to know whether he's done the right thing. Should he dance with a girl or go to Asia and fight communism?

It's possible to see the rest of the film as the story of how Kovic realized he'd made the wrong choice and then learned to live with the consequences. I could go into detail; but rather than regale you with the rest of the eighteen pages of notes I scribbled so frantically in the dark, let me just encourage you to go. The film is long, overbearing, brutal, and indispensable. It gives you more of one man's reality than you can easily handle, combined with more political honesty than anyone could expect from Hollywood. Just how far does it go to get things right? Put it this way: In the big campus demonstration scene, the main speaker is Abbie Hoffman. May the dear man rest in peace—he finally made it into that major motion picture.

The Nation, January 1, 1990

BORN ON THE FOURTH OF JULY

Hal Hinson

Oliver Stone's *Born on the Fourth of July* unfurls itself with an ambitious flourish, like a stirring, patriotic anthem. It's his Main Street symphony, and in every frame, you feel his passion to make a grandiose social statement, to unload the movie equivalent of the Great American Novel and to define our age. In every frame you feel him empty-ing out his heart and soul.

This is an impassioned movie, made with conviction and evangelical verve. It's also hysterical and overbearing and alienating. Using Ron Kovic's autobiographical account of his lower-middle-class, small-town American upbringing, Stone stretches an epic canvas and splatters onto it all his beliefs about Vietnam, America, family, patriotism, and just about everything that's happened here in the last quarter century.

This is not new territory for Stone. The film could almost be called *Platoon, Part II;* it establishes the social and political context that led to Vietnam, plus its thundering aftershocks.

He begins Kovic's saga before Kovic enlists in the marines for a tour in Vietnam that ultimately leaves him paralyzed from the chest down and leads him to overturn his cradle-born beliefs in God and country. It's easy to see why Stone chose Kovic's story to tell — it isn't simply about the war; it's about the disenchantment over the loss of the American dream. It's about how Kovic — who's played with diligence here by Tom Cruise and who stands in for millions of others like him — is betrayed by the Fourth of July parades he's watched as a boy, by the John Wayne movies and the Yankee Doodle hoopla. About how everything in the culture, from playing war games in the woods as a boy to high school wrestling, draws this American Everyman to fight in Southeast Asia and lose all that matters to him — his body, his values, his family, his country.

Kovic's book — which he and Stone adapted for the screen — tells of younger days wall-to-wall with dreams of glory and heroism. His father — who's played by Raymond J. Barry and comes off as more of a weakling than in the book — works at the A&P. The son wants more, and in Cruise's portrayal, his determination to succeed makes him seem grim and slightly haunted. Cruise is effective early as a square-shouldered, intensely disciplined boy dominated by his sternly devout mother (Caroline Kava).

These opening scenes — which are set in Kovic's hometown of Massapequa, New York — are loaded with farm-fresh normalcy. But the camera-flexing, emphatic style that Stone uses gives them a kind of spooky burn. Stone, of course, can't help signaling that this all-American existence is going to turn into a horror show. The techniques he employs, in fact, are those of horror movies. When the scene shifts to Vietnam and Kovic and his unit mistakenly fire on a village of women and children, Stone and his cinematographer

Robert Richardson give the carnage a maddened frenzy. They make sure the screaming baby sprawled next to its dead mother is burned into our minds and lock us inside the young soldier's confused thought processes as, struggling with the blinding sun and the chaos of moving bodies, he kills one of his own men.

This is the film's pivotal moment, and it's shot with a searing dynamism. In it, all the moral underpinnings of Kovic's life are destroyed. Later, when a bullet severs nerves, leaving him without feeling in his lower body and unable to walk, the point is underscored. In body and mind, he has been ravaged.

Dramatically, the long following section, in which Kovic is forced through the hell of recovery in pigsty conditions in an understaffed veterans' hospital, doesn't contribute anything essential, but in Stone's view that is probably the reason the picture was made. He didn't include the treatment of veterans in *Platoon,* and he presents Kovic's ordeal as a kind of septic immersion — a sordid rite of passage.

Here Stone is more an advocate for social justice than an artist. The scenes in Mexico — where Kovic escapes after being kicked out of his parents' house and finds acceptance among a clot of disaffected vets led by a Manson-like figure played by Willem Dafoe — are, in their own fevered, hallucinatory terms, the film's best.

Afterward, the movie shifts, first to Kovic's purifying confession of his sins to the parents of the boy he killed, and then to his transformation into an antiwar activist. This metamorphosis culminates in his speech before the 1980 Democratic National Convention, where his mother's dream is realized and the film comes full circle. It's hard to imagine, though, that audiences will feel similarly transformed. *Born on the Fourth of July* is nettlesome work. Stone has gifts as a filmmaker, but subtlety is not one of them. In essence, he's a propagandist, and, as it turns out, the least effective representative for his point of view. Stone wants desperately to effect a radical transformation in his audience. But it's this panicky drive to convert us to his way of thinking that undermines Stone's message.

It's not so much that what he puts on screen is negligible. The perceptions are valid, but they're not particularly original, and his personal investment in his issues and his vivid, hyperbolic style camouflage just how commonplace his ideas are. His major failing, though, is that he's not interested in any emotional state that doesn't include fireworks and strobe effects. Cruise's work in front of the camera is as ardent as his director's behind it. But Stone doesn't give his actors much room to work. He's too busy filling in all the details himself.

There's another problem: Because there have now been so many films about Vietnam, because we've seen so many innocent villagers gunned down, so many accidental deaths, so much tragedy and pain, unless a radically different perspective is presented — as in De Palma's *Casualties of War* — a numbing sense of familiarity sets in. If we're going to have to endure these tortures again, there had better be an urgent and essential need for it. In *Born on the Fourth of July,* the urgency is there, but ultimately, urgency alone is not good enough.

Washington Post, December 20, 1989

GET REAL!

Documentaries have a bum rap with moviegoers — the result for us, no doubt, of too many dozy sessions in high school science seminars watching films about the life cycle of the basic food groups, or some such. Documentaries carry the "educational" taint.

For the general public, they also exist now almost solely on television, where financing is more available (though still a dribble) and audiences are more built-in (though still minuscule).

And yet some of the most highly charged and provocative theatrical features have been documentaries. They raise issues ranging from the highfalutin (What is "real"?) to the low-down (Is Madonna going to spear someone with her conical outerwear?).

Perhaps one reason documentaries have been making such a welcome impact in the past few years is that, by comparison, most fictional films seem to be concerned with nothing at all. Documentaries, even self-promoting ones, are frequently *about* something — a true-crime conundrum (*The Thin Blue Line*); General Motors plant closings (*Roger & Me*); a material girl (*Truth or Dare*). They feed our desire to get beyond the dopey star turns and tricked-up, seen-it-all-before plots. (Environmentalists take note: Hollywood is the largest recycling plant in the country!)

But should one go to these movies expecting the truth? For a documentarian like *Roger & Me*'s Michael Moore, who was accused of juggling the chronology of events in his movie, what constitutes the breaking of faith with the audience? Just as dramatic films like *JFK* incorporate documentary footage (both actual and pseudo), documentaries like Errol Morris's *The Thin Blue Line* offer up reenactments. (Morris's reenactments were generally believed to have been a factor in his film's snub for a best documentary Oscar in 1988.) The core of the debate in the following pieces is the maddening, mysterious linkage between fiction and documentary.

ROGER & ME

Stuart Klawans

You might recall Michael Moore as the fellow from Flint, Michigan, who lasted about four months as editor of *Mother Jones*. After getting canned, he returned with empty pockets to his hometown and sued the magazine for wrongful discharge. This brought him an out-of-court settlement of $58,000 — a turn of events so inspirational that he decided, without the encumbrance of experience, to put his money into making a film. The result, titled *Roger & Me,* is so good that I wish *Mother Jones* had fired Moore twice, so he could have made two movies.

Though its subject — the destruction of a once-prosperous town by factory closings — could hardly be more wrenching, *Roger & Me* is one of the funniest, most invigorating movies you're likely to see this year. "I figured, who wants to sit in a dark theatre and watch people collect free federal surplus cheese?" Moore says. "How's that going to be entertaining? How's that going to change anything?" He decided his documentary would have to be accessible and funny — *The Atomic Café* is the model he cites — and to some degree, Moore has followed that example. *Roger & Me* is crammed with found footage: home movies, promotional films, TV shows, and stock clips, most of them used with deadpan humor. (This might be the place to mention the editors, Wendey Stanzler and Jennifer Beman; amazingly, they too are novice filmmakers.)

But the mocking use of found footage is already a bit too familiar a technique; though well employed here, it would not have been effective in itself. The real delight of *Roger & Me* comes from Michael Moore's personality—his dry, commonsense wit as a narrator, his shambling on-camera presence, his interest in the people he encounters as he knocks around Flint. In his amused sympathy with all sorts of human oddity he reminds me of such gonzo documentarians as Les Blank and Tony Buba. Moore also brings to mind Harvey Pekar, the auteur of *American Splendor* comics, another autobiographer of the dead industrial heartland.

As the Me of the title, Moore represents not only himself but a long line of industrial laborers. His father used to work on the line at AC Spark Plugs; his uncle was among the sit-down strikers who founded the United Automobile Workers. On behalf of them and everybody else he knew in Flint, Moore thought he should invite Roger to visit his hometown—that being Roger Smith, chair of General Motors. Under Smith's leadership, GM had been closing its U.S. factories and relocating the assembly lines to more favorable climates, such as Mexico. Moore therefore thought it would be a good thing for the GM chair to pass through town, so he could see for himself how the loss of thirty thousand jobs might cause some inconvenience. Strangely enough, Smith declined the invitation. In fact, he wouldn't even talk with Moore.

A large part of *Roger & Me* thus consists of a hilarious series of failed efforts to meet Roger Smith. Moore—a portly young man with long, dirty-blond hair and radar-scanner eyes—keeps turning up with his camera crew at GM headquarters in Detroit, at the Grosse Pointe Yacht Club, at the Detroit Athletic Club, at the annual GM stockholders' meeting. Usually, he is dressed in an old blue windbreaker and a baseball cap bearing the message "I'm out for Trout." He sometimes augments this costume with the accessory of a toothpick stuck between his lips. People keep asking him if he has an appointment. When one of Roger Smith's guardians requests his credentials, Moore hands over a discount card from a pizza establishment. "I didn't have a business card," he explains on the sound track.

Since these near-encounters with Roger happened at long intervals, Moore had a lot of time on his hands. He filled it by taking his crew around Flint to see how the neighbors were coping with the economic equivalent of occupying ground zero under the Enola Gay. In their own grim way, these meetings are as funny as the hunt for Roger Smith. GM had put some money into a job-retraining program, so its former employees could learn to work at Taco Bell. All of them dropped out, though: A Taco Bell manager explains that they couldn't take the challenge of the fast-food environment. Other former autoworkers and their families started selling Amway products door to door, though this, too, proved full of unexpected risks. One of Moore's informants, trained as a color consultant for makeup and clothing, suffered a shocking loss of faith when she discovered that the instructors had classified her incorrectly — they had called her an autumn, but she was really a spring.

Some of the others captured by Moore get a little closer to the bone. At the Flint Plasma Company, Moore talks with a man who makes a living selling blood. "They're open Monday, Tuesday, Wednesday, Thursday, and Friday," the man says, going over it carefully in his mind. "They're closed Saturday and Sunday." It's sidesplitting, unless you think about why the man can no longer remember how to say "weekdays."

And then there is the remarkable young woman Moore encounters when he sees a sign by the road: "Rabbits and Bunnies — Pets or Meat." He knocks on the door and asks about the rabbits. "Pets or meat?" asks the woman. It turns out that she makes $10 or $15 a week at this business, her only supplement to Social Security, and no doubt eats a hell of a lot of fried bunny. Of the working-class people in Moore's film, she is one of the survivors, a rare example of someone who actually gets by as an entrepreneur, the route to self-sufficiency touted by the ruling-class people and their shills.

The latter provide *Roger & Me* with its most outrageously funny moments, turning some sections of the film into a fantasia of misguided optimism and all-American puffery. Keep in mind that the rats in Flint had started to outnumber the humans; entire blocks were boarded up or burned down; the city had one of the highest homicide rates in the nation; and one of the few growth industries was in evictions. (Moore got close to Sheriff's Deputy Fred Ross and filmed him practicing this trade.) The civic leaders' response was to try turning Flint into a tourist center — you can't make this stuff up — spending millions to put up a luxury hotel and a quaint marketplace (designed by the people who built New York City's South Street Seaport) and topping it off with an indoor theme park called AutoWorld, celebrating the industry that had left town. GM built a $1 million exhibit for AutoWorld in which a puppet autoworker sang a love song to the robot that was replacing him on the assembly line. The song was titled

"Me and My Buddy." AutoWorld, the marketplace, and the hotel are all closed now. I assume the rats are doing fine.

The Nation, October 30, 1989

POSTSCRIPT: Michael Moore's *Roger & Me,* the movie America has been waiting for, opens at the end of December, bringing its tale of corporate rapacity and working-class pain to screens across the country, though not, as Moore notes, to Flint, Michigan, where it was shot. All the movie houses there have closed. Through a special arrangement with the film's distributor, Warner Brothers, *Roger & Me* will be shown as close to Flint as possible, at a multiplex three miles outside of town.

Given the rapturous welcome the film already has received at festivals, it's not surprising that some revisionist criticism has started to appear. You can't make a funny, angry, persuasive documentary about the depredations of capitalism and expect everyone just to smile.

The most recent focus of debate has been an article by Harlan Jacobson in the November/December 1989 issue of *Film Comment,* challenging Moore about how he selected and arranged the material in his film. Though I doubt Jacobson intended to harm either Moore or the movie, it's easy to see how other commentators might use the article as a weapon. Already, I've heard people speak with ill-disguised glee about how Moore has been "exposed."

So let me note that Moore has indeed given an accurate account of the trials of Flint with all the details fully explained in their proper order. He published it in *The Nation* of June 6, 1987. And yet, strangely enough, Warner Brothers did not beg him on that occasion for permission to bring Flint's story to the world. That had to wait for the film festival triumph of *Roger & Me.* My advice, then, is to ignore the phony controversy and see the movie twice. That way, you can catch the jokes you missed because of laughing so hard the first time.

The Nation, January 1, 1990

ROGER & ME

Pauline Kael

I've heard it said that Michael Moore's muckraking documentary *Roger & Me* is scathing and Voltairean. I've read that Michael Moore is "a satirist of the Reagan period equal in talent to Mencken and [Sinclair] Lewis," and "an irrepressible new humorist in the tradition of Mark Twain and Artemus Ward." But the film I saw was shallow and facetious, a piece of gonzo demagoguery that made me feel cheap for laughing.

Roger is Roger Smith, the chairman of General Motors, who, in Moore's account, closed eleven GM plants in Flint, Michigan, in 1986 (despite big profits), laid off thirty thousand workers, and set up plants in Mexico, where the wage rate was seventy cents an hour. In the film, he's directly responsible for bringing about the city's (unconvincingly speedy) deterioration. Flint, GM's birthplace, is also Michael Moore's hometown, and Moore, a journalist, previously inexperienced in film, set out, with a camera crew, ostensibly to persuade Roger Smith to come to Flint and see the human results of his policies. This mock mission is the peg that Moore hangs the picture on: He pursues Roger Smith over a span of two and a half years, from February 1987 to August 1989. Moore, who directed, produced, and wrote the film, and is its star, has defined his approach: "I knew the theme would be 'looking for Roger' and showing what was happening in Flint during this time period."

What happens is that Moore, a big, shambling joker in windbreaker and baseball cap, narrates his analysis of the ironies and idiocies of what's going on, and deadpans his way through interviews with an assortment of unlikely people, who are used as stooges, as filler. He asks them broad questions about the high rate of unemployment and the soaring crime rate, and their responses make them look like phonies or stupes; those who try to block his path or duck his queries appear to be flunkies. Low-level GM public-relations people make squirmy, evasive statements; elderly women on a golf course are confused as to what's wanted of them; visiting entertainers are cheery and optimistic; Miss Michigan, who is about to take part in the Miss America Pageant, tries to look concerned and smiles her prettiest. What does Moore expect? Why are these people being made targets for the audience's laughter? The camera makes brutal fun of a woman who's trying to earn money as an Amway color consultant, and it stares blankly at a woman who's supplementing her government checks by raising rabbits. (For a minute or two, we seem to be watching an Errol Morris movie.) Moore's final jab is at a woman with a Jewish name, whose job promoting the attractions of the city has been eliminated. He asks her what she's going to do next. When she says she's going to Tel Aviv, Moore seems to be drawing the conclusion that the rats are deserting the ship; something distasteful hovers over the closing credits.

Moore is the only one the movie takes straight. (Almost everybody else is a fun-house case.) This stand-up crusader appears to be the only person in town who's awake to the destruction of what used to be a thriving community. And we in the audience are expected to identify with his puckish sanity. The way he tells it, the people who run the town are incompetent twerps. (That's always popular with movie audiences.) He reports that the civic leaders have been thinking about solutions for the decay of the city and have come up with lamebrained fantasy schemes to attract tourism: a Hyatt Regency hotel and convention center; AutoWorld, a theme park; the Water Street Pavilion, a mall. The three projects are actually built; roughly $150 million is poured in, and all three are fiascoes.

I had stopped believing what Moore was saying very early; he was just too glib. Later, when he told us about the tourist schemes, I began to feel I was watching a film version of the thirties best-seller *A Short Introduction to the History of Human Stupidity,* and I began to wonder how so much of what was being reported had actually taken place in the two and a half years of shooting the film. So I wasn't surprised when I read Harlan Jacobson's article in the November/December 1989 *Film Comment* and learned that Moore had compressed the events of many years and fiddled with the time sequence. For example, the eleven plant closings announced in 1986 were in four states; the thirty thousand jobs were lost in Flint over a period of a dozen years; and the tourist attractions were constructed and failed well before the 1986 shutdowns that they are said to be a response to. Or let's take a smaller example of Moore at play. We're told that Ronald Reagan visited the devastated city, and we hear about what we assume is the President's response to the crisis. He had a pizza with twelve unemployed workers and advised them to move to Texas; we're told that during lunch the cash register was lifted from the pizza parlor. That's good for a few more laughs. But Reagan visited the city in

1980, when he wasn't yet president—he was a candidate. And the cash register had been taken two days earlier.

Whatever the reasons for the GM shutdowns, the company had a moral and financial responsibility to join with government agencies and the United Automobile Workers in arranging for the laid-off workers to reenter the labor force. Moore doesn't get into this—at least, not directly. Possibly he thought that he'd lose the audience's attention if he did. Maybe he thought that it was implicit in the gimmick of his wanting to show Roger the damage the company has done, but it's almost perverse of him to pretend that what's happened is all Roger Smith's fault, and to tell the story in cartoon form.

The movie is an aw-shucks, cracker-barrel pastiche. In Moore's jocular pursuit of Roger, he chases gags and improvises his own version of history. He comes on in a give-'em-hell style, but he breaks faith with the audience. The picture is like the work of a slick ad exec. It does something that is humanly very offensive: *Roger & Me* uses its leftism as a superior attitude. Members of the audience can laugh at ordinary working people and still feel that they're taking a politically correct position.

The New Yorker, January 8, 1990

TRUTH OR DARE

David Ansen

In the world of Madonna, Kitty Kelleys are superfluous—she's her own Kitty Kelley. During her inexorable climb from teeny-bopper tramp to international legend, the queen of self-exploitation has dropped media bombshells with a surgical precision the Pentagon would envy. Every season brings fresh outrage: the breakup with Sean Penn, the scandal over her "Like a Prayer" video, the hint of a lesbian affair with Sandra Bernhard, the new scandal over the racy "Justify My Love" video, and her current ribald interview in the *Advocate,* a gay biweekly. Miraculously, she seems immune to overexposure: Indeed, the more she wallows in the media mud the higher her stock rises, to the point where she is now often hailed as a political and feminist heroine. All of this has surprisingly little to do with talent, and everything to do with attitude. As she freely concedes in her dishy, down-and-dirty new documentary, *Truth or Dare,* she is not the world's greatest singer or dancer. "I'm interested in pushing people's buttons," she says. In *Truth or Dare* she lights up a whole console.

Madonna has broken the first role of celebrity: that mystery is an essential ingredient of stardom. From the days of Garbo on, it was what you kept hidden that nourished your mystique. *Truth or Dare* is intent on proving otherwise — or so it seems. For one of the most fascinating things about this behind-the-scenes, no-holds-barred document of her 1990 worldwide Blond Ambition concert tour is Madonna's Pirandellian gift for revealing everything and nothing simultaneously. When a natural-born exhibitionist exhibits herself, is it the "real" Madonna you are watching or an artful imitation of reality?

That conundrum is part of the fun of Alek Keshishian's provocative film. Whether you are wowed by Madonna's honesty or appalled by her shamelessness doesn't really matter: In either event, the movie turns you into a happy voyeur, eagerly awaiting the star's next outrageous move. See Madonna greet Kevin Costner in her dressing room and dismiss him with a gagging put-down. Watch her frolic in bed with her gay dancers. Listen to her X-rated description of what she did in bed with her childhood girlfriend. Gaze, amazed, as she accepts the dare to demonstrate her oral lovemaking technique on a bottle of mineral water. Observe her bossing her then-boyfriend Warren Beatty around the room.

Beatty's role in the movie is small but telling. As a member of the old school of publicity dodging, he is naturally horrified that she would let a documentary crew invade her own privacy (not to mention his) with such zest. He draws the line when she permits the camera to watch a doctor examine her damaged throat. With exquisite irony he mocks her lust for self-exposure. "She doesn't want to live off camera. Why would you bother to say something if it's off camera?" Beatty scores major points as the voice of sanity, but of course Madonna gets the final credit for including it in her film.

The unifying theme of Keshishian's movie is the notion of family. We see Madonna with her real family — her brother Christopher, with whom she's closest, her troubled brother Marty, just out of an alcohol-rehab program, and at the grave of her mother. When her father comes to her Detroit concert, she suffers a rare outbreak of modesty, admitting she toned down her infamous "masturbation number" because he was in the audience. But it's the Blond Ambition "family" that's the real subject—and Madonna's vision of herself as the nurturing mommy to the young, multiracial touring company. Leading her troops in a prayer circle before each show, soothing tensions between the homophobic dancer Oliver Crumes and his gay colleagues, reading a birthday poem to her assistant Melissa, this Madonna presents herself as a wound-licking, spirit-raising matriarchal dynamo. But it's just one of myriad contradictory impressions we come away with: crass/sensitive, selfish/generous, spontaneous/rigid, sensual/mechanical.

That's the second rule of celebrity Madonna has always broken: Instead of cultivating a single persona, she's reveled in changing masks, in contradiction, in putting ironic quotation marks around her various identities. The jest of her appropriation of Marilyn Monroe's image is that she is Monroe's antithesis: There's little that's vulnerable, and nothing of the victim, about her. As a performer, she's closer to Marlene Dietrich, all premeditated theatricality. (The concert footage is in color, the rest in black and white.) The role she plays least confidently is that of serious artist: When she holds a press conference after the Vatican condemns her show, she loses her natural voice and lapses into rote banalities about freedom of expression.

But if *Truth or Dare* is on its shakiest ground when Madonna is taking herself seriously, you come away feeling that only a fool *wouldn't* take her seriously. She has put herself on the cutting edge of celebrity, and the questions she poses about sexuality, power, and personas have made her the most stimulating pop icon around—and the most fun to follow. Whether you regard her as a symptom or a cure for a culture still locked in its eternal battle between the puritanical and the prurient, she's out there at the barricades. In *Truth or Dare,* she's at her button-pushing best.

Newsweek, May 13, 1991

TRUTH OR DARE

Michael Sragow

The Mae West one-liner "It's better to be looked over than overlooked" could serve as Madonna's motto. She's an inspired impresario of one act—her own—and when she's packaging her energy in concert or on video, it can be formidable. Her dancing has an engaging signature bounce—a kinetic squiggle that ends up rolling through her shoulders. Her thin, wiry voice is all-purpose pop—not a fatal flaw for a performer who remakes herself every time out, often as an outré update of time-honored show-biz legends.

What's impossible to buy about Madonna is exactly what *Truth or Dare,* the backstage chronicle of her Blond Ambition tour, is trying to sell: that she's not just a self-promoting entertainer—a combination gadfly and chanteuse—but also a serious person.

Under the influence of the deep-dish pop criticism hailing her as an imagistic genius and provocateur, she's decided to deliver a movie that would live up (and down) to her reputation. She's been acclaimed for her blasphemous, ribald, race-spanning, gender-bending videos—even though (like Spike Lee) she doesn't do anything with incendiary material except slick it up and throw it in your face. The banality of the lyrics in most of her hit songs could be contrived to afford the greatest possible flexibility for visual interpretation. Her best video is probably "Vogue," partly because it acknowledges that what she does is pose.

Yet in *Truth or Dare,* she speaks of herself as an artist fighting for integrity. The concert's most controversial number is a masturbatory rendition of "Like a Virgin" performed with two male dancers wearing cone-breasts. You can defend Madonna's right to free expression without dragging "art" into the description of this new-wave burlesque turn. When the film and the concert grow presumptuous, non-Madonnaholics will experience withdrawal before they get addicted.

In *Truth or Dare,* Madonna tries to show herself living a life true to her videos—and molds a self-portrait that's as slender as a cathode ray. You see her acting as den mother to her mostly gay backup dancers, dealing amiably with her straight-arrow dad and stepmom, goading Warren Beatty and gagging on Kevin Costner when he tells her that her act is "neat." You see her praying before each concert—and practicing fellatio on a bottle of mineral water. All that emerges from this voyeur's delight is a girl who cain't say no to the spotlight. Even her sympathy for gays—which she's backed up offscreen—seems faintly patronizing in the movie. Madonna's method is to imitate what other idols have done, only more all-out and consciously. It makes sense that she'd become the first pop diva to recruit a gay audience this openly—and relentlessly.

In the film's most agitating incident (for Madonna), she talks of experimenting sexually with her best teenage girlfriend, but when confronted with the friend (who asks her to be godmother to her next child), she's panicky and evasive. She thinks that dedicating a song to her former pal will make her feel all right. Moments like that are calculated to be "frank" and "revealing." But all they do is present another charade — a Bette Davis mask to place next to the well-used one of Marilyn Monroe. *Truth or Dare* is like *All About Eve* without Eve; Madonna is a Margo Channing who sniffs out competition on any front (even the emotional front) before it can get dangerous.

☆

In Madonna's previous film work, she never demonstrated the ability to merge her personality with a character. She was sensationally effective in *Dick Tracy* only because Warren Beatty shaped her into a cartoon icon — a postmodern Mae West. In *Truth or Dare,* which purports to deliver the unvarnished goods behind her Blond Ambition tour, she doesn't project a rich personality even when she's "acting herself." She comes off as a movie star only because everybody in back and in front of the camera treats her as if she already is one.

When her *Tracy* director and one-time lover, Beatty, shows up here as a reluctant supporting character, he asks a central question: Why hasn't anybody remarked on the insanity of her intention to film everything (including an appointment with a throat doctor)? She says people just "accept" the craziness. The real answer is that everyone knows Madonna is in charge — and, as Beatty also wryly comments, "She doesn't want to live off camera, much less talk. . . . What would you say if it's off camera? What point is there in existing?"

The teasing snippets of concert footage display Madonna in top form as a singer-prancer. Otherwise, *Truth or Dare* amounts to pictures of a professional exhibitionist. The movie doesn't even have the entertainment value of gossip. Its pretentiousness gets in the way. So does the advance press: You can't separate the movie from the "coverage." If you've perused the profiles and interviews, the movie itself is superfluous. What passes for "revelation" has already been reported ad nauseam.

It may be hard for observers to remember which supposed "bombshells" were launched in the movie, and which were unloaded in *Vanity Fair* or *The Advocate* or on television. Was it in *Truth or Dare* or on MTV that she named Sean Penn as the love of her life? Maybe it was on "Live with Regis and Kathie Lee" (an interview that, at Madonna's wish, was actually taped, at 6 P.M., in black and white, on the terrace of a sixteenth-story apartment at LA's Four Seasons Hotel). Of course, she revealed that I'm-just-an-average-Catholic-girl headline everywhere.

The newspaper and magazine profiles, and the TV interviews, function as advertisements for the movie; the movie is an advertisement for herself. The only reason to see it is to round off a hype experience that's virtually without precedent—unless you count Reagan's second presidential campaign.

If you check your gullibility at the door, there's a low-level intrigue to seeing how Our Mother of the Media operates. It starts with proclaiming the movie to be an innovation, and then—with twenty-six-year-old director Alek Keshishian as her partner—going down the trail blazed decades ago by *Don't Look Back*. The supposedly gritty human-interest scenes are shot in grainy, jittery black and white; the concert bits are in MTV color. The result is about as believably vérité as those wavering, hand-held camera commercials (for coffee and jeans) that came into fashion in the late eighties. Keshishian turns rough visuals into chic clichés.

That's what Madonna does verbally—she makes a show of candor, with the emphasis on show. There's no suggestion of a complex character beneath her multiplex of images; what exudes from the core is determination. *Truth or Dare* is made up of half-truths and quarter-dares. The real Madonna, if there is one in this movie, is a tough businesswoman. The only time she turns the camera away is when she's about to talk business.

☆

The movie begins with a quintessential fan-mag vignette: Madonna cleaning up (she's so down-to-earth!) after an end-of-tour party, and talking wistfully about how she has to distance herself from the conclusion of the experience as she would from a friend's death (she's so sensitive!). That sets the movie's tone of insane yet covert adulation. After clips of the kickoff in Japan, where her troupe encounters horrendous weather, *Truth or Dare* goes back to the United States, with the star's avowal to come home and do things right.

That statement implies that we'll be able to see the work and organization that go into a blockbuster multi-city marathon. Instead, we get only a self-centered soap opera on the general theme of—

What's a female superstar to do! You can't get a rest, and you can't get a man with a grenade-gun bra. When you do win a feller, like Warren, you grow competitive about whose celebrityhood is bigger. (She dreams of making Warren jealous by meeting Gorbachev first.) Even sardonic Sandra Bernhard seems to be having a better time than Madonna. When our poor little superstar lands in Spain and gets to meet her personal heartthrob—Antonio Banderas, the star of Pedro Almodóvar's movies—he turns out to be married!

☆

Madonna is a superstar devoted to being a gal of a thousand faces—fun loving and vivacious in a deliberately sassy, naughty-girl way, but also alone in a crowd of her own making; alternately loving and Machiavellian, needy and ferociously independent. Madonnaphiles interpret her fractured personality, and her constant urge to remake herself, as a grand new form of personal expressionism for the MTV era. Is she a conqueror of this age, or an unknowing victim of it? In *Truth or Dare* she's the human equivalent of the tin kaleidoscopes you used to be able to buy at five-and-dime stores—good for a turn or two, then boring.

When Madonna wins accolades for reactivating the sexual imagery of Marilyn Monroe's calendar art, her fans say she transcends any taint of exploitation because she's the one in control. Has the word "control" ever been used so often in praise of a performer? When Bette Davis fought for more control over her parts, she was fighting for the chance to be instinctive.

For Madonna, control is an end in itself. *Truth or Dare* is a demonstration of manipulation at its most total—and shallow. The star isn't much of a movie subject, but as a media ringmaster she's phenomenal. She sets off the buzz; then she modulates the spin.

San Francisco Examiner, May 17, 1991

THE THIN BLUE LINE

Terrence Rafferty

Errol Morris's documentaries have a luxuriant weirdness, a deep unfamiliarity. In his first two films — *Gates of Heaven* (1978), a report on pet cemeteries in California, and *Vernon, Florida* (1981), a loosely assembled collection of tales from a small southern town, told by rambling coots and half-demented good old boys — his choice of material and his fondness for lingering on the cracked discourse of his interview subjects identified him as a true connoisseur of native eccentricity, a hoarder of oddball Americana. His new movie, *The Thin Blue Line,* shows that he's more than an inspired believe-it-or-not artist. Telling the story of a 1976 cop killing in Dallas, and detailing the process by which a man who is almost certainly innocent was convicted and sentenced to death for the crime (with the likely killer as the prosecution's star witness), Morris burrows into a nightmarish realm of duplicity, faulty perception, and bottomless ambiguity. The movie is both detached and fanatically intense. Its materials have the heterogeneity, the heedless comprehensiveness, of documents in a dossier: There are interviews with the principals, close-ups of key words and paragraphs from the newspaper accounts, courtroom sketches, maps, family-album snapshots of the suspects, diagrams of the crime scene and of the entry and exit wounds in the victim's body, and a series of eerie reenactments of witnesses' different versions of the murder and the events that led up to it. But this stuff isn't organized in ways that we're used to. *The Thin Blue Line* doesn't have the structure either of "60 Minutes"–style investigative journalism or of detective fiction, though it borrows elements from both; its form is circular, spiraling, its obsessive, repetitive visual motifs echoed in Philip Glass's hauntingly monotonous score. This is documentary as epistemological thriller; Morris seems to want to bring us to the point at which our apprehension of the real world reaches the pitch of paranoia — to induce in us the state of mind of a detective whose scrutiny of the evidence, whose search for the connections between stubbornly isolated facts, has begun to take on the feverish clarity of hallucination.

The movie is a trancelike, almost lyrical rendering of a small, messy murder case — the kind of story that's usually found only in local newspapers and, sensationalized, in true-detective magazines—and it's as hypnotic as *Vertigo*. Although Morris himself doesn't appear in *The Thin Blue Line*, he is this film's true detective, the investigator whose insomniac consciousness keeps reshuffling the evidence, generating ambiguous images of the crime from the contradictory testimony of witnesses, swerving constantly between words and pictures, between facts and hypotheses. He came upon the story by accident. In 1985, Morris was interviewing prisoners in a Texas penitentiary for a documentary on Dr. James P. Grigson, a Dallas psychiatrist who is known as Dr. Death, because his expert testimony in capital cases virtually guarantees that the defendant will be sentenced to death. One of the filmmaker's interview subjects was a man named Randall Adams, who claimed to have been wrongly convicted of a policeman's murder. Morris did some digging into the records of the case and the trial, became convinced that Adams was innocent, and wound up on a long detour from the Dr. Death movie; the question of how Randall Adams could have landed in jail for something he probably didn't do took over the filmmaker's mind. Undoubtedly, the urgent, compulsive quality of *The Thin Blue Line* is, at least in part, a consequence of the film's unusual origin. The subject seems to have seized Morris's imagination unexpectedly—in much the same way that another Dallas murder, the Kennedy assassination, has drawn people, almost against their will, into its labyrinth of half-truths and contradictions, closed files and intimations of conspiracy.

Officer Robert Wood was killed on a cold night in November 1976. He and his partner had stopped a car in a bad section of town just to tell the driver to turn his headlights on; when Wood reached the window on the driver's side, he was shot, several times, by the man at the wheel. Since the crime was apparently so senseless, and since the only known witness, Wood's partner, wasn't very observant (the movie suggests that she may have violated procedure by remaining seated in the patrol car, drinking a milkshake, while Wood approached the killer's car), the Dallas police had no leads and hardly any clues. A month later, they questioned sixteen-year-old David Harris, who had been bragging to his buddies in the small town of Vidor that he had killed a Dallas cop. He admitted to the police that he had been in the car that Wood pulled over, but claimed that the person who had done the shooting was Randall Adams, a hitchhiker he had picked up earlier that day. After interrogating Adams—who insisted that the teenager had dropped him off at his motel a couple of hours before the time of the murder, and who refused to sign a

The roadside murder of Officer Robert Wood is reenacted on the set of Errol Morris's *Thin Blue Line*. (Photo by Mark Lipson, courtesy of Miramax Films.)

confession—the police decided that they would believe Harris, despite what might have seemed fairly strong circumstantial evidence pointing to him as the killer: Both the murder weapon and the car had been stolen by Harris in Vidor; since he knew that the car was stolen, he would have had far more reason than Adams to panic at being stopped by a patrol car; he had a substantial criminal record, and was facing charges in Vidor at the time he gave his evidence, whereas Adams had no record at all and no history of violence. So why, the movie asks, was Adams prosecuted, much less convicted and sentenced to death?

Morris's answers, or suggestions of answers, are complex, and whirl by us at such speed that we're barely able to keep up. We register one fact, and then another comes at us, then another and another, until, finally, we seem to be taking it all in on an almost subliminal level—our attention is so intensely focused that everything resonates, everything connects, with a logic we have stopped even trying to articulate. In showing us the lies, the fears, the social pressures, the cultural influences, the unwarranted assumptions, the ulterior motives, the stubbornness, and the plain confusion that combined to produce the case against Randall Adams, Morris—who has a degree in philosophy, and who once worked as a private detective—seems to be investigating not just this squalid murder but the very nature of untruth. It's hard to think of another movie (let alone another documentary) that has such a richly developed sense of the *texture* of falsehood, that picks out so many of the strands that, woven together, blind us. The Dallas police, their anger stirred and their pride challenged by the murder of one of their own, needed to arrest someone: If they believed Harris, they had a crime with a witness; if they believed Adams, then Harris was alone in the car, and they had nothing. The District Attorney, Douglas Mulder, who had never lost a capital case, needed a conviction and a death sentence: Harris, as a juvenile, couldn't be tried for first-degree murder; Adams, who was twenty-seven, could. At the trial, the victim's partner, who was feeling the heat of a departmental investigation of her conduct on the night of the killing and therefore may have been especially eager to cooperate, changed her testimony from her original report: Having initially said that there was only one person in the car, she now claimed to have seen two; the driver was now described as having had bushy shoulder-length hair (like Adams), rather than short hair and a fur-collared jacket (like Harris). The judge, the son of an FBI agent, was a man with a passion for law enforcement; he admits that he "welled up" during the DA's closing argument about "the thin blue line" of police risking their lives to protect society. One of the prosecution's chief witnesses, sprung on the defense at the last moment, was a woman named Emily Miller, who "used to watch all the detective shows on TV" and loved to make herself useful to the authorities—particularly in this case, since there was a twenty-one-thousand-dollar reward involved, and her daughter had just been arrested for a felony. (The charges were quietly dropped.)

Morris sucks us into the process by which a man, Randall Adams, becomes a kind of fictional character in a story whose momentum seems unstoppable. Adams, labeled a "drifter" by the police and the press (although he had been holding down a decent job ever since he arrived in Dallas, two months before the murder), is, when we see him interviewed in prison, a wan, ghostly, soft-spoken man. He's much thinner than the mustached hippie we've seen in newspaper photos from the time of his arrest, and he has a flat, weary voice. Although Adams isn't on Death Row anymore—in a complicated legal maneuver, the State of Texas commuted his sentence to life imprisonment in 1977 (after the Supreme Court struck down his death penalty), so that it wouldn't have to give him a new trial—he looks and sounds like someone on the verge of disappearing. He seems barely real, a shadowy image animated only sporadically by glints of bitter humor. The recreations of the murder and the events surrounding it have a stronger presence than Adams himself. Even when these scenes are representing accounts that are probably false, they're compelling. We watch the same actions occur over and over again, with slight but significant variations, on the same dark stretch of road—a setting that Morris endows with an unearthly vividness, composed of the piercing beams of headlights, silhouetted figures, flashes of gunfire, the revolving red light on top of the police car, and rich, enveloping nighttime blackness—and we think, against all reason, that one more detail, a different angle of vision, will suddenly reveal the truth, that these reconstructions somehow have the power to take us to the heart of things. Once David Harris had told his story, Randall Adams's life was obliterated, to be replaced by an endless series of constructions and reconstructions of a single moment (a moment at which he was most likely asleep in his motel room). It's as if time had simply stopped for him the instant the image of him shooting Robert Wood lodged in the minds of the Dallas police, and he had been condemned to live the rest of his life exclusively in the minds of others: cops, judges, juries, lawyers, newspaper readers, Errol Morris, audiences watching this movie—all of us, for our various reasons, rehearsing that terrible moment, with the figure of Randall Adams flickering in and out of the picture.

Adams's fate is worthy of a Borges hero, one of those melancholy spirits trapped in infinite loops of metaphysical treachery. It's no small feat for Morris to have made a documentary that evokes this kind of existential unease in its audience. There are times, though, when things get all muddy and confused, and that's not because reality is, you know, hopelessly ambiguous; it's because the filmmaker's style is too fancy and elliptical, or because he just hasn't bothered to give us information we need. The legal proceedings, in particular, are almost never entirely lucid. The flowering absurdity of Adams's experiences with the courts wouldn't lose its horror if Morris troubled to explain a few crucial points of law. But this is a powerful and thrillingly strange movie, and Morris's occasional excess of artiness shouldn't be taken as an indication of indifference to the reality of Randall Adams's plight. In fact, the filmmaker himself uncovered several pieces of new evidence, testified in Adams's behalf at hearings on motions for retrial, and coaxed a near-confession out of David Harris, which we hear, on tape, in the movie's final scene. (Harris has since, in a recent interview with a newspaper reporter, come even closer to an outright admission of guilt. He's on Death Row for another murder, and Adams is still petitioning for a new trial.) [Editor's Note: On March 24, 1989, the Texas Court of Criminal Appeals overturned Adams's conviction.] Morris, who clearly has a very sophisticated understanding of the relationship between art and reality, did a thorough, painstaking investigation in the real world, and then did something different on film: He turned the case into a kind of tabloid poetry, a meditation on uncertainty and the fascination of violence. If we quibble every now and then with his presentation of the facts, it's his own fault; *The Thin Blue Line* makes us all obsessed detectives.

The New Yorker, September 5, 1988

THE THIN BLUE LINE

Dave Kehr

In the night of November 29, 1979, Dallas police officer Robert Wood pulled over a car that was traveling without headlights. He was immediately shot and killed, and a hitchhiker named Randall Adams was later sentenced to death for his murder.

Those are the facts of the case as they are laid out in *The Thin Blue Line,* an insistently unconventional documentary directed by Errol Morris (*Gates of Heaven*).

But *The Thin Blue Line* is less concerned with laying out facts than with kicking them around—with coaxing out the ambiguities, contradictions, and pockets of the purely inexplicable that seem to surround any human event when it is examined closely enough.

In this case, those ambiguities appear to have led to the conviction of an innocent man, or so Morris argues. His candidate for the killer is David Harris, a troubled sixteen-year-old who had picked up Adams in a stolen car and, Morris suggests, panicked when Officer Wood approached.

Although Harris had a history of violent crimes, and had even bragged of killing the policeman to his friends, Adams—who had no previous record—was charged with the crime because, Morris argues, as an older man from out of state he was easier to prosecute.

It's the stuff of a superior "60 Minutes" segment, but Morris has something more ambitious in mind, though it's hard to say exactly what.

Drawing on an eerie Philip Glass score, interspersing interviews with spooky (and maddeningly repetitious) "re-creations" of the crime scene, and amassing a mountain of maps, diagrams, and transcripts, Morris gives the material a morbid, expressionistic charge.

Aided by the understandably gloomy Adams (whose sentence was eventually transferred to life), Morris suspends the dark, sinister hand of fate over the entire incident, as if Adams were the protagonist in a real-life film noir.

But at the same time that Morris is driven to dramatize the material—to turn it into a parable of cruel destiny—he also seems to be condescending to it, finding a smug, hipster's comedy in the perceived gaucheries of the southwestern characters.

When Morris wants to discredit interviewees, he allows them to ramble on until they become ridiculous. He then further undermines their authority by cutting away to clips from old B movies, which are meant to indicate the witnesses' exaggerated notions of themselves.

The Thin Blue Line begins to gather some interest when, out of restlessness or sheer paranoia, it begins to wander off from the immediate facts of the case. The film finds a strange significance in the fact that, for example, Harris's hometown is also the state headquarters of the Ku Klux Klan, or that Harris and Adams had been to see a drive-in double bill of *The Swinging Cheerleaders* and *The Student Body* before the killing. As in the better detective novels, the investigation of a murder leads to a more general scrutiny of a society.

But Morris's interests ultimately seem highly particular and perhaps a little obsessive. As the director of *Gates of Heaven,* a study of pet cemeteries and their middle-American patrons, Morris seems to be fascinated by our culture's ways of dealing with death. It is an intriguing subject, though so far all that Morris has brought to it is a combination of the morbid and the cruel; he needs to develop some sympathy, too.

Chicago Tribune, September 16, 1988

ABOUT THE CONTRIBUTORS

David Ansen is a movie critic and senior writer at *Newsweek*. He wrote the documentary *The Divine Garbo,* which appeared on TNT in 1990, and *The One and Only . . . Groucho* for HBO in 1991. He has won three Page One awards from the Newspaper Guild of New York. He was formerly the movie critic at *The Real Paper.*

Gary Arnold has been senior movie critic of *The Washington Times* since March 1989. He was the movie critic of *The Washington Post* from April 1969 to September 1984, and he has contributed movie reviews and essays on popular culture to many other publications.

Sheila Benson, currently a free-lance critic, was the *Los Angeles Times* film critic from 1981 to 1991, and also, for a portion of 1991, its critic-at-large columnist. From 1974 to 1981 she was one of the two film critics for the *Pacific Sun* in Marin County.

Jay Carr is the *Boston Globe's* film critic. He was previously the theater and music critic for the *Detroit News* and won the 1971–72 George Jean Nathan Award for Dramatic Criticism.

Kathleen Carroll is movie critic for the *New York Daily News.* She has been chairperson of the New York Critics Circle three times. She was formerly associate professor in the Communication Arts Division of St. John's University. She ran a program at Toronto's Festival of Festivals, while regularly reporting on the Cannes Film Festival.

Charles Champlin was principal film critic for the *Los Angeles Times* from 1967 to 1980 and retired as arts editor and critic-at-large columnist in April 1991. He presently hosts "Champlin on Film" and "The Great Directors" series on Bravo cable. His latest book is *George Lucas: The Creative Impulse* (Abrams).

Richard Corliss is a film critic for *Time* magazine and contributing editor of *Film Comment*. He is the author of *Talking Pictures*.

Judith Crist, an adjunct professor at the Columbia Graduate School of Journalism, began her career in film criticism at the *New York Herald Tribune* and has reviewed movies for a variety of publications and on television. She is the author of *The Private Eye, The Cowboy and the Very Naked Girl, Judith Crist's TV Guide to the Movies,* and *Take 22: Moviemakers on Moviemaking,* now in paperback.

David Denby is film critic of *New York* magazine and writes the "Rear Window" column for *Premiere*. His articles and reviews have also appeared in *The New Republic, The Atlantic,* and *The New York Review of Books.* He is currently working on a nonfiction book for Simon and Schuster on core education.

Morris Dickstein's film criticism has appeared in *American Film, Chaplin, The Bennington Review, In These Times, Grand Street, The Nation,* and *Partisan Review,* of which he is currently a contributing editor. He teaches literature and film at Queens College, CUNY, and is the author of *Gates of Eden* (Penguin). With Leo Braudy, he edited *Great Film Directors: A Critical Anthology* (Oxford). His new book is *Double Agent: The Critic and Society* (Oxford).

Roger Ebert is the Pulitzer Prize–winning film critic of the *Chicago Sunday Times,* co-host of television's "Siskel & Ebert," and author of *Roger Ebert's Movie Home Companion* and *Two Weeks in the Midday Sun,* a journal of the Cannes film festival.

Joseph Gelmis has reviewed movies for *Newsday* since 1964. His articles on film and filmmakers are syndicated to publications in the United States and Britain by the Los Angeles Times/Washington Post News Wire. He has taught at the State University of New York at Stony Brook, hosted a weekly radio show on WBAI FM, and is the author of *The Film Director as Superstar*.

Owen Gleiberman is the movie critic for *Entertainment Weekly*. He reviewed movies for the *Boston Phoenix* from 1981 to 1989. He has also written for *Premiere* and is heard on National Public Radio's "Fresh Air."

Hal Hinson is a film critic for *The Washington Post.*

J. Hoberman has reviewed movies for the *Village Voice* since 1978. He is a contributing writer to *Premiere* and has a regular column in *Artforum.* He is coauthor (with Jonathan Rosenbaum) of *Midnight Movies* and the author of *Bridge of Light,* a history of Yiddish-language cinema, published by the Museum of Modern Art and Schocken Books in 1991. He is also the author of *Vulgar Modernism,* a collection of pieces written in the eighties from the *Village Voice* and elsewhere.

Richard T. Jameson has written for the *Seattle Weekly, Pacific Northwest,* and *7 Days* and edited the Seattle Film Society's journal, *Movietone News,* from 1971 to 1981. He has been the editor of *Film Comment* since the beginning of 1990.

Pauline Kael began reviewing movies for *The New Yorker* in 1967 and retired from regular reviewing in February 1991. Her work has been compiled in *Going Steady, Deeper into Movies* (National Book Award winner, 1973), *Reeling, When the Lights Go Down, 5001 Nights at the Movies, Taking It All In, State of the Art, Hooked,* a 1991 expanded version of *5001 Nights at the Movies,* and *Movie Love.* Her first two collections, *I Lost It at the Movies* and *Kiss Kiss Bang Bang,* include essays and reviews written for *Partisan Review, Sight and Sound, Film Quarterly,* and *The Atlantic,* as well as *The New Yorker. The Citizen Kane Book* contains her long essay "Raising Kane," and she also wrote the introduction to *Three Screen Comedies by Samson Raphaelson.*

Dave Kehr has been the movie critic of the *Chicago Tribune* since 1986. From 1975 to 1986, he was the movie critic of the *Chicago Reader.*

Stuart Klawans reviews films for *The Nation* and WBAI radio. His commentaries and fiction have appeared in the *Village Voice, Grand Street, The Threepenny Review, Entertainment Weekly,* and the *Times Literary Supplement.*

John Powers is a film critic for the *LA Weekly* and writes a regular Hollywood column for *Sight and Sound.* He is currently at work on a book about mosquitoes and history.

Terrence Rafferty is film critic for *The New Yorker.* His movie writing has also appeared in *The Nation, Sight and Sound, The Atlantic, The*

Threepenny Review, and *Film Quarterly.* His book *The Thing Happens: Ten Years of Writing about the Movies,* will be out in January 1993 from Grove Press.

Peter Rainer, the chairman of the National Society of Film Critics, writes film criticism and commentary for the *Los Angeles Times.* From 1981 until its demise in 1989, he was film critic for the *Los Angeles Herald Examiner.* Rainer's writing has also appeared in *The New York Times Magazine, Vogue, GQ, Newsday, Premiere, Connoisseur, American Film,* and *Mademoiselle.* Rainer has appeared as a film commentator on such television shows as "Nightline," "ABC World News Tonight," and "CBS Morning News." He has also taught criticism at the University of Southern California Graduate Film School.

Carrie Rickey is currently on two-year leave as a film critic for the *Philadelphia Inquirer* to serve as an editor on its op-ed pages. She was previously the film critic for the *Boston Herald* and the *Village Voice.*

Jonathan Rosenbaum has written for over fifty periodicals, including the *Chicago Reader* (where he has been film critic since 1987), *Cahiers du Cinéma, Elle, Film Comment, Sight and Sound,* and *Tikkun.* His books include *Moving Places: A Life at the Movies* and *Film: The Front Line 1983.* He edited Orson Welles's *The Big Brass Ring* and *The Cradle Will Rock* and Peter Bogdanovich's *Conversations with Orson Welles.*

Julie Salamon is the film critic for the *Wall Street Journal.* She is the author of the novel *White Lies* and the book *The Devil's Candy: The Bonfire of the Vanities Goes to Hollywood.*

Andrew Sarris is film critic for the *New York Observer* and professor of film at the School of the Arts at Columbia University. He is also the author of ten books, including *The American Cinema, Confessions of a Cultist, The John Ford Movie Mystery,* and *Politics and Cinema.* He was a movie reviewer for twenty-nine years at the *Village Voice.*

Richard Schickel has reviewed movies for *Time* magazine since 1972; before that he was *Life's* film critic. He is the author of many books, most notably *The Disney Version, His Picture in the Papers, D. W. Griffith: An American Life, Intimate Strangers: The Culture of Celebrity, Schickel on Film,* and his latest, *Marlon Brando: A Life in Our Times.* He is also a producer-writer-director of television documentaries, the latest of which, *Barbara Stanwyck: Fire and Desire,* appeared in summer 1991 on TNT. He has held a Guggenheim Fellowship and has won the British Film Institute book prize.

Stephen Schiff is a cultural critic at *The New Yorker* and a film critic on National Public Radio. A former correspondent on CBS-TV's "West 57th," and a Pulitzer Prize finalist in 1983, he was critic-at-large at *Vanity Fair* from 1983 to 1992 and has written film criticism for *The Atlantic,* the *Boston Phoenix, Film Comment, Glamour,* and *American Film.*

Henry Sheehan is the film critic of *L.A. Style* and a contributing critic to *The Hollywood Reporter* and the *LA Weekly.* From 1986 to 1991 he was film critic of the *Los Angeles Reader.* He has written on film and related subjects for *Film Comment, Sight and Sound,* the *Boston Globe,* the *Boston Phoenix, Premiere,* and *The New York Times Book Review.*

Michael Sragow was the editor of *Produced and Abandoned: The Best Films You've Never Seen,* the first in this National Society of Film Critics series. He is currently a movie critic for *The New Yorker.* He was previously movie critic for the *San Francisco Examiner,* the *Boston Phoenix,* the *Los Angeles Herald Examiner,* and *Rolling Stone* magazine. His book, television, and movie criticism has appeared in *Esquire, The Atlantic, Mother Jones, Harper's, The Nation, The New Republic, New York* magazine, *Film Comment, American Film,* and *Sight and Sound.*

Kevin Thomas has been a movie critic of the *Los Angeles Times* since 1962. He has served on the juries of the Tokyo, Chicago, Berlin, Montreal, and Tehran film festivals. A fourth-generation California newspaperman and native Angeleno, he was named a chevalier in France's Order of Arts and Letters for his "contributions to French cinema."

Peter Travers is the film critic for *Rolling Stone* magazine.

Kenneth Turan is the chief film critic for the *Los Angeles Times.* He has been a staff writer for *The Washington Post* and *TV Guide* and film critic for GQ and National Public Radio's "All Things Considered." He is the coauthor of *Call Me Anna: The Autobiography of Patty Duke.* He is on the board of directors of the National Yiddish Book Center.

Armond White is the film critic and arts editor of the Brooklyn-based weekly, the *City Sun*. He is the author of the forthcoming Brian De Palma study, *Total Illumination*.

Bruce Williamson has been *Playboy*'s movie critic (and a contributing editor there) for more than two decades. He was a former chairman of the New York Film Critics Circle, a movie critic at *Time* magazine from 1963 to 1967, and, for a brief period, a movie–media critic for *Life*.

Michael Wilmington has been a movie reviewer for the *Los Angeles Times* since 1984. He contributes regularly to *L.A. Style, Film Comment,* and *Sight and Sound,* and was formerly a film editor at *LA Weekly*. He is coauthor of *John Ford* (British Film Institute, 1973) and has won five Milwaukee Press Awards for art criticism while working at *Isthmus*.

PERMISSIONS

Every effort has been made to identify the holders of copyright of previously published materials included in this book. The publisher apologizes for any oversights that may have occurred; any errors that may have been made will be corrected in subsequent printings upon notification to the publisher.

Grateful acknowledgment is made to the following for permission to reprint copyrighted material:

Sheila Benson: for her *Los Angeles Times* reviews of *Thelma & Louise* (May 31, 1991), *Ishtar* (May 15, 1987), *One from the Heart* (January 22, 1982, March 1, 1990), and *Under the Volcano* (July 6, 1984).

Boston Globe: for Jay Carr's reviews of *sex, lies, and videotape* (August 11, 1989), *Pretty Woman* (March 23, 1990), *Batman* (June 23, 1989), *Naked Lunch* (January 10, 1992), and *Hannah and Her Sisters* (February 7, 1986).

Boston Phoenix: for Owen Gleiberman's reviews of *River's Edge* (May 22, 1987), *Fatal Attraction* (September 25, 1987), *Hail Mary* (November 26, 1985), and Eddie Murphy (December 24, 1987); for Stephen Schiff's reviews of *Dressed to Kill* (July 29, 1980, August 26, 1980), *Reds* (December 1, 1981), *Ordinary People* (September 23, 1980), and *The Deer Hunter* (February 13, 1979); for Michael Sragow's review of *The Wild Bunch* (January 8, 1985).

Chicago Reader: for David Kehr's review of *The Exorcist II: The Heretic* (June 24, 1977); for Jonathan Rosenbaum's reviews of *Mississippi Burning* (December 16, 1988) and *Do the Right Thing* (August 4, 1989).

Chicago Tribune: for David Kehr's reviews of *The Silence of the Lambs* (March 10, 1991), *Vincent & Theo* (November 16, 1990), Julia Roberts (March 24, 1991), *Boyz N the Hood* (July 12, 1991), and *The Thin Blue Line* (September 16, 1988). Copyrighted © 1988, 1990, 1991, Chicago Tribune Company, all rights reserved, used with permission.

City Sun: for Armond White's reviews of *Wild at Heart* (August 22–28, 1990),

The Adventures of Ford Fairlane (July 25–31, 1990), Michelle Pfeiffer (October 25–31, 1989), *The Color Purple* (January 15–21, 1986), and *Driving Miss Daisy* (January 10–16, 1990).

The Connection Newspapers: for Gary Arnold's review of *The Last Temptation of Christ* (August 17, 1988).

Judith Crist: for her *New York* magazine reviews of *Last Tango in Paris* (February 5, 1973), *Straw Dogs* (January 24, 1972), *A Woman Under the Influence* (November 25, 1974); and for her *Saturday Review* review of *Swept Away* (November 1, 1975).

David Denby: for his *New York* magazine reviews of *The Big Chill* (September 26, 1983), *Places in the Heart* (October 1, 1984), *Veronika Voss* (November 1, 1982), *Jungle Fever* (June 17, 1991), *Boyz N the Hood* (July 22, 1991, July 29, 1991), and *JFK* (January 6, 1992).

Roger Ebert: for his *Chicago Sun-Times* reviews of *Blue Velvet* (September 19, 1986), *The Accused* (October 14, 1988), *Field of Dreams* (April 21, 1989), and *Vincent & Theo* (November 16, 1990); and for his essay "On Violence" (July 1, 1990).

Entertainment Weekly: for Owen Gleiberman's review of *Dances with Wolves* (November 16, 1990).

In These Times: for Morris Dickstein's essay "Steven Spielberg and George Lucas: On Peter Panavision" (June 15–28, 1983).

Richard Jameson: for his *Seattle Weekly* reviews of *Places in the Heart* (October 3, 1984), *Indiana Jones and the Temple of Doom* (June 6, 1984), and *Apocalypse Now* (October 17, 1979).

Pauline Kael: for her reviews in *The New Yorker* of *Terms of Endearment* (December 12, 1983), *A Woman Under the Influence* (December 9, 1974), *Get Out Your Handkerchiefs* (October 16, 1978), *Under Fire* (October 31, 1983), *Platoon* (January 12, 1987), and *Roger & Me* (January 8, 1990).

Los Angeles Times: for Charles Champlin's review of *Last Tango in Paris* (March 11, 1973); for Peter Rainer's essays "On Actresses" (June 3, 1990) and "On Male Weepies" (August 19, 1991), and his review of Eddie Murphy (November 24, 1989); for Kevin Thomas's reviews of *Heaven's Gate* (April 25, 1980) and *Pink Flamingos* (December 13, 1974); for Kenneth Turan's review of *The Doctor* (July 24, 1991). Copyright 1973, 1974, 1980, 1989, 1990, 1991. *Los Angeles Times.* Reprinted by permission.

Terrence Rafferty: for his reviews in *The New Yorker* of *Cape Fear* (December 2, 1991), *Henry: Portrait of a Serial Killer* (April 23, 1990), *The Cook, the Thief, His Wife and Her Lover* (May 7, 1990), *Do the Right Thing* (July 24, 1989), and *The Thin Blue Line* (September 5, 1988).

Peter Rainer: for his *Los Angeles Herald Examiner* reviews of *Blue Velvet* (September 19, 1986), *Under the Volcano* (July 5, 1984), and *Indiana Jones and the Temple of Doom* (May 23, 1984).

Rolling Stone: for Michael Sragow's review of *Reds* (January 21, 1982); for Peter Travers's reviews of *Wild at Heart* (September 6, 1990), *Basic Instinct* (April 16, 1992), and *Barton Fink* (August 22, 1991).

Jonathan Rosenbaum: for his *Take One* review of *The Deer Hunter* (March 1979).

San Francisco Examiner: for Michael Sragow's reviews of *Henry & June* (September 30, 1990), *Hannah and Her Sisters* (February 7, 1986), Michelle Pfeiffer (November 17, 1991), and *Truth or Dare* (May 17, 1991). The Michelle Pfeiffer article appeared in the *San Francisco Examiner*'s *Image* magazine.

Henry Sheehan: for his *Los Angeles Reader* reviews of *Henry: Portrait of a Serial Killer* (April 13, 1990), *Tie Me Up! Tie Me Down!* (May 11, 1990), and *It's a Wonderful Life* (December 8, 1989).

Sight and Sound: for J. Hoberman's review of *Cape Fear* (February 1992); for Terrence Rafferty's review of *The Unbearable Lightness of Being* (Summer 1988).

Time: for Richard Corliss's reviews of *The Big Chill* (September 12, 1983) and *Batman* (June 19, 1989); for Richard Schickel's reviews of *Thelma & Louise* (June 24, 1991), *Ordinary People* (September 22, 1980), *Terms of Endearment* (November 28, 1983), *Mississippi Burning* (December 5, 1988), *Under Fire* (November 7, 1983), and *Casualties of War* (August 21, 1989). Copyright 1980, 1983, 1988, 1989, 1991 Time Inc. Reprinted by permission.

Kenneth Turan: for his *New West* review of *Absence of Malice* (December 1981); for his *GQ* essay "On Colorization" (January 1987); for his *California Magazine* review of *Brazil* (December 1985).

Vanity Fair: for Stephen Schiff's review of *Cry Freedom* (December 1, 1987).

Village Voice: for J. Hoberman's reviews of *The Silence of the Lambs* (February 19, 1991), *The Unbearable Lightness of Being* (February 9, 1988), *First Name:*

Carmen (August 14, 1984), and *JFK* (December 31, 1991); for Andrew Sarris's essay "On Families" (November 11, 1980) and his review of *The Marriage of Maria Braun* (October 22, 1979). Reprinted by permission of the author and the *Village Voice*.

Wall Street Journal: for Julie Salamon's reviews of *The Accused* (October 20, 1988), *Field of Dreams* (April 27, 1989), *The Godfather Part III* (December 27, 1990), and *The Color Purple* (December 19, 1985).

The Washington Post: for Gary Arnold's review of *Swept Away* (February 4, 1976); for Hal Hinson's reviews of *Hudson Hawk* (May 24, 1991), *Naked Lunch* (January 10, 1992), *Casualties of War* (August 18, 1989), and *Born on the Fourth of July* (December 20, 1989).

The Washington Times: for Gary Arnold's reviews of *sex, lies, and videotape* (August 11, 1989), *Crimes and Misdemeanors* (October 13, 1989), and *Barton Fink* (August 21, 1991).

Michael Wilmington: for his *Isthmus* reviews of *Absence of Malice* (December 18, 1981), *The Cook, the Thief, His Wife and Her Lover* (May 4, 1990), *The Last Temptation of Christ* (September 16, 1988), and *Platoon* (January 16, 1978).

INDEX OF FILMS, DIRECTORS, AND ACTORS

ABOUT THE EDITOR

Kirk McKoy

Peter Rainer, the chairman of the National Society of Film Critics, writes film criticism and commentary for the *Los Angeles Times.* From 1981 until its demise in 1989, Rainer was film critic for the *Los Angeles Herald Examiner.*

Rainer's writing has also appeared in *The New York Times Magazine, Vogue, GQ, Newsday, Premiere, American Film, Connoisseur,* and *Mademoiselle.* In book form, his essays have been published in *The National Society of Film Critics on the Movie Star, Resolution: A Critique of Video Art, Produced and Abandoned: The Best Films You've Never Seen, Foreign Affairs,* and the college writing textbook *The Writer's Roles.* His 1990 *Los Angeles Times* essay "Hollywood's Lost Generation of Women," reprinted in *Love and Hisses* as "On Actresses," won a 1991 Breakthrough award from the journalists organization Women, Men and Media.

Rainer has appeared as a film commentator on such television shows as "Nightline," "ABC World News Tonight," "CBS Morning News" and CNN; and, on radio, for National Public Radio and the Pacifica Network. He has taught film criticism in the Graduate Division of the University of Southern California Film School, where he received a master's degree. He also served on the jury for the 1990 Montreal Film Festival.